PSALMS III
101-150

VOLUME 17A

THE ANCHOR BIBLE is a fresh approach to the world's greatest classic. Its object is to make the Bible accessible to the modern reader; its method is to arrive at the meaning of biblical literature through exact translation and extended exposition, and to reconstruct the ancient setting of the biblical story, as well as the circumstances of its transcription and the characteristics of its transcribers.

THE ANCHOR BIBLE is a project of international and interfaith scope: Protestant, Catholic, and Jewish scholars from many countries contribute individual volumes. The project is not sponsored by any ecclesiastical organization and is not intended to reflect any particular theological doctrine. Prepared under our joint supervision, THE ANCHOR BIBLE is an effort to make available all the significant historical and linguistic knowledge which bears on the interpretation of the biblical record.

THE ANCHOR BIBLE is aimed at the general reader with no special formal training in biblical studies; yet, it is written with the most exacting standards of scholarship, reflecting the highest technical accomplishment.

This project marks the beginning of a new era of co-operation among scholars in biblical research, thus forming a common body of knowledge to be shared by all.

William Foxwell Albright
David Noel Freedman
GENERAL EDITORS

THE ANCHOR BIBLE

PSALMS III

101–150

INTRODUCTION, TRANSLATION, AND NOTES

WITH AN APPENDIX

THE GRAMMAR OF THE PSALTER

BY

MITCHELL DAHOOD, S. J.

Doubleday & Company, Inc.

Garden City, New York

Library of Congress Catalog Card Number 66–11766

Printed in the United States of America
First Edition
Fifth Printing
1979

PREFACE

Ten years have passed since that August afternoon of 1959 when my tranquil study in the library of the Biblical Institute in Jerusalem was interrupted by an intruder who sat himself opposite me at the table and began approximately thus: "For a number of years you have been publishing for *Biblica* potboilers on the Psalter, and it seems to me that you should now devote your energy to something more substantial." "What do you have in mind?" I asked. Today, a decade and one hundred and fifty psalms later, I thank Professor D. N. Freedman both for his intrusion and for his subsequent help and counsel. I consider myself fortunate to have had a General Editor whose predilection for archaic Hebrew poetry enabled him constantly to offer penetrating and constructive criticism. It is also a pleasure to express gratitude to my colleagues and students, to my relatives and friends, for their encouragement and, perhaps more importantly, for their long suffering. Finally, I am indebted to the typist, Signorina M. Grazia Franzese who, in addition to such foreign tongues as Ugaritic and Biblical Hebrew, had also to contend with longhand English.

Scholars should be just toward their materials. And they have the further duty of being kind toward their readers. Their methods may be in themselves the perfection of scholarship, and yet may ask too much of readers. The decision whether I have been just toward my materials is inevitably restricted to professional scholars, but more than one popular reviewer has suggested that I have been less than kind to my readers. This may well be due to an "abandonment of simple common sense," as one critic complained, or to the refractory nature of the ancient materials. One thinks of the ability described by Matthew Arnold, "to divest knowledge of all that was harsh, uncouth, difficult, abstract, professional, exclusive; to humanize it, to make it efficient outside the clique of the cultivated and the learned." Perhaps the most practical solution to the problem of access and intelligibility was found by the reviewer who proposed skipping the notes and concentrating on the translation itself, which he described as "literal and preserving many features of Hebrew poetry usually lost in English versions." And yet, this proposal cannot be fully endorsed. The reviewer who evaluated the letters of the English poet Edward Thomas (died 1917) to Gordon Bottomley could in good conscience close his review with the judgment, "for the scholarly student, the Bottomley letters will be useful, . . . but the readers of the poems will not really need any of them—the poems are enough."* The biblical scholar would like to be able to say the same about the psalms, but they are nearly three thousand years old and would not be self-explanatory even in the most perfect translation.

If Coleridge was correct in stating that "poetry gives most pleasure when only generally and not perfectly understood," the Psalter should continue to afford considerable pleasure to its readers. To be sure, the number of verses on which new light is shed by non-biblical texts may not be equaled by the number of problems uncovered. Nonetheless, the number of questions raised that demand further study may give the impression that I have started numerous hares and too soon abandoned the chase. One readily understands the meaning of Hermann Gunkel's introduction to his *Die Psalmen* (Göttingen, 1926): "Bin ich zu Ende, beginne ich" ["When I am finished, I begin"].

It will, however, be personally satisfying if this work, conceived in Jerusalem and realized in Rome, elicits a creative response within the religious traditions emanating from these two cities, and leads to the discovery and appreciation of doctrinal and spiritual treasures still hidden in the Psalter.

Easter, 1969

* *The Times Literary Supplement*, 16 January 1969, p. 62.

CONTENTS

PRINCIPAL ABBREVIATIONS

1. Publications

BASOR	Bulletin of the American Schools of Oriental Research
BCCT	*The Bible in Current Catholic Thought,* ed. J. L. McKenzie (New York, 1962)
BDB	F. Brown, S. R. Driver, and C. A. Briggs, eds., *A Hebrew and English Lexicon of the Old Testament* (Boston, 1906)
BH^{3}	*Biblia Hebraica,* ed. R. Kittel, 3d ed. (Stuttgart, 1937)
BHS	*Biblia Hebraica Stuttgartensia,* eds. K. Elliger and W. Rudolph (Stuttgart, 1968–)
BibOr	Bibbia e Oriente
BO	Bibliotheca Orientalis
CAD	*The Assyrian Dictionary,* Oriental Institute of the University of Chicago (1956–)
CBQ	Catholic Biblical Quarterly
CECBP	*A Critical and Exegetical Commentary on the Book of Psalms,* by C. A. Briggs (see Selected Bibliography)
CIS	*Corpus Inscriptionum Semiticarum* (Paris, 1881–)
CML	*Canaanite Myths and Legends,* by G. R. Driver (Edinburgh, 1956)
CPBP	*Canaanite Parallels in the Book of Psalms,* by J. H. Patton (Baltimore, 1944)
DISO	*Dictionnaire des inscriptions sémitiques de l'ouest,* by Charles F. Jean and Jacob Hoftijzer (2 vols.; Leiden, 1960)
EA	*Die El-Amarna Tafeln,* ed. J. Knudtzon (Leipzig, 1915)
EPT	*Ezekiel's Prophecy on Tyre (Ez. 26, 1–28, 19): A New Approach,* by H. J. van Dijk (Rome, 1968)
ETL	Ephemerides Theologicae Lovanienses
GB	Gesenius-Buhl, *Handwörterbuch,* 17th ed. (Leipzig, 1921)
GHB	*Grammaire de l'Hébreu Biblique,* by P. Joüon, 2d ed. (Rome, 1947)
GK	*Gesenius' Hebräische Grammatik,* ed. E. Kautzsch, 28th rev. ed. (Leipzig, 1909)
HALAT	*Hebräisches und aramäisches Lexikon zum Alten Testament,* by W. Baumgartner, 3d ed. (fasc. 1; Leiden, 1967)

HUCA Hebrew Union College Annual
HWFB *Hebräische Wortforschung: Festschrift zum 80. Geburtstag von Walter Baumgartner,* ed. by Benedikt Hartmann and others (VTS, XVI; Leiden, 1967)
ICC International Critical Commentary (Edinburgh, 1901–)
IDB The Interpreter's Dictionary of the Bible (4 vols.; New York, 1962)
IEJ Israel Exploration Journal
JAOS Journal of the American Oriental Society
JBL Journal of Biblical Literature
JCS Journal of Cuneiform Studies
JNES Journal of Near Eastern Studies
JSS Journal of Semitic Studies
JTS Journal of Theological Studies
KAI *Kanaanäische und aramäische Inschriften,* by H. Donner and W. Röllig (3 vols.; Wiesbaden, 1962–64)
KB L. Koehler and W. Baumgartner, *Lexicon in Veteris Testamenti Libros* (Leiden, 1951; Grand Rapids, 1953)
LKK *The Legend of King Keret,* by H. L. Ginsberg (New Haven, 1946)
PCTNT *The Psalms Chronologically Treated with a New Translation,* by M. Buttenwieser (see Selected Bibliography)
PMS *The Psalms in Modern Speech,* by R. M. Hanson (3 vols.; Philadelphia, 1968)
PNWSP *Proverbs and Northwest Semitic Philology,* by M. Dahood (Rome, 1963)
PPG *Phönizisch-Punische Grammatik,* by Johannes Friedrich (Rome, 1951)
1QIs^a The St. Mark's Isaiah Scroll, ed. M. Burrows (New Haven, 1950)
1QM Qumran War Scroll
1QS Qumran Manual of Discipline
11QPs^a *The Psalms Scroll of Qumran Cave 11,* ed. James A. Sanders (Discoveries in the Judaean Desert of Jordan, IV; Oxford, 1965)
RB Revue Biblique
TS Theological Studies
UHP *Ugaritic-Hebrew Philology,* by M. Dahood (Rome, 1965)
UT *Ugaritic Textbook,* 4th ed. (Rome, 1965) of C. H. Gordon's *Ugaritic Grammar* (Rome, 1940)
VD Verbum Domini
VT Vetus Testamentum
VTS Vetus Testamentum Supplements (Leiden, 1953–)
WuS *Wörterbuch der ugaritischen Sprache,* by Joseph Aistleitner (Berlin, 1963)

YGC *Yahweh and the Gods of Canaan: A Historical Analysis of Two Contrasting Faiths,* by W. F. Albright (Garden City, N.Y., 1968)

ZLH F. Zorell, *Lexicon Hebraicum* (Rome, 1965)

2. Versions

AB	The Anchor Bible, 1964–
AT	The Bible, an American Translation, 1931
ATD	Das Alte Testament Deutsch, 1949–
BJ	Bible de Jérusalem, 2d ed., 1951–
CCD	Confraternity of Christian Doctrine Version, 1944–69
JB	The Jerusalem Bible, 1966
JPS	The Jewish Publication Society of America: The Holy Scriptures, 1917, The Torah, 1962
KJ	The King James, or Authorized Version of 1611
LXX	The Septuagint
LXX^{A}	Codex Alexandrinus
MT	Masoretic Text
RSV	The Revised Standard Version, 1946, 1952
Symm.	Ancient Greek translation of the Old Testament by Symmachus
Syr.	Syriac version, the Peshitta
Targ.	Aramaic translations or paraphrases
Vulg.	The Vulgate

3. Other Abbreviations

Akk.	Akkadian
Ar.	Arabic
Aram.	Aramaic
Heb.	Hebrew
NT	New Testament
OT	Old Testament
Phoen.	Phoenician
Ugar.	Ugaritic

GLOSSARY OF TERMS

aleph, the first letter of the Phoenician-Hebrew alphabet, whose symbol is ', e.g., *'ādām,* "man."

prothetic aleph, an *aleph* placed before a root or a word to modify its form and/or meaning.

aphel (masc. singular imperative, etc.), a causative conjugation formed by placing an *aleph* before the verb; e.g., *pā'al,* "he did," but *'ap'ēl,* "he caused to do."

primae aleph nouns, nouns whose first consonant is *aleph.*

athnach, a symbol used by the Masoretes to indicate the principal pause in a verse.

asseverative or *kaph veritatis,* the particle *kī* when it emphasizes the following word; e.g., *kī ṭōb,* "truly good."

beth comparativum, the preposition b^e when employed to express comparison; e.g., Ps li 9, *b^e'āzōb,* "than gushing water."

beth essentiae, the preposition b^e when used to state identity of subject and predicate; e.g., Ps xcix 6, "Moses and Aaron were his priests" (*b^ekōh^{a}nāyw*).

bilabials, consonants such as *b* and *m* that are pronounced by pressing the two lips together.

by-form, an alternate form or spelling of a word.

chiasm or *chiasmus, chiastic,* the arrangement of words in an "x" pattern.

construct, the shortened form that a noun assumes before another noun or verb in the genitive case. E.g. Absolute *dābār,* "word," but in construct *d^ebar yhwh,* "word of Yahweh."

copulative conjunctions, conjunctions which connect words rather than, say, contrast them.

dativus commodi, the dative of advantage.

dislegomenon, a word or form that occurs only twice.

hapax legomenon, a word or form occurring only once.

haplography, the accidental omission by a scribe of a letter or a word.

hendiadys, literally "one through two," hendiadys is a rhetorical figure using two words to express one idea.

hiphil elative, a causative verb form that is employed to heighten the root idea, e.g., Ps li 9, *'albīn,* "I'll be much whiter."

hiphil energic, a causative verb form ending in *-annāh.*

hithpoel participle, a participle of reflexive conjugation.

ketiv, literally "what is written," *ketiv* is a term of the Masoretes which indicates that what is written in the received text is at variance with their vocalization; see *qere.*

lamedh, the twelfth letter of the Phoenician-Hebrew alphabet, our "l."

merism or *merismus,* a rhetorical figure in which totality is expressed by mentioning the two extremes of a class; e.g., Ps viii 8, "small and large cattle," or xxxvi 8, "gods and men," namely, all creatures dependent upon Yahweh.

nota accusativi, the particle *'ēt,* which introduces the accusative object.

partitive construction, the use of the prepositions *min* or *b*[e] to express the notion of part; e.g., Prov ix 5, "Eat some of my bread" (*b*[e]*laḥmī*).

piel, the third Hebrew conjugation which often intensifies the root idea of the verb, but which can also express other nuances; see *piel privative.*

piel participle, the participle of the intensive conjugation.

piel privative, the third conjugation of the verb when used to negate the root idea.

postpositive verb, a verb placed at the end of its clause under the influence of an emphatic particle such as *kī,* "indeed."

precative perfect, a verb form, often balanced by an imperative, that states an ardent wish or prayer.

preterit verb, a verb expressing past action.

pual, the passive of the piel or intensive conjugation.

pual participle, the participle of the passive of the intensive verb form.

qal, the light form, that is the simplest form, of the verb; e.g., *rādap,* "to pursue," whereas the intensive or piel form *riddēp* means "to pursue closely."

qal imperfect, the prefixed verb form of the simple (as opposed to the intensive or causative) conjugation.

energic qal imperative, the imperative of the simple conjugation, followed by the ending *-annāh* which serves to intensify the imperative idea.

qere, a term employed by the Masoretes to indicate that their pointing or vocalization is at variance with the consonants of the received text.

qtl verb, the suffixed form of the verb, to be distinguished from the *yqtl* or prefixed verb form.

scriptio defectiva, literally "defective or incomplete spelling," this manner of writing does not indicate long vowels by the use of vowel letters such as *-h, w* or *y;* see *scriptio plena.*

scriptio plena, literally "full or complete spelling," this manner of writing employs vowel letters such as *-h, w,* and *y* to indicate long vowels.

shaphel causatives, semantically equal to the hiphil conjugation, the shaphel causatives prefix *sh-* to the root to form a causative verb; e.g., *pā'al,* "he did," but *shaph'ēl,* "he caused to do."

stichometric, referring to the division of stichs or cola in a verse.

terminus technicus, literally "a technical expression," often employed in the original language because it has no perfect equivalent in other languages.

waw emphaticum or *emphatic waw,* the particle *wᵉ* or *wa* used, not as a connecting conjunction, but rather as an emphasizing word.

waw explicativum, a technical expression which means that the particle *wᵉ* or *wa* explains the preceding word; in English it would usually be rendered by the relative pronoun "who" or "which."

yod, the tenth letter of the Phoenician-Hebrew alphabet, whose symbol is *y.*

primae yod, a root whose first letter is *yod.*

yqtl verb, the prefixed form of the verb, to be distinguished from the *qtl* or suffixed verb form.

LIST OF ANCIENT NEAR EASTERN TEXTS

Aḥiram, a three-line Phoenician inscription of the eleventh century B.C. It was inscribed on the rim of a sarcophagus discovered in 1923 at Byblos in the Lebanon.

El Amarna Correspondence, a corpus of Akkadian letters discovered in 1887 in central Egypt. They were written around 1350 B.C. by kings and princes in Syria-Palestine to the Egyptian Pharaoh, and are of special significance for the biblical scholar because of the numerous Canaanite expressions (Canaanisms) interspersed throughout the letters.

Arslan Tash Incantation, an eighth-seventh century B.C. Phoenician inscription found in Syria.

Eshmunazor, a Phoenician inscription of the sixth century B.C., discovered in 1855 near Sidon in the Lebanon. Next to the great Karatepe inscription, it is the longest Phoenician text discovered to date.

Hadad Inscription, an Aramaic inscription of the eighth century B.C. discovered at Zincirli (or Zenjirli) in southeastern Turkey. Though commonly described as Aramaic, the language of the inscription contains many similarities to Phoenician.

Karatepe Inscriptions, discovered in 1946 in southeastern Turkey, are bilingual inscriptions written in Phoenician and hieroglyphic Hittite. Running to more than sixty long lines, the Phoenician text is the longest yet discovered in this language. It describes the achievements of a certain King Azitawaddu, who ruled in the second half of the eighth century B.C.

The Keret Legend, one of the important Ugaritic texts preserved in three broken tablets. It tells of a Syrian king who has lost his family and is heartbroken.

Kilamuwa, a Phoenician inscription of the ninth century B.C., discovered in 1902 at Zincirli.

Mari texts, a corpus of more than twenty thousand tablets discovered in 1935 in northern Mesopotamia. Written in the Amorite dialect of Akkadian, these tablets date to the period 1700 B.C., the era of Hammurapi.

Mesha Inscription, found in 1868 at Diban in Transjordan; also called the Moabite Stone. It was set up by King Mesha of Moab in the ninth century B.C., and contains the longest text in the Moabite dialect discovered till now.

The Sayings of Aḥiqar, a composition of the Wisdom genre preserved on eleven sheets of papyrus of the late fifth century B.C. Discovered in Elephantine in Upper Egypt in 1906–7, this composition in Aramaic contains both the story of the man Aḥiqar as well as his sayings.

Sefîre Inscriptions, long Aramaic inscriptions of the eighth century B.C., discovered in 1932 near Aleppo, Syria.

INTRODUCTION

The lively critical reaction to *Psalms I, 1–50* and *Psalms II, 51–100* (AB, vols. 16 and 17) belies the apologetic dictum of Saint Jerome that of all the gifts or graces bestowed by Heaven, that of the translator ranks lowest in the scale of importance. Modern scholars know better; they realize that the soundness of biblical theology and anthropology depends upon the soundness of the translation on which these disciplines are based. Try as we will, we cannot escape words, in themselves, or the subtle grammatical structures that build up sentences and paragraphs. "In theology," writes Stephen Neill,[1] "no one renders us more valuable service than the scholar who helps us understand the words better, who guides us through the subtleties of idiom, who heads us off from the blind alleys of false etymology or false interpretation of usage." Thus scholars are obliged to cast a critical eye upon a new translation of Psalms which upends current assumptions and urges a basic reorientation.

This volume trusts to have profited from the comments of critical reviewers; their questions have helped shape the following paragraphs. The Prophet announced that if two texts of the Koran appeared inconsistent, the later one was to be taken as authoritative. And I should wish the reader to apply the same principle when judging these volumes that were ten years a-borning. Some revisions presented below are necessitated by the author's faulty judgment in the past, and some arise from his failure to have adhered consistently to the enunciated canons of Northwest Semitic grammar.

Translating the Psalms

A statement of principles governing this version should logically have been presented in the Introduction to *Psalms I;* indeed, such was the original plan. Actual translation was preceded by the study of various

[1] *The Interpretation of the New Testament, 1861–1961: The Firth Lectures, 1962* (London, 1964), p. 335.

theories of translation, but it was not possible to apply any of these theories consistently. In fact, as the work progressed it became evident that the theoreticians, whatever experience they may have had translating other languages, had never tested their theories against Hebrew poetry. Thus it gradually became necessary to modify, if not to jettison completely, the received rules and techniques, and to work out in the psalms themselves some guiding principles of translation. Hence an explanation of the principles of translation had to be deferred.

Three centuries ago Dryden distinguished between paraphrase or "translation with latitude," and metaphrase or "turning an author word by word, and line by line, from one language into another." Current scholarship prefers to use the terms "formal" and "dynamic equivalence." Formal equivalence focuses attention on the message itself in both form and content. It seeks to reproduce the original source as faithfully as possible in terms of its formal elements, namely, grammatical constructions, consistency in word usage, difference of words in the target language when the original uses different words, etc. Thus formal equivalence would keep, say, John xii 26 in the active voice, *timēsei auton ho patēr,* "The Father will honor him," and not transmute it into passive "He will be honored by the Father," as read by *The New English Bible* (Oxford-Cambridge, 1961). Or again, formal equivalence would discountenance the transformation of the active voice in the first colon of Ps cxviii 22, *'eben mā'ᵃsū habbōnīm hāyᵉtāh lᵉrō'š pinnāh,* "The stone the builders rejected became the head of the corner," into the passive voice of *The Jerusalem Bible* [abbr. JB], "It was the stone rejected by the builders that proved to be the keystone."

In contrast, dynamic equivalence seeks to produce identity of thought without any attempt to retain the forms of the original. Its chief concern is to create in the contemporary reader a response as close as possible to that of the original reader. The trend over the past fifty years has been toward dynamic translations aiming at a complete naturalness of style, expressed in language that fits the cultural pattern of readers today. Recent exponents of dynamic equivalence include *The New English Bible* (New Testament) and JB (complete Bible).

Though the translation presented here differs sharply from traditional versions, it adheres, paradoxically, to the method of formal equivalence. In Dryden's terminology it might be called a metaphrase. Yet the differences result less from the theory of translation adopted than from different conceptions of Hebrew grammar and style. Since the grammar of Hebrew poetry is being rewritten in the light of emerging Northwest Semitic grammar,[2] it was deemed wise to propose a formally equivalent version, one that would permit the reader who understands some Hebrew to follow word by word this new translation which so frequently, and often radically, diverges from the well-known versions. For example, the Hebrew of Ps xxxii 5b reads, *'āmartī 'ōdeh ʿᵃlēy pᵉšāʿay layhwh,* rendered by *The Revised Standard Version* [abbr. RSV], "I said, 'I will confess my transgressions to the Lord,'" and by JB, "I said, 'I will go to Yahweh and confess my fault.'" Both make good sense, but are they fully faithful to the original? RSV, which normally follows the principles of formal equivalence, glosses over the serious difficulty posed by the Masoretic Text [abbr. MT] *ʿᵃlēy,* "upon," which is not reflected in RSV. Alive to the syntactic problem created by *ʿᵃlēy,* "upon," JB seeks to reproduce it, but at a price; it is obliged to bring in the verb "I will go," not found in the Hebrew, and then translates *ʿᵃlēy,* "to." The textual critic, however, who employs the new grammar constructed from the data of Ugaritic and Phoenician texts as well as from the Hebrew Bible, asks whether the consonants *ʿly* underlying MT *ʿalēy,* "upon," may not submit to another analysis. Cognizant that Canaanite poetry avoids otiose prepositions, he suspects the prepositional nature of *ʿly.* At the same time he turns to *Ugaritic Textbook* [abbr. UT], 126:III:5–6, *larṣ mṭr bʿl wlšd mṭr ʿly,* "For the earth was the rain of Baal, and for the field the rain of the Most High," where the parallelism between *bʿl,* "Baal," and *ʿly,* "the Most High," opens up the possibility that non-malleable *ʿᵃlēy,* "upon," might in reality be the divine appellative *ʿēlīy,* "the Most High." The Hebrew text would read:

'āmartī 'ōdeh ʿēlīy
pᵉšāʿay layhwh

I said, "I shall confess, O Most High,
my transgressions, O Yahweh!"

Once *ʿly,* "O Most High," is identified, the vocative function of *la* in *layhwh,* "O Yahweh!" comes to light. At the same time an interlocking verse emerges, revealing the composite divine name or binomial Most High Yahweh, here separated over the parallel cola. Thus the syntactic

[2] See the Appendix: THE GRAMMAR OF THE PSALTER; T. F. McDaniel, "Philological Studies in Lamentations," *Biblica* 49 (1968), 27–53, 199–220; H. J. van Dijk, EPT; Anton Blommerde, *Northwest Semitic Grammar and Job* (Rome, 1969); N. J. Tromp, *Primitive Conceptions of Death and the Nether World in the Old Testament* (cited hereafter as *Primitive Conceptions*) (Rome, 1969); W. A. van der Weiden, *Le Livre des Proverbes: Notes philologiques* (Rome, 1970).

problem posed by MT *ʿalēy,* "upon," appears solved, and the poetic flavor of the line is notably improved.

This version attempts to reflect in English the differences between the synonyms employed in Hebrew. Thus cxlvii 12, *šabbeḥī,* "Laud!" is balanced by *halelī,* "Praise!" but RSV renders both by "Praise!" leading the unsuspecting reader to believe that the psalmist repeated the same imperative twice. Ps cxxxix 2 reads *rēʿī,* "my thought(s)," whose counterweight at the end of the psalm (vs. 23) is the rare noun *śarʿappāy,* "my cares," or "my anxious thoughts." The Jewish Publication Society [abbr. JPS] version (1917) renders *rēʿī* as "my thought" and *śarʿappāy* as "my thoughts," creating the impression that the only difference between the two is number.

In some cases, however, the problems grow more complex. Hebrew possesses some two dozen words for the notion of sin; in English there are currently about a dozen. This means that the translator must reduce this wealth of Hebrew synonyms to half their number in English, forcing some of the former to give up their distinctive character. Hebrew is almost equally rich in words for "strong" and "strength"; if the translator tries to work out a one-to-one formula, he is obliged to mobilize words that were discharged from English centuries ago.

Nonetheless, the principle retains its validity in the formally equivalent approach to biblical translation. Thus its application to Ps lxvi 2, *śīmū,* parallel to *zammerū,* "Sing!" (Hebrew has many synonyms to express this action), produced, in view of its etymology, "Indite!" as the nearest English equivalent of *śīmū* (*Psalms II,* NOTE ad loc.). One can sympathize with the complaint of a reader who wrote to ask that this choice be reconsidered. Not many words of this kind, he observed, would be needed to spoil an otherwise good translation. His assumption was held by most English classical translators until a very short time ago. Their central and unquestioned tenet was that the convenience of readers came first, an honest adherence to the original a very poor second. In this version, which attempts to be as faithful (but not servile) to the original as English idiom permits, an uncommon word in Hebrew will normally be reproduced by an uncommon word in English. Hence the rare imperative *śīmū* is rendered "Indite!" One reviewer has questioned the wisdom of rendering Ps li 9, *teḥaṭṭeʾēnī,* "Unsin me," because "translations are not the place to coin new words like 'unsin.'" Yet if one accepts its parsing as a piel privative jussive verb, one will accept "Unsin me" as an excellent equivalent of the Hebrew form. What is more, "unsin" has existed in English since the middle of the seventeenth century. On grounds of unfamiliarity, an objection has been raised against *māgān,* "suzerain," but better-known cognates such as "king" and "ruler" have already been impressed to translate *melek* and *mōšēl,* and do not really answer to *māgān,* a special type of overlord whose character has been delineated by the publication and study of suzerainty treaties in recent decades. P. Reymond,[3] the editor of the French Ecumenical Bible, must therefore be commended for his decision to find separate synonyms for *ḥēn,* "grace, charm," *ḥesed,* "kindness," *raḥᵃmīm,* "compassion," and *'ᵃhābāh,* "love," all of which appear as "amour" in some French versions.

Where possible, the grammatical construction of the Hebrew has been carried over into English. For example, JB translates Ps cxlvii 20, *lō' 'āśāh kēn lᵉkol gōy ūmišpāṭīm bal yōdī'ūm* (MT *yᵉdā'ūm*), "He never does this for other nations, he never reveals his rulings to them," but *Psalms III* proposes "He has not dealt thus with any nation, / and has never taught them his ordinances." In the second colon the double accusative construction of the Hebrew is preserved, but JB chose a verb ("reveals") which does not govern two direct objects.

Poetry, again according to Coleridge, has its own logic with a reason assignable for the position of every word. Chiasmus, or diagonal word order, was surely one of the psalmists' preferred devices. This translation attempts to transmit this word order to the English reader. Thus the chiastic order of Ps cvii 32, *wīrōmᵉmūhū biqhal 'ām ūbᵉmōšab zᵉqēnīm yᵉhalᵉlūhū* is retained in "Let them extol him in the popular assembly, / and in the session of elders praise him." Contrast The King James Version [abbr. KJ], "Let them exalt him also in the congregation of the people, and praise him in the assembly of the elders." Similarly in Ps cix 30, *'ōdeh yhwh mā'ēd* (MT *mᵉ'ōd*) *bᵉpī ūbᵉtōk rabbīm 'ᵃhalᵉlennū,* "I will thank Yahweh the Grand with my mouth, / amid the aged will I praise him." In KJ the chiasmus is disregarded, "I will greatly praise the Lord with my mouth; yea, I will praise him among the multitude." A palpable difference can be felt when the translation mirrors the chiasmus of Ps xci 13, *'al šaḥal wāpeten tidrōk tirmōs kᵉpīr wᵉtannīn,* "On lion and adder you will tread / and trample young lion and serpent." Compare KJ, "Thou shalt tread upon the lion and adder: the young lion and the dragon shalt thou trample under feet."

[3] In HWFB, p. 238.

Relationships between Ugaritic and Hebrew

In his review of *Psalms I,* F. I. Andersen[4] remarked that many Old Testament scholars may not be prepared to accept the general presuppositions underlying many of these results. These volumes assume that Israelite poetry continues the poetic tradition of the Canaanites, borrowing Canaanite poetic techniques, parallelism, vocabulary, imagery etc. The psalms are translated with an eye more to the meaning given the words in an earlier period than to the sense attributed them by post-Exilic Jewish culture or by Christian interpretation. In this approach the ancient versions play a very minor role. Andersen correctly sensed the mood of some scholars, to judge from Samuel Terrien's[5] review of *Psalms II.* I quote Professor Terrien at some length because his opinion is shared by a number of Old Testament scholars: "To study the first-millenium Hebrew Psalms in the light of the second-millenium Ugaritic texts is a little as if a Patagonian translator in A.D. 2968 attempted to elucidate Shakespearean vocabulary and syntax in the light of the Beowulf epic, or Ezra Pound's convolutions with the help of the Piers Plowman. The comparison is unfair, of course, but it may suggest both the possibilities and the dangers involved in such a procedure. . . . Biblical Hebrew must be checked first with the help of rabbinical and mediaeval Hebraists (who were not as ignorant or misinformed as Dahood's general disregard of them implies), and then with all cognate forms and usages that are available in other Semitic languages, including especially Ugaritic, but not Ugaritic exclusively."

Two recent developments in ancient Near Eastern studies can, however, provide a better vantage point from which to view the supposed chronological gap between Ugaritic and Hebrew poetry that disquiets Professor Terrien. The facts are that the Ugaritic tablets date from *circa* 1375–1195 B.C., the earliest biblical poems belong to the period 1250–1100 B.C., and the vast majority of psalms may be ascribed to the period 1000–539 B.C. So the time differential between Ugaritic and Hebrew poetry should not be exaggerated.

During the past decade a number of articles and monographs have examined the rapports between the elements of prophetism found in the Mari texts of the eighteenth century B.C. and the prophetic movement in the Bible. The earliest references to biblical prophetism con-

[4] *Anglican Theological Review* 49 (1967), 98.
[5] *Union Seminary Quarterly Review* 33 (Summer 1968), 391.

cern Saul and Samuel (eleventh century B.C.), and the earliest prophetic book in the Bible is that of Amos (ca. 750 B.C.). Though there is an interval of seven hundred fifty to a thousand years, and though the Mari texts are written in a language different from Hebrew, Orientalists seem not to be disturbed by the chronological chasm, and no protests have yet been voiced against this procedure. In fact, the validity of these comparative studies is sustained by the growing recognition that prophetism was introduced from the west, that is, Syria-Canaan, into central Mesopotamia by the Amorites. For this institution in Mesopotamian culture there is no evidence before the Mari period. This basic insight into the origins of Mari prophetism accords with the proposition of the Assyriologist W. G. Lambert[6] that the recovery of the Ugaritic texts has shown that the allusions to Yahweh's battle with Leviathan and the *tannīn* are derived from Canaanite Baal myths,[7] which betray no signs of dependence on Mesopotamian sources. Accordingly, Lambert concludes, one of the main supports for assuming the dependence of Genesis has gone, and the whole question needs reconsideration. Yet not all Old Testament scholars have faced these facts.[8]

Another leading Assyriologist, A. Leo Oppenheim, the editor of *The Assyrian Dictionary* [abbr. CAD], writes in a similar vein[9]: "Whatever the native and alien components on the shore of the Mediterranean may have been, they exercised considerable influence toward the south, in Palestine, a region that was apparently only slightly touched by the radiations of Mesopotamian civilization. . . . While Mesopotamian influence on the Old Testament is either secondary (via Ugarit or other, still unknown, intermediaries) or accidental, the Old Testament itself serves as a vehicle for the transmission to the West of a number of literary concepts and cultural traits of Mesopotamian extraction." Oppenheim's distinction between "Ugarit or other, still unknown, intermediaries" is a valid one and may serve to handle the difficulty of the reviewer[10] of *Psalms I,* who writes, "To see him at work one would almost suppose that the psalms arose in the suburbs of fourteenth-century Ras Shamra." As Oppenheim has rightly observed, Ras Shamra happens to be the single Canaanite city which as yet has yielded up to archaeologists a substantial part of its literary treasures. If excavations were carried out on the Late Bronze (1500–

[6] See JTS 16 (1965), 290.
[7] Cf. M. H. Pope, *Job* (AB, vol. 15), NOTES on Job vii 12.
[8] See below the NOTES on Ps cxxxv 6.
[9] *Ancient Mesopotamia: Portrait of a Dead Civilization* (Chicago, 1964), pp. 72–73.
[10] John Stek in *Calvin Theological Journal* 2 (1967), 251.

1200 B.C.) or Early Iron (1200–1000 B.C.) levels of other prominent Canaanite coastal cities such as Byblos, Sidon, or Tyre, the probability is very great that the literary texts unearthed would be similar in language and content to the Ugaritic tablets. A careful examination of their contents reveals that the Ugaritic mythological texts were not composed in Ugarit (or its suburbs). Their more southern provenance is evidenced by references to the Lebanon, the Anti-Lebanon, Apheq, just north of Beirut, Tyre, Sidon, and Semachonitis (=Lake of Huleh in northern Galilee). Few would contest the conclusion of F. M. Th. De Liagre Böhl[11] regarding the Canaanite psalms that are fragmentarily quoted in the El Amarna Correspondence. De Liagre Böhl argues that when the scribes of Phoenicia quoted hymns and psalms in the El Amarna Letters, they were actually quoting native compositions. Why, he asks, should we deny to the southern Phoenicians a literary genre that precisely in this period reached the apex of its evolution among their northern neighbors of Ugarit?

The second recent development in Near Eastern studies that may help scholars assess the bearing of Ugaritic on biblical poetry concerns the lexical rapport between Ugaritic and Late Hebrew (i.e., post-Biblical and Mishnaic Hebrew).[12] The Ras Shamra tablets, especially those published during the past decade, contain a number of words with no biblical counterpart which do occur in Late Hebrew. Here the chronological chasm is about twelve to fifteen centuries. The following are some of the Ugaritic words not found in the Bible but which appear in Late Hebrew: *bnš bnny,* "middleman"; *gbṯt,* "humps (of animals)"; *ḥḏr,* "lettuce"; *ḫtr,* "to sift"; *ym prʿ,* "the first day"; *kmt,* "thus"; *mlg,* "dowry"; *spu,* "to feed, eat"; *pqr yḥd,* "overseer of the community"; *šḥlt,* "a certain vegetable"; *ššrt,* "chain (of gold)." Of particular interest is the short article entitled "Jerusalem—A City of Gold," published in 1967 by S. M. Paul[13] of the Jewish Theological Seminary in New York. In the Akkadian texts from Ras Shamra (published in 1955 by Jean Nougayrol) occurs the expression *âlu ḫurâṣu,* "a city of gold," weighing 215 shekels. It is found in an inventory of the trousseau of Queen Aḫatmilku of Ugarit. Nougayrol could translate the phrase but was at a loss to explain it, since it is not encountered elsewhere in the vast Akkadian literature preserved. Professor Paul, however, related the unique phrase to Rabbinic Hebrew *ʿīr šel zāhāb,* "a city of gold," the name of a piece of jewelry worn by women.

[11] Consult *Opera Minora* (Groningen, 1953), pp. 376, 517.

[12] Cf. B. A. Levine, *Ancient Survivals in Mishnaic Hebrew* (Brandeis University Dissertation; University Microfilms, 1964); UT, Glossary, *passim.*

[13] In IEJ 17 (1967), 259–63.

Despite the fifteen hundred years separating the two texts, the identification appears convincing.

We may close this discussion with a further example of lexical stability in the Canaanite milieu. In a Phoenician inscription from Kition in Cyprus occurs the sentence *mzbḥ 'z w'rwm 'šnm 'š ytn bd' khn ršp ḥṣ,* "this altar and two *'rwm* which BD', priest of Resheph *ḥṣ,* presented." Two of the terms are uncertain, namely, *'rwm* and *ḥṣ*. The meaning of the divine title *ršp ḥṣ* was clarified by the 1956 publication of a Ugaritic text with the expression *b'l ḥẓ ršp,* "Resheph the Archer"; hence Phoenician *ršp ḥṣ* probably means literally "Resheph of the Arrow." The sense of the other doubtful Phoenician word *'rwm* has recently been settled by the publication of the Ugaritic text, *pn arw d š'ly nrn l ršp gn,* "the lion's face which NRN erected to Resheph of the Garden." The Ugaritic association of *arw,* "lion," with Resheph urges that the two *'rwm* offered by the Cypriote priest of Resheph were also lions. That a fourth-century B.C. Phoenician inscription had to await the publication of fourteenth-century B.C. Ugaritic texts for clarification betokens a remarkable continuity of Canaanite religious terminology and practice which biblical scholars should not overlook when appraising Ugaritic-Hebrew relationships.

Poetic Techniques

From the attempt to translate the biblical psalms in view of their Northwest Semitic ambience rather than according to their interpretation by later tradition and the versions one must conclude that the Psalter contains extremely difficult poetry. In the summer of 1948, while I was a student at the University of Chicago, the late Professor Benno Landsberger asked me what was in my view the most difficult Semitic language. After some hesitation I replied, "Arabic," and gave my reasons. Landsberger disagreed; to my surprise, he said that he found biblical poetry, especially the Prophets, the most difficult. The lack of case endings that would serve to show the relationship between words, the compact construct chains that could express innumerable rapports between the construct and the genitive, the poetic vocabulary, and the highly elliptical character imposed by metrical considerations conspired to make biblical poetry the greatest challenge to Landsberger. At the time I was in no position to appreciate fully what he had in mind; today, I fully agree with him.

The poetry of the Psalter can be highly sophisticated, subtle, full of nuances. Often its conciseness results in ambiguity, and in some cases the ambiguity seems willed. All know that its dominant structural feature is parallelism, but the innumerable devices employed by the psalmists to ensure that the second colon would elaborate, not merely repeat, the thought of the first are still being discovered. The poets' consistency of metaphor and subtlety of wordplay bespeak a literary skill surprising in a people recently arrived from the desert and supposedly possessing only a rudimentary culture. The following five texts illustrate some of the psalmists' techniques.

In revised form (contrast *Psalms I,* ad loc.), Ps xlvi 2 reads:

'^{e}lōhīm lānū maḥseh (MT *maḥ^{a}seh*) *wā'ōz* (4 beats + 9 syllables)
'ezrāh b^{e}ṣārōt nimṣā' mā'ēd (MT *m^{e}'ōd*) (4 beats + 9 syllables)

God for us is refuge and stronghold,
liberator from sieges have we found the Grand.

When MT *maḥ^{a}seh,* "refuge," is repointed to the more frequent form *maḥseh,* the syllable count evens at 9:9, and if *mā'ēd,* "the Grand," is read for MT *m^{e}'ōd,* "much," there emerges an inclusion formed by the composite divine name *'^{e}lōhīm mā'ēd,* "God the Grand." The verse thus opens with "God" and closes with "Grand"; cf. Pss xxi 2, lviii 7, lxxvii 14. The word order is recognized as chiastic, following an A+B+C//Ć+B́+Á pattern (as in Ps vii 17), and the consistency of metaphor comes to light when the expression *'ezrāh b^{e}ṣārōt* is analyzed in the light of UT, 3 Aqht:rev.:14, *wy'ḏrk byd btlt* [*'nt*], "Or will he liberate you from the hand of the Virgin Anath?" The abstract Hebrew noun *'ezrāh,* "liberation," takes on a concrete meaning by reason of its parallelism with concrete "refuge and stronghold," while generic *ṣārōt,* "straits," becomes more specific "sieges" within the context of the military metaphor. Compare Prov iii 10 with its chiastic A+B+C//Ć+B́+Á sequence, its balancing abstract *śābā',* "satiety (=grain)," with concrete *tīrōš,* "wine," and its 10:10 syllable count.

Chiasmus, consistency of metaphor, and a composite divine name functioning as a double-duty modifier characterize Ps cix 14:

yizzākēr '^{a}wōn '^{a}bōtāyw (3 beats + 8 syllables)
'ēl (MT *'el*) *yhwh* (2 beats + 3 syllables)
w^{e}ḥaṭṭa't 'immō 'al timmāḥ (3 beats + 8 syllables)

Recorded be the iniquity of his father
by El Yahweh
And his mother's sin not be erased.

As will be noted in the body of the volume, the metaphorically ambivalent verb *yizzākēr* is rendered "Recorded be" by reason of its chiastic balance with *'al timmaḥ,* "not be erased," which describes the action of a bookkeeper. The formally plural noun *'^{a}bōtāyw,* "his father," parallel to singular *'immō,* "his mother," must accordingly be parsed as a plural of majesty with a singular meaning, a usage which this same noun exhibits in Phoenician.

Though Ugaritic serves to clarify numerous constructions, it also adds to the translator's problems. Thus the simply written consonant *l* may represent four different particles with different meanings. Three of these particles are illustrated by the translation and analysis proposed for Ps xxxi 3:

h^{e}yēh lī l^{e}ṣūr mā'ōz
l^{e}bēt m^{e}ṣūdōt l^{e}hōšī'ēnī

Be mine, O Mountain of Refuge!
O Fortified Citadel, save me!

Thus *lī* contains prepositional *l,* "mine"; *l^{e}ṣūr,* "O Mountain," and *l^{e}bēt m^{e}ṣūdōt,* "O Fortified Citadel," illustrate vocative *l,* while *l^{e}hōšī'ēnī,* "save me!" parses well when *l^{e}* is explained as emphatic *lamedh.*

The difficulty created by the elliptical nature of Hebrew poetry can be shown by Ps lxxxi 6b where four ordinary well-known words do not readily yield up their meaning:

ś^{e}pat lō' yāda'tī 'ešmā'

I heard the speech of one unknown to me.

Contrast RSV, "I heard a voice I had not known," JB, "I can hear a voice I no longer recognise," and LXX, "He caused him to hear a tongue which he knew not." These divergencies stem in large part from the poet's apparent omission of the relative pronoun after construct *ś^{e}pat,* "the speech of," and from his use of the *yqtl* form *'ešmā',* "I heard," to express an event of the past.

The concision permitted by the dative-suffix construction may account for the mispointing and consequent misunderstanding of Ps cii 17:

kī bānāh yhwh ṣiyyōn
nir'āhā (MT *nir'āh*) *bik^{e}bōdō*

When Yahweh builds Zion anew,
appears to her in his glory.

Proposals to insert in the second colon a prepositional phrase such as *b^{e}qirbāh,* "in her midst," or *'ālehā,* "over her," may prove superfluous with the recognition of the datival suffix of consonantal *nr'h;* the resultant 7:7 syllable count sustains the syntactic analysis.

From these random examples the textual method pursued in these volumes becomes evident. First and foremost is respect for the consonantal text. No more than eight consonantal changes are encountered in the NOTES to the one hundred and fifty psalms. But at once to maintain consonantal integrity and to elicit sense from the text, one must often cut free from the Masoretic vowels, most of which were inserted more than a millennium after the completion of the Psalter.[14] The notion that consonantal freedom exists inside the text is rather novel and difficult for many scholars, who would prefer the same consonants to mean the same thing everywhere. They are unwilling to concede that Hebrew, like all other languages and perhaps more than most, teems with ambiguities, due partly to the nature of the language and partly to the several methods of transcription employed during the long formation of the Hebrew text. Though the Masoretic points should not be dismissed out of hand, one must, for example, be duly suspicious of the innumerable instances of prepositons such as *'el,* "to," *'al* and *'ᵃlē,* "upon." As prepositions they often contribute little or nothing to the sense, being thus at odds with a fundamental quality of biblical (and Canaanite) poetry: concise intensity. When, however, these purported prepositions are revocalized, they are freighted with meaning; cf. the list of composite divine names given below, many of which have been recovered from purported prepositions. In many of these divine binomials one of the two components was camouflaged as a Masoretic preposition, such as *'el,* "to," which in reality should often be read *'ēl,* "El." When adverbial *mᵉ'ōd,* "much," is revoweled *mā'ēd* (Ugar. *mid,* "great, grand"), "the Grand One," the sense of numerous passages is sharply improved; cf., for example, Pss xxi 2, xlvi 2, xcii 6, xcvii 9, cix 30. Such reinterpretations can be controlled, not by improved sense alone, but by the other text-critical principles sketched in *Psalms II,* pp. XVII–XXII.

If progress in Northwest Semitic grammar and prosody entails some devaluation of the Masoretic vocalization, it considerably weakens the authority of the ancient versions, at least in the poetic books of the

[14] Thus E. Ullendorff, *Bulletin of the School of Oriental and African Studies* 32 (1969), 147, rightly criticizes James Barr, *Comparative Philology and the Text of the Old Testament* (Oxford, 1968), p. 221, who accords the Masoretic vocalization a status comparable to the consonantal or written text. Ullendorff observes that "not even the most complete chain of transmission and the most scrupulous attention to detail could have prevented very material alterations in the pronunciation of the text over a period of 1000–1500 years."

Bible.[15] Ugaritic, for instance, illustrates various senses of the preposition *l*, "to," "from," which are not normally appreciated by the versions of antiquity, and numerous cases of vocative and emphatic *lamedh*, "surely," go unrecognized. Emphatic *kī* finds no response in the versions; their grasp of the functions of the *yqtl* verb form is unsteady. The significance of the precative and energic modes was generally lost on them, and dative suffixes proved a constant source of embarrassment. (For a further catalogue, the interested reader can examine the phenomena classified under THE GRAMMAR OF THE PSALTER and compare the proposed translation with the versional understanding of the respective texts.[16])

With the appropriate changes, one may criticize the scribes of Qumran, whose understanding of poetic grammar seems comparable to that of the LXX. *Psalms III* frequently cites 11QPs[a] (published in 1965), but very rarely adopts its variant readings. Generally speaking, 11QPs[a] is distinctly inferior to the Hebrew consonantal text transmitted by MT. Thus at Ps cxlvii 20 the monks of Qumran changed consonantal *yd'wm*, "taught them," to *hwdy'm*, with the same meaning, evidently unaware that the *yqtl* verb could also express the past time of the *qtl* form *hwdy'm*. The suspicion that Qumran did not understand the past function of the *yqtl* form is borne out at Isa liii 7, *welō' yiptaḥ pīū*, "And he did not open his mouth." This statement, which clearly describes a past event, is repeated twice, but the second time the St. Mark's Isaiah scroll 1QIs[a] reads *ptḥ* for MT *yiptaḥ*. In Ps cxxxix 23 Qumran's two-syllabled reading *lby* (=*libbī*), "my heart," for three-syllabled MT *lebābī*, also "my heart," turns a 4:5::4:5 line into a less gainly 4:4::4:5 syllabic sequence. Though their reading *m'rṣ*, "from the earth," in Ps cxix 87 can be defended as correct, it must be judged less original than MT *bā'āreṣ*, "from the earth." W. F. Albright[17] has observed that there are many examples where the preposition *la* should be translated "from," and he notes that this meaning seems to have been forgotten by the time of the LXX. The same obtains regarding Qumran's understanding of *ba*, "from." Occasionally the sectarianism of the scribes of Qumran renders them untrustworthy, as in Ps cxxxiii 3, *kī šām ṣiwwāh yhwh 'et habberākāh*

[15] A recent illustration of versional limitations can be seen in the writer's note, "HDK in Job 40, 12," *Biblica* 49 (1968), 509–10, especially n. 3.

[16] P. Reymond in HWFB, p. 234, reports that the committee preparing the French Ecumenical Bible has decided to follow the Hebrew text closely, convinced that a reading based on the LXX, Vulgate, Syriac, or Targum can rarely lose its hypothetical character.

[17] In *Hebrew and Semitic Studies Presented to Godfrey Rolles Driver*, eds. D. W. Thomas and W. D. McHardy (Oxford, 1963), p. 2.

ḥayyīm ʿad hāʿōlām, "For there Yahweh confers the blessing—life for evermore." 11QPs[a] omits *ḥayyīm,* a clear reference to eternal life, and substitutes *šlwm ʿl yśrʾl,* "peace upon Israel."

However, the clash between Qumran and Northwest Semitic grammar is perhaps pinpointed best at Ps cxxxix 11, where MT presents the hapax legomenon preposition *baʿᵃdēnī,* "all round me," but 11QPs[a] offers the ordinary form *bʿdy,* with the same meaning. Which to choose? Witnessed in Ugar. *bʿdn,* "all round me," and being assonant with first-colon *yᵉšūpēnī,* "he observes me," MT *baʿᵃdēnī,* possesses the ring of originality, whereas *baʿᵃdī* betrays a scribe insensitive to cadences.

Conservative or Radical?

During the past half century the approach of scholars to the text of the Hebrew Old Testament has changed considerably. To supplant the earlier skepticism, which regarded much of the text as needing serious emendation, has arisen an increasing respect for it, coupled with the belief that many of its puzzles can be solved by an appeal to comparative philological evidence from allied languages and dialects. The recovery of Akkadian, Ugaritic, and Phoenician has greatly encouraged this procedure. While most biblical scholars welcome this change of attitude toward the Hebrew text, some are concerned that an increasing acceptance of this method is leading to excessive boldness in its use.

Though the treatment of some verses in the first two volumes may be censured for audacity, excessive caution may be blamed for the failure to elicit sense from many other verses. In Ps xxii 17b, for example, acceptance of the prevailing view produced the translation of *kʾry yāday wᵉraglāy,* "Piercing my hands and my feet." Properly studied within the framework of Northwest Semitic morphology, consonantal *kʾry* would have been analyzed into *kī,* "because," followed by *ʾry,* the third-person perfect plural with the final radical *-y* preserved, as in Ugaritic regularly and sporadically in Phoenician and Hebrew; the verb *ʾārāh,* "to pick, pluck," occurs in Song of Sol v 1 and, more significantly, in Ps lxxx 13, *ʾārūhā,* where it describes picking clean a vineyard. Thus Ps xxii 17b–18a would read:

> *kī ʾārᵉyū yāday wᵉraglāy*
> *ʾᵃsappēr kol ʿaṣmōtāy*

> **Because they picked clean my hands and my feet,**
> **I can number all my bones.**

This derivation from *'araya* further commends itself because of the allusion to vs. 14, *'aryēh ṭōrēp,* "a ravening lion," and to vs. 22, *pī 'aryēh,* "the lion's mouth." Moreover, the explicit identity in this translation of *yāday wᵉraglāy,* "my hands and my feet," and *kol 'aṣmōtāy,* "all my bones," reveals the former to be an example of merismus, that is, a twofold expression of totality.

The documentation at Ps xviii 28 of the root *'mm,* "to be strong," should have led to a recognition of this root in Ps xlvi 8 (also in vs. 12):

> *yhwh ṣᵉbā'ōt 'ammēnū* (MT *'immānū,* "with us")
> *miśgāb lānū 'ᵉlōhē ya'ᵃqōb*
>
> Yahweh of Hosts is our fortress,
> our stronghold is the God of Jacob.

H. J. van Dijk[18] has recognized from the inner parallelism, and one might add from the emergent chiasmus of the four components, that MT *'immānū,* "with us," in reality conceals a noun from *'mm,* "to be strong," comparable to *'ōz,* "fortress," from *'zz,* "to be strong."

The identification of *ḥokmōt,* "wisdom," as a Phoenician feminine singular form should have resulted in retaining MT *hāgūt* as a second Phoenician form in Ps xlix 4:

> *pī yᵉdabbēr ḥokmōt*
> *wᵉhāgūt libbī tᵉbūnōt*
>
> My mouth shall speak wisdom,
> and my throat[19] shall proclaim insight.

Psalms I, in the second NOTE ad loc., proposed the repointing of MT *hāgūt,* "shall proclaim," to classical infinitive absolute *hāgōt,* but failed to draw the correct inference from the presence of Phoen. *ḥokmōt,* "wisdom," and *tᵉbūnōt* "insight," both nouns with the Phoenician singular ending *-ōt.* Since in the Phoenician dialect *ō* is transmuted to *ū,* MT *hāgūt* can be parsed as an infinitive absolute of the class discussed in the second NOTE on Ps ciii 14.

In 1964 and again in 1965 the writer[20] proposed to read *hāribbāh* "Rain down!" for MT *harbeh* (Ketiv), "much," in Ps li 4, but caution overcame boldness in *Psalms II.* Since then C. Schedl,[21] W. H.

[18] EPT, p. 6.
[19] For this definition of *libbī,* see H. L. Ginsberg in HWFB, p. 80.
[20] In *Mélanges E. Tisserant* (Vatican City, 1964), I, p. 85; UHP, p. 51.
[21] *Psalmen im Rhythmus des Urtextes: Eine Auswahl* (Klosterneuburg, 1964), p. 80.

Irwin,[22] and L. Sabottka (oral communication) have expressed a preference for the earlier proposal, which may be adopted. At once a fine associate of *kabb^{e}sēnī,* "wash me," *hāribbāh,* "Rain down!" also forms an inclusion with a similar energic hiphil in vs. 20, *hēṭībāh,* "make beautiful."

In *Psalms I* and *Psalms II* considerable stress was laid on the need to recognize composite divine names that are often concealed by erroneous Masoretic pointing. A new example can be recovered in Ps xcii 6:

mah gād^{e}lū ma^{ʿa}śekā	(3 beats + 8 syllables)
yhwh mā'ēd (MT *m^{e}'ōd*)	(2 beats + 4 syllables)
'ām^{e}qū maḥš^{e}bōtekā	(3 beats + 8 syllables)

How great your works,
  Yahweh the Grand,
How deep your thoughts!

In this reconstruction the composite divine title *yhwh mā'ēd,* "Yahweh the Grand," is suspended as a double-duty vocative between the two longer cola and semantically looks to both, while the interjection *mah,* "How," extends its force from the first to the third colon, much as in Ps iii 2–3.

Verification of Proposals

In *Psalms II,* p. XXVII, the author wrote that increased interest in Ugaritic and its bearing on the Bible would hasten the ratification or rejection of new proposals based on data supplied by Northwest Semitic. Since that opinion was expressed, a new journal named *Ugarit-Forschungen* has been founded at Münster by O. Loretz and M. Dietrich. In California the Claremont Graduate School has announced a twelve-part Ugaritic-Hebrew parallels project that, when completed, will enable both Ugaritic specialists and Old Testament scholars to form a more adequate idea of the rapports existing between these two literatures.

The continual publication of new texts in Northwest Semitic dialects facilitates the testing of new proposals which cannot be controlled by means of direct biblical evidence. Thus the force of context, coupled with the awareness that Hebrew tended no less than Ugaritic to coin denominative verbs, prompted the repointing of nominal *kis'^{a}kā,*

[22] In CBQ 29 (1967), 35.

"your throne," in Ps xlv 7 to verbal *kissēʼᵃkā*, "has enthroned you." The proposal now appears less venturesome with the publication by A. Mahjoubi and M. H. Fantar[23] of a Punic text from Carthage containing the piel participle *hmksʼm*, probably denoting "chairmakers," though the editors also suggest "chair-merchants." For our discussion, however, the essential point is that we now have a non-biblical attestation of a denominative form based on *kissēʼ*, "throne." Some scholars have raised their eyebrows at the frequent appeal to the conditioned interchange between *b* and *p* sounds in Hebrew words with no change of meaning, but the validity of the appeal is upheld anew by the discovery of a Hebrew ostracon at Tell Arad in southern Palestine. In this inscription, from about 600 B.C., Biblical Hebrew *hipqīd*, "he commanded," is written *hbqyd*, with *b* instead of *p*, while the word for "your life" is written *nbškm* instead of *napšᵉkem*.[24]

The recognition of the composite divine name *ʼēl yhwh*, "El Yahweh" (the sequence *yhwh ʼēl*, "Yahweh El," is more frequent) in such texts as Pss xxxi 7, lxix 34, cix 14, led to its recognition in Ps xxii 28 and may well be present in difficult Ps xxii 9:

> *gōl ʼēl* (MT *ʼel*) *yhwh yᵉpallᵉṭēhū*
> *yaṣṣīlēhū kī ḥāpēṣ bō*
>
> Let El Yahweh rejoice to deliver him,
> let him rescue him since he delights in him.

Unexplained MT *gōl* may be retained and parsed as the precative perfect of *gīl*, "to rejoice"; the pronunciation *gōl* for classical Heb. *gāl* would reflect the Phoenician or Northern dialect in which long *a* was pronounced as long *o*. This proposal also sheds light on the crux in Prov xvi 3, which may be rendered, "If El Yahweh rejoices in your works, your plans will be realized."

The novel scansion of Ps xi 4a, "Yahweh—in the temple is his holy seat, / Yahweh—in the heavens is his throne," into an A+B+C// A+B́+Ć pattern no longer appears singular alongside Ps cxxxv 13, "Yahweh—your name is eternal, / Yahweh—your title is for all generations," a verse also scanning as A+B+C//A+B́+Ć.

The eschatological interpretation of Pss l 15, "I will rescue you and you will be feasted by me" (*tᵉkubbᵉdēnī*), and xci 15, " . . . will I rescue him and I will feast him" (*ʼᵃkabbᵉdēhū*), is borne out by New Testament usage. The recognition that the verb which literally means

[23] *Atti dell' Accademia Nazionale dei Lincei, Rendiconti della classe di scienze morali, storiche e filologiche* 21 (1966), 207.

[24] For fuller discussion, consult *Biblica* 50 (1969), 75, and Y. Aharoni, *Eretz-Israel* 9 (1969), 11.

"to honor" also pregnantly signifies "to honor with a feast" on the other side of the grave affects the exegesis of John xii 26, a passage dealing with eternal life: "If anyone would serve me, let him follow me; and where I am, my servant will also be. Whoever serves me, the Father will honor him." The Greek verb *timēsei,* "will honor," reflects Heb. *yᵉkabbēd* in its pregnant sense "he will feast." New Testament scholars[25] have been unable to pinpoint the meaning of *timēsei,* but since the preceding verse (xii 25) explicitly discusses *zōēn aiōnion,* "eternal life," *timēsei* evidently refers to the celestial banquet. It may further be noted that modern translations of the New Testament into Hebrew reproduce *timēsei* by *yᵉkabbēd.*

The Dating of the Psalms

Since the introductory Notes to each psalm discuss the date of composition (where there is some tangible evidence), the present consideration is limited to the general impact of Northwest Semitic studies on the question of dating the psalms. The earlier judgment (*Psalms I,* p. xxx) that most of the psalms are pre-Exilic, and that some may have been composed in the Davidic period, is corroborated by new evidence deriving from the textual study of the last hundred psalms. This view contrasts in part with the position of Richard S. Hanson (to cite but one recent work), *The Psalms in Modern Speech: For Public and Private Use* [abbr. PMS] I, p. xxvii, who writes, "There are psalms which quite likely go back, in their original form at least, to the time of the united kingdom if not earlier and there are psalms from as late as the third or second century B.C."

What virtually rules out a third–second century date is the increasing disparity, created by progress in Northwest Semitic, between the meaning of the Hebrew psalms and their comprehension by the LXX, whose translation of the psalms was prepared in precisely the third–second century B.C. When the supposedly late psalms are translated in the light of Northwest Semitic, the number of differences between the new translation and the LXX appreciably increases. This means that these psalms were composed in a period employing poetic techniques that were no longer appreciated. Had they been composed contemporaneously with the LXX, these psalms would not have presented so many features incomprehensible to the translators of the LXX. For example, scholars widely agree that Ps cxxviii is a late

[25] Cf. R. E. Brown, *The Gospel According to John, i–xii* (AB, vol. 29, 1966), p. 467.

composition, yet vs. 2a reads, *yᵉgīaʿ kappekā kī tō'kal,* "The toil of your hands indeed shall you eat." In this statement the particle *kī* parses as the emphatic particle which forces the verb *tō'kēl,* "shall you eat," to the end of the clause; this usage was first recognized in the Bible with the publication of Ugaritic texts exhibiting this usage. In our passage, however, *kī,* "indeed," finds no equivalent in the LXX translation. Is this omission due to the translator's incompetence or to the fact that he worked in a period when such poetic niceties were long forgotten? The manifold evidence registered in the NOTES points to the latter conclusion. To be sure, one may hazard the opinion that the psalmist was indulging in post-Exilic archaizing, but then it becomes difficult to explain why so many archaizing usages were lost upon the contemporary translators of the LXX.

To appreciate the full force of this argument, one must couple it with an assessment of how familiar the Qumranic community was with the poetic elements found in the Hebrew Psalter. This evaluation is based both on original compositions of the monks of Qumran, namely, the Hodayot or Psalms of Thanksgiving, which belong to the second–first centuries B.C., and on their copies of biblical psalms. A study of both sources must conclude that a considerable period of time had elapsed between the composition of the latest canonical psalms and of the Hodayot and the copying of the canonical psalms by the monks at Qumran. Though parallelism, for example, still characterizes the Hodayot, the conciseness and intensity which marks the biblical psalms is largely missing. The numerous interlocking devices by which the canonical poets melded the members of the parallel cola seem to have been unknown to the men of Qumran. Thus one does not find double-duty suffixes, double-duty modifiers, double-duty prepositions and negatives, devices all designed to create tension, concision, and poetic strength; alongside the biblical psalms, the Qumran hymns appear prolix and sluggish. The *qtl–yqtl* verbal sequence, a rich source of stylistic variety in the Psalter, and the pairing of imperatives with jussive and precative forms do not characterize Qumranic style. The frequent recurrence of the poetic breakup of stereotyped phrases and composite divine names sharply distinguishes the Psalter from Qumranic compositions. To account for these differences of style and taste one must, it seems, posit a wide chronological gap between the two collections of poems. Since both originate in Palestine, cultural differences hardly account for the sharp differences in structure and manner of composition.

An examination of the biblical psalms or fragments of psalms preserved in the scrolls from Qumran sustains this conclusion. For example, biblical psalmists rendered their verses more direct and graphic by the use of the vocative *lamedh,* but in Ps cxxii 4, supposedly a late poem, *'ēdūt lᵉyiśrā'ēl lᵉhōdōt lᵉšēm yhwh,* "It is a decree, O Israel, to give thanks to Yahweh's name," the monks of Qumran omitted the vocative *lamedh,* reading simply *yśr'l* for MT *lᵉyiśrā'ēl,* "O Israel!" Evidently they did not grasp its function and accordingly dropped it from their text. Similarly in Ps cxxiii 1, no trace of the genitive ending of MT *hayyōšᵉbī,* "who are enthroned," appears in 11QPs[a] *hywšb.* A good idea of Qumranic limitations vis-à-vis biblical prosody can be gained from Ps cxxxix 23, where their substitution of bisyllabic *lby* (=*libbī*), "my heart," for MT trisyllabic *lᵉbābī,* also "my heart," results in a 4:4::4:5 syllable count, destroying the preferable MT 4:5::4:5 sequence.

This strong argument against late dating is positively supported by the identification of many psalms as royal (hence pre-Exilic) in character through a more precise translation on the basis of Northwest Semitic data; consult, for example, the introductory NOTES to Pss liv, lvi, lvii, lix, lxi, cxviii, cxxvii, cxxxviii. Again, it has been argued that those psalms, such as xxvii 4 and xxviii 2, which imply the existence of a temple, cannot belong to the Davidic period because the first temple was not built until the reign of Solomon. The Ugaritic use of *bt* or *hkl* to designate the celestial temple of the gods reveals that biblical *bēt,* "temple," often refers to the heavenly temple, so that its presence in a psalm does not *ipso facto* brand the poem as post-Davidic.

The Northwest Semitic data which accentuate the literary differences between the biblical psalms and those of Qumran seem to preclude a late date of composition (i.e., after the sixth century B.C.) for the biblical Psalter. Do these data permit a more precise dating within the earlier period (i.e., between the eleventh and sixth centuries B.C.)? For many years W. F. Albright[26] has championed the view that, just as a literary revival and interest in earlier institutions flourished during the Saite Dynasty in Egypt (660–525 B.C.) and among the Neo-Assyrian and Neo-Babylonian rulers in Mesopotamia, so a similar revival of interest in the past grew up in Phoenicia at about the same time. On this hypothesis he sought to account for the flood of allusions to Canaanite-Phoenician literature in Job, Proverbs, Isaiah (the Exilic sections and Deutero-Isaiah), Ezekiel, Habakkuk, the Song of Songs, and Ecclesiastes, works presumably composed between the seventh and third centuries B.C.[27] Albright's opinion has gained considerable currency

26 *From the Stone Age to Christianity* (Baltimore, 1940), pp. 241–44.

27 Albright's latest views on the dating of Job (seventh century) and Ecclesiastes (fifth century) can be found in his volume YGC, pp. 258–59.

in recent years,[28] but advances in comparative literary studies suggest that it may have been too narrowly based. It is increasingly evident that the eighth-century prophets Isaiah, Hosea, Amos, and Micah were quite familiar with Canaanite literature and poetic devices, so that this criterion loses some of its value for purposes of dating. Words, images, and constructions that were once considered to be typically Canaanite, appear throughout the five Books of the Psalter and, generally speaking, are rather evenly distributed.

This amounts to saying that what was once labeled Canaanite or Phoenician influence is more correctly described as natively Hebraic but elucidated chiefly by Ugaritic and Phoenician discoveries. These elements clarified by Northwest Semitic studies actually form part of Hebrew language and literature and should not ordinarily be termed "borrowings"; cf. *Psalms II,* pp. XV–XVI. Hence the rather even distribution throughout the Psalter of elements formerly thought by scholars to be Canaanisms, deprives us of a criterion for dating psalms more precisely within the period spanning the eleventh–sixth centuries B.C.

Nor can Aramaisms any longer be used indiscriminately as proof for a late date. The gradual chronological extension of the Aramaic corpus of inscriptions renders more hazardous a post-Exilic dating of psalms that contain typically Aramaic roots. Thus the occurrence of *slq,* "to ascend," in the mid-eighth-century Aramaic Inscription of Sefîre urges caution against assigning Ps cxxxix to the post-Exilic period simply because vs. 8 witnesses this verb. The customary comments on Ps cxlvi 4 *'eštōnōtāyw,* "his projects," which identify this word with an Aramaic and Late Hebrew root, must now take cognizance of this root in the Sefîre Inscription, as well as in the Sayings of Aḥiqar which, though preserved on late fifth-century B.C. sheets of papyrus, contain older material.

LITERARY GENUS AND SITZ IM LEBEN

As observed in *Psalms I,* p. XXXII, the absence of psalms among the published texts from Ras Shamra limits their direct contribution to the problems of literary genus and situation in life of the biblical psalms. Since Gunkel these questions have overshadowed purely philological considerations. The important commentaries of the past two generations have thus concentrated on trying to classify the individual psalms and to fix their place in the cult. As a result, the philological

[28] Cf. R. Tournay, RB 70 (1963), 591–92, with bibliography.

treatment of the text has been, generally speaking, quite perfunctory. Hence the predominantly philological bent of the present volumes, imposed by the need to profit from the grammatical and lexical riches presented by the Ugaritic tablets, may serve as an antidote to some recent speculations. What emerges from the philological approach to the text is the impression that many recent proposals regarding literary genus and the reconstruction of the *Sitz im Leben* have not been based on a firsthand control of the Hebrew text.

The study of the Hebrew text within the milieu of Northwest Semitic contributes little directly to the speculative reconstruction of the cultic setting in which the psalms are supposed to have arisen. It does, however, advance our knowledge of their literary classification at a number of points. Sometimes it provides a subtler appreciation of the accepted classification of a particular psalm, and not infrequently it calls for a reclassification. Further particulars can be found in the introductory NOTE to each psalm. Here one may single out the principal contribution made by the philological method.

Scholars generally classify eleven psalms as royal, that is, psalms sung on festive occasions for or in honor of the king and the royal house. These are ii, xviii, xx, xxi, xlv, lxxii, lxxxix, ci, cx, cxxxii, cxliv. To this list the following may now be added: iii, xxii, xxvii (though not yet recognized in *Psalms I*), xli (possibly), liv, lvii, lix, lxi, lxiii, lxxxvi, xci, xcii, cii, cxxvii, cxxx, cxxxviii, cxliii.

Some of the verbal clues that help identify these psalms as royal are: *šēm,* "name"; *'ānāh,* "to conquer"; *'ebed,* "servant"; *ḥesed we'ᵉmet,* "kindness and fidelity"; *'ᵃdōnay,* "my Lord"; *kābōd,* "glory"; *māgān,* "Suzerain" (divine title); *ṣūrī,* "My Mountain"; *nāgīd,* "Leader" (divine title); the composite divine name *yhwh 'elyōn,* "Yahweh Most High"; the parallelism of *ṣārāh,* "my adversaries," and *'ōyᵉbay,* "my foes"; *yāmīn,* "right hand." In several of these psalms (xxii 28, lxxxvi 9, cii 16, 23, cxxxviii 4) the note of universalism coheres with the phrasal evidence to strengthen the royal classification.

BIBLICAL THEOLOGY

The psalmists' conception of God and his attributes clearly appears in the titles they employ to describe him. What Northwest Semitic philology contributes to this branch of biblical theology can be gauged from the following list of composite divine names:

'ēl 'elōhīm "The God of gods"

Jointly: Ps l 1 and in Pss lxii 2, lxxvii 2(bis), lxxxiv 8, where the MT reads *'el-'elōhīm*

Separated: Pss lix 10 *'ēli kī* (MT *'ēlēkā*) // *'elōhīm,* lxii 11–12 *kī yānūb 'ēl* (MT *'al* // *'aḥat dibber 'elōhīm,* cxviii 28 *'ēlī* // *'elōhay*

'elōhīm 'ēl "God El"

Separated: Ps xliii 4 *'elōhīm* // *'ēl*

'ēl yhwh "El Yahweh"

Jointly: Ps cxviii 27 and in Pss xxii 9, 28, xxxi 7, cix 14; in all these verses MT reads *'el-yhwh*

Separated: Pss xviii 31 *hā'ēl* // *yhwh,* lxviii 21 *hā'ēl* // *wlyhwh,* lxix 34 *'ēl* (MT *'el*) // *yhwh,* lxxxv 9 *mah yedabbēr hā'ēl* // *yhwh kī yedabbēr šālōm*

yhwh 'ēl "Yahweh God"

Jointly: Pss x 12, xxxi 6

Separated: Pss xviii 3 *yhwh* // *'ēlī,* xxix 3 *qōl yhwh* // *'ēl hakkābōd,* xxxix 13 *šim'āh tepillātī yhwh* // *wešaw'ātī ha'azīnāh 'ēl* (MT *'el*), cii 24 *yhwh* (transferred from the preceding verse) // *'ēlī,* cxli 8 *kī 'ēlēkā yhwh* // *bekāh ḥāsītī 'ēl* (MT *'al*), cxliii 1 *yhwh šema' tepillātī* // *ha'azīnāḥ 'ēl* (MT *'el*) *taḥanūnay,* 7 *yhwh* // *'ēl* (MT *'al*), 9 *yhwh* // *'ēlī kī kussētī* (MT *'ēlēkā kissītī*)

'ēl 'elyōn "The Most High God"

Jointly: Gen xiv 18–20, 22; Ps lxxviii 35

Separated: Pss lxxiii 11 *'ēl* // *'elyōn,* lxxvii 10–11 *'ēl . . . 'elyōn,* lxxviii 17–18 *'elyōn . . . 'ēl,* cvii 11 *'ēl* // *'elyōn*

'elōhīm 'elyōn "God Most High"

Jointly: Ps lvii 3

Separated: Pss xlvi 5, lxxviii 56, *'elōhīm* // *'elyōn*

yhwh 'elyōn "Yahweh Most High"

Jointly: Pss vii 18, xlvii 3

Separated: *yhwh* // *'elyōn* in Pss xviii 14, xxi 8, xci 9, xcii 2

'al yhwh "The Most High Yahweh"

Jointly: Pss xviii 42 // *mōšīa',* lv 23, cxlvi 5

Separated: *yhwh* // *'al* in Pss cxxi 5, cxli 3

'al 'elōhīm "The Most High God"

Jointly: Pss vii 11, lxii 8 // *kebōdī,* "my Glorious One"

'ēlī 'elōhīm "God Most High"

Jointly: Ps lvi 13 (MT *'ālay*)

ʿēlī yhwh "Most High Yahweh"
  Separated: *ēlī // yhwh* in Ps xxxii 5 (MT *ʿ^{a}lē*)
    yhwh // ʿēlī (MT *ʿālāy*) in Pss vii 9, xiii 6, xvi 5–6

ʿēlī šadday "Most High Shaddai"
  Separated: Ps xxxii 4 *ʿēlī* (MT *ʿālay*) // *l^{e}šadday* (MT *l^{e}šaddī*)

ʿelyōn šadday "Most High Shaddai"
  Separated: Ps xci 1 *ʿelyōn // šadday*

yhwh mā'ēd "Yahweh the Grand"
  Jointly: Pss xcii 6, cix 30 (MT *m^{e}'ōd*)
  Separated: *yhwh // mā'ēd* (MT *m^{e}'ōd*) in Pss xxi 2, xlviii 2, xcvi 4, xcvii 9, cxlv 3

'ēl mā'ēd "El the Grand"
  Separated: Ps cxlii 7 *'ēl* (MT *'el*) // *mā'ēd* (MT *m^{e}'ōd*)

'^{e}lōhīm mā'ēd "God the Grand"
  Separated: *'^{e}lōhīm // mā'ēd* (MT *m^{e}'ōd*) Pss xlvi 2 (revised translation), lxxviii 59 (revised translation)

ṣaddīq mā'ēd "The Just Grand One"
  Separated: *ṣaddīq* (MT *ṣedeq*) // *mā'ēd* (MT *m^{e}'ōd*) in Ps cxix 138

yhwh '^{a}dōnāy "Yahweh my Lord"
  Jointly: Pss lxviii 21, cix 21, cxl 8, cxli 8
  Separated: *yhwh // '^{a}dōnēnū* in Ps cxxxv 5
    'adōnāy // yhwh in Ps lxxi 5, 16

yhwh '^{e}lōhīm "Yahweh God"
  Jointly: Pss lxxii 18, cix 26, cxxiii 2
  Separated: Ps cxxxv 2 *yhwh // '^{e}lōhēnū*,
    '^{e}lōhīm // yhwh in Pss xlvii 6, lv 17, lviii 7

yhwh yārūmū "Yahweh the Exalted"
  Separated: Ps cxl 9 *yhwh // yārūmū*

yhwh maḥsī "Yahweh my refuge"
  Jointly: Ps xiv 6, xci 9
  Separated: Ps cxlii 6 *yhwh // maḥsī*

yhwh ʿōzēr "Yahweh the Helper"
  Separated: Ps xxx 11 *yhwh // ʿōzēr*

'^{e}lōhīm ʿōzēr "God the Helper" (revised translation)
  Jointly: Ps liv 6

yhwh ʿōlām "Yahweh the Eternal"
Separated: Pss xxxi 2=lxxi 1 *yhwh // leʿōlām*, cx 4
yhwh // leʿōlām

ʾēl qedem "El the Primeval" (cf. Prov viii 22; M. Dahood, CBQ 30 [1968], 513–14)
Separated: *ʾēl // qedem* Ps lv 20

melek ʿōlām wāʿed "The Eternal and Everlasting King"
Jointly: Ps x 16
Separated: Ps cxlv 1 *hammelek // leʿōlām wāʿed*,
"O King // O Eternal and Everlasting"

ṣaddīq weyāšār "The Just and Upright One"
Jointly: Deut xxxii 4
Separated: Pss xi 7 *ṣaddīq // yāšār*, cxix 137 *ṣaddīq // weyāšār*

Death, Resurrection, and Immortality

Psalms I, p. XXXVI, remarks that the psalmists gave much more thought to the problem of death and the afterlife than earlier commentators could have suspected. The psalmists' preoccupation with death becomes evident from the numerous names of the nether world in the Psalter, some of which are first identified in this commentary or in the recently published study of Nicholas J. Tromp, *Primitive Conceptions of Death and the Nether World in the Old Testament* (Rome, 1969). Since the latter is a systematic treatment of the subject, there is no need to review the evidence here. Moreover, the Index of Subjects in *Psalms III* will help the interested reader locate the pertinent texts and interpretations.

None of the many and vigorous reactions of scholars to *Psalms I* and *Psalms II* has been more spirited than their reaction to my insistence that a deep and steady belief in resurrection and immortality permeates the Psalter. Thus B. K. Waltke comments in the conservative *Bibliotheca Sacra*[29]: "The most shocking result of the writer's approach is its effect upon the theology of the Psalms. He writes: 'Perhaps the most significant contribution to biblical theology that flows from the translation based on the new philological principles concerns the subject of resurrection and immortality. . . . The opinion of Sigmund Mowinckel that neither Israel nor early Judaism knew of a faith in any resurrection nor is such a faith represented in the Psalms will not survive serious scrutiny.' However, it seems that the author is too zealous in this regard, for even now Psalm 1:3 and Psalm 23:2

[29] Volume 123 (1966), 176.

have reference to the Elysian Fields along with a score of other passages." For R. Doermann,[30] "One of the most startling suggestions set forth by Dr. Dahood is that the psalms are full of references to resurrection and immortality. On the basis of the mythological motif of the Elysian Fields in Ugaritic texts, the word 'life' is rendered 'eternal life' in Pss 16:11; 27:13, and 'upon waking' is translated 'at the resurrection' in Ps 17:15. One wonders if the existence of parallels is sufficient warrant for translations of this kind." Finally, S. Sandmel[31] comments on *Psalms I:* "I have personally suspected that there has been something wrong in the interpretation of Scripture which has assumed that immortality or resurrection awaited the very late post-exilic period to be expressed, and I am not startled by Dahood's statement that after-life is demanded by the context. What I am puzzled by is the absence of any significant excursus by him in the book to justify this remarkable shift in scholarly appraisal. He touches on the matter, as one can see from the Index, in the words Afterlife, Immortality, and Resurrection. But I am aghast at his procedure in handling the matter only by dismissing as 'incapable of surviving serious scrutiny' the judgment of Mowinckel that 'neither Israel nor Judaism knew of a faith in any resurrection or such a faith represented in the Psalms.' "[32]

As may be seen from the last citation, prevailing psalms scholarship does not concede to early Israel a belief in resurrection and immortality. To go back no further than the beginning of this century, the conservative commentary of A. F. Kirkpatrick[33] maintained that only four psalms (xvi, xvii, xlix, lxxiii) might be considered as possibly

[30] *The Lutheran Quarterly,* August 1966, p. 279.

[31] *Central Conference of American Rabbis* 15, No. 2 (April 1968), 90.

[32] The prevailing consensus that late Judaism in general entertained no hopes for a continued existence beyond the grave is now being questioned. Cf. M. F. Thelen, "Jewish Symbols and 'Normative' Judaism," in JBL 83 (1964), 361–63, who concludes from the symbolism on the tombs and in the synagogues that the Jews shared the pervasive longing for immortal life after death or for mystical experience (as with Philo), while having faith that these desires were to be realized through the religion of the Torah; W. Wirgin, "The *Menorah* as Symbol of After-Life," in IEJ 14 (1964), 102–4, maintains that "it would be inaccurate to think that Judaism places little stress on a future life, as has been sometimes asserted with regard to the Jews buried in the catacombs. Interest in a future life is particularly evident in those representations in which the Menorah was intended to symbolize the continuation of life after death."

[33] *The Book of Psalms* (Cambridge, 1903), p. xcv. It seems ironic that while Kirkpatrick warns against reading Christian ideas back into the Psalter, M. Himmelfarb in *Commentary,* February 1968, p. 75, cautions against reading Canaanite concepts of immortality into the Old Testament. Is one to conclude that Himmelfarb considers the Israelites inferior to the Late Bronze Age Canaanites (ca. 1500–1200 B.C.) in this regard?

expressing this belief. Even about these Kirkpatrick had reservations because "reading these passages in the light of fuller revelation we may easily assign to them a more precise meaning than their original authors and hearers understood. They adapt themselves so readily to Christian hope that we are easily led to believe that it was there from the first." The present commentary runs no such risk, seeking as it does to elucidate the meaning of Hebrew terms in view of the earlier Ugaritic pagan usage. Some reviewers of *Psalms I* and *Psalms II* have in fact lamented this avoidance of New Testament references as a weakness in the discussion of immortality there. Had not J. Hempel flatly stated in 1961 in the authoritative *Interpreter's Dictionary of the Bible* [abbr. IDB], III, p. 951, that the aim of the laments in the Psalter is "liberation from the cruelties of this life, health, strength, freedom from persecution by enemies, grace of his God, but never (except perhaps the two uncertain cases in Pss. 49:15; 73:24) salvation after death"? Had not J. H. Eaton assured us in his 1967 commentary on Psalms,[34] "But for most of their course, the Old Testament people had to suffer and trust without a hope of future life for themselves, apart from a continuation in their descendants. The religion that was thus forged was marked by an urgent seriousness about life on this earth"? Against this background the lively reaction to my insistence on the concept of a future life in the Psalter may be understood.

Before citing the relevant texts from the Psalter, it may be useful to examine the attitudes and methods of scholars vis-à-vis the question of afterlife as revealed by their treatment of three texts in Proverbs. The first is Prov xiv 32:

b^erā'ātō yiddāḥēh rāšā'
w^eḥōseh b^emōtō ṣaddīq

For his evil the wicked will be flung headlong,
but at his death the just man will find refuge.

This appears to be the plain meaning of the text, but many scholars refuse to accept its implications. Thus C. H. Toy[35] writes: "This, however, is but another way of saying that they had the hope of immortal life. We must either suppose that Proverbs here announces a doctrine which is ignored in the rest of the book, or we must recognize an erroneous reading in the Hebrew text. A slight change gives the reading of the Greek." Here the LXX probably reads *b^etummō,* "in his

[34] *Psalms: Introduction and Commentary* (Torch Bible Commentaries; London, 1967), p. 40.

[35] *A Critical and Exegetical Commentary on the Book of Proverbs* (ICC; Edinburgh, 1904), p. 300.

integrity," for MT *bᵉmōtō*, "at his death." W. O. E. Oesterley,[36] when commenting on Heb. *bᵉmōtō*, "at his death," expresses the same opinion: "This cannot be right, as it would imply hope in a future life, and such a hope had not yet come into existence in Israel." The latest Hebrew lexicon, the *Hebräisches und aramäisches Lexikon zum Alten Testament* [abb. HALAT], by W. Baumgartner (Leiden, 1967), I, p. 324a, likewise emends MT *bᵉmōtō* to LXX *bᵉtummō*. However, MT *bᵉmōtō*, "at his death," will no longer submit to emendation because of the recognition that first-colon *yiddāḥeh*, "will be flung headlong," is used pregnantly in a number of texts cited at Ps lvi 14 to denote flinging into the nether world. In biblical usage this verb has eschatological overtones which make it an apt parallel to *ḥōseh bᵉmōtō*, "at his death . . . will find refuge." Toy's statement above that the doctrine of immortality is not encountered elsewhere in Proverbs ignores the correct understanding of Prov xii 28, cited in *Psalms II*, p. XXVII, and when R. B. Y. Scott[37] correctly renders Prov xii 28, "On the road of righteousness there is life, / And the treading of its path is deathlessness," he shows little consistency when altering *bᵉmōtō*, "at his death," to *bᵉtummō*, "in his innocence," in xiv 32.

Scholars resort to similar expedients to explain away the implications of Prov xvi 2:

> *kol dᵉrākēy* (MT *darkē*) *'īš zak bᵉ'ēnāyw*
> *wᵉtōken rūḥōt yhwh*

> In all his ways a man is pure in his own eyes,
> but the weigher of spirits is Yahweh.

R. N. Whybray[38] comments on this verse: "While the statement in Prov 16.2 that 'Yahweh weigheth the spirits' probably shows that the author was familiar with the Egyptian belief that a man's heart is weighed before Osiris at the judgment after death, the Egyptian doctrine of the after-life, which was a very prominent feature of Egyptian religious belief and appears fairly frequently in Egyptian wisdom literature, has no place in Proverbs with this single exception, which may be a slip." Of course, it is nothing of the sort because Prov xxi 2 and xxiv 12 attest *tōkēn libbōt*, "the weigher of hearts," in similar contexts. It would strain credulity to maintain that all three texts are slips.

36 *The Book of Proverbs: With Introduction and Notes* (London, 1929), p. 116.

37 *Proverbs • Ecclesiastes* (AB, vol. 18, 1965), ad loc.

38 *Wisdom in Proverbs: The Concept of Wisdom in Proverbs 1–9* (London, 1965), p. 24.

The third text illustrating ancient and modern methods is Prov xv 24:

> *'ōraḥ ḥayyīm l^ema'lāh l^emaśkīl*
> *l^ema'an sūr miššᵉ'ōl l^emaṭṭāh* (MT *maṭṭāh*)
>
> The path of life eternal is upward for the prudent,
> thus escaping Sheol below.

Once again, the commentary of Oesterley[39] clearly exposes both the problem and the method chosen to burke the consequences of the plain meaning of the text. He writes, "As this verse stands it is difficult to get away from the impression that 'upward' and 'beneath' imply a somewhat advanced conception of the hereafter; but *Proverbs,* and especially this earlier collection, nowhere contains a developed conception[40] of this kind; hence the efforts of commentators to explain away what these expressions seem to imply. The probability, however, is that these two words do not belong to the original text, but were added later when more developed ideas regarding the future life had arisen. The two lines are each quite long enough without these words, which do not occur in the Septuagint." As was noted above in connection with Prov xiv 32, the LXX betrayed a certain tendentiousness, so it would be ill-advised to appeal to its omission of two embarrassing phrases here. Our reading *l^emaṭṭāh,* "below," for MT *maṭṭāh* with the same meaning, assumes that the final *l* of *šᵉ'ōl* was meant to be shared by the next word. With this reading the syllable count evens at 10:10. On shared consonants in Hebrew, see Wilfred Watson, *Biblica* 50 (1969), 525–33.

These examples should suffice to show how preconceptions can prevent scholars from grasping the obvious meaning of a text. They may likewise enable the non-professional reader to understand why psalms scholarship has been slow to recognize the belief in resurrection and immortality which the present commentary would identify in some forty texts.[41] Hence it may not be amiss to cite here the more important

[39] *The Book of Proverbs,* p. 123.

[40] Oesterley, like Brown cited in note 41, is impaled on the assumption that belief must be sought only in measured formulas.

[41] There are, however, some signs of a change in attitude. Thus R. E. Brown, *John, i–xii,* p. 506, writes that "The rarity of the expression ["eternal life"] is explained by the fact that only in the very late era of OT thought is there explicit attestation of a belief in a life that transcends death (although the roots of the concept in Israelite theology may be older than hitherto believed)." It seems to me that the implicit assumptions underlying an affirmation like Prov xiv 32, "but at his death the just man will find refuge," tell us more about Israelite theology and beliefs than an explicit attestation like "I firmly believe in a future life that transcends death," which most scholars require (wrongly) before recognizing the

texts explicitly affirming or implying a belief in immortality and resurrection. For details of translation and exegesis the reader must consult the NOTES on the respective texts.

The first group of texts contains the term *ḥayyīm,* translated both "life" and "life eternal." L. Swain[42] has observed that "for the Hebrew mind human life is such an absolute and positive value that it involves eternity. Thus it would be superfluous for the Hebrew to qualify what he knew to be human life in its fulness with the epithet." The philological breakthrough for the definition of *ḥayyīm,* "life eternal," was afforded by the description of everlasting happiness in UT, 2 Aqht:VI:27–29:

Ask for life eternal (*ḥym*) and I will give it to you,
    immortality (*blmt*) and I will bestow it upon you.
I will make you number years like Baal,
    like the gods you will number months.

Ps xvi 11 — You will make me know the path of life eternal,
    filling me with happiness before you,
    with pleasures at your right hand forever.

Ps xxi 5 — The life eternal he asked of you
    you gave him
Length of days, eternity, and everlasting.[43]

Ps xxvii 13 — In the Victor do I trust,
    to behold the beauty of Yahweh
    in the land of life eternal.

Ps xxx 6 — For death is in his anger,
    life eternal in his favor;
In the evening one falls asleep crying,
    but at dawn there are shouts of joy.

Ps xxxvi 10 — Truly with you is the fountain of life,
    in your field we shall see the light.

Ps lvi 14 — Would that you rescue me from Death,
    keeping my feet distant from Banishment,

---

existence of such a belief. Cf. also E. B. Smick, "The Bearing of New Philological Data on the Subjects of Resurrection and Immortality in the Old Testament," in *Westminster Theological Journal* 21, No. 1 (November 1968), 12–21.

[42] In *Clergy Review* 52 (1967), 105.

[43] This revised translation follows from interpreting the first colon as a relative clause with the relative pronoun omitted, and the identification of the second phrase as a double-duty verb predicated of both parts of the verse. The resultant syllable count is 7:4:8 instead of the current 11:8 scansion.

That I might walk before God
in the Field of Life.

Ps lxix 29 Let them be erased from the scroll of life eternal,
and not enrolled among the just.

Ps cxvi 8–9 For you, my soul, have been rescued from Death,
you, mine eye, from Tears,
you, my foot, from Banishment.
I shall walk before Yahweh
in the Fields of Life.

Ps cxxxiii 3 For there Yahweh confers
the blessing—
life for evermore.

Ps cxlii 6 My portion in the land of life eternal.

Prov iv 22 For they are life eternal to those who find them,
and to all who preach them, healing.

Prov viii 35–36 Indeed, who finds me finds life eternal for himself,
and wins favor from Yahweh;
But he who misses me harms himself;
all who hate me love death.[44]

Prov xii 28 In the way of virtue is life eternal,
and the treading of her path is immortality.

Prov xv 24 The path of life eternal is upward for the prudent,
thus escaping Sheol below.

The following texts have in common the term *'aḥ^{a}rīt,* "the future," or "future life," whose eschatological overtones were brought out more clearly by UT, 2 Aqht:VI:35–36:

mt uḫryt mh yqḥ
mh yqḥ mt aṯryt

Man—what will he receive as future life?
what will man receive as afterlife?

Ps xxxvii 37b–38 For there is a future for the man of integrity.
But perverse men shall wholly be destroyed,
and the future of the wicked shall be cut off.

[44] For details, consult the writer's article "The Phoenician Contribution to Biblical Wisdom Literature," in *The Role of the Phoenicians in the Interaction of Mediterranean Civilizations,* ed. W. A. Ward (Beirut, 1968), pp. 123–52, especially 130–31.

Ps cix 13 May his future life be cut off,
from the age to come his name erased.

Num xxiii 10b May his soul die the death of the just man,
and may his future life be like his.[45]

Prov xxiii 18 For surely there is a future life,
and your hope will not be cut off.

Prov xxiv 14b If you find her, there will be future life,
and your hope will not be cut off.

Prov xxiv 20 Because there shall not be a future life for the evil man,
the lamp of the wicked will go out.

Ecclus vii 36 In all your works remember the future life,
and never shall you descend the Pit.

That eternal life will be graced by festive banqueting is known from the New Testament (Luke xiv 16–24), but the Canaanite description of the celestial banquet as an essential component of the blessed after-life permits the exegete to interpret certain passages of the Psalter in the light of UT, 2 Aqht:VI:30–32:

For Baal, when he gives life gives a feast,
gives a feast to the life-given and bids him drink;
The Gracious chants and sings in his presence.

Ps xxiii 4 Even though I should walk
in the midst of total darkness,
I will not fear the Evil One
since you are with me.
Your rod and your staff—
behold, they will lead me.

5 You will prepare before me my table
far from my Adversary.
You will generously anoint my head with oil,
my cup will overflow.

6 Surely goodness and kindness will attend me
all the days of my life;
And I shall dwell in the house of Yahweh
for days without end.

[45] For the grammatical explication of this new version, consult M. Dahood, in ETL 44 (1968), 39, n. 18.

This revision of translation and interpretation follows from the recognition that vs. 4, *rāʿ*, earlier translated "danger," is in reality the epithet of Death identified in Ps cxl 12, and that vs. 5, *ṣōrᵉrāy*, "my Adversary," is a plural of majesty designating the psalmist's chief enemy. It should be observed that *rāʿ*, "the Evil One," forms a theological wordplay with Yahweh's title in vs. 1, *rōʿī*, "my Shepherd." From these identifications we may infer that vss. 5–6 describe the heavenly banquet awaiting the psalmist in the afterlife and that the two demythologized attendants, goodness and kindness, belong to the theme that recurs in Pss xliii 3, lxi 8; Prov iii 3—all descriptions of celestial life.

Ps xliii 3 Send forth your light and your truth;
behold, let them lead me;
Let them bring me to your holy mountain
and to your dwelling,
4 That I might come to the banquet of God,[46]
to El, the joy of my life;
That I might praise you with the lyre,
O God, my God!

Ps xci 15–16 From his anguish will I rescue him,
and I will feast him.
With length of days will I content him,
and make him drink deeply of my salvation.

Particularly surprising is the number of references to the beatific vision, the beholding of God throughout eternity, in the afterlife.

Ps xvii 15 At my vindication
I will gaze upon your face;
At the resurrection
I will be saturated with your being.

Ps xxi 7 Indeed you will give him blessing forever,
you will make him gaze with happiness upon your face.

Ps xxvii 4 One thing I have asked
of Yahweh[47]
This do I seek,
To dwell in Yahweh's house
all the days of my life,

[46] It appears more probable that messengers would be dispatched to conduct one to a banquet (cf. Matt xxii 3) than to the altar.

[47] Parsing *mēʾēt yhwh* as a double-duty modifier in a verse now scanning as a 5:4:5 tricolon.

Gazing upon the loveliness of Yahweh,
awaking each dawn in his temple.

13 In the Victor do I trust,
to behold the beauty of Yahweh
in the land of life eternal.

Ps xli 13 But I in my integrity—
grasp me
And set me before you forever!

Ps lxi 8 Let him sit enthroned before God forever,
may kindness and fidelity be appointed to safeguard him.

Ps lxiii 3 So in your sanctuary may I gaze upon you,
beholding your power and glory.

Ps cxl 14 Indeed, the just shall give praise to your Name,
the upright shall dwell before your face.

In a number of texts the full connotation of the verb *nāḥāh,* "to lead," is clearly recognized as "to lead into Paradise."

Ps v 9 Lead me into your meadow.

Ps xxiii 3 He will lead me into luxuriant pastures.

Ps lxi 3 From the brink of the nether world
I call to you as my heart grows faint;
From it lead me to the Lofty Mountain.

Ps lxxiii 24 Lead me into your council,
and with glory take me to yourself.

Ps cxxxix 24b and lead me into the eternal dominion.

Ps cxliii 10b With your good spirit
lead me
Into the level land.

Several texts witness the verb *qīṣ,* "to awake, arise," with reference to resurrection; in addition to Ps xvii 15, cited above, these include:

Ps cxxxix 18 May I rise and my continuance be with you!

Isa xxvi 19 But your dead will live,
their bodies will rise.
Arise and sing, O you who dwell in the slime!

Dan xii 2 And many of those who sleep
in the land of slime will arise,

Some to everlasting life,
and others to everlasting reproach and contempt.

Prov vi 22 During your lifetime she will guide you,
when you fall asleep she will watch over you,
and when you arise she will converse with you.

A related concept is expressed by the verb *lāqaḥ,* "to take, snatch," when predicated of God in Gen v 24; II Kings ii 3, 5, 9. Cf. also:

Ps xlix 16 But God will ransom me,
from the hand of Sheol will he surely snatch me.

Ps lxxiii 24 Lead me into your council,
and with glory take me to yourself.

The last text cited implies reward after death, a concept which modern scholarship hesitates to admit. Thus Sheldon Blank[48] insists that "The idea of reward after death does not belong in the book of Psalms." The following texts seem to contradict this view:

Ps ciii 4–5 Who will redeem your life from the Pit,
who will crown you with kindness and mercy,
Who will imbue your eternity with his beauty,
when your youth will be renewed like the eagle's.

Ps cxix 112 I incline my heart
to perform your statutes;
eternal will be my reward.

In view of the texts stating a belief in the afterlife, the psalmist's affirmation "eternal will be my reward" should doubtless be understood literally.

A study of the language of the texts presumably professing a faith in the afterlife reveals the recurrence of certain words, some of which became technical terms. Those of more frequent recurrence are *ḥayyīm,* "life" or "life eternal"; *'aḥarīt,* "future" or "future life"; *ḥāzāh,* "to gaze upon"; *ṭōb,* "beauty"; *kibbēd,* "to feast"; *lāqaḥ,* "to take, assume"; *nāḥāh,* "to lead" or "to lead into Paradise"; *ṣedāqāh,* "meadow"; *śāba',* "to sate"; *qīṣ,* "to arise"; *šātal,* "to transplant"; *tāmak,* "to grasp."

Several years ago an American scholar suggested a moratorium on the writing of major works attempting to synthesize the theology of the Old Testament. He maintained that our generation should concentrate

48 In *To Do and to Teach: Essays in Honor of Charles Lynn Pyatt,* ed. R. M. Pierson (Lexington, 1953), p. 1.

on monographic studies of individual problems put in a new light by textual and archaeological discoveries of recent decades. The foregoing observations on the theology of the Psalter seem to corroborate the wisdom of his suggestion. The new readings and analyses—grammatical and prosodic—disclose numerous concepts, motifs, and attitudes that require a more thorough and systematic treatment than is feasible here. I would be gratified if this heavily philological commentary were to elicit monographic studies of some of the ideas uncovered by the systematic application of Northwest Semitic philological principles to the text of the Psalter.

SELECTED BIBLIOGRAPHY

Commentaries

Briggs, C. A., *A Critical and Exegetical Commentary on the Book of Psalms* (abbr. CECBP) (International Critical Commentary, 2 vols.). Edinburgh, 1906.

Buttenwieser, Moses, *The Psalms Chronologically Treated with a New Translation* (abbr. PCTNT). University of Chicago Press, 1938.

Castellino, Giorgio, *Libro dei Salmi.* Torino-Roma, 1955.

Delitzsch, Franz, *Biblischer Kommentar über Die Psalmen.* Leipzig, 5th rev. ed., 1894. Edited by Friedrich Delitzsch.

Gunkel, H., *Die Psalmen* (Handkommentar zum Alten Testament). Göttingen, 1926.

———, and Begrich, J., *Einleitung in Die Psalmen. Die Gattungen der religiösen Lyrik Israels* (Handkommentar zum Alten Testament). Göttingen, 1933.

Kraus, H. J., *Psalmen* (Biblischer Kommentar Altes Testament, 2 vols.). Neukirchen Kreis Moers, 2d ed., 1961.

Mowinckel, Sigmund, *Psalmenstudien* I–VI. Kristiania, 1921–24.

———, *The Psalms in Israel's Worship. A Translation and Revision of* Offersang og Sangoffer, by D. R. Ap-Thomas, 2 vols. Oxford, 1963.

Nötscher, F., *Die Psalmen* (Echter-Bibel). Würzburg, 1947.

Podechard, E., *Le Psautier. Traduction littérale et explication historique. Psaumes 1–75,* 2 vols. Lyon, 1949.

Schmidt, H., *Die Psalmen* (Handbuch zum Alten Testament). Göttingen, 1934.

Weiser, Artur, *The Psalms: A Commentary* (Old Testament Library). London-Philadelphia, 1962.

Articles

Albright, W. F., "The Old Testament and Canaanite Literature and Language," CBQ 7 (1945), 5–31.

———, "The Psalm of Habakkuk," in *Studies in Old Testament Prophecy. Essays presented to Theodore H. Robinson,* ed. H. H. Rowley (Edinburgh, 1950), pp. 1–18.

———, "A Catalogue of Early Hebrew Lyric Poems (Psalm LXVIII)," HUCA 23 (1950), 1–39.

———, "Notes on Psalms 68 and 134," *Norsk teologisk Tidsskrift* 56 (1955), 1–12.

Coppens, J., "Les parallèles du Psautier avec les textes de Ras-Shamra-Ougarit," *Muséon* 59 (1946), 113–42.

Cross, F. M., Jr., and Freedman, D. N., "A Royal Song of Thanksgiving: II Samuel 22=Psalm 18," JBL 72 (1953), 15–34.

Dahood, M., "Ugaritic Studies and the Bible," *Gregorianum* 43 (1962), 55–79.

Jirku, A., "Kana'anäische Psalmenfragmente in der vorisraelitischen Zeit Palästinas und Syriens," JBL 52 (1933), 108–20.

Johnson, A. R., "The Psalms," in *The Old Testament and Modern Study*, ed. H. H. Rowley (Oxford, 1951), pp. 162–209.

O'Callaghan, Roger T., "Echoes of Canaanite Literature in the Psalms," VT 4 (1954), 164–76.

Robinson, T. H., "Basic Principles of Hebrew Poetic Form," in *Festschrift für Alfred Bertholet*, eds. W. Baumgartner and others (Tübingen, 1950), pp. 438–50.

Stamm, J. J., "Ein Vierteljahrhundert Psalmenforschung, *Theologische Rundschau* 23 (1955), 1–68.

PSALMS III

101–150

PSALM 101

(ci 1–8)

1 *A psalm of David.*

Your love and justice will I sing,
to you, Yahweh, will I chant,
2 I will rhapsodize about your dominion complete.
When will you come to me?
I have walked with blameless heart
within my palace.
3 I have never set before my eyes
any worthless object;
the making of images
Have I so detested it never clung to me.
4 The perverse heart turned away from me,
the evil man I befriended not.
5 Whoever by backbiting slandered his neighbor—
him I reduced to silence;
The one of haughty looks and proud heart,
of such I made an end indeed.
6 My eyes were upon my faithful countrymen,
that they might dwell with me.
The man of blameless conduct—
he alone ministered to me.
7 There never dwelt within my palace
an artist of deceit;
a speaker of lies
Never lingered before my eyes.
8 Like cattle I destroyed
all the wicked in the land,
Cutting off from the city of Yahweh
the evildoers one and all.

NOTES

ci. After Gunkel's (*Die Psalmen,* p. 433) demonstration, few current commentators would question the royal character of this psalm. Scholarly opinion divides sharply, though, when a more specific classification must be proposed. Some label the poem the vow of the ideal king, others classify it as the royal proclamation on the day of the new king's enthronement, while Mowinckel, followed by A. R. Johnson, describes the composition as the king's vow which formed part of the Autumn Festival liturgy. *La Bible de la Pléiade* (ed. É Dhorme; Paris, 1959), II, p. 118, categorizes this psalm among didactic writings. The application to the text of the principles of Northwest Semitic philology (see the Introduction) brings to light the following: the psalm is distinctly royal, the work of a king or for a king; secondly, the psalm is a lament composed in a uniform 3+2 or *Qinah* meter, commonly found in laments. The king complains that Yahweh has not adequately responded to his devotion and blameless conduct. "When will you come to me?" the poet asks in vs. 2, an embarrassing question which many modern commentators prefer to delete, since it does not accord with their classification of the poem. God's failure to grant the king a vision or some palpable form of spiritual comfort is the ground for the king's complaint. This classification is sustained by the recognition, on the basis of Canaanite and biblical poetic usage, and on the authority of the LXX, that all the imperfect or *yqtl* verb forms in vss. 2c–8 describe past activity, not future promises as construed by the leading modern commentators.

When asserting that this past behavior has been irreprehensible, the psalmist employs terms that bring the psalm into close relationship with the psalms of innocence, such as Pss v, xxvi, cxxxix.

To reconstruct the original cultic setting of this lament is unhappily beyond the reach of current psalms scholarship, and attempts to fit the composition into its cultural or historical setting must remain subjective and conjectural. As it is of royal nature, the psalm dates to the pre-Exilic period, but a more precise dating within the period of the Israelite monarchy (1000–586 B.C.) cannot be given on the basis of contents or language.

1. *Your love and justice.* Not "My song is about kindness and justice" (JB), because suffixless *ḥesed ūmišpāṭ* receive their determination from *l^ekā,* "to you," which refers to Yahweh. This use of the double-duty suffix (see Index of Subjects) compares closely with that examined in Ps liv 8, "For your nobility I will sacrifice to you," where undetermined *n^edābāh* receives its determination from *lāk,* "to you."

By resorting to the poetic device of the double-duty suffix, the psalmist could perfectly balance his line with eight syllables in each colon.

The terms *ḥesed ūmišpāṭ,* "your love and justice," belong to covenant language. Thus in Ps l 5 those who have made a covenant with Yahweh are called *ḥᵃsīdēy,* "his devoted ones," i.e., those bound by covenant obligations. But Yahweh, too, is bound by covenantal obligations to maintain his loyalty to the king; cf. Ps lxxxix 29, "I shall keep my love (*ḥasdī*) for him eternal, / and my covenant shall endure for him." Thus Nelson Glueck, *Das Wort ḥesed* (Giessen, 1927), p. 66, correctly concludes that God's *ḥesed* is the consequence of his covenant with his king or his people.

Your love and justice . . . to you, Yahweh. The poet balances two direct objects in the first colon with two indirect objects in the second (courtesy D. N. Freedman). Compare the first NOTE on Ps lxxvi 12, and UT, 602:3–4, *yšr wydmr bknr wṯlb,* "He sings and chants upon lyre and lute," where two verbs are followed by two nouns of a prepositional phrase.

will I sing . . . will I chant . . . 2. *I will rhapsodize.* The three synonymous verbs *'āšīrāh, 'ᵃzammērāh,* and *'aśkīlāh* suggest that the lament is introduced by a tricolon rather than by a bicolon, as in most versions. In other words, vs. 2b, "When will you come to me?" stands as an independent question, metrically and semantically distinct from the first three cola, which have an 8:8:8 syllable count.

The syntax of *ḥesed ūmišpāṭ 'āšīrāh,* "your love and justice will I sing," where *ḥesed ūmišpāṭ* are the direct object of the verb, resembles the construction of UT 603:rev.:7–8 *tšr dd al[iyn] b'l,* "She sings the affection of Victor Baal," while the biblical parallelism between *šīr,* "to sing," and *zāmar,* "to chant," in Pss xxvii 6, lvii 8 etc., is now joined by the Ugaritic pairing of *šr* and *ḏmr* (see the fourth NOTE on Ps lvii 8) to upset Gunkel's emendation of *'āšīrāh* "will I sing," to *'eᶜᵉśāh,* "I will practice," and of *'ᵃzammērāh,* "will I chant," to *'ešmᵉrāh,* "I will heed." See also the second NOTE on Ps lxxxix 2.

2. *I will rhapsodize.* Rendered "I will behave myself wisely" by KJ, and "I will give heed" by RSV, *'aśkīlāh* belongs rather to the same conceptual category as vs. 1, "will I sing" and "will I chant." This is indicated not only by the structure of the psalm's first three cola, but by the concurrence of *šīr, mizmōr,* and *maśkīl* in the heading of Ps lxxxviii; cf. also Ps xlvii 8, *zammᵉrū maśkīl.*

your dominion complete. The NOTES on Ps xviii 31, 33, examine this definition of *derek tāmīm.* Like suffixless *ḥesed ūmišpāṭ* in vs. 1, *derek tāmīm* receives its determination from *lᵉkā yhwh,* "to you, Yahweh," in the central colon, vs. 1b. A related stylistic phenomenon at Prov viii 30 and UT, 51:IV:41–43 is discussed in the writer's article, "Proverbs 8, 22–31: Translation and Commentary," in CBQ 30 (1968), 512–21.

When will you come to me? Doubtless the most contested phrase of the psalm, *mātay tābō' 'ēlāy* (which *La Bible de la Plēiade,* among others, emends away because "It has no connection with the context") becomes reasonably germane when the following verbs are taken in the past tense. The psalmist wants to know "When am I going to be rewarded by God's presence for my perfect conformity to his will in the past?" Compare the use of *mātay* in the cognate context of Ps xlii 3, "When shall I begin to drink in deeply the presence of God?"

I have walked. With the LXX, understanding the imperfect or *yqtl* form *'ethallēk* as describing past action; see the introductory NOTE to Ps lxxviii. The appreciation of the Canaanite-biblical employment of the *yqtl* form in poetry to describe past activity will surely have far-reaching consequences for Bible translation and exegesis. For example, Isa xliii 2, *kī taʿabōr bammayim 'ittekā 'ānī,* should now be rendered, "When you passed through the waters, I was with you," a reference to the Exodus, and not, "When you pass through the waters I will be with you," as read by RSV. This becomes reasonably evident from vs. 3, *nātattī koprekā miṣrayim,* "I gave Egypt as your ransom," where preterit *nātattī* designates a completed action. Having translated *yqtl* form *taʿabōr* as a present tense, RSV is obliged to compound the error and reproduce *nātattī* in the present tense, "I give Egypt as your ransom."

my palace. Since the speaker is a king, *bētī* takes on a nuance attested in other biblical texts, e.g., I Kings iv 6, xvi 9; Isa xxii 15. RSV's "my house" falls short of the intended meaning. This usage recurs in vs. 7, with which it forms an inclusion.

3. *I have never set.* Again following the LXX, which understood *'āšīt* as a *yqtl* form referring to the past.

before my eyes. Forms an inclusion with the same phrase in vs 7.

any worthless object. Probably an idol, since it is something held up to view; consult the second NOTE on Ps xl 5. Cf. Ezek xviii 15, "[But if] he does not raise his eyes to the idols of the house of Israel."

the making of images. Parsing *ʿaśōh sēṭīm* as the infinitive construct (GK, § 75n, especially Prov xxi 3) followed by the direct object *sēṭīm,* which is an alternate spelling of *śēṭīm,* "images," discussed in NOTE on Ps xl 5.

Have I so detested. Since this verse was apparently structured to create an inclusion with vs. 7 (see second NOTE on this verse above), it too should be analyzed chiastically, with the first colon corresponding to the fourth, and the second pairing with the third; thus, A:B:B:A. Hence the MT *athnach* under *śānē'tī* should be transferred to the preceding word *ṣēṭīm,* "images," so that the syllable count of the four-cola chiasmus becomes 8:6:4:7.

As observed in the third NOTE on Ps v 6, *śānē'tī* became a technical term employed in the formula abjuring idols and idol worship. The significance of this disclaimer comes out more clearly with the knowledge that in the seventh–sixth century B.C. citadel and palace of the king of Judah at Ramat Rahel, four kilometers south of Jerusalem, representations of the Canaanite fertility goddess Astarte were found during the 1954–1962 excavations. See Yohanan Aharoni, "The Citadel of Ramat Rahel," in *Archaeology* 18 (1965), 15–25.

it never clung. Another instance of the imperfect (*yidbaq*) or *yqtl* verb describing past action.

4. *the evil man.* Though many versions interpret ambivalent *rāʿ* as neuter "evil" (RSV, "I will know nothing of evil"), I prefer, on the basis of parallelism, to understand *rāʿ* as an evil person; see the next NOTE.

I befriended not. Interpreting the clause *rāʿ lōʾ ʾēdāʿ* in the light of Pss v 5, *lōʾ yegūrekā rāʿ*, "No evil man can be your guest," and xv 4, "The despicable man is rejected from his presence, / but those who fear Yahweh he feasts." For this nuance of *yādaʿ*, "to care for, be a friend," in Ugaritic, Hebrew, and Punic, see my discussion in *Biblica* 45 (1964), 403, and UHP, p. 61.

5. *Whoever . . . slandered.* Parsing *melōšenī* as a poel participle whose final *-ī* is the third-person singular suffix expressing the dative of advantage, as set forth in first NOTE on Ps xcvii 10. By adding the dative suffix the psalmist managed to even at 10:10 the syllable count of vs. 5a and 5c. Like vs. 6, "The man of blameless conduct," *melōšenī* stands as *casus pendens,* a stylistic mechanism studied at Ps ciii 15.

The denominative verb *lāšan,* "to use the tongue," specifically "to slander," occurs in UT, 2 Aqht:VI:51, *tlšn aqht ǵzr,* "She slanders the lad Aqht," and belongs to the impressive list of Northwest Semitic denominative verbs that are derived from names of parts of the body. Consult NOTES on Pss xv 3, xviii 48, and lxiv 9, *slanderers.* The use of this verb with the specific denotation "to slander," a usage not found in other Semitic languages, serves to illustrate the close lexical relationship between Hebrew and Ugaritic.

by backbiting. Or "in secret," with both ancient and modern versions, but Prov xxv 23, *lešōn sāter,* "a backbiting tongue" (RSV), and the juxtaposition with *melōšenī* in our verse sustain this translation of *bassāter.*

I reduced to silence. With *ʾaṣmīt* expressing past time, as in Ps xviii 41, where the balance with preterit *nātattāh,* "You gave," leaves little doubt concerning the tense of *ʾaṣmītēm.*

I made an end. Reading *ʾakalle* (MT *ʾūkāl*) the piel imperfect form of *kālāh,* "to come to an end." This etymology creates a fine parallel to *ʾasmīṭ,* "I reduced to silence." For other instances of Masoretic mispointing of this verb, cf. Ps x 4 (see NOTES there); Hos xi 6; Josh xviii 7. One may also read the apocopated form *ʾakal,* as in Ezek xliii 8.

In the royal Phoenician inscriptions from Karatepe, King Azitawaddu avers (I:8) that *šbrt mlṣm,* "I shattered the critics."

indeed. Understanding consonantal *lʾ* as an alternate spelling of the emphatic *lamedh.* Cf. Jer iv 27, "The entire earth will become a desolation" *wekālāh lʾ ʾeʿeśeh,* "and I will indeed make a full end." Contrast RSV, ". . . I will not make a full end." Other examples of *lʾ* as an alternate writing of *le,* "indeed," have been studied by F. Nötscher in

VT 3 (1953), 375; G. Glanzman in CBQ 23 (1961), 231 f.; H. Neil Richardson in JBL 85 (1966), 89; F. C. Fensham in *The Bible Translator* 18 (1967), 73; J. Alberto Soggin in *Biblica* 46 (1965), 56–59; BibOr 9 (1967), 42.

6. *blameless conduct.* The phrase *derek tāmīm* harks back to vs. 2 where it is predicated of God in quite a different sense; the second NOTE on Ps civ 8 comments on such usage. Cf. also Leon J. Liebreich in HUCA 27 (1956), 184, who points out that in Ps xxxiv 9, *ṭōb* has reference to the goodness (better, tenderness) of God, whereas in vs. 11, *ṭōb* designates material or worldly goods of man. These divine and human connotations of *ṭōb* nicely illustrate the divine and human senses of *derek tāmīm.*

he alone. An attempt to bring out the emphatic nature of *hū'*.

ministered to me. The appearance in Ugaritic of the term *ṯrtnm* (phonetically equals Heb. *šērēt,* "to minister"), who are members of a certain professional guild ("ministers"?), definitely weakens the position of those (e.g., Aistleitner) who equate Heb. *šērēt* with Ugar. *šrd* in UT, Krt:77, *šrd b'l bdbḥk,* and favors the parsing of *šrd* as the shaphel imperative of *yrd,* "to descend." Hence translate: "With your sacrifice make Baal descend."

7. *There never dwelt . . . Never lingered.* The four cola of this verse exhibit an interesting chiastic arrangement that closely resembles the structure of vs. 3 with which they establish an inclusion. Thus the first and fourth cola are rigorously parallel in meaning, in number of words (4:4), and in syllable count (8:8), with *lō' yēšēb,* "never dwelt," corresponding to *lō' yikkōn,* "never lingered"; *b^{e}qereb,* "within," to *l^{e}neged,* "before"; and *bētī,* "my palace," to *'ēnāy,* "my eyes." The second and third cola are likewise carefully balanced. Thus *'ōśēh r^{e}miyyāh,* "an artist of deceit," balances *dōbēr š^{e}qārīm,* "speaker of lies," both in form (two qal active participles with corresponding nouns) and in syllable count (8:8).

within my palace. b^{e}qereb bētī forms an inclusion with this phrase in vs. 3; see next NOTE.

before my eyes. l^{e}neged 'ēnāy creates an inclusion with the identical phrase in vs. 3, while the thought evokes Ps xv 4, "The despicable man is rejected from his presence."

8. *Like cattle.* The customary translation of MT *labb^{e}qārīm* "morning by morning" (RSV) creates the impression that the king was singularly ineffectual; an oriental king who each morning had to rid his land of undesirable citizens was destined for a very short reign. Accordingly, I explain the prepositional phrase in the light of Ps xlix 15, *labbāqer,* "like a calf," which is parallel to *k^{e}ṣō'n,* "like sheep." For fuller discussion see fifth NOTE on Ps xlix 15.

all the wicked in the land. Comparing Phoenician Karatepe I:9, *wtrq 'nk kl hr' 'š kn b'rṣ,* "And I removed all the evil that was in the land."

Cutting off. The use of the circumstantial infinitive *l^{e}hakrīt* (cf. the third NOTE on Ps cxi 6) recalls Phoenician Eshmunazor, lines 9–10, "And may the holy gods imprison them with the Mighty King [=Death] who will rule over them by cutting down [circumstantial infinitive *lqṣtnm*] that king or commoner who would open the cover of this sarcophagus."

the city of Yahweh. Comparing Ps cxxii 3, "Jerusalem which was built as his city." Occurring only in the first and the last verses, the divine name *yhwh* enfolds the intervening lines.

PSALM 102

(cii 1–29)

1 *The prayer of one afflicted, when he grew faint*
and poured out his complaint before Yahweh.

2 Yahweh, hear my prayer,
let my cry come to you.
3 Turn not your face from me [2]*
on the day of my anguish;
Incline your ear toward me
on the day I call,
Hasten to answer me.
4 For my days pass more quickly than smoke, [3]
and my bones burn like a brazier.
5 Scorched like grass, my heart has withered indeed, [4]
I am utterly wasted by the Devourer.
6 My jaws fester from my groaning, [5]
my skeleton clings to my flesh.
7 I resemble a vulture in the wilderness, [6]
I have become like an owl in desolate places.
8 I stay awake and have become like a sparrow, [7]
like a chatterer on the roof all day long.
9 My Foe taunts me, [8]
my Mocker feasts on me.
10 Ashes I eat as my food, [9]
and from my tears I draw my drink.
11 Because of your fury and your wrath, [10]
you lifted me up and threw me down.
12 My days are like a tapering shadow, [11]
and I wither like grass.
13 But you, Yahweh, [12]
from eternity have sat enthroned,
and your throne endures from age to age.

* Verse numbers in RSV.

14 You will arise to show compassion to Zion, [13]
because it is time to have pity on her;
indeed the appointed time has come.
15 How your servants love her stones, [14]
by her dust are moved to pity!
16 Then will the nations revere your name, Yahweh, [15]
and all kings of the earth your glory,
17 When Yahweh builds Zion anew, [16]
appears to her in his glory,
18 If he regards the prayer of the destitute, [17]
and does not despise their prayer.
19 Let this be written for the next generation, [18]
that a people yet to be created might praise Yah:
20 "From his holy height looked down, [19]
From heaven to earth gazed Yahweh
21 To hear the groans of prisoners, [20]
to release those condemned to die;
22 That Yahweh's name be proclaimed in Zion, [21]
and his laudation in Jerusalem,
23 When peoples gather together [22]
with kings to serve him."
24 Yahweh humbled my strength by his power, [23]
and my God cut short my vigorous days.
25 "Do not take me away before half my days, [24]
when your years last generations!"
26 Long ago you laid earth's foundations, [25]
and the heavens are your handiwork.
27 They will perish, but you will remain, [26]
all of them will wear out like clothes.
You change them like a garment,
and they pass away.
28 But you remain the same, [27]
and your years will never end.
29 The children of your servants will dwell secure, [28]
and their seed shall endure in your presence.

NOTES

cii. In this lament of an individual, three different themes can be readily discerned. In vss. 2–12 the psalmist graphically describes his illness and his being taunted by approaching Death. In the second stanza (vss. 13–18) he shifts his attention to Zion, which has been destroyed, and to her children, (vss. 19–23), while in the final stanza (vss. 24–29) the psalmist contrasts the brevity of his life with the permanence of Yahweh.

Current psalms scholarship tends to label the psalm a compilation from older laments and hymns, but the pervasive oneness of diction and spirit points to a single author. For example, the collocation of *mamlākōt*, "kings," in vs. 23, the last line of the third stanza, and *darkō*, "his power," in vs. 24, the first line of the fourth stanza, recalls the parallelism between *mlk*, "kingship," and *drkt*, "dominion," often found in Ugaritic. Surely such careful collocation bespeaks unity of authorship.

Who is the speaker in this lament? We have several indications of the royal character of the psalmist. On a purely phrasal level, vs. 1 *ya'ᵃṭōp* recalls royal Ps lxi 3, *ba'ᵃṭōp libbī*, "as my heart grows faint," and vs. 24 *wᵉqiṣṣar yᵉmay 'emār 'ēlī*, "and my God cut short my vigorous days," aligns itself to royal Ps lxxxix 46, "You cut short the days of his youth." The rare parallelism between *bᵉnē*, "children," and *zar'ām*, "their seed," in vs. 29, is reminiscent of their juxtaposition in royal Ps xxi 11, *wᵉzar'ām mibbᵉnē 'ādām*, "and their children from the sons of men"; the equally uncommon balance of *'ōyᵉbay*, "my Foe," and *mᵉhōlālay*, "my Mocker," in vs. 9 betrays a kinship with royal Ps xviii 4, *mᵉhullāl*, "when mocked," that is associated with *'ōyᵉbay*, "my Foe" (in revised translation). The poet shares a common concern for the name of Yahweh (vss. 16, 22) with the authors of royal Pss xx 2, 6, 8, liv 9, lxxxvi 9, 12, cxxxviii 2, and his universalistic aspirations in vss. 16, 23 show an affinity with royal Pss xxii 28, lxxxvi 9, and cxxxviii 4. Equally significant for the identification of the psalmist's status is the contrast he limns between his own fleeting days (vss. 4–12) and the enduring kingship of Yahweh (vs. 13). For a king to depict Yahweh precisely as enthroned would have been appropriate.

1. *he grew faint and poured out.* Both ancient and modern versions customarily render *ya'ᵃṭōp* and *yišpōk* in the present tense, but sense and poetic practice (see introductory NOTE to Ps ci) are equally sustained by a rendition in the past. The expression *ba'ᵃṭōp libbī*, "as my heart grows faint," occurs in royal Ps lxi 3.

2. *hear . . . come.* The pairing of the energic imperative (*šim'āh*) with the jussive (*tābō'*) is a stylistic trait of psalms noticed in the second NOTE on Ps li 14.

3. *Turn not . . . Incline . . . Hasten.* Reading vs. 3 as a run-on line, with a 9:4:7:4:5 syllable count, a pattern in which the major units descend in length (9:7:5) while the interludes remain the same (4:4) In other words, the phrases *bᵉyōm ṣar lī*, "on the day of my anguish," and *bᵉyōm 'eqrā'*, "on the day I call," are suspended between the longer units, serving as double-duty modifiers. I have noticed this poetic pattern at Ps lvii 5 and have formally studied it in "A New Metrical Pattern in Biblical Poetry," CBQ 29 (1967), 574–79.

Turn not. LXX *mē apostrépsēs*, Vulg. *non avertas*, and the proposed emendation of *tastēr* to *tāsēr*, registered in the critical apparatus of BH[3], merely confirm the correctness of parsing consonantal *tstr* as an infixed *-t-* form of *sūr*, "to turn aside"; cf. second NOTE on Ps x 11. The contrary of *'al tastēr pānekā mimmennī* "Turn not your face from me," is expressed by the prayer in the next line, *haṭṭēh 'ēlay 'oznekā*, "Incline your ear toward me." A new instance can be made out in Ecclus vi 11, *'m tśygk r'h yhpk bk wmpnk ystr*, "If tragedy befalls you, he will recoil from you and turn away from your face"; cf. T. Penar, "Job 19,19 in the Light of Ben Sira 6,11," in *Biblica* 48 (1967), 293–95.

my anguish. Like *ṣar* in Ps xviii 7, where the preceding verse mentions Sheol and Death, and like *ṣārāh* with the same connotation in Pss xci 15, cxlii 3, *ṣar* here signifies the agony of death.

4. *pass more quickly*. For this nuance of *kālū*, see last NOTE on Ps xxxvii 20, and BDB, p. 478a, who observe that the added idea of transitoriness attaches to this verb in Ps xc 9. Cf. Job xvii 7, *wīṣūray kaṣṣēl kālū-m* (*mem* is enclitic; MT *kullām*), "And my limbs tapered like a shadow."

than smoke. The evident parallelism with comparative *k*^{e}*mōqēd*, "like a brazier," points to the comparative function of *b*^{e} in *b*^{e}*'āšān*, "than smoke," a usage discussed in the last NOTE on Ps xxxvii 20, the second NOTE on Ps li 8, and the third NOTE on Ps li 9. On the strength of the ancient versions, many commentators emend *b*^{e}*'āšān* here and in Ps xxxvii 20 to *k*^{e}*'āšān*, "like smoke," but Northwest Semitic philology discourages such an emendation. For a list of passages where emendation may be scouted, see the Index of Subjects in both *Psalms II* and *Psalms III.*

burn. Occurring several times in Ugaritic, the verb *ḥrr*, "to burn, be hot," appears in a context not unlike that of the psalm in UT, 75:II:38–39, *anpnm yḥr* [ ] *bmtnm yšḫn*, "His face is flushed, in his loins he is feverish."

like a brazier. Biblical *mōqēd* probably finds its Canaanite counterpart in UT, 1127:19, *ḫmš mqdm*, "five braziers," one of the items mentioned in a list of silver and commodities, with their prices.

5. *Scorched.* Literally "struck," *hūkkāh* contains the root predicated of the sun in Ps cxxi 6, "By day the sun will not strike you." The obscurity of the context unfortunately precludes the certain identification of this root in Ugar. *nkyt.*

has withered indeed. Parsing the *waw* of *wayyībaš* as the emphatic particle, discussed in the second NOTE on Ps li 9.

I am utterly wasted. The clear parallelism with *yībaš*, "has withered," shows that *šākaḥtī* must be dissociated from *šākaḥ*, "to forget" (JB's "my appetite has gone" glosses over the problem), and identified with Ugar. *ṯkḥ*, "to wither," examined in the first NOTE on Ps xxxi 13, the fourth NOTE on Ps lix 12, and the second NOTE on Ps lxxvii 10. Gunkel's (*Die Psalmen*, p. 438) emendation of *šākaḥtī* to *kāḥaštī*, "I have grown lean," need not, therefore, enlist further attention. RSV incongruously accepts this root in Ps cxxxvii 5 and hesitates here. In his report, "The Revised Standard Version of the Old Testament," in VTS, VII (Congress volume, Oxford, 1959; Leiden, 1960), pp. 206–21, Millar Burrows writes (p. 218), "Nor has 'I forget to eat my bread' in Ps cii 4 been changed to 'I am too wasted away to eat my bread,' though the parallelism as well as the Ugaritic evidence favor the change, and this meaning has already been given to the same verb in Ps cxxxvii 5."

utterly. In the phrase *kī šākaḥtī*, "I am utterly wasted," *kī* parses as the emphatic particle, here reproduced by "utterly."

The present association of *libbī*, "my heart," and *šākaḥtī*, "I am too wasted," sustains the translation of Ps xxxi 13, *niškaḥtī kᵉmēt millēb*, "I have shriveled up like a dead man, senseless."

by the Devourer. Repointing MT *mē'ᵃkōl* to *mē'ōkēl*, and identifying "the Devourer" with Death who is said in vs. 9 to feast on the psalmist. Cf. Job xviii 12–13, *yᵉhī rā'ēb 'ōnō wᵉ'ēd nākōn lᵉṣal'ō yō'kal baddēy 'iwwērū* [MT *'ōrō*] *yō'kal baddāyw bᵉkōr māwet*, "The Ravenous One confronts him, Calamity ready at his side. The Blind One devours his limbs, Death devours the limbs of his first-born." The suffix of *baddēy*, "his limbs," is that of third-person singular (*Psalms I*, third NOTE on ii 6), while the phrase *baddāyw bᵉkōr*, "the limbs of his first-born," parses as a construct chain with interposed pronominal suffix (as in the following verse, Job xviii 14), a usage documented in THE GRAMMAR OF THE PSALTER.

The title *'ōkēl*, "the Devourer," falls in with the motif of *rā'ēb*, "the Hungry One," and of Death's insatiable appetite, both discussed in the NOTE on Ps xxxiii 19. The translation of Ps xlii 10, "because of the Assassin within my bones," is of a pattern with the present description of Death.

6. *My jaws*. Transferring MT *laḥmī*, "my bread," from vs. 5 and vocalizing it *leḥēm*, the contracted Northern dual (Ugar. *lḥm*) of *lᵉḥī*, "cheek, jaw," studied in the seventh NOTE on Ps lvi 2. The final yod of *laḥmī* becomes the preformative of the following verb. Being the name of a part of the body, *leḥēm* need not be furnished with a suffix to denote "my jaws"; cf. the fourth NOTE on Ps lvi 8.

fester from my groaning. Redividing the consonants to read *yāmaqqū lᵉ'anḥātī* for MT hapax legomenon *miqqōl 'anḥātī*, "at the voice of my groaning"; as proposed in the preceding NOTE, the preformative *yā-* of *yāmaqqū* is forthcoming from the final syllable of MT *laḥmī*. The appearance of *nāmaqqū* in the individual lament Ps xxxviii 6 and of *mōq* in the national lament Ps xliv 20 shows that *māqaq*, "to rot, fester," belongs to the language of laments, while Zech xiv 12, *ūlᵉšōnō timmaq bᵉpīhū-m* (*mem* is enclitic), "And his tongue shall fester in his mouth," sustains the authenticity of the expression *leḥēm yāmaqqū*, "My jaws fester." With this reading the line, whose first colon has long been thought to lack a word (cf. apparatus in BH³ which reads *vb prb exc, prps yāga'tī, l frt kāḥaštī*), divides into two balanced cola, each numbering three words and nine syllables. The resultant parallelism between the *yqtl* verb form *yāmaqqū* and *qtl dābeqāh* also deserves mention; in vs. 15 the poet employs the *qtl–yqtl* sequence.

These observations seem to bear on the translation of Ps lxxiii 7–8, where we should probably attach the first word of vs. 8, unexplained *yāmīqū,* to the end of vs. 7 to recover the expression *lēbāb yāmīqū,* "Their heart festers." As a result of this scansion, a clear case of inclusion comes to light in vs. 8 that now begins with *wīdabbērū,* "and (they) speak," and closes with *yedabbērū,* "they speak." Verses 7–8 now scan into five cola with an 8:6:5:8:6 syllable count.

from my groaning. The causal force of the preposition *le* (*le'anḥātī*) comes across in G. R. Driver's (CML, p. 35) translation of UT, Krt:119–22, *wl yšn pbl mlk lqr ṯigt ibrh lql nhqt ḥmrh lg't alp ḥrṯ,* "King Pabil slept not for the rumble of the roaring of his buffaloes, for the sound of the braying of his asses, for the lowing of the plowing ox." Cf. further Isa xv 5, xvi 7, 11; Jer xxxi 20; Hos x 5; Job xxxvii 1.

Feminine in Hebrew, *'anāḥāh,* "groaning," appears as masculine *anḫ,* "groaning," in Ugaritic.

8. *I stay awake . . . all day long. šāqadtī* and *kol hayyōm* are an instance of merismus, signifying "night and day." Consult the fourth NOTE to this verse.

like a sparrow. MT and the versions read *keṣippōr bōdēd,* "like a lonely sparrow/bird," with masculine *bōdēd* modifying normally feminine *ṣippōr.* In his study of the gender of Hebrew nouns, Karl Albrecht (ZAW 16 [1896], 41–121) concludes his discussion of the gender of *ṣippōr* with the observation that Ps cii 8 is the only text where *ṣippōr* is arguably masculine, but even here he remains skeptical because the unsatisfactory parallelism hints at some disorder in the transmission of this verse. The consonantal text is quite sound; proper balance and agreement of gender can be restored by terminating the first colon with feminine *ṣippōr* and beginning the second colon with the masculine substantive *bōdēd,* "chatterer"; see the next NOTE.

like a chatterer. Comparative *ke* of *keṣippōr* extends its comparative force to parallel *bōdēd;* other instances of double-duty prepositions are registered in the third NOTE on Ps xc 4. I parse *bōdēd* as a participle of **bādad,* preserved in the substantive *baddīm,* "chatter, idle talk," Phoen. *bdm* in Eshmunazor, line 6, *'l tšm' bdnm,* "Heed not their idle talk." That *bōdēd,* "chatterer," aptly describes a bird is sustained by the analogy of English "chatterer," any of several passerine birds having a chattering cry, as certain waxwings and cotingas. Whether this root *bdd* relates to Ugar. *bd//šr,* "to sing," is uncertain for lack of Ugaritic vocalization.

all day long. Attaching the first two words of vs. 9 to the end of vs. 8 which now reads:

šāqadtī wā'ehyeh keṣippōr (3 beats—9 syllables)
bōdēd 'al gāg kol hayyōm (3 beats—7 syllables)

As observed in the first NOTE to this verse, this reading uncovers an example of merismus, while at the same time bringing the syllable count of vs. 9 into better balance with seven syllables in the first colon and eight in the second.

9. *My Foe . . . feasts on me.* By detaching *kol hayyōm,* "all day long," from vs. 9 and joining them to vs. 8, we effectuate a balanced chiastic verse with seven syllables in the first colon and eight in the second.

ḥēr^{e}pūnī 'ōy^{e}bāy (2 beats—7 syllables)
m^{e}hōl^{e}lay bī niśbā'ū (2 beats—8 syllables)

The chiasmus proves especially interesting. The plural verb plus suffix *ḥēr^{e}pūnī* are balanced by prepositional phrase *bī* followed by the plural verb *niśbā'ū* (MT *nišbā'ū*), "feasts on me," and the two epithets of Death, chiastically paired, are a good example of assonance.

My Foe. The uncommon parallelism between *'ōy^{e}bāy* and *m^{e}hōlālay* suggests a relationship with the revised translation of Ps xviii 4, *m^{e}hullāl 'eqrā' yhwh ūmin 'ōy^{e}bay 'iwwāšē^{a}',* "When mocked, I called Yahweh, and from my Foe I was saved" (contrast *Psalms I*). See also the cognate parallelism in Ps cxxxvii 3. Since there can be little doubt in Ps xviii 4 about the identity of the plural of majesty *'ōy^{e}bay,* "my Foe,"—Death, Sheol, and Belial being mentioned in vss. 5–6—one should seek to identify the parallel substantives *'ōy^{e}bāy* and *m^{e}hōlālay* in our verse in the same manner. This is rendered possible, first, by the contents of the lament in vss. 2–12; second, by the fact that the plural of majesty *'ōy^{e}bīm,* "Foe," designates Death in Pss xviii 4, 49, xxx 2, xli 3, lxix 19, cxliii 9; third, the verb *ḥēr^{e}pūnī,* "taunts me," is predicated of Death in Ps xlii 11, *ḥēr^{e}pūnī ṣōr^{e}rāy,* "My Adversary taunts me," where *ṣōr^{e}rāy* is now seen to be synonymous with *reṣaḥ,* "the Assassin," and with *'ōyēb,* "the Foe," in the preceding verse. In Pss xiii 5, xxvii 12, the plural of majesty *ṣāray,* "my Adversary," denotes Death.

taunts me. Comparing Pss xiii 3, "How long must my Foe rejoice over me?", xiii 5, "Lest my Foe should boast, 'I overcame him!' Lest my Adversary should exult when I stumble," and revised xlii 11, *ḥēr^{e}pūnī ṣōr^{e}rāy,* "My Adversary taunts me." Thus the plural verb agrees with the plural form of the subject, as in Ps xiii 5, *ṣāray yāgīlū,* "Lest my Adversary should exult," and Ps xlvi 5; see fourth NOTE on Ps xiii 5, and below on Ps cxlii 7.

Though the psalmist does not give the text of Death's taunt, it may tentatively be supplied from Ps xlii 11, "Where is your God?"

my Mocker. Pointing *m^{e}hōl^{e}lay,* the plural poel participle, for MT poal *m^{e}hōlālay.* In the poel conjugation *hōlēl* specifically signifies "to make a fool of, to mock," the nuance desired by the context. Like its counterpart *'ōy^{e}bay,* "my Foe," plural *m^{e}hōl^{e}lay* is a plural of majesty referring to the supreme mocker, Death.

Among the more curious attempts to interpret this word, one might cite A. B. Ehrlich's (*Randglossen zur hebräischen Bibel,* VI [Leipzig, 1913], p. 6) translation of *mᵉhōlᵉlay:* "those who Hellenize me."

feasts on me. Reading *niśbā'ū* for MT *nišbā'ū;* since the pre-Masoretic consonantal text used but one symbol for both *śin* and *shin,* the proposed reading assumes no emendation of the consonantal text. This repointing produces a version that accords with vs. 5, "I am utterly wasted by the Devourer," and is more explicable (cf. the commentaries) than traditional "those who deride me use my name for a curse" (RSV).

For the construction *śāba' bᵉ,* "to be sated with, to feast on," cf. Pss lxv 5, lxxxviii 4; Lam iii 30, and for the niphal form, see Job xxxi 31, *mī yittēn mībbᵉśārō lū'* (MT *lō'*) *niśbā',* "O that we might feast on his flesh!" and the comments of Pope, *Job* ad loc. In the following verse of the psalm, the preposition *bᵉ* again denotes "from."

10. *Ashes.* The emphatic nature of *kī* in *kī 'ēper* is reproduced by the emphatic position of "Ashes" in translation.

my food. Suffixless *leḥem* shares the suffix of its opposite number *šiqqūway,* "my drink" (cf. first NOTE on Ps iii 4); hence RSV's "For I eat ashes like bread" obscures the point. For the Ugaritic parallelism between the roots *lḥm* and *šqy,* see UT, 2 Aqht:I:22–23, *uzrm ilm ylḥm uzrm yšqy bn qdš,* and for their juxtaposition, 2 Aqht:V:29, *tšlḥm tššqy ilm,* "She dines and wines the god." Cf. also Ps lxxx 6, "You have fed us tears as our food (*leḥem*), and given us tears to drink (*wattašqēmō*) by the bowl," and the fourth NOTE on Ps lvii 8, which discusses parallel words as a criterion for evaluating the proximity of Hebrew and Ugaritic.

from my tears. Assigning to the preposition *bᵉ* of *bibᵉkī* its frequent (see vss. 4, 9) sense of "from"; the Indexes and THE GRAMMAR OF THE PSALTER refer to numerous passages where this sense occurs.

I draw my drink. The psalmist continues the hyberbolic metaphor, depicting himself as drawing his drink from an amphora or vat filled with his tears. As observed in the fifth NOTE on Ps lxxv 9, the definition of *māsak,* "to draw," is finding wide acceptance; cf., for example, R. B. Y. Scott's translation of Prov ix 2, *māsᵉkāh yēnāh,* "She has poured out her wine," in AB, vol. 18. The syntax of *bibᵉkî māsaktī,* "from my tears I draw," is identical with that found in UT, 'nt:I:15–17, *alp kd yqḥ bḫmr rbt ymsk bmskh,* "A thousand pitchers he took from his bowl, ten thousand he drew from his vat."

Canaanite poets, too, resort to extravagant language when comparing King Kirta's tears to shekels: UT, Krt:28–29, *tntkn udm'th km ṯqlm arṣh,* "His tears are poured out like shekels toward the ground."

In fact, the proposed translation of the biblical metaphor may shed light on UT, 62:I:10, where the sorrowing goddess Anath is described: *tšt kyn udm't,* "She drinks tears like wine." So far as I know, no Ugaritic specialist has explained the nature of her action, but from the biblical description it appears that the goddess' copious tears filled an amphora from which she drank tears as wine. Thus the translation "and from my tears I draw my drink" and the explanation of the Ugaritic figure of speech sustain the translation of *šālīš*, "bowl," in Ps lxxx 6, quoted in the second NOTE on this verse.

my drink. Biblical *šiqqūway* (cf. Hos ii 7; Prov iii 8) equals Ugar. *šqym*, an exceptionally strong or exceptionally refreshing drink; see Otto Eissfeldt, JSS 5 (1960), 45.

11. *your wrath*. The root of *qeṣep*, "wrath," appears as a Canaanite gloss in the niphal conjugation in EA 82:51, *naqṣapu*, "He is wroth," and 93:5, *naqṣapti*, "I am wroth."

your fury and your wrath. The poet balances the line by placing the two nouns in the first colon and the two verbs "you lifted me up and threw me down" in the second; cf. the comments on Pss lxxvi 12, ci 1, cvii 39. A prose writer would say, "You lifted me up because of your fury, and threw me down in your wrath."

12. *a tapering shadow*. The psalmist, because of his sickness, has reached the evening of life; cf. Jer vi 4, "The day wanes, the shadows of evening taper."

13. *But you, Yahweh*. Scanning the line into three (5+5+8 syllables) cola, instead of the traditional two-cola division.

from eternity. The second NOTES on Pss ix 8, xxix 10, and the third NOTE on Ps lxxviii 69 examine the ambivalent phrase *leʻōlām*, "from eternity," or "to eternity." From the context one can generally see which meaning is intended.

have sat enthroned. The most instructive parallel to this locution comes from Ps ix 8 where the balance with preterit *kōnēn*, "has established," points up the past nature of *yēšēb*, "has reigned," and where the pairing with *kiseʼō*, "his throne," brings out the majestic meaning of the verb *tēšēb*: "Behold Yahweh who has reigned from eternity, has established his throne for judgment."

your throne. Textual critics and commentators, along with a number of Hebrew scribes, have doctored the reading *zikrekā* to bring it into line with Lam v 19, *'attāh yhwh leʻōlām tēšēb kis'akā ledōr wedōr*, "You, Yahweh, have sat enthroned from eternity; your throne endures from age to age." Unfortunately this alteration slights the observation made at Pss liii (introductory NOTE) and lv 23 that variant readings in a doubly transmitted line or poem are often synonyms, so that one reading should not be emended on the basis of the other variant. Applying this rule to the present case we must conclude that *zikrekā* (preferably read *zakrekā*; see also Ps cxv 12) is synonymous with *kis'akā*, "your throne." This conclusion would seem to bear on Ugaritic text 51:VI:51–54, *špq ilm kḥṯm yn špq ilht ksat* [*yn*] *špq ilm rḥbt yn špq ilht dkrt* [*yn*], "He sates the chair-gods with wine, he sates the throne-goddesses [with wine], he sates the couch-gods with wine, he sates the seat-goddesses [with wine]." The meaning of *kḥṯm* and *ksat* is clear, but uncertainty attends *rḥbt* and *dkrt*. The series of four corresponding nouns in immediately preceding lines 47–50: *ilm krm*, "he-lamb gods," *ilht ḫpr̠t,* "ewe-lamb goddesses," *ilm alpm,* "bull-gods," *ilht arḫt,* "cow-goddesses," permits one to argue that the four components of the present list also belong to one class, namely, furniture. In UT, 128: IV:5, 16, *rḥbt yn* seems to signify "cask of wine," here it appears to refer to a wide divan or bed; cf. Isa lvii 8, *hirḥabtā miškābēk,* "You widened your bed." Accordingly the final noun of the series *dkrt* (singular *dkr*) would be synonymous with *ksat,* "thrones," as in the psalm text.

14. *You will arise.* That is, from your throne, as in Pss ix 20, lxxvi 10; Zeph iii 8; and Job xxxi 14, as noted in *Psalms I* on Ps ix 20; cf. also BDB, p. 878a.

to show compassion. Parsing *teraḥēm* as subjunctive expressing purpose after *tāqūm;* cf. RSV, "Thou wilt arise and have pity." In vs. 19, *yehallēl,* we recognize another subjunctive. The root is witnessed in UT, 125:33, *yd't krḥmt,* "I know that she shows compassion."

indeed. Understanding *kī* as an emphasizing particle.

15. *love . . . are moved to pity.* The psalmist achieves poetic variation by pairing the *qtl* form *rāṣū* (Ugar. *rṣy*) with *yqtl yeḥōnēnū* (Ugar. *ḥnn*), and by arranging the verbs and their accusative objects ("her stones," "her dust") in a chiastic pattern.

her stones, by her dust. Zion has been leveled by the foe; her buildings are in ruin, mere stones and rubble. Cf. the description of the destruction of Tyre in Ezek xxvi 12, "Your stones, your timbers, your dust they poured into the sea."

16. *revere.* A number of manuscripts read *weyire'ū,* "They will see," for MT *weyiyre'ū,* "They will revere," but the Masoretic reading is vindicated by the observation that it forms a wordplay with vs. 17, *nir'āhā* from *rā'āh,* "to see." The same play on roots is noticed at Ps lii 8, *weyire'ū ṣaddīqīm weyiyrā'ū,* "The just will look on in dread," and at Ps lxiv 5–6, while the second NOTE on Ps lx 5 shows that punning was not out of place in Canaanite and biblical laments. Another pun recurs in vss. 17–18.

your name. Though unsupplied with a pronominal suffix, *šēm* must be rendered "your name" because of its parallelism with *kebōdekā,* "your glory"; cf. the first NOTE on Ps lxxxix 2. In fact, Ps lxxii 19, *šēm kebōdō,* literally "the glory of his name," shows that the poet, when placing *šēm* in the first colon and *kebōdekā* in the second, employed the figure known as the breakup of composite phrases. Consult first NOTE on Ps xi 4, and THE GRAMMAR OF THE PSALTER.

17. *builds Zion anew.* As noticed at Ps li 20, biblical *bānāh,* like Ugar. *bny,* denotes both "to build" and "to build anew." The knowledge that *b* and *p* were closely related sounds, that often interchange with no semantic difference (THE GRAMMAR OF THE PSALTER), facilitates appreciation of the psalmist's punning on *bānāh,* "builds anew," and *pānāh,* "he regards," in vs. 18.

appears to her in his glory. To many scholars the final colon, *nir'āh bikᵉbōdō,* seems defective. Thus *La Bible de la Pléiade,* II, p. 1120, states that a word has disappeared from the second colon, and accordingly restores *bᵉqirbāh,* "in her midst." The revision of the tract on dative suffixes necessitated by Northwest Semitic epigraphical discoveries permits the textual critic to forgo such drastic expedients. Suffice it to add one syllable to MT *nir'āh,* reading *nir'āhā* and explaining the suffix *-hā* as the original feminine singular suffix that is often written in the Qumran Scrolls *-hāh;* in Ugaritic the suffix is *-hā.* Its syntactic function here would be as the dative suffix, an alternate construction to Jer xxxi 3, *mērāḥōq yhwh nir'āh lī,* "From afar Yahweh appeared to him" (the third-person suffix of *lī* referring to Israel). Hence the reading *nir'āhā bikᵉbōdō,* with its seven syllables, balances the seven syllables of the first colon, *kī bānāh yahweh ṣiyyōn,* "When Yahweh builds Zion anew."

In Gen xvi 11 the author, by employing the Canaanite form of the second-person feminine singular suffix *-kī,* was able perfectly to balance his cola of five syllables each: *kī yišma' yahweh 'ēl 'ᵃnāyākī,* "For Yahweh has heard you, El has answered you." For this reading and the grammatical details, see M. Dahood, *Biblica* 49 (1968), 87–88.

18. *he regards.* The pun on *pānāh* and *bānāh* in vs. 17 is noticed in the first NOTE on vs. 17.

the prayer. Briggs, CECBP, II, p. 328, deletes *tᵉpillat* as a gloss because it is improbable that the poet would use the same noun in parallel cola. His deletion, however, destroys the 9:9 syllable count (cf. the second NOTE on vs. 17), and at the same time slights the well-attested Ugaritic and biblical practice of using the same noun in both halves of the verse. See the fourth NOTE on Ps lxxiii 8.

the destitute. KB, p. 738a, derive the present *'ar'ār* and the name of the tamarisk in Jer xvii 6 from the same root *'ārar,* "to lay bare," a by-form of *'ārāh,* also "to lay bare, strip." If both nouns derive from the same root, then the citation of Ugar. *'r'r,* "tamarisk," parallel to *'ṣ mt,* "the tree of death," is not irrelevant, especially since the poet speaks of the *bᵉnē tᵉmūtāh,* literally "the sons of death," in vs. 21.

Like *'āsīr,* "prisoners," in vs. 21, *'ar'ār* is a singular noun with collective meaning.

19. *Let this be written.* Namely, vss. 20–23, which are here placed between inverted commas.

Yah. A shortened form of Yahweh.

20. *From.* Reproducing *kī,* literally "that," by inverted commas; see the comment on a similar usage at Ps lii 2, in the NOTE on "and told Saul," where the words "and he said" are taken as the equivalent of our quotation marks.

Yahweh. The position of the divine name within the verse has been the object of controversy, with some critics placing it after first-colon *hišqīp,* "looked down." D. N. Freedman, however, has correctly seen that MT *yhwh* stands precisely between the two longer cola and serves as the subject of both. A literal translation, preserving the Hebrew word order, would read, "From his holy height looked down / Yahweh / From heaven to earth gazed." The syllable count thus becomes 8:2:9 (following MT; with the archaic vocalization the count could also be 7 instead of 9). Lending further conviction to this scansion is the chiastic arrangement of the longer cola in an A+B//B́+Á sequence. The double-duty modifier (see the first NOTE to vs. 3) plus chiasmus is discussed at Ps cix 14.

height . . . heaven. In *mārōm* and *šāmayim* the psalmist balances two roots that are juxtaposed in one of the goddess Anath's titles, *b'lt šmm rmm,* "mistress of the high heavens," in Phoen. *šmm rmm* and in *samēroumos,* mentioned by Sanchunyaton; cf. the second NOTE on Ps lxxviii 69.

From heaven to earth. The pairing of *šāmayim* and *'ereṣ* is well attested in Ugaritic (see the first NOTE on Ps lxxiii 9), and a recently published tablet speaks of an animal being sacrificed to the divinities *arṣ wšmm,* "Earth and Heaven" (RŠ 24.643). The fourth NOTE on Ps lvii 8 deals with parallel pairs as a criterion for establishing the linguistic and literary classification of Ugaritic; to date 290 such parallel pairs in Ugaritic and in Hebrew have been identified, an increase of 50 since *Psalms II* was published in 1968. See the list in THE GRAMMAR OF THE PSALTER.

gazed. Synonymous with *hišqīp,* with which it forms the poetic figure of chiasmus, *hibbīṭ,* probably occurs in UT, 51:III:21, *kbh bṯt ltbṭ,* "For therein shame is seen."

21. *prisoners.* As in Ps lxxix 11, singular *'āsīr* bears a collective meaning, a usage also witnessed in Ugar. *kp,* "hands," and *riš,* "heads," as noticed at Ps lxviii 22.

those condemned to die. Literally "sons of death," the second element of *bᵉnē tᵉmūtāh* probably occurs twice in UT, 2059:16, 22. The latter text reads *w[k]lhm bd rb tmtt lqḥt* "And I snatched all of them from the hand of the Master of Death," where "the Master of Death" would be an epithet of Death himself. M. Dietrich and O. Loretz in BO 23 (1966), 132, reject the equation of *tmtt* with biblical *tᵉmūtāh,* and postulate a substantive denoting "crew, gang"; hence their translation "Mannschaftführer" ("leader of the crew"). But this derivation neglects the mention of death in line 13 (*mtt*) and the biblical idiom which often speaks of rescue from the hands of Death and bestows upon Death such titles as *melek ballāhōt,* "the King of Terrors" (Job xviii 14).

22. *be proclaimed.* Cf. Ps lxvii 3, where the qal infinitive construct *lāda'at* is translated passively, just as the piel infinitive construct here, *lᵉsappēr,* must be turned passively.

23. *with kings.* For this definition of *mamlākōt,* see the first NOTE on Ps lxviii 33. The Vatican and Sinaitic codices of the LXX read *basileís,* "kings," as do Aquila, and Theodotion, a reading followed by the Vulgate. This lection appears superior to *basileías,* "kingdoms," adopted in their editions of the LXX by Henry Swete and by Alfred Rahlfs. Cf. Alfred

Rahlfs, *Septuaginta—Studien I–III,* 2d ed. (Göttingen, 1965), 2. Heft, *Der Text des Septuaginta—Psalters,* p. 49.

him. I read *'ōtō* for MT *'et* and transfer *yhwh* to the next colon where, as Gunkel (*Die Psalmen,* p. 440) has acutely observed, the lack of a divine name is surprising. With this reading, the three words and nine syllables of the second colon balance better the three words and eight syllables in the first colon than do the four words and ten syllables of MT. What is more, the transposition of *yhwh* to the next verse restores the word and syllable equilibrium hitherto lacking. For other instances of *'ōtōh,* see the second NOTES on Pss lxix 27 and xci 9. Cf. also Eccles iv 10, *kī 'im yippōl* (MT *yippelū*) *hā'eḥād yāqīm 'ōtō* (MT *'et*) *ḥabērō,* "For if one should fall, his companion will lift him up," as proposed by M. Dahood, *Biblica* 49 (1968), 243. Contrast RSV, "For if they fall, one will lift up his fellow." How?

24. *Yahweh.* Once transposed to vs. 24 (see second NOTE on vs. 23), *yhwh* supplies the divine name desired in the first colon, brings the number of words in the verse into equilibrium (4:4) and the syllables into perfect balance (9:9). The verse (including first two words of vs. 25) reads:

yahweh 'innāh bedarkō kōḥī
weqiṣṣar yāmay 'emār 'ēlī

Noteworthy too is the emergent inclusion formed by the composite divine name *yahweh 'ēlī,* whose first component stands as the first word of the line, while the second element ends the verse. On *yahwēh 'ēl* see NOTES on Pss x 12, xxxix 13, and cxliii 1, 7, 9, and my articles in *Biblica* 46 (1965), 317–18; 47 (1966), 410. The second NOTE on vs. 16 discusses the separation of composite phrases into parallel cola.

my strength. Vocalizing *kōḥī* (Ketiv *kōḥw*), with defective spelling of the final suffix *-ī,* and attaching the *waw* of consonantal *kḥw* to the next word as the conjunction "and." As a result, the syllable count becomes 9:9 instead of 9:8. A similar instance of defective spelling is noticed in the preceding word *bedarkō,* "by his power," MT *badderek.*

by his power. Reading *bedarkō* (MT *badderek*), an instance of defective spelling; the next word *kōḥī,* "my strength," is also written defectively. Cf. Job xxvi 14, *qeṣōt darkō,* "bits of his power," as rendered by Pope, *Job* and his NOTE ad loc. This definition of *derek* is discussed in the third NOTE on Ps i 1, in the first NOTE on Ps lxvii 3, and in the second NOTE on Ps lxxvii 14. Such an interpretation of *derek* accords with vs. 23, *mamlākōt,* "kings," and brings out the parallelism between the roots *drk* and *mlk* that occurs in UT, 68:10, *tqḥ mlk 'lmk drkt dt drdrk,* "You will receive your eternal kingship, your everlasting dominion," in Pss cxxxviii 4–5, cxlvi 9–10, and Job xxix 25. In other words, the pair *'ammīm,* "peoples," and *mamlākōt,* "kings," semantically equals the parallelism of *gōyīm,* "nations," and *malkē hā'āreṣ,* "kings of the earth," in vs. 16.

The association of *darkō,* "his power," with *mamlākōt,* "kings," in vs. 23, roots elsewhere occurring in parallelism, surely suggests that the third stanza (vss. 13–23) and the fourth stanza (vss. 24–29) come from the same hand. The collocation of these cognate roots can hardly be ascribed to the accidental juxtaposition of two stanzas composed by different poets.

and. The conjunction *wᵉ* has been transposed to *qiṣṣar* from the preceding cluster *kḥw.*

my God. In the Hebrew text *'ēlī,* the last word of the verse, forms an inclusion with *yhwh,* the first word in the line, and with *kōḥī,* the last word of the first colon, an instance of assonance. The poignancy of the psalmist's suffering is brought out by the thought that *'ēlī,* "my God," has caused his sufferings.

cut short. Piel *qiṣṣār* balances in vocalic sequence and in the number of syllables piel *'innāh,* "humbled." The observation that the poet carefully structured the verse prepares the textual critic for the uncertain elements of the line.

The root of *qiṣṣār* occurs in the Ugaritic phrase *qṣr npš,* "the wretched."

my vigorous days. Literally "my days of vigor." With *yhwh* balancing *'ēlī* and *'innāh* matching *qiṣṣār,* one may infer that disputed *ymy 'mr* answers to *kōḥī,* "my strength." This inference becomes defensible thanks to the well-documented Northwest Semitic root *mrr,* "to strengthen, commend." On Ugar. *mrr* consult UT, Glossary, No. 1556, and for biblical occurrences, M. Dahood, *Biblica* 39 (1958), 308–10; 47 (1966), 276. The proposed translation of Eccles vii 26 in *Biblica* 39 (1958), 308–10, *mar mimmāwet,* "stronger than death" (cf. Song of Sol viii 6), has been adopted by G. R. Driver in *Studia semitica philologica necnon philosophica Ioanni Bakoš dicata,* ed. S. Segert (Bratislava, 1965), p. 102, and by Svi and Sifra Rin in *Biblische Zeitschrift* 11 (1967), 189. Consonantal *'mr* would accordingly be explained as a noun with prothetic *aleph* from *mrr;* the third NOTE on Ps li 9 examines other members of this noun formation. One may accordingly argue that unexplained Hab iii 9, *maṭṭōt 'emār* (MT *'ōmer*), "powerful shafts," is semantically cognate to Ps cx 2, *maṭṭēh 'uzzᵉkā,* "your victorious mace."

One may vocalize consonantal *ymy 'mr* as *yᵉmēy 'emār,* "the days of vigor," whose pronominal suffix would be supplied by its opposite number *kōḥī,* "my strength," on the principle of the double-duty suffix; or one may read *yᵉmay 'emār,* literally "my days of vigor," and parse the phrase as a construct chain with interposed pronominal suffix, a poetic usage widely attested in the Psalter; cf. the second NOTE on Ps lxi 5. New bibliography includes J.-E. David, "*Tò haimá mou tēs diathēkēs* MT 26,28: Un faux problème," *Biblica* 48 (1967), 291–92.

In summary, *wᵉqiṣṣar yᵉmay 'emār 'ēlī,* "And my God cut short my vigorous days," states the same sentiment as Ps lxxxix 46, *hiqṣartā yᵉmē 'ᵃlūmāyw,* "You cut short the days of his youth."

This reconstruction and reinterpretation clarifies four obscure cola in Job xxxvi 22–23, *hēn 'ēl yaśgīb bᵉkōḥō ūmī kāmōhū mōreh mī pāqad 'alāyw darkō ūmī 'āmar pā'altā 'awlāh,* "Look, El is supreme in his strength, and who is puissant like him? Who entrusted him with his power? And who can say, 'You have done wrong?' " In these two verses occur three of the key words witnessed here in vs. 24: *kōḥō,* "his strength," *mōreh,* "puissant," a by-form of *mrr,* "to be powerful," and *darkō,* "his power." In vs. 22 the final *w* of *kḥw* (*kōḥō*) should also be read as the first letter of *ūmī* (on single writing of two successive like consonants, see the third NOTE on Ps lx 11 and THE GRAMMAR OF THE PSALTER), so that both cola perfectly balance with seven syllables each.

25. *when your years last generations.* Reading *b^{e}dūr* (MT *b^{e}dōr*) *dōrīm š^{e}nōtekā,* with "years" the subject of the infinitive construct *dūr* (as in Ps lxxxiv 11), and *dōrīm* an accusative of time.

26. *you laid earth's foundations.* The phrase *hā'āreṣ yāsadtā* collocates the two roots of the Ugaritic expression *msdt arṣ,* "the foundations of the earth." The cosmogonic nuance of *yāsadtā* appears only in hymnal passages of the Bible: Pss xxiv 2, lxxviii 69, lxxxix 12, civ 5, 8; Amos ix 6; Zech xii 1; Prov iii 19; Isa xlviii 13, li 13, 16. This cosmogonic overtone in hymnal passages probably reflects archaic cultic traditions which the Israelites inherited from their Canaanite predecessors in Palestine. According to this Canaanite theme, the earth was created by some divinity and set like a building upon foundations that reached to the bottom of the ocean. Cf. Paul Humbert, "Note sur YĀSAD et ses dérivés," in HWFB, pp. 135–42, especially 138.

earth's . . . heavens. The parallelism between *'ereṣ* and *šāmayim* has Canaanite antecedents in Ugaritic *arṣ wšmm š,* "Earth and Heaven, one sheep"; NOTE on Ps l 4, and for parallel pairs, the discussion in the fourth NOTE on vs. 20.

your handiwork. Literally "the works of your hands." Cf. Isa xlviii 13, *'ap yādī yās^{e}dāh 'ereṣ wīmīnī ṭipp^{e}ḥāh šāmāyim,* "Yes, my left hand laid the foundation of the earth, my right hand spread out the heavens," as correctly rendered by Carroll Stuhlmueller in CBQ 29 (1967), 196.

27. *will wear out.* Cf. Job xiv 12, *'ad b^{e}lōtī* (MT *biltī*) *šāmayim,* "until the wearing out of the heavens," where the reading *b^{e}lōtī,* the infinitive construct of *bālāh,* Ugar. *bly,* followed by the genitive ending, smoothes the syntax of the phrase.

According to Isa lxv 17 and lxvi 22 new heavens and a new earth will take their place.

28. *you remain the same.* The new translation of Ps lv 20 also affirms the immutability of God.

29. *The children . . . their seed.* The parallel pair *b^{e}nē,* "the children," and *zar'ām,* "their seed," recurs juxtaposed in Phoenician Eshmunazor, line 8, *bn wzr',* "son or seed." Cf. also Pss xxi 11, cv 6.

in your presence. Namely, in the land of Palestine. Ps lxxxv 10 may serve as commentary on the present verse: "Truly near is his prosperity to those who fear him; / Indeed his glory dwells in our land."

PSALM 103

(ciii 1–22)

1 *Of David.*

Bless Yahweh, O my soul!
and all my inmost parts his holy name.
2 Bless Yahweh, O my soul,
and forget not all his benefits,
3 Who forgives all your iniquity,
who heals all your diseases,
4 Who will redeem your life from the Pit,
who will crown you with kindness and mercy,
5 Who will imbue your eternity with his beauty,
when your youth will be renewed like the eagle's.
6 Yahweh, who secures vindication
and justice for all the oppressed,
7 Made known his ways to Moses,
to Israel's sons his deeds.
8 Merciful and gracious is Yahweh,
slow to anger and rich in kindness.
9 He will not always scold,
nor eternally nourish his anger.
10 Not according to our sins does he deal with us,
nor as fits our crimes does he punish us.
11 But as the height of heaven above the nether world,
strong is his kindness for those who fear him.
12 As distant as east from west,
has he made distant from himself our rebellious acts.
13 As a father has compassion upon his children,
Yahweh has compassion upon those who fear him.
14 For he knows our form,
mindful that we are clay.
15 Man, his days are like grass,
like a wild flower, so he flowers.

16 If a wind passes over him, he is no more,
and his home knows him no longer.
17 But Yahweh's kindness is from eternity,
and to eternity toward those who fear him;
And his generosity to children's children,
18 to those who keep his covenant,
and remember to fulfill his precepts.
19 Though Yahweh set his throne in heaven,
by his royal power he rules over all.
20 Bless Yahweh, his angels,
warriors mighty to execute his command,
heeding the sound of his word.
21 Bless Yahweh, all his soldiers,
his ministers who do his will.
22 Bless Yahweh, all his works,
in all places, you his subjects.
Bless Yahweh, O my soul!

NOTES

ciii. This hymn may fairly be described as an Old Testament *Te Deum.* In vss. 1–5 the psalmist urges his innermost being to thank Yahweh for five blessings: the forgiveness of sins, the healing of illnesses, rescue from Sheol, admittance to a blessed afterlife, the eternal enjoyment of God's beauty in heaven. In this catalogue of blessings the poet employs five participles—five as half of the basic number ten is important in the Bible (I Kings vii 39, 49; Matt xxv 2)—that recall the ten participles in the Canaanite catalogue enumerating the duties of a son toward his father (2 Aqht:II:16–21). The psalmist then (vss. 6–10) recounts some historical instances of Yahweh's generosity toward Israel, and in vss. 11–18 he offers some reflections on the nature of God, his justice, love, and eternity, compared with the frail and transient condition of man. Verses 19–22 form a conclusion, with a summons to all created beings to join the psalmist in praise of Yahweh.

Critics customarily signalize the putative Aramaic suffix *-kī* in vss. 3–5 and the supposed literary dependence of vss. 15–16 on Second Isaiah (xl 6–8) as arguments for a post-Exilic dating (cf., e.g., Kraus, *Psalmen,* II, p. 702). The possibility, though, that the suffix *-kī* might be a Canaanite archaism (see the second NOTE on vs. 3), and that both the psalmist and Second Isaiah might have borrowed from a common literary source (cf. *Psalms I,* pp. XXIX f., 161; *Psalms II,* introductory NOTE to Ps lv) drains such arguments of much of their cogency; a post-Exilic date of composition thus appears very unlikely.

1. *Bless Yahweh, O my soul. bār*^{a}*kī napšī 'et yhwh* forms an inclusion with this same phrase in the final verse.

O my soul. The psalmist employs the literary genre known as "the dialogue of a man with his soul," commented upon at Pss xlii 6 and lxii 2.

my inmost parts. Since the plural form *q*^{e}*rābay* is a hapax legomenon, critics (e.g., Kraus, BH^3 apparatus) generally prefer to read the well-attested singular form *qirbī.* The three-syllable plural form (against two-syllable *qirbī*) does have its *raison d'être,* namely, to bring the syllable count of the second colon to nine syllables; thus the second colon perfectly matches the nine syllables of the second colon in vs. 2. Since the eight-syllable first colon of vs. 1 is repeated in vs. 2, the syllable count in vss. 1–2 becomes 8:9, thanks to the poet's use of plural *q*^{e}*rābay.* On the utility of syllable counting, see the Index of Subjects in *Psalms II,* and the first NOTE on Ps cxxxix 15.

3. *forgives . . . heals.* Inasmuch as sickness was believed to be caused by sin (second NOTE on Ps xli 7, third NOTE on lxix 27), the psalmist mentions the forgiveness of sin before the healing of disease.

your iniquity . . . your diseases. Coinciding with the second-person feminine singular suffix *-kī* of Aramaic, the suffix of *'*^{a}*wōnēkī* and *taḥ*^{a}*lū'āy*^{e}*kī* is usually termed an Aramaism (cf. GK, § 91e) and cited as an argument for post-Exilic dating of the psalm. While this inference may be correct, feminine *-kī* possibly may be a Canaanite archaism. This was the form in Ugaritic (UT, § 6.7), and some early biblical poets may have used this form to achieve certain poetic effects. Thus the desire for syllabic equilibrium and an inclusion points to the vocalization *'*^{a}*nāyākī* (MT *'onyēk*) in Gen xvi 11, *kī yišma' yhwh 'ēl '*^{a}*nāyākī,* "For Yahweh has heard you, El has answered you," where the syllable count is 5:5, and initial *kī* forms an inclusion with final second-person feminine suffix *-kī.* For further details, see Dahood, *Biblica* 49 (1968), 87–88.

4. *redeem your life.* When the psalmist dies and goes down to Sheol, Yahweh will ransom him from the hand of Death and bring him to Paradise; cf. NOTES on Pss xxxiv 23 and lv 18–19. The use of *gō'ēl,* "redeem," here recalls Job xix 25, "I know that my Redeemer lives," in a passage dealing with the afterlife.

your life. On the feminine suffix *-kī* of *ḥayyāykī,* consult the second NOTE on vs. 3.

the Pit. Heretofore unattested in other Semitic languages, *šaḥat,* "the Pit," a key word in Psalms (vii 16, ix 16, xvi 10, xxx 10, xxxv 7, xlix 10, lv 23, xciv 13), makes its first non-biblical appearance in UT, 607:64–65, published by C. Virolleaud in *Groupe Linguistique d'Etudes Chamito-Semitiques* 10 (1963–66), 64. The lines read: *ydy b'ṣm 'r'r wbšḥt 'ṣ mt,* "He hurled the tamarisk into the Hole, and into the Pit the tree of death." Its parallelism with *šḥt,* "the Pit," shows that *'ṣm* is an alternate spelling of *'ẓm,* "to burrow," in UT, 75:I:23–25, discussed in *Psalms I,* second NOTE on x 10. The pairing of the Ugaritic roots *'ṣm* and *šwḥ* (*šḥt*) recalls the association of *yāšō^aḥ*, "tumbles," and *'^aṣūmāyw*, "his pit," in Ps x 10. The meaning of Ugar. *šḥt*, completely missed by Virolleaud, who tentatively connected it with Akk. *šaḫatu*, the name of a plant (see the writer's strictures on Virolleaud's methodology in *Psalms I*, p. XXVIII), has been correctly seized by C. H. Gordon, *Supplement to the Ugaritic Textbook* (Rome, 1967), pp. 554–55.

Though some commentators (e.g., Briggs) understand the Pit of Sheol metaphorically, namely as Israel's exile in Babylon, I take the term literally. Like the author of Ps xvi 10, "Since you will not put me in Sheol, nor allow your devoted one to see the Pit," the psalmist is confident that he will be removed from the Pit and transferred to Yahweh's eternal abode.

who will crown you. Exegetes conventionally explain this action in worldly terms—they imagine the psalmist celebrating his recovery with a festive turban on his head (so Gunkel)—but the mention of *šaḥat*, "the Pit," in the first colon and the use of three eschatological terms in the following verse show that the psalmist is describing the afterlife wherein Yahweh will place crowns on the heads of the just admitted to Paradise. Ps v 13, collocating *ṣaddīq*, "the just man," and *ta'ṭ^erennū*, the same verb of our context, probably refers to the same practice of crowning the blessed in heaven.

with kindness and mercy. As noticed at Pss viii 6 and lxv 12, *'iṭṭēr*, "to crown," likewise governs a double accusative in Phoenician. In the description of Paradise found in Ps xxiii 6, personified goodness and kindness are said to accompany the blessed in heaven; here kindness and mercy will form the crown of the psalmist in Paradise.

5. *Who will imbue*. As noted at Ps lxv 5, the root of *maśbī^a'* belongs to the diction of passages describing the joys of eternal life.

your eternity. Vocalizing *'ōdekī*, "your eternity," for unexplained MT *'edyēk*, which KJ renders as "thy mouth." Accustomed to the *scriptio plena* (*'wd*) of this substantive, the Masoretes again fail to recognize this word in Pss iii 4 and cxxxviii 8, reading *ba'^adī*, "on my behalf," for *b^e'ōdī* (Ugar. *b'd*), "as long as I live." Cf. also second NOTE on Ps iii 4. Thus the synonymy of *'ōdekī* and *ḥayyāykī*, "your life," in vs. 4, recalls the parallelism of these two nouns in Pss civ 33 and cxlvi 2.

The archaic feminine suffix of *'ōdekī* is assonant with its opposite number *n^e'ūrāykī*, "your youth," precisely as in vs. 3. The balance of these two nouns elicits not only the motif of "eternal youth," but in a context mentioning "life" and "Pit" suggests the everlasting enjoyment of the divine presence in the afterlife. Cf. the third NOTE on Ps cxxxix 18, which states a similar idea.

with his beauty. With no consonantal changes, reading *b^eṭūbō* for MT *baṭṭōb*. In defective orthography *bṭb* could be read either *baṭṭōb* (MT) or *b^eṭūbō*. The problems stemming from MT *'edyēk*, it has been noticed, can be traced to an original employing defective spelling. By adding two syllables to the first colon, the lection *b^eṭūbō 'ōdekī* evens the syllable count of both cola at ten syllables each; in MT the count stands at 8:10. Consult the third NOTE on vs. 1.

Like *maśbīaʿ*, *ṭūb*, "beauty," also figures in descriptions of celestial afterlife; see third NOTE on Ps xxvii 13 and fifth NOTE on Ps lxv 5. The exegesis of our phrase is forthcoming from Pss xxvii 13, "to behold the beauty of Yahweh [*beṭūb yhwh* equals our *beṭūbō*] in the land of life eternal," xvii 15, "At the vindication I will gaze upon your face; At the resurrection I will be saturated with your being."

like the eagle's. An allusion to the fable of the eagle's renewing its youth in old age. Gunkel (*Die Psalmen,* p. 445) is probably right (contrast the note in CCD and Kraus, *Psalmen,* II, p. 703) in seeing here a reference to the story of the phoenix; cf. Job xxix 18, *wāʾōmar ʿim qinnī ʾegwāʿ wekaḥōl ʾarbeh yāmīm,* "And I thought, 'Though I perish like its nest, I shall multiply days like the phoenix.'" For details, see M. Dahood, *Biblica* 48 (1967), 542–44. These allusions fit in most naturally with the interpretation of vss. 4–5 as a description of immortality.

6. *vindication.* Following BDB, p. 842b and RSV's translation of *ṣedāqāh,* and consulting *Psalms II,* first NOTE on Ps lxv 6, for other instances of this nuance in the root *ṣdq.* Cf. also J. Bright, *Jeremiah* (AB, vol. 21), second NOTE on Jer xxiii 6.

This vindication will take place in the future life when the inequities and inconsistencies of this life will find their resolution.

all the oppressed. Comparing Matt v 10, "Blessed are those who have endured persecution for the sake of justice, for the Kingdom of Heaven belongs to them."

7. *Made known.* In *yōdīaʿ* we recognize the *yqtl* form in one of its normal functions in poetry, viz., to express the past; see THE GRAMMAR OF THE PSALTER. Contrast Briggs, CECBP, II, pp. 324–25: "He used to make known His ways to Moses."

his ways . . . his deeds. An example of chiasmus (A+B+C//Ć+B́) in a syllabically balanced line with nine syllables in each colon.

10. *with us . . . punish us.* The proposal of BH[3] to delete the balancing prepositions *lānū* and *ʿālēnū* (see vs. 17) is implausible in the light of two recent discoveries. The Qumran fragment 2Q 14, 1 contains the final four letters of this verse [ʿ]*lynw* (M. Dahood, *Biblica* 45 [1964], 131), and the recently published Ugaritic tablet 608:7 balances the same prepositions as the psalmist: *isp špš lhrm ǵrpl ʿl arṣ,* "the obscuring of the sun upon the mountains, dark clouds upon the earth." Regarding parallel pairs as a text-critical criterion, see the fourth NOTE on lvii 8, the third NOTE on Ps cii 20, and for another instance of Ugaritic and Qumran conspiring to secure the reading and meaning of a biblical verse, consult Dahood, "Ugaritic *ušn,* Job 12,10 and 11QPs[a] Plea 3–4," in *Biblica* 47 (1966), 107–8.

11. *heaven above the nether world.* Traditionally rendered "heaven above the earth," *šāmayim ʿal hāʾāreṣ* assumes greater significance when

interpreted against Prov xxv 3, *šāmayim lārūm wā'āreṣ lā'ōmeq,* "the heavens for height, and the nether world for depth" (cf. PNWSP, p. 52; Scott, *Proverbs • Ecclesiastes,* ad loc., and Ps lxxiii 9, *šattū baššāmayim pīhem ūlᵉšōnām tihᵃlak bā'āreṣ,* "They set their mouth against heaven, and their tongue swished through the nether world," a version indebted to UT, 52:61–62, *št špt larṣ špt lšmm,* "They set one lip against the nether world, the other lip against heaven," and 'nt:III:21, *tant šmm 'm arṣ,* "the meeting of heaven with the nether world." Compare likewise Isa lv 9, "For as heaven is higher than the nether world (*šāmayim mē'āreṣ*), so are my ways higher than your ways."

12. *west.* Biblical *ma'ᵃrāb* equals Ugar. *m'rb* in *m'rb špš,* "setting of the sun," and Phoen. *m'rb,* "west."

from himself. MT *mimmennū* being ambivalent, capable of denoting "from himself" or "from us," I follow A. B. Ehrlich, *Die Psalmen,* (Berlin, 1905), p. 245, who maintains that the traditional version "from us" results in an affirmation unexampled in the OT, whereas the proposed translation states the opposite of Ps xc 8, "You have kept our iniquities before you, the sins of our youth in the light of your face."

14. *our form.* The metaphor of the potter and his jar which evokes Job x 9, *zᵉkor nā' kī kaḥōmer 'ᵃśītanī wᵉ'el 'āpār tᵉšībēnī,* "Remember that you formed me like a jar, and to clay will make me return."

mindful. MT *zākūr,* which is a hapax legomenon, can be parsed either as the qal passive participle (cf. Willy Schottroff, *'Gedenken' im Alten Orient und im Alten Testament* [Neukirchen, 1964], p. 240) or as the infinitive absolute with Phoenician vocalization; in the Phoenician dialect Heb. *zākōr* would be pronounced *zākūr.* Cf. Eccles xii 10, *wᵉkātūb,* "and he wrote," a Phoenician infinitive absolute that is often needlessly repointed to *wᵉkātōb,* and also the second NOTE to Ps cxii 7, and the third NOTE to Ps cxxxix 20. It thus becomes unnecessary to repoint Ps xlix 4 *hāgūt,* "shall proclaim," to infinitive absolute *hāgōt* (second NOTE ad loc.), since MT *hāgūt* may now be explained as the Phoenician form of the infinitive absolute. The presence of the Phoenician forms *ḥokmōt,* "wisdom," and *tᵉbūnōt,* "insight," in this verse sustains this analysis.

clay. The psalmists' consistency in their use of metaphors (cf. M. Dahood, "Congruity of Metaphors," in HWFB, pp. 40–49; fourth NOTES on Pss li 9 and xci 2, and NOTES on Pss xciv 9 and xcvii 11) suggests that the conventional translation of *'āpār* here (RSV, "we are dust") in Gen ii 7, iii 19, and Job x 9 is misleading. A potter normally works with clay, not dust. On *'āpār,* "mud, slime," consult last NOTES on Pss vii 6, xxii 16, xxx 10. Unless sustained by Yahweh, man, who is fashioned of clay, is ever in danger of returning to the slime of Sheol. The psalmist brilliantly associates two distinct images.

15. *Man, his days are like grass.* The psalmist employs the construction known as *casus pendens* (GK, § 143). CCD's "Man's days are like those of grass," obliterates the Hebrew construction and obscures the reflective

style of the original. UT, 2 Aqht:vi:35 presents a close parallel: *mt uḫryt mh yqḥ,* "Man, what will he receive as afterlife?" Ugaritic specialists have, however, misconstrued this usage in UT, 52:39, *il aṯtm k ypt,* usually rendered "El indeed seduces the two women," but which should more probably read, "El, his two wives are indeed beautiful," with *il* analyzed as *casus pendens.* In other terms, the phrase *aṯtm k ypt* semantically approaches *'iššāh yāpāh,* "a beautiful woman," an expression well attested in the Bible. Cf. also UT, 67:vi:16–17, *lpš yks mizrtm,* "For clothes, he is covered with a double garment," another illustration of *casus pendens.*

like . . . like . . . so. The series *k*ᵉ . . . *k*ᵉ. . . *kēn* (cf. Pss lxxxiii 15–16, cxxiii 2) recalls the sequence in UT, 49:ii:28–30, *klb arḫ l'glh klb ṯat limrh km lb 'nt aṯr b'l,* "Like the heart of a wild cow for her calf, like the heart of a wild ewe for her lamb, such was the heart of Anath toward Baal."

a wild flower. Literally "a flower of the field"; cf. Matt vi 28, "Study the wild lilies," literally "the lilies of the field," erroneously translated by the *New English Bible,* "Consider how the lilies grow in the fields."

The root of *ṣīṣ,* "flower," which means "to shine, glisten," occurs in *ṣṣ,* the Ugaritic term for "salt mine."

16. *over him.* Not "over it," as translated by RSV, since *m*ᵉ*qōmō* in the second colon refers to his human domicile. See next NOTE.

his home. Literally "his place," *māqōm* often bears the nuance "home, abode"; cf. second NOTE on Ps xxvi 8; *Biblica* 48 (1967), 431. For the present consideration, the most relevant text might be Job vii 10, *lō' yāšūb 'ōd l*ᵉ*bētō w*ᵉ*lō' yakkīrennū 'ōd m*ᵉ*qōmō,* "He returns to his house no more, and his home knows him no more."

17. *and to eternity.* Splitting the stereotyped phrase *mē'ōlām w*ᵉ*'ad 'ōlām,* and attaching *w*ᵉ*'ad 'ōlām* to the second colon, whose eight syllables nicely match the eight syllables of the first colon; cf. Ps cvii 25.

19. *his throne . . . his royal power.* The biblical collocation *kis'ō ūmalkūtō* echoes such Canaanite expressions as UT, 127:23, *yṯb lksi mlk,* "He sits upon his royal throne," where *ksi mlk* juxtaposes the same two roots found in the biblical diction.

by his royal power. Parsing *malkūtō* as an accusative of means preceding its verb, a stylistic feature of frequent occurrence in the Psalter; see fifth NOTE on Ps v 10, last NOTE on Ps lvi 2. The versions make it the subject of the colon: "And his kingdom rules over all" (RSV).

he rules. Parsing *māšālāh* not as the third-person singular feminine whose subject is *malkūtō* (so the standard grammars and lexicons), but rather as the archaic masculine *qatala* form whose subject is *yahweh,* as in the first colon. An examination of biblical texts containing the verb *māšal,* "to rule," reveals that the subject is always a living being, such as God, man, or animal. Outside this text there is no attestation of an abstract noun like *malkūt,* "royal power," serving as the subject of this verb; cf. *Biblica* 48 (1967), 434. JB fudges the difficulty by ignoring *māšālāh* altogether: "his empire is over all." To lengthen the second colon that would otherwise be too short, the psalmist employed an archaic *qatala* form. Other examples of this archaism are listed in THE GRAMMAR OF THE PSALTER. See below on Ps cxiii 9, and cf. Deut xxxiii 23, *yām wᵉdōrō-m yārāšāh* (MT *yᵉrāšāh*), "he (Naphtali) inherited the lake and environs."

20. *heeding the sound of his word.* The Hebrew expression *lišmōᵃʿ bᵉqōl dᵉbārō* finds its Phoenician counterpart in CIS, I, 123:5–6, *šmʿ ql dbry,* "He heard the sound of his words."

21. *his soldiers.* Not "his hosts/armies" with the versions, because the plural of *ṣābāʾ*, "host, army," is always *ṣᵉbāʾōt*. Here and in Ps cxlviii 2 the masculine plural suggests a nuance different from the feminine plural. The parallelism here with "his ministers" and with "his angels" in Ps cxlviii 2 sustains this observation. In Ugaritic, *ṣbu* denotes both "soldier" and "army."

The "soldiers" refer to Yahweh's angels. Consult further Patrick D. Miller, "The Divine Council and the Prophetic Call to War," in VT 18 (1968), 100–7, especially p. 104, n. 1, where references to Qumranic designations of angels may be found.

his ministers. Another expression for the angels, described as ministerial servants ready to execute the sovereign will.

22. *you his subjects.* The parallelistic structure of vss. 21–22 (his soldiers . . . his ministers . . . his works) suggests that abstract *memšaltō,* "his dominion," carries here a concrete denotation, namely, men ruled by God. Consult *Psalms II,* third NOTE on Ps li 16, second NOTES on Ps lxxxix 9 and 14, and Index of Subjects, s.v. Isa xi 14 furnishes an illuminating analogy: *bᵉnē ʿammōn mišmaʿtām,* "The Ammonites will be their subjects," literally "their obedience"; cf. Mesha Inscription, line 28.

This concrete meaning of *memšaltō,* "his subjects," may shed some light on Ecclus x 1, *šwpṭ ʿm ywsr ʿmw wmmšlt mbyn sdyrh,* "A sagacious ruler educates his people, and his subjects he makes understand order."

Bless Yahweh, O my soul. The three occurrences of this command (vss. 1, 2, 22) match the triple command "Bless Yahweh" (vss. 20–22). The last member of the former group, namely vs. 22b, has been detached and put at the end of the poem to form an inclusion with vss. 1–2 (D. N. Freedman).

PSALM 104

(civ 1–35)

1 Bless Yahweh, O my soul!
Yahweh my God, you are very great indeed,
with splendor and majesty are you clothed!
2 Who is robed with the sun as his garment,
who stretched out the heavens like a tent,
3 Who stored with water his upper chambers,
who set his chariot on the clouds,
Who travels on wings outstretched,
4 who makes the winds his messengers,
fire and flame his ministers,
5 Who placed the earth upon its foundations,
lest it should ever quake.
6 You covered it with the ocean like a garment,
and upon the mountains stood the waters.
7 At your roar they fled,
at the sound of your thunder they took flight.
8 They went up to the mountains,
they went down to the nether chasm,
to the place which you appointed for them.
9 You marked a border they should not cross,
lest they cover the earth again.
10 Who released springs and torrents
to flow between the mountains,
11 To supply all beasts with water,
that wild asses might quench their thirst.
12 Near them the birds of heaven dwell,
from their midst the ravens give forth their voice.
13 Who waters the mountains from his upper chambers;
with supplies from his storehouses
the earth is fully provided.
14 Who makes grass grow for the cattle,
and fodder for beasts plowing the land.

Indeed he brings forth grain from the earth,
15 and with wine he gladdens the heart of man.
Truly he makes the full face resplendent,
and with food sustains the heart of man.
16 Well watered are Yahweh's trees,
the cedars of Lebanon, which he planted;
17 Where the birds build their nest,
the stork—the junipers are her home;
18 The high mountains belong to the wild goats,
the sheltering crags to the badgers.
19 The moon acts according to the seasons,
the sun knows its setting.
20 It grows dark and night comes on,
then all the beasts of the forest prowl.
21 The young lions roar for their prey,
seeking their food from God.
22 The sun rises, they steal away,
and in their dens stretch out.
23 Man goes forth to his labor,
and to his tilling until evening.
24 How manifold are your works, Yahweh!
With Wisdom at your side you made them all;
the earth is full of your creatures.
25 The One of the Sea,
tall and broad of reach,
Who put gliding things past counting,
living creatures, small and large,
26 Who made ships for travel,
Leviathan whom you fashioned to sport with—
27 All of them look to you
to give them food in due season.
28 When you give to them, they gather;
when you open your hand, they fill up, O Good One!
29 Should you turn away your face, they would expire;
Take back your spirit, they die,
and return to their clay.
30 Send forth your spirit, they are created anew,
and you renew the surface of the land.
31 May Yahweh's glory last for ever,
may Yahweh find joy in his works!
32 He who gazes upon the earth and it trembles,
touches the mountains and they smoke!

33 May I sing to Yahweh throughout my life,
chant to my God while I have being.
34 When my hymn enters his presence,
I shall rejoice in Yahweh.
35 Let sinners vanish from the earth,
and the wicked exist no more.
Bless Yahweh, O my soul!

NOTES

civ. A hymn to God the Creator. In recent decades commentators have stressed the resemblances between this psalm and the Egyptian Hymn to the Aton, the solar disc, of Pharaoh Amen-hotep IV (ca. 1375–1357 B.C.). Some, in fact, have argued for a direct relation between the two, e.g., James Breasted, *The Dawn of Conscience* (New York, 1933), pp. 366–70. One is on safer ground, though, in following the opinion of Georges Nagel, "À propos des rapports du psaume 104 avec les textes égyptiens," in *Festschrift für Alfred Bertholet*, eds. O. Eissfeldt et al. (Tübingen, 1950), pp. 395–403, who maintains that in the present state of documentation it would be more prudent to envisage an indirect Egyptian influence through Canaanite mediation, more specifically through Phoenician intervention. The Phoenicians were regularly in close commercial and cultural contact with Egypt. Nagel's assessment is borne out by the fresh identification in the subsequent NOTES of numerous typically Phoenician forms, expressions, and parallelisms. One may endorse, too, Nagel's statement that this influence was probably exercised during the period of the Israelite monarchy; the psalm would be, then, of pre-Exilic composition.

The following comments bring out a number of literary usages, but an especially striking practice is noticed at vs. 6, namely the shifting from second person to third person and back again to second person.

1. *Bless Yahweh, O my soul!* Though enclosing the poem by way of an inclusion with vs. 35, this phrase stands apart from the body of the poem.

with splendor and majesty. Comparing Job xl 10, and xl 12, *hōd^{e}kā r^{e}šā'īm t^{e}ḥittēm* (MT *taḥtām*), "By your splendor terrify the wicked."

majesty . . . 2. Who is robed. As pointed out by Gunkel, the sequence *hōd . . . 'ōṭeh* collocates the two roots of the Phoenician personal name *'ṭhd*.

2. *Who is robed . . . who stretched out*. In *'ōṭeh* and *nōṭeh* are present fine rhyme and assonance. Hence the recommendation of BH^{3} to add the article to *nōṭeh* (*hannōṭeh*) may be declined without qualms.

with the sun. Grammatically an accusative of material-with-which, *'ōr*, "light," is taken in the sense documented at Ps xxxvii 6 and by Pope, *Job,* NOTE on xxxi 26; see also Neh viii 3 and below on Ps cxii 4. By identifying *'ōr* with the sun, we recover the image of Yahweh clothed with the sun, an image evoking the description of Rev xii 1, "Then a great wonder appeared in the heavens, a woman clothed with the sun." It will be noted that the psalmist balances *'ōr,* "sun," and *šāmayim,* "heavens," just as the NT writer collocates "heavens" and "sun."

as his garment. MT *kaśśalmāh* literally reads "as the garment," but as observed at Pss lv 23, lxxxv 13, lxxxix 48, xc 16, the article occasionally serves as a stylistic substitute for the pronominal suffix.

who stretched out. Cf. Isa xl 22, "He stretches out the heavens like a veil; he spreads them like a tent to dwell in" (J. L. McKenzie, *Second Isaiah,* AB, vol. 20).

3. *Who stored with water his upper chambers.* The traditional rendition of *hamᵉqāreh bammayim ʿᵃliyyōtāyw,* "who hast laid the beams of thy chambers on the waters" (RSV), produces a blurred image that exegetes have not succeeded in clarifying. Ugar. *qryt* "granary," Akk. *qarītu,* "granary" (especially in the Code of Hammurapi), which W. F. Albright, in "Some Canaanite-Phoenician Sources of Hebrew Wisdom," in *Wisdom in Israel and in the Ancient Near East* (the H. H. Rowley sixty-fifth anniversary volume), eds. M. Noth and D. W. Thomas, VTS, III (Leiden, 1955), p. 11, n. 4, believes to be ultimately identical with Heb. *qōrāh,* "plank, boarding," supplies the meaning which helps focus the picture drawn by the psalmist. There is, in fact, one text where *qōrāh* specifically designates "storeroom," illustrating the nuance found in our piel denominative participle *mᵉqāreh,* "Who stored." The text is Job xxxvii 9, *min haḥeder tābō' sūpāh ūmēm zārīm miqqōrāh* (MT *mimmᵉzārīm qārāh*), "Out of the chamber comes the tempest, and flowing waters out of the storeroom." Here *mēm zārīm* is the contracted Northern form of Jer xviii 14, *mayim zārīm* "flowing waters," studied in ZAW 74 (1962), 207–8. The parallelism of *sūpāh,* "tempest," and "flowing waters," recalls the pairing of *sūpāh* and *mayim* in Job xxvii 20, "Terrors will overtake him like a flood, Night will kidnap him like a tempest." Our reading *miqqōrāh,* "from the storeroom," does not assume the haplography of *mem* since the preceding word ends with *mem,* another instance of shared consonants, discussed at Ps lx 11 and by Watson, "Shared Consonants in Northwest Semitic," *Biblica* 50 (1969), 525–33.

From this proposed translation naturally follows the sequel in vs. 13, "Who waters the mountains from his upper chambers; / with supplies from his storehouses / the earth is fully provided." Cf. the cognate motif in Ps xxxiii 7, "He puts the deeps into storehouses."

his chambers. The rooms of Yahweh's heavenly palace.

on the clouds. The force of the preposition *'al,* "on," in the parallel colon "on wings outstretched," extends to *'ābīm,* "on the clouds." This insight necessitates a departure from the currently accepted version "who makest the clouds thy chariot" (RSV). It urges the adoption of S. Mowinckel's thesis, propounded in his article "Drive and/or Ride in O.T.," VT 12 (1962), 278–99, that phrases such as *rōkēb šāmayim* or *rōkēb ba'ᵃrābōt* mean that Yahweh drives his chariot across the heavens, not that Yahweh, sitting on a cloud, is thus transported through the air. This description is related to the description of Yahweh's chariot in the first chapter of Ezekiel. Mowinckel did not discuss our verse, apparently because he did not recognize the use of the double-duty preposition *ba,* which yields a translation confirming his proposition.

on wings outstretched. The third NOTE on Ps xviii 11 discussed the reading *'al kanᵉpē rewaḥ* (MT *rūᵃḥ*), literally "wings of broadness." As pointed out there, the outstretched wings are those of the Cherubs. The picture that emerges is one of Yahweh's chariot, set upon clouds, whose front and sides are in some fashion carved in the shape of winged cherubs or decorated with such figures. According to Mowinckel, the motive power is supplied not by the Cherubim but by the horses.

4. *fire and flame.* Plural or dual *mᵉšārᵉtāyw,* "his ministers," requires that *'ēš lōhēṭ* (or *lāhaṭ*) be taken as two distinct nouns.

The Psalms fragment from Qumran recently published by Y. Yadin, "Another Fragment (E) of the Psalms Scroll from Qumran Cave 11 (11QPsᵃ)," *Textus* 5 (1966), 1–10, attempts to remove the putative gender disagreement between feminine *'ēš* and masculine *lōhēṭ* by reading feminine participle *lwhṭt,* but this does not eliminate the disagreement of number.

The poet's omission of the conjunction *wᵉ,* "and," technically termed asyndeton, may well have been prompted by his desire to keep the parallel cola perfectly balanced at seven syllables each. The poetic pattern chosen by the psalmist, A+B+C//B́+Ć, is a frequently recurring one in the Ugaritic poems; e.g., UT, 51:VI:22–23, *tšt išt bbhtm nblat bhklm,* "Fire is set on the house, flame on the palace." See the first NOTE on vs. 14.

Originally two minor divinities in the Canaanite pantheon, "fire and flame" have been demythologized and reduced to servitors of Yahweh. Cf. Ps xcvii 3 and Joel ii 3, "Before him fire devours, and behind him blazes flame."

5. *Who placed.* Repointing MT qal perfect *yāsad* to participial *yōsēd,* with the Targum and *Juxta Hebraeos.* With this vocalization emerges the last of the seven participles employed in vss. 2–5. Compare *'attā,* "you," repeated seven times in Ps lxxiv 13–17.

the earth. The expression *yōsēd 'ereṣ* collocates the roots of the Ugaritic phrase *msdt arṣ,* "the foundations of the earth."

lest. This nuance of *bal* recurs in vs. 9.

6. *You covered it.* Reading *kissītā* (MT *kīssītō*) and attaching the final *w* to the next word as the conjunction. The desired suffix "it," namely the earth, is forthcoming from vs. 5, *mᵉkōnehā,* "its foundations."

With this reading the poet shifts from the third-person participles in vss. 2–5, returns to the second person of vs. 1, and prepares for the second-person suffixes of vs. 7.

with the ocean. Parsing *tᵉhōm* as an accusative of means preceding its verb, a frequent stylistic trait of the psalmists; cf. vs. 15. This analysis is supported by Exod xv 5, *tᵉhōmōt yᵉkussayū-m* (with *mem* enclitic), "By the ocean were they covered." The chiastic arrangement, though, suggests another possible version; the first and final positions of *tᵉhōm,* "the ocean," and *māyim,* "waters," permit the inference that both fulfill identical grammatical functions. If so, then translate "The ocean covered it like a garment, the waters stood upon the mountains," as proposed by Giuseppe Leonardi, "Note su alcuni versetti del Salmo 104," in *Biblica* 49 (1968), 238–42. Biblical *tᵉhōm* equals Ugar. *thm,* and does not derive directly from Babylonian sources, as urged by earlier generations of scholars.

like a garment. The phrase *kallᵉbūš kissītā* juxtaposes the two roots juxtaposed in UT, 67:VI:16–17, *lpš yks mizrtm,* "For clothing, he is covered with a doubled garment."

7. *At your roar.* As observed at Ps lxxvi 7, *ga'ᵃratᵉkā,* usually rendered "your rebuke," denotes here the roar of Yahweh's thunder.

they fled. Namely, the primeval waters that had engulfed the earth, even its highest mountains. Heb. *nūs,* "to flee," now appears in UT, 2063:13–16, *wht mlk syn* (UT, *syr*) *ns wṯm ydbḥ,* "And behold the king of Siyanna fled and was then slain" (translation of W. F. Albright).

8. *They.* Namely, the chaotic waters that flooded the earth. In the translation and exegesis of this verse I received valuable help from Giuseppe Leonardi.

went up to the mountains. The translation and parsing of much-contested *ya'ᵃlū hārīm* are linked with Ps cvii 26, *ya'ᵃlū šāmayim,* "They (i.e., the waves) went up to heaven." Cf. also Jer li 53; Amos ix 2; Prov xxx 4. Where are these mountains situated? The phrase cited from Ps cvii 26 suggests that *hārīm* and *šāmayim* are synonymous, that is, the poet speaks of the celestial mountains. This inference accords with the discussion of *har* and *hārīm* as terms for mountains in heaven (last NOTE on Ps lxi 3), and with the description in Gen i 7, "And God made the vault and separated the waters which were under the vault from the waters which were above the vault." Before God created the vault of heaven, all the waters were united upon the surface of the earth.

This interpretation of *hārīm* assumes that in vs. 6 the psalmist uses this noun to designate mountains on earth, and in vs. 8 uses the same noun in reference to the celestial mountains. The assumption is not unreasonable, for, as G. R. Driver, VT 4 (1954), 228, has pointed out, "The use of the same root with different senses in neighboring clauses is not uncommon." In addition to the biblical examples cited by Driver (pp. 225 ff., 242 f., not all of which, though, are equally compelling), one might quote UT, 67:VI:8–10, *mǵny lb'l npl larṣ mt aliyn b'l ḫlq zbl b'l arṣ,* "We came upon Baal who had fallen into the nether world. Dead is Victor

Baal, perished is the Prince, Lord of Earth!" where the first *arṣ* designates the nether regions and the second denotes the visible earth.

they went down to the nether chasm. Comparison with Ps cvii 26, *yērᵉdū tᵉhōmōt,* "They went down to the depths," reveals that in the phrase *yẹrᵉdū bᵉqā'ōt,* "they went down to the nether chasm," *bᵉqā'ōt* and *tᵉhōmōt* bear cognate meanings. Other texts employing *yārad* plus accusative include Isa xiv 11, xxxviii 18; Ps xxii 30, and UT, 67:v:15–16, *tspr b yrdm arṣ,* "Be numbered among those who have descended to the nether world." Very illuminating is the juxtaposition of their roots in Prov iii 20, *tᵉhōmōt nibqā'ū,* "The abyss was cleft open." Morphologically, both *tᵉhōmōt* and *bᵉqā'ōt* appear to be Phoenician feminine singulars ending in *-ōt* (GRAMMAR OF THE PSALTER, s.v.). The psalmist describes the action set forth in such texts as Gen vii 11, viii 2; Prov iii 20, viii 28, which distinguish between the waters above the vault of heaven and the waters beneath the surface of the earth. In other words, my proposed translation of vs. 8 seeks to explain what became of the waters that covered the earth in vs. 6.

The observations above lend support to the proposition of J. A. Emerton, "'Spring and Torrent' in Psalm LXXIV 15," in VTS, XV (Congress volume, Geneva, 1965; Leiden, 1966), pp. 122–33, that *'attāh bāqa'tā ma'yān wānāḥal* means that God cleft open springs so that water might descend through them. I would now read piel *biqqa'tā* for MT qal *bāqa'tā* and render, "You sent spring and torrent to the chasm." This agrees with the parallel colon, "It was you who turned primordial rivers into dry land." That both springs and torrents are found in the subterranean regions is clear from Gen vii 11, *ma'yᵉnōt tᵉhōm,* "the springs of the abyss," and Ps xviii 5, *naḥᵃlẹ̄ bᵉliyya'al,* "the torrents of Belial."

which. On the use of the relative pronoun *d* in Ugaritic and *z* in Phoenician, see last NOTE on Ps lxxiv 2. Relative *zeh* recurs in vs. 26.

9. *You marked.* For this nuance of *śamtā,* see fourth NOTE on Ps lvi 9. The new orientation in biblical literary studies, seeking a rapprochement between Old Testament poetry and Canaanite literature, no longer permits the exegete to state with Briggs (CECBP, II, p. 333) that "The poet evidently had in mind Job xxxviii 8–11, Prov viii 29." All three poets may have drawn from a common literary source; consult, in *Psalms II,* Ps lv, introductory NOTE and first NOTE on vs. 7.

10. *springs and torrents.* The clause *hamᵉšallēᵃḥ ma'yānīm bannᵉḥālīm* has been traditionally rendered "Thou makest springs gush forth in the valleys," but the apparent relationship between our phrase and the revised translation of Ps lxxiv 15, *biqqa'tā ma'yān wānāḥal,* "You sent spring and torrent to the chasm" (see second NOTE on vs. 8), suggests that the psalmist is referring to the same mythical motif. The destructive springs and torrents which Yahweh imprisoned in the subterranean chasm at the time of creation he now releases for the benefit of his creatures. The springs and torrents are those waters which in vs. 8 are said to have descended to the nether chasm.

This new interpretation stems from recognizing in *ma'yānīm bannᵉḥālīm* (or *binᵉḥālīm*) the *beth* of accompaniment, as in Ps lxviii 31; cf. below on vs. 24 and Ezek xxvii 7, *šēš bᵉriqmāh,* "linen with embroidered work," that appears in the Targum as *šēš wᵉriqmāh,* "linen and embroidered work." For the *beth comitatus* in Qumran, see M. Dahood, *Biblica* 44 (1963), 229.

to flow. The collocation of *nᵉḥālīm,* "torrents" and *yᵉhallēkūn,* literally "They flow," recalls UT, 49:III:7, *nḫlm tlk nbtm,* "The torrents flow with honey." Syntactically, *yᵉhallēkūn* is subjunctive, expressing the purpose for which God released the subterranean springs and rivers.

11. *To supply . . . with water. yašqū* (Ugar. *šqy, ššqy*) fulfills the function of a subjunctive; see preceding NOTE.

beasts. Literally "beasts of the field"; cf. the third NOTE on Ps ciii 15.

might quench their thirst. Literally *yišbᵉrū ṣᵉmā'ām* reads "that they might break their thirst," an idiom which some lexicographers (e.g., BDB) correctly compare with Latin *frangere sitim.* This neat analogy undermines BJ's alteration of *yišbᵉrū* to *yᵉśabbᵉrū* and of *ṣᵉmā'ām* to *ṣᵉmē'īm,* "Les onagres assoiffés les espèrent," and the freewheeling rendition of JB, "attracting the thirsty wild donkeys."

12. *Near them.* Namely, near the springs and torrents. For this nuance of *'al,* consult the second NOTE on Ps xxiii 2, *'al mē mᵉnūḥōt,* "Near tranquil waters," the fourth NOTE on Ps lxxxi 8, *'al mē mᵉrībāh,* "near Meribah's waters," and UT, 1 Aqht:152–53, *ylkm qr mym d'lk mḫṣ aqht ġzr,* "Woe to you, O fountain of waters, since near you was struck down Aqhat the hero." See also Judg v 19, *'al mē mᵉgiddō,* "near Megiddo's waters."

the birds of heaven. Comparing *'ōp haššāmayim* with UT, 124:11, *'pt šmm.*

dwell. The apparatus of BH³ recommends reading plural *yiškᵉnū* for MT singular *yiškōn* because the parallel verb, whose subject is presumably the same "birds of heaven," is plural *yittᵉnū,* "give forth." I suspect that a difference in number of verbs points to two different subjects in the corresponding cola; see the NOTE after next.

from their midst. Namely, of the fountains and springs. Prepositional *mibbēn* shares the suffix of its first-colon counterpart *'ᵃlēhem,* "near them" (D. N. Freedman).

the ravens. The hapax legomenon *'p'ym* has been customarily identified as an Aramaism (most recently by Max Wagner, *Die lexikalischen und grammatikalischen Aramäismen im alttestamentlichen Hebräisch* [cited hereafter as *Aramäismen*] [Berlin, 1966], pp. 92–93) signifying "dense foliage," but what is symmetrically needed in this second colon is a new subject to balance first-colon *'ōp haššāmayim,* "the birds of heaven." Hebrew knows the root *'w/yp,* "to be dark," in *tā'ūpāh* (Job xi 17) and in the well-attested noun *'ēpāh,* "darkness, gloom." The posited root *'p'* would thus be cognate (*Nebenform*) with *'w/yp*, and consonantal *'p'ym* would parse as plural participle. Compare *'ōrēb*, "raven," from the root *'rb*, "to be black."

their voice. Reading *qōlām* (MT *qōl*), a lection which does not assume the haplography of an *m* because the next word (*mašqeh*) begins with *m;* under such conditions the single writing of the letter was permitted, as noted at Pss lxxxiv 6, lxxxviii 6. Another striking instance can be seen in Job iv 19–20, *yidkeʾū* (MT *yedakkeʾūm*) *millipnē 'ōśām mibbōqer* (MT *'āš mibbōqer*), "Can they be pure in the sight of their Maker? From morning etc."

On the other hand, one may urge the correctness of MT *qōl*, without the suffix, because "voice" may be considered a part of the body, *sensu lato*, and thus free to forgo the determining suffix (see the fourth NOTE on Ps lii 7), precisely as in UT, 76:III:33, *ql lb'l ttnn*, "She gives forth her voice to Baal." There is thus no need to put "her" between parentheses as read by C. H. Gordon (*Ugarit and Minoan Crete* [New York, 1966], p. 90), "She gives forth (her) voice to Baal." All the same, the former reading (*qōlām*), defensible on orthographic grounds, commends itself for sonic and syllabic (each colon would number ten syllables) reasons.

13. *Who waters the mountains*. Comparing Ps lxv 12, "Crown the peaks with your rain."

the mountains . . . the earth. For the Ugaritic pair *hrm*, "the mountains," and *arṣ*, "the earth," see the fourth NOTE on Ps lxxii 16. The same nouns occur in vs. 32 and in reverse order in vss. 5–6 above.

his upper chambers. How to reconcile the third-person singular suffix of *'aliyyōtāyw*, "his upper chambers," with the second-person singular suffix of MT *ma'aśekā*, "your works," is the thorniest problem bedeviling this verse. From *ma'aśekā* I detach *kā* and vocalize it as the emphatic particle *kī*, "fully," the procedure employed in Pss liv 7, lix 10, lxviii 29, 36, lxxxix 3. On Jer xvii 13 see Dahood, *Biblica* 48 (1967), 109–10. This *kī* introduces a new colon, so that the verse now scans as a tricolon with a 9:6:6 syllable count; see below on vss. 17–18.

his storehouses. Explaining *ma'aśēy* (consult preceding NOTE) as a substantive from *'āśāh* in its well-attested meaning "to gather, harvest" (e.g., Ps cvii 37; Jer xvii 11; Eccles x 19). There is no need then to accept Gunkel's attractive emendation (*Die Psalmen*, p. 455) to *'asāmekā*, "your storerooms." The Phoenician third-person suffix *-y* of consonantal *m'śy* answers to the suffix of *'aliyyōtāyw*, "his upper chambers," a sequence observable in, e.g., Job xviii 13 and Eccles viii 1–2.

The motif of celestial storehouses of rain is documented in the NOTE on Ps xxxiii 7.

fully. Explaining *kī* (MT *-kā*) as the emphatic particle.

14. *for beasts plowing the land*. From the poetic sequence of this verse (A+B+C//B́+Ć) one may conclude that *l'bdt h'dm* is synonymous with *labbehēmāh* (Ugar. *bhmt*), "for the cattle." See the NOTE on vs. 4. Hence vocalize as qal participle *le'ōbedōt* (MT *la'abōdat*) *hā'ādām*. In

several passages (Exod xxi 4; Ezek xxxvi 9, 34; Eccles v 8) *'ābad* specifically denotes "to plow, till," but for present purpose the most relevant line is Zech xiii 5, *'īš 'ōbēd 'ᵃdāmāh 'ānōkī kī 'ādām hiqnanī minnᵉ'ūrāy*, "I am a man who tills the land, because the land has owned me since my youth," where the prophet plays on the two forms *'ᵃdāmāh* and *'ādām*, both signifying "the land."

The evidence for *'ādām*, "land," is impressive. Texts where this meaning is found include Gen xvi 12; Josh iii 16; Isa xxix 19, xliii 4; Jer xxxii 20; Ezek xxxvi 37, 38; Hos vi 7; Mic v 5, vii 2; Zech ix 1, xiii 5; Job xi 12, xxi 4, xxxvi 28; Prov xxviii 2, xxx 14. Recent bibliography: M. Dahood, PNWSP, pp. 57–58; "Zacharia 9,1, 'EN 'ADAM," in CBQ 25 (1963), 123–24; *Biblica* 44 (1963), 292; W. F. Albright in *Interpretation* 18 (1964), 196; A Barucq, *Le Livre des Proverbes* (Paris, 1964), p. 222; Pope, *Job*, NOTE on xi 12; C. T. Fritsch, *Journal of Religion* 46 (1966), 71; Walter Baumgartner, HALAT, p. 14.

The Phoenician personal name *'bd'dm*, "servant of the god(dess) Earth" (cf. II Sam vi 10–12), collocates the same roots occurring in our phrase *'ōbᵉdōt hā'ādām;* consult A. Dupont-Sommer, *Revue d'Assyriologie* 41 (1947), 206–8. As noted in PNWSP, p. 58, n. 5, *'dm*, "land," probably recurs in the Aramaic Inscription of Sefîre I, Face A, line 10. In his discussion of this passage, J. A. Fitzmyer, *The Aramaic Inscriptions of Sefîre* (Rome, 1967), p. 36, suggests the emendation of *'ādām* to *'ᵃdāmāh* in Josh iii 16, but this emendation should be rejected.

Indeed he brings forth. Analyzing *lᵉhōṣī'* into the emphatic *lamedh* (*Psalms II*, Index of Subjects, s.v.), and the hiphil preterit verb *hōṣī'*. The standard parsing of this congeries as the preposition followed by the hiphil infinitive construct to express purpose ("to bring forth") can scarcely be fitted into the context, since it does not logically follow from the preceding statements.

The sequence participle-emphatic *lamedh* plus finite verb can likewise be seen in Job v 10–11, *hannōtēn . . . šōlēᵃḥ . . . lāśām* (MT *lāśūm*), where MT *lāśūm* is often emended to participial *haśśām*.

grain. As observed by some commentators and lexicographers (BDB, p. 537a; GB, p. 384a), *leḥem* here denotes "grain" or "breadcorn" rather than "food" (so RSV). This observation is validated by Ugar. *lḥm*, "grain." Cf. the second NOTE on Ps xiv 4 and Gr. *sītos*, which signifies both "grain" and "food."

grain . . . 15. wine . . . oil. The sequence of the substantives *leḥem, yayin,* and *šemen* perfectly corresponds to the noun sequence in UT, 126:III:13–16, *kly lḥm [b] dnhm kly yn bḥmthm k[l]y šmn bq[bthm]*, "Spent was the grain from their jars, spent the wine from their skin-bottles, spent the oil from their vats."

the earth. With *hā'ādām*, "the land," in the preceding colon, *hā'āreṣ* exhibits the same parallelism seen in Prov xxx 14, *le'ᵉkōl 'ᵃnīyīm mē'ereṣ w^e'ebyōnīm mē'ādām,* "Devouring the oppressed from the earth, and the needy from the land." Cf. also Mic vii 2.

15. *with wine.* As remarked at Ps lxxv 9, *yayin* parses here as the accusative of means preceding the verb, a stylistic trait of the psalmists repeatedly noted; see the second NOTE on Ps ciii 19. From this analysis, whereby Yahweh continues to be the subject as in the preceding verses, issues an assertion more vigorous and grammatically defensible than traditional "and wine to gladden the heart of man" (RSV).

he gladdens . . . makes . . . resplendent. The parallelism between *y^eśammaḥ* and *hiṣhīl* here and in UT, 2 Aqht:II:9, *pnm tšmḫ w'l yṣhl pi[t],* "(Daniel's) face is full of gladness, while above his brow is resplendent," supports a new translation of Jer xxxi 7, where both these roots appear juxtaposed: *ronnū l^eya'^aqōb śimḥāh w^eṣah^alū b^erō'š haggōyīm,* "Sing aloud, O Jacob, songs of gladness [the second NOTE on Ps li 10, on *śimḥāh,* "song of gladness"]; let your heads be resplendent [literally "be resplendent on your heads"], O nations!" Hitherto *ṣah^alū* has been derived from *ṣāhal,* "to cry shrilly"; e.g., RSV, "Sing aloud with gladness for Jacob, and raise shouts for the chief of the nations." Cf. also Esther viii 15, *w^ehā'īr šūšān ṣāh^alāh w^eśāmēḥāh,* "And the city of Susah was resplendent and gay."

Truly he makes . . . resplendent. Vocalizing *l^ehiṣhīl* (MT *l^ehaṣhīl*), and taking *l^e* as the emphatic particle followed by the hiphil finite form, as in the former verse.

full. Consonantal *mšmn* (MT *miššāmen,* "with oil") has been pointed pual participle *m^ešumman,* from *šāmēn,* "to be fat," and the colon rendered, "Truly he makes the full face resplendent." In Semitic idiom the full or fattened face symbolizes glowing health; see Leonardi, *Biblica* 49 (1968), 241–42.

with food. The grammatical function of *leḥem,* like that of *yayin,* "with wine," is accusative of means; the versions usually make it the subject of the verb. For identical usages with the verb *sā'ad,* "to support, sustain," cf. Ps xviii 36, *wīmīn^ekā tis'ādēnī,* "with your right hand you sustained me."

Just as in vss. 6 and 8 the psalmist uses *hārīm* in two senses, so here *leḥem* denotes "food," whereas in the preceding verse it signifies "grain." This exegesis meets Gunkel's (*Die Psalmen,* p. 455) objection to having *leḥem* repeated in the same context; he consequently emends vs. 14 *leḥem* to *lē^aḥ,* "moisture, greenness."

the heart of man. In this final colon of vs. 15 the psalmist uses the same phrase *l^ebab 'enōš,* "the heart of man," that he employed in the first colon of this verse. Some critics find this repetition inelegant and propose reading *l^ebābō,* "his heart," for MT *l^ebab 'enōš,* "the heart of man." This proposal is cited in the latest edition of the Hebrew Psalter by H. Bardtke, *Liber Psalmorum* (BHS; Stuttgart, 1969). This proposal should be declined in view of the Ugaritic-Hebrew word pattern which may be symbolized A+B+A. For example, UT, 67:VI:20–22 reads, *yṯlṯ qn ḏr'h yḥrṯ kgn aplb k'mq yṯlṯ bmt,* "He harrows his forearms, he plows his chest like a garden, like a valley he harrows his back." In the first and third cola the poet uses the same verb *yṯlṯ,* "he harrows," and in between he sets the synonymous verb *yḥrṯ,* "he plows." In our text the psalmist begins with *lᵉbab 'ᵉnōš* "the heart of man," follows with *pānīm,* "the face," and in the third colon he repeats *lᵉbab 'ᵉnōš,* "the heart of man." This stylistic observation should serve to safeguard the Masoretic text against the proposed emendation. Other texts exhibiting this A+B+A pattern, such as Job x 1, 22, xii 4, xiii 27, xv 30, are discussed by the writer in his article, "Ugaritic-Hebrew Syntax and Style," in *Ugarit-Forschungen* 1 (Neukirchen-Vluyn, 1969), 15–36, especially pp. 32–34.

17. *the stork.* The awkward English translation of this colon faithfully reflects the awkward *casus pendens* construction of the original Hebrew.

18. *The high mountains.* The lack of article with *hārīm* in the phrase *hārīm haggᵉbōhīm* would seem to reflect Phoenician syntax. As Z. S. Harris (*A Grammar of the Phoenician Language* [New Haven, 1936], p. 66) points out, "In the use of the article, Phoenician goes its own way. There is no agreement between noun and adjective or noun and demonstrative pronoun." In line 9 of the Eshmunazor Inscription, for instance, the scribe writes *h'lnm hqdšm,* "the holy gods," but in line 22, *'lnm hqdšm,* whose syntax coincides with biblical *hārīm haggᵉbōhīm.*

the wild goats. It may be pure coincidence that the uncommon noun *yā'ēl* (three biblical occurrences) appears in a context mentioning Lebanon (vs. 16). In the famous description of the composite bow, *lbnn* and *y'lm* appear together: *adr 'qbm dlbnn adr gdm brumm adr qrnt by'lm,* "Cut yew trees [?] of Lebanon, cut tendons from wild buffaloes, cut horns from wild goats" (UT, 2 Aqht:VI:20–22).

the sheltering crags. Since the first colon consists of only two thought units which can be represented as A+B (high mountains + wild goats), the second colon should be construed to yield only two units of meaning Á+B́. The traditional version, "The rocks are a refuge for the badgers" (RSV), introduces a third element that finds no correspondent in the first colon. The Á+B́ pattern emerges when MT *sᵉlā'īm maḥseh* is read *sal'ē-mi maḥseh,* literally "the crags of shelter," a construct chain with interposed enclitic *mēm* (THE GRAMMAR OF THE PSALTER). Cf. Ps xciv 22, *ṣūr maḥsī,* "my mountain of refuge."

19. *the moon . . . the sun.* The balance between *yārēᵃḥ* and *šemeš* has counterparts in UT, 5:11.14; 77:3–4 and 602:11, *špš wyrḫ,* "the Sun and the Moon" (cf. C. H. Gordon, *Supplement to the Ugaritic Textbook,* § 19.2447, pp. 555–56), and in Phoenician Karatepe IV:3, *šmš wyrḥ,* "the sun and the moon."

acts. For the absolute use of *'āśāh,* see the second NOTE on Ps lii 11. The versions make Yahweh the subject of *'āśāh* (RSV emends third-person *'āśāh,* "he/it acts," to second-person *'āśītā,* "Thou hast made"), but parallelism is better served and the consonantal text upheld when "the moon" and "the sun" are construed as the subjects (courtesy of Werner Quintens) of the two qal third-person verbs *'āśāh,* "acts," and *yāda',* "knows."

the seasons. Heb. *mō'ēd,* "season, assembly," appears in the latter sense in Ugar. *m'd* (third NOTE on Ps lxxv 3).

its setting. Comparing *m^ebō'ō* with Karatepe I:4–5, *lmmṣ' šmš w'd mb'y,* "from the rising of the sun right to its setting."

20. *It grows dark.* For the two words of MT, *tāšet ḥōšek,* "If you put darkness," I read the single word *tištaḥšēk,* the *ishtaphel* conjugation of the verb *ḥāšak,* "to be or grow dark." This formation may now (contrast *Psalms I*) be identified in Ps xviii 12, *yištaḥšēk sitrō s^ebībōtāyw* (MT *yāšet ḥōšek*), "Dark grew his canopy around him." In our verse, two advantages derive from this new reading. First, it restores the 3+3 rhythm that is the prevailing beat of the surrounding verses. Second, it eliminates the dissonant shift from the third to the second person. From vs. 10 to vs. 24 God is spoken of in the third person, so there seems to be no reason for introducing here the second person of MT *tāšet ḥōšek,* "If you put darkness," that is also followed by the versions. The proposed reading and analysis retain the third person of the preceding and following verses, so that there is no direct address of Yahweh until vs. 24. The feminine prefix of *tištaḥšēk* is often used when the subject is impersonal "it."

then. Ascribing to *bō* a consequential meaning (cf. *bāh,* "thereupon," in Ps lxviii 15, and *bāhem,* "then," in Ps xc 10) rather than a merely temporal ("when all the beasts of the forest creep forth," RSV) sense. Once night falls the wild beasts leave their lairs in search of prey; cf. the first NOTE on Ps lix 7, and the translation of Gen xlix 27 proposed there.

21. *their prey.* Suffixless *ṭārep* shares the suffix of its opposite number *'oklām,* "their food," on the principle of the double-duty suffix. Contrast CCD, "Young lions roar for the prey and seek their food from God."

seeking. Unwitnessed in other Semitic languages *biqqēš,* "to seek," appears twice in Ugaritic as *bqṯ,* which reveals the original quality of the third radical.

22. *The sun rises.* In the diction *tizraḥ haššemeš,* the word for "sun" is of feminine gender, but in vs. 19 masculine. Some commentators accordingly propose the hiphil vocalization *tazrī^aḥ,* "You (namely God) make rise," but this reasoning is no longer compelling. The frequent concurrence in Ugaritic and Hebrew of the same noun in both masculine and feminine gender cautions the Semitist against treating a noun as always masculine or always feminine; cf. the last NOTE on lvi 9. In Ugaritic, *špš,* "sun" is, in the texts hitherto published, always feminine. The psalmist's use of masculine *šemeš* in vs. 19 and of feminine *šemeš* in our verse may be compared with masculine *trbṣ,* "courtyard," in UT, Krt:56, but feminine *trbṣt* in the duplicate passage Krt:141.

23. *his tilling.* For this nuance of *'^abōdātō,* see the first NOTE on vs. 14. CCD correctly renders "to his tillage."

until evening. Scholars (e.g., É. Dhorme, *Le Livre de Job* [Paris, 1926], p. 326) may no longer cite the phrase *ʿadē ʿāreb* to justify their emendation of consonantal *ʿrbh* to *ʿadē ʿāreb* in cognate Job xxiv 5, "seeking their prey till evening." Consonantal *ʿrbh* can now be pointed *ʿarbāh*, with the final syllable *-āh* explained as temporal *hē* as in Ugaritic *ʿlmh*, "to eternity." Cf. BCCT, p. 59.

24. *With Wisdom at your side.* D. N. Freedman suggests parsing *b^e* of *b^eḥokmāh* as the *beth comitatus* which occurs above in vs. 10; see Pss lxvi 13, lxviii 31, cxli 4; 1QM X6 (*Biblica* 44 [1963], 229), and possibly Job v 13, *lōkēd ḥakāmīm baʿarūmīm* (MT *b^eʿormām*), "Who catches the wise along with the crafty."

What emerges from this grammatical analysis is the motif so well known from Prov iii 19, *yhwh b^eḥokmāh yāsad ʾāreṣ kōnēn šāmayim bit^ebūnāh*, "With Wisdom at his side Yahweh founded the earth, with Understanding at his side he established the heavens," viii 26–27, 30 (see Dahood in CBQ 30 [1968], 512–21), and Job xxxvii 18, *tarqīaʿ ʿimmō liš^eḥāqīm ḥazāqīm kir^eʾī mūṣāq*, "Did you hammer out with him the vault itself, hard as a molten mirror?"

the earth . . . your creatures. In the juxtaposed words *hāʾāreṣ qinyānekā* one recognizes the roots found in Phoenician Karatepe III:18, *ʾl qn ʾrṣ*, "El, the Creator of the Earth" (cf. Gen xiv 19, 22), and in a neo-Punic inscription from Leptis Magna; cf. KAI, II, p. 43.

25. *The One of the Sea.* Recognizing in *zeh hayyām* a divine epithet that is syntactically identical with Ps lxviii 9, *zeh sīnay*, "the One of Sinai," studied in NOTE ad loc. Cf. Exod xxxii 1, "When the people saw that Moses delayed to come down from the mountain, the people gathered before Aaron and said to him, 'Up, make us a god who will go before us because The One of Moses [*zeh mōšeh*], the man who brought us up out of the land of Egypt, we do not know what has happened to him.'" In Mic v 4 it is said of the ruler who will go forth from Bethlehem, *w^ehāyāh zeh šālōm*, "And he shall be The One of Peace." In Canaanite religion, the goddess Asherah was called *aṯrt ym*, "Asherah of the Sea." As noticed in the sixth NOTE on Ps xxvii 4 and the fourth NOTE on Ps xxxvi 8, biblical poets appropriated terms and images depicting Canaanite goddesses and used them to describe attributes of Yahweh.

tall. For the nuance of length in *gādōl*, here usually rendered "great," consult the discussion on *gōdel*, "length," the sixth NOTE on lxxix 10. Yahweh does not suffer from the physical shortcoming which led to the rejection of Canaanite Athtar's claim to occupy the vacant throne of Baal. Cf. UT, 49:I:30–32, "He sits on the throne of Victor Baal, but his feet do not reach the footstool, his head does not reach the top." In Ps xcix 3, Yahweh is called *gādōl w^enōrāʾ*, "Great and Awesome One." Cf. NOTE on Ps lvii 6, "Your stature is above the heavens."

broad of reach. Literally "broad of hands," *r^eḥab yādāyīm* (some commentators, e.g., Briggs, unable to explain *yādāyīm*, simply delete it as a gloss) parses as an adjective followed by an accusative of specification or limitation. The same construction appears in a description of the Canaanite artisan god Skillful and Cunning, who is termed *dḥrš ydm*, "the one skillful of hands" (UT, 2 Aqht:v:24–25), while in 125:9 Baal is depicted as *rḥb mknpt*, "broad of wingspan."

Who put. Reading, as in vs. 17, *śām* for MT *šām*, but parsing it here as qal participle whose antecedent is to be found in the second-person suffixes of vs. 24.

26. *Who made.* As in vs. 25, read qal participle *śām* for MT *šām*.

ships. Heb. *'oniyyōt* equals Ugaritic plural *anyt*. On first reading, "ships" appears to be an ill-matched partner to second-colon "Leviathan," an unusual parallelism that has encouraged critics to try their hand at emendation. But the highly mythical passage UT, 125:7–9, seems to associate *any*, "ship, bark," with *ḥl*, "phoenix," a collocation that, for the moment, dissuades alteration of the biblical text. See W. F. Albright in *Festschrift für Alfred Bertholet*, pp. 1–14, on Ugar. *any*, "bark," and *ḥl*, "phoenix." 11QPs[a] frag. E, with its reading *'wnywt*, likewise urges caution.

for travel. Heb. *yehallēkūn* literally reads "that they might travel," a subjunctive usage.

Leviathan. The mention of this Canaanite monster, well known from Ps lxxiv 13–14 and such Ugaritic texts as UT, 67:I:1–3 (see first NOTE on Ps lxxiv 13) which reads, "When you smite Lotan [=Leviathan], the primeval dragon, when you destroy the twisting dragon, the mighty one of the seven heads," further points up the Canaanite-Phoenician background of this psalm, which in recent decades has been widely interpreted in terms of Egyptian mythology. See also Pope's long and fascinating NOTE on Job xli 1 (AB, vol. 15, § 39).

whom. As in vs. 8, *zeh's* function is that of a relative pronoun.

to sport with. *leśaḥeq bō* is admittedly ambivalent, so that RSV's "to sport in it" cannot be discounted. The expression, however, in Job xl 29, *hateśaḥeq bō*, "Will you sport with him [namely Leviathan]?" serves to remove much of the ambivalence, *pace* Buttenwieser, PCTNT, p. 169, and G. R. Driver in JSS 7 (1962), 19.

27. *to give them food.* The diction *lātēt 'oklām* literally reads "to give their food," but as noticed in the first NOTE on Ps xx 3, the pronominal suffix (*'oklām*) not infrequently bears a dative meaning. For present purposes, Exod ii 9 provides the most relevant parallel: *'ettēn 'et śekārēk*, literally "I shall give your salary," but really "I shall pay you a salary." This usage, well attested in Ugaritic, was lost on the monks of Qumran who inserted *lāhem*, "to them," reading *ltt lhm 'wklm b'tw*, "to give to them their food in its season" (11QPs[a] frag. E).

28. *When you give.* *tittēn* begins a temporal or conditional sentence without a morphological indicator, such as *'im* or *kī* (first NOTE on Ps iii 8, second NOTE on Ps xxvii 7), that may be compared with UT, 1019:12–14,

ttn wtn wlttn wal ttn, "When you give, then give; and if you don't give, then don't give!" Cf. further PNWSP, p. 6.

O Good One! The Syriac version drops *ṭōb* completely, evidently feeling that it contributes nothing to the thought of *yiśbeʻūn.* The parallelism, too, between the latter and *yilqōṭūn,* "they gather," with no object expressed, would sustain the Syriac. Understood as a divine title in the vocative case, *ṭōb* does add to the thought and at the same time serves a metrical function by bringing the syllable count of the second colon to nine syllables as against seven in the first colon. This seemingly unbalanced 7:9 syllable count does chiastically fit in with vs. 27 which consists of a 9:7 syllable count. Another instance of syllabic chiasmus occurs in Ps cxxxviii 1–2. On the syllabic chiasmus in Prov viii 22–23, see CBQ 30 (1968), 516. The second NOTE on Ps lxxxvi 17 discusses the divine titles *ṭōbāh* and *ṭōb;* see also Ps cxi 10; Prov xiii 21–22.

29. *Should you turn away.* Deriving *tastīr* from *sūr,* "to turn away," and parsing the conjugation as infixed *-t;* cf. first NOTE on Ps cii 3, and below on Ps cxliii 7.

they would expire. This nuance of *yibbāhēlū,* traditionally rendered "They are dismayed," is discussed in the third NOTE on Ps xc 7.

your spirit. One of the firmest, clearest statements of the divine origin of life is Job xii 10, "That from his hand is the soul of every living being, and the spirit in all flesh is his gift," as read and explained in *Biblica* 47 (1966), 107–8. Consonantal *rwḥm* (MT *rūḥām,* "their spirit") breaks down into *rūḥ* plus the enclitic *mem,* which serves here as a stylistic surrogate for the pronominal suffix. That "your spirit" is intended appears from the balance with *pānekā,* "your face." This literary device for eschewing parallelistic monotony is commented upon in the third NOTE on Ps x 17, and at Pss lxv 10, lxxx 6, lxxxi 13, lxxxiv 6, lxxxix 38. Ps x 17 is especially relevant, balancing *lbm* with *'oznekā* when speaking of Yahweh's heart and ear. That the copyists of Qumran were innocent of this literary nuance is probably the conclusion to be drawn from their reading *rwḥkh* (11QPs^a frag. E). Aware that "your spirit," best fits the context, the men of Qumran did not recognize that the enclitic *mem* could pair off with the pronominal suffix and express possessive "your (spirit)." And so they altered *rwḥm* to *rwḥkh.*

Biblical poets may well have learned this device from their Canaanite predecessors. One reads in UT, Krt:96–99, *yḥd bth sgr . . . zbl 'ršm yšu,* "Let the solitary man close his house . . . the invalid carry his bed"; contrast C. H. Gordon (*Ugarit and Minoan Crete,* p. 104), "[Let] the invalid carry the bed." H. L. Ginsberg approaches a correct understanding in his version, "The sick man is carried in (his) bed," but in his well-annotated edition (LKK, p. 16) he offers no explanation of *'ršm,* which he renders "(his) bed." The recognition that the enclitic *m* of *'ršm* serves as a stylistic substitute for the suffix of *bth,* "his house," permits the translator to dispense with Ginsberg's parentheses. The Canaanite origin of this usage whereby a pronominal suffix is balanced by an enclitic *mem* would deal the *coup de grâce* to the theory of Raphael Weiss, "On Ligatures in the Hebrew Bible (*m=nw*)," JBL 82 (1963), 188–94, that the enclitic *mem* in many of these cases resulted from scribal confusion of the ligature *nw* and *m*. In Ugaritic cuneiform writing, such confusion would have been virtually impossible because of the sharp dissimilarity of the characters involved.

and return. The psalmist evokes the motif of the return to the nether slime from which all living creatures were fashioned; cf. Gen iii 19; Ps cxxxix 15; Job xxx 23; Eccles xii 7.

to their clay. Namely, the clay out of which all living creatures were modeled. For this nuance of *ʿapārām*, consult the third NOTE on Ps ciii 14, and compare Ps cxlvi 4, "When his spirit departs he returns to his earth."

32. *the earth . . . the mountains.* See the second NOTE on vs. 13.

it trembles. Earthquakes and volcanic eruptions are also the work of God.

they smoke! Volcanic activity doubtless inspired this metaphor; cf. Pss cxliv 5, cxlviii 8.

33. *sing . . . chant.* Consult the second NOTE on Ps ci 1.

throughout my life. Comparing Phoenician Tabnit, lines 7–8, *ʾl ykn lk zrʿ bḥym tḥt šmš*, "May you have no offspring throughout your life under the sun." Scholars usually translate *bḥym* "among the living," but the temporal notion in biblical *beḥayyāy* favors the temporal interpretation of the Phoenician expression.

34. *my hymn.* This nuance of *śîḥī*, suggested by the two preceding verbs here and by the sequence in Ps cv 2, has been noticed in the second NOTE on Ps lxix 13. In his recent study, "Die Hebräische Wurzel ŚYḤ," in VT 19 (1969), 361–71, Hans Peter Müller argues that this root, which he relates to *ṣwḥ*, "to cry out," describes loud, enthusiastic, emotional speech. On p. 363, however, where he discusses our verse, he admits that *śîḥī*, "my hymn," designates activity closely akin to singing and music-making.

enters his presence. Usually translated "[May my meditation] be pleasing to him" (RSV), *yeʿerab ʿālāyw* is preferably identified with the expression in UT, 125:11–12, *ʿl abh yʿrb*, "He enters his father's presence." The verb *ʿārab*, "to please," elsewhere takes the preposition *le*, "to." Cf BCCT, p. 69, n. 68, and UHP, pp. 31, 68. On Qumranic *ʿrbh bʾp tšbḥtk ṣyyn mʿlh lkl tbl*, "May your praise, O Zion, enter into his presence, extolment from all the world," see my remarks in *Biblica* 47 (1966), 143; below on Ps cvi 35, and W. A. van der Weiden, "Radix hebraica *ʿrb*," in VD 44 (1966), 97–104, who establishes the presence of this root in Ezek xvi 37; Jer xxxi 26; Prov iii 24 (qal forms); Hos ix 4 (hiphil); Ezra ix 2; Prov xiv 10, xx 19, xxiv 21 (hithpael).

35. *vanish . . . exist no more.* The psalmist chiastically balances the jussive form *yittammū* with the precative perfect verb *ʾēnām*.

Bless Yahweh, O my soul! Forms an inclusion with the identical phrase in vs. 1. MT adds *halᵉlū-yāh,* "Praise Yah!" but this disrupts the perfect inclusion with vs. 1. Transferred to the beginning of Ps cv, it forms a perfect inclusion with Ps cv 45, *halᵉlū-yāh,* "Praise Yah!"

PSALM 105

(cv 1–45)

1 Praise Yah!
Give thanks to Yahweh, invoke his name,
make known his actions among the peoples!
2 Sing to him, chant to him,
make songs of all his wonders!
3 Glory in his holy name,
let your heart rejoice, O seekers of Yahweh!
4 Search for Yahweh and his strength,
seek his perpetual presence.
5 Recall his wonders that he wrought,
his prodigies, and the judgments from his mouth,
6 O seed of Abraham, his servant,
sons of Jacob, his chosen one!
7 For he is Yahweh our God,
over all the earth is his authority.
8 He remembers ever his covenant,
the pact he imposed for a thousand generations;
9 Which he made with Abraham,
and was sworn by him to Isaac,
10 Since he confirmed it as a statute for Jacob,
for Israel as an eternal covenant,
11 Saying, "To you will I give the land,
Canaan will be your upland patrimony."
12 When they were few in number,
a mere handful and strangers therein,
13 Wandering from nation to nation,
from one kingdom to another people,
14 He let no man oppress them,
and on their behalf rebuked kings.
15 "Touch not my anointed,
and to my prophets do no harm!"
16 Then he called down famine upon the land,
he broke every stalk of grain.

17 He sent a man before them,
Joseph, sold as a slave.
18 They pressed his feet with shackles,
and his neck passed through irons,
19 Till the moment his word came to him,
Yahweh's promise was proved true by him.
20 He sent the king to release him,
the ruler of peoples to set him free.
21 He made him master of his palace,
the ruler of all his possessions,
22 To instruct his princes personally,
and that he might teach his elders wisdom.
23 Then Israel came to Egypt,
Jacob sojourned in the land of Ham.
24 The Grand One made his people prolific,
made it too numerous for its adversaries.
25 He turned their heart to hate his people,
to double-dealing with his servants.
26 He sent Moses his servant,
and Aaron whom he had chosen.
27 They wrought his miracles in the wilderness,
and his prodigies in the land of Ham.
28 He sent darkness and it darkened,
so that they could not see his actions.
29 He changed their waters to blood,
and caused their fish to die.
30 He made frogs swarm in their land,
in the chambers of their king.
31 He spoke and brought flies,
gnats within all their territory.
32 He gave them hail for rain,
he produced lightning in their land.
33 He blighted their vine and their fig tree,
and shattered their hillside trees.
34 He spoke and brought the locust,
grasshoppers beyond number,
35 Which devoured every blade in their land,
devoured the fruit of their soil.
36 He struck every first-born in their land,
the first fruit of all their vigor.
37 Then he led them forth with silver and gold,
and no one in his tribes stumbled.

38 Egypt rejoiced at their exodus,
for dread of them had fallen upon them.
39 He spread a cloud as covering,
and fire to light up the night.
40 They asked and he brought them quails,
with the wheat of heaven he gratified them.
41 He opened the rock and water gushed forth;
it flowed like a river through the arid land.
42 For he remembered his sacred pact
with Abraham his servant.
43 So he led forth his people with songs of joy,
his chosen ones with singing.
44 Then he gave to them heathen lands,
the wealth of nations they seized,
45 Providing they keep his statutes,
and his laws observe.
Praise Yah!

NOTES

cv. An historical psalm resembling Ps lxxviii and, like the latter, probably composed for one of the major Israelite festivals. The psalmist recalls the basic events (save, strangely, the giving of the Law or any other event at Sinai) that fashioned the nation of Israel. Internal evidence for dating the psalm is meager indeed, though the citation of part of the poem by I Chron xvi 18 ff. points to a pre-Exilic date of composition.

The number of literary subtleties uncovered in this hymn by the application of Northwest Semitic criteria makes it difficult to subscribe fully to Gunkel's (*Die Psalmen,* p. 458) view that "the poem is certainly no great work of art." Thus the pairing of the third-person singular suffixes *-ō* and *-ī* in vs. 6, the use of singular and plural suffixes in relation to the same antecedent in vs. 11, the effective separation of composite phrases in parallel verse members in vss. 11 and 18, the competent use of chiasmus in vss. 15, 22, 43–45, all bespeak uncommon literary artistry. Another literary trait which might be mentioned is the "explicitation" of the subject in the final colon of a sentence, a device noticed at vss. 3, 5–6, 17, 19.

1. *Praise Yah!* See the second NOTE on Ps civ 35.

2. *Sing . . . chant.* Cf. the second NOTE on Ps ci 1.

make songs of. For this nuance of *śîḥû,* consult the second NOTE on Ps lxix 13 and the first NOTE on Ps civ 34.

3. *Glory . . . let . . . rejoice.* For stylistic variation the psalmist pairs

imperative *hithalᵉlū,* "Glory," with jussive *yiśmaḥ,* "let rejoice" This nuance is lost in CCD, which treats both as imperatives: "Glory in his holy name; rejoice, O hearts that seek the Lord."

your heart. Recognizing in *lēb* the name of a part of the body not determined by a suffix; cf. *Psalms II,* Index of Subjects, s.v., and UT, 1 Aqht:I:34, *tbky pǵt bm lb,* "Pughat wept from her heart" (courtesy D. N. Freedman). Thus *lēb mᵉbaqqᵉšē yhwh* breaks down not as a three-word construct chain but rather as a subject followed by a phrase in the vocative case; in this periodic sentence the subject of the first three verses is "O seekers of Yahweh." The poet employs a similar structure in vss. 5–6, 17, 19, placing the subject at the end of the sentence. As noticed at vs. 17, biblical poets may have been indebted to their Canaanite predecessors for this literary technique, which might be termed "explicitation," in the last colon of a periodic structure.

4. *his perpetual presence.* Though God is ever present, man must search for him. Parsing *pānāyw tāmīd* as a construct chain with pronominal suffix interposed; compare, especially, Ps lxxi 6, *tᵉhillātī tāmīd,* "my perpetual praise," and Nah iii 19, *rā'ātᵉkā tāmīd,* "your unceasing evil" (RSV). This analysis sustains the translation of Ps xvi 8, *nᵉgīdī tāmīd,* "my perpetual Leader," proposed in NOTE on Ps liv 5. To be sure, this grammatical analysis reverses the versions' meaning (RSV, "seek his presence continually") that it is the seeking which must be perpetual, but the psalmists' use of *tāmīd* in the passages cited, and the parallelism with "Yahweh and his strength," suggest that both the presence and the perpetuity are Yahweh's.

5. *his wonders that he wrought.* Though it seems awkwardly redundant, this version is a literal reproduction of the original Hebrew. RSV's "the wonderful works that he has done" involves the emendation (albeit silent) of *niplᵉ'ōtāyw,* "his wonders," to *niplᵉ'ōt,* "the wonderful works" (RSV).

the judgments from his mouth. RSV's "the judgments he uttered" needlessly tones down the anthropomorphism of the Heb. *mišpᵉṭē pīū* by substituting "he uttered" for Hebrew "from his mouth."

6. *seed . . . sons of.* Consult the first NOTE on Ps cii 29 for this parallelism in Phoenician. As in vss. 3, 17, the psalmist withholds the subject (here in vocative case) till the end of the sentence.

his servant. In order to achieve identity of number, the LXX took MT singular *'abdō,* "his servant," referring to Abraham, as plural *'ᵃbādāyw,* "his servants," referring to the Israelites. See the next NOTE. Verse 42 *'abdō,* however, ensures MT *'abdō* here.

his chosen one. MT plural *bᵉḥīrāyw,* "his chosen ones," induced the LXX to read first-colon *'abdō* as plural *'ᵃbādāyw,* "his servants." The identification of third-person singular suffix *-y* in consonantal *bḥyryw* permits a more satisfactory solution; by reading *bᵉḥīrī,* "his chosen one," and attaching final *waw* to the next verse, we preserve the numerical balance of *'abdō* and *bᵉḥīrī* and, at the same time, even the syllable count of vs. 7 at eight syllables in each colon. The grammatical structure of our verse now stands out clearly: construct-genitive-singular noun of apposition // construct-genitive-singular noun of apposition.

For other instances of parallelism between the third-person suffixes -ō and -ī(y), see the fourth NOTE on Ps civ 13; Job xix 28, *kī tō'merū mah nirdop lō wešōreš dābār nimṣā' bī*, "If you say, 'How shall we pursue him, seeing that the root of the matter is found in him?' " where the ancient versions and some hundred manuscripts read *bō* for MT *bī*. Cf. also Job xxxvii 11, "His shining one (*bārī*) dispels the mist, and his sun (*'ōrō*) scatters the clouds," as proposed in *Biblica* 45 (1964), 412. Cf. also Pss cix 31, cxiii 8, cxiv 2.

7. *For he.* Once detached from *bḥyryw,* the final word of vs. 6, *w* serves both a semantic and syllabic function in our verse. It serves as a connecting word, giving the reason for the series of commands in vss. 1–5, and, at the same time, evens the syllable count of each colon at eight syllables. Some copyist of Qumran also felt the need of a causal conjunction between vss. 6–7, since 11QPs[a] frag. E inserts *ky* after its reading *bḥyrw* which is a correction of original *bḥyry* with third-person suffix *-y.*

his authority. This nuance of the root *špṭ* has been annotated at Ps ii 10.

8. *ever . . . generations.* For the Ugaritic brace *'lm//dr,* see the first NOTE on Ps lxxxv 6.

the pact. This nuance of *dābār* recurs in vs. 42; cf. also Deut ix 5 and George Mendenhall in IDB, I, p. 716a, who points out that since the term for "covenant" (*berīt*) is quite rare in the earliest sections of the Old Testament, the tradition of the covenant with Yahweh must have been designated by other words than *berīt*. Mendenhall holds that the oldest designation of the Ten Commandments, *'eśtrat debārīm,* "the ten words," rests on this early tradition, since covenants were regarded and called the "words" of the suzerain.

he imposed. That *ṣiwwāh* is the right word to be used with *dābār,* "the pact," may be inferred from Ps cxi 9, *ṣiwwāh le'ōlām berītō,* "He imposed his covenant for ever."

This translation, which implies that the pact contains provisions or stipulations that are binding upon the human party (Abraham's descendants), runs counter to the prevailing scholarly opinion that in the Abrahamic covenant (Gen xv 18–21, xvii 1–14, xxvi 1–5) only God is bound. Of course, scholarly opinion must interpret circumcision (Gen xvii 9–14) not as an obligation made binding by the covenant but only as a "sign" of the covenant. The proposed translation casts serious doubt on this distinction between an obligation and a "sign," and calls for a re-examination of the problem.

9. *Which he made.* The antecedent of *'ašer kārat* being *dābār* in the immediately preceding colon, Kraus (*Psalmen,* II, p. 720) denies that *dābār* is the object of *kārat,* "he made," and must consequently treat vs. 8b as a parenthesis. This procedure must be termed arbitrary. The psalmist

is evidently using *dābār* in a double sense. As the direct object of *ṣiwwāh*, "he imposed" (RSV "he commanded"), *dābār* connotes the terms of the treaty dictated by the suzerain (in this case God) to his vassal (Abraham). As the direct object of vs. 9, *kārat*, "he made" (literally "he cut"), *dābār* connotes an agreement reached freely by two parties (God and Abraham). As noted at Ps civ 8, biblical poets sometimes employ one word in two different senses.

with Abraham. The psalm fragment from Qumran (11QPs[a] frag. E) reads *'m 'brhm* for MT *'et 'abrāhām.* The Qumran lection must be considered inferior to MT both in view of vs. 42, where the psalmist again uses *'et*, "with," and because *'et* is in fact the more difficult reading.

and was sworn by him. Construing feminine *b[e]rītō*, "his covenant," in vs. 8a as the antecedent of *š[e]bū'ātō.* In other words, the psalmist arranges the four cola of vss. 8–9 in a diagonal or chiastic pattern. Traditionally rendered as the noun "his sworn promise" (RSV), *š[e]bū'ātō* can also be parsed as the qal feminine passive participle followed by the dative suffix expressing the agent, exactly like Ps lxxxvii 1, *y[e]sūdātō*, "[city] founded by him," and vs. 19 (below), *ṣ[e]rūpathū*, "was proved true by him."

11. *Saying.* The authenticity of *lē'mōr*, missing in a few manuscripts and deleted by some critics, is vouched for by the syllable count (9:10) that proceeds from the proposed division of the verse.

To you. Proposals to emend singular *l[e]kā* to plural *lākem*, in order to align it numerically with plural suffix of *naḥ[a]lat[e]kem*, receive new support from the 11QPs[a] frag. E reading *lkm.* In first NOTE on Ps xxvii 8, the plural imperative pointing *l[e]kū*, "Come!," was proffered on the basis of Pss xxvii 8 and xlv 15. Here we further observe that biblical poets, possibly to eschew monotony, occasionally use both singular (to be understood collectively, like *zera'*, "seed," in vs. 6) and plural forms when dealing with the same subject, as witness Ps cxlv 4; Isa xli 6, xliii 9b, liv 3b–c; Hos viii 3, *zānaḥ yiśrā'ēl ṭōb 'ōyēb yird[e]pū* (MT *yird[e]pō*) *hēm*, "Israel has rejected the Good One, they have followed the Foe" (cf. ETL 44 [1968], 45); Deut xxxii 7, *z[e]kōr y[e]mōt 'ōlām bīnū š[e]nōt dōr wādōr*, "Recall the days of old, consider the years of ages past."

This stylistic observation provides a satisfactory explanation of Ps lxxxi 13, "So I repudiated him for his stubbornness of heart, they followed their own designs." In the third NOTE ad loc. appears this comment: "This disconcerting shift between third person singular and plural forms when referring to Israel is not amenable to a satisfactory explanation. The recurrence of the same phenomenon in vss. 15–16 dissuades one from assuming textual corruption." The identification of new examples of this stylistic device now makes it more amenable to successful analysis and effectively rules out the likelihood of textual corruption.

the land, Canaan. Most versions translate *'ereṣ k[e]nā'an* as "the land of Canaan," but I propose shifting the *athnach*, the symbol of principal pause in the verse, to *'āreṣ;* hence read *'āreṣ kᵉna'an* for MT *'ereṣ kᵉnā'an.* In MT the syllable count of the two cola is 12:7, but, on recognition of the breakup of composite phrases (second NOTE on Ps cii 16 and below on vs. 18), it becomes a more balanced 9:10. Another striking instance is recorded at Ps cvii 25, again misconstrued by MT.

your upland patrimony. The phrase *ḥebel naḥᵃlatᵉkem* sounds too much like Exod xv 17, *har naḥᵃlātᵉkā,* "your mountain of patrimony," and UT, 'nt:III:27, *ǵr nḥlty,* "my mountain of patrimony," to be translated "the lot of your inheritance" (KJ). In other words, *ḥebel* is a metathetic form of Ugar. *ḫlb//ǵr,* which signifies "hill" and is frequent in place names. The long-standing crux in Prov xxiii 34 can now be coaxed into yielding excellent sense: *wᵉhāyītā kᵉšōkēb bᵉleb yām ūkᵉšōkēb bᵉrō'š ḥebel* (MT *ḥibbēl*), "You will be like one asleep in the depths of the ocean, like one asleep on top of the mountain." This definition calls for a retranslation of Ps lxxviii 55, *wayᵉgārēš mippᵉnēhem gōyīm wayyappīlēm bᵉḥebel naḥᵃlāh,* "He drove out the nations before them, and felled them (the Canaanites) on their upland patrimony." Cf. likewise Deut xxxii 9.

12. *When they were.* The doublet in I Chron xvi 19 reads second-person plural *bihyōtᵉkem,* "When you were," but the present reading appears preferable because the two cola are perfectly balanced with seven syllables each, whereas in I Chron xvi 19 the syllable count is 8:7.

a mere handful. Parsing *kī* of *kīmᵉ'aṭ* as emphatic.

therein. Namely, in Palestine or the Land of Canaan.

14. *no man . . . kings.* Heb. *'ādām . . . mᵉlākīm* is a "polar" expression or a kind of merismus (first NOTE on Ps viii 8 and last NOTE on Ps xxxvi 7) whereby the poet represents totality by mentioning two extremes. A similar locution can be seen in UT, 51:VII:43, *umlk ublmlk,* "whether king or commoner." Cf. A. Schökel, "Poésie hebräique," in *Supplément au Dictionnaire de la Bible,* ed. by H. Cazelles and A. Feuillet, fasc. 42, (Paris, 1967), col. 69. The fact that in Pss xlix 3 and lxii 10 *bᵉnē 'ādām* connotes "men of low birth" in contradistinction to *bᵉnē 'īš,* "men of high degree," sustains the psalm reading *'ādām* against the variant *'īš* in I Chron xvi 21.

15. *Touch not . . . do no harm.* Maintaining the chiastic or diagonal arrangement of the words in the original Hebrew.

my anointed. The patriarchs Abraham, Isaac, and Jacob who only here are given this title. In a metaphorical sense they were "anointed," that is, consecrated to God, and received from him special revelations.

The Ugaritic phrase *šmn mšḥt,* "oil for anointing," discloses the origin of the biblical term *māšaḥ,* "to anoint."

my prophets. Another surprising designation of the patriarchs; in Gen xx 7 alone is Abraham called a *nābī',* "a prophet."

16. *famine upon the land.* A reference to the event described in Gen xli 56, "So when the famine had spread over all the land, Joseph opened all the storehouses, and sold to the Egyptians."

stalk of grain. Usually translated "staff of bread" and frequently explained as a stave passed through a series of ring-shaped loaves and suspended to preserve them from mice, etc., the Hebrew expression *maṭṭēh leḥem* (Lev xxvi 26; Ezek iv 16, v 16, xiv 13) becomes susceptible to a literal interpretation with the acknowledgment that in Ugaritic and Hebrew *leḥem* often signifies "grain, wheat" (second NOTE on Ps xiv 4, third NOTE on Ps civ 14). In Ezek xix 11, 12, 14 *maṭṭeh* denotes "vine branches" and in Hab iii 9, 14 the "shaft" of an arrow, so that the meaning "stem, stalk" would comport with Hebrew usage. The use of the verb *šābar,* "he broke," also accords with the proposed explanation, because in vs. 33 the psalmist employs it with *'ēṣ gᵉbūlām,* "their hillside trees."

17. *a man . . . Joseph.* The poet creates suspense by mentioning indefinitely "a man" in the first colon and reserving his specific name "Joseph" to the end of the second colon. The antecedents of this biblical stylistic artifice (see above on vss. 3, 6) can be observed in, say UT, 'nt:II:23–24, *mid tmtḫṣn wt'n tḫtṣb wtḥdy 'nt,* "Much does she smite and behold, battle and gaze does Anath," where the subject of the action is not made explicit until the last word. See the second NOTE on Ps cxii 6. The author of Job is especially fond of this artistic device; cf. Job vi 2, xix 26, xx 23, xxii 21, xxvii 3, xxix 18, xxxiv 17.

sold. the root of *nimkar* occurs frequently in Ugaritic texts, especially in *mkrm,* "merchants," and in Punic *mkr,* "merchant."

18. *his feet.* Reading *raglēy* (MT *raglāyw*), with third-person suffix *-y,* and the final *w* of MT transferred to the next word as the conjunction "and." Another instance of this suffix and transfer of *w* to the following word is noted at vs. 6.

shackles. The root of *kebel* probably appears in the frequent Ugaritic personal name *kbln;* see Frauke Gröndahl, *Die Personennamen der Texte aus Ugarit* (Rome, 1967), pp. 276–77.

and. With the transfer of final *waw* of MT *rglyw* to the next word (*barzel*), the two cola become even with seven syllables each.

his neck. For this definition of *napšō,* consult the second NOTE on Ps lvii 7, where *napšī,* "my neck," balances *pᵉ'āmay,* "my feet," the same semantic pairing as in our verse. In IDB, IV, p. 428, N. W. Porteous writes, "The meaning 'throat, neck' is suggested, not always convincingly, for sundry passages of the OT—e.g. Isa. 5:14; 29:8; Jonah 2:6; the clearest case is possibly Ps 105:18." Had he adverted to the frequent occurrences of *npš,* "throat, neck," in Ugaritic, Porteous would doubtless have been less tentative in his biblical appraisal. Cf. also J. A. Emerton, VT 17 (1967), 135, n. 1, and *The Torah* (JPS: Philadelphia, 1962), p. 266, which correctly translates Num xi 6, *napšēnū yᵉbēšāh,* "Our gullets are shriveled." Cf. *Biblica* 49 (1968), 368, for further examples of *nepeš,* "throat, gullet."

passed. That *bā'āh* is the *mot juste* to express this action appears upon comparison with Jer xxvii 12, *hābīʾū ʾet ṣawwᵉʾrēkem bᵉʿōl melek bābel,* "Pass your necks through the yoke of the king of Babylon."

through irons. Or possibly "a collar of iron," an allusion to Joseph's imprisonment described in Gen xxxix 20. A number of critics, e.g., Gunkel, would insert the preposition *ba* before *barzel* to read *babbarzel,* but this insertion proves unnecessary, first because *barzel* begins with *ba* and is preceded by labial *ū* (*ūbarzel,* see third NOTE on verse), and hence would tend to eschew the preposition, much like *bayit,* "in the house," for *babbayit,* and second because *barzel* is entitled to share the preposition of its opposite number *bakkebel,* "in shackles," on the basis of the poetic principle of the double-duty preposition. A similar set of considerations can be observed in UT, 125:14–15, *bḥyk abn nšmḫ blmtk ngln,* "In your life eternal, our father, we rejoice; in your immortality we exult," where *blmtk,* "your immortality," which begins with *b,* shares the preposition of *bḥyk,* "in your life eternal."

Heb. *barzel* appears in Ugaritic as *brḏl,* a word of non-Semitic origin, most likely derived from Hittite *barzillu.* It is widely believed that iron was introduced into Palestine by the Philistines ca. 1190 B.C. The mention, however, of iron in a tablet listing the items of tribute sent by a ruler of Ugarit either to the Hittite suzerain or to the king of Carchemish in the fourteenth century B.C. bespeaks the earlier use of the metal in Syria-Palestine.

J. Brinktrine in ZAW 64 (1952), 251–58, proposes, on the basis of Luke ii 35, and some OT passages, the translation "A sword entered his soul," a reading countenanced by Kraus (*Psalmen,* II, p. 718), though not adopted in his translation. Attractive though this version might appear, it does not impose itself because, among other reasons, it disturbs the parallelism between "his feet" and "his neck" and slights the expression *kablē barzel,* "iron shackles," in Ps cxlix 8. In other terms, by placing *kebel* in the first colon and *barzel* in the second, the psalmist employs the figure called the breakup of a composite phrase, annotated above at vs. 11. Joseph's feet and neck were put in iron chains (*kebel barzel*), and there is no mention of "a sword." See the second NOTE on Ps cxix 55.

19. *his word.* Namely, Yahweh's word. When setting up the parallelism between *dᵉbārō//ʾimrat yhwh* ("his word//Yahweh's utterance"), the psalmist employs the artistic device which may be termed second-colon explicitation, a usage noticed in the second NOTE on vs. 3. The psalmist doubtless refers to Gen xli 25, "God has revealed to the Pharaoh what he is about to do."

came to him. Namely, to the Pharaoh, who is mentioned in the next verse. This translation assumes that *bōʾ,* "came to him," shares the dative suffix of its second-colon fellow, *ṣᵉrūpathū,* "was proved true by him."

Yahweh's promise. To Joseph, that he would become greater than his brothers and would rule over them; cf. Gen xxxvii 8 ff.

was proved true by him. Namely, by the Pharaoh. Syntactically one of the more troublesome expressions in the psalm, consonantal *ṣrpthw* yields to ready parsing if pointed *ṣ*ᵉ*rūpathū,* the qal passive participle followed by the dative suffix of agency; cf. third NOTE on vs. 9. God used the Egyptian ruler to forward the plans he had made for Joseph.

20. *He sent.* Understanding Yahweh as the subject of *šālaḥ,* exactly as in vss. 17, 26, 28; the versions take as subject *melek,* "the king" (RSV, "The king sent and released him"). The ambivalent Hebrew original permits both interpretations.

the king. Pharaoh, king of Egypt. Scholars have yet to determine the date of Joseph's sojourn in Egypt, and are presently unable to identify the Pharaoh alluded to.

to release him . . . to set him free. Explaining the *waw* preceding the two verbs as *waw finale,* introducing purpose clauses; cf. the second NOTE on lxxvii 7.

21. *He made.* The subject being the Egyptian Pharaoh who appointed Joseph the administrator of his kingdom.

master. Cf. Gen xlv 8. The association of *'ādōn* with vs. 20, *melek,* "king," recalls the titles of King Kirta in 125:56–57, *mlk//adnk,* and the colophon in UT, 62:56–57, *nqmd mlk ugr*[*t*] *adn yrgb,* "Niqmad, the king of Ugarit, master of Yrgb."

Gen xli 33 ff. records that Pharaoh raised Joseph to the highest post to reward his correct interpretation of dreams and his wise advice.

his palace. This nuance of *bētō* also occurs in royal Ps ci 2, 7. The expression *'ādōn l*ᵉ*bētō* recalls the title *'ᵃšer 'al bētō,* "he who is over the palace" (Gen xliv 1; I Kings xvi 9, etc.) that is found in the epitaph of a royal steward from Siloam (Silwan) near Jerusalem, studied by N. Avigad in IEJ 3 (1953), 137–52.

22. *To instruct.* Vocalizing *l*ᵉ*'ōsīr,* the aphel infinitive construct of *yāsar,* "to discipline, instruct." The first NOTE on Ps lv 3 cites other instances of aphel conjugation in the Psalter. The aphel infinitive construct to express purpose after the preposition *l*ᵉ finds a syntactic analogue in Job xxxiii 17, *l*ᵉ*hōsīr* (MT *l*ᵉ*hāsīr*) *'ādām ma'ᵃśeh w*ᵉ*gōhū-m* (enclitic *mem;* MT *w*ᵉ*gawāh m*) *geber y*ᵉ*kasseh,* "To teach men his work, and he discloses his voice to mortals."

That consonantal *'sr* derives from *ysr* can be certified from the *Wortfeld* or verbal context. Three of the five roots—*'sr, z*ᵉ*qēnāyw,* and *y*ᵉ*ḥakkēm*—recur in UT, 51:v:65–66, *rbt ilm lḥkmt šbt dqnk ltsrk,* "You are aged, O El, and truly wise; your hoary beard has truly instructed you."

personally. Not through subordinates. The phrase *b*ᵉ*napšō* has been variously rendered, but a literal understanding "in his own person" comports nicely with the context.

*teach . . . wisdom. y*ᵉ*ḥakkēm* forms an inclusion with *l*ᵉ*'ōsīr,* "to instruct." The psalmist varies the manner in which he expresses purpose; in the first colon he uses *l*ᵉ with the aphel infinitive construct, but in the second half-verse he resorts to the imperfect form.

23. *to Egypt.* This use of *miṣrayim* in the accusative case finds an interesting counterpart in UT, 2059:10–11, *any kn dt likt mṣrm,* "the sturdy ship that you sent to Egypt." In Ugaritic the verb *lik,* "to send," is usually followed by the preposition *'m,* "to, toward," but here it directly governs accusative *mṣrm.* Cf. also UT, 1084:27, *tb' mṣrm,* "They departed for Egypt." This similarity of syntax further points up the close linguistic connection between Hebrew and Ugaritic; cf. UT, § 13.45.

the land of Ham. Another name for Egypt; Gen x 6 ff.

24. *The Grand One.* The lack of an explicit subject has presented translators with a problem. Thus RSV inserts "the Lord" ("And the Lord made his people very fruitful"), but both the translational and grammatical ambiguity can be resolved by repointing the adverb *m*[e]*'ōd,* "very," to the stative adjective *mā'ēd,* "the Grand One," a divine appellative documented at Ps cix 30. The verse thus acquires an explicit subject.

too numerous. Cf. Exod i 8 and Gunkel, *Die Psalmen,* p. 460. Commentators often translate "and made them stronger than their adversaries," then charge the poet with an inappropriate exaggeration. If accurate, this translation would seem to render divine intervention unnecessary. But as Gunkel, following A. Ehrlich, rightly points out, *ya'*[a]*ṣīmēhū miṣṣārāyw* need mean no more than "they became too numerous" for the comfort of the Egyptians.

25. *to double-dealing.* A new instance of the root in *hitnakkēl* has been identified in Prov xiii 15, *śēkel ṭob yittēn ḥēn w*[e]*derek bōg*[e]*dīm 'yt nēkel* (MT *'ēytān kol*), "The intelligence of a good man breeds charm, but the conduct of the faithless, craftiness"; for details, M. Dahood in HWFB, pp. 42–43. This root probably occurs in the Ugaritic personal names *nkl* and *nklb;* the latter, in fact, doubtlessly juxtaposes *nkl* and *lb,* "heart," both of which roots concur in the psalm verse, and may well be rendered "wily-hearted." This concurrence seems to reduce the options in explaining *nklb,* about which Gröndahl, *Die Personennamen der Texte aus Ugarit,* p. 166, writes "various interpretations are possible."

27. *They wrought.* MT plural *śāmū* proves correct against the ancient versions that read singular *śām,* "He (Moses) wrought," with the realization that the psalmist is referring to Exod xvi 1–12, which narrates events whose protagonists are Moses and Aaron. See the next NOTE.

in the wilderness. With no consonantal changes, reading *b*[e]*midbārī* (MT *bām dibrē*), with the genitive ending; cf. the sixth NOTE on Ps lxv 6; *Biblica* 47 (1966), 414; van Dijk, EPT, p. 80. In vs. 30, *malkīhem,* "their king," one encounters another genitive ending. Here *midbārī* probably refers to Exod xv 22, *midbar šūr,* "the wilderness of Shur," and Exod xvi 1, *midbar sīn,* "the wilderness of Sin," where Moses and Aaron placated the grumbling Israelites by assuring them that God would supply them with food by nightfall. On the other hand, "the wilderness" may refer to Egypt itself, an interpretation that finds support in I Sam iv 8 and Ezek xx 36, texts which speak of *midbar 'ereṣ miṣrāyim,* "the wilderness of the land of Egypt." This latter view is defended by H. J. van Dijk in VT 18 (1968), 28.

his prodigies. Suffixless *mōpᵉtīm* shares the suffix of its opposite number *'ōtōtāyw,* "his miracles." In Ps lxxxviii 43, however, both nouns are determined by pronominal suffixes. This fact alone does not warrant the emendation to *mōpᵉtāyw* registered in the apparatus of BH³ because, as observed in the introductory NOTE to Ps liii, variant readings in doubly transmitted texts may reflect two equally valid traditions. See the next NOTE.

the land of Ham. The related verse Ps lxxxviii 43 reads "the plain of Zoan," but, as noticed above, variant readings do not of themselves justify emendation.

28. *so that they could not see.* Reading *wᵉlō'āmᵉrū* (MT *wᵉlō' mārū*), and equating the verb *'āmᵉrū* with Ugar. *amr,* "to see," discussed in the first NOTE on Ps liii 3, second NOTE on Ps iv 5, first NOTE on Ps xi 1, NOTE on Ps lxxi 10, third NOTE on Ps xciv 4, and *Biblica* 44 (1963), 295–96. There is no need to assume the haplography of an *aleph* (*l' 'mr*), because the negative particle here may simply be the Ugaritic form *l,* without *aleph,* followed by the verb *'āmᵉrū.* Or we may have here an instance of the single writing of *aleph* where morphology calls for two.

There is a growing recognition among Hebraists that *'āmar* often describes visual activity, as in Ugaritic, Akkadian, and Ethiopic. See Hanson, PMS, I, p. 74, on Ps xi 1; W. L. Holladay, VT 18 (1968), 485–86, on Isa iii 10–11; E. Lipiński, RB 75 (1968), 350, n. 23, on Ps cxlv 11; E. Ullendorff, *Ethiopia and the Bible: The Schweich Lectures of 1967* (London, 1968), p. 127, on Deut xxvi 17–18. Hence F. I. Andersen, JBL 88 (1969), 210, belabors the obvious with his cautionary remark, "The meaning 'see' for *'mr* should be invoked only when 'say' is hopeless." It is precisely because "say" is hopeless in all these texts that the above-named scholars have invoked Ugar. *'mr,* "to see." See below on Ps cxix 82.

The subject of *'āmᵉrū* is, of course, the Egyptians. The incident alluded to comes from Exod xi 22–23, "So Moses stretched out his hand toward heaven, and there was thick darkness in all the land of Egypt for three days; they did not see one another, nor did any rise from his place for three days."

his actions. Since Yahweh had hardened the hearts of the Egyptians, they were unable to appreciate the meaning of his miraculous intervention on behalf of the Israelites. One encounters a similar use of language in John xiii 30, "It was night," a pregnant expression which describes the physical night outside and the spiritual darkness within the soul of Judas.

30. *He made . . . swarm.* Vocalizing piel *šērēṣ* for MT qal *šāraṣ.* This reading keeps Yahweh the subject (cf. vss. 28, 29, 31, 32, 34, 36) and preserves the ever feminine gender of *'arṣām,* "their land," which in the versions (RSV, "Their land swarmed with frogs") is treated as a masculine noun. Thanks to advances in Northwest Semitic philology, the modern

Hebraist can show that the majority of purported examples of gender disagreement listed in standard Hebrew grammars do not violate the rule of agreement in gender between subject and predicate. Cf., for example, Exod xv 5 as translated at Ps civ 6, and Ehrlich, *Die Psalmen,* pp. 258–59, on the present passage. On the other hand, MT qal *šāraṣ* might be retained and given a causative meaning, since a number of verbs in qal express both an intransitive and causative meaning; see the NOTE on vs. 31; M. Noth, *Die israelitischen Personennamen* (Stuttgart, 1928), p. 36; S. E. Loewenstamm, IEJ 15 (1965), 124–25, n. 13.

in their land. With *'arṣām* sharing the preposition of its second-colon opposite number *bᵉḥadrē,* "in the chambers of." See the first NOTE on Ps cxx 4.

chambers. Ugar. *ḥdr,* "chamber," supplies the Semitic root as against Arabic-Ethiopic *ḫdr.*

their king. MT plural *malkēhem,* "their kings," has long constituted a problem, inasmuch as Moses addresses one Pharaoh and speaks of singular *bētᵉkā,* "your palace" (Exod vii 28). One viable explanation emerges from the reading *malkīhem,* the singular form with the genitive ending *-ī,* followed by plural suffix *-hem.* The genitive ending of *midbārī* has been noted in vs. 27; cf. also Ps xliv 13 as read in *Psalms II,* p. XXVI.

One should not, however, discount the possibility of parsing MT *malkēhem* as a plural of majesty; the translation would remain singular "their king." Consult the second NOTE on Ps cxviii 26.

31. *and brought.* The qal verb *wayyābō'* need not be repointed to the hiphil or causative conjugation (cf. Targ., Syr.), given that the qal of this verb often (twelve occurrences) denotes "bring"; cf. fifth NOTE on Ps xliii 3; second NOTE on Ps lxv 3; Isa lx 5; Mic i 15; Hag ii 7.

32. *He gave them hail for rain.* A literal translation of the Hebrew would read, "He gave hail as their rain," but the suffix of *gišmēhem,* "their rain," is really datival, "rain for them," like UT 51:v:89, *bšrtk yblt,* "I bring you good tidings," but literally "I bring your good tidings."

rain. Ugar. *gšm,* "rain," discloses that the second radical of this root is *š,* not *ṯ* as assumed by some lexicographers.

he produced. Vocalizing *'āš* (MT *'ēš,* "fire"), qal perfect of *'wš,* "to donate, bestow," though the well-established phrase *'ēš lehābāh,* literally "fire of flame," can be invoked in defense of MT. On the other hand, the parallelism between *nātan* and *'āš* is unfaultable, especially since these roots are found in tandem in UT, Krt:135–36, *udm ytnt il wušn ab adm,* "Udum is the present of El and the gift of the Father of Mankind." That the Masoretes were unfamiliar with the root *'wš* follows from their vocalization in Job xii 10, *'ᵃšer bᵉyādō nepeš kol ḥāy wᵉrūᵃḥ kol bāśār* (MT *bᵉśar*) *'ōšō* (MT *'īš*), "That from his hand is the soul of every living being, and the spirit in all flesh is his gift," a version nicely sustained by 11QPsᵃ Plea 3–4, *ky bydk npš kwl ḥy nšmt kwl bśr 'th ntth,* "For from your hand is the soul of every living being, the breath in all flesh have you given." See *Biblica* 47 (1966), 107–8, and UHP, p. 16. This root is further attested in Ps cxii 5, as proposed below, Jer xxvii 1, *y'wšyhw*, to be pointed *yā'ūšyāhū* in the light of Amorite personal names *ya'uš-il* and *ya'uš-addu* and *y'wš* in the Lachish Letters; cf. M. Noth, JSS 1 (1956), 326–27, and F. M. Cross, Jr., BASOR 184 (1966), 7–10. P. F. van Zyl in *Proceedings of the Ninth Meeting of Die Ou-Testamentiese Werkgeneenskap in Suid-Afrika, 26–29 July 1966*, p. 160, denies that this root appears in the Ugaritic personal name *išb'l*, which probably means "given by Baal," because "it nowhere agrees with Baal." Van Zyl unfortunately overlooks the Amorite personal name from Mari, *ya-uš-IM=ya'uš-addu*, and his identifying of Ugar. *iṯb'l* with *išb'l* flouts the phonetic laws of permutation.

lightning. Cf. Exod ix 18 ff.

33. *and shattered*. As recorded in Exod ix 25.

their hillside trees. Ehrlich (*Die Psalmen*, p. 259) is right in questioning the traditional rendition of *'ēṣ gᵉbūlām*, "the trees within their boundary," but wrong in proposing that *gᵉbūlām* be changed to *yᵉbūlām*, "their produce." The evidence for *gᵉbūl*, "hill," is given in the first NOTE on Ps lxxviii 54.

34. *and brought*. As in vs. 31, qal *wayyābō'* carries the same meaning as the hiphil; see also the comments on vs. 30, *šāraṣ*.

37. *with silver and gold*. Exod xi 2, 35–36, records that the Israelites, before leaving Egypt, "despoiled the Egyptians."

no one . . . stumbled. Yahweh so strengthened the Israelites that none of them stumbled under the heavy burden of booty that each carried out of Egypt.

40. *They asked and he brought*. The consonantal sequence *š'lwyb'*, to be pointed *šā'ᵃlū wayyābē'*, illustrates the single writing of *waw* where morphology requires two; cf. the third NOTE on Ps lx 11, and CBQ 29 (1967), 577–78.

he brought them. With *wayyābē'* sharing the suffix of *yaśbī'ēm*, "he gratified them."

with the wheat of heaven. Another term for "manna," which in Ps lxxviii 24 is called *dᵉgan šāmayim*, "the grain of heaven." On *leḥem*, "wheat, grain," see the second NOTE on vs. 16. Stylistically, our phrase, with the accusative of material preceding its verb, is of a pattern with the semantically similar phrases in Ps civ 15.

42. *his sacred pact*. For this nuance of *dābār*, consult the third NOTE on vs. 8.

with Abraham. Understanding *'et* as the preposition "with," precisely as in vs. 9, where 11QPsᵃ frag. E reads *'m*, "with," for MT *'et*. Most versions translate *'et* as the *nota accusativi*, with the resultant version "and Abraham his servant" (RSV). This verse forms an inclusion with vs. 8, beginning and ending the body of the poem with references to Abraham and the eternal covenant with him.

43. *songs of joy.* The second NOTE on Ps li 10 examines this definition of *śāśōn,* whereas the first colon of our verse served to interpret the difficult phrase in Ps lxviii 7.

44. *Then he gave to them.* Many prefer the reading *wayyitt^{e}nēm,* with a dative suffix, to MT *wayyittēn lāhem,* but the present 9:9 syllable count should counsel the critic to stay his hand. Were the emendation accepted, the syllable count would be 8:9.

44. *the wealth.* This shade of meaning in *'āmāl* is especially frequent in the Book of Ecclesiastes; cf. Eccles ii 10–11, 18, 24, iv 6, v 14, and O. Loretz, *Qohelet und der Alte Orient* (Freiburg, 1964), p. 280, n. 273.

they seized. Preserving the chiastic arrangement of the Hebrew. This denotation of *yīrāšū,* often rendered "they inherited," has been studied in *Biblica* 47 (1966), 404–5, and finds confirmation in UT, 'nt:III:43–44, *imtḫṣ w itrṯ ḫrṣ,* "I battled and seized the gold."

45. *they keep . . . observe.* Again the Hebrew word order is chiastic, but it cannot be gracefully reproduced in English.

Praise Yah! hal^{e}lū-yāh forms an inclusion with this command which has been shifted from the end of Ps civ to the beginning of Ps cv.

PSALM 106

(cvi 1–48)

1 Praise Yah!
Give thanks to Yahweh for he is good,
for eternal is his kindness.
2 Who can express Yahweh's might,
sound all his praise?
3 How blest the alert to what is right,
the doer of justice at all times!
4 Remember me, Yahweh,
with your powerful favor;
Visit me with your saving help,
5 That I may enjoy the prosperity of your chosen,
rejoice in the joy of your nation,
glory in your patrimony.
6 We have sinned like our fathers,
we have done wrong, committed crimes.
7 After Egypt our fathers
considered not your wonders,
remembered not your abounding kindness,
And from the Reed Sea they defied the Most High,
8 though he saved them because of his name,
to make known his might.
9 He rebuked the Sea,
the Reeds he dried up,
He marched them through the deep as through a desert.
10 He saved them from the hand of the enemy,
and freed them from the hand of the foe.
11 The waters covered their adversaries,
not one of whom survived.
12 Then they believed his words,
and they sang his praise.
13 But they quickly forgot his works,
and did not wait for his advice.

14 They complained bitterly in the desert,
and tested El in the barrens.
15 Yet he gave them what they requested,
and cast out leanness from their throats.
16 They envied Moses in the camp,
and Aaron the holy one of Yahweh.
17 The earth opened up
and swallowed Dathan,
It covered over the faction of Abiram.
18 Fire blazed up against their faction,
flames devoured the wicked.
19 They made a young bull at Horeb,
and worshiped a molten image.
20 They bartered their adoration
for the figure of a grass-eating bull.
21 They forgot El their Savior,
who had worked great deeds in Egypt,
22 wonders in the land of Ham,
awesome happenings near the Reed Sea.
23 Then he decided to exterminate them,
were it not for Moses his chosen,
Who stood in the breach before him
to keep his fury from ravaging them.
24 Then they rejected the coveted land,
they did not believe his word;
25 They grumbled in their tents,
heeded not the voice of Yahweh.
26 So he raised his hand against them
to fell them in the desert,
27 To cast their seed among the nations,
and disperse them throughout the lands.
28 They yoked themselves to Baal Peor,
and ate banquets of the dead.
29 They so angered him by their doings
that a plague erupted among them.
30 Then Phinehas stood up and interceded,
and the plague was checked.
31 This was credited to his virtue,
from generation to generation, forever.
32 They infuriated him at the waters of Meribah,
so that Moses fared ill on their account,

33 Because they defied his spirit,
and he spoke rashly with his lips.
34 They did not exterminate the peoples
as Yahweh had commanded them,
35 But they intermarried with the nations
and learned their customs.
36 They served their idols
which became a lure for them.
37 They sacrificed their sons
and their daughters to demons.
38 They shed innocent blood,
the blood of their sons and daughters,
Whom they sacrificed to the idols of Canaan,
and they desecrated the land with torrents of blood.
39 They defiled themselves by their actions,
and whored in their doings.
40 Then Yahweh's anger was kindled against his people,
and he abhorred his patrimony.
41 He put them into the hand of the nations,
so that their enemies ruled over them;
42 Their foes oppressed them,
they were humbled under their hand.
43 Many times he rescued them,
but they hardened in their purpose,
and so collapsed in their iniquity.
44 Yet he looked upon them in their distress,
listening to their cry.
45 He remembered his covenant with them,
and led them in his abounding kindness.
46 He granted them untold mercies
in the sight of all their captors.
47 Save us, Yahweh our God,
and gather us from among the nations,
That we may give thanks to your holy Name,
to be extolled when you are praised.
48 Praised be Yahweh, the God of Israel,
from eternity and to eternity!
And let all the people say, "Amen!"
Praise Yah!

Notes

cvi. A national confession of sins in vss. 1–6 and a prayer for help in vs. 47 frame an historical poem (vss. 7–46) which in a somber tone sets Yahweh's deeds on Israel's behalf against Israel's repeated response of rebellion and ingratitude. Whatever God has done, Israel has always proved unfaithful; nonetheless, he has constantly forgiven her defiance (the verb *mārāh,* "to rebel, defy" recurs in vss. 7, 33) and shown her unlimited mercy.

A noteworthy stylistic trait of the psalmist is his fondness for the usage known as the breakup of stereotyped or composite phrases (vss. 9, 14, 18, 19, 38, 40). Cf. The Grammar of the Psalter for full listing. In his omission of pronominal suffixes (vss. 24, 29) he resembles the author of Ps lxxviii.

From the prayer in vs. 47 scholars infer that the psalm, at least in its present form, dates from after the time when the Israelites entered the Babylonian captivity (587 B.C.). The psalm is older than the partial recension in I Chron xvi and contains some arresting archaic grammatical constructions.

2. *can express.* The widely received opinion that *y*ᵉ*mallēl* is here an Aramaism (*La Bible de la Pléiade.* II, p. 1133) may need modification in view of eighth-century attestation of *mll* on the Phoenician Karatepe Statue, *wbl kn mtmll bymty ldnnyn,* "And there was no one speaking against the Dananians in my days"; cf. Dahood, *Biblica* 44 (1963), 71–72.

Yahweh's might. Commonly rendered "the mighty doings of the Lord" (RSV), *g*ᵉ*būrōt* makes a finer parallel to singular *t*ᵉ*hillātō,* "his praise," if explained as a singular noun (cf. vs. 8) with the Phoenician ending *-ōt* (second Note on Ps liii 7). The same form is encountered in Job xli 4, *lē'* (MT *lō'*) *'aḥ*ᵃ*rīš baddāyw ūd*ᵉ*bar g*ᵉ*būrōt w*ᵉ*ḥīn 'erkō,* "I the Almighty fashioned his limbs, his powerful back and graceful build." Cf. also Job xxvi 14 and Pss cxlv 4, 11, 12, cl 2.

his praise. To bring it into numerical agreement with the putative plural *g*ᵉ*būrōt,* some ancient versions read singular MT *t*ᵉ*hillātō* as plural *t*ᵉ*hillōtāyw,* "his praises." The analysis proposed in the preceding Note permits the retention of singular *t*ᵉ*hillātō.*

3. *the doer of justice.* Often changed to plural *'ōśē,* MT singular *'ōśēh* may well refer to the poet himself. This interpretation may help explain vs. 4, *zokrēnī,* "Remember me," frequently altered to *zokrēnū,* "Remember us." It has been noted that in Ps iv 4 the psalmist calls himself a *ḥāsīd,* "a devoted one," and refers to himself in Ps v 13 as *ṣaddīq,* "the just man," parallel to plural "they who love your name" in vs. 12.

4. *Remember me . . . Visit me.* The defense of the singular reading

'ōśēh in vs. 3 proves equally valid in upholding *zokrēnī* and *poqdēnī* against the emendators who follow LXX "Remember us . . . visit us."

Yahweh. Some critics (cf. BH³ apparatus) would delete *yhwh* for overloading the verse, but this objection can be met by scanning the line as a 2+2+3 tricolon (Gunkel scans it as 4+3), the sequence repeated in vss. 9 and 17 and Ps cvii 4.

with your powerful favor. The hapax legomenon phrase *birᵉṣōn 'ammekā* must obviously be accounted for on the basis of context and parallelism. The stress of Yahweh's might in vss. 2 and 8 points up the fittingness of appealing here to his "powerful favor." Note the juxtaposition of *'am* and *gᵉbūrāh* in Ps lxxxix 14, "Yours is a powerful arm, O Warrior!" Balance with "your saving help" recalls the collocation of the roots *'āmam*, "to be strong," and *hōšīaʿ*, "to save," in Ps xviii 28, *kī 'attāh 'am 'ānī tōšīaʿ*, "Indeed you are the Strong One who saves the poor," whereas the construction *birᵉṣōn 'ammekā* resembles Ps lxxvii 16, *bizᵉrōaʿ 'ammekā*, "With your powerful arm." Powerful fittingly describes God's favor, as we may infer from the metaphor in Ps v 13, "As with a shield you will surround him with your favor."

with your saving help. As Gunkel has observed, *bīšū'ātekā*, receives two beats, so that the final two words are read as a three-beat colon.

5. *enjoy*. This seems to be the force of the idiom *rā'āh bᵉ*, rather than mere "see"; RSV's "That I may see the prosperity" is too weak. Cf. Pss liv 9, cxxviii 5, and Job iii 9, and below on Pss cxii 8, cxviii 7.

6. *like our fathers*. Implying that the sinful behavior of the Israelites is due partially to the bad example of their forebears. This implication is obscured in RSV's faulty rendering "Both we and our fathers have sinned," a version which fudges the import of *'im*, "like." This frequently attested meaning of *'im*, "like" (second NOTE on Ps lxxii 5; BDB, pp. 767–68) is confirmed by Ugar. *'m*, "like," and serves to clarify the famous crux in Job xxix 18, *wā'ōmar 'im qinnī 'egwāʿ wᵉkaḥōl 'arbeh yāmīm*, "And I thought, 'though I perish like its nest, I shall multiply days like the phoenix.'" Cf. Ps lxxviii 57, "They turned away and broke faith like their fathers."

7. *After Egypt*. Hardly "in Egypt," with both ancient and modern versions and expositors. Cf. Deut ix 7, "Remember, never forget, how you angered Yahweh your God in the wilderness: from the very day that you left the land of Egypt until you reached this place, you have continued defiant toward Yahweh." This temporal sense of *bᵉ* recurs in the final phrase of the verse, in Ps xxvii 5; Prov xiv 23; Eccles xi 1, *bᵉrōb hayyāmīm*, correctly rendered "after many days" by RSV, and in UT, 1 Aqht:179, *bšbʿ šnt*, "after seven years," as rightly understood by Gordon, UT, § 10.5, p. 95.

your abounding kindness. Many critics (see the sound observations of Briggs, CECBP, II, p. 355) would read singular *ḥasdekā* for MT plural *ḥᵃsādekā*, but the parsing of consonantal *ḥsdyk* as a singular noun with the genitive ending—*ḥasdīkā*—achieves the same result without changing any consonants; see vs. 45 and Ps lxxxix 20.

And from the Reed Sea. Joining the fourth colon of vs. 7 to vs. 8, which becomes a tricolon in which Yahweh is referred to in the third person, whereas the tricolon in vs. 7 addresses God in the second person.

As in the phrase *bemiṣrayim, be* in *beyam sūp* carries the temporal meaning "after." It was after their passage through the Sea of Reeds that the Israelites provoked the Most High. KJ and RSV translate *yam sūp*, "the Red Sea," but recent scholarship favors the identification with "the Reed Sea" in northeastern Egypt.

the Most High. With no consonantal changes reading *'ēlīm* for MT *'al yam* (cf. vs. 32). Virtually all commentators emend *'al yam* to *'elyōn*, "the Most High," on the basis of Ps lxxviii 17, 56, but this change proves needless, given biblical *'ēlī*, "the Most High," in the passages listed in NOTE on Ps vii 9. Morphologically, *'ēlīm* can be explained as singular *'ēlī* plus enclitic *mem*, or as a plural of majesty, like *'elōhīm* and *'ēlīm*, "God," *rāmīm*, "the High One" (Job xxi 22), *qedōšīm*, "the Holy One," *yešīšīm*, "the Venerable" (Job xii 12), *gebōhīm*, "the Lofty One" (Eccles v 7), and, most relevantly, *'elyōnīn*, "the Most High," in Dan vii 18, 22, 25. The latter explanation appears preferable.

8. *his might.* Singular *gebūrātō* harks back to vs. 2 *gebūrōt*, a singular form of Phoenician type. This variation is analogous to Ps cvii where in vs. 6 the psalmist uses the verb *yiṣ'aqū*, but *yiz'aqū*, with the same meaning, in vs. 13.

9. *He rebuked . . . he dried up.* Departing from traditional "He rebuked the Red Sea, and it became dry" (RSV), and reading the first four words of the line as two cola instead of one:

wayyig'ar bayyām (5 syllables+2 beats)
sūp wayyaḥrēb (5 syllables+2 beats)

The verse thus scans into a 2+2+3 tricolon, much like vss. 4 and 17, and Ps xlvi 10. With its chiasmus the bicolon closely resembles Ps cvii 4.

The psalmist pictures the sea as a servant who was rebuked for having exceeded his authority. The construction *g'r b* occurs in UT, 137:24, *bhm yg'r b'l*, "Baal rebukes them."

the Sea, the Reeds. Just as Ps cv 11 (also Ps cvi 38) surprisingly breaks up the conventional phrase *'ereṣ kena'an*, "the land of Canaan," so our psalmist separates into chiastically arranged cola the components of the fixed term *yam sūp*, "the Reed Sea." By employing this pattern, he keeps the Most High as the subject of both verbs in this bicolon and of all three verbs in the verse, just as "earth" is the subject of all three verbs in the 2+2+3 tricolon in vs. 17. Consult the comments on Ps lxxx 10 where our parsing retains Yahweh as the subject of the three parallel verbs.

he dried up. Repointing the MT qal form to hiphil *wayyaḥrēb*, and explaining the *waw*, not as consecutive, but as emphatic; as stated in the second NOTES on Ps li 9 and 18, third NOTE on Ps lxxvii 2, and second NOTE on Ps cii 5, the emphatic *waw* often forces the verb to the end of its clause. With three of the same roots and the emphatic *waw* construction, Nah i 4 presents the most illuminating parallel: *gō'ēr bayyām wayyabbᵉšēhû wᵉkol hannᵉhārōt heḥᵉrīb*, "Rebuking the sea, he made it dry; all the rivers he dried up."

the deep. Heb. *tᵉhōmōt* equals Ugar. *thmt*.

as through a desert. Alluding to Exod xiv 21–22, "Yahweh drove the sea back by a strong east wind all the night, and made the sea dry land, and the waters were divided. And the Israelites went into the midst of the sea on dry ground."

10. *the hand of the enemy . . . the hand of the foe.* Gunkel finds the repetition of *yad*, "hand," in both cola "unschön" [ugly] and alters the second *yad* to *kap*, "fist." A comparison of the matching construct chains *yad śōnē'* and *yad 'ōyēb* with UT, 2 Aqht:vi:43–44, *ntb pš'*, "the path of rebellion," which is parallel to *ntb gan*, "the path of presumption," where *ntb*, like *yad*, is repeated, makes one less enthusiastic for Gunkel's emendation and at the same time warns against imposing modern Western tastes upon ancient Semitic poetry.

enemy . . . foe. The balance of *śōnē'*, "enemy," with *'ōyēb*, "foe," finds a counterpart in the Ugaritic brace *ib*, "foes," and *šnu*, "enemies," in UT, 51:VII:35–36. See the list in THE GRAMMAR OF THE PSALTER.

12. *his words, and they sang.* The present syllabic imbalance (9:7) between the cola can partially be corrected by transferring the final *waw* of MT *dᵉbārāyw* to the next word *yāšîrū*, where it becomes the conjunction "and," and then repointing to *dᵉbārēy* with the third-person suffix *-y;* see the second NOTE on the next verse and the third NOTE on Ps cv 18. The line now reads 9:8 syllables.

his praise. The singular form *tᵉhillātō*, "his praise," might be cited in defense of the singular reading in vs. 2, where some ancient versions read plural "his praises" instead of MT *tᵉhillātō*, "his praise."

13. *they quickly forgot.* Literally "they hastened, they forgot," *mihᵃrū šākᵉḥū* is an example of hendiadys.

his works. Detaching the final *waw* of *maᶜᵃśāyw* and joining it to the following word as the conjunction "and." Hence vocalize *maᶜᵃśēy*, "his works," as in Ps civ 13, with the third-person suffix *-y*.

and did not. With the transfer of *w* from the preceding word to the second colon (*wᵉlō'*), the syllable count becomes 9:8 (MT 9:7), precisely as in vs. 12.

14. *They complained bitterly.* Usually translated "They had a wanton craving" (RSV), the expression *yit'awwū ta'ᵃwāh*, borrowed from Num xi 4, takes on a contextually more satisfactory meaning when derived from the root *'āwāh*, "to sigh, complain," examined at Pss ix 13 and

lxxviii 30. The traditional version does not bring out the nexus with the parallel statement "they tempted God," and a perceptive expositor like Briggs betrays uneasiness when commenting on his own translation *they desired a desire:* "This under the circumstances *tested 'El,* tried him by questioning His ability to provide for them."

the desert . . . the barrens. The juxtaposition of *midbār,* "desert," and *y*[e]*šīmōn,* "barrens," in Ps cvii 4 suggests that the psalmist here employs the breakup of composite phrases by which the components are separated and placed in the parallel cola. Cf. Ps lxxviii 40; Deut xxxii 10; Isa xliii 19–20.

15. *and cast out.* Commentators are agreed that the second colon, *way*[e]*šallaḥ rāzōn b*[e]*napšām,* is probably the most puzzling of the psalm. At first blush it seems to say "And he sent leanness into their throats," the opposite of the first colon, "But he gave them what they requested." Since the prevailing pattern is one of synonymous rather than antithetical parallelism, critics suspect that a scribe mistakenly wrote *rāzōn,* "leanness, wasting disease," for *māzōn,* "food." The LXX, Vulg., and Syr. all read "satiety." If, on the other hand, the sense "from" is recognized in the phrase *b*[e]*napšām,* "from their throats" (cf. Ps cxv 7), then *y*[e]*šallaḥ* signifies "he cast out," a denotation found in Gen iii 23; Lev xviii 24, xx 23; Jer xxviii 16, etc. For cognate terminology regarding disease, compare UT, 126:v:20–21, *my bilm ydy mrṣ gršm zbln,* "Who among the gods will cast out the sickness, driving out the malady?"

leanness. The result of their prolonged hunger. Compare Ps cvii 9, "and filled with good things the hungry throat."

from their throats. As so often in biblical and Canaanite poetry, *b*[e] denotes "from." But compare Isa x 16, *y*[e]*šallaḥ 'ādōn . . . b*[e]*mišmannāyw rāzōn,* "The Lord will send . . . leanness among his stout warriors."

17. *The earth . . . Dathan.* Reading the first four words as a bicolon numbering 5:5 syllables, and the entire line as a 2+2+3 beat tricolon, the pattern of vss. 4, 9.

opened up. With LXX, Syr., and *Juxta Hebraeos,* reading trisyllabic niphal *tippātaḥ* for MT bisyllabic qal *tiptaḥ.* With this vocalization the first colon numbers five syllables that match the five of the second colon.

Dathan. In referring to the historical event expressed in demythologized language in Num xvi 25 ff., the psalmist omits mention of Korah, who in Num xvi is described as the leader of the rebellion in the wilderness. Some would attribute this omission to the psalmist's desire to avoid possible confusion with "the sons of Korah" to whom ten psalms are ascribed.

Abiram. A member of the tribe of Reuben; together with Dathan he led a revolt against Moses. They complained that Moses had misled the people by bringing them out of Egypt, "a land flowing with milk and honey," to kill them in the wilderness (Num xvi 13).

18. *Fire . . . flames.* The poet separates the elements of the composite phrase *'ēš lehābāh,* literally "fire of flame" (Isa iv 5; Hos vii 6), placing

one in each colon, a poetic practice recurring in vss. 9, 14, 19, 40. Cf. especially Ps lxxxiii 15.

devoured. The *tqtl* verb *t^elahēṭ* expresses past time; see the next NOTE.

19. *They made.* Like vs. 18 *t^elahēṭ*, "devoured," *ya'^aśū* describes the past history first recorded in Exod xxxii 1–6. The meaning of the two cola is: They made a molten bull in Horeb and worshiped it.

a young bull. The discovery at Ras Shamra, at Enkomi in Cyprus, and in the environs of Tyre in Phoenicia, of Late Bronze Age (1500–1200 B.C.) molten statues of young bulls representing the Canaanite gods El or Baal provides good commentary on vss. 19–20. Consult C. F. A. Schaeffer, "Nouveaux témoignages du culte de El et de Baal a Ras Shamra-Ugarit et ailleurs en Syrie-Palestine," in *Syria* 43 (1966), 1–19, and Plates I–IV; Norbert Lohfink, "Neue kanaanäische Götterbronzen und die Bibel," in *Stimmen der Zeit* 179 (1967), 62–64.

at Horeb. An alternative name for Mount Sinai.

a molten image. Again the psalmist distributes over the two parallel cola the elements of the unit phrase *'ēgel massēkāh*, "a molten young bull" (Exod xxxii 4); see vss. 9, 14, 18, 40. In the Phoenician Karatepe Inscription the king relates that he offered sacrifices *lkl hmskt*, "to all the molten images" (III:1).

20. *They bartered.* In describing the Canaanite image worship to which the Israelites succumbed, the poet fittingly chooses the economic term *yāmīrū*, "they bartered, exchanged," to capture the commercial flavor of Canaanite-Phoenician life. Cf. Hos iv 7, *k^ebōdām b^eqālōn 'āmīrū* (MT *'āmīr*), "They bartered their adoration for dishonor," where defectively spelled *'āmīrū* parses as the aphel causative that is the equivalent of hiphil *hēmīrū* in the psalm.

their adoration. Or, their religion. The Israelites exchanged their worship of invisible Yahweh for the worship of a taurine bronze. The Hebrew form *k^ebōdām* has invited needless emendation. The parallelism in Ps lxxxvi 9 and in UT, 51:viii:28–29, *tštḥwy wkbd hwt*, "Worship and adore/honor him," between the verbs *ḥwy* and *kbd* suggests that the subject of vs. 19, *yištaḥ^awū*, "they worshiped," is also the subject of the suffix *-ām* of *k^ebōdām*, "their adoration," while the object of the verbal action in *kābōd* is Yahweh. The chiastic order of vss. 19–20 points to the same conclusion. The problem recurs in Jer ii 11, *w^e'ammī hēmīr k^ebōdō b^elō' yō'īl*, "My people has bartered its adoration for something of no avail." The standard correction of *k^ebōdō* to *k^ebōdī*, "my Presence" (Bright, AB, vol. 21, NOTE ad loc.) no longer commends itself.

bull. In the Ugaritic texts *ṯr* (=Heb. *šōr*), "bull," is one of the god El's epithets. Second-colon *šōr*, it might be noted, chiastically balances first-colon *'ēgel*, "young bull," in vs. 19.

21. *El their Savior.* Who is contrasted with the bronze statue of Canaanite El in vss. 19–20.

23. *from ravaging them.* The hiphil infinitive construct *hašḥīt* shares

the suffix of the synonymous hiphil infinitive construct *hašmīdām,* "to exterminate them," on the principle of the double-duty suffix. The grammatically indefensible version read in CCD, "to turn back his destructive wrath," can be traced back to the failure to recognize this poetic usage. CCD treats *mēhašḥīt* as though it were a participle. RSV rightly translates "from destroying them," but the lack of an apposite note prevents our knowing how this reading was reached.

B. Duhm (*Die Psalmen* [Freiburg i. B., 1899], p. 248) terms vs. 23 a four-liner so badly constructed that one is tempted to consider it a prosaic insertion. However, the 7:7//8:9 syllable count, the use of the double-duty suffix, and the chiastic arrangement of the four cola make it difficult to credit Duhm's assessment.

24. *they rejected the coveted land.* This strange statement becomes fully intelligible only when we reach the end of the verse. What the Israelites spurned was in reality Yahweh's promise to give them the pleasant land of Canaan.

they did not. Proposals to insert the conjunction *w*ᵉ before *lō'* should be scouted as disrupting the present 9:9 syllable count.

26. *he raised his hand.* In the gesture of an oath; cf. Ps cxliv 8; Exod vi 8; Deut xxxii 40; and for the event, Num xiv 28–35.

28. *They yoked themselves to Baal.* The phrase *yiṣṣamᵉdū lᵉba'al* collocates the two roots found in the Phoenician divine name *b'l ṣmd,* "Baal of the Yoke." Ugar. *ṣmd,* "yoke," is well attested and underlies the noun *mṣmdt>mṣmt,* "bond, treaty," as shown by Manfred Weippert in *Göttingische Gelehrte Anzeigen* 216 (1964), 193.

Baal Peor. A deity worshiped at Mount Peor in Moab, to whom the Israelites apostatized (Num xxv). His Hebrew name *ba'al pᵉ'ōr* recalls UT, 68:18, *yp'r šmthm,* "He declaimed their names," an expression found in a scene that describes the naming of two clubs used by Baal to drive the god Sea from his throne.

banquets of the dead. That is, funeral banquets, which must have been regarded with great disfavor, not only because of the apparent Canaanite cultic associations, but also because they must have involved something close to ancestor worship and the deification of the dead that is found in, say, UT, 2 Aqht:II:16–17. The phrase *zibḥē mētīm* is hapax legomenon and must therefore be explained on the basis of the present context and that of Num xxv, which also reports this incident. The prevailing interpretation of this expression sees here a reference to sacrifices offered to pagan gods who, in the psalmist's mind, are as dead as their images. The corresponding passage in Num xxv 2 reads, "These [namely, the Moabite women] invited the people [i.e., the Israelites] to the sacrifices of their gods [*zibḥē 'ᵉlōhēhen*], and the people ate, and bowed down to their gods." From this confrontation emerges the equation *zibḥē mētīm=zibḥē 'ᵉlōhēhen,* "banquets of their gods." The question to be decided is whether the gods were considered "dead" or whether "the dead" were believed to be gods or preternatural beings. No biblical text calls the gods *mētīm*, "the dead," but II Sam xxviii 13 and Isa viii 19 use the term *'elōhīm*, "gods," to describe the deceased. It follows then that *zibḥē mētīm* denotes "funeral banquets." Upon the "high places" the Canaanites are known to have shared meals with their dead. Both Ugar. *dbḥ* and Heb. *zebaḥ* sometimes denote "banquet" rather than "sacrifice" in our sense of the word. Cf. also W. F. Albright in VTS, IV (Congress volume, Strasbourg, 1956; Leiden, 1957), 252–56; T. H. Gaster in IDB, IV, p. 153b; R. T. O'Callaghan in VT 4 (1954), 174–75.

29. *They so angered him.* The omission of the accusative suffix with *yak'īsū* (see vs. 43) may have been prompted by syllabic considerations (9:7); the addition of the suffix would result in a 10:7 syllable count; cf. cognate Ps. lxxviii 6, 21, 28, 38, 51, 59 where the expected suffixes are wanting.

32. *Moses fared ill.* Because he was not allowed to enter the Promised Land, as reported in Num xx 12.

33. *his spirit.* Namely, the spirit of Yahweh. According to Isa lxiii 14, it was Yahweh's spirit in Moses which led the Israelites through the wilderness: *rūaḥ yhwh tenīḥennū kēn nihagtā 'ammekā*, "Your spirit, Yahweh, you made rest on him [namely, Moses]; thus did you lead your people."

he spoke rashly. The subject being Moses, though it is not clear what the rash utterance was, nor wherein his guilt lay.

35. *they intermarried.* Deriving the root of *yit'ārebū* from *'ārab*, "to enter," discussed in the second NOTE on Ps civ 34. Current translations assume that the root is *'rb*, "to go surety for." The nuance "to enter into marriage" is implied in the description of King Kirta's attempt to bring home a bride in UT, Krt:203–4, *hm ḥry bty iqḥ aš'rb ǵlmt ḥẓry*, "If I receive Ḥurrai into my house, make the young lady enter my court." Cf. also UT, 77:17–19, *tn nkl yrḫ ytrḫ ib t'rbm bbhth*, "Give Nikkal that Moon may wed, that Ib may enter his house."

the nations. The Canaanites and Amorites who lived in Canaan.

37. *to demons.* Another occurrence of the noun *šēd*, "demon," has been recognized in Amos ii 1, *'al śorpō 'aṣmōt mōlek* (MT *melek*) *'ādām laššēd* (MT *laśśīd*), "Because he burns the bones . . . of a human sacrifice to a demon," by W. F. Albright, YGC, p. 240.

38. *the idols of Canaan . . . the land.* The proposal to delete the two middle cola of the verse as a gloss would obliterate an instance of the breakup of the composite phrase *'ereṣ kena'an* (see Ps cv 11), though here the order is reversed, and eliminate the wordplay on *kena'an* and vs. 42, *yikkāne'ū*, "they were humbled." The Israelites were brought into subjection precisely because they adopted Canaanite mores.

they desecrated. Retaining the Israelites as the subject of all three verbs in this verse, so that *teḥenap* (perhaps to be vocalized as defectively spelled *teḥenepū*) parses as the third person with preformative *t-*; see third NOTE on Ps lxviii 3.

torrents of blood. The traditional rendering "blood" (RSV) does not bring out the full force of plural *dāmīm,* which seems to convey something more than what is expressed by singular *dām,* "blood." This shade of meaning may well be present in the threat of the sanguinary goddess Anath: *aškhlk šbtk dmm šbt dqnk mm'm,* "I shall make your hoariness flow with torrents of blood, your hoary beard with gore" ('nt:v:32–33).

39. *they . . . whored.* Biblical writers not infrequently use the verb *zānāh,* "to be a harlot," to describe idolatry; cf. especially Hos i–iii.

40. *his people . . . his patrimony.* In the distribution over parallel cola of *'ammō,* "his people," and *naḥªlātō,* "his patrimony," we have the breakup of the composite phrase *'am naḥªlāh,* "the people of patrimony," that occurs in Deut iv 20. This phrase is split in Pss xxviii 9, lxxviii 62, 71, xciv 5, and here.

41. *into the hand . . .* 42. *under their hand.* The chiastic arrangement of vss. 41–42 should be noted.

42. *they were humbled.* The verb *yikkānᵉ'ū* contains the same root as vs. 38, *kᵉnā'an,* "Canaan." By this play on roots the poet alludes to the fact that the humiliation of the Israelites was due to their humbling themselves before the idols of Canaan.

43. *Many times.* Biblical *pᵉ'āmīm rabbōt* sheds light on an obscure Punic phrase, *kšm' ql' 'd p'mt brbm,* "For he heard his voice very many times," in which baffling *brbm* is analyzed into *rabbīm* preceded by the intensifying *b,* discussed in NOTE on Ps xxix 4 and fourth NOTE on lv 4. Cf. M. Lidzbarski, *Ephemeris für semitische Epigraphik,* III (Giessen, 1915), p. 281.

he rescued them. The *yqtl* form *yaṣṣīlēm* describes past action.

he rescued them . . . they hardened . . . so collapsed. This tricolon presents an unusual verbal arrangement: in the first colon the verb comes last, in the second it stands in the middle, but in the third colon it heads the clause.

they hardened. Repointing to *yēmārū* (MT *yamrū*) and ascribing the verb to the root *mrr,* "to strengthen, harden," discussed in the seventh NOTE to Ps cii 24. This etymology is suggested by the cognate motif expressed in Ps lxxxi 13, "So I repudiated him for his stubbornness of heart, they followed their own designs." The concurrence of *šᵉrīrūt,* "stubbornness," and *mō'ªṣōtēhem,* "their own designs," renders it likely that our verse expresses a related idea.

in their purpose. Which was not God's design for them. As observed in preceding NOTE, this translation leans heavily on Ps lxxxi 13, "they followed their own designs."

and so collapsed. The proposal to emend *yāmōkkū* to *yimmaqqū* may be firmly declined in the light of UT, 68:17, *nhr 'z ym lymk,* "River is strong, Sea does not collapse, "which collocates the same two ideas as biblical *yēmārū,* "they hardened," and *yāmōkkū,* "they collapsed."

As pointed out in UHP, p. 46, Gordon's emendation of Ugar. *ymk* to *ymr* founders upon the observation that in this same line occurs *ydlp* to set up a rare parallelism between the verbs *mkk,* "to sink, collapse," and *dlp,* "to sag, totter," that also appears in Eccles x 18.

Finally, the suggestion that the third colon of our verse, *yamōkkū ba'*^{a}*wōnām,* "and so collapsed in their iniquity," be deleted (cf. BH^{3} apparatus) need enlist no further attention in view of the 8:10:8 syllable count.

44. *he looked upon them.* With first-colon *yar'* sharing the suffix of second-colon *rinnātām,* "their cry." This analysis makes for a more convincing translation than the customary "He regarded their distress" (RSV). Other texts predicating *rā'āh,* "to look upon (with favor)," of Yahweh include Pss cxxxviii 6, cxlii 5, and Job xxxvii 24.

45. *his covenant with them.* Generally rendered "for their sake," *lāhem* appears to modify *b*^{e}*rītō* and to bear the sense found in the frequent expression *kārat lāhem b*^{e}*rīt,* "He made a covenant with them" (cf. Jer xxxii 40; Ezek xxxiv 25).

and led them. With the Syr., vocalizing *wayyanḥēm,* from *nāḥāh,* "to lead, guide," instead of MT *yinnāḥēm,* "he relented." Even though the Israelites, through their rebellion and apostasy, had forfeited their rights to further guidance from Yahweh, he in his mercy continued to direct their steps.

his . . . kindness. Reading singular *ḥasdō* for MT fusion of Ketiv and Qere *ḥ*^{a}*sādāw,* and comparing singular *ḥasdīkā,* the lection adopted in vs. 7.

46. *them.* Parsing *'ōtām* as the first of the two accusatives governed by the verb *yittēn;* see the next NOTE.

untold mercies. Grammars and commentaries scant their explanation of the function of *l*^{e}*raḥ*^{a}*mīm,* but a comparison with Gen xliii 14, *w*^{e}*'ēl šadday yittēn lākem raḥ*^{a}*mīm lipnē hā'īš,* "May El Shaddai grant you mercies in the sight of the man," reveals that the *lamedh* of *l*^{e}*raḥ*^{a}*mīm* in our verse and in I Kings viii 50 is the emphatic particle, here reproduced by "untold." In other words, *raḥ*^{a}*mīm* is the second accusative object after *yittēn.* Briggs' translation, "And He gave them for compassion," borders on gibberish.

their captors. Namely, the Babylonians who led the Israelites into the captivity of Babylon in 587 B.C. In Exilic Ps cxxxvii 3, the Babylonians are termed *šōbēnū,* "our captors."

47. *from among the nations.* A clear indication of the *Sitz im Leben* of the psalm; this is the prayer of the Israelite community in the diaspora or dispersion after the destruction of Jerusalem in 587 B.C.

give thanks . . . when you are praised. l^{e}*hōdōt* and *bit*^{e}*hillātekā* form an inclusion with vss. 1–2, *hōdū,* "Give thanks," and *t*^{e}*hillātō,* "his praise."

to be extolled. The hapax legomenon form *l*^{e}*hištabbē*^{a}*ḥ,* usually translated "to glory in," is an infinitive of a passive or reflexive conjugation. My translation sets up a distinction between Yahweh and his holy Name, a distinction validated by such texts as Pss lii 11, liv 3, 8–9, lxix 31. On the supposed Aramaicity of *šbḥ,* see the annotation to Ps liii 4.

when you are praised. Literally "in your praise."

48. *And let . . . say.* The verb *'āmar* parses as precative perfect. The doublet in I Chron xvi 36 reads the *yqtl* form *yō'mᵉrū,* a reading which suggests that by the time of the Chronicler the precative mode was no longer understood. From this variant one may infer that the Psalm is the earlier recension.

Amen! Praise Yah! This doxology or benediction closes the fourth of the five books of the Psalter; cf. Pss xli, lxxii, lxxxix, and *Psalms I,* pp. XXX–XXXII.

PSALM 107

(cvii 1–43)

1 Thank Yahweh, for he is good,
for eternal is his mercy.
2 Let those redeemed by Yahweh tell
that he redeemed them from the oppressor's hand,
3 And from the lands gathered them:
from the east and from the west,
from the north and from the southern sea.
4 They wandered in the wilderness,
in the barrens they trod,
A town to dwell in they did not find.
5 Hungry and thirsty,
their life ebbed from them.
6 Then they cried to Yahweh in their distress,
from their straits he rescued them.
7 He marched them on a straight road
till they came to a town to dwell in.
8 Let these confess to Yahweh his mercy,
and his wonders to the children of men,
9 Because he satisfied the throbbing throat,
and filled with good things the hungry throat.
10 As for those who dwelt in gloomy darkness,
fettered by torturing irons,
11 Because they defied the commands of El,
the counsel of the Most High spurned,
12 He humbled their mind by hardship,
they stumbled with none to help them.
13 Then they cried to Yahweh in their distress,
from their straits he saved them.
14 He brought them out of gloomy darkness,
and their bonds he snapped.
15 Let these confess to Yahweh his mercy,
and his wonders to the children of men,

16 Because he shattered doors of bronze,
and bars of iron he cut in two.
17 Enfeebled by their rebellious conduct,
they were afflicted for their iniquities.
18 All food their throats found so loathsome
that they reached the gates of Death.
19 Then they cried to Yahweh in their distress,
from their straits he saved them.
20 He sent his word to heal them,
to relieve them of their boils.
21 Let these confess to Yahweh his mercy,
and his wonders to the children of men.
22 Let them offer sacrifices of thanks
and recount his deeds in joyful song.
23 As for those who cross the sea in ships,
carry on trade over the great waters,
24 They saw the works of Yahweh,
and his wonders with the abyss.
25 He commanded and raised the wind,
a storm which lifted high his waves;
26 They went up to heaven,
they went down to the depths.
Their throats trembled from peril.
27 They gyrated and teetered like a drunkard,
and all their skill was swallowed up.
28 Then they cried to Yahweh in their distress,
and from their straits he brought them forth.
29 He stilled the storm to a whisper,
the waves that roared were hushed.
30 They rejoiced when they grew calm,
when he guided them to their port of trade.
31 Let these confess to Yahweh his mercy,
and his wonders to the children of men;
32 Let them extol him in the popular assembly,
and in the session of elders praise him.
33 He changed rivers into desert,
and springs of water into parched ground,
34 A land of fruit into salt flats
because of the wickedness of those who dwelt therein.
35 He changed desert into pools of water,
and parched earth into springs of water.

36 He settled the hungry there,
and they established a town to dwell in.
37 They sowed fields,
and planted vineyards,
They harvested a fruitful yield.
38 He blessed them, and they greatly multiplied,
and their cattle he never let diminish,
39 But diminished and declined from them
oppression, peril, and sorrow.
40 He who poured contempt upon princes,
and sent them astray into a trackless waste,
41 Set the pauper in his habitation secure,
and made his clans like lambs.
42 Let the upright see and rejoice,
and every evil man clap shut his mouth.
43 Whoever is wise will heed these things,
and they will consider the mercies of Yahweh.

NOTES

cvii. A hymn of national thanksgiving that begins the fifth and final Book of the Psalter (Pss cvii–cl). It consists of a prologue (vss. 1–3) inviting those who have assembled from all parts to thank Yahweh for his eternal kindness to Israel; of four stanzas and a closing hymn (vss. 33–43) which, in the style of Wisdom literature, develops the theme of reversal of fortunes. Each of the four stanzas is divided by a refrain (vss. 8, 15, 21, 31) that urges the Israelites not only to acknowledge to Yahweh his goodness but also to announce before all men the divine wonders of Israel's salvation history. This strong international note of the recurrent refrain is unfortunately lost in most modern translations. The first three stanzas (vss. 4–9, 10–16, 17–22) describe the Israelites' hunger and sickness as they roamed in the desert, while the fourth stanza (vss. 23–32) relates the experiences of storm-tossed seafarers who were saved by divine intervention.

A serious problem of interpretation is created by the psalmist's disconcerting interchange of *qtl* and *yqtl* verb forms. Weiser (*The Psalms*, p. 687) sees in this interchange of perfect and imperfect tenses an attempt to express the actualization of past events in the cult of the present. I understand these *yqtl* forms as merely stylistic variants expressing the same time as the *qtl* verbs, namely the past. This stylistic variation is placed in a clear light by Ugaritic poetry; consult the introductory NOTE to the historical Ps lxxviii, which makes wide use of it.

The psalmist uses chiasmus effectively (vss. 4, 9, 11, 14, 16, 19, 32), and the three instances of wordplay (vss. 9, 11) are equally skillful.

1. *Yahweh . . . his mercy.* The words *yhwh* and *ḥasdō* sound the theme of this psalm which ends, by way of an inclusion, with the phrase *ḥasdē yhwh,* "the mercies of Yahweh."

2. *those redeemed by Yahweh.* Most expositors take the phrase *g^{e}'ūlē yhwh* as referring to redemption from Exile in Babylonia, echoing Second Isaiah. But the use of the verb *gā'al* to describe Yahweh's redemption of Israel from bondage in Egypt in Exod vi 8, xv 13; Pss lxxiv 2, lxxvii 16, lxxviii 35 permits one to interpret the present phrase accordingly. The Israelite community assembled to thank Yahweh for his favors throughout its history can appropriately be termed "those redeemed (from Egypt) by Yahweh." Redemption from the Babylonian Exile will be recorded in the next verse.

tell that he redeemed them. Reading the verse as an instance of enjambment, and analyzing *'^{a}šer* as introducing the discourse implied by *yō'm^{e}rū,* "Let . . . tell." Contrast RSV, "Let the redeemed of the Lord say so, whom he has redeemed from trouble," which unwarrantedly inserts "so" after *yō'm^{e}rū,* "say." Nor can one agree with Robert C. Culley, *Oral Formulaic Language in the Biblical Psalms* (Toronto, 1967), p. 97, that enjambment is rarely if ever present in the Psalter; cf. *Psalms II,* Index of Subjects, s.v., and the numerous examples of double-duty modifiers (CBQ 29 [1967], 574–79) which show that enjambment was one of the psalmists' standard devices.

from the oppressor's hand. If we understand *g^{e}'ūlē yhwh* in the first colon as those redeemed from Egypt, then the oppressor par excellence would be Pharaoh. RSV renders *miyyad ṣār* impersonally "from trouble," omitting all reference to "hand," but Ehrlich, *Die Psalmen,* p. 267, has already shown that the personal translation is indicated.

3. *from the lands.* Plural *'^{a}rāṣōt* suggests a widespread diaspora, doubtless that of the Babylonian Exile which in several verses is implicitly likened to the Egyptian oppression.

the southern sea. Usually emended to *yāmīn, yām* in the phrase *miṣṣāpōn ūmiyyām* (it recurs in Isa xlix 12, so emendation is ruled out) can alone bear the meaning "the southern sea," i.e., the Gulf of Aqabah (II Chron viii 17). This follows from the antithetic parallelism and from the consideration that in the vocabulary of the psalmists some words can take on a conditioned meaning (second NOTES on Ps lxxiv 11 and 16). Thus *yād* comes to mean "left hand" when contrasted with *yāmīn,* "right hand" (see below on Ps cxxxviii 7), just as Ugar. *alp* designates "bull" when contrasted with *gdlt,* "cow," and *š* signifies "ram" or "buck" when contrasted with *dqt,* "ewe" or "nanny goat," as noted by Baruch Levine in JCS 17 (1963), 108.

The motif of the four cardinal points of the compass, discussed in second NOTE on Ps xlviii 8, sixth NOTE on Ps lxxiv 12, and third NOTE on Ps lxxv 7, recurs in Ps cxxxix 9–10.

4. *They wandered.* Namely the Israelites after the Exodus from Egypt, as recorded in Exod xiii 17–22. Commentators usually understand "caravans" as the subject of *tāʻū*.

in the barrens they trod. Reading the first four words of the line as a 2+2 bicolon with a 5:5 syllable count: *tāʻū bammidbār // bīšīmōn dārōk* (MT *derek*). From this stichometric division emerges a neat instance of chiasmus that closely resembles the analysis of Ps cvi 9. Thus our verse, like vss. 3, 26, 37, reads as a tricolon instead of a bicolon, as scanned by most versions.

they trod. Repointing MT *derek,* "way," to infinitive absolute *dārōk.* In vs. 7 the psalmist uses the hiphil of this verb, *yadrīkem,* "He marched them."

5. *Hungry and thirsty.* Heb. *rᵉʻēbīm gam ṣᵉmāʼīm* is a parallel pair appearing also in UT, 51:IV:33–34, *rġb rġbt . . . ġmu ġmit,* "Hungering you hunger . . . thirsting you thirst." The third NOTE on Ps cii 20 mentions the importance of the 290 pairs of parallel words in classifying Ugaritic in relation to Hebrew.

This verse alludes to the hunger and thirst of the Israelites, described in Exod xvi 3 and xvii 3, as they wandered in the Sinai Peninsula.

their life ebbed from them. Often translated "Their soul fainted within them" (RSV), this clause contains the expression *bāhem titʻaṭṭāp* that is hapax legomenon. Its correct translation and analysis would seem to be linked to Isa lvii 16, "For I shall not quarrel for ever, nor always be angry, *kī rūᵃḥ millᵉpānay yaʻᵃṭōp,* "but my fury will subside from me." Hence *bāhem* would signify "from them," much like UT, 1 Aqht:145–46, *wyqḥ bhm aqht,* "And he took Aqhat from them," namely from the gizzard of the eagle. From this translation proceeds the metaphor similar to the biblical description of one's life oozing like a liquid; cf. Ps xxii 15.

As so frequently in this historical poem, the *yqtl* verb form *titʻaṭṭāp* narrates an event of the past.

6. *Then they cried.* The psalmist's use here and in vs. 28 of *yiṣʻᵃqū* with *ṣadē,* but *yizʻᵃqū* with *zayin* in vss. 13 and 19, sustains the observation made at Ps lxviii 4–5 concerning *ʻālaṣ* and *ʻālaz,* "to exult."

he rescued them. Recognizing in *yaṣṣīlēm* another instance of a *yqtl* form expressing the past.

7. *He marched them.* Hiphil *yadrīkēm* forms an inclusion with vs. 4, *dārōk,* "they trod." The refrain in vs. 8 also shows that vs. 7 concludes the description of the first incident chosen by the poet to illustrate the working of divine providence.

a town to dwell in. The phrase *ʻīr mōšāb* harks back to the same phrase in vs. 4, with which it creates an inclusion.

8. *Let these confess.* Since versions and commentators diverge in their construction of this refrain (vss. 15, 21, 31), its syntactic analysis becomes

imperative: *yōdū layhwh ḥasdō wᵉniplᵉʾōtāyw libnē ʾādām.* When chiastically placed *ḥasdō,* "his mercy," and *niplᵉʾōtāyw,* "his wonders," are parsed as direct objects of *yōdū,* "confess," and parallel *layhwh* and *libnē ʾādām* construed as the persons to whom the confession (in different senses, to be sure) should be made, the refrain emerges as a summons to a vertical dialogue with Yahweh and to a horizontal proclamation before the other nations of God's miracles on behalf of Israel. This refrain thus strikes a strong apostolic and universalistic note that is lost in such versions as RSV, "Let them thank the Lord for his steadfast love, and for his wonderful works to the sons of men!" Consult Ehrlich, *Die Psalmen,* p. 267; Weiser, *The Psalms,* p. 685, and compare the curious translation of the Vulgate, *confiteantur Domino misericordiae ejus,* "Let his mercies confess to the Lord." The strictures made in *Psalms I,* pp. XXIV ff. and *Psalms II,* pp. XVIII ff., on the versional competence vis-à-vis Hebrew poetic syntax appear justified.

9. *the throbbing throat.* Often translated "the longing soul" (KJ), *nepeš šōqēqāh,* which also occurs in Isa xxix 8, cleverly collocates the names of two parts of the body. Here *nepeš* designates "throat," as clearly recognized by Gunkel (*Die Psalmen,* p. 47) on the authority of L. Dürr—consult the fourth NOTE on Ps cv 18—whereas *šōqēqāh,* from *šqq,* "to leap, spring," is related to *šōq,* "thigh." A similar collocation of names of parts of the body is noticed in the fourth NOTE on Ps lxxvii 5.

filled with good things. Comparing Eccles vi 7 for similar phraseology: *kol ʿᵃmal hāʾādām lᵉpīhū wᵉgam hannepeš lōʾ timmālēʾ,* "All a man's toil is for its (Sheol's) mouth, and yet its throat is never filled."

In this verse the psalmist resumes the theme of vs. 5, which describes the Israelites' hunger and thirst in the wasteland.

the hungry throat. The psalmist arranges the verse chiastically: verb + object//object + verb. The 9:9 syllable count of the line is also noteworthy.

10. *As for those who dwelt . . . fettered.* The two participles *yōšᵉbē* and *ʾᵃsīrē* in *casus pendens* (cf. Ps ciii 15) correspond to the two participles of vs. 23, also in *casus pendens,* and just as vs. 10 is completed by vs. 11, so vs. 23 is completed by vs. 24 (courtesy D. N. Freedman).

gloomy darkness . . . torturing irons. Usually translated "darkness and gloom," *ḥōšek wᵉṣalmāwet* is better treated as hendiadys because it balances *ʿonī ūbarzel,* literally "affliction and iron," which, though difficult, does yield good sense when treated as hendiadys; cf. Job xxxvi 8, *ḥablē ʿōnī,* "torturing cords." D. Winton Thomas in JTS 16 (1965), 444–45, has recourse to Ar. *ʿaniya,* "to become a captive," to explain these two passages along with Ps cv 18, but such an etymology does not impose itself nor is it really necessary.

Where is the prison to which the psalmist alludes? If the background is the Exodus and Wanderings (cf. Ps cvi 7, 33), then the imprisonment is probably a reference to the nether world to which the Israelites were banished and from which they were released. The motif of Sheol the Prison, discussed at Ps lxxxviii 9, recurs in Ps cxlii 8, whereas the theme of torture in Sheol, found in Job xv 33; Prov xi 31; Luke xvi 23, will be touched upon at Ps cxl 11. The episode of Dathan and Abiram (Ps cvi 17) may be relevant to the present exegesis, which is also sustained by the presence of the term *ṣalmāwet* which alludes to the shadow of Death in Job x 21, xxxviii 17. See Tromp, *Primitive Conceptions*, Index, *sub voce*.

11. *they defied the commands*. The expression *himrū 'imrē*, which contains a play on words, recalls such statements as Pss lxxviii 40, *yamrūhū bammidbār*, "They defied him in the wilderness," and cvi 7, *wayyamrū 'ēlīm*, "And they defied the Most High," which describe the rebellious conduct of the people of Israel after their exodus from Egypt. Our poet doubtless refers to these incidents.

they defied . . . spurned. As in vs. 9, the word order is diagonal or chiastic.

El . . . the Most High. Placing *'ēl* in the first colon and *'elyōn* in the second, the psalmist achieves the breakup of the composite divine name *'ēl 'elyōn* (Gen xiv 18); consult third NOTE on Ps xlvi 5 and second NOTE on Ps lxxviii 56.

13. *he saved them*. Another instance of the *yqtl* verb expressing past time. The psalmist eschews monotony by varying the final word of the refrain: in vs. 6 he uses *yaṣṣīlēm*, "he rescued them," here and in vs. 19 he offers *yōšī'ēm*, "he saved them," and in vs. 28 he again surprises with *yōṣī'ēm*, "he brought them forth." A number of modern translations (AT, CCD, RSV, BJ, JB, *The Grail Psalms* [London, 1962]) can be criticized for their rendition of the three different verbs used by the psalmist. These versions render all three verbs in the same manner, as though the poet employed the same verb in all four refrains! Thus all four times AT and RSV read "he delivered them," CCD, JB and *The Grail Psalms* offer "he rescued them," while BJ translates, *il les a délivrés*. *Etiam Homerus dormitat*. It would be interesting to establish which version first (my limited inquiry goes back to the 1931 edition of AT) perpetrated this howler that has been repeated by subsequent translators.

14. *He brought them out . . . he snapped*. The *yqtl* verbs expressing happenings of the past open and close a chiastically patterned verse; compare vs. 16 and NOTE thereto.

16. *he shattered . . . he cut in two*. The psalmist varies his style by beginning and ending a chiastically arranged verse with the *qtl* verbs *šibbar* and *giddēa'*; see the preceding NOTE.

doors of bronze, and bars of iron. The strong gates of the prison implied in vss. 10 and 14.

17. *Enfeebled*. Often emended to *ḥōlīm*, "sick," consonantal *'wlym* can

be defended as a qal passive participle of a posited root *'wl,* a by-form of *'ll,* Akk. *ulālu,* "to be weak."

their rebellious conduct. Literally "the way of their rebellion," *derek piš'ām* might be compared with Ugar. *ntb pš',* "the path of rebellion."

for their iniquities. The causal relationship between sin and sickness in the mind of the Israelites, still held in NT times (cf. John ix 2), has been commented upon at Pss xli 7 and lxix 27. It remains to be pointed out that this Israelite belief, combated by the Book of Job, has roots in Canaanite culture as now appears from a clearer understanding of UT, 127:44–52, "You have let your hand fall into malice. You judge not the cause of the widow, adjudicate not the case of the wretched, nor drive out those preying on the poor. You do not feed the fatherless before you, the widow behind your back. *Thus* have you become a brother of the bed of sickness, a companion of the bed of disease." In their translation of lines 50–51, *km aḫt 'rš mdw,* Ugaritic specialists either ignore *km* or misconstrue it. That it signifies "thus" is clear from such texts as UT, 49:II:28–30, "Like the heart of a wild cow toward her calf, like the heart of a wild ewe toward her lamb, thus [*km*] was the heart of Anath toward Baal." In other words, Ugar. *km* is the equivalent of Heb. *kēn,* "so" (first NOTE on Ps lxxiii 15 describes the phonetic development), which sometimes leads to the logical outcome of an action. King Kirta's aforementioned crimes inexorably resulted in his mortal illness.

18. *their throats.* This denotation of *napšām* is noted at vs. 9. RSV's "They loathed any kind of food" has eased out nettlesome *napšām.*

found so loathsome. Sickness causes loss of appetite; cf. UT, 127:11, *npšh llḥm tpth̩,* "She sharpened his appetite for food," the first action performed by King Kirta's youngest daughter after she cast out the fever from her father's body. Cf. Albright, YGC, p. 148, n. 104.

the gates of Death. The nether abode of the dead was often depicted as a city with walls and gates; third NOTE on Ps ix 14; fourth NOTE on Ps lxxiii 20; Dahood, in HWFB, p. 47, on Jon ii 7 and Jer xv 7.

20. *his word.* The psalmist pictures the word of Yahweh as an angel sent to heal the Israelites. Compare Ps xliii 3, where God is asked to send his light and truth to lead the psalmist to the holy mountain; Isa xl 8, lv 10–11, and Luke vii 7, "Say but the word and my servant will be healed." Cf. also the Johannine concept of Logos.

to heal them. Parsing the *waw* of *weyirpā'ēm* as the final *waw,* which introduces the purpose clause; cf. second NOTE on Ps lxxvii 7, where biblical and Ugaritic references are given. The identity of syntax here and in Ps cv 20, "He sent the king to release him," supports the view that both psalms were written by the same poet.

to relieve them. MT *wīmallēṭ* can be parsed either as sharing the suffix of *yirpā'ēm,* "to heal them," or read *wīmalleṭēm,* with the final *mem* explained as a shared consonant, since the next word begins with *mem.* The latter reading evens the syllable count at 9:9 and uncovers the assonance of *yirpā'ēm,* "to heal them," and *wīmalleṭēm,* "to relieve them."

their boils. Much-canvassed *šeḥītōtām* can convincingly be derived from *šḥn,* "to be inflamed," *šeḥīn,* "boil," with the assimilation of the third radical *nun: šḥnt>šḥt.* Hence read *šeḥītōttām.* Cf. Ps xlvi 9, *šmt,* "fertility," from *šmnt;* Ugar. *ypt,* "cow," from *ypnt;* Phoen. *'lmt,* "widow," but Ugar. *almnt;* Ugar. *ytnt,* "I have given," but also *ytt* (UT, Glossary, No. 1169). Consult PNWSP, p. 28, n. 2, which examines Lam iv 2, *nilkad bišeḥītōt-m,* "We are seized by boils."

The psalmist probably refers to some incident during the Israelite wandering in the desert after leaving Egypt; cf. Num xi 33; Deut xxviii 35; and Ps lxvi 11, "You brought us into the wilderness, put ulcers on our thighs."

22. *offer sacrifices.* Comparing *yizbeḥū zibḥē* with UT, 125:39–40, *krtn dbḥ dbḥ,* "Our Kirta is offering a sacrifice."

23. *As for those who cross . . . carry on.* The participles *yōredē* and *'ōśē* stand in *casus pendens,* a construction discussed in the first NOTE on Ps ciii 15, and above at vs. 10. These participles lose their suspended state in vs. 24 when they are introduced by *hēmāh,* "these," as subjects of the verb *rā'ū,* "saw." It is also possible to translate *hēmmāh* a "Look! Behold!", as tentatively proposed by Patton, CPBP, p. 37. RSV translates the participle *yōredē* "Some went down," as though it were a finite verb, but such a version takes liberties with Hebrew grammar.

the sea in ships. The expression *hayyām bā'onīyōt* collocates two roots appearing in the Ugaritic phrase *anyt ym,* "sea-ships," (2061:13–14), and discussed by van Dijk, EPT, pp. 60 ff., 72. Also consult Jack Sasson, "Canaanite Maritime Involvement in the Second Millennium B.C.," in JAOS 86 (1966), 126–38, whose study of Ugaritic texts reveals that by 1400 B.C. Ugarit carried on a far-flung and prosperous trade in the Mediterranean. He also cites the statement of Jean Nougayrol, based on data supplied by a Ras Shamra tablet, that the king of Ugarit had at his service ships capable of carrying 500 tons, or perhaps even more, if one takes into account the cargo of grain and oil. Columbus' largest ship, the *Santa Maria,* was only 233 tons.

This new information regarding Canaanite maritime activity in the Late Bronze Age (1500–1200 B.C.), and such texts as Judg v 17 and I Kings ix 27 ff., which describes King Solomon's overseas commercial enterprises, make it difficult to infer, with some scholars, a post-Exilic date for the psalm.

trade. This economic nuance of *melā'kāh* occurs in economic texts from Ras Shamra (*mlakt*), as first observed by W. F. Albright, BASOR 150 (1958), 38, n. 14. Albright also finds this meaning in Prov xxii 29. On 1QIsa xxiii 2, *ml'kyk,* "your salesmen," see present writer in CBQ 22 (1960), 403–4, and UT, Glossary, No. 1344.

the great waters. The psalmist's term for the Mediterranean.

24. *with the abyss.* Following Ehrlich (*Die Psalmen*, p. 268), who takes the preposition of *bimᵉṣûlāh* as instrumental. A related notion is expressed by Ps civ 26, "Leviathan whom you fashioned to sport with." D. N. Freedman proposes to see a hostile meaning in *bimᵉṣûlāh*, "against Abyss," since the relationship between Yahweh and Abyss (//Leviathan) is essentially combative. The second NOTE on Ps cxxiv 3 examines other instances of *b*, "against."

25. *the wind, a storm.* Not conversant with stereotyped phrases broken up for metrical and parallelistic purposes, MT (as well as the versions) puts the composite phrase *rûᵃḥ sᵉʿārāh* (cf. Ps cxlviii 8; Isa xli 16) in the first colon with the resultant syllabic imbalance 12:6. By shifting *sᵉʿārāh* to the second colon, the syllable count becomes 9:9! The same poetic device occurs in Job iv 15, "A wind (*rûᵃḥ*) passed before my face / A storm (*śᵉʿārāt*) made my body bristle," as proposed in *Biblica* 48 (1967), 544–45.

which lifted high. Parsing the *waw* of *wattᵉrômēm* as explicative, a usage annotated in the fourth Note on Ps iii 4 and second and third NOTES on Ps lxix 36.

his waves. Expositors have puzzled before the suffix of *gallāyw*, because it has no apparent antecedent in the verse. Thus some go back to vs. 23 and identify *hayyām*, "the sea," as its antecedent. RSV's "the waves of the sea" evidently derives from an unwarranted emendation to *gallē hayyām*. If, however, the first (*yōʾmer*) and last (*gallāyw*) words of the verse are understood as forming an inclusion—and hence speaking of the same person—the rendition of *gallāyw*, "his waves," becomes attractive. Just as "the abyss" of vs. 24 is pictured as a mere instrument of Yahweh, so "the waves" might appropriately be termed "his."

26. *They went up . . . went down.* Commentators may correctly understand sailors as the subject of *yaʿᵃlû* and *yērᵉdû*, but a comparison with Ps civ 8, "They [the chaotic waters] went up to the mountains, they went down to the nether chasm," allows one to propose that the waves not the seamen swell and sink. Thus vss. 25–26a-b describe the storm, and the next three cola depict the affects of the storm on the sailors.

All three *yqtl* verbs of this tricolon narrate past incidents.

heaven . . . depths. The parallelism of *šāmayim* and *tᵉhômôt* echoes their collocation in UT, ʿnt:III:21–22, *tant šmm ʿm arṣ thmt ʿmn kbkbm*, "the meeting of heaven with the nether world, of the depths with the stars," and UT, 607:1, *bt šmm wthm*, "the daughter of heaven and the depths."

Their throats. Scholars disagree widely in their translation of the final colon *napšām bᵉrāʿāh titmôgāg;* I retain the sense of *napšām* found in vss. 9 and 18.

trembled. For this nuance of *titmōgāg,* a *yqtl* narrative form, see first NOTE on lxxv 4; compare Ezek xxi 20, where *mūg* describes the heart's palpitation and Ecclus xlviii 19 where *nāmūgū* parallels *yāḥīlū,* "they writhed."

27. *They gyrated.* Repointing MT *yāḥōggū,* "They kept festival," to *yāḥūgū.*

like a drunkard. In several biblical texts (e.g., Jer xxv 27) "drunkenness" and "helplessness" are coterminous; consult CBQ 22 (1960), 404–6, and Phoenician Kilamuwa, lines 7–8, *wškr 'nk 'ly mlk 'šr,* "And I was drunk (i.e., helpless) before him, the king of Assyria."

was swallowed up. The psalmist chooses the apt word in *titballā',* which is predicated of *mᵉṣūlāh* (see vs. 24) in Ps lxix 16, "or the abyss swallow me."

28. *he brought them forth.* Not "He delivered them," with RSV and some other modern versions.

29. *He stilled.* Ascribing hiphil *yāqēm* (cf. vs. 33, *yāśēm,* "He changed") to *qwm,* "to become still," a root needed to explain Eccles xii 4 as well: *wᵉyāqūm lᵉqōl haṣṣippōr,* "And even the voice of the birds will become still," a difficult Hebrew clause which becomes intelligible when *lᵉ* of *lᵉqōl* is parsed as the emphatic *lamedh.*

the waves that roared. The word apparently missing in the second colon can be supplied by reading, with no consonantal changes, *gallē hāmū* (MT *gallēhem*) and parsing the phrase as a construct noun (*gallē*) dependent on a verb (*hāmū*). The first NOTE on Ps lxv 5, and the NOTES on Pss cxvi 2 and cxli 9 examine other instances of this construction while Jer v 22, *hāmū gallāyw,* "his waves roar," establishes the authenticity of the phrase. With this reading, the syllable count evens at 8:8 against MT 8:7. One may, to be sure, also explain the final *yod* of *gly* as third-person singular suffix, "his waves" (see vs. 25 *gallāyw,* "his waves") and assume that consonantal *hm* shares the *w* of the following word, an orthographic practice discussed at Ps lx 11.

30. *they grew calm.* Given the hundreds of *yqtl* verb forms describing completed events, the proposed emendation of BH³ of *yištōqū* to *šātāqū* can safely be dropped from future editions.

their port of trade. The port to which they were headed when the storm blew up. This is a literal translation of *mᵉḥōz ḥepṣām,* a phrase containing the hapax legomenon *māḥōz,* Akk. *maḫāzu,* "city," (cf. *Ugaritica V,* ed. C. F. A. Schaeffer [Mission de Ras Shamra, XVI; Paris, 1968], p. 351) which occurs in a first-century A.D. Punic Inscription from North Africa with the meaning "forum, market place." Cf. J. Friedrich, VT 11 (1961), 355, and KAI, II, pp. 130, 134. Professor B. Mazar discovered some years ago a sixth-century B.C. inscription at Ein Gedi on the west bank of the Dead Sea containing the word *mḥz,* "forum, market."

Also Phoenician is the nuance of *ḥepṣām,* "their business, trade," a favorite word of the Phoenicianizing Book of Ecclesiastes. See W. E. Staples, "The Meaning of *ḥēpeṣ* in Ecclesiastes," JNES 24 (1965), 110–12.

32. *extol him . . . praise him.* Another fine example of chiasmus. This verse provides a clue to the original setting in which the psalm was sung, namely, the community's thanksgiving service.

33. *He changed.* With the *yqtl* verb *yāśēm* describing the past. This may be inferred from MT's vocalization of vs. 36, *wayyōšeb,* "He settled," and vs. 37, *wayyizrᵉʿū,* "They sowed," both with *waw* consecutive. This shows that the Masoretes took all the verbs of 33–41 as narrating past history.

Most modern commentators translate all the verbs as present and see in vss. 33–43 a hymn praising God for his bounty. They maintain that the psalmist alludes to no particular historical incidents, but refers to Yahweh's providential care in general. Consequently, they argue that vss. 33–43 were not originally composed to go with the preceding verses.

As the following notes will attempt to show, the hymn in vss. 33–43 contains historical allusions and refers back to some of the earlier verses, so that the entire psalm is a unity composed by one psalmist.

He changed rivers into desert. This and the two following clauses are metaphorical for reversing the fortunes of a prosperous people.

34. *because of the wickedness.* Namely, of the Canaanites who were decimated or driven out of Canaan because of their sinfulness. Cf. Deut ix 5, "It is not because of your virtue or your rectitude that you are coming to occupy their land, but because of the wickedness of those nations that Yahweh your God is dispossessing them before you."

therein. The last word of the verse, *bāh,* has as its antecedent *'ereṣ,* "a land," the first word in the line, thereby forming an inclusion.

35. *He changed.* That *yāśēm,* as in vs. 33, describes the past is the inference to be drawn from MT's pointing of next verb *wayyōšeb,* "He settled."

desert into pools of water. This metaphor describing the Israelite change of fortunes is particularly apt inasmuch as the Israelites exchanged the desert for a "land flowing with milk and honey."

36. *He settled.* With the *waw* consecutive construction *wayyōšeb* continuing the description of past *yāśēm,* "He changed."

the hungry. Namely, the Israelites. The poet uses the same term as in vs. 5 to describe the Israelites: *rᵉʿēbīm.* This reprise points to unity of authorship; see the next NOTE.

a town to dwell in. In addition to creating an inclusion with *wayyōšeb,* "He settled," *ʿīr mōšāb* harks back to vs. 4 and sustains the unity of authorship defended in preceding NOTE.

37. *They sowed.* To wit, the Israelites after their entry into the Promised Land.

fields . . . vineyards. The psalmist employs the parallel pair *śādōt* and *kᵉrāmīm,* the same brace written by his Canaanite predecessor in UT,

77:22, *atn šdh krmm,* "I shall make her fields vineyards," and 1079:6, *ṯlṯ šd w krm,* "three fields and a vineyard."

They harvested. For this shade of meaning in *'āśū,* consult the fourth NOTE on Ps civ 13.

39. *But diminished.* Verses 38b and 39a are arranged in a chiastic pattern. The versions make the object "them" of vs. 38 the subject of vs. 39 (RSV, "When they are diminished and brought low through oppression, trouble, and sorrow"), but the chiastic sequence suggests that the three nouns in vs. 39b are the subjects of the two verbs in vs. 39a.

declined from them oppression. Reading *wayyāšōḥūm 'ōṣer* instead of MT *wayyāšōḥū me'ōṣer,* and parsing the *-m* as the dative of advantage. Another instructive use of the dative suffix of advantage can be seen; MT misses it in Job xv 18, "That which wise men have announced, and their fathers did not hide from them" (*kiḥ^{a}dūm '^{a}bōtām;* MT *kiḥ^{a}dū mē'^{a}bōtām*). H. D. Hummel in JBL 76 (1957), 104, would explain the *-m* as the enclitic *mem* with the following three nouns analyzed as adverbial accusatives ("They are brought low by oppression, evil, and sorrow"). One may also adopt this explanation of the *m* ending while keeping the three nouns as subjects of the verse: "While diminished and declined oppression, peril, and sorrow."

oppression, peril, and sorrow. Construing *'ōṣer rā'āh w^{e}yāgōn* as subjects of the preceding two verbs, and ascribing to generic *rā'āh* the nuance found in vs. 26.

40. *He who poured.* Translating the participle *šōpēk* as a participle and not as a finite verb with many versions. It belongs to Yahweh to reverse the fortunes of peoples.

princes. A probable reference to the Canaanite leaders driven out of Canaan by the Israelites.

41. *the pauper.* Within the context of this psalm *'ebyōn* probably designates the people Israel.

in his habitation. Some expositors have directed attention to the unusual full spelling *'wny,* "affliction," instead of *'ny.* Hence I vocalize consonantal *m'wny* as *m^e'ōnī,* the substantive *mā'ōn* followed by the third-person suffix *-ī;* syntactically it parses as accusative of place. Here "his habitation" doubtless means Palestine.

his clans. With *mišpāḥot* sharing the suffix of *m^e'ōnī,* "his habitation."

like lambs. The clans of pauper Israel were rendered as prolific as a flock of sheep. Compare Job xxi 11, "They give birth to their young like lambs."

42. *every evil man.* If vss. 42–43 are considered chiastic or diagonal in their disposition (and chiasmus characterizes this psalm), with plural *y^{e}šārīm,* "the upright," serving also as the subject of plural *yitbōn^{e}nū* "they will consider," in vs. 43b, then singular and abstract *kol 'āwlāh,* literally "all evil," pairs with singular and concrete *mī ḥākām,* "Whoever is wise," in vs. 43a. In other words, the psalmist here employs the poetic

device wherein an abstract noun is balanced by a concrete vocable, but both of which are to be rendered concretely; consult third NOTE on Ps v 8, second NOTE on Ps lxxviii 61, and THE GRAMMAR OF THE PSALTER.

clap shut. Balancing two jussive verbs in the first colon, *qāpᵉṣāh* parses as a precative perfect.

43. *Whoever is wise.* The indefinite pronoun in the phrase *mī ḥākām* appears quite frequently in the Phoenician Inscriptions; e.g., Kilamuwa, line 11, *wmy bl ḥz pn š šty bʿl ʿdr,* And who never saw the face of a sheep, I made him the owner of a flock."

these things. All the divine manifestations of mercy enumerated throughout the psalm.

they. Recognizing from the chiastic arrangement of vss. 42–43 that plural "the upright" of vs. 42 is the subject of plural *yitbōnᵉnū.*

the mercies of Yahweh. The phrase *ḥasdē yhwh* creates an inclusion with vs. 1, *yhwh . . . ḥasdō,* an observation that undermines the contention that vss. 33–43 are a later addition to the psalm.

PSALM 108

(cviii 1–14)

1 *A song. A psalm of David.*

2 Firm is my resolve,
O God;
I will sing and chant.
Awake, my heart!
3 Awake, O harp and lyre! [2]*
that I might awaken Dawn!
4 I will thank you among peoples, Yahweh, [3]
I will sing to you among nations, O truly Great One!
5 Above the heavens is your kindness, [4]
and to the sky your fidelity.
6 Your stature is above the heavens, O God, [5]
over all the earth your glory.
7 That your beloved may be delivered [6]
give me victory with your right hand,
and grant me triumph!
8 God spoke from his sanctuary: [7]
"Exultant will I divide up Shechem,
the Valley of Succoth measure off.
9 Gilead is mine, and Manasseh is mine; [8]
Ephraim is my helmet,
Judah my commander's staff.
10 Moab is my washbasin, [9]
upon Edom will I plant my sandal,
over Philistia will I give a cry of conquest."
11 Who will bring me the Fortress City? [10]
Who will offer me Edom's throne as tribute?
12 But you, O God—will you be angry with us, [11]
and go forth no more, O God, with our armies?

* Verse numbers in RSV.

13 Grant us liberation from the adversary, [12]
since the aid of man is futile.
14 With God we will achieve victory, [13]
and he will trample on our adversaries.

Notes

cviii. This psalm was probably compiled for liturgical purposes from ancient religious poems that are also used in Pss lvii 8–11 and lx 7–14. To describe the psalm as a compilation from two other psalms (so CCD) goes beyond the available evidence. The following annotations are limited chiefly to the variant readings and to several modifications of the translations of Pss lvii and lx proferred in *Psalms II.*

2. *O God.* In Ps lvii 8, *nākōn libbī,* "Firm is my resolve," is repeated a second time, but this fact alone does not permit us to insert it here, as recommended by BH³ on the basis of LXX, Syr., and five manuscripts. Doubly transmitted texts contain too much random variation (is this a sign of original oral composition? cf. Culley, *Oral Formulaic Language in the Biblical Psalms, passim*) to warrant standardization by the textual critic. What is more, the extremely literal *Juxta Hebraeos* witnesses no repetition of *nākōn libbī.* On doubly transmitted texts, consult introductory Notes to Pss liii and xcvi.

Awake, my heart! At this point in the line Ps lvii 9 reads *ʿūrāh k^{e}bēdī,* "Awake, my heart!" Applying the principle examined at Pss lv 23 and lxxi 6, one should conclude that MT *ʾap k^{e}bōdī,* "also my glory," conceals the same thought and should be re-voweled *ʾ^{a}pē k^{e}bēdī,* with *ʾ^{a}pē* parsed as the imperative of **ʾāpāh,* "to arouse, inflame." Whether such a root should be identified with well-known *ʾāpāh,* "to bake," cannot be established on such slender evidence, but Hos vii 4 proves instructive with its possible play on roots: *mē ʾōpeh yišbōt mēʿīr,* a subtle pun which collocates *ʾōpeh* and *mēʿīr,* the two roots apparently underlying the variant readings *ʿūrāh k^{e}bēdī* in Ps lvii 9 and *ʾ^{a}pēh k^{e}bēdī* posited in our verse.

4. *O truly Great One!* The A+B+C sequence in the first colon is not fully matched in MT's second colon which only contains Á+B́. Accordingly *kī gādōl,* the first two words of vs. 5, should be attached to vs. 4 to supply the vocative element needed to balance vocative *yhwh* of the first colon. Verse 4 now scans as A+B+C//Á+B́+Ć, while vs. 5 reads A+B//Á+B́.

The divine epithet *kī gādōl,* with its emphatic *kī,* compares with *kī ṭōb,* "truly good," which modifies the name of Yahweh in Pss lii 11, liv 8, while *gādōl* appears as a divine appellative in Ps xcix 3, *gādōl w^{e}nōrāʾ,* "O Great and Awesome One." One may also render *kī gādōl,* "O truly Tall One," the meaning found in Ps civ 25, and suggested by vs. 6 of our psalm which speaks of Yahweh's "stature." Ps lvii 10 should now be translated according to this analysis: "I will thank you among peoples, O Lord / I will sing to you among nations, O truly Great One."

5. *Above.* Commentators experience difficulty with *mē'al* (Ehrlich, *Die Psalmen*, p. 271, stoutly labels it *unhebräisch;* others emend it to *'ad* as in Ps lvii 11), but it may be accepted as another instance of heaped-up prepositions (second NOTE on Ps xvii 2). The psalmist needed another syllable in the first colon (syllable count now 8:9), so he used two prepositions where one would have sufficed. Job iv 19 supplies a new example of compound prepositions that were thought to be an exclusive prerogative of the Phoenician dialect: *yidkᵉ'ū millipnē 'ōśām,* "Can they be pure before their Maker?" MT reads *yᵉdakkᵉ'ūm lipnē 'āš m,* which yields no coherent statement.

6. *over.* With Ps lvii 12, omitting the conjunction *wᵉ,* "and," before *'al.* The chiastic structure and the resultant 9:9 syllable count likewise favor its deletion.

8. *Exultant . . . measure off.* Departing from the wording of Ps lx 8 in *Psalms II,* in order to bring out the chiastic word order in the Hebrew. Stylistically noteworthy, too, is the poet's positioning of two verbs followed by one noun in the first colon, but of two nouns followed by one verb in the second colon.

Exultant. In VT 17 (1967), 242–43, Christopher R. North proposes to emend *'e'lōzāh* to *'a'al zeh,* "I will go up forthwith," because "It is perhaps decisive that nowhere else except in Ps lx 8//Ps cviii 8 is Yahweh said to exult." In pre-Ugaritic days such a proposal might have found some endorsers, but North's argumentation is hardly convincing in the face of such texts as UT, 'nt:II:23–28, "Much does she smite and look; battle and gaze does Anath. Her liver swells with laughter, her heart is filled with joy, Anath's liver with victory. Then knee-deep she plunges into the blood of soldiers, to her neck into warrior's gore." Since North accepts the blood-stained warrior motif of Yahweh in Isa lxiii 1–6, he will doubtless admit the concomitant motif of exultation over enemy blood. There is a growing consensus among biblical scholars that for poetic and theological imagery the Old Testament poets were deeply indebted to their Canaanite predecessors. See the annotations to Pss xviii 11, xxxvi 9, lxviii 24, civ 25.

10. *will I give a cry of conquest.* The principle of random variation, discussed in the first NOTE on vs. 2, obviates the need to alter *'etrō'ā'* to Ps lx 10, *hitrō'ā'ī,* "my cry of conquest." See the next NOTE.

11. *the Fortress City.* Perhaps Petra, which is called *'īr-m ṣūr,* "the Rock City," in Ps lx 11. By grace of the principle cited in the preceding NOTE, *'īr mibṣār* need not be emended to align it with its counterpart in Ps lx 11.

will offer me . . . as tribute. Closer attention to the parallelistic elements in the verse would have discouraged the derivation of MT *nāḥanī* from *nwḥ,* "to rest, sit," as proposed in third NOTE on Ps lx 11.

Texts such as Zeph iii 10, *yōbīlūn minḥātī,* "[My suppliants] will offer me tribute" (see the first NOTE on Ps ii 8, on function of genitive suffix), and UT, 137:37–38, *hw ybl argmnk kilm* [ ] *ybl kbn qdš mnḥyk,* "He himself shall bring you imposts like the gods, he shall bring you tribute like the sons of holiness," both of which collocate the roots *ybl* and *nḥh,* show that *nāḥanī,* the opposite number of *yōbīlēnī,* parses as *qtl nāḥā* followed by the dative suffix. Thus we have a perfect A+B+C// A+B́+Ć sequence as well as the *yqtl–qtl* verbal succession. Cf. also Hos x 6 and Job xxix 25. On the importance of parallel or associated pairs as a text-critical criterion, consult the third NOTE on Ps cii 20.

Consequently it becomes difficult to appreciate the stricture (gratuitous in my opinion) of J. T. Milik, who in *Biblica* 48 (1967), 565, writes: "La méthode, en vogue depuis peu, qui considère les éléments parallèles dans les passages poétiques comme rigoureusement identiques ou peu s'en faut, et qui cherche, à partir de ce critère mécanique et arbitraire, à construire un lexique, une grammaire ou un panthéon nouveaux, ne m'inspire guère confiance." ["The method, recently become fashionable, which considers the parallel elements in poetic passages as rigorously or almost identical, and which, setting out from this mechanical and arbitrary criterion, seeks to construct a lexicon, a grammar, or a new pantheon, hardly fills me with confidence."] These remarks bespeak a limited familiarity with the latent possibilities of poetic parallelism for Northwest Semitic philology. In fact, the present parallelism between *yōbīlēnī* and *nāḥanī* builds up the case of those philologists who would derive *minḥāh,* "gift, tribute," from *nāḥāh,* "to lead, bring," as against those lexicographers who posit the root *mnḥ* as the base of *minḥāh.*

13. *liberation from the adversary. Psalms II* renders *'ezrat miṣṣār,* "help against the adversary"; this is the traditional version of Ps lx 13. Ugaritic usage, however, suggests a philologically more precise translation and analysis of the phrase. UT, 3 Aqht:rev.:12–14 reads *w* [ ] *aqht wypltk bn* [*dnil*] *wy'ḏrk byd btlt* [*'nt*], "Then [call] Aqhat to save you, Daniel's son to liberate you from the hand of the Virgin Anath." Normally signifying "to help," *'ḏr* denotes "to rescue, liberate from" when employed with the preposition *b,* "from," in Ugaritic or *min* in Hebrew. This observation considerably improves our understanding of Ps xlvi 2 as translated in the Introduction to *Psalms III,* and Ecclus li 2–3, *ngd qmy hyyth ly 'zrtny krwb ḥsdk mmwqšy ṣwpy sl' wmyd mbqšy npšy,* "In the presence of my assailants you were on my side. You liberated me in your abounding kindness from the snares of those watching my cave, from the claw of those seeking my life." Here the construction *'zrtny . . . myd* recalls Ugar. *y'ḏrk byd.* Cf. also Deut xxxiii 8, *we'ēzer miṣṣārāyw tihyeh,* "And be the liberation from his adversaries"; Ezra viii 22, "For I was ashamed to request a contingent of cavalry from the king to liberate us from the foe [*le'ozrēnū mē'ōyēb*]" (courtesy of T. Penar). In this direction too may be found the clearer translation of Zech i 15, "For my part I

was only a little angry, and so they escaped disaster [*'āzᵉrû lᵉrā'āh*]," and Job xxx 13, *lō' 'ōzēr lāmō,* "There is no one to liberate from them." The two ideas residing in *'zr,* namely "to help" and "to liberate," depending upon the prepositions used, recall the similar concepts expressed by *yš'*, "to save," but also "to help." The same usage may be recognized in 1QH 2:34–35, *w'th 'ly 'zrth npš 'ny wrš myd ḥzq mmnw,* "But you, my God, liberated the life of the afflicted and poor from the grasp of one stronger than he" (courtesy T. Penar). It should be observed that T. H. Gaster, *The Dead Sea Scriptures,* rev. ed. (Doubleday Anchor Books, 1964), p. 142, in order to translate the line, inserted the verb "snatched from"—not found in the Hebrew: "But ever, O my God, hast Thou holpen the needy and weak and snatched him from the grasp of him that was stronger than he."

PSALM 109

(cix 1–31)

1 *For the director. A psalm of David.*

My God, be not deaf to my song of praise,
2 Because the mouth of the wicked
and the mouth of the deceitful
are opened wide against me.
They pursue me with a lying tongue,
3 and with words of hate surround me.
They attack me without reason:
4 in return for my love
they slander me, even me.
5 My prayer they set down to my debit,
evil in return for my good,
and hatred for my love.
6 Appoint the Evil One against him,
and let Satan stand at his right hand.
7 When he is judged, let him come forth guilty,
may his prayer become a sin.
8 May his days be few,
let another assume his office.
9 May his children become fatherless,
and his wife a widow.
10 Let his children ever roam and beg,
may their houses be investigated by the appraiser.
11 May the creditor seize everything he has,
and strangers plunder his earnings.
12 Let there be no one extending him kindness,
no one pitying his fatherless children.
13 May his future life be cut off,
from the age to come his name erased.
14 May his father's iniquity be recorded
by El Yahweh
And his mother's sin not be erased.

15 May they be continually before Yahweh,
while he cuts off his memory from the earth,
16 Because he does not remember to show kindness,
but hounds the poor and needy man,
and the broken-hearted he seeks even to slay.
17 Since he has loved cursing,
it has come to him,
Has taken no delight in blessing,
it has gone far from him.
18 He clothed himself with cursing as his cloak,
and it entered his entrails like water,
like oil into his bones.
19 So let him have it as a garment which enfolds him,
and as a sash, daily let him gird it on.
20 Ignominy as the recompense of my slanderers
increase a hundredfold, Yahweh,
Of those speaking evil about me.
21 So come, Yahweh, my Lord,
work a miracle for me,
For the sake of your Name, truly good.
By your kindness rescue me,
22 for I am poor and needy,
and my heart has been pierced within me.
23 Like a shadow indeed have I tapered,
and am passing away;
I have lost my youth, truly I have aged.
24 My knees wobble from fasting,
and my well-fed body has grown gaunt.
25 Those who meet me—
I have become a taunt to them,
they see me, shake their heads.
26 Help me, Yahweh my God,
save me as befits your kindness,
27 That they may know that this hand of yours
nay, that you, Yahweh, have worked it.
28 So let them curse,
as long as you bless;
Let them rise up, only to be humiliated,
while your servant rejoices.
29 May my slanderers wear their disgrace,
may they put on their humiliation as a garment.

30 I will thank Yahweh the Grand with my mouth,
amid the aged will I praise him,
31 Because he will stand at the right hand of the needy
to save his life from his judge.

Notes

cix. A perplexing Hebrew text makes it difficult to identify with certainty the dramatis personae and the sequence of action in this lament of an individual. From the proposed translation this succession can be traced: Verse 1 contains the usual invocation of the divine name. In vss. 2–5 the poet describes the activity of his ingrate enemies who accuse him of an unidentified capital crime (cf. vss. 16, 31) and bring him to trial. In vss. 6–19, the psalmist directs a series of dreadful imprecations against the venal judge (see vs. 31) who, instead of throwing out the indictment as preposterous, agrees to hear the case. It is apparently while awaiting trial by a court filled with perjurers and presided over by a knavish judge that the psalmist composed this charged lament. In vs. 20, the poet briefly curses his slanderers, and in vss. 21–27 he prays for deliverance and help. Interestingly, vs. 28 reflects the psychological effects of the psalmist's prayer, whereas vs. 29 is a reprise of the curse against the slanderers. The poem concludes (vss. 30–31) with the public confession of the help the psalmist is sure Yahweh will send.

The psalmist, an aged man (vss. 23, 30), was a very able poet. Good examples of chiasmus (vss. 2–3, 14, 16), double-duty modifiers (vss. 14, 20), congruency of metaphors (vss. 2–3, 13–14), inclusions (vss. 1 and 30, 7 and 31, 21 and 26, 22 and 30, 26 and 31), careful syllable counting (e.g., vss. 2–3, 19, 26, 28–29), and the balance between abstract and concrete nouns in vs. 2 witness to his high poetic gifts. What is more, the uniformly excellent poetic quality bespeaks unity of authorship and composition, obliging one to dismiss Briggs' (CECBP, II, p. 366) description of vss. 6–15 as an inserted Maccabean psalm containing little real poetry. The psalm probably dates to the early pre-Exilic period.

The poet's use of composite divine names deserves comment, especially since two of them have been the victims of deletion at the hands of textual critics. Thus *'ēl yahweh* (vs. 14) and *yahweh 'ᵃdōnāy* (vs. 21) have, from time to time, been expunged. In vs. 26, *yahweh 'ᵉlōhāy* has escaped such a fate, though vs. 30, *yahweh mā'ēd,* probably to be read for *yahweh mᵉ'ōd,* has been misunderstood.

1. *My God.* Vocalizing *'ᵉlōhay* for MT *'ᵉlōhēy.*

be not deaf to my song of praise. The prayer *tᵉhillātī 'al teḥᵉraš* is syntactically, and in word order, identical with Ps xxxix 13, *dim'ātī* *'al teḥ^{e}raš,* "Be not deaf to my tears," as translated and parsed in *Psalms I,* ad loc.

my song of praise. t^{e}hillātī forms an inclusion with vs. 30, *'^{a}hal^{e}lennū,* "will I praise him." Though the burden of the psalm is a lament, the poet is so confident that his complaint will be heard (cf. vss. 30–31) that he proleptically calls it a "song of praise."

2. *the mouth.* The psalmist contrasts, by way of inclusion with vs. 30, the maligning mouth of the wicked with his own mouth singing God's praises. Though most versions read this line as a bicolon, I scan it as a tricolon with a 4:4:5 syllable count.

the wicked . . . the deceitful. The pairing of concrete *rāšā'* with abstract *mirmāh,* "deceit," illustrates the poetic practice examined in the first NOTE on Ps cvii 42. Hence the frequent repointing of concrete *rāšā'* to abstract *reša'* (see BH^{3} apparatus and BHS) is no longer necessary. Cf. Prov xiv 25, where concrete *'ēd '^{e}met,* "a truthful witness," is balanced by abstract *mirmāh,* "deceit," but which, thanks to the parallelism, denotes "the deceiver."

are opened wide. As of wild beasts in full pursuit of quarry. Cf. Lam iii 46–47, "All our foes open wide their mouths against us; a pack and a trap await us"; Ps xxii 14, "They open their mouths against me, like a ravening and raging lion." Perhaps the best-known biblical comparison of the tongue to an untamed beast was penned by James iii 7, "For every kind of animal and bird, reptile and sea creature, can be tamed and has been tamed by man, but no human being can tame the tongue." The qal active pointing of MT is preferably read as qal passive *pūtāḥū,* since the active form usually has a transitive meaning. See vs. 22 *ḥūlal* for MT *ḥalal,* further proof that the Masoretes were strangers to the qal passive conjugation as observed in the first NOTE on Ps xvii 10.

They pursue. For this meaning of *dibb^{e}rū,* first NOTE on Ps ii 5, NOTE on Ps xxxviii 13, and Rabbi Qimḥi, *Sefer Ha-shorashim,* s.v. *dbr,* col. 134 (courtesy of S. Speier). The psalmist resumes this imagery in vs. 16.

They pursue me . . . surround me. A masterfully constructed line characterized by chiasmus, syntactic, and syllabic balance. Thus the first-colon verb + direct object (*dibb^{e}rū 'ōtī*) diagonally matches second-colon verb + suffix (*s^{e}bābūnī*), while the accusative of means *l^{e}šōn šāqer,* "with a lying tongue," is counterbalanced by accusative of means *w^{e}dibrē śin'āh,* "and with words of hate." Each colon numbers nine syllables.

me. Repointing to *'ōtī,* the *nota accusativi* plus suffix, instead of MT *'ittī,* "with me," which, as most commentators admit, is not readily explicable.

3. *surround me.* Cf. Pss xxii 17, where *s^{e}bābūnī* describes the action of dogs encircling their victim, and xxxv 16, "My encircling mockers gnashed their teeth at me."

They attack me. Scanning vss. 3b–4 as a tricolon with a 7:6:7 syllable count.

4. *they slander me, even me.* Construing *yiśṭᵉnūnī wāʼānī* (MT *waʼᵃnī*) as the final colon of vs. 4, and transferring *tᵉpillāh,* "my prayer," to the next verse. Syntactically, *wāʼānī,* the *waw emphaticum* plus the independent pronoun, emphasizes the verbal suffix, a construction familiar from Ugar. *šmk at,* "your own name"; Pss lxxxiii 19, lxxxvi 2, and especially Gen xxvii 34, *bārᵃkēnī gam ʼānī,* "Bless me, also me!" The reason for the double emphasis in *wāʼānī* is apparent from the preceding and the following cola. Stylistically, emphatic *ʼānī,* harks back to vs. 2, *ʼōtī,* "me," which is also emphatic.

5. *My prayer.* Once *tᵉpillāh* has been transferred, vs. 5 scans into a tricolon with a 9:6:9 syllable count. Though suffixless, *tᵉpillāh* shares the suffix of *ʻālāy* (pausal for MT *ʻālay*), "to my debit."

they set down. Parsing the *waw* of *wayyāśīmū* as emphatic, and ascribing to *yāśīmū* the meaning discussed at Ps lvi 9, namely "to set down in writing." To those who thrive on cursing (vs. 17), prayer is considered a crime. But the poet hurls the curse back at his enemies in vs. 7, "may his prayer become a sin."

to my debit. This nuance of *ʻālāy,* placed in a clear light by economic texts from Ras Shamra (second NOTE on Ps xl 8), finds further confirmation in Gen xxx 28 and xxxiv 12, as orally pointed out to me by J. Swetnam.

my good. With *ṭōbāh* sharing the suffix of preceding *ʻālay,* "to my debit," and following *ʼahᵃbātī,* "my love." Note that in Prov viii 30, central *šaʻᵃšūʻīm,* "his delight," receives its determination from preceding *ʼeṣlō,* "beside him," and from following *lᵉpānāyw,* "in his presence," a sequence recognizable in UT, 51:IV:41–43, *tḥmk il ḥkm ḥkmt ʻm ʻlm ḥyt ḥẓt tḥmk,* "Your message, O El, is wise: your wisdom is eternal sagacity, felicitous life your message," in which centrally placed *ḥkmt,* "your wisdom," shares the suffix of preceding and following *tḥmk,* "your message."

6. *Appoint.* As his prosecutor during the trial to be held after death; see the next NOTE. Other Psalter texts speaking of a trial after death include i 5, xvii 15, lxv 3–4, lxxv 3, lxxvi 10–11.

the Evil One . . . Satan. The identification of *rāšāʻ* and *śāṭān* is a long-standing puzzler, but a measure of coherence can be won if vss. 6–7 are seen as referring to judgment after death and vss. 8–19 as invoking terrestrial misfortunes upon the unprincipled judge. In three biblical texts Satan appears as a superhuman celestial figure whose role is that of prosecutor. I Chron xxi 1 states, *wayyaʻᵃmōd śāṭān ʻal yiśrāʼēl,* "Satan took the stand against Israel," and in our text it is said *wᵉśāṭān yaʻᵃmōd ʻal yᵉmīnō,* "and let Satan stand at his right hand." In Zech iii 1–2, the celestial being who challenges the fitness of Joshua ben Jozadak to function as the high priest is called "the Satan," and is described as *ʻōmēd ʻal yᵉmīnō lᵉśiṭᵉnō,* "standing on his right to accuse him," language similar to the psalmist's. In the prose monologue to the Book of Job (i–ii), Satan is depicted as one of the *bᵉnē ʼēlīm,* a member of the divine entourage, who impugns the integrity of Job. These descriptions warrant, then, the interpretation of the Evil One and Satan as one personage who will serve as the prosecutor at the trial of the psalmist's adversary before the divine judge after death.

If this analysis proves correct, the widely held view that the designation of Satan as the Evil One is a development of the intertestamental period will need to be reexamined.

The evidence reviewed in the first NOTE on Ps xxxviii 21, for *śāṭan,* "to slander, traduce," supplies a good etymology for the disputed meaning of *śāṭān,* "Satan," who is termed "a liar and the father of lies" in John viii 44, while Victor Hugo writes "Satan a deux noms, il s'appelle Satan et il s'appelle Mensonge" (*Les Misérables,* Pléiade ed., p. 247).

against him. In vss. 2–5, the beleaguered psalmist describes the behavior of his (plural) enemies who falsely accuse him and have him brought to trial. In vss. 6–19, however, he curses the judge who thought the charges warranted a hearing. Thus no grammatical or exegetical difficulty presents itself, and it is difficult to appreciate Weiser's assertion (*The Psalms,* p. 691) that "The change from the plural in vv. 1–5 and 20 ff. to the singular in vv. 6–19 is satisfactorily accounted for only if vv. 6–19 are interpreted as a quotation of the imprecations directed against the psalmist." In other words, Weiser places vss. 6–19 between quotation marks. If his solution were correct, the burden of Jewish and Christian apologists, who must explain these horrendous imprecations within the framework of revelation, would be greatly lightened. Unfortunately, the burden remains.

stand at his right hand. Namely to accuse him, as may be inferred from the more explicit statement about Satan in Zech iii 1, "standing on his right to accuse him." In vs. 31, however, the psalmist hopes that Yahweh will stand at his right in order to save his life from the judge.

7. *When he is judged.* In the afterlife.

come forth guilty. An exemplification of the *lex talionis,* the OT theological principle of retaliation whereby a punishment should correspond in degree and kind to the offense of the wrongdoer. Just as the knavish judge intends to pronounce the psalmist guilty, so may he likewise be found culpable by the higher judge.

his prayer. His plea for clemency. Just as the poet's enemies considered his prayer a crime (vs. 5), so may the judge's plea be charged against him.

8. *his office.* The high position held by the accursed serves to explain the use of the plural of excellence *'ᵃbōtāyw,* "his father," in vs. 14.

9. *his children . . . his wife.* The parallel pair *bānāyw//'ištō,* now registered in UT, 2068:19, *'bdn watth wbnh,* "Abdanu and his wife and his children," brings to 290 the pairs of parallel words in Ugaritic and in Hebrew; see the third NOTE on Ps cii 20. The same parallelism recurs in Ps cxxviii 3.

fatherless . . . a widow. The first NOTE on Ps lxviii 6 cites the Ugaritic text with *ytm*, "the fatherless," parallel to *almnt*, "the widow."

his wife. Given the present 7:6 syllable count, the proposal to insert *t^{e}hī* after *'išto* is not compelling.

10. *his children . . . their houses.* The parallelism of *bānāyw* and *bōtēhem* echoes the juxtaposition of these words in UT, 2 Aqht:I:26–27, *wykn bnh bbt šrš bqrb hklh*, "And his son shall be in his house, his offspring inside his palace" (notice the two dual-purpose suffixes).

their houses be investigated by the appraiser. Sense can be wrested from the consonantal cluster *dršw mḥrbwtyhm* by reading qal passive *dūr^{e}šū*, followed by the accusative of agency *mōhēr* (see vs. 14), the participle of **māḥar*, the root of *m^{e}ḥīr*, "price, hire," attested in Ps xliv 13. The resultant parallelism between *mōḥēr* and vs. 11, *nōšeh*, "the creditor," is unfaultable. The final consonants *bwtyhm*, to be vocalized *bōtēhem*, reflect the newly published Ugaritic plural form *bwtm*, "houses," whose importance for the correct interpretation of Heb. *bottīm*, and not the unlikely *bāttīm*, has been stressed by Gordon, UT, Glossary, No. 463. In the present context, the appraisal would be either for forced sale, to satisfy a debt, or for purposes of assessing taxes that were likely to be confiscatory.

11. *seize.* On *y^{e}naqqēš*, see GB, p. 522a, and Pss ix 17, xxxviii 13; it seems to be a by-form of *yāqaš*, "to snare, seize with a snare."

everything. Since elsewhere the verb *y^{e}naqqēš* governs a direct object, a strong case can be made for analyzing *l^{e}kol* into the emphatic *lamedh* and the accusative object *kol*. Another instance of emphatic *lamedh* is noticed in vs. 16 and in *l^{e}kol* at Pss cxxxv 11, cxlv 16. Cf. also I Sam xxii 7, *l^{e}kull^{e}kem yāśīm śārē 'alāpīm w^{e}śārē mē'ōt*, "Every single one of you he will make commanders of thousands and commanders of hundreds" (courtesy of W. Kuhnigk); Eccles x 3, *l^{e}kol*, "every single one," as proposed by me in *Biblica* 33 (1952), 193; and II Chron vii 21, *l^{e}kol*, as analyzed by A. Kropat, *Die Syntax des Autors der Chronik* (Giessen, 1909), pp. 4–5.

his earnings. Like *'āmāl*, "trouble, toil," but also "wealth" (cf. the first NOTE on Ps cv 44), *pā'al*, "to work," and *pō'al*, "wages of work," *y^{e}gīa'* too makes the semantic transition from the root idea "to toil, grow weary" to "gain, earnings."

12. *extending him kindness.* The bearing of the construction *lō mōšek ḥāsed* on the translation of disputed Jer xxxi 3 received comment at Ps xxxvi 11. The expression *māšak yādō* in Hos vii 5 makes it very probable that UT, 128:I:2, *yd mṯkt* contains the same root; UT, Glossary, No. 1582, is surely being overcautious when forgoing all comment.

13. *his future life.* For this nuance of *'aḥarītō*, see second NOTES Pss xxxvii 37 and lxxiii 17. This sense also occurs in the Aramaic Inscription of Agbar, lines 9–10, *w'ḥrth t'bd*, "And may his future life perish"; cf. S. Gevirtz, VT 11 (1961), 147. The Aramaic sentiment

closely resembles the biblical curse. A recognition of this meaning brings forth meaning from Num xxiii 10b, *tāmōt napšī mōt yᵉšārī-m* (MT *yᵉšārīm*) *ūtᵉhī 'aḥᵃrītī kāmōhū*, "May his (Jacob's) soul die the death of the just man, and may his (Israel's) future life be like his." In his article "The Death of the Upright and the World to Come," *Journal of Jewish Studies* 16 (1965), 183–86, S. E. Loewenstamm cites the opinion of the medieval Jewish commentator Nahmanides who saw in *'aḥᵃrīt* a reference to life in the world to come. Loewenstamm rejects this interpretation because "the world to come" is an idea entirely foreign to the time of Balaam. His rejection, however, conveniently ignores Ugar. *uḫryt*, "future life," and the texts speaking of immortality.

from the age to come. Understanding *dōr 'aḥēr* as synonymous with first-colon *'aḥᵃrītō*, "his future life." In other words, this verse closely relates to Ps lxix 29, "Let them be erased from the scroll of life eternal, / and not enrolled among the just."

his name. In consonantal *šmm* we probably have the substantive *šēm* followed by the enclitic *mem* serving as a stylistic substitute for the suffix. In this case, *šēm* would share the singular suffix of its counterpart *'aḥᵃrītō;* this stylistic phenomenon is documented in the third NOTE on Ps x 17. Hummel, JBL 76 (1957), 100, proposes the analysis *šᵉmō* (with suffix) plus enclitic *mem*, which is possible but less elegant.

erased. The construction *māḥāh bᵉ*, "to erase from," occurs in the Phoenician Inscription of Azitawaddu, cited in the second NOTE on Ps lxix 29.

14. *his father's.* As proposed in *Biblica* 44 (1963), 70, 291, and *Orientalia* 34 (1965), 86, and adopted by HALAT, p. 2a, *'ᵃbōtāyw* parses as a plural of excellence, doubtless because "his father" refers to the father of a notable; see the NOTE on vs. 8. This is precisely the usage encountered in Isa xiv 21, *hākīnū lᵉbānāyw maṭbēᵃḥ ba'ᵃwōn 'ᵃbōtām*, "Prepare the slaughter for his sons because of the iniquity of their father," where plural of excellence *'ᵃbōtām* refers to the king of Babylon. In Phoenician, plural *'bt* describes King Azitawaddu in Karatepe I:12, *w'p b'bt p'ln kl mlk*, "And every king considered me even as a father." This plural of majesty helps explain the Cypriote Greek gloss *abát*, "schoolmaster," studied by Emilia Masson, *Recherches sur les plus anciens emprunts sémitiques en grec* (Paris, 1967), pp. 71–72.

be recorded. The consistency of the metaphor of the divine bookkeeper (*Psalms II*, Index of Subjects, s.v.) is better maintained when *yizzākēr*, usually translated "be remembered," is given the nuance examined at Ps lxxix 8, "Do not record to our debit, O Scribe, the iniquities of our forefathers."

by El Yahweh. Reading *'ēl* (MT *'el*) *yhwh*, whose syntactic function is that of accusative of agency with passive *yizzākēr*, "be recorded." Similar syntax is noted at vs. 10 and can be documented in Phoenician in CIS, I, 3783:5–7, *wkl 'dm 'š gnb tmtnt z nkst tnt pn b'l*, "And any man who would steal this gift, may your throat be cut by Tinnit, the Presence of Baal!" This scansion and grammatical analysis, it may be noted, oblige us to scout the deletion of *'l yhwh* suggested by Gunkel, who cites its omission in the Syriac version. As repeatedly observed, the ancient versions must be reassessed in the light of the new Northwest Semitic grammar and prosody.

Metrically, *'ēl yahweh* is suspended between two longer, chiastically arranged cola (8:3:8) and modifies both; see below on vs. 20 and the second NOTE on Ps cii 20. Similar chiastically patterned lines with suspended double-duty modifiers can be recognized in Jer iv 2, 30b (identified by Jack Lundbom), in Jon ii 6 (6:3:7), Pss cxix 149, 166, 174, cxxi 6, and in Ps xxii 26 which should now be read as an 8:4:8 line:

mī'ētikā tehillātī	8
beqāhāl rab	4
nedāray 'ašallēm nāgīd	8

One hundred times will I repeat to you my song of praise
in the great congregation
I will fulfill my vows, O Prince.

With the transfer of MT *yerē'āyw*, "those who fear him," to the next line, vs. 27 scans into 6:6:9.

his mother's. Singular *'immō* confirms the analysis of *'abōtāyw* as plural in form but singular in meaning.

not be erased. The negative wish *'al timmāḥ* continues the bookkeeping metaphor begun in the first word of the verse, *yizzākēr;* on congruency of metaphors as a text-critical and exegetical criterion, see fourth NOTES on Pss li 9 and xci 2, first NOTE on Ps xciv 9, and NOTE on Ps xcvii 11.

15. *they.* Namely, the iniquity of his father and the sin of his mother. This is a three-pronged curse, aimed at three generations: the targets are the crooked judge and his possessions, his children (vss. 9–10), and his parents. Compare the three periods of the curse in UT, 1 Aqht:161, *'nt brḥ p'lmh,* "now, primordially, and to eternity."

continually before Yahweh. That is, inscribed on a tablet or written on parchment that Yahweh should constantly read. Cf. Ps xc 8, "You have kept our iniquities before you, the sins of our youth in the light of your face," and its exposition in *Psalms II,* in the NOTES ad loc.

his memory. Reading *zikrō-m* (with enclitic *mem*) for MT *zikrām,* "their memory"; cf. Hummel in JBL 76 (1957), 100, and the third NOTE on vs. 13.

16. *but hounds . . . he seeks even to slay.* The second and third cola of this verse are chiastically arranged in the pattern verb + object // object + verb.

poor and needy . . . the broken-hearted. As correctly seen by Gunkel and others, these terms describe the psalmist; cf. vss. 22, 31.

he seeks even to slay. Usually emended with the Syriac to *lemāwet,* "to death," MT *lemōtēt* easily parses as the emphatic *lamedh* intensifying the polel verb *mōtēt,* which also figured in the discussion on the quadriliteral verb in Ps lxxxviii 17. Though polel in form because of its deriving from a *mediae waw* root, *mōtēt* carries the meaning inherent in the poʻel conjugation which properly expresses an aim or endeavor to perform an action, especially with hostile intent; cf. GK, § 55c. On postposition of verb with emphatic *lamedh,* see second NOTE on Ps xxv 14, and below on Ps cxix 128.

17. *Since he has loved cursing.* Considerable debate centers about the Masoretic vocalization of the conjunction *waw* as the *waw* consecutive with five verbs in vss. 17–18. *Juxta Hebraeos* and many modern expositors prefer to point all these *waws* as merely conjunctive and not consecutive, that is, as expressing wishes in the present context. The latter view gains plausibility from vs. 19 where the jussive verb *t*ᵉ*hī,* "May it be," implies that the foregoing verbs are also jussive. The Masoretic pointing may be retained throughout vss. 17–19; see below on vs. 19.

The metrical scansion has also been a source of difficulty, leading to considerable excision of what appear to be metrically objectionable words. Again, MT proves sound when read as a line of four cola (2+2//2+2), with a syllable count of 7:5//7:6.

it has come to him. As a welcome guest. Compare the similar use of a dative suffix in *watt*ᵉ*bōʼēhū* in Job xxii 21, *bāhem t*ᵉ*bōʼāt*ᵉ*kā ṭōbāh,* "Then will the Good One come to you," where *ṭōbāh* is the divine title discussed at Ps lxxxvi 17. For other instances of dative suffixes with *bōʼ,* "to come," see NOTE on xxxv 8, with bibliography.

18. *He clothed himself.* Cursing became his outer fabric. The expression *yilbaš q*ᵉ*lālāh* bears on the translation of UT, 75:II:47–48, *km lpš dm a[ḫh] km all dm aryh,* "Like clothing was the abuse of his brothers, like vesture the abuse of his kinsmen," where ambivalent *dm,* usually rendered "blood," makes better sense when derived from the attested Ugaritic verb *dmm,* "to abuse" (UT, Glossary, No. 675). See first NOTE on Ps cxix 22.

like water, like oil. Cursing also became his inner fiber. He drank curses like water, and imprecations healed and soothed his frame like oil. Cf. Job xxxiv 7, "What man is like Job? He gulps mockery like water." The nouns *mayim* and *šemen* are collocated in UT, ʻnt:IV:86–87, *tḥspn mh wtrḥṣ ṭl šmm wšmn arṣ,* "She drew her water that she might wash with the dew of heaven and the oil of earth."

19. *So let him have it.* Since in the psalmist's view the unprincipled judge is incorrigible, let him continue in his evil ways.

which enfolds him. MT reads *yaʻṭeh ūl*ᵉ*mēzaḥ* with the result that the syllable count of the two cola is 8:10. By reading (with no changes of the consonantal text) *yaʻṭēhū l*ᵉ*mēzaḥ,* we obtain a 9:9 syllable count. Cf. Ps lxxi 13, which expresses a similar curse.

the sash. Perhaps an insigne of the judicial office.

20. *Ignominy.* The evidence for this meaning of *zōʼt* is reviewed in NOTE on Ps vii 4.

increase a hundredfold, Yahweh. Often deleted as contributing little to the verse, consonantal *m't yhwh* becomes instinct with meaning when vocalized *mī'ētā yahweh* and *mī'ētā* parsed as precative. The denominative verb *mī'āh,* studied at Ps xxii 26, can also be identified in Ps lxvi 20 (contrast *Psalms II,* ad loc.), *wᵉḥasdō mī'ētī* (MT *mē'ittī*), "And his kindness will I retell a hundred times." What lends conviction to this derivation in Ps lxvi 20 is the emergent inclusion with vs. 13, *'ᵃšallēm lᵉkā nᵉdāray,* "I shall pay to you my vows." In Ps xxii 26 *mī'ētīkā* and *nᵉdāray 'ᵃšallēm* stand in parallelism. Metrically, five-syllable *mī'ētā yahweh* is suspended between two longer cola (see next NOTE), creating the pattern of the double-duty modifier (7:5:9) noticed in vs. 14.

evil. Job ii 11, *hārā'ah hazzō't,* "the evil, the ignominy," juxtaposes the two roots found in parallelism here.

21. *So come.* Repointing MT *'attāh,* "you," to *'ᵃtēh,* the imperative of *'ātāh,* "to come." The present Masoretic vocalization lends support to the note in the BH[3] critical apparatus recommending deletion of the entire first colon *wᵉ'attāh yahweh 'ᵃdōnāy,* "But you, Yahweh my Lord," but the proposed repointing and the scansion of the line as an 8:4:8 tricolon allow us to reject this deletion.

a miracle for me. Nothing less than a miracle will save the psalmist from condemnation at the hands of an unjust judge and skillful slanderers. For MT *'ittī,* "with me," I read *'ōtī* whose genitive suffix has a datival meaning (the first NOTE on Ps civ 27), and refer to a similar prayer in Ps lxxxvi 17, *'ᵃśēh 'immī 'ōt,* "Work a miracle for me." In vs. 2, it has been observed, MT mispointed *'ittī,* "with me," for the *nota accusativi 'ōtī.*

your Name, truly good. The identical phrase *šimᵉkā kī ṭōb* in Pss lii 11 and liv 8 greatly facilitates the stichometric division of the final words in vs. 21; see the next NOTE.

By your kindness rescue me. Attaching *ḥasdᵉkā haṣṣīlēnī* to vs. 22 to form a tricolon (7:9:8), and parsing *ḥasdᵉkā* as an accusative of means preceding the imperative, much as in Pss xxxii 10, li 14 etc.

22. *poor and needy.* Clarifies vs. 16 as to the person meant by the psalmist, namely himself.

has been pierced. Repointing MT qal active and transitive *ḥālal* to qal passive *ḥūlal,* a conjugation unknown to the Masoretes, as noted at vs. 2. Contrast the explanation set forth by M. Z. Kaddary, VT 13 (1963), 486–89, who translates, "My heart trembles within me."

23. *indeed have I tapered.* Reading *kī nāṭawtī* instead of MT *kinᵉṭōtō,* and joining the final *w* (*ō*) to the next word as part of the conjunction *w.* The reading *nāṭawtī* preserves the original third consonant *-w* (Arabic attests *nṭy* and *nṭw*), as in such verbs as *šālawtī,* "I am at ease," while the emphatic *kī* balances emphatic *kī* in the second colon. Cf. the phrase *ṣēl nāṭūy,* "a tapering shadow."

and am passing away. After the transfer of final *w* of *nṭwtw* to the next word, the verse scans into three cola with a 6:4:6 syllable count;

currently the line is read as a 10:6 bicolon. For the signification "to pass away" of *hālak,* see third NOTE on Ps lviii 9 and references given there, as well as the standard lexicons.

I have lost my youth. Explaining *nin'artī* as a denominative verb of *na'ar,* "boy, lad," and ascribing to the niphal form a privative sense; cf. possibly Ezek xix 5, *nwḥlh* (read *nāḥōlāh*), "She had lost her strength," and Ps xxxvii 25, "I have been young and now am grown old."

truly I have aged. The translation of the preceding words and the emerging parallelistic structure ease out traditional *kā'ārbeh,* "like a locust," which more sensibly reads *kī 'erbeh,* thus becoming the stylistic counterpart of first-colon *kī nāṭawtī,* "indeed have I tapered." Balancing *qtl* verb *nāṭawtī,* the *yqtl* form *'erbeh* carries the nuance born by cognate *rabbīm,* "the elders," in vs. 30. In Job xxxiii 12, this temporal nuance appears in LXX's rendition of *yirbeh* by *aiōnios estin,* "He is eternal."

24. *from fasting.* While awaiting trial the psalmist has been fasting.

well-fed. Since MT *miššāmen,* "without oil," is scarcely viable, the repointing to pual participle *m^{e}šummān* or a similar adjectival form modifying *b^{e}śārī,* "my body," seems indicated. Another possible grammatical analysis (the sense remains the same) is suggested by Isa xvii 4, *ūmišman b^{e}śārō yērāzeh,* "And the fat of his body will grow lean." Thus one might read *ūb^{e}śārī kāḥaš mišmān,* "and my fat body has grown gaunt," in which the verb *kāḥaš* interposes in a construct chain, a poetic construction recognized by Qimḥi in Hos viii 2, xiv 3, and by Blommerde in Job xvii 11, *Northwest Semitic Grammar and Job, ad locum.*

25. *Those who meet me.* Often deleted, consonantal *w'ny* (MT *wa'^{a}nī,* "and I") acquires a *raison d'être* when vocalized *w^{e}ōnay,* the qal participle of *'ānāh,* "to meet," discussed at Ps li 5. Grammatically, *w^e'ōnay* is an example of *casus pendens* that is resumed in *lāhem,* "for them"; cf. the first NOTE on Ps ciii 15, and for a similar sentiment, Ps xxxi 12, "I have become an object of scorn even to my neighbors."

to them. lāhem refers back to the *casus pendens 'ōnay,* "those who meet me." Having missed the *casus pendens* construction, RSV must find an antecedent to *lāhem.* Unable to locate one, RSV ends up with, "I am an object of scorn to my accusers," and we are left unenlightened as to how *lāhem,* "for them," comes to denote "my accusers."

26. *save me as befits your kindness. hōšī'ēnī k^{e}ḥasdekā,* with eight syllables, forms an inclusion with vs. 21, *ḥasd^{e}kā haṣṣīlēnī,* "By your kindness rescue me," while *hōšī'ēnī,* "save me," looks ahead as well to link up this verse with vs. 31, *l^{e}hōšī^a',* "to save."

as befits. Proposals to alter *k^{e}ḥasdekā* to *b^{e}rōb ḥasdekā* (LXX), "in your abounding kindness," or to *k^{e}ṭōb ḥasdekā,* "according to the goodness of Thy kindness" (Briggs), disturb the present 8:8 syllable count and must consequently be declined.

27. *this hand of yours.* The syntactic function of *yād^{e}kā zō't* awaits a satisfactory explanation, but it seems that the poet had intended to

make "this hand of yours" the subject of the second-colon verb. Instead, he broke the grammatical construction (anacolouthon) and made Yahweh the subject of the verb. D. N. Freedman suggests that the second-colon verb also serves in the first colon, where *yādekā* becomes instrumental "with your hand." Hence, "That they may know that with your hand [you did] this, / you, Yahweh, achieved it."

you, Yahweh, have worked it. To wit, the miracle requested in vs. 21, *ʿaśēh ʾōtī*, "work a miracle for me."

28. *So let them curse.* The psalmist appears no longer disturbed, since he feels confident of divine assistance after his prayer in vss. 26–27. This carefully constructed line scans into four cola (2+2//2+2), each of which numbers six syllables.

Let them rise up. As in Ps xxvii 12, where *qāmū* describes the action of false witnesses, precative perfect *qāmū*, which balances jussive *yeqalelū*, "So let them curse," relates procedure of witnesses in court.

29. *wear . . . their humiliation.* The rootplay evident in *yilbešu* and *boštām* (as in Ps cxxxii 18) is of a piece with the wordplays that wryly characterize many biblical and Canaanite laments; see second NOTE on Ps lx 5.

their disgrace. Suffixless *kelimmāh* shares the suffix of its opposite number *boštām*, "their humiliation." Had the poet furnished *kelimmāh* with a suffix (=*kelimmātām*), he would have added another syllable to the first colon, upsetting the present 9:9 syllable count; consult the second NOTE on vs. 19. Compare Isa lxi 7, *boštekem*, "your humiliation," balanced by suffixless *kelimmāh*, to be rendered "your disgrace."

30. *Yahweh the Grand.* An analysis of the verse's components discloses the chiastic A+B//B́+Á pattern that is found in Ps xxii 23, which expresses a similar idea. If *bepī*, "with my mouth" (B), and *betōk rabbīm*, "amid the aged" (B́), pair off, then *ʾōdeh yhwh m'd* (A) should answer to *ʾahallelennū*, "will I praise him." This means that *ʾōdeh yhwh m'd* should consist of a verb of praise plus its direct object. Hence vocalize *yahweh mā'ēd* (MT *me'ōd*), "Yahweh the Grand," and compare the Ugaritic adjective *mid*, "great, grand." This identification clears up the difficulty bedeviling Ps xxi 2, *yhwh beʿozzekā yiśmaḥ melek ūbīšūʿātekā mah yāgīl* (MT *yāgel*) *mā'ēd* (MT *me'ōd*), "O Yahweh, in your triumph the king rejoices, and in your victory how he exults, O Grand One!" (contrast *Psalms I*, ad loc.). See also Ps xcii 6, to be read as an 8:4:8 tricolon, Ps xlvi 2, and the revised translation of Ps xcvi 4, *kī gādōl yhwh ūmehūllāl mā'ēd* (MT *me'ōd*), "For great is Yahweh and worthy of praise the Grand." The emergent inclusion shaped by the two vocatives *yhwh* and *m'd* (similar inclusions recur in Pss lviii 7 and lxxvii 14) renders this analysis compelling. See below on Pss cxix 96, 138, 140, cxlii 7, cxlv 3, and cf. Job viii 7.

with . . . amid. The pairing of *be* with *betōk* can be seen in UT,

75:I:19–22, *wẓi baln tkn btk mlbr ilšiy* where the parallelism between *b* and *btk* is clearer than the meaning of most of the adjacent words.

my mouth. While his foes spew lies, the psalmist's mouth is full of thanks and praise. Thus *pī* can be said to create a contrasting inclusion with *pī* in vs. 2.

the aged. An indication (see vs. 23) that the psalmist belonged to the *mōšāb zeqēnīm,* "the session of elders," mentioned in Ps cvii 32. Though most versions render *rabbīm* by "the throng" or "the multitude," the Targum approached the correct meaning when translating *ḥakāmīm,* "the sages." The close nexus between these two roots appears in UT, 51:v:65–66, *rbt ilm lḥkmt šbt dqnk ltsrk,* "You are aged, O El, and truly wise; the grayness of your beard has truly instructed you," and in Job xxxii 9, *lō' rabbīm yeḥkāmū ūzeqēnīm yābīnū mišpāṭ,* "It is not the aged who are wise, nor the elders who understand what is right." Cf. also Job iv 3, xxvi 3; Gen xxv 23; Eccles x 6; and Dahood, UHP, p. 71; *Biblica* 48 (1967), 425. It thus develops that *betōk rabbīm,* "amid the aged," probably refers to an institution similar to Qumranic *bmwšb hrbym,* "in the session of the aged," repeatedly mentioned in the Manual of Discipline; cf. Col VII:13, *twk mwšb hrbym,* "amid the session of the aged."

31. *he will stand.* The poet is confident that Yahweh the Grand will come to his defense. The ancient versions divide sharply in their interpretation of the tense of *ya'amōd.* Thus the LXX, Vulg., and 11QPsa, which reads perfect *'md* for MT *ya'amōd,* all took it as past tense, while *Juxta Hebraeos* understood it as referring to the future. As noticed repeatedly elsewhere, the time expressed by *qtl* and *yqtl* forms must be deduced from context, and here the *yqtl* verb must refer to the future if the description of the poet's imminent danger in vss. 1–14, 16, and 21–26 has been correctly interpreted.

at the right hand. Just as he had prayed (vs. 6) that Satan would stand at the right hand of the unjust judge to accuse him, the psalmist hopes that Yahweh will stand at his right side to defend him.

the needy. Referring to the psalmist, *'ebyōn* creates an inclusion with vs. 22 where the poet likewise styles himself an *'ebyōn.*

to save his life. *lehōšia'* harks back to vs. 26, "save me!"

from his judge. In vss. 27–29, the psalmist spoke of his slanderers; here he refers to the judge before whom he has been called. Good sense can be wrested from much-canvassed *miššōpeṭē* if it is repointed to *miššōpeṭī,* whose suffix designates the third person. Stylistic considerations can account for the juxtaposition of two different third-person singular suffixes in *miššōpeṭī napšō.* Similar juxtaposition recurs in, say, Isa liii 10, *weyhwh ḥāpēṣ dakke'ō heḥillī* (MT *heḥelī*) *'emet śīmā* (MT *'im tāśīm*) *'āšām napšō,* "But Yahweh enjoyed smiting him, piercing him; truly was his life made a sin-offering," where consonantal *hḥly* parses as the hiphil infinitive construct of *ḥll,* "to pierce," followed by the third-person singular suffix *-y.* The correctness of this analysis receives confirmation from 1QIsa, *wyḥllw,* "and he pierced him," showing that the Qumran scribe understood that the suffix should be third-person singular. The reading *'ᵉmet śīmā* appeals to Heb. *'ᵉmet,* Phoen.-Ugar. *'mt,* "truly," while *śīmā* parses as the qal perfect passive (cf. Ar. *qīla,* "it was said") of *śīm,* "to place, make." Cf. Obad 4. For a full discussion of Isa liii 10, see M. Dahood, "The Phoenician Elements in Isa 52:13 – 53:12," in the *W. F. Albright Anniversary Volume* (Baltimore, 1971).

PSALM 110

(cx 1–7)

1 A *psalm of David.*

Yahweh's utterance to my lord:
"Sit enthroned at my right hand.
A seat have I made your foes,
a stool for your feet."
2 He has forged your victorious mace,
Yahweh of Zion has hammered it.
3 In the battle with your foes he was your Strong One,
your Valiant on the day of your conquest.
When the Holy One appeared he was your Comforter,
the dawn of life for you,
the dew of your youth.
4 Yahweh has sworn
and will not change his mind:
"You are a priest of the Eternal
according to his pact;
His legitimate king, my lord,
5 according to your right hand."
He smote kings in the day of his wrath,
6 he routed nations;
he heaped corpses high,
He smote heads across a vast terrain.
7 The Bestower of Succession set him on his throne,
the Most High Legitimate One lifted high his head.

NOTES

cx. A royal psalm, probably composed to celebrate a military victory. Its many verbal and conceptual resemblances to royal Ps ii suggest a tenth-century date of composition; cf. *Psalms I,* introductory NOTE. Though the Hebrew text teems with difficulties, and the consequent interpretation of some details remains uncertain, it should not be described as "unusually corrupt," an evaluation put upon it by *The Oxford Annotated Bible* the RSV, ed. by H. G. May and B. M. Metzger (Oxford, 1962). Jerome's *Juxta Hebraeos* witnesses to the same consonantal text as MT, so the modern textual critic must come to grips with this text; emendation of the consonants will no longer suffice.

The hypothesis that the psalmist employed no vowel letters improves the sense in vss. 2 (*rdh=rādāhū*), 6 (*yᵉdannēb* for MT *yādīn ba-*), 7 (*manḥīl* for MT *minnaḥal; yšth=yᵉšītēhū; r'š=rō'šō*), and the recognition of the third-person suffix *-y* in vss. 3–7 enables the critic to forgo textual alteration of these verses. A study of the psalm's vocabulary and style within the Northwest Semitic ambience brings to light new words in vss. 1 (*'ad,* "seat"), 2 (*šlḥ,* "to forge"), 3 (*'ammekā,* "your Strong One"), 7 (*derek,* "throne"), and figures of speech such as chiasmus and the balance of concrete with abstract nouns in vs. 3, and the multiple inclusions which bind the final vs. 7 to vs. 1. A curious feature is the frequency of names of parts of the body. The poet mentions "right hand" (vss. 1, 5), "feet" (vs. 1), "his wrath" (vs. 5, *'appō,* originally "his nostril"), "routed" (vs. 6, the proposed reading *yᵉdannēb* being derived from *dnb,* "tail"), "corpses" (vs. 6), and "head" (vss. 6–7).

The psalm divides into two stanzas, vss. 1–3 and 4–7. D. N. Freedman has strikingly observed that each stanza contains 74 syllables. Thus vs. 1 contains 24 syllables (7:4:7:6), vs. 2 is a 7:7 bicolon, and vs. 3 falls into a 10:8:8:10 pattern; a total over all of 74. Verse 4 is a 9:7:8 tricolon, while vss. 5–7 run 17:19:13 or 14 (if we read *rō'šō*), with a total of 50; the sum total of the second stanza is thus 74, just matching strophe I. From these figures based on MT flows the conclusion that the text is basically intact, at least so far as meter is concerned. The new readings and interpretations proposed below do not alter his syllable count; for example, in vss. 2–3, I read *rādāhū biqrab* (5 syllables) for MT *rᵉdāh bᵉqereb,* also 5 syllables, and in vs. 6 the proposed reading *yᵉdannēb gōyīm* contains the same number of syllables as MT *yādīn baggōyīm.*

1. *Yahweh's utterance.* Unlike the opening of the second oracle in vs. 4, with its 2+2 meter, this utterance begins with the 3+2 meter.

to my lord . . . at my right hand. The Hebrew words *la'dōnī* and *līmīnī* illustrate both alliteration and assonance.

my lord. Namely, the Israelite king who is addressed as *'ᵃdōnī* by the court prophet or poet. The Hebrew expression exemplifies *Hofstil* or polite address, equivalent to "you," and used by a subject when addressing a superior. Cf. I Sam xxii 12, xxv 25, xxvi 18; I Kings i 13, 17. This title recurs in vs. 5.

Sit enthroned. The first NOTE on Ps ii 4 cites biblical and Ugaritic evidence for the majestic sense of imperative *šēb;* cf. also Ps cii 13, and van Dijk, EPT, pp. 50–51, 66–69.

at my right hand. The place of honor next to the throne of the Supreme King. During the coronation ceremony the Israelite king was considered to be enthroned at the right of the invisible but nonetheless present Lord. Ehrlich's (*Die Psalmen,* p. 278) vigorous protest that from the Old Testament viewpoint it was wholly unthinkable, even in metaphor, to describe a mortal as seated on Yahweh's right, cannot be sustained as a result of literary discoveries revealing the source of much biblical imagery. Cf. UT, 51:v:108–10, *t'db ksu wyṯṯb lymn aliyn b'l,* "A chair is placed and he is seated at the right hand of Victor Baal."

A seat. Preceded by *šēb,* "Sit enthroned," and followed by *hadōm,* "stool," consonantal *'d* must denote something like "throne, seat," especially since MT adverbial *'ad,* "until," is grammatically difficult as recognized by many commentators. Ugar. *'d,* "seat, throne" (fourth NOTE on Ps lx 11 and first NOTES on Pss lxxxix 30, xciii 5, and xciv 15; C. H. W. Brekelmans in BO 23 [1966], 308, and L. Sabottka, *Biblica* 51 [1970], 225–29), supplies the missing vocable needed to balance *hadōm,* "stool." Syntactically, the result is excellent, because the verb *šīt,* "make," often governs two accusatives.

Archaeological discoveries of ancient Near Eastern art amply illustrate this literary picture. From the palace of Sennacherib (705–681 B.C.) in Nineveh comes a relief showing Sennacherib, king of Assyria, sitting upon his throne while the spoil from the city of Lachish near Jerusalem in Palestine passes before him. So runs the cuneiform inscription above him. On the visible side of the throne twelve captives are carved in three registers; two registers support the throne seat, while one supports the arm rest. From their pointed beards and clothing, the prisoners on whom Sennacherib sits can be identified as the Israelites taken captive during the siege of Lachish ca. 700 B.C. For a reproduction of this throne, see James B. Pritchard, *The Ancient Near East in Pictures Relating to the Old Testament* (Princeton, 1954), p. 129, No. 371, and D. J. Wiseman, *Illustrations from Biblical Archaeology* (London, 1958), Plate 57.

In the El Amarna Letters (ca. 1375 B.C.) one encounters affirmations like "Behold, I am a servant of the king my lord, and the stool of his feet" (141:39–40), and "I am the dust of your feet" (195:5–10). The motif employed by the psalmist was widespread and durable.

have I made. Like its counterpart in vs. 7, *yešītēhū,* with which it forms an inclusion, *'āšīt* is a *yqtl* form expressing past activity. This follows from Yahweh's command that the king sit at his right hand; there must be a throne to sit on—one fashioned of their mutual enemies.

your foes . . . your feet. Another instance (see the second NOTE above) of assonance is observable in *'ōyebekā* and *raglekā.*

a stool. Concerning *hadōm,* Ugar. *hdm,* NOTE on Ps xcix 5, and F. Gössmann, "Scabellum pedum tuorum," in *Divinitas* 11 (1967), 30–53. On Tutankhamen's footstool or hassock are representations of foreign captives, prostrate, with their hands behind their backs.

2. *He has forged.* The verb *yišlaḥ* is here ascribed to *šlḥ*, "to forge, hammer," as distinct from *šlḥ*, "to send," a distinction presented in the first NOTE on Ps xviii 15. In parallelism with the *qtl* verb *rādāhū*, "has hammered it," *yqtl* form *yišlaḥ* expresses past time. The motif of the divine forger of weapons is noted in *Psalms I*, in the first and second NOTES on Ps xviii 35.

By reading this line as a 3+3 bicolon, we uncover a stylistic feature quite common in the Book of Job, namely, the explicitation of the subject in the second colon. The psalmist merely states in the first colon "He has forged," and only in the second colon does he specify who "He" is. Consult the first NOTE on Ps cv 17, and below on Ps cxlvi 7.

your victorious mace. This nuance of *ʿōz* in the phrase *maṭṭēh ʿuzzᵉkā* is discussed in the first NOTES on Pss xxi 2 and xxix 11, and is found also in Ps lxviii 36. The association of "mace" and royal "seat" recalls the similar parallelism in the Phoenician tenth-century Inscription of Aḥiram, *tḥtsp ḥṭr mšpṭh thtpk ksʾ mlkh*, "May the scepter of your governance be stripped, your royal throne upset!"

Yahweh of Zion. Explaining *yhwh miṣṣīyōn* (cf. Pss cxxviii 5 and cxxxiv 3) as a construct chain of the type discussed at Ps viii 9, and at Ps lxxiv 12, *malkē miqqedem*, "the kings from the East," or reading *yhwh-m ṣīyōn* and analyzing it as a construct chain with interposed enclitic *mem*, like Ps lix 6, *ʾᵉlōhē-m ṣᵉbāʾōt*, "God of Hosts." See below on Ps cxxxv 21, where *yhwh miṣṣīyōn* balances *šōkēn yᵉrūšālāim*, "the Resident of Jerusalem."

An interesting occurrence of the expression *ʾlhy yršlm*, "the God of Jerusalem," was found in a Hebrew inscription in a burial cave near Lachish, dating to about 700 B.C. The text reads, *yhwh ʾlhy kl hʾrṣ hry yhd lw lʾlhy yršlm*, "Yahweh is the God of the whole earth; the mountains of Judah belong to him, to the God of Jerusalem." J. Naveh, "Old Hebrew Inscriptions in a Burial Cave," IEJ 13 (1963), 74–92, finds the appellation "the God of Jerusalem" somewhat surprising (p. 84), but titles like "Yahweh of Zion" and "the Resident of Jerusalem" create an ambience in which this appellation appears quite normal.

has hammered it. Repointing MT *rᵉdēh* to *rādāhū*, a lengthened reading which evens the syllable count of the two 3-beat cola at seven each. The standard lexicons recognize the verb *rādad*, "to beat, hammer," but it seems necessary to postulate a by-form *rādāh* to explain this verse and Isa xiv 6, *rōdeh bāʾap gōyīm mᵉraddēp* (MT *murdāp;* contrast *Biblica* 48 [1967], 432) *bᵉlī ḥāšāk*, "Hammering nations in his anger, pursuing without cessation." When attached to the second colon of vs. 2, the *qtl* form *rādāhū* becomes the counterpart of the *yqtl* verb *yišlaḥ*, "He has forged," and at the same time restores balance to the third and fourth cola of vs. 2 which also become 3-beat cola.

3. *In the battle.* Repointing MT *bᵉqereb*, "in the midst of," to *biqrab;* thus the emergent parallelism of *biqrab* and *bᵉyōm*, "on the day of,"

actually splits a composite phrase witnessed in Ps lxxviii 9 and Zech xiv 3, *b^{e}yōm q^{e}rāb*, "on the day of battle." The first two cola of vs. 3 exhibit a neat example of A+B//B́+Á chiasmus. The appearance of *q^{e}rāb*, "battle," in such ancient psalms as lxviii 31 and cx 3(2) raises doubts about the Aramaicity of *q^{e}rāb*, the Aramaic vocalization (if correct) notwithstanding; contrast Wagner, *Aramäismen*, p. 103.

your Strong One. Vocalizing pausal *'ammekā* (MT *'amm^{e}kā*), the last word of the first colon, whose assonance with *ḥēlekā* resembles that of *'ōy^{e}bekā*, "your foes," and *raglekā*, "your feet," in vs. 1. The divine appellative *'ammekā* derives from the root *'mm*, "to be strong," documented at Pss xviii 28, xlvii 2, and lxii 9.

your Valiant. Explaining *n^{e}dābōt*, which shares the suffix of synonymous *'ammekā*, "your Strong One," as an abstract noun assuming a concrete denotation by reason of its pairing with a concrete noun; consult first NOTE on Ps cvii 42. Or the plural form *n^{e}dābōt* may be simply a plural of majesty comparable to the divine epithets *t^{e}hillōt yiśrā'ēl*, "the Glory of Israel," in Ps xxii 4, or *z^{e}mīrōt yiśrā'ēl*, "the Sentinel of Israel," in II Sam xxiii 1. The present attribution of the root *ndb*, "to be noble, generous, valiant," to God sustains the proposed exegesis of *n^{e}dābāh* in Ps liv 8.

your conquest. For this nuance of *ḥēlekā*, see Ps lx 14.

When the Holy One appeared. The phrase *b^{e}hadrē qōdeš* is apparently a by-form of *b^{e}hadrat qōdeš*, discussed at Ps xxix 2 and by P. R. Ackroyd in JTS 17 (1966), 393–96. Like abstract *n^{e}dābōt*, "the Valiant," in the preceding colon, and Jewish Aramaic *qudšā*, also used of God, abstract *qōdeš* here designates Yahweh. On Ugar. *qdš*, an appellation of the goddess Asherah, see Albright, YGC, pp. 121–22.

It would seem that Yahweh appeared to the king the night before the crucial battle.

your Comforter. Adopting the suggestion of D. N. Freedman, who repoints MT *mēreḥem* to *m^{e}raḥem*, a divine title occurring in Ps cxvi 5. Its suffix would be forthcoming from *'amm^{e}kā*, "your Strong One."

the dawn of life. Disputed MT *mišḥar* yields a measure of sense when compared with Lam iv 8, *ḥāšak mšḥwr to'^{o}rām*, "The freshness of their beauty has dimmed," and when the present collocation of *mišḥar* and *yaldūtekā*, "your youth," is set alongside Eccles xi 10, *hayyaldūt w^{e}haššaḥ^{a}rūt*, "youth and the dawn of life" (RSV). It may be relevant to direct attention to Isa xl 28–31, verses which describe the freshness of the Eternal's (occurring in vs. 4) youth, which he bestows on those who invoke him.

4. *Yahweh has sworn.* Balancing vs. 1, *n^{e}'ūm yhwh*, the formula *nišba' yhwh* begins the second stanza.

Yahweh . . . the Eternal. Placing *yhwh* in the first colon and *'ōlām* in the third, the psalmist effects the poetic figure known as the breakup of divine composite names, so clearly illustrated by Ugaritic examples cited in *Psalms I*, p. xxxv, and UT, § 8.61. Cf. also Ps xxxi 2 (=lxxi 1), where the same composite divine name is separated into its components.

You are a priest. Here begins the second oracle pronounced by the court poet or prophet.

a priest. The new king, like all early Israelite kings, enjoyed the privileges of a priest; II Sam viii 18; I Kings iii 4. The frequency of the term *khn* in Ugaritic lists of religious classes confutes the last-century view of J. Wellhausen that Heb. *kōhēn* is derived from Ar. *kāhin*, "seer, diviner," an opinion uncritically accepted by many scholars and still found in some recent manuals of biblical theology.

of the Eternal. Parsing *leʿōlām* into the *lamedh* of property or ownership, noticed in vs. 3, and the divine appellation studied at Pss xxiv 6, 7 and lxxv 10. The most relevant text employing the *lamedh* of property occurs in Gen xiv 18, "Melchizedek king of Salem brought bread and wine; since he was *kōhēn leʾēl ʿelyōn*, a priest of El Elyon." In Gen xxi 33, however, El Elyon is called *ʾel ʿōlām*, "El the Eternal." The case does not rest here. The traditional rendering, "You are a priest for ever after the order of Melchizedek," creates problems of interpretation that have proved insoluble. As J. A. Fitzmyer has pointed out in CBQ 25 (1963), 317, nothing in Genesis indicates that Melchizedek will remain a priest forever. But to account for *leʿōlām* in Ps cx, Fitzmyer labels the phrase a midrashic element introduced into the psalm; our translation, however, eliminates the necessity of appealing to later interpretive insertions—always a risky procedure.

according to his pact. The present state of knowledge concerning this colon was summarized by Fitzmyer, CBQ 25 (1963), 308, with his remark "whatever the puzzling Hebrew phrase *ʿal dibrātī malkī-ṣedeq* means." A step toward clarity is taken when the ending of *dibrātī* is isolated as the third-person singular suffix *-y*, whose antecedent is the Eternal, and the substantive given the nuance of *dābār*, "pact," in Ps cv 8, 42; Deut ix 5, etc. Eccles viii 2–3 juxtaposes two roots that are also collocated in our verse: *pī melek šemōr ʿal* (MT *weʿal*) *dibrat šebūʿat ʾelōhīm ʾal tibbāhēl*, "Observe the command of the king according to the pact; with an oath to God be not hasty."

His legitimate king. Parsing *malkī ṣedeq* as a construct chain with the third-person singular suffix *-y* interposed; cf. the seventh NOTE on Ps cii 24. It is significant that cognate Ps ii 6 also employs this suffix in *malkī:* "But I have been anointed his king (*malkī*)." For the meaning of *ṣedeq*, "legitimate," see the first NOTE on Ps li 21; E. A. Speiser, *Genesis* (AB, vol. 1), the first NOTE on Gen xiv 18, and Robert Houston Smith in ZAW 77 (1965), 145, n. 36, who acutely asks if the name "Melchizedek" might not yield to analysis as something other than a proper name. Smith also cites a footnote of W. F. Albright in *Annual of the American Schools of Oriental Research* 6 (1924–25), 63, n. 172, in which Albright expresses the opinion that *malkī ṣedeq* could be interpreted as "Legitimate King."

By his covenant the Suzerain Yahweh has named his vassal, the Israelite King, the legitimate ruler of Israel.

my lord. Revocalizing MT *'ᵃdōnāy* as *'ᵃdōnī,* the term designating the human king in vs. 1. Structurally, *'ᵃdōnī* corresponds to *'attāh,* "you," so that the following parallel elements stand forth in a chiastic pattern: You // my lord; priest of the Eternal // His legitimate king; according to his pact // according to your right hand.

5. *according to your right hand.* As pointed out by D. N. Freedman, *'al yᵉmīnᵉkā,* commonly rendered "at your right hand," describes the gesture by which the king ratified the divine pact; cf. Isa lxii 8, *nišba' yhwh bīmīnō,* "Yahweh swore by his right hand," and Ps cxliv 11.

He smote kings. The subject of *māḥaṣ,* an ancient Canaanite verb, as observed by Patton, CPBP, and by H. Jefferson, JBL 73 (1954), 154, is Yahweh. The psalmist resumes the motif of the discomfiture of the Israelite king's enemies depicted in vss. 1c–4. The chiastic arrangement of these four cola might be noted, with *māḥaṣ* serving as the verb of the first and fourth cola. The syllable count of these cola is 9:5:5:8.

in the day of his wrath. A literal rendition of *bᵉyōm 'appō,* which might also be translated "when he raged," in order to show identity of phrase in vs. 3.

6. *he routed nations.* MT *yādīn baggōyīm,* "He judges among nations," being contextually difficult and the construction *yādīn bᵉ* elsewhere unexampled, I propose reading *yᵉdannēb gōyīm,* with *yᵉdannēb* the Canaanite (cf. Ugar. *ḏnb,* "tail") form of *yᵉzannēb.* Literally "to 'de-tail,' attack the rear," this verb occurs in the military contexts of Deut xxv 18 and Josh x 19 signifying "to rout, discomfit." The number of biblical roots in which etymological *ḏ* did not become *z* (cf. PNWSP, p. 31; *Biblica* 45 [1964], 403) continues to grow. Identified as dialectal for *yizkā'ū,* "to be pure," in Job xxii 9, *yidkā'ū,* for example, can now be isolated in Job iv 19, "How then can those who dwell in clay houses, whose foundations are in the dust be pure before their Maker (*yidkā'ū milpᵉnē 'ōśām*)?" On *dē'āh*=*zē'āh,* "sweat," in Isa liii 10, see HALAT, p. 220a.

This etymology accords with the Ugaritic-Hebrew penchant for coining verbs from names of members of the body (*Psalms II,* Index of Subjects, s.v.) and with the frequent mention of same in this brief poem. The verse scans as a 2+2+3 tricolon with a 5:5:8 syllable count.

he heaped . . . high. MT qal *mālē'* should perhaps be pointed as piel *millē',* a *qtl* verb matching *yqtl* from *yᵉdannēb,* a verbal sequence characteristic of Ugaritic poetry. For this meaning of *millē',* consult the standard lexicons and D. Winton Thomas in *Journal of Jewish Studies* 3 (1952), 47–52, and for a similar description, Ezek xxxii 5, "I will strew your flesh upon your mountains, *ūmillē'tī haggᵉ'iyyōt* (MT *haggē'āyōt,* "the valleys") *rāmūtekā,* and will heap your corpses upon your heights."

heads. The second NOTE on Ps lxviii 22 cites the Ugaritic and biblical use of *rō'š* with a collective meaning. See likewise UHP, p. 37, which observes that conversance with Ugaritic practice would have forestalled J. de Savignac's description (*Oudtestamentische Studiën* 9 [1952], 132) of *rō'š* as being strangely employed here.

7. *The Bestower of Succession.* To elicit a measure of sense from this baffling line, traditionally rendered, "He shall drink of the brook in the way; therefore shall he lift up the head" (KJ), the critic must prescind from the Masoretic vowels in the first colon while preserving the consonants. Proposed vocalization: *manḥīl badderek yᵉšītēhū* (MT *minnaḥal badderek yišteh*).

The divine appellative *manḥīl*, "The Bestower of Succession," creates an inclusion with Yahweh in vs. 1 who commands the king to be enthroned. Of course, a number of texts make Yahweh the subject of the verb *nāḥal* in the hiphil conjugation, so that the attribution of the hiphil participle *manḥīl* to God falls in with biblical usage.

set him. The repointing of MT *yišteh* to *yᵉšītēhū* (an original with purely consonantal *yšth* lends itself to such ambiguity; see vs. 2 *rādāhū* for MT *rᵉdēh*) uncovers the second inclusion with vs. 1, namely, with *'ašīt*, "will I set." In vs. 1 the poet employs court style when addressing his king in the third person; he reverts to the third-person address which contrasts with the direct second-person address of the two intervening oracles.

his throne. With *derek* sharing the suffix of *yᵉšītēhū*, "set him." As Aistleitner, WuS, No. 792, pp. 82–83, has rightly seen, Ugar. *drkt* signifies "throne" in UT, 127:37–38, *rd lmlk amlk ldrktk aṯbnn*, "Descend from your royal seat that I may reign, from your throne that I may sit thereon"; see also third NOTE on Ps i 1 for other nuances of this root, and Anton Jirku, *Kanaanäische Mythen und Epen aus Ras Schamra-Ugarit* (Gütersloh, 1962), p. 113, who renders *drktk* by *Herrschersitz*, "the ruler's seat."

This translation of *derek* uncovers the third inclusion with vs. 1, *'ad*, "a seat," and recalls the association of *'d*, "seat," and *drkt*, "authority," in UT, 127:22–24, *yṯb krt l'dh yṯb lksi mlk lnḫt lkḥṯ drkt*, "Kirta sits upon his seat, he sits upon his royal throne, upon the peaceful bench of his authority." Thus the reinterpretation of the three words of this colon splices three new bonds with vs. 1.

the Most High Legitimate One. The identification of the divine title *manḥīl* suggests that prosaic *'al kēn*, "therefore," conceals the homonym studied at Ps cxix 104. There, by reason of context, *kēn* is translated "Honest One," but here the context desiderates rather the Akkadian sense of *kēnu*, "legitimate."

lifted high. Namely, he made the king triumphant over his adversaries. The phrase *yārīm rō'šō* evokes Ps iii 4, *mērīm rō'šī* in a partially similar context: "But you, O Yahweh, are my Suzerain as long as I live, my Glorious One who lifts high my head."

his head. MT *rō'š* appears highly improbable because in its reading (*yārīm rō'š*) two accents fall on two successive syllables. Hence vocalize *rō'šō;* in *scriptio defectiva* both *rō'š*, "head," and *rō'šō*, "his head," would be written simply *r'š* as Phoenician specialists know only too well from the much-disputed Kilamuwa Inscription, lines 15–16, *my yšḥt hspr z yšḥt r'š b'l*, "Whosoever shall smash this inscription, may Baal smash his head." Defectively written *r'š* is almost certainly to be vocalized *rō'šō* precisely as in the psalm. The Syriac and two Hebrew manuscripts also read *rō'šō*.

In vs. 1, Yahweh promises to abase the king's enemies, making them the stool for the king's feet. Here, in sharp contrast to the prostrate foes, the Israelite king is pictured with head lifted high in triumph.

PSALM 111

(cxi 1–10)

1 Praise Yah!
I will thank Yahweh
with all my heart,
In the council of the upright and the assembly.
2 Great are the works of Yahweh,
to be pondered by all who enjoy them.
3 Splendor and majesty are his work,
and his generosity endures for ever.
4 A memorial he made by his wonders,
the Compassionate and Merciful Yahweh.
5 Nourishment he gave to those who fear him,
he remembered his covenant of old.
6 His power by his works
he manifested to his people,
By giving to them
the patrimony of nations.
7 The works of his hands
are truth and justice,
Trustworthy are all his precepts,
8 Supported by everlasting and by eternity,
made of truth and uprightness.
9 Ransom he sent to his people,
he imposed his covenant for ever;
Holy and awesome is his Name.
10 The beginning of wisdom
is the fear of Yahweh;
The understanding of the Good One
belongs to all those who acquire it.
May his praise endure for ever!

NOTES

cxi. A hymn of praise to Yahweh for his great works in nature and in history. Verses 2–9 are a compact version of the traditional recitals (cf. Pss lxxviii, cv, cvi, cxxxvi), with references to the Exodus, Sinai, and the Conquest of Canaan.

The psalmist has effectively employed the acrostic pattern, beginning every line with a successive letter of the Hebrew alphabet; see *Psalms I*, introductory NOTE to Ps ix. Such a pattern naturally requires some inversion of word order. The present translation tries to reproduce, as nearly as possible, the word order dictated by the acrostic scheme.

A stylistic trait which might be singled out is the use of the passive participle (vss. 2, 7, 8) followed by a preposition, a construction which has baffled many translators and has caused divergencies in translation.

Though contents and style do not permit the dating of this psalm with any precision, they are sufficiently similar to those of Ps cxii to justify the conclusion that both psalms proceed from the same stylus or pen.

1. *with all my heart.* Usually read as a one-colon line with three beats, this line scans better as a 2+2 bicolon with four syllables in each colon; cf. vss. 6, 7, 10. This scansion naturally rules out Ehrlich's (*Die Psalmen*, p. 281) emendation of *lēbāb*, "my heart," to monosyllabic *lēb*. Being the name of a part of the body, *lēbāb* needs no suffix; consult *Psalms II*, Index of Subjects, s.v., and compare UT, 1 Aqht:34, *tbky pġt bm lb*, "Pughat wept from her heart."

2. *the works of Yahweh.* Sometimes interpreted as God's acts on behalf of his people, the phrase *ma'ᵃśē yhwh* might also refer to the works of creation and providence. The mention of "majesty and splendor" in the next verse echoes Ps civ 1, a hymn celebrating Yahweh the Creator.

to be pondered. dᵉrūšīm is the first of four passive participles employed by this psalmist. The works of nature are to be contemplated and respected; cf. Ps xvii 4, "My mouth has not transgressed against the works of your hands."

by all. Some versions and commentators (e.g., LXX, Gunkel) experienced difficulty with the prepositional phrase *lᵉkol*, but following a passive participle, *lᵉ* naturally parses (also in vs. 8) as the *lamedh* of agency. See BDB, p. 514a, and compare Isa lvi 7c, *kī bētī bēt tᵉpillāh yiqqārē' lᵉkol hā'ammīm*, "Because my house will be called by all peoples [RSV, 'for all peoples'] a house of prayer," and Isa liii 8, *mippešaʿ 'ammī nagūᵃʿ* (MT *negaʿ*) *lāmō*, "Because of the rebellion of his people he was struck by him."

who enjoy them. Repointing MT *ḥepṣēhem*, "their delights," to adjectival *ḥ^a^pēṣēhem.* From the Masoretic vocalization it is evident that the Masoretes did not construe *l^e^* of *l^e^kol* as the *lamedh* introducing the agent. Other texts with *ḥāpēṣ* followed by the accusative include Ps lxviii 31; Isa lviii 2; Eccles viii 3. It is also possible that MT *ḥepṣēhem* is merely a contraction of *ḥ^a^pēṣēhem,* rather than a different word.

3. *Splendor and majesty.* He who contemplates nature sees the splendor and glory of God manifested in his works.

his generosity. The catalogue of divine benefactions in the following verses suggests that this is the meaning of *ṣidqātō* (NOTE on Ps xxiv 5 and NOTES on Ps xxxvi 7, 11) rather than "his righteousness" (RSV).

4. *A memorial.* The psalmist probably has in mind the Feast of the Passover as the occasion when the tradition of the deliverance from Egypt, to which the following verses allude, was especially commemorated.

by his wonders. Interpreting the *lamedh* of *l^e^nipl^e^'ōtāyw* as expressing means, i.e., "by means of his wonders." Contrast RSV, "He has caused his wonderful works to be remembered," which is difficult to justify grammatically. By his miracles on behalf of his people in Egypt, God created the feast when these miracles were recalled and rehearsed. Note the use of *nipl^e^'ōtay,* "my wonders," in Exod iii 20.

the Compassionate and Merciful Yahweh. Usually construed as an independent nominal sentence—"the Lord is gracious and merciful" (RSV)—*ḥannūn w^e^raḥūm yhwh* may also be taken as the subject of the first-colon verb *'āśāh,* precisely as in Ps cxii 4. Which is to say that the verse is read as an example of enjambment (as in vs. 6a) with the explicitation of the subject (see the first NOTE on Ps cv 17) in the second colon.

5. *Nourishment.* The need for a word beginning with the letter *ṭeth* helps explain the choice of *ṭerep,* "prey," but also "food, nourishment" in Mal iii 10; Prov xxxi 15.

he gave. The perfect form *nātan* refers to a past event (not "he gives" with RSV), which some scholars correctly identify with the miraculous feeding of the Israelites in the wilderness as handed down in the tradition of salvation history.

he remembered. With the *yqtl* verb *yizkōr//nātan* expressing past history.

his covenant. The covenant which God made with the patriarchs, which forms the theological foundation of the Exodus event.

of old. Literally "from eternity," when *l^e^* in *l^e^'ōlām* is understood as "from"; see second NOTE on Ps xxix 10. Thus in the clause *yizkōr l^e^'ōlām b^e^rītō, l^e^'ōlām* modifies *b^e^rītō,* "his covenant," much like Ps cvi 45, *wayyizkōr lāhem b^e^rītō,* "He remembered his covenant with them," wherein *lāhem* modifies *b^e^rītō,* "his covenant," rather than *wayyizkōr,* "He remembered."

6. *His power.* Suffixless *kō^a^ḥ* shares the third-person suffix of *ma'^a^śāyw,* "his works," and *'ammō,* "his people."

by his works. The hapax legomenon phrase *kō^a^ḥ ma'^a^śāyw* has hitherto (at least when it has not been emended, as, e.g., by Briggs) been construed as a construct chain, "the power of his works," but equally viable syntactically is the analysis of *kōaḥ* as the direct object of *higgīd*, "he manifested," with *ma'aśāyw* the accusative of means. Cf. vs. 4 for a similar idea. These divine works include the events of the early period of the nation's history, especially the Conquest of Canaan.

By giving. Parsing *lātēt* as a circumstantial infinitive modifying the main verb *higgīd*, "he manifested." Gunkel, in *Einleitung in die Psalmen* (Göttingen, 1933), p. 53, sees a sign of lateness in this usage, but the presence of the same construction in the eighth-century Phoenician Inscription of Karatepe makes serious inroads into his conclusion. Cf. III:2–6, *wbrk b'l krntryš 'yt 'ztwd ḥym wšlm w'z 'dr 'l kl mlk ltty b'l krntryš wkl 'ln qrt l'ztwd 'rk ymm wrb šnt*, "May Baal-KRNTRYŠ bless Azitawadda with life, prosperity, and mighty power over every king, by Baal-KRNTRYŠ and all the gods of the city giving to him, namely Azitawadda, length of days, numerous years." Phoen. *ltty*, like biblical *lātēt*, is a circumstantial infinitive.

7. *his precepts.* The laws of the Pentateuchal Codes.

8. *Supported.* A literal rendition of the qal passive participle *semūkīm*.

by everlasting and by eternity. Parsing the two *lamedhs* of *lā'ad* and *le'ōlām* as expressing agency (see vs. 2), and identifying *'ad* and *'ōlām* with two demythologized figures.

of truth. The grammatical function of the preposition *be* in *be'emet* is to express the material out of which something is made. Compare Exod xxxviii 8; Ezek vii 20; I Kings xv 22, and the related usage in UT, 1122:2, *ṣpyt bḫrṣ*, "plated with gold." The recognition of this usage requires a modification of the traditional version of Job iv 19, *'ašer be'āpār yesōdām*, "whose foundation is in the dust" (RSV). Better: "whose foundation is of dust."

and uprightness. MT reads *weyāšār*, literally "and the upright man," but in tandem with abstract *'emet*, "truth," concrete *yāšār* takes on an abstract meaning. Numerous instances of the poetic transition from abstract to concrete have been noticed throughout the Psalter; this is one of the few instances where the semantic movement is in the opposite direction. Not a few commentators seek to avoid the problem by repointing *yāšār* to abstract *yōšer*, "uprightness," but Judg ix 16, *be'emet ūbetāmīm*, where LXX renders the adjective *tāmīm* as an abstract noun, "with truth and uprightness," counsels the would-be repointer to stay his hand here.

The four poetically personified attributes "everlasting, eternity, truth, uprightness" find their closest counterpart in Ps lxxxix 15, "Justice and right are the foundation of your throne, / love and truth stand before you."

9. *Ransom . . . covenant.* In this verse the psalmist sums up the thoughts of the hymn, alluding once more to the Exodus from Egypt (vs. 4) and to the covenant at Sinai.

Holy and awesome is his Name. The psalmist speaks in one and the same verse of God's generosity in ransoming his people and of the terrifying nature of his Name, much as the poet addresses El the Forgiver who dealt severely with his people in Ps xcix 8 (third NOTE ad loc.).

10. *The beginning of wisdom . . . who acquire it.* The chiastic arrangement of the first four cola in the verse should be noticed.

The understanding of the Good One. Traditionally translated "a good understanding," *śēkel ṭōb* may also be analyzed as a construct chain, whose genitive *ṭōb* would be the divine appellation discussed in the second NOTE on Ps civ 28. A similar construct chain can be identified in Prov xiii 15, *śēkel ṭōb yittēn ḥēn wᵉderek bōgᵉdīm 'yt nēkel* (MT *'eytān kol*), "The understanding of a good man breeds charm / But the conduct of the faithless, craftiness." For details, see *Biblica* 49 (1968), 363–64.

Of course, the construct chain *śēkel ṭōb,* "The understanding of the Good One," in which *ṭōb* is an objective genitive, makes an excellent chiastic parallel to the construct chain *yir'at yhwh,* "the fear of Yahweh," where *yhwh* is also an objective genitive. From this analysis likewise emerges the composite divine name *yhwh ṭōb,* "Yahweh the Good One," whose components are separated and placed in successive cola. In a hymn praising Yahweh's generosity (vs. 3) and mercy (vs. 4), such a title brings the poem to a fitting conclusion.

who acquire it. Namely, wisdom. Critics have been hard pressed to locate the antecedents of the putative masculine suffix in MT *'ōśēhem.* The opinion that one must seek its antecedents in vs. 7, "his precepts," has not been widely endorsed. The proposal to make feminine *ḥokmāh,* "wisdom," and *yir'at,* "fear," the antecedents of masculine *-hem,* though not grammatically objectionable since there are some clear instances of suffixal gender discord (GK, § 135), creates an exegetical problem and slights the chiastic pattern which apparently connects *ḥokmāh,* "wisdom," with the suffix of consonantal *'śyhm.* Hence vocalize the latter *'ōśēhā-m,* with *mem* enclitic attached to the feminine singular suffix *-hā,* a Ugaritic-Hebrew phenomenon documented at Ps lxviii 24. LXX, *Juxta Hebraeos,* and Syr. all read a feminine singular suffix *'ōśehā.* The nuance "acquire" of *'āśāh* is documented in BDB, p. 795a, and in the fourth NOTE on Ps civ 13.

From the didactic or Wisdom ending of the hymn Gunkel (*Die Psalmen,* p. 488) concludes a late date of composition, but this inference may no longer be valid because of the healthy tendency in recent years to push back the beginnings of the Wisdom tradition in Israel to the early centuries of Israel's settlement in Canaan.

May his praise endure. Forming an inclusion with the summons in vs. 1, *halᵉlū yāh,* "Praise Yah!", *tᵉhillātō 'ōmedet* is more logically interpreted as a prayer rather than as the assertion "His praise endures for ever!" (RSV). In other words, *'ōmedet* parses as a precative participle, exactly like Ps cxv 15, *bᵉrūkīm 'attem layhwh,* "May you be blessed by Yahweh." See also Ps cxix 21.

PSALM 112

(cxii 1–10)

1 Praise Yah!
How happy the man
who fears Yahweh,
Who greatly delights in his commands.
2 Numerous in the land
shall be his seed;
The abode of the upright shall be blessed.
3 Wealth and riches are in his house,
and his generosity endures for ever.
4 In the Darkness will dawn
the Sun for the upright,
The Merciful and Compassionate and Just One!
5 The good man is generous, open-handed in lending,
he conducts his affairs with justice.
6 For never shall he stumble;
in eternal memory
shall be the just man.
7 Of an evil report
he has no fear;
Firm his heart,
he trusts in Yahweh.
8 Steadfast his heart,
he fears not;
Perpetually happy,
he rejoices over his adversaries.
9 He gives lavishly to the needy,
his generosity endures for ever,
his head will be raised in glory.
10 The wicked looks with envy and is vexed,
gnashes his teeth and pines away;
The lodging of the wicked shall perish.

Notes

cxii. A Wisdom psalm so closely related in its alphabetical or acrostic structure and diction to the preceding psalm that modern scholars find themselves in rare agreement when crediting both poems to the same psalmist. Here, however, the poet ascribes to the just man some of the attributes he assigned to Yahweh in Ps cxi. What was a hymn now becomes a Wisdom psalm, similar in content to Ps i, affirming in Wisdom style the contrasting destinies of the godly and the wicked. Ps cxii is, though, more concerned with the rewards of virtue (vss. 1–9), which include a blessed afterlife (vs. 4) as in Ps i 5 (second NOTE ad loc.), than with the punishment of ungodliness (vs. 10).

2. *Numerous.* This nuance of the root *gbr* is considered at Ps lxv 4; see also the remarks of Speiser, *Genesis,* ad loc., on synonymous *'āṣūm,* "powerful," but in Gen xviii 18, "populous."

in the land. Proposals to delete *bā'āreṣ* founder upon the observation that vss. 2–3 are a neat example of syllabic chiasmus; the 5:4//7 syllable count of vs. 2 balances the 7//9 count of vs. 3. Consult the second NOTE on Ps. civ 28.

The abode of the upright. dōr yešārīm forms an inclusion of contrast with vs. 10, *ta'awat rešā'īm,* "the lodging of the wicked." Traditionally rendered "generation," *dōr* bears rather the Canaanite sense of "family, assembly," examined at Ps xiv 5. In the Ugaritic place name *dr khnm,* "Abode of Priests," *dr* possesses a meaning similar to Ar. *dayr,* "monastery."

4. *In the Darkness.* This name of the nether world is documented at Ps xxxv 6; cf. further Ps cxxxix 11–12. At death the upright will pass to the infernal regions, but they will not remain in the Darkness because Yahweh, the Sun of Justice, will come to deliver them. In addition to prosperity and numerous progeny in this life, the virtuous will enjoy happiness with Yahweh in the life to come. This sentiment accords with the thought of Ps i 3, another text affirming immortality for those who observe the Torah. Failure to recognize that *ḥōšek,* "Darkness," refers to the next life helps to explain the commentary of Briggs (CECBP, II, p. 386) on this phrase: "The gloss 'in darkness' was introduced through a similar mistake, at the expense of the measure; for the context would make it altogether inappropriate to the man who is the theme of the Psalm."

will dawn. Compare the prayer from the Requiem Mass, *et lux perpetua luceat eis,* "And may perpetual light shine upon them."

the Sun . . . Just One. A probable allusion to the motif attested in Mal iii 20 (iv 2 RSV), and Isa li 6 *weṣidqātī lō' tēḥāt,* "But my justice shall not set." That *'ōr,* literally "light," may specifically denote the light par excellence has been noted as Pss xxxvii 6 and civ 2, but attention must be directed to Ps cxxxix 11 and Job xxiv 13, where *'ōr*, "Sun," designates Yahweh. In the Joban text, Ibn Ezra and others likewise understood light to refer to God as the light of the world.

The Merciful and Compassionate and Just One. These divine appellations (see Ps cxi 4) stand grammatically in apposition with *'ōr*, "the Sun."

and Just One. The annotations to Pss xi 3, xxxi 19, lxxv 11 comment on the divine title *ṣaddīq*. Some critics would delete, with the Syriac, the conjunction *wᵉ* of *wᵉṣaddīq* and make "the just one" refer to the godly man praised by the psalm, but this deletion entails the deletion of either *ḥōsek*, "Darkness," or *'ōr*, "Sun," in the first half of the verse.

5. *The good man is generous.* Critics widely recognize that MT *ṭōb 'īš* can scarcely be parsed in the present context, and rightly label as ungrammatical the translation "a good man" found in KJ and other versions. If, however, one repoints *'īš* to *'āš*, the participle or third-person singular of *'wš*, "to donate," discussed at Ps cv 32, the colon becomes grammatically unexceptionable. Thus the three words predicated of the good man—*'āš ḥōnēn ūmalweh*, "is generous, merciful, and obliging"—correspond to the three adjectives predicated of Yahweh in vs. 4b, namely, *ḥannūn wᵉraḥūm wᵉṣaddīq*, "The Merciful and Compassionate and Just One." From this analysis also emerges the chiastic arrangement of vss. 4–5. It might further be noted that in Ps xxxvii 21, *lōweh* and *ḥōnēn* are radically identical with *ḥōnēn* and *malweh*, "merciful and obliging," while *nōtēn*, "who gives," in Ps xxxvii 21 is synonymous with *'āš* "is generous." Cf. the synonymy of these two words in Ps cv 32, and the Masoretic confusion between *'īš*, "man," and *'ōšō*, "his gift," in Job xii 10, as proposed in *Biblica* 47 (1966), 107–8.

6. *he stumble.* With its translation of the first colon, "For the righteous will never be moved," the RSV obliterates the literary figure which has been termed at Ps cv 3, 6, 17 the explicitation of the subject in the second colon. The Hebrew poet places last the subject of the line, *ṣaddīq*, "the just man," but RSV ill-advisedly brings it to the head of the sentence.

the just man. When placing *ṣaddīq*, "the just man," at the end of the verse, the psalmist employs the poetic figure of rendering explicit in the final colon what a prose writer would have made explicit in the first colon. See the discussion in the first NOTE on Ps cv 17. At the same time he realizes an inclusion between vs. 5 *ṭōb*, "the good man," and *ṣaddīq*, "the just man."

7. *Of an evil report.* Unlike the characters who in Ugaritic and biblical literature are pictured as breaking out into sweat at the sight of an oncoming messenger, a motif documented at Pss xlvi 7 and lx 4.

he trusts. MT *bāṭūᵃḥ* can be parsed either as the qal passive participle, or, with LXX, as the qal infinitive absolute with the Phoenician pronunciation (Heb. *ō* becomes *ū* in Phoenician), a phenomenon examined in the second NOTE on Ps ciii 14. Compare Isa xxvi 3 where critics generally repoint *bāṭūaḥ* to *bāṭōaḥ* since an infinitive absolute is manifestly desired; an appeal to Phoenician pronunciation renders vocalic alteration unnecessary.

8. *Perpetually happy.* MT *'ad 'ašer* and the traditional interpretation of the second and third cola, "He will not be afraid, until he sees his desire on his adversaries" (RSV), is logically unsatisfactory. Hence the proposed reading *'ōd 'āšēr,* "Perpetually happy," with consonantal *'d* understood as defective spelling for *'ōd* (see Ps iii 4 and Job i 18), and *'āšēr* as an adjective found in the tribal name Asher and in Ps x 6, *ledōr wādōr 'āšēr,* "forever happy." See below on Ps cxix 48. Thus *'ōd 'āšēr,* "Perpetually happy," nicely balances *sāmūk libbō,* "Steadfast his heart."

he rejoices over. As noted at Ps cvi 5, *yir'eh be* is an idiom to be rendered according to the needs of context; cf. Ps lix 11, "God . . . will let me gloat over my defamers." The wordplay on *yīrā',* "he fears (not)," and *yir'eh,* is one of the commonest puns in biblical poetry; cf., for example, Pss lii 8, lxiv 5–6, cii 16–17, cxviii 6–7, cxix 74; Job xxxvii 24.

9. *He gives lavishly.* Literally "he scatters, he gives," Heb. *pizzar nātan* is an instance of hendiadys, with two verbs expressing one idea. Predicated of the good man here, *pizzar* and *nātan* describe the generosity of God in Ps cxlvii 16. Since in this poem the psalmist transfers to the godly man attributes he ascribed to Yahweh in the preceding psalm, the apparatus of BH³ would do well to exorcise the suspicion that *nātan* is a gloss, especially in view of Ps cxlvii 16, where these two verbs stand in parallelism.

his head. Literally "his horn."

10. *looks with envy.* The first NOTE on Ps xlix 17 cites the evidence for this nuance of *yir'eh,* which most versions render simply "sees."

The lodging. The current dissatisfaction (cf. BH³ apparatus) with *ta'awat,* "desire," is registered by the frequent emendation to *tiqwat,* "hope," but the apparent contrast between vs. 2, *dōr yešārīm,* "the abode of the upright," and *ta'awat rešā'īm* suggests a definition of *ta'awat* consonant with "abode." In VT 2 (1952), 113, the late Joseph Reider, on the basis of Ar. *'awā,* "to lodge, take shelter in," proposed to translate Gen xlix 26 *ta'awat gebā'ōt 'ōlām,* "the abode of the everlasting hills" instead of "the desire of the everlasting hills." He also sought to identify this root in Num xxiv 7, 10, correctly it would appear. With our phrase *ta'awat rešā'īm tō'bēd* might be compared Ps i 6, *wederek rešā'īm tō'bēd,* "While the assembly of the wicked shall perish."

PSALM 113

(cxiii 1–9)

1 Praise Yah!
Praise the works of Yahweh,
 praise the name of Yahweh.
2 May the name of Yahweh be blessed
 from now unto eternity;
3 From the rising of the sun to its setting,
 praised be the name of Yahweh.
4 High above all nations is Yahweh,
 above the heavens his glory.
5 Who is like Yahweh our God,
 the One who is enthroned on high,
6 The One who stoops to look
 from heaven to earth?
7 He lifts up the poor from the dust,
 from the dunghill he raises the needy
8 To seat him with princes,
 yes, with the princes of his people.
9 He founds a family for the sterile,
 a happy mother of children.
Praise Yah!

Notes

cxiii. A hymn celebrating the Lord as helper of the lowly. With this hymn began the Hallel or Hymn of Praise (Pss cxiii–cxviii), sometimes called "the Egyptian Hallel" to distinguish it from "the Great Hallel" (Pss cxx–cxxxvi) and from another "Hallel" in Pss cxlvi–cl. At the Passover, Pss cxiii–cxiv are sung before the meal, cxv–cxviii afterwards.

This poem is characterized by genitive case endings (vss. 5, 6, 7, 9), third-person suffix *-y* (vs. 8), and meaningful chiasmus (vss. 2–3, 9). It divides into three stanzas, namely, vss. 1–3, 4–6, and 7–9.

1. *the works of Yahweh.* In the phrase *halᵉlū ʿabdē yhwh,* which recurs in Ps cxxxv 1, *ʿabdē yhwh,* "the servants of Yahweh," does not readily parse (hence the ancient versions simply read *ʿᵃbādīm,* "the servants," in the absolute rather than construct form). Moreover, Ps cxxxiv 1, *kol ʿabdē yhwh,* "all the servants of Yahweh," does not lend itself to easy analysis. The meaning and grammar of all three texts becomes clear when MT *ʿabdē* is repointed *ʿᵃbādē,* "the works of," a noun instanced in Eccles ix 1, "The just and the wise and their works (*ʿᵃbādēhem*) are from the hand of God." See the discussion at Ps cxxxv 1.

2. *name of Yahweh* 3. *name of Yahweh.* The identification of the chiastic arrangement bears on the interpretation of the first colon in vs. 3; see the next NOTE.

3. *From the rising of the sun to its setting.* This phrase closely resembles Phoenician Karatepe, I:4–5, *lmmṣʾ šmš wʿd mbʾy,* literally, "from the going forth of the sun to its entering in." The dispute whether the biblical phrase should be understood temporally, "from morning to evening," or spatially, "from the east to the west" (Mal i 11), is apparently resolved by the stylistic observation that in the diagonally arranged cola of vss. 2–3, the temporal dimension finds expression in "from now to eternity," so that one would expect our phrase to designate geographical limits in the main.

the sun . . . the name. The wordplay on *šemeš,* "sun," and *šēm,* "name," evokes the pun in Eccles vii 1, *ṭōb šēm miššemen ṭōb,* "Better a good name than good oil," while the sequence *ʿōlām,* "eternity" (vs. 2), *šemeš,* and *šēm* shows a striking kinship to Karatepe, Lion:6–7, *lʿlm km šm šmš wyrḥ,* "to eternity like the name of the sun and the moon."

5. *the One who is enthroned on high.* The ending of *hammagbīhī,* an elative, not causative, hiphil participle, parses as genitive, since the participle depends on first-colon *ka,* "like," which governs the genitive case; see the next NOTE.

6. *the One who stoops.* Another genitive ending, to add an extra beat to the first colon, has been preserved by *hammašpīlī,* also an elative hiphil participle.

from heaven to earth. Ascribing to the preposition *ba* of *baššāmayim* its frequent meaning "from," so that the spatial phrase *baššāmayim ūbāʾāreṣ* might profitably be compared with the temporal expression in vs. 2, *mēʿattāh wᵉʿad ʿōlām,* "from now unto eternity." This translation of *baššāmayim* affects the long-standing dispute regarding the possible displacement of vs. 6b. Some scholars propose to rearrange the four cola of vss. 5–6 thus: 5a, 6b//5b, 6a: "Who is like Yahweh our God, in heaven and on earth//The One who is enthroned on high, the One who stoops to look?" It will be seen that our translation renders this dispute academic; the present Hebrew text has been correctly transmitted. Contrast C. J. Labuschagne, *The Incomparability of Yahweh in the Old Testament* (Leiden, 1966), p. 77, n. 1.

7. *He lifts.* Identifying the ending of *m^eqīmī* as genitival, as in vss. 5, 6, and 9.

8. *To seat him.* The well-established existence of the third-person suffix *-y* in Biblical Hebrew obliges the critic to forgo the widely accepted emendation of *l^ehōšībī* to *l^ehōšībō*. Thus the third-person suffix *-ī(y)* balances the suffix of *'ammō,* "his people," a stylistic variation noted at Ps cv 6.

his people. The Syriac reading *'ām* for MT *'ammō* gives a good insight into the limitations of this version regarding meter and accent. By reading *n^edībē 'ām,* the Syriac places the accent on two successive syllables, whereas this harsh sequence is avoided by MT *n^edībē 'ammō,* "the princes of his people."

9. *the sterile.* The importance of large families in ancient Israel encouraged the belief that a barren wife was cursed by God; cf. Gen xvi 4 f.; I Sam i 5 f., ii 5; Luke i 25.

PSALM 114

(cxiv 1–8)

1 After Israel went out of Egypt,
the house of Jacob from a barbaric people,
2 Judah became his sanctuary,
Israel his dominion.
3 When the sea saw him, it fled,
the Jordan turned back.
4 The mountains leaped like rams,
the hills like lambs of the flock.
5 What ailed you, O sea, that you fled?
O Jordan, that you turned back?
6 O mountains, that you leaped like rams?
O hills like lambs of the flock?
7 In the presence of the Lord writhe, O land,
in the presence of Jacob's God,
8 Who turned rock into a pool of water,
flint into a flowing spring.

NOTES

cxiv. The current descriptions of this psalm as "unusual in form" (*The Oxford Annotated Bible*) or "original and peculiar in character" (Gunkel, Weiser) derive, in large measure, from what appears a mistaken translation and interpretation of its contents. The prevailing exegesis isolates four symmetrically constructed strophes; the first (vss. 1–2) speaks of the Exodus and the Election of the peope of Israel at Mount Sinai, the second (vss. 3–4) describes the miracles attending the Exodus and the Crossing of the Jordan, the third (vss. 5–6) contains the psalmist's question regarding the cause of these miracles, and the final strophe (vss. 7–8) reports the psalmist's answer to his own question. The translation and interpretation proposed here offer a more orderly sequence of ideas and a greater unity of theme. Verse 2 states the central theme of the poem: Yahweh has chosen Palestine as his sacred kingdom and abode. The remaining verses embroider this main proposition.

The skillful use of double-duty prepositions (vss. 2, 8), the breakup of composite phrases (vss. 2, 8), ballast variants (vss. 1, 4, 6, 7), and the metrically balanced verses attest to the psalmist's poetic skill.

The designation in vs. 2 of all Palestine by political terms that were particularly significant in the period between the death of King Solomon in ca. 922 B.C. and the destruction of Israel by the Assyrians in 721 B.C. suggests a ninth–eighth century date of composition. The one purported sign of a late composition, *lō'ēz* in vs. 1, can no longer be cited, in view of the new explanation proffered in the critical NOTES below.

1. *After.* The logical nexus between vs. 1 and vs. 2 emerges more clearly when *b*^{e} of *b*^{e}*ṣē't,* customarily rendered "When (Israel) went out," is given the sense discussed at Ps cvi 7. It was *after* the Exodus from Egypt that Palestine became the abode of Yahweh.

barbaric. The MT hapax legomenon *lō'ēz* has usually been translated "of strange language" on the basis of Late Hebrew *lā'az,* "to speak a foreign tongue." It is sometimes cited as the only linguistic evidence for late composition of the poem. Exodus i–ii, which stress the cruelty of the Egyptians rather than their speaking a tongue unintelligible to the Israelites, suggest, however, a different analysis of the consonants *l'z.* These letters yield better sense if vocalized *l*^{e}*'āz,* the emphatic *lamedh* plus *'āz,* "strong, cruel, barbaric." Thus the AT renders Isa xxv 3, *'al kēn y*^{e}*kabb*^{e}*dūkā 'am 'āz,* "Therefore will barbarous peoples honor thee." Cf. also Lam iv 3, *bat 'ammī l*^{e}*'akzār,* "The daughter of my people is really cruel," where Nötscher, VT 3 (1953), 380, has identified *l*^{e} in *l*^{e}*'akzār* as the emphasizing particle.

2. *Judah . . . Israel.* Designating the entire land of Palestine. Exegetes who understand Judah as referring to the Southern Kingdom and Israel to the Northern Kingdom, political states that came into existence after the death of King Solomon (ca. 922 B.C.), must assume here a striking anachronism. According to those commentators (e.g., Kraus), the psalmist dates the divine election of tenth-century political states to the period of the Exodus in the mid-thirteenth century. Our proposed translation of vs. 1 and exegesis of vs. 2 create no such chronological problem.

his sanctuary . . . his dominion. The division of the verse is rhythmical, not logical. The whole of Palestine became Yahweh's sanctuary and dominion. In other terms, the parallel pair *qodšō* and *mamš*^{e}*lōtī* expresses one composite idea, "sanctuary of dominion," and the separation of the component elements in the parallel cola creates the poetic figure known as the breakup of composite phrases, a poetic device recurring in vs. 8. This usage thus forbids us to look for an essential difference between the terms which are here used, or to understand the term "sanctuary" as a reference to the temple, showing preference for Judah over Israel. Similar terminology and poetic structure can be seen in UT, 'nt:III:27–28, in these terms: *bqdš bǵr nḥlty bn'm bgb' tliyt,* "in my sanctuary on where the Canaanite god Baal describes his sacred abode, Mount Zaphon, the mountain of my patrimony; in the pleasance on the hill of my dominion."

his dominion. Often emended to singular *memšāltō*, "his dominion," MT *mamšelōtāyw* is capable of a morphological analysis which at the same time respects the consonantal text. The cluster *mmšlwtyw* can be vocalized *memšelōtī(y)*, the Phoenician form of the feminine singular (also in Ps cxxxvi 9), followed by the Phoenician pronominal suffix *-y*, which provides a stylistic variant to the suffix of its opposite number *qodšō*, "his sanctuary." The third NOTE on Ps cv 6 cites other instances of the *ō*//*ī* sequence. The final *w* of *mmšlwtyw* would then be attached to vs. 3 as the conjunction.

Some critics propose to insert the preposition *le* before *memšelōtī*, but the poetic use of dual-purpose prepositions permits it to share the preposition of *leqodšō*, especially since these parallel nouns form one composite concept. The present 9:7 syllable count tells against those who seek to correct the 9:7 syllable count in vss. 4 and 6.

3. *When the sea.* Having been transferred from the end of vs. 2, *we* of *wehayyām* introduces a statement of the concomitant conditions under which the action denoted by the principal verb takes place; BDB, p. 253b, lists other examples of this very frequent usage, e.g., Gen xxiv 62; I Kings xix 19.

the sea . . . the Jordan. Commentators agree that *hayyām* designates the Reed Sea, which parted to permit the passage of the Israelites at the time of the Exodus, and that the poet fused into a single event two different incidents occurring at different times. But the two parallel cola of vs. 1 refer to the Exodus from Egypt, and the two cola of vs. 2 also describe a single event, namely, the choice of Judah and Israel as Yahweh's sacred habitation. This indicates that the parallel cola of vs. 3 likewise allude to a single historical event, the entry into Canaan across the Jordan River. Hence *hayyām* should designate the Salt or Dead Sea, which is explicitly mentioned in the biblical account of the entry into Canaan in Josh iii 14–16, "So, when the people set out from their tents, to pass over the Jordan with the priests bearing the ark of the covenant before the people . . . the waters coming down from above stood and rose up in a heap far off, at Adam, the city that is beside Zarethan, and those flowing down toward the sea of the Arabah, the Salt Sea, were wholly cut off." In Isa xvi 8 and Jer xlviii 32, *yām* alone designates the Dead Sea.

saw him. MT *rā'āh* desiderates a direct object which is forthcoming when the *w* of the next word *wayyānōs* is taken as the singly written consonant that serves two words, an orthographic practice documented at Ps lx 11. Hence read *rā'āhū wayyānōs*, and interpret the suffix as referring either to Yahweh or to the ark of the covenant, which contained his presence. Cf. Job ix 11 where critics agree that MT *'er'eh weyaḥalōp* should be read *'er'ēhū yaḥalōp*, and Job xxxvii 24, *lākēn yerē'ūhū 'ᵃnāšīm lō' yir'ūhū* (MT *yir'eh*) *kol ḥokmē lēb,* "Therefore let men fear him, even though none of the wisest minds see him."

it fled. Parsing *wa* of *wayyānōs* as introducing the apodosis of the conditional sentence discussed in the first NOTE on this verse.

turned back. As in vs. 5, the *yqtl* verb *yissōb* describes a single event of the past.

4. *The mountains leaped.* Current exegesis sees here a poetical description of the earthquake which accompanied the giving of the Law at Sinai. The fact, however, that the only other predication of *rāqad,* "to leap" of mountains is predicated of Lebanon and Sirion in Ps xxix 6 leads one to think that the mountains and hills in our verse are located in Canaan or Palestine, not in the Sinai Peninsula. The mountains of pre-Israelite Palestine were the dwellings of Canaanite gods; well might they leap in fright at the approach of the awesome God of Israel.

like. Proposals to read *kᵉmō* for MT *kī,* in order to bring the present 9:7 syllable count into more perfect equilibrium, slight the 9:7 syllable count of vs. 2.

lambs of the flock. The phrase *bᵉnē ṣō'n* is a ballast variant of first-colon *'ēlīm,* "rams," in a line patterned A+B+C//B́+Ć. Compare UT, Krt:77–79, *šrd b'l bdbḥk bn dgn bmṣdk,* "Make Baal descend by your sacrifice, the son of Dagan by your victuals," where the A+B+C//B́+Ć scheme and the ballast variant *bn dgn* point up the close kinship of Ugaritic and biblical poetry.

5. *that . . . that . . .* 6. *that.* The force of *kī,* "that," in vs. 5a extends to vss. 5b and 6a as well. We have here an example of triple-duty *kī* which enables the psalmist to balance vss. 5–6 with sixteen syllables each.

you fled . . . you turned back. The LXX correctly saw that the *yqtl* verbs, like *yissōb* in vs. 3, described past events.

7. *the Lord.* It might be noted that in the account of the crossing of the Jordan, Yahweh is called *'ᵃdōn kol hā'āreṣ,* "Lord of all the earth" (Josh iii 11, 13).

writhe. Imperative *ḥūlī* signifies here to writhe for fright at the approach of Israel's awesome Lord.

O land. The Promised Land of Canaan, which trembled at the approach of her new *'ādōn,* "Lord."

in the presence of Jacob's God. Another instance of a ballast variant in a verse following an A+B+C//Á pattern. Though the second colon contains only the Á component, the syllable count evens at 10:10. Compare UT, 51:IV:14–15, *yštn aṯrt lbmt 'r lysmsmt bmt pḥl,* "He set Asherah on the back of the ass, on the beautiful back of the donkey," where the metrical pattern is A+B+C//Ć. Cf. also UT, Krt:116–18.

8. *Who turned.* Explaining as genitive the ending of *hahōpᵉkī,* which stands in apposition with genitives *'ādōn* and *'ᵉlōᵃh* in vs. 7. The psalmist alludes to the event described in Exod xvii 6 and Num xx 8 ff. which

relate that Yahweh made water flow from the rock in Rephidim and the cliff in Kadesh.

rock . . . flint. Deut viii 15, *ṣūr haḥallāmīš,* Deut xxxii 13, *ḥalᵉmīš ṣūr,* "flinty rock," and Job xxviii 9–10 reveal that by placing *haṣṣūr* in the first colon and *ḥallāmīš* in the second, the psalmist employed the poetic figure commented upon at vs. 2.

into a pool. Heb. 'ᵃgam shares the preposition of second-colon *lᵉma'yᵉnō,* "into a (flowing) spring"; cf. vs. 2.

spring. For the case ending of *ma'yᵉnō,* see GK, § 90o. As in Pss cxx 1 and cxxii 3, the poet uses an accusative ending where correct grammar requires the genitive. In the Phoenician dialect, too, one observes a similar confusion of case endings; see KAI, II, p. 8.

PSALM 115

(cxv 1–18)

1 Not because of us, Yahweh,
not because of us,
But because of your name
display your glory,
On account of your kindness,
on account of your fidelity,
2 Lest the nations say,
"Where, indeed, is their God?"
3 Though our God is in heaven,
whatever he wills, he does.
4 Their idols are silver and gold,
the work of men's hands.
5 A mouth have they,
but they do not speak;
6 Eyes have they,
but do not see.
They have ears,
but do not hear;
They have a nose,
but do not smell.
7 They have hands,
but do not feel;
They have feet,
but do not walk;
They emit no sound from their throats.
8 Like them shall their makers become,
everyone who trusts in them.
9 Israel, trust in Yahweh,
Helper and Suzerain is he!
10 House of Aaron,
trust in Yahweh,
Helper and Suzerain is he!

11 You who fear Yahweh,
trust in Yahweh,
Helper and Suzerain is he!
12 Our throne may Yahweh bless,
may he bless the house of Israel,
may he bless the house of Aaron.
13 May he bless those who fear Yahweh,
the small with the great.
14 May Yahweh increase you,
you and your children.
15 May you be blessed by Yahweh,
who made heaven and earth.
16 The heaven of heavens belongs to Yahweh,
but the earth he has entrusted to the children of men.
17 It is not the dead who praise Yah,
none of those who have gone down to the Fortress.
18 But we will bless Yah
from now to eternity.
Praise Yah!

NOTES

cxv. A liturgical psalm contrasting the omnipotence of Israel's God with the utter ineffectuality of heathen deities. It was probably sung antiphonally, though the exact distribution of verses between choirs or soloists cannot be fixed with certainty. One proposed breakdown: vss. 1–2, a choral supplication asking God to vindicate his good name; vss. 3–8, a solo proclamation of God's power and of the impotence of pagan idols; vss. 9–11, a choral plea that Israel therefore maintain its trust in Yahweh's sovereignty; vss. 12–15, a blessing given by the priests; vss. 16–18, a concluding hymn of praise.

Current scholarship tends to date this psalm in the post-Exilic period, but the proposed translation of certain expressions in vss. 9–12 suggests that Israel still had a king. Thus a pre-Exilic date of composition would be indicated.

1. *Not because of us.* This verse is not self-deprecation, as implied by many current versions, but protest; we do not ask for our own sakes, but out of concern for your honor. If the pagans despise us, they will condemn your name as well.

because of your name. Comparing *l*^{e}*šim*^{e}*kā* with Josh ix 9; Jer iii 17, *l*^{e}*šēm yhwh*, "because of Yahweh's name," and with Isa lv 5 and Ezek xxxvi 22 where *l^e*, "because of," is balanced by *l^ema'an*, "for the sake of." BDB, p. 514b, handles this definition well.

display. Though you dwell in heaven, your control extends over the earth as well. The Israelites admit this, the nations do not. Hence Yahweh is asked to manifest himself in some physical way upon the earth. Other texts attesting *nātan*, "to show, display," include Exod vii 9; Ezek xxvii 10, *nāt^enū h^adārēk*, "They display your splendor"; and Prov xxiii 31.

your glory. With *kābōd* sharing the pronominal suffix of *šim^ekā*, "your name," precisely as in Ps cii 16. The 5:3//5:3 syllable count of the first four cola will explain why the suffix with *kābōd* is omitted. A suffix would have added two syllables to the fourth colon.

On account of . . . on account of. The repeated prepositions *'al . . . 'al* are meant to counterbalance twice repeated *lānū*, "because of us." Hence proposals to delete the final four words as a reminiscence of Ps cxxxviii 2 should be declined. What is more, the sequence *l^e . . . 'al* recurs in Ugaritic, as observed at Ps ciii 10.

your kindness . . . your fidelity. Not content with appealing to the honor of Yahweh's name, the psalmist cites two other divine attributes to induce Yahweh to intervene on behalf of his people.

2. *Lest*. Better than "Why?" (RSV). Cf. Ps lxxix 9–10, "Because of your glorious name rescue us, / forgive us our sins for your name's sake, / Lest (*lammāh*) the heathen should say, 'Where is their God?' "

3. *in heaven*. The 8:7 syllable count (as in vs. 2) secures the MT against the addition, "above in heaven and on earth," found in LXX.

4. *Their idols*. *'^aṣabbēhem* is but one of eight Hebrew synonyms denoting "idols"; the paucity of corresponding terms in English prevents the translator from reproducing the variety of Hebrew designations for man-made gods.

7. *They have hands*. For the syntax of *y^edēhem*, consult the fourth NOTE on Ps xvi 4. This concise construction shows the possibilities inherent in dative suffixes; one can even form nominal sentences with them.

they have feet. See the preceding NOTE.

They emit no sound. On the various nuances of *hāgāh*, Ugar. *hgy*, see the discussion of Pss i 2 and ii 1, where it is noted that the verb *hāgāh* denotes some sort of oral activity which must be further specified from the parallelism and context.

from their throats. Recognizing in *bi* of *big^erōnām* the frequent meaning "from," and comparing UT, 51:VII:47–48, *yqra mt bnpšh*, "Mot called from his throat." Contrast RSV, "They do not make a sound in their throat." Ehrlich (*Die Psalmen*, p. 289) rightly renders, "Sie bringen keinen Laut aus ihrer Kehle hervor."

D. N. Freedman raises the interesting question how this inability to emit sounds differs from the statement of vs. 5 that idols cannot speak. He submits that the difference has to do with the kind of sounds: the mouth is used for articulate speech, while the throat (prescinding from the actual physiology of the matter) is used for making rudimentary sounds to express elemental emotions; even mutes can generally make throat sounds to express various feelings and desires. So the psalmist ridicules the heathen gods for their inability to do even what any mortal can do.

8. *shall . . . become.* Non-sentient gods reduce their worshipers to the same level of obtuseness.

their makers. The psalmist contrasts the heathen gods whose existence depends on "their makers" (*'ōśēhem*) with the Israelite God "who made (*'ōśēh*) heaven and earth" (vs. 15).

9. *trust in Yahweh.* In vss. 9–11, MT vocalizes the root *bṭḥ* as imperative, therefore in the second person. But this vocalization consorts oddly with the third-person suffixes in the second cola of vss. 9–11. To avoid this discord, many versions read *bṭḥ* as third-person finite verbs. Thus CCD translates, "The house of Israel trusts in the Lord; he is their help and their shield." The next NOTE proposes a compromise solution, retaining the Masoretic vocalization in the first colon and discarding it in the second.

Helper and Suzerain. Repointing MT *'ezrām ūmaginnām,* "their helper and their shield," to *'ōzᵉrīm* (or *'ᵉzārīm*) *ūmᵉgānīm,* and explaining both forms as plurals of majesty. The final *mems* could also be enclitic, but the sense would remain the same. On *māgān,* "Suzerain," see first NOTES on Pss iii 4 and lxxiv 10. This interpretation fits the description of Israel's God in vs. 3 as one who achieves whatever he decides, and entails the correction of the translation of Ps xxxiii 20 given in *Psalms I.* In our verse the verbal idea is "trust" and in Ps xxxiii 20 the verb is *ḥikkᵉtāh,* "waits for"; one more properly waits for a person, here Suzerain, than for a shield.

In TS 28 (1967), 177, Eric May objects to the term "Suzerain" as rather unfamiliar, and the point is well taken. But since Hebrew uses so many synonyms for "king," the translator must find corresponding synonyms in English. Conceding that "Suzerain" is slightly unfamiliar in English, one feels obliged to observe that *māgān* was not exactly current in Biblical Hebrew; witness the early versions and the later Masoretic punctuation which obliterated the word. In biblical circles today the word has gained considerable currency due to numerous recent studies on suzerainty treaties. Cf. the *Elenchus Bibliographicus* in recent numbers of *Biblica.*

10. *House of Aaron.* The priests or religious leaders of Israel.

12. *Our throne.* If this definition of *zakrēnū* (MT *zᵉkārānū*), examined in the fourth NOTE on Ps cii 13, proves correct, the psalm would date to the period when Israel still had a king. The first colon, as it now stands in MT, *yhwh zᵉkārānū yᵉbārēk,* "Yahweh has remembered us, may

he bless," presents syntactic as well as stylistic problems, whereas the proposed version is syntactically unfaultable and stylistically reveals the chiasmus of the first two cola: *zakrēnū yebārēk//yebārēk 'et bēt yiśrā'ēl,* "Our throne may (Yahweh) bless//may he bless the house of Israel." The prayer for the king is of course quite fitting after the proclamation at the end of vs. 11, "Helper and Suzerain is he!"

15. *May you be blessed.* As correctly rendered by RSV in contrast to KJ's indicative mode, "Ye are blessed." Other instances of precative participles (here *berūkīm*) are cited in the fourth NOTE on Ps cxi 10.

heaven and earth. See the list of parallel pairs in THE GRAMMAR OF THE PSALTER for the Ugaritic parallel pair *šmm//arṣ.*

16. *The heaven of heavens.* Probably intending the highest heaven conceived as an indefinite ascending series. Though the ancient versions such as LXX, Vulg., Syr., Targ., and *Juxta Hebraeos* all understood the phrase *haššāmayim šāmayim* as "the heaven of heavens," they doubtless would have been hard put to explain the syntax of the phrase. Compare Ps cxlviii 4, *šemē haššāmāyim,* "the heaven of heavens." The modern philologist's task is made considerably easier by the Phoenician-Punic phrase *hkkbm 'l,* "the stars of El," discussed in *Psalms II,* p. xx; *Biblica* 47 (1966), 413, in Albright, YGC, p. 232, n. 69, and by Phoenician Yeḥimilk (tenth century B.C.), 2–3, *h't ḥwy kl mplt hbtm 'l,* "He restored all the ruins of the temple of El." The syntax of Num xxi 14, *hannaḥalē-m 'arnōn,* "the wadis of the Arnon," was established by Hummel in JBL 76 (1957), 97.

Nor need one search long for a reason behind the psalmist's choice of this alternate construction: the syllable count is now 10:11. Had the poet written *šemē haššāmāyim,* as in Ps cxlviii 4, the first colon would have added up to only nine syllables.

The heaven of heavens . . . the earth. Compare Deut x 14, "Mark, the heaven and the heaven of heavens belong to Yahweh your God, the earth and all that is on it." In view of this affirmation, the contention of Bernard Cardinal Alfrink, "L'expression *'Šamaim ou Šemei Haš-šamaim,'*" in *Mélanges E. Tisserant,* I, pp. 1–7, that our phrase means "le ciel est le ciel de Jahvé" (p. 3) becomes more difficult to sustain.

he has entrusted. Perhaps a more faithful rendition of the expression *nātan le* than RSV's "he has given," since it is clear from Deut x 14 that earth also belongs to God and that his "giving" of it to men is temporary, not final. Man has not received title to earth but only the right and responsibility to tend it for the true owner. Other texts displaying this nuance of *nātan* include Gen xxx 35, xxxix 4, 8, 22; Exod xxii 6, 9; Song of Sol viii 17; cf. BDB, p. 679b.

The heaven of heavens . . . the earth 17 . . . *the dead.* This reference to the tripartite division of the cosmos might be added to the Ugaritic and biblical texts exemplifying this theme cited at Ps lxxvii 19. See also Ps cxxi 2–3.

17. *who praise Yah.* On the lack of praise of God in Sheol, see NOTE on Ps lxxxviii 11.

the Fortress. The NOTE on Ps xciv 17 studies this definition of *dūmāh.* Cf. the collocation of similar ideas in Ps cxlii 8, "Lead my life out from the Prison that I might praise your name."

PSALM 116

(cxvi 1–19)

1 Out of love for me Yahweh did hear
my plea for his mercy;
2 Truly he inclined his ear to me
even as I called.
3 The bands of Death encompassed me,
and emissaries of Sheol overtook me.
By anguish and grief was I overtaken,
4 but I invoked the name of Yahweh:
"I beg you, Yahweh,
deliver my soul!"
5 Gracious is Yahweh and just,
and our God is merciful.
6 Yahweh is the defender of the innocent;
I was brought low but he saved me.
7 "Return, my soul, to your rest,
for Yahweh has treated you kindly,
8 For you, my soul, have been rescued from Death,
you, mine eye, from Tears,
you, my foot, from Banishment.
9 I shall walk before Yahweh
in the Fields of Life."
10 I remained faithful though I was pursued,
though I was harried by Calamity.
11 I thought in my alarm,
"Every man is unreliable."
12 How can I return to Yahweh
all his favors to me?
13 I will take the chalice of salvation,
and invoke the name of Yahweh.
14 I will fulfill my vows to Yahweh
in front of all his people.
15 Yahweh considers precious in his eyes
the death of his devoted ones.

16 "O Yahweh,
truly am I your servant;
I am your servant,
your faithful son;
Loose my fetters!
17 To you will I offer
the sacrifice of thanksgiving,
And your name, Yahweh, invoke."
18 I will fulfill my vows to Yahweh
in front of all his people,
19 In the courts of Yahweh's house,
in the midst of Jerusalem.
Praise Yah!

Notes

cxvi. A hymn of thanksgiving sung in the temple by an individual whom Yahweh had saved from impending death. The psalmist does not specify the cause of his peril; most likely it was sickness. No clear-cut evidence permits the closer identification of the person performing the thanksgiving rites, though several features follow the royal tradition and the whole assembly of Israel is in attendance (vss. 14, 18). In several points the psalm recalls Hezekiah's thanksgiving (Isa xxxviii).

Verses 1–6 were recited or sung before the congregation, vss. 7–11 are the text of the psalmist's dialogue with his soul, vss. 12–15 are addressed to the religious assembly, vss. 16–17 are the prayer uttered by the psalmist *in extremis,* while vss. 18–19 turn once again to the congregation.

Critics tend to assign this poem to the post-Exilic period, but the dense syntax of several verses (1, 8, 12), frequent enjambment (vss. 1, 9, 12, 14, 15, 18), the use of *yqtl* verbs to describe completed past action (vss. 1, 3, 4, 6), rare forms such as energic *-nā'* in vss. 14, 18, double-duty particles in vss. 10, 17, bespeak a much earlier period of composition. The Qumran poems, for example, show scant familiarity with these poetic devices.

1. *Out of love for me.* About vs. 1 Ehrlich (*Die Psalmen,* p. 291) writes, "Here we encounter one of the most difficult passages in the Psalms," but progress in Northwest Semitic philology enables the Hebraist to elicit sense from the poet's crowded syntax. If MT *'āhabtī,* "I have loved," is repointed to the substantive *'ahᵃbātī,* the critic can explain the latter as an accusative of cause (third Note on Ps lxxvi 11) followed by the objective genitive ending of the first-person singular; cf. Joüon, GHB, § 129c. Or he may analyze the ending as the third-person singular and com-

pare Isa lxiii 9, *beʾahabātō . . . hūʾ geʾālām,* "In his love . . . he avenged them," and Jer xxxi 3, *weʾahabat ʿōlām ʾāhabtīk,* "With an eternal love I love you." Cf. also I John iv 19, "We love, because he first loved us." In this case, the first colon would read, "In his love Yahweh did hear." That MT elsewhere experienced difficulty with the accusative of cause construction is evidenced by Prov xii 25, *deʾāgāh belēb* (MT *beleb*) *ʾīš yešūḥannāh* (MT *yašḥennāh*), "Because of anxiety of heart a man is greatly depressed."

did hear. Identifying *kī* of *kī yišmaʿ* as emphatic.

my plea for his mercy. Earlier commentators, such as Baethgen, explain the ending of *qōlī* in the phrase *qōlī taḥanūnāy* (cf. Ps xxxi 23, *qōl taḥanūnay*) as an archaic genitive ending. True, the case is wrong (one expects the accusative), but critics ascribe this confusion to the fact that the poets who affected their use no longer fully understood the subtleties of case endings. The correct employment, however, of the accusative ending in vs. 15 belies this line of reasoning. Hence one may propose, with due reserve, the repointing to *taḥanūnēy,* with the third-person suffix *-y* expressing the objective genitive. The emergent inclusion of the objective genitives in initial "Out of love for me" and final "my plea for his mercy" would seem to sustain this grammatical analysis.

2. *Truly.* Understanding *kī,* as in vs. 1, as emphatic.

even as I called. Consonantal *wbymy ʾqrʾ* (MT *ūbeyāmay ʾeqrāʾ* becomes semantically and syntactically defensible when vocalized *ūbīmēy ʾeqrāʾ*. The initial *waw* would parse as emphatic and *bīmēy* as the plural construct before the verb *ʾeqrāʾ*, a construction examined at Pss lxxxi 6, xc 15, and cvii 29. Cf. Gen xiv 1 and Speiser's comments thereto in AB, vol. 1, as well as Ps lxxvii 3, *beyōm ṣartī,* "When I implore" (second NOTE on Ps lxxvii 3).

3. *The bands of Death.* The ambivalent translation "bands" has been chosen to reflect the ambivalence of Heb. *ḥeblē,* which can mean either "bonds, cords," or "companies of persons or animals," as in I Sam x 5, 10 and Job xxxix 3, "They crouch, bring forth their young (*yaldēhem*), their bands (*ḥeblēhem*) they send out."

encompassed me . . . overtook me. Good chiasmus marks this verse.

emissaries of Sheol. The traditional rendition "the pangs of Sheol" can scarcely be reconciled with the predicate *meṣāʾūnī,* which is consequently distorted to "laid hold on me" (RSV). Consonantal *mṣry* is easily related to *ṣīr,* "messenger, emissary," from the root *ṣw/yr,* "to beckon," described at Ps lxxvii 3. Hence *mṣry* would parse as a noun or passive participle. That Death employed messengers to execute his will is well known from the phrase of Prov xvi 14, *malʾakē māwet,* "the (two) messengers of Death."

overtook me. Ascribing to *meṣāʾūnī* the only sense it possesses in Ugar. *mṣa-mẓa,* "to reach," a meaning touched upon in second NOTE on Ps xxxii 6; see Job iii 22, xi 7, xxviii 12, xxxi 29, xxxiv 11, and S. Iwry in *Textus* 5 (1966), 36–39.

By anguish and grief. These being interpreted as the names of two of Death's minions; see below on Ps cxix 143. As noted at Pss xci 15 and cii 3, *ṣārāh* connotes the anguish of death. Syntactically, *ṣārāh wᵉyāgōn* are accusatives expressing the agents, a construction studied in the third NOTE on Ps cix 14; cf. also Job xxvii 15 and Prov v 22. As so frequently in psalms, nouns in the accusative precede their verb; cf. *Psalms II*, Index of Subjects, s.v., and THE GRAMMAR OF THE PSALTER.

was I overtaken. Repointing MT qal *'emṣā'* to niphal *'immāṣē'*, and comparing Job xxviii 12 with xxviii 20.

6. *the innocent.* That is, of the inexperienced.

but he saved me. The *yqtl* verb *yᵉhôšîaʿ*, in tandem with the *qtl* form *dallōtī*, "I was brought low," states a single completed action.

7. *Return, my soul.* In the next verse the psalmist will expand this dialogue of a man with his soul (first NOTE on Ps xlii 6; fourth NOTE on Ps lxii 2) to include other members of his body. That the Canaanites were familiar with this literary convention appears from UT, 127:25–28, *ap yṣb yṯb lhkl wywsrnn ggnh lk labk yṣb lk [la]bk wrgm*, "Then Yaṣṣib returned to the palace, and his innards instructed him: 'Go to your father, Yaṣṣib, go to your father and say.' "

to your rest. Indicating more a condition of rest than a place of rest. The opposite condition is described by the verb *hāmāh*, "to sigh, be disquieted," predicated of the soul in the dialogue of Ps xlii 6, 12. Scholars puzzle over the unique plural form *mᵉnūḥaykī*, "your rest," but a satisfactory explanation is supplied by the desire for assonance with the corresponding final word of the second colon, *'ālāykī*, "you." A similar phenomenon is noted in Ps ciii 1, where the need for another syllable is alleged as the reason behind the choice of the hapax legomenon plural form *qᵉrābay*, "my inmost parts." On the second-person feminine suffix *kī* (also in vs. 19), see introductory NOTE to Ps ciii 3.

8. *have been rescued.* Often emended with the ancient versions to third-person *ḥillēṣ*, "he has rescued," consonantal *ḥlṣt* can be upheld if vocalized as pual second-person feminine *ḥullaṣt* (MT piel *ḥillaṣtā* as in related passage of Ps lvi 14). This reading, then, continues the dialogue begun by feminine *šūbī*, "Return," in the preceding verse.

from Death. The local meaning of *māwet*, documented at Pss vi 6 and lvi 14, has likewise escaped attention in Job xxx 23, where the synonymy with *bēt mō'ēd*, "the meeting house," indicates that *māwet tᵉšībēnī* is most correctly rendered, "You will return me to Death"; contrast RSV, "Thou wilt bring me to death," an inaccurate version because *tᵉšībēnī* means "You will bring me back," not simply "You will bring me."

you. Repointing MT *'et* to pronominal *'att*, a vocalization that also protects the MT singular readings *'ēnī*, "mine eye," and *raglī*, "my foot," against the dual vocalization of some ancient versions.

mine eye. The psalmist addresses his eye in an unusual dialogue beyond the grasp of the Syriac version which conveniently dropped this colon.

Tears. The local sense ascribed to parallel *māwet*, "Death," suggests that *dim'āh* is another poetic name for the infernal regions depicted in Matt viii 14 as a place "of weeping and gnashing of teeth." Cf. Ps. li 16, "Deliver me from the tears of death."

you. Again reading the feminine second-person *'att* for the *nota accusativi* of MT, *'et*.

Banishment. The evidence for this name of the nether world, given at Ps lvi 14, is further validated by the eschatological overtones of *yiddāḥeh* in Prov xiv 32, a passage studied by van der Weiden in *Le Livre des Proverbs: Notes philologiques*.

9. *the Fields of Life*. Having been rescued from Sheol, the psalmist is convinced that his future life will be spent in the presence of Yahweh in heaven. In the cognate verse Ps lvi 14, the text reads *'ūr* (MT *'ōr*) *haḥayyīm*, discussed in last NOTE on Ps lvi 20.

10. *I remained faithful*. This appears to be the straightforward meaning of hiphil *he'emantī*, and it is reassuring to see HALAT, p. 62a, accept this definition here in contrast to KB, p. 61b, which labeled our text "unexplained." From vss. 7–9 it is clear that faith in Yahweh was the sustaining force of the psalmist's life.

though. BDB, p. 474b, cites many instances of adversative *kī* followed by the *yqtl* verbal form, as here.

I was pursued. Namely, by the emissaries of Sheol, as expressly stated by vs. 3. This meaning of pual *'adubbār* (MT piel *'adabbēr*), discussed in first NOTE on Ps ii 5 and NOTE on Ps xxxviii 13 is adopted in a number of texts by the latest Hebrew lexicon, HALAT, p. 201a.

though. With first colon adversative *kī* extending its force to the second colon.

I was harried. Repointing MT *'ānītī* to pual *'unnētī*, a more fitting counterpart to pual *'adubbār*.

Calamity. Consonantal *m'd* (MT *me'ōd*, "much, greatly," scarcely meets contextual requirements) can be analyzed into the preposition *min*, expressing the cause or agent, and the well-known noun *'ēd*, "calamity, distress"; text would then read *mē'ēd*. It was observed at Ps xviii 19 that *yōm 'ēdī*, "the day of my calamity," signified the day of death. The present poem too bristles with names and designations of the inferno. There are also newly interpreted texts, such as Pss vi 4, 11, xxxviii 7, 9, lxxix 8, cxix 107, where the substantive *m'd* with preformative *mem* of place, has come to light; in this case the vocalization would probably be *mā'ēd*.

11. *"Every man is unreliable."* All the more reason, then, for the psalmist to rely on God.

12. *How*. When used adverbially as an interrogative, *mah* especially expresses what is regarded as an impossibility, obviously true of the

present context. Cf. Gen xliv 16; Exod x 26; Mic vi 3; Job ix 2 and BDB, p. 553b.

The classic translation of this verse, Voltaire's favorite from the Psalter (see Arnold Ages, "Voltaire et les Psaumes, un livre admiré," in *Revue de l'Université d'Ottawa* 36 [1966], 61–65, especially 64), "What shall I render unto the Lord *for* all his benefits toward me?" (KJ), is grammatically difficult to justify. The commentators alive to the grammatical problem (e.g., Baethgen, Gunkel) insert *k^e*, "according to," before *kol tagmūlōhī*, "all his favors," a procedure equally difficult to justify.

all his favors. Syntactically, *kol tagmūlōhī* is the direct object of hiphil *'āšīb*, "can I return," or, in other terms, we have an instance of enjambment. *Die Zürcher Bibel* (based on Zwingli's translation; Zürich, 1954) correctly translates, "Wie soll ich dem Herrn vergelten alles Gute, das er an mir getan." Cf. I Sam xxvi 23; Deut xxxii 43; Hos xii 15. Though the suffix of *tagmūlōhī* is normally labeled a "purely Aramaic form" (GK, § 91l), the frequency of the Phoenician third-person *-y* suffix in poetic Hebrew may require a reassessment of this description.

13. *the chalice of salvation.* The cup to be drunk as a part of the thanksgiving sacrifice (vs. 14) for a major deliverance. Apparently plural *y^ešū'ōt*, usually explained as an intensive plural abstract, may also be parsed as the Phoenician singular form with the *-ōt* ending. Cf. Matt xxvi 27 and I Cor x 16.

14. *I will fulfill my vows.* In a neo-Punic inscription studied by J. Février in *Journal Asiatique* 254 (1966), 306, occurs the same phrase *šlmty 't ndry*, "I have fulfilled my vows."

in front of. Some commentators (e.g., J. Halévy, *Recherches bibliques*, III, p. 314) find the addition of *-nā'* to *negdāh* very enigmatic, but the enigma disappears in the light of Northwest Semitic whose dialects display a double set of prepositions, one a simple form and the other an intensive form reinforced by the ending *-n;* thus we have *b* + *bn; b'd* + *b'dn; l* + *ln; 'l* + *'ln; tḥt* + *tḥtn*. See first NOTE on Ps xlvii 5, and UT, p. 72, n. 2, which sees a survival of Ugar. *-anna,* in Heb. *g^ešāh-nnā'* and *haggīdāh-annā'*. In our verse the extended form is doubtless used for metrical purposes.

15. *considers precious.* Since MT *yāqār*, "precious," leaves *hmwth*, "death," without a grammatical explanation, one is obliged to repoint *yqr* as the piel verb *yiqqar*. In MT the verse lacks a verb. For analogous use of the piel, compare *giddēl*, "to consider great."

This statement that Yahweh puts great value on the death of his faithful assumes that he will take them to himself when they die. This belief accords with the oft-expressed conviction of the psalmists that the just will enjoy Yahweh's presence after death.

in his eyes. Parsing the ending of *'ēnēy* as the third-person singular suffix.

the death. The unexplained MT hapax legomenon *hammāwtāh* may simply be masculine *mōt* plus the accusative ending *-āh;* hence vocalize *hammōtāh.* Being the second-colon object of first-colon *yiqqar,* "considers precious"—thus another example of enjambment as in vs. 12—the accusative form evens the syllable count at 7:7.

of his devoted ones. Literally *laḥᵃsīdāyw* reads either "by his devoted ones" or "for his devoted ones." Cf. Ps cxxiii 4.

16. *O Yahweh.* Verses 16–17 are a longer recension of the short prayer in vs. 4a uttered by the psalmist when threatened by death. Both prayers begin with the words *'ānnāh yhwh.* Compare UT, 49:IV:46, *an lan yšpš,* "Alas, alas, O Shapsh!"

truly. Often omitted by the versions (e.g., RSV, "O Lord, I am thy servant"), *kī* parses as the emphatic particle.

am I your servant. Comparing *'ᵃnī 'abdekā* with the protestation of Baal before Death in UT, 67:II:12, *'bdk an,* "Your servant am I."

your faithful son. For this translation of *ben 'ᵃmittekā,* literally "the son of your fidelity" (MT and versions, "the son of your handmaid"), see the second NOTE on Ps lxxxvi 16. Interpreted thus, this phrase forms an inclusion with vs. 10, *he'ᵉmantī,* "I remained faithful." For a recent defense of the traditional translation, see F. C. Fensham, VT 19 (1969), 312–21.

Loose. The problem presented by perfect *pittaḥtā,* rendered "Thou hast loosed" by RSV, is not glossed over by Kirkpatrick, *The Book of Psalms,* p. 691, who writes, "The precative interjection [i.e., *'ānnā,* "Oh"] would naturally be followed by an imperative, as in v. 4b [*'ānnāh yhwh mallᵉṭāh napšī*]; but the Psalmist breaks off into thanksgiving." Given the large number of precative perfects in the Psalter, unrecognized by earlier translators, *pittaḥtā* can convincingly be parsed as a precative perfect, that is, as a stylistic variant of the imperative following *'ānnā* in vs. 4b. Consult the second NOTE on Ps iv 2 and *passim;* H. Ewald, *Ausführliches Lehrbuch der hebräischen Sprache* (6th ed.; Leipzig, 1855), § 223, recognized the precative mode of *pittaḥtā.*

my fetters. The psalmist harks back to vs. 3, "the bands of Death."

17. *will I offer the sacrifice.* The biblical expression *'ezbaḥ zebaḥ* recalls the Ugaritic phrase *dbḥ dbḥ,* "He is offering a sacrifice," in UT, 125: 39–40.

your name. Suffixless *šēm* shares the suffix of first-colon *lᵉkā,* "to you." The same phenomenon is noted at Ps cii 16, where suffixless *šēm* is modified by the suffix of parallel *kᵉbōdekā,* "your glory."

19. *In . . . in the midst of.* The sequence *bᵉ . . . bᵉtōkēkī* corresponds to the Ugaritic parallelism of *b//btk* cited at Ps cix 30.

courts . . . house. The phrase *ḥaṣᵉrōt bēt* collocates two words found in parallelism in Ugaritic and Phoenician, as pointed out at Ps lxxxiv 11. See also the list of parallel words in THE GRAMMAR OF THE PSALTER.

in the midst of Jerusalem. Explaining the final *-kī* of *bᵉtōkēkī* as the emphatic particle in a construct chain discussed in the second Note on Ps lxviii 25, and by van Dijk, EPT, pp. 69–70; see below on Pss cxxii 2, cxxxv 9.

PSALM 117

(cxvii 1–2)

1 Praise Yahweh, all you nations,
  laud him, all you gods!
2 For mighty is his kindness toward us,
  and the fidelity of Yahweh is eternal.
Praise Yah!

Notes

cxvii. The shortest of all the psalms is theologically one of the grandest. Its invitation to all nations and their gods to join in praising Yahweh for his goodness to Israel virtually recognizes that Israel's vocation was the salvation of the world. Cf. Rom xv 11.

This hymn cannot be dated with any precision. The description of *šabbᵉḥūhū*, "laud him," in vs. 2 as an Aramaism is, however, no longer valid and hence no longer an argument for a late date. The occurrence, on the other hand, of vs. 1 *'ēmīm*, "gods," in Jer l 38 might suggest composition in the seventh–sixth century B.C.

The two verses are arranged chiastically: the divine name *yhwh* appears in the first and fourth cola, but in the second and third cola he is present in the suffixes of *šabbᵉḥūhū*, "laud him," and *ḥasdō*, "his kindness."

1. *laud him.* On the supposed Aramaicity of *šabbᵉḥūhū*, see the fifth NOTE on Ps lxiii 4.

you gods. MT *'ummīm*, traditionally translated "you peoples," is unexampled; the plural of *'ummāh*, "clan, people," is elsewhere feminine *'ummōt*. Hence some scholars emend to *lᵉ'ummīm*, "peoples," but the repointing to *'ēmīm*, "gods," literally "frightful ones," in Jer l 38, yields excellent sense in view of other Psalter texts, that extend similar invitations to pagan deities. Thus Ps xlvii 2–3, "All you strong ones, clap your hands, / acclaim, you gods, with shouts of joy. For Yahweh Most High is awesome, / the Great King over all the earth."

Scholars are perplexed by the presence of the definite article in *hā'ēmīm*, whereas parallel *gōyīm*, "nations," lacks it. The reason for this difference seems to be metrical, not semantic; the psalmist needed another syllable in the second colon, and by using the definite article brought the syllable count to a more balanced 9:8.

2. *For mighty.* Duhm and other commentators find the logical nexus between the two verses extremely puzzling. The psalmist invites the pagans and their gods to praise Yahweh (this implies conversion) because he has been good to Israel. "How naïve of the psalmist" is the comment of some critics, and yet the same sentiment is encountered in Pss xxii 28, lxvii 2–6, and lxxxvi 9, "If you act, all the pagans will come / to prostrate themselves before you, my Lord, / And they will glorify your name." See also Ps cxv 1–3.

kindness . . . fidelity. As in Ps xl 11b, the poet breaks up the customary pair *ḥesed* and *'emet,* placing one in each colon.

the fidelity of Yahweh. The diagonal arrangement of the two verses in the original text (see introductory NOTE) is obliterated in the deplorably careless translation of *'ᵉmet yhwh* by *The Grail Psalms,* "he is faithful."

is eternal. This ambivalent version of *lᵉʿōlām* attempts to reflect the ambiguity of the original in which it can signify "to eternity" or "from eternity," according to the context. And sometimes the context precludes certainty. Those versions, such as RSV, which render "endures for ever" may exceed the intent of the poet.

PSALM 118

(cxviii 1–29)

1 Give thanks to Yahweh for he is good,
for his kindness is eternal.
2 Let Israel say,
"His kindness is eternal!"
3 Let the house of Aaron say,
"His kindness is eternal!"
4 Let those who fear Yahweh say,
"His kindness is eternal!"
5 From Confinement I called Yah,
Yah answered me from the Broad Domain.
6 Yahweh is for me, I fear not;
what can man do against me?
7 Yahweh is for me, my Great Warrior,
so I shall gloat over my enemies.
8 It is better to seek refuge in Yahweh
than to trust in man.
9 It is better to seek refuge in Yahweh
than to trust in princes.
10 All nations surrounded me,
but in Yahweh's name indeed I cut off their foreskins.
11 They surrounded me, surrounded me completely,
but in Yahweh's name indeed I cut off their foreskins.
12 They surrounded me like bees,
they crackled like a fire of thorns,
but in Yahweh's name indeed I cut off their foreskins.
13 You grimly thrust me to the point of falling,
but Yahweh helped me.
14 My fortress and my sentinel was Yah,
who became the victory for me.
15 The sound of rejoicing and victory
was in the tents of the triumphant.
16 Yahweh's right hand achieved victory,
Yahweh's right hand was exalted,

Yahweh's right hand achieved victory.
17 I did not die but lived
that I might recount the works of Yah.
18 Though Yah chastised me sorely,
he did not hand me to Death.
19 Open for me the gates of victory
that I may enter them to thank Yah.
20 This is the gate that belongs to Yahweh,
let the triumphant enter it!
21 I thank you because you granted me triumph,
and became the victory for me.
22 The stone the builders rejected
became the cornerstone.
23 From Yahweh this has come to pass,
it is wondrous in our eyes.
24 This is the day Yahweh acted,
let us exult and rejoice in him!
25 We beg you, Yahweh, give victory!
we beg you, Yahweh, send prosperity!
26 Blessed be he who enters in the name of Yahweh,
we bless you in the house of Yahweh.
27 El Yahweh has truly shone upon us!
Deck the shrine with leafy boughs,
adorn the horns of the altar.
28 You are my God and I thank you,
my God, I extol you.
29 Give thanks to Yahweh for he is good,
for his kindness is eternal.

Notes

cxviii. A king's hymn of thanksgiving for delivery from death and for a military victory. Some critics claim that this psalm is best understood as part of the annual liturgy in which the Davidic king was prominent, but this reconstruction must symbolically interpret the psalmist's references to an encounter with death, which seem to be literal.

In vss. 1–4 a singer calls for thanksgiving from the companies of the laity, of the priests, and of all together (cf. Ps cxv 9–11). Verses 5–18 contain the king's description of the battle in which through divine intervention he escaped sure death. Verses 19–22 describe the entry of the procession, first, into the city and then into the temple. In vss.

23–29 the king and the worshipers celebrate their common salvation in alternating voices.

The several striking verbal similarities between this hymn and the ancient victory hymn in Exod xv (compare vs. 14 with Exod xv 2; vss. 15–16 with Exod xv 6; and vs. 28 with Exod xv 2) indicate an early date of composition. This inference is further sustained by the economy of language (e.g., the relative clauses without relative pronouns in vss. 22, 24), and by the reference to a very primitive custom in vss. 10–12. The contents and the probable use of the verb *'ānāh*, "to conquer," in vs. 21 point to the royal, hence pre-Exilic, nature of the victory hymn.

1. *is eternal.* Consult the third NOTE on Ps cxvii 2 for the possible ambivalence of the phrase *l^e'ōlām,* "to/from eternity."

2. *Israel.* The proposal to insert, with LXX, *bēt,* "house," before "Israel" is not compelling, especially since the present syllable count is perfectly balanced at 6:6.

"His . . . eternal." Heb. *kī* which introduces the quotation, is here, and in vss. 3–4, reproduced by quotation marks.

5. *From . . . from* The first NOTE on Ps lv 12 cites other instances of the *min//b^e* sequence in which both prepositions denote "from."

Confinement. Being hapax legomenon, the singular form *mēṣar,* usually rendered "straits, distress," must be defined from the over-all context of the psalm. Since the psalmist was in immediate danger of death (vss. 10–14, 17–18), *mēṣar* should designate a place from which he called for divine help, much as in Ps lxi 3, where the poet pictures himself on the edge of the abyss, and in Ecclus li 9, which reads, "And I raised my voice from the City, and from the gates of Sheol my cry." The motif of Sheol as a place of confinement (see third NOTE on Ps lxxxviii 9 on Sheol as Prison) accords with the verb *sabbūnī,* "They surrounded me." The preformative *m,* then, expresses place, precisely as in the second-colon antonym *merḥāb,* "Broad Domain."

answered me from. Cf. Pss lx 8 and xcix 7.

the Broad Domain. In Pss xviii 20 and xxxi 9, *merḥāb* designates the vast expanses of the nether world, but here it refers to Yahweh's celestial abode. The subsequent contrast between the psalmist's confined existence on earth and the freedom of heaven recalls the sequence of ideas in Pss iv 2, *baṣṣār hirḥabtā lī,* "in distress set me at large," and xviii 7–8.

Failure to recognize that both *mēṣar* and *merḥāb* are place names produced the indefensible translation of KJ, which transmutes the eight words of the Hebrew original into eighteen in English: "I called upon the Lord in distress: the Lord answered me, *and set me* in a large place."

6. *Yahweh . . . man.* The poet sharpens the contrast between God and man by placing *yahweh* at the beginning of the verse and *'ādām* at the end.

for me. Compare Ps lvi 10, "Then will I know / that God is for me." The ancient versions found difficult the nuance of *lī;* thus *Juxta Hebraeos* strays far afield with *Dominus meus es,* "You are my Lord."

for me . . . against me. The use of *lī* in two opposite senses effectively illustrates the aspect of Hebrew style noticed at Ps civ 8.

against me. The second NOTE on Ps xvii 4 cites Ugaritic-Phoenician-Hebrew texts witnessing this nuance of *lī.*

7. *my Great Warrior.* Like Ps liv 6, *b^{e}sōm^{e}kē,* "the true Sustainer," *b^e'ōz^{e}rāy* may be analyzed into the emphatic *beth* followed by the plural of majesty. The psalmist evidently chose the plural form *'ōz^{e}ray,* "my Great Warrior," to effect assonance and rhyme with second-colon *śōn$^{e'}$āy,* "my enemies." The numerous enemies of the poet were no match for the unique and majestic God of the psalmist. The root of *'ōz^{e}ray* occurs in Ugaritic as *'ḏr,* "lad, warrior," discussed in NOTE on Ps xxxv 2.

I shall gloat over. See Ps cxii 8 for this idiom and for the play on the verbs *yārē',* "to fear," and *rā'āh,* "to see."

8. *in man* 9. *in princes.* As in Ps cxlvi 3, the balance between *'ādām,* "man," and *n^{e}dībīm,* "princes," may be an instance of merismus expressing "all men." A similar usage can be found in the Phoenician Inscription of Eshmunazor, line 4, *kl mmlkt wkl 'dm,* "every king and every man," and in UT, 51:VII:43, *umlk ublmlk,* "whether king or commoner."

10. *indeed.* As pointed out by R. T. O'Callaghan, VT 4 (1954), 175, this *kī* is emphatic, forcing the verb to the end of the sentence; consult the second NOTE on Ps xlix 16. Briggs, CECBP, II, p. 408, correctly observes that the LXX and *Juxta Hebraeos* do not translate *kī,* but he erroneously concludes that it is probably a gloss of asseveration. From a study of other passages with emphatic *kī* it is clear that the versions did not appreciate the function of this particle; from the postposition of the verb it appears certain that *kī* is not a gloss.

I cut off their foreskins. Many translators and commentators fight shy of the obvious meaning of MT *'^{a}mīlēm,* the hiphil of *mūl,* "to circumcise," but BDB, p. 558, correctly defines it "I will make them to be circumcised," though it misunderstood the tense of the verb. The *yqtl* form expresses the past, since from vss. 5 and 13 it is clear that the crisis was past and the victory won. Whether the hiphil should be taken with BDB as causative or as elative does not change the meaning substantially.

The poet doubtless alludes to the practice mentioned in I Sam xviii 25–27, "The king desires no marriage present except a hundred foreskins of the Philistines, that he may be avenged of the king's foes. . . . David arose and went, along with his men, and killed two hundred of the Philistines; and David brought their foreskins, which were given in full number to the king, that he might become the king's son-in-law." The reference to the "nations" and the "foreskins" suggests further that the psalmist had the Philistines in mind; most of Israel's neighbors practiced circumcision, but the Philistines did not.

12. *they crackled.* The first NOTE on Ps lxxiv 5 seeks to establish this meaning of *d'kw,* probably to be vocalized as piel privative *dē'ᵃkū.* The verb "crackled" replaces "blazed" as a more accurate description of the burning of thorns.

13. *You grimly thrust me.* One of the more difficult expressions in the poem, unexplained *dāḥōh dᵉḥītanī* assumes a measure of intelligibility when taken as a direct address of the psalmist to Death. This exegesis consorts well with the observations made at Pss v 11, xxxv 5, xxxvi 13, lvi 14, cxvi 8, that biblical poets often used the verb *dāḥāh* specifically to describe casting someone into the infernal abyss.

to the point of falling. Namely, into Sheol. This pregnant sense of *linpōl,* documented at Ps lxxxii 7, sustains the interpretation proposed in the preceding NOTE and at vs. 5.

but Yahweh helped me. As in Pss xiii 5 and lxi 3, the psalmist is dramatically caught in the struggle between Yahweh and Death.

14. *My fortress.* This nuance of *'ozzī,* usually rendered "my strength," is inferred from the military metaphor the poet employs in this verse; cf. the first NOTE on Ps lix 10.

my sentinel. With *zimrāt* sharing the suffix of *'ozzī;* one might also read *zimrātī,* with the single writing of *-y* (the next word being *yāh*). The latter reading would result in a 7:7 syllable count. This composite phrase recurs in Exod xv 2 and Isa xii 2.

The third NOTE on Ps lix 18 cites the evidence for this definition of *zimrāt,* now confirmed by Ugar. *'zk ḏmrk;* see UT, Supplement, p. 551.

victory. The valid assumption that the poet composed a congruent metaphor indicates this nuance of *yᵉšū'āh,* studied at Ps lxvii 3.

15. *the tents of the triumphant.* The army of the Israelite king celebrating the king's delivery from death. Ehrlich (*Die Psalmen,* p. 299) appears to be correct when translating *ṣaddīqīm,* "the victors," since the context is military. Other texts where this shade of meaning is pronounced include Isa xli 2, 10, xlix 24, where *ṣaddīq//gibbōr* must not be emended to *'ārīṣ,* "the violent" (*pace* 1QIsᵃ and McKenzie, *Second Isaiah,* § 27, Isa xlix 24, n. *b*); Jer xxiii 6; consult BDB, p. 842a.

16. *Yahweh's right hand.* The threefold repetition of *yᵉmīn yhwh* corresponds to the threefold repetition of vss. 10–12 and of Ps cxv 9–11.

17. *I did not die but lived.* Like vs. 10, *'ᵃmīlam, 'āmūt* and *'eḥyeh* are *yqtl* forms expressing past events, namely, the result of vs. 13, *yhwh 'ᵃzārānī,* "Yahweh helped me." The parallelism with the *qtl* verbs *yissᵉrannī,* "chastised me," and *lō' nᵉtānānī,* "he did not hand me," reveals the past nature of these two verbs.

that I might recount. The inability to sing God's praises in Sheol being one of the most painful privations of the Israelite dead; see NOTE on Ps lxxxviii 11.

19. *Open for me.* The triumphant king at the head of his army commands that the gates be thrown open.

the gates of victory. For this nuance of *ṣedeq,* see the NOTE on vs. 15. Most modern commentators see here a reference to the gates of the temple, but comparison with the processional hymn in Ps xxiv 7–10 suggests rather the gates of Jerusalem. The singular form *šaʻar* in the next verse probably refers to the door of the temple.

20. *This is the gate.* Words spoken by the priest to the king.

the gate. In contradistinction to plural "gates" in vs. 19, singular *šaʻar* probably designates the entrance to the temple.

that belongs to Yahweh. Interpreting *l* as the *lamedh* of ownership, noticed in eighth NOTE to Ps cx 3.

21. *you granted me triumph.* Consonantal *ʻnytny* (MT *ʻănītānī*) is capable of several valid interpretations, but a piel pointing *ʻinnētanī* and the definition examined at Pss xviii 36, xx 2, 7, 10, lx 7, lxxxix 23 yield a convincing meaning consonant with the immediate context and with the royal genre of the psalm. As the introductory NOTE points out, *ʻnw,* "to conquer, triumph," occurs only in royal psalms.

22. *The stone.* Namely, Israel. Though considered unimportant by the great empires, Israel received an honorable and important place in the building of Yahweh's kingdom.

the cornerstone. Literally "the head of the corner." Placing *'eben,* "stone," at the beginning of the verse and *pinnāh,* "corner," at the end, the psalmist effects the breakup of a composite phrase. The phrase *'eben pinnāh,* "the cornerstone," occurs in Jer li 26 and Job xxxviii 6. See the list of breakup of stereotyped phrases in THE GRAMMAR OF THE PSALTER. This literary analysis thus supports the interpretation of the stone as the cornerstone, not the keystone as maintained by some commentators.

23. *From Yahweh.* The order of words emphasizes "From Yahweh," who, as stated in vs. 5, "answered me from the Broad Domain."

24. *This is the day Yahweh acted.* Not "This is the day which the Lord has made" (RSV). Cf. Mal iii 21 (iv 3 RSV), *bayyōm 'ăšer 'ănī ʻōśeh,* "on the day when I act"; fourth NOTE on Ps xxii 32, second NOTE on Ps xxxvii 5, NOTE on Ps xxxix 10; and Eaton, *Psalms: Introduction and Commentary,* p. 272.

let us exult and rejoice. Comparing UT, 125:14–15, *bḥyk abn nšmḫ blmtk ngln,* "In your life eternal we rejoice, our father, in your immortality we exult."

in him. Not "in it." Compare Pss xxxiii 21, "For in him our heart rejoices," and lxvi 6, *niśmeḥāh bō,* "let us rejoice in him."

25. *We beg you, Yahweh.* The choir or the congregation implores God to carry forward the work which he began by bringing the Israelite forces victory.

26. *Blessed be he.* Namely, the king.

we bless you. The plural suffix *-kem* can be parsed as a plural of majesty referring to the king (see fourth NOTE on Ps cv 30), or it may be numerically plural, addressing the king's troops.

in the house. Usually rendered "from the house," *mibbēt* more probably denotes "in the house"; in numerous texts *min* means "in" (second NOTE on Ps lxviii 27), and here parallelism with *b*ᵉ, "in," and the desire to avoid the sequence *b*ᵉ*bēt* point to this definition.

27. *El Yahweh.* Interpreting *'ēl yhwh* as the composite divine name encountered in Pss xviii 31, lxix 34, lxxxv 9, cix 14, not as a nominal sentence, with the versions; e.g., RSV translates, "The Lord is God." This latter translation became inevitable once the *waw* of *wayyā'er* was taken as the conjunctive *waw* and not as the emphasizing particle. In vs. 28 recurs another composite divine title, but with the components placed in the parallel cola.

has truly shone. By granting our king and troops victory over the foes. Given the numerous instances of *waw* emphatic in biblical poetry, the proposed deletion of *wa* in *wayyā'er* no longer commends itself.

the shrine. Redividing the consonants to read *ḥgb 'btym* (MT *ḥag ba'*ᵃ*bōtīm*), and identifying *ḥgb* with Syr. *ḥugbā,* "shrine," Ar. *ḥijāb,* "screen." The appropriateness of the emergent parallelism "shrine//horns of the altar" is evident. Less apparent, however, is the feast and the rites to which the psalmist alludes. Most probably this line refers to thanksgiving rites celebrating the recent victory. In VT 5 (1955), 266–71, J. J. Petuchowski has made the attractive suggestion that this verse is a prayer for rain, a part of the specific Sukkoth rites and rainmaking ceremonies, but he does not satisfactorily explain how it arrived here.

with leafy boughs. *'*ᵃ*bōtīm* now parses as the accusative of means, a very frequent construction in the Psalter; cf. Ps cxi 6.

adorn. Repointing MT *'ad,* "up to," to plural imperative *'*ᵃ*dū,* from *'ādāh,* "to adorn, deck oneself," a fine counterpart to imperative *'is*ᵉ*rū,* "Deck!"

the horns of the altar. The phrase *qarnōt hammizbē*ᵃ*ḥ* may profitably be compared with UT, 613:30–31, *qrnt ṯlḥn,* "horns of the (cultic) table"; see UT, Supplement, p. 555.

28. *I thank you.* As in vs. 21, these are the words of the king. Each word in this verse, it might be noted, begins with the letter *aleph,* and though the first colon numbers three words against the two of the second colon, the poet perfectly balanced the syllables at eight apiece. D. N. Freedman notes the similar sequence of five words beginning with *aleph* in Exod xv 9.

29. *Give thanks.* To complete an inclusion this line repeats the sentiment of the opening verse.

PSALM 119

(cxix 1–176)

ALEPH

1 How happy those of blameless way,
who walk in Yahweh's law!
2 How happy those who observe his stipulations,
and with all their heart search for him,
3 Who also do no wrong,
but walk in his ways.
4 It was you who commanded
your precepts to be diligently observed.
5 Oh that my ways were ordered
to observe your statutes!
6 Then I should not be humiliated,
if I gazed upon all your commandments.
7 I praise you for your upright heart,
as I learn your just ordinances.
8 I will observe your statutes;
do not forsake me, Everlasting Grand One!

BETH

9 How can a young man keep himself pure?
By guarding his path according to your word.
10 With all my heart I search for you;
make me not stray from your commandments.
11 Within my heart I treasure your promise,
that I might not sin against you.
12 May you be blessed Yahweh!
teach me your statutes.
13 With my lips I proclaim
all the ordinances from your mouth.
14 In the way of your stipulations
I rejoice in you more than in all riches.
15 On your precepts may I meditate,
and gaze upon your paths.

16 In your statutes I delight myself,
I never forget your words.

GIMEL

17 Requite your servant that I may live,
and that I may observe your word.
18 Open my eyes that I may behold
the wonders of your law.
19 I am a sojourner on earth,
hide not from me your commandments.
20 My soul craves, truly longs
for your ordinances at all times.
21 Rebuke the accursed presumptuous,
who have strayed from your commandments.
22 Strip me of reproach and scorn,
for I observe your stipulations.
23 Though corrupt men sit to gossip about me,
your servant meditates on your statutes.
24 Yes, your stipulations are my delight,
they are the men of my council.

DALETH

25 My neck cleaves to the dust,
restore me to life according to your word.
26 I declared your ways, and you answered me;
teach me your statutes.
27 Make me understand the ways of your precepts,
that I may meditate on your wonders.
28 My frame sags from sorrow;
raise me according to your word!
29 Put far from me the way of falsehood,
and through your law show me your favor.
30 The way of truth have I chosen,
your ordinances I consider supreme.
31 I have clung to your precepts;
Yahweh, do not humiliate me!
32 I shall run the way of your commandments,
if you enlarge my understanding.

HE

33 Teach me, Yahweh,
the way of your statutes,
That I may guard it as a reward.
34 Give me insight that I may observe your law,
that I may keep it with all my heart.
35 Direct me in the path of your commandments,
for I delight in it.
36 Incline my heart toward your stipulations,
and not to unjust gain.
37 Keep my eyes from looking at idols,
but by your power give me life.
38 Maintain your promise to your servant,
because truly I fear you.
39 Remove my reproach because I revere you,
since your ordinances are good.
40 Mark how I long for your precepts;
in your justice give me life.

WAW

41 Let your kindness come to me, Yahweh,
your salvation according to your promise.
42 I shall have an answer for my taunter,
for I trust in your word.
43 So do not remove the true word from my mouth,
Everlasting Grand One!
Indeed I wait for your ordinances,
44 That I may keep your law,
Perpetual One, for ever and ever;
45 That I may walk at liberty,
while I seek your precepts;
46 That I may proclaim your stipulations
before kings,
And not be humiliated.
47 I shall delight myself in your commandments
which I love,
48 And I shall raise my hands
according to your commandments which I love,
And I shall meditate on your statutes.

ZAIN

49 Remember your word to your servant
upon which you made me rest my hope.
50 This is my comfort during my affliction,
that your word sustains my life.
51 The presumptuous derided me, Everlasting Grand One,
but from your law I have not strayed.
52 When I remember your ordinances of old,
truly am I comforted, Yahweh.
53 Indignation seizes me
because of the wicked who have forsaken your law.
54 Your statutes have been my defenses,
in the house of my sojourning.
55 I remember your name in the night,
Yahweh,
And during the watch your law.
56 Indignity became mine
because I observed your precepts.

ḤETH

57 My Creator, Yahweh, I promise
to observe your commandments.
58 I entreat your favor with all my heart;
have pity on me according to your promise.
59 I considered your ways,
and retraced my steps to your stipulations.
60 I hastened and did not delay
to observe your commandments.
61 Though bands of the wicked encircled me,
I did not forget your law.
62 The middle of the night,
I rise to thank you
for your just ordinances.
63 I am a companion
to all who fear you,
and to all who observe your precepts.
64 With your kindness, Yahweh,
the earth is full;
Teach me your statutes.

ṬETH

65 Do good to your servant,
Yahweh, according to your good word.
66 Teach me judgment and knowledge,
because I believe in your commandments.
67 Before I had answered I went astray,
but now I keep your word.
68 You are good and the cause of good;
teach me your statutes.
69 The presumptuous besmear me with lies,
but I—
With all my heart I observe your precepts.
70 Gross as lard is their heart,
but I—your law is my delight.
71 It was good for me that I was afflicted,
that I might learn your statutes.
72 More precious to me the law from your mouth
than thousands of shekels of gold and silver.

YODH

73 Your hands made me and fashioned me;
give me insight that I may learn your commandments.
74 Those who fear you will see me and rejoice,
because I wait for your word.
75 I know, Yahweh,
that you are just in your judgments,
and for the sake of truth you afflicted me.
76 Let your kindness be my comfort,
according to your promise to your servant.
77 Let your mercies come to me that I may live,
since your law is my delight.
78 Let the presumptuous be humiliated,
because with guile they sought to pervert me;
but I meditated on your commandments.
79 Let those who fear you turn to me,
that they may know your stipulations.
80 May my heart be blameless in your statutes,
that I may not be humiliated.

KAPH

81 My soul languishes for your salvation,
for your word I wait.
82 My eyes grow bleary watching for your word,
"When will it comfort me?"
83 For I have become like one weeping from smoke,
yet I have not forgotten your statutes.
84 How many are the days of your servant?
When will you execute judgment on my persecutors?
85 The presumptuous have dug pits for me,
who are not in conformity with your law.
86 All your commandments are truth,
but by falsehood they persecute me;
Help me!
87 They nearly exterminated me from the earth,
but I did not forsake your precepts.
88 In your kindness preserve my life,
that I may keep the stipulation of your mouth.

LAMEDH

89 Yahweh, your word is eternal,
more stable than the heavens!
90 For generation after generation
you established your truth,
more firmly than earth will it stand!
91 By your appointment they stand firm today,
because all things are your servants.
92 Had your law not been my delight,
I should have perished in my affliction.
93 Never will I forget your precepts,
for by these you have kept me alive.
94 I am yours, save me,
since I search your precepts.
95 For me the wicked lie in wait to destroy me,
but I consider your stipulations.
96 Than all the perfection I have seen, O End,
your commandment is more extensive, O Grand One!

MEM

97 Oh, how I love your law!
all day long it is my meditation.
98 Your commandment makes me wiser than my foes,
because it is ever with me.
99 I have more understanding than all my teachers,
because your stipulations are my meditation.
100 I understand more than the old,
because I observe your precepts.
101 I restrain my feet from every evil path,
in order to keep your word.
102 I do not turn aside from your ordinances,
since you yourself have taught me.
103 How tasty to my palate
your words,
How sweet to my mouth!
104 Through your precepts I acquire insight,
Most High Honest One,
I hate every false way.

NUN

105 Your words are a lamp to my feet,
and a light upon my path.
106 I have sworn and will persevere
in keeping your just ordinances.
107 I am afflicted to Calamity,
Yahweh,
Preserve my life according to your word.
108 Oblige me, Yahweh, with noble utterances of your mouth,
and teach me your ordinances.
109 My life is in your eternal hands,
so I do not forget your law.
110 The wicked have set a trap for me,
but from your precepts I do not stray.
111 I have inherited your stipulations,
O Eternal One,
Truly they are my heart's joy.
112 I incline my heart
to perform your statutes;
eternal will be my reward.

SAMEKH

113 I hate the double-minded,
but love your law.
114 You are my Protector and my Suzerain;
I await your word.
115 Depart from me, you wicked,
that I may observe the commandments of my God.
116 Support me according to your promise that I may live,
and do not make me ashamed of my hope.
117 Uphold me that I may be saved,
that I may respect your statutes, O Perpetual One.
118 Make a mound of all who stray from your precepts,
because their idolatry is false.
119 You reject as dross all the wicked of earth;
therefore I love your stipulations.
120 My body bristles out of awe of you,
and I fear your judgments.

AIN

121 Defend for me my right and my just cause,
do not leave me to my oppressors.
122 Assure your servant, O Good One,
lest the presumptuous oppress me.
123 My eyes languish for your salvation,
and for your promise of justice.
124 Deal with your servant according to your kindness,
and teach me your statutes.
125 I am your servant; give me insight,
that I may know your stipulations.
126 Time to act, O Yahweh!
they have broken your law.
127 Most High Honest One,
I love your commandments
more than gold, and more than fine gold.
128 Most High Honest One,
all your precepts I consider truly right,
I hate every false way.

PE

129 Your stipulations are wonderful,
Most High Honest One,
My soul observes them.
130 Unfold your words which illuminate,
give the innocent insight.
131 With gaping mouth I panted,
because I longed for your commandments.
132 Turn to me and have pity on me,
as you do toward those who love your name.
133 Steady my steps by your word,
and let no iniquity dominate me.
134 Redeem me from the oppression of men,
that I may keep your precepts.
135 Make your face shine upon your servant,
and teach me your statutes.
136 My eyes shed streams of tears;
Most High, they do not keep your law.

ṢADE

137 You are just, Yahweh,
and upright in your judgments.
138 You justly imposed your stipulations,
and fidelity to you, O Grand One.
139 My antagonists sought to annihilate me,
because my adversaries ignored your commandments.
140 Your word is tested,
O Grand One,
And your servant loves it.
141 Though I am young and despised,
I do not forget your precepts.
142 Your justice is just,
O Eternal One,
And your law is truth.
143 Though anguish and distress overtook me,
your commandments were my delight.
144 Into the justice of your stipulations,
O Eternal One,
Give me insight that I may live.

QOPH

145 I called with all my heart,
answer me, Yahweh,
that I may observe your statutes.
146 I called you, save me,
that I may keep your stipulations.
147 I looked toward you at dawn and cried for help,
for your words I waited.
148 Throughout the watches my eyes looked toward you,
as I meditated on your promise.
149 In your kindness hear my voice,
Yahweh,
In your justice preserve my life.
150 Pursuers of idols draw near,
from your law they have gone far.
151 But you are the Near One, Yahweh,
and all your commandments are truth.
152 O Primeval One, I acknowledge your stipulations,
because you established them from eternity.

RESH

153 See my affliction and rescue me,
for I have not forgotten your law.
154 Plead my cause and redeem me;
according to your promise, preserve my life.
155 Keep distant from the wicked your salvation,
because they do not study your statutes.
156 Your mercies are numerous, Yahweh;
according to your ordinances preserve my life.
157 Though my persecutors and adversaries are numerous,
I do not turn away from your stipulations.
158 I looked at the faithless and was disgusted,
because they did not keep your command.
159 See how I love your precepts!
in your kindness preserve my life.
160 The essence of your word is your truth,
O Eternal One,
The content of your judgment is your justice.

SHIN

161 Corrupt men persecuted me without cause,
and my heart indeed dreaded my pursuers,
162 But I rejoiced at your word
because your utterance was my great boon.
163 I hate and abhor falsehood,
but I love your law.
164 Seven times a day I praise you
for your just ordinances.
165 Great prosperity for those who love your law,
no stumbling blocks for them!
166 I hope for your salvation,
Yahweh,
And your commandments I perform.
167 My soul keeps your stipulations,
and I love them deeply.
168 I keep your precepts and stipulations,
because all my ways are before you.

TAU

169 May my cry reach your presence,
Yahweh,
According to your word, give me insight.
170 May my supplication come before you;
according to your promise, rescue me.
171 May my lips pour forth your praise,
because you have taught me your statutes.
172 May my tongue repeat your word,
because the content of your commandments is justice.
173 May your hand be ready to help me,
since I have chosen your precepts.
174 I long for your salvation,
Yahweh,
And your law is my delight.
175 Long live my soul to praise you,
and let your ordinances help me.
176 If I should stray like a lost sheep,
seek your servant,
For I have not forgotten your commandments.

Notes

cxix. This great "Psalm of the Law," the longest poem in the Psalter, is the literary composition of a psalmist whose earnest desire is to make God's law the governing principle of his conduct. He has arranged his meditations in an elaborate acrostic form (compare Pss ix–x, xxv, xxxiv, xxxvii, cxi, cxii, cxlv), adopted perhaps as an aid to memory. For each letter of the Hebrew alphabet there is a stanza of eight verses which all begin with that letter; thus there are twenty-two stanzas. One encounters a similar framework in an Akkadian "Dialogue about Human Misery," a poem sometimes called "The Babylonian Ecclesiastes"; see *Ancient Near Eastern Texts Relating to the Old Testament,* ed. J. B. Pritchard, 2d ed. (Princeton, 1955), pp. 438–40.

This artificiality of structure seems to have hindered many commentators from appreciating the variety of the contents of the psalm. Some have denied that any real connection or progress of thought is to be found in it. Thus Weiser (*The Psalms,* p. 739) writes that the formal external character of the psalm stifles its subject matter. For him this poem is a many-colored mosaic of thoughts which are often repeated in a wearisome manner. The present writer shared this evaluation until a careful analysis of the Hebrew text revealed, in verse after verse, a freshness of thought and a felicity of expression unnoticed and consequently unappreciated in earlier versions. Weiser (*The Psalms,* p. 740) appears mistaken in his conviction that "The simple form of the diction makes it unnecessary to expound the psalm in detail." The reader will recognize how frequently and how sharply the present translation differs from other editions.

The following Notes register numerous new interpretations and stylistic features, but one prosodic pattern must be mentioned as especially characteristic of this acrostic. For want of a better term, it has been labeled "the double-duty modifier" and would probably be classified in classical prosody as a type of zeugma. Cf. Édouard des Places, "Constructions grecques de mots à fonction double (APO KOINOU)," in *Revue des Études Grecques,* Tome 75, No. 354–55 (1962), 1–12. The desire to avoid homophony and the law of economy seem to be the principal factors behind the APO KOINOU construction that is witnessed in numerous Greek writers and poets beginning with Homer. This poetic arrangement has already been noticed at Ps lvii 5, but no poet employs it more frequently or more effectively than this psalmist. He suspends between two longer cola a divine name or title addressed by both the preceding and the following cola. This pattern recurs in vss. 43, 55, 62, 111, 140, 142, 144, 149, 160, 166, 169, 174.

Of all the psalms, Ps cxix benefits most from the Qumran discoveries. Of its verses, 114 are preserved wholly or partially in the Psalms Scroll labeled 11QPs[a]. Many of its significant variants will be cited and commented upon in the following NOTES. Cf. also J. A. Sanders, *The Dead Sea Psalms Scroll* (Ithaca, 1967), pp. 17–18.

Current scholarship tends to assign a late date of composition to this psalm, but the view that the psalm was composed for a ruler—even, perhaps, a Davidic king who stood in special relation to God's law (cf. Deut xvii 18 ff.; Ps xl 6–8)—does not seem improbable. Numerous poetic usages that were rarely employed in the post-Exilic period have been uncovered in the poem. These strongly favor a pre-Exilic date of composition. The period of the Deuteronomic reform (late seventh century B.C.) provides a likely background for the spirit and legal language that pervades throughout.

1. *Yahweh's law*. Here, as in Pss i and xix, *tōrāh* signifies "law" in its widest sense, including all divine revelation as the guide of life and prophetic exhortation as well as priestly direction. Compare the use of "the law" to denote the whole OT in John x 34, which quotes Ps lxxxii 6 as "your law."

2. *who observe*. Comparing the phrase *nōṣ^e^rē 'ēdōtēy* with Aramaic Sefîre (eighth century B.C.), I B:7–8, *w'dy' ['ln kl 'lhy'] yṣrn*, ["All the gods] will guard these stipulations"; cf. also J. C. Greenfield in *Acta Orientalia* 29 (1965), 9.

his stipulations. Traditionally translated "his testimonies," *'ēdōtēy* belongs rather to the terminology of covenant; cf. Ps xxv 10, *b^e^rītō w^e^'ēdōtāyw*, "his covenant stipulations"; Aramaic Sefîre *'dy*, "treaty stipulations" (Fitzmyer, *The Aramaic Inscriptions of Sefîre*, pp. 24–25); Albright, YGC, pp. 92–93; H. Cazelles, ETL 44 (1968), 63.

The present 8:7 syllable count can be brought into perfect equilibrium if consonantal *'dtyw* is broken down into *'ēdōtēy*, with the third-person suffix *-y*, and the final *w* attached to the next phrase as the conjunction "and." Other instances of like analysis are cited at Pss cv 6, 18 and cvi 12–13.

and with all their heart. See the preceding NOTE for "and." Since *lēb* signifies a member of the body, it need not be supplied with a suffix, as frequently noted in *Psalms II* (Index of Subjects, s.v.), and more recently by M. C. Astour in JNES 27 (1968), 26, n. 78. Contrast KJ, "with the whole heart," and see below on vs. 58.

4. *who commanded*. KJ renders "Thou hast commanded *us*," inserting *us* as the first object of transitive *ṣiwwītāh*. The verse becomes syntactically explicable when read as a run-on line, that is, as an instance of enjambment; see the next NOTE.

your precepts to be diligently observed. In the infinitival phrase *piqqūdekā lišmōr* (which is the direct object of the verb *ṣiwwītāh*), *piqqūdekā*, "your precepts," parses as the direct object of the construct infinitive *lišmōr*. In this unusual piece of syntax we have the object preceding the infinitive expressing the idea of obligation (GK, § 114l), but this usage is not as uncommon as previously thought. See the same construction in vs. 9, and cf. Ps viii 3; Isa xxiii 9, xlix 6b; C. Brockelmann, *Grundriss* (Berlin, 1908), II, pp. 438–39, n. 1, and J. Carmignac, "L'infinitif placé après son object," in *Revue de Qumrân* 5 (1966), 503–20. Thus the objection to my rendering of Ps viii 3 raised by J. A. Soggin, *Biblica* 47 (1966), 422, can no longer be upheld. Soggin claims that the infinitive should precede its object; this may be generally true in prose, but hardly in poetry, as shown by Carmignac.

5. *Oh that.* Heb. *'aḥᵃlay,* occurring only twice in the Bible, probably finds its counterpart in Ugar. *aḥl,* as pointed out by U. Cassuto; cf. UT, Glossary, No. 127.

7. *for your upright heart.* Usually rendered "with uprightness of heart," a version savoring of self-righteousness on the part of the psalmist, the phrase *bᵉyōšer lēbāb* shares the suffix of second-colon "your just ordinances." Thus the uprightness in question is an attribute of God, not of the psalmist; consult the first NOTE on Ps liv 8.

8. *Everlasting Grand One.* At a loss to explain *'ad-mᵉ'ōd,* critics often transpose it after *'ešmōr,* "I will observe." Consonantal *'d m'd,* coming at the end of the first stanza (notice *yhwh* at end of first verse), can be upheld if distinguished from adverbial *'ad mᵉōd,* "exceedingly," and repointed *'ad mā'ēd,* a composite divine title whose second component is documented at Ps cix 30. Lending conviction to this analysis is the inclusion which emerges. The final phrase of the first strophe, *'ad mā'ēd* creates an elegant inclusion with *yhwh* in the first line of this strophe, a phenomenon repeated in the *lamedh* strophe (vss. 89–96).

Its first element *'ad,* "everlasting, perpetual," would thus be categorized with such titles as *'ōlām,* "Eternal One." On the possible Ugaritic correspondent in such composite titles as *'d w šr, 'd mlk, 'd ršp,* see M. C. Astour in JAOS 86 (1966), 282. This composite title of Yahweh is probably verified in vss. 43 and 51, where it has proved equally troublesome to ancient and modern versions. Thus the prayer, "do not forsake me, Everlasting Grand One!" is identical in form to Ps xxxviii 22, "Do not forsake me, O Yahweh!"

9. *keep himself pure.* Retaining MT piel *yᵉzakkeh* but repointing *'et* to *'ōtō,* "himself." The second NOTE on Ps cii 23 lists other instances of confusion between *'et* and *'ōtō.* This reading solves the syntactic problem of identifying the direct object of transitive *yᵉzakkeh,* often emended to qal *yizkeh,* as well as the stichometric difficulty (Briggs, for example, deletes *na'ar,* "young man") by placing four words in each colon with a 9:9 syllable count. The new analysis of vs. 2 results in an 8:8 line, a further confirmation of syllable counting as a text-critical criterion.

By guarding his path. In the phrase *'orḥō lišmōr* we have another (see vs. 4) instance of an infinitive construct placed after its object.

11. *Within my heart I treasure.* With *bᵉlibbī ṣāpantī* comparing Job xxiii 12, *miṣwōt* (MT *miṣwat*) *śᵉpātāyw wᵉlō' 'ᵃmīšēm* (MT *'āmīš m-*)

ḥēqī (MT *ḥuqqī*) *ṣāpantī 'imrē pīū,* "The commandments from his lips—I have certainly not veered from them; in my bosom I have treasured the words from his mouth." For the nuance "treasure" in *ṣāpantī* (KJ, "I hid"), see the fourth NOTE on Ps xvii 14.

12. *May you be blessed.* Interpreting *bārūk 'attāh* as precative mode (the fourth NOTE on Ps cxi 10) with RSV, rather than the indicative mode of KJ, "Blessed *art* thou." This mode better comports with second-colon imperative mode "teach me," which is sometimes emended to indicative *kī tᵉlammᵉdēnī,* "because you teach me."

13. *With my lips I proclaim.* The phrase *biśᵉpātay sippartī* juxtaposes two roots collocated in UT, 77:45–47, *bpy sprhn bšpty mnthn,* "In my mouth is their number, on my lips their count."

my lips . . . your mouth. The frequent Ugaritic-Hebrew parallelism between these two words (cf. second NOTE on Ps lix 8) and the contrast obviously intended by the psalmist, who forms an inclusion with them, argue against the emendation of *pīkā,* "your mouth," to *ṣidqekā,* "your justice," a reading found in six manuscripts and in the Syriac version.

14. *I rejoice in you.* Reading *śaśtīkā* (MT *śaśtī kᵉ*), and parsing the suffix as datival, expressing the cause of joy. As noted at Ps lxxvii 14, the Masoretes were unversed in the dative function of suffixes. Cf. Jer xx 15, *śᵉmaḥ śimḥēhū* (MT *śammēᵃḥ śimmāḥāhū*), "Rejoice, rejoice over him!" where the suffix is datival, expressing the source of joy; cf. M. Dahood, "Ugaritic and the Old Testament," in ETL 44 (1968), 35–54, especially 39 for further details on Jer xx 15. In UT, 125:6, *tbkyk,* "They weep for you," the poet uses the dative suffix *-k* to state the cause of grief. Another instance of dative suffix recurs in vs. 41.

more than. There is now no need to emend consonantal *k'l* to *mē'al,* once initial *k-* has been attached to the preceding word as dative suffix.

15. *On your precepts . . . upon your paths.* This word order has been adopted to reflect the excellent chiasmus of the Hebrew.

16. *In your statutes . . . your words.* Another instance of chiasmus. Parallelism with plural "your statutes" suggests that consonantal *dbrk* is defective spelling for plural "your words," an inference sustained by 11QPsᵃ *dbrykh,* by many manuscripts, and by LXX, Syr., and *Juxta Hebraeos.*

your statutes. The widely accepted emendation of MT *ḥuqqōtekā* to *tōrātᵉkā,* "your law," is checkmated by 11QPsᵃ *ḥwqykh,* which, though masculine as against MT feminine, still means "your statutes."

17. *Requite.* Namely, to make repayment of return for service. The close semantic relationship between the roots *gml,* "to requite," and *gmr,* "to avenge," stressed in my article, "The Root GMR in the Psalms," TS 14 (1953), 595–97, is further evidenced by 11QPsᵃ which reads *gmwr,* "Avenge!" instead of MT *gᵉmōl,* "Requite!"

18. *the wonders of your law.* Usually rendered "wondrous things out of thy law" (KJ), MT *niplā'ōt mittōrāteka* should preferably be read *niplᵉ'ōt-m tōrāteka,* with an enclitic *mem* in a construct chain. Compare Isa lviii 12,

ḥōr^{e}bōt ʿōlām, "ancient ruins," with Ezek xxvi 20, *ḥōr^{e}bōt-m* (with enclitic *mem*) *ʿōlām,* where MT reads *ḥ^{o}rābōt mēʿōlām,* "ruins from antiquity."

20. *truly longs.* Commonly understood as "for the longing," MT *l^{e}taʾ^{a}bāh* can also be analyzed into emphatic *lamedh* plus the third-person feminine singular verb *taʾ^{a}bāh* from *tāʾab,* "to long for, crave." Both LXX and Vulg. understood a verb here; what is more, the putative noun *taʾ^{a}bāh* is a hapax legomenon, whereas the verb *tāʾab* has good credentials, recurring in vss. 40 and 174. The two verbs of the first colon, *gār^{e}sāh* and *tāʾ^{a}bāh,* are thus balanced in the second colon by two prepositional phrases *ʾel mišpāṭekā,* "for your ordinances," and *b^{e}kol ʿēt,* "at all times." The verse reads, like vs. 18, as a run-on line (enjambment).

21. *Rebuke.* Recognizing the precative mode in *gāʿartā,* exactly as in Ps ix 6, *gāʿartā gōyīm,* "Rebuke the nations!" This is further indicated by imperative *gal,* "Strip," in the next verse.

the accursed presumptuous. Proposals to shift the MT *athnach* so that *ʾ^{a}rūrīm,* "accursed," would modify *haššōgīm,* "those who have strayed," disarrange the present 8:8 syllable count; see the second NOTE on vs. 22 below.

22. *Strip me.* MT piel imperative *gal* from *gālāh,* "to uncover," has often been repointed, on the basis of Josh v 9, to *gōl,* from *gālal,* "to roll away." This repunctuation finds new support in 11QPs[a] *gwl;* cf. HALAT, p. 186a. The recognition, however, that the underlying metaphor may be that of reproach and scorn pictured as garments, a metaphor witnessed in Ugaritic as observed in the NOTE on Ps cix 18, permits the retention of MT *gal.* Cf. Ps lxxviii 66, *ḥerpat ʿōlām nātan lāmō,* "he covered them with everlasting shame," and NOTE thereto.

and scorn. The note in the critical apparatus of BH^3 recommending the deletion of *wābūz,* with the Syriac, overlooks the 8:8 syllable count (see preceding NOTE) and would convert the line into 6:8. The second NOTE on Ps cxiii 8 comments upon the Syriac version's limitations regarding Hebrew metrics.

23. *corrupt men.* The inability of commentators to explain convincingly why *śārīm,* traditionally rendered "princes," should malign the psalmist, and the Syriac understanding of *śārīm* as "evil men" suggest that *śārīm* is a homonym of "princes" that denotes "corrupt men." The name of the Ugaritic maleficent deity *mt wšr,* "Death and Corruption" (cf. UT, Glossary, No. 2479; CML, p. 148s) contains the root (Ar. *šarra,* "to be evil") which may underlie MT *śārīm;* see below on vs. 161. In fact, biblical *yāš^{e}bū śārīm,* "corrupt men sit," sounds strikingly like UT, 52:8, *mt wšr yṯb,* "Death and Corruption sits enthroned."

to gossip. For this nuance of *nidbārū,* see the second NOTE on Ps lvi 5. Again the syllable count is perfectly balanced at 10:10.

24. *men of my council.* Hebrew for "my counselors."

25. *My neck cleaves.* Comparing the similar description in Ps xliv 26, "For our neck is bowed down to the dust, / our belly cleaves to the

ground." RSV follows KJ when translating *napšī* as "my soul," a version made dubious by the context and by Ugar. *npš,* "throat, neck."

26. *your ways.* MT read first person *dᵉrākay,* "my ways," but the apparent inclusion with final *ḥuqqekā,* "your statutes," favors LXX "your ways." Nor is it required to alter consonantal *drky;* it may vocalized as construct *darkēy* dependent upon the suffix of its opposite number *ḥuqqekā.* The same phenomenon, which may be classified with the double-duty suffixes in a construct chain (cf. first NOTE on Ps lxxxix 2), recurs in vss. 59 and 109.

28. *My frame.* As in vs. 25, *napšī* has a physical sense. There it is translated "my neck," but here this definition might be too detailed. The underlying metaphor asks a meaning such as "my frame" or "my person," the latter an especially well-documented usage.

sags. Heb. *dālᵉpāh* has been translated in many ways (RSV reads "My soul melts away for sorrow"; CCD "My soul weeps for sorrow"), but I follow a suggestion of William L. Moran, "A Note on Ps 119:28," in CBQ 15 (1953), 10, who relates *dālᵉpāh* to Ugar. *dlp* in UT, 68:17–18, *ym lymk ltnǵṣn pnth lydlp tmnh,* "Sea did not sink, his corners did not vibrate, his frame did not sag." Moran's suggestion has been adopted by J. C. Greenfield, HUCA 29 (1958), 208–9, who cites the Midrash that made the same point concerning the parallelism of the verbs. In *Biblica* 33 (1952), 212, and 46 (1965), 311–12, the present writer interpreted the Ugaritic terms and metaphor in the light of Eccles x 18 which displays in parallelism *mkk//dlp,* two of the verbs found in the Ugaritic sequence *mkk//ngṣ//dlp: bᵉʿaṣlūtī-m yimmak hammᵉqāreh ūbᵉšiplūt yādayim yidlōp habbāyit,* "When there is laziness, the rafters sink; when hands are slack, the house sags." This text reveals that in all three passages the underlying metaphor is that of a building. Second-colon *qayyᵉmēnī,* "raise me," and the well-established assumption that biblical poets employed metaphors congruently (fourth NOTE on Ps li 9, second NOTE on Ps cix 14) sustain this interpretation. The metaphor likening the body to a building passes over into NT imagery; e.g., Eph iv 12, "for the building up [*oikodomēn*] of the body of Christ."

This translation and exegesis, it may be observed, point up the danger of defining Ugaritic and Hebrew words on the basis of the nuance borne by the corresponding term in Akkadian. Thus E. A. Speiser, JCS 5 (1951), 66, on the basis of Akk. *dalāpu* ascribes to Ugar. *dlp* the Akkadian meaning "to be disquieted, agitated," and A. Haldar, BO 21 (1964), 275, lists Ugar. *dlp* as one of the pure Akkadian loanwords in Ugaritic, a conclusion upset by Hebrew usage in Eccles x 18 and Ps cxix 28.

raise me. Whom sorrow has made like a sagging roof. In Isa xliv 26 and lxi 4, polel forms of *qūm* (here piel *qayyᵉmēnī*) signify "to raise, repair" dilapidated buildings.

30. *I consider supreme.* Deriving *šiwwītī,* often emended with the Syriac to *'iwwītī,* "I desire," from the root discussed at Ps lxxxix 20, and

assigning the piel form to the "piel of consideration"; see the first NOTE on Ps cxvi 15 and below on vs. 128, *yiššārtī*, "I consider right."

33. *Teach me*. Gunkel (*Die Psalmen*, p. 520) is surely correct when scanning this line as a 2+2+2 tricolon, and not as a 3+3 bicolon with RSV and other versions. Which is to say that a 5:5:7 syllable count is preferable to a 10:7 bicolon.

reward. Parsing *'ēqeb* as the second (predicate) accusative with *'eṣṣ^e^rennāh*, "I will guard it." Contrast RSV, "I will keep it to the end." Heb. *'ēqeb*, "reward," which recurs in vs. 112, Ps xix 12, and Prov xxii 4, equals Phoen. *'qb*.

34. *Give me insight that I may observe*. The syntax of *h^a^bīnēnī w^e^'eṣṣ^e^rāh*, an imperative followed a verb in the subjunctive mode, recalls EA, 123:25–27, *uššira 3 awīli u ibluṭa u inaṣṣira ala šarri*, "Send three men that I may live and guard the city for the king."

with all my heart. As in vs. 2, *b^e^kol lēb* requires no pronominal suffix, being the name of a part of the body. KJ here translates *b^e^kol lēb* "with *my* whole heart," but did not supply the apposite suffix at vs. 2, "with the whole heart."

37. *idols*. The third NOTE on Ps xxiv 4 and *Biblica* 46 (1965), 78, substantiate this meaning of *šāw'*; Ps ci 3 expresses a similar idea.

by your power. The newest Hebrew lexicon, HALAT, concedes (p. 222a) that in a number of passages *derek* may well bear the Ugaritic denotation "power, dominion," and in the very next line ill-advisedly recommends the emendation of *d^e^rākekā* in our verse to *d^e^bārekā*, "your word." But the prayer "by your power give me life" asks no emendation, especially since it conforms to the pattern of vs. 40, "in your justice give me life." In other words, the poet appeals to a divine attribute for a fuller life. Consult *Biblica* 49 (1968), and PNWSP, p. 40, n. 2.

38. *because*. Interpreting *'^a^šer* as a causal conjunction (BDB, p. 83b; HALAT, p. 95b) rather than as the relative pronoun "which." Ditto for the next verse. The Ugaritic relative pronoun *d*, "who," displays the same semantic range in UT, 1 Aqht:157–59, *ylk mrrt tǵll bnr d'lk mḫṣ aqht ǵzr*, "Woe to you . . . because near (*d'lk*) you Aqhat the lad was struck down."

truly I fear you. The awareness that the psalmist occasionally used defective spelling (for example, vss. 14, 16–17, 43) prompts an analysis of consonantal *lyr'tk* (MT *l^e^yir'ātekā*) differing from that proposed in the third NOTE on Ps v 8. Vocalized *lirē'tīkā* and parsed as the emphatic *lamedh* (cf. vs. 128) followed by the verb, this clause becomes synonymous with vs. 39, *'^a^šer yāgōrtī*, "because I revere you," and states the reason why God should honor his promise to his servant.

39. *because*. As in preceding verse, *'^a^šer* is a causal conjunction, an inference sustained by the parallelism with *kī*, "since."

I revere you. With *yāgōrtī* sharing the suffix of *mišpāṭekā*, "your ordinances." Failure to appreciate this poetic usage leads RSV into a highly dubious rendition, "Turn away the reproach (MT has "my reproach") which I dread." In the new translation the psalmist repeats in substance the petition of vs. 22, "Strip me of reproach and scorn, for I observe your stipulations."

41. *your kindness.* Parallelism with singular "your salvation" supports the singular vocalization *ḥasdekā* against MT plural *ḥ*ᵃ*sādekā.*

come to me. Consonantal *yb'ny* may be repointed to singular *y*ᵉ*bō'ēnī,* as in LXX, or MT plural explained as serving both "kindness" and "salvation."

In either case, the suffix is dative, precisely as in Pss xliv 18, cix 17, and probably in UT 76:II:21, *qrn dbatk btlt 'nt,* "Meet me that I may come to you, O Virgin Anath," as analyzed by several scholars, most recently by Kjell Aartun in *Die Welt des Orients* 4 (1968), 289.

43. *Everlasting Grand One.* Frequently deleted (most recently by BHS) on the basis of the Syriac, where it is missing, *'d m'd* (present in 11QPsᵃ) finds a *raison d'être* if repointed *'ad mā'ēd,* as proposed at vs. 8. Metrically, the three-syllable composite title is suspended between two longer cola as a double-duty modifier in a tricolon with a 10:3:9 syllable count; see introductory NOTE.

Indeed. Taking *kī* as emphatic rather than causal, in order to explain the subjunctive verbs in vss. 44–46.

your ordinances. Pointing consonantal *mšpṭk* as plural *mišpāṭekā* (MT singular), another instance of *scriptio defectiva.* 11QPsᵃ reads plural *dbrykh,* "your words."

44. *That I may keep.* Parsing *'ešm*ᵉ*rāh* as a subjunctive or volitive form with the *-āh* ending. Contrast RSV, "I will keep." Ditto for the verbs in vss. 45–46.

Perpetual One. Interpreting *tāmīd* as a divine title synonymous with vs. 43. *'ad mā'ēd,* "Everlasting Grand One." Understood adverbially—"continually" (RSV)—*tāmīd* merely repeats what is expressed by *l*ᵉ*'ōlām wā'ed,* "for ever and ever." This tautology was felt by 11QPsᵃ, which reads *tmyd w'd,* omitting *l'wlm* altogether. This divine epithet probably recurs in vs. 117.

46. *And not be humiliated.* Briggs, CECBP, II, p. 438, maintains that the measure requires that *lō'* be united with *'ēbōš* in one tone; he concludes that *w* is a gloss. But 11QPsᵃ likewise reads *wlw' 'bwš,* so we must come to terms with the present text which can be scanned as a 2+2+2 tricolon, especially when the *w* of *w*ᵉ*lō'* is parsed as emphatic assuring *w*ᵉ*lō'* of a full accent.

48. *which I love.* 11QPsᵃ confutes the proposal to delete *'*ᵃ*šer 'āhabtī* as dittographic of the same phrase in vs. 47.

49. *your word.* Suffixless *dābār* shares the suffix of immediately following *l*ᵉ*'abdekā,* "to your servant." The present 8:7 syllable count would have become 10:7 had the poet employed the suffix which is, however, witnessed by 11QPsᵃ plural *dbrykh,* "your words."

51. *Everlasting Grand One.* Again missing in the Syriac (see vs. 43),

'ad-mā'ēd (MT *m^{e}'ōd*) proves its authenticity by contributing to both sense and measure; with its three syllables the verse numbers 9:9.

52. *truly am I comforted.* Explaining the *wā* of *wā'etneḥām* as emphatic with the consequent postposition of the verb; consult second NOTE on Ps li 9 and below on vs. 90.

54. *my defenses.* For this meaning of *z^{e}mīrōt,* which could also denote "my songs," see second NOTE on Ps cxviii 14.

in the house of my sojourning. During the earthly existence of the psalmist; cf. vs. 19.

55. *Yahweh.* Scanning vocative *yahweh* as a double-duty modifier, suspended between the longer cola to form a 9:2:8 syllabic pattern; see the introductory NOTE.

And during the watch. Repointing with Ehrlich (*Die Psalmen,* p. 308) to *w^{e}ašmūrāh* (MT *wā'ešm^{e}rāh,* "and I keep"), and comparing Ps xc 4, *w^{e}'ašmūrāh ballaylāh,* "like a watch in the night." This phrase discloses that the present psalmist, when placing *laylāh* in the first colon and *'ašmūrāh* in the second, employed the poetic device called the breakup of composite phrases. In fact, the association here is so close that *'ašmūrāh* (which recurs in vs. 178) shares the preposition of *ballaylah,* "at night." The same phenomena, namely the breakup of a composite phrase and the use of a double-duty preposition, are noticed at Ps cv 18.

56. *Indignity.* The NOTE on Ps vii 7 documents this denotation of *zō't,* which RSV translates "this blessing," though on what basis we are not told. That observance of God's law invites derision is the gravamen of vss. 22–23, 51, 69.

57. *My Creator, Yahweh.* MT *ḥelqī yhwh,* "My portion, Yahweh," or "My portion is Yahweh," does not adequately accord with the thought of the rest of the verse, "I promise to observe your commandments." This lack of a tight semantic connection can be felt, say, in RSV, "The Lord is my portion; I promise to keep thy words." In this version there is even the lack of personal accord, the first colon speaking of Yahweh in the third person, and the second colon directly addressing him in the second person. Both problems can be resolved, it would seem, by repointing to *ḥōl^{e}qī,* "My Creator," and parsing *yhwh* as the vocative standing in apposition with *ḥōl^{e}qī,* "My Creator." The close semantic bond between the parts of the verse comes to light. Since the psalmist recognizes Yahweh as his Creator, he promises to observe his commands.

Lexicographers admit that *ḥlq,* "to create," Ar. *ḫalaqa,* occurs in Ecclus xxxi 13 and xxxviii 1. It remains to point out this root in Jer x 16 (=li 19), *lō' k^{e}'ēlleh ḥōlēq* (MT *ḥēleq*) *ya'^{a}qōb kī yōṣēr hakkōl hū',* "Not like these is the Creator of Jacob, because the Fashioner of All is he." The parallelism between *ḥōlēq ya'^{a}qōb* and *yōṣēr hakkōl* semantically equals the balance of Isa xliii 1, *bōra'^{a}kā ya'^{a}qōb w^{e}yōṣer^{e}kā yiśrā'ēl,* "your Creator, O Jacob, and your Fashioner, O Israel." Cf. also Job xxxviii 24 and Lam iii 24, *ḥōlᵉqī yhwh 'āmᵉrāh napšī 'al kēn 'ōḥīl lō*, "My Creator is Yahweh," says my soul, "therefore I will hope in him."

your commandments. Literally "your words," *dibrekā* is here, as well as in vs. 139, taken as the Ten Commandments which elsewhere are termed "the ten words."

58. *with all my heart.* Cf. the second NOTE on vs. 2.

59. *your ways.* Repointing MT *dᵉrākāy*, "my ways," to construct *darkēy*, which shares the suffix of *'ēdōtekā*, "your stipulations," as in vss. 26 and 109. LXX saw that "the ways" in question belonged to God, and RSV likewise renders, "When I think of thy ways," without any note that the text was being emended.

61. *bands of the wicked.* Ambivalent *ḥeblē rᵉšā'īm* is interpreted in line with the observations at Ps cxvi 3, *'ᵃpāpūnī ḥeblē māwet*, "The bands of Death encompassed me."

encircled me. The sense of *'iwwᵉdūnī*, a hapax legomenon in the piel of uncertain meaning, is derived from the parallel passage in Ps cxvi 3 which reads *'ᵃpāpūnī*, "encompassed me"; see preceding NOTE. This inference, happily, is sustained by Ethiopic usage.

62. *The middle of the night.* An attempt to reproduce the accusative of time construction in Heb. *ḥᵃṣōt laylāh*, that is lost in RSV, "at midnight." Cf. UT, 1019:4–5, *t'zzk alp ymm wrbt šnt*, "May (the gods) strengthen you a thousand days and ten thousand years," and 2062:A:1o, ed. 1, *wymym*, "and every day."

63. *to all who fear you.* Critics who would alter MT, omitting relative pronoun *'ᵃšer* and reading participle *yᵉrē'ekā* for MT imperfect *yᵉrē'ūkā*, must now reckon with 11QPsᵃ which supports MT fully.

65. *Do good.* Preceded by imperative *lammᵉdēnī*, "teach me," in vs. 64, and followed by the same imperative in vs. 66, the phrase *ṭōb 'āśītā* is logically interpreted not as a statement of fact, "Thou hast dealt well" (RSV), but as a prayer. Hence *'āśītā* preferably parses as a precative (see vs. 21) perfect, as in Pss ix 5, xxxix 10, and below in vs. 121.

your good word. Some critics propose deletion of *ṭūb*, "goodness," the first word of vs. 66, since the poet already has a pivot word beginning with *ṭeth;* another solution is available. With the transfer of *ṭūb* to vs. 65 and its repointing to *ṭōb*, "good," to form an inclusion with initial *ṭōb*, vs. 65 now numbers eight syllables in each colon, and the 4:2 word count becomes a more balanced 4:3. The phrase *dābār ṭōb* recurs in Ps xlv 2 and Prov xii 25, whereas MT *ṭūb ṭa'am*, "goodness of judgment," remains unwitnessed elsewhere. For another inclusion involving *ṭōb*, cf. Song of Sol i 2–3, *kī ṭōbīm dōdekā miyyāyin lᵉrēᵃḥ šamnī kī* (MT *šᵉmānekā*) *ṭōbīm*, "How much sweeter your love than wine, than the scent of oil how much sweeter!"

66. *Teach me.* Failing to recognize the precative mode of vs. 65, *'āśītā*, "Do!" Ehrlich (*Die Psalmen*, p. 309) proves to be at least consistent in

emending MT imperative *lamm^{e}dēnī* to preterit *limmadtānī,* "you have taught me."

69. *but I.* Scanning *'^{a}nī* as a double-duty modifier, with a resultant 9:2:9 syllable count (courtesy D. N. Freedman).

70. *gross as lard.* Hebraic for rebellious and arrogant; cf. second NOTE on Ps xvii 10, and Pope, AB, vol. 15, NOTE on Job xv 27.

but I. Parsing *'^{a}nī,* as *casus pendens;* consult the first NOTE on Ps ciii 15 and contrast RSV, "But I delight in thy law," which obliterates the Hebrew syntax of the clause. By juxtaposing the plural suffix of *libbām,* "their heart," and *'^{a}nī,* the psalmist evidently intended to sharpen the contrast between the two attitudes.

72. *More precious.* Generic *ṭōb,* customarily rendered here "better," assumes a more precise denotation in this context. As noted at vs. 28, the psalmists were consistent in their development of a metaphor. Cf. PNWSP, pp. 10–11, on *ṭōb* in Prov iii 27, xxxi 18, and Prov viii 11, *kī ṭōbāh ḥokmāh mipp^{e}nīnīm,* "For wisdom is more precious [RSV 'better'] than jewels" (van der Weiden, *Le Livre des Proverbes,* ad loc.).

thousands of shekels. The psalmist merely writes "thousands of gold and silver," omitting to mention the unit of weight. In this he adopts a usage of Ugaritic scribes who sometimes omitted mention of the unit of measure as well as of the product measured or weighed. Thus in UT, 1082:18, 21, *ṯlṯ,* "three," means "three jars of oil." See UT, § 7.5, and 51:I:27–28, *yṣq ksp lalpm,* "He smelted silver by thousands (of shekels)," and the study by S. E. Loewenstamm, "The Numerals in Ugaritic," in *Proceedings of the International Conference on Semitic Studies, Jerusalem 1965,* p. 8.

74. *who fear you will see me.* Heb. *y^{e}rē'ekā yir'ūnī* being one of the more common puns, as pointed out at Ps cxii 8.

75. *you are just.* Repointing to *ṣaddīq* (MT *ṣedeq*) and comparing *ṣaddīq mišpāṭekā* (accusative of specification) with vs. 137, *yāšār mišpāṭekā,* "upright in your judgments."

and for the sake of truth. Heb. *we'^{e}mūnāh* is taken as an adverbial accusative explaining the reason why God afflicted the psalmist.

77. *come to me.* The suffix of *y^{e}bō'ūnī* being datival, as in vs. 41.

79. *that they may know.* Adopting the Ketiv reading *w^{e}yēd^{e}'ū* as against the participial form *w^{e}yōd^{e}'ē* of the Qere. Cognizant of his own rich knowledge of the Law, the psalmist is eager to share it with his coreligionists.

82. *watching.* MT *lē'mōr,* lacking in the Syriac and Sahidic versions, stems otiose when understood as "saying." But when assigned the meaning of Ugar. *amr,* "to see, watch," documented in the first NOTE on Ps cv 28, it explains how the psalmist's eyes grew bleary. Cf. Ps lxix 4. In the phrase *l^{e}imrāt^{e}kā lē'mōr,* "watching for your word," we recognize the same root bearing two different nuances, and observe that the resultant

11:7 syllable count nicely balances its companion vs. 81 which numbers 11:8 syllables.

will it comfort me. Or, "will you comfort me," since *tᵉnaḥᵃmēnī* can be parsed either as third-person feminine singular or as second-person masculine singular.

83. *one weeping from smoke.* In the long history of psalms interpretation no commentator has proposed an acceptable explanation of the quaint simile "like a bottle in smoke" (KJ), or "like a wineskin in smoke" (RSV). Hence I take consonantal *n'd* (MT *nō'd*) as a participle from *nūd*, "to grieve, weep," with secondary *aleph.*

At least by the first century B.C. the *aleph* was introduced into the orthography as a vowel letter for long *a* in the medial position; on the use of *aleph* as a vowel letter in the Genesis Apocryphon of Qumran, see D. N. Freedman and A. Ritterspach, *Revue de Qumrân* 6 (1967), 293–300.

For the imagery, cf. Prov x 26, "As vinegar to the teeth, smoke to the eyes, so the sluggard to those who send him." In the preceding verse, it might be noted, the psalmist describes his eyes growing weak from watching for a word from God.

85. *pits.* MT *šīḥōt,* with long *i* in the first syllable, should be upheld against 11QPsᵃ *šḥt* (=*šaḥat*), just as the questioned validity of MT Ps cxxvi 1, *šībāt* has been vouched for by Aramaic Sefîre *šybt,* "restored fortunes."

87. *from the earth.* The long-standing emendation of *bā'āreṣ* to *mē'āreṣ* is sustained by 11QPsᵃ *m'rṣ,* but both the emendation and the Qumranic lection are confuted by the growing documentation of *bā,* "from." Gunkel (*Die Psalmen,* p. 527) notes that *bā'āreṣ* does not well fit the context, and that one expects, in view of Pss xxi 11, xxxiv 17, lii 7, cix 15, *mē'āreṣ,* "from the earth." MT *bā'āreṣ* remains the more difficult reading and still to be maintained. What 11QPsᵃ proves is that *b,* "from," was no longer understood in the first century B.C. For further bibliography on *b,* "from," see third NOTE on Ps lxxviii 26 and Index of Hebrew Words in *Psalms II;* Soggin, BibOr 9 (1967), 87–88; Dahood in ETL 44 (1968), 47, and consult THE GRAMMAR OF THE PSALTER.

89. *eternal.* On the ambiguity of *lᵉʿōlām,* "to/from eternity," consult the third NOTE on Ps cxvii 2.

more stable than the heavens. The frequently adopted emendation of *baššāmāyim* to *kaššāmāyim,* "[stable] like the heavens," becomes needless with the recognition of the comparative meaning of *ba,* "than," documented at Ps lxxxix 3, a passage voicing a sentiment similar to that of our verse. Cf. also HALAT, p. 100, and Matt xxiv 35, "Heaven and earth will pass away; my words will never pass away."

90. *more firmly than earth will it stand!* The phrase *'ereṣ wattaʿᵃmōd* may be considered synonymous with vs. 89, *niṣṣāb baššāmāyim,* "more stable than the heavens," so that *'ereṣ* shares comparative *ba-* of its opposite number *šāmāyim,* "heavens," and the *wa-* of *wattaʿᵃmōd* parses as

the emphatic *waw* with the postposition of the verb; cf. the NOTE on vs. 52. For the nuance of *ta'ᵃmōd,* see Ps xxx 8, "By your favor you made me more stable than the mighty mountains," and for double-duty prepositions consult the second NOTE on vs. 55.

91. *they stand firm.* The subject of plural *'āmᵉdū* being vs. 89 "your word" and "your truth" in vs. 90. For *'āmad,* "to stand firm," see the first NOTE on Ps xxx 8.

94. *your precepts.* The proposed substitution of *piqqūdekā* by *ḥuqqekā,* "your statutes," since the former already occurs in vs. 93, is opposed both by the present 8:8 syllable count (it would become 8:7 with the alteration) and by 11QPsᵃ *pqwdykh.* Cf. vss. 117–118, where *ḥuqqekā,* "your statutes," occurs twice in successive verses.

96. *Than all the perfection.* This radical departure from traditional "I have seen an end of all perfection" (KJ) recognizes, first, in *lᵉkol,* not the particle introducing the accusative object, but the comparative *lamedh,* discussed in the second NOTE on Ps xxx 8, and more recently by R. Meyer in *Orientalistische Literaturzeitung* 62 (1967), col. 371. In vs. 89, the psalmist employs the *beth* of comparison.

I have seen. A relative clause not introduced by *'ᵃšer,* "which," as in vs. 130; cf. *Psalms II,* Index of Subjects, s.v.

O End. MT *qēṣ* can be saved from the deletion decreed by BH³ if taken as a divine epithet, hitherto unattested elsewhere though enjoying an instructive analogy in *'aḥᵃrōn,* "the Last," a divine title in Isa xli 4, xliv 6, xlviii 12; Job xix 25. The deletion of *qēṣ* proposed by BH³ is further challenged by 11QPsᵃ which reads *qṣ.*

O Grand One! Repointing MT *mᵉ'ōd,* "much," to *mā'ēd,* the divine title discussed at Ps cix 30 and above at vs. 8. Just as vs. 8, *'ad mā'ēd,* "Everlasting Grand One," closing the first stanza, forms an inclusion with vs. 1, *yahweh,* so here *mā'ēd,* "O Grand One," the final word of the stanza, sets up an inclusion with *yahweh* in the first line (vs. 89) of this stanza.

98. *Your commandment.* The seeming numerical inconsistency between apparently plural *miṣwōtekā,* "your commandments," and second-colon singular *hī',* "it," can be eliminated by parsing *miṣwōtekā* as a Phoenician feminine singular ending in *ōt.*

The sentiment expressed in this verse may be compared with UT, 51: IV:41–42, *tḥmk il ḥkm ḥkmt 'm 'lm,* "Your message, El, is wise; your wisdom is eternal sagacity."

103. *your words.* MT singular *'imrātekā,* "your word," read as plural *'mrtyk* by some manuscripts and ancient versions, looks like another instance of defective spelling. Here we may read, with no consonantal changes, plural *'imrōtekā,* "your words."

How sweet. Vocalizing consonantal *mdbš* (MT *middᵉbaš,* "than honey") *ma-dābᵉšū,* the counterpart to *mah-nimlᵉṣū,* "How tasty." This postulated denominative verb would thus manifest the same semantic development from Akk. *dišpu,* "honey," to *dašāpu,* "to be sweet."

104. *Most High Honest One.* Usually understood as the conjunction "therefore," *'al kēn* can also be interpreted as a composite divine name, whose first component, *'al,* "Most High," is documented at Ps lv 23, while *kēn,* "Honest One," explains further why the psalmist repudiates "every false way." Metrically, *'al kēn* is a double-duty vocative, belonging to both longer cola in an 8:2:8 pattern that recurs in vss. 149 and 177. While "therefore" yields good sense in our verse, it does not in vs. 127, where *'al kēn* is often emended. Cf. also vss. 128–129, Ps cx 7, and Job vi 3, xxxiv 27, xlii 6.

107. *Calamity.* This name of the nether world, *mā'ēd* (MT *me'ōd*), is studied in the sixth NOTE on Ps cxvi 10.

Yahweh. Scanning the line as a 7:2:8 tricolon, with vocative *yahweh* in the middle.

108. *Oblige me.* The poet gains stylistic variety when balancing emphatic imperative *reṣēh-nā'* with second-colon *lammedēnī,* "teach me." The psalmist apparently meant energic *-nā'* (missing in 11QPs[a], which seems not to have appreciated its function) to match the suffix of *lammedēnī.*

noble utterances of your mouth. Being hapax legomenon, the diction *nedābōt pī,* customarily rendered "my offerings of praise" (RSV), must be evaluated on a contextual basis. It seems to be the opposite number of second-colon *mišpāṭekā,* "your ordinances," and thus ascribable to Yahweh, not the psalmist. Which is to say that it shares the suffix of the latter, much like Ps liv 8, "For your nobility [*binedābāh*] I will sacrifice to you." With *nedābōt,* "noble utterances," might be compared Prov viii 6, *negīdīm,* probably "princely sayings."

109. *your eternal hands.* Vocalizing dual *kappē* (MT *kappī,* "my hand"), and explaining the syntax of *kappē tāmīd* according to the principle enunciated in the NOTE on vs. 26. The LXX saw that the hands were the hands of God. Cf. Ps xxxi 6, "Into your hand I entrust my life."

111. *O Eternal One.* Traditionally rendered as the prepositional phrase "for ever, to eternity," *le'ōlām* preferably parses as vocative *lamedh* followed by the divine epithet *'ōlām,* "Eternal One." This analysis uncovers the "pivot" pattern of the verse, which now scans into 7:3:7 syllables. See below on vss. 142 and 144.

Truly. Recognizing in *kī* the emphatic particle; RSV agrees, but 11QPs[a] simply omits it, apparently unaware of its asseverative function.

112. *eternal will be my reward.* MT *le'ōlām 'ēqeb* makes the accent fall on two successive syllables. In view of the numerous cases of *scriptio defectiva* in this psalm, one may be permitted to vocalize consonantal *'qb* as *'iqbī,* "my reward," thus avoiding two beats on successive syllables. This meaning of *'iqbī,* also found in vs. 33, is adopted by a number of scholars and receives negative support from such versions as RSV, "for ever, to the end," a very unlikely reproduction of *le'ōlām 'ēqeb.* The

NOTES on Pss xvi 10, lxxiii 24, ciii 5–6 discuss the concept of eternal reward; cf. also Ps xix 12. This exegesis clashes with the opinion of Sheldon Blank in *To Do and to Teach,* p. 1, that "The idea of reward after death does not belong in the book of Psalms."

114. *my Protector and my Suzerain.* MT *sitrī ūmāginnī,* "my hiding place and my shield" (RSV), oddly comports with second-colon "I rely on your word." Congruency of metaphor suggests, nay, requires that consonantal *mgny* be pointed *m^e^gānī,* "my Suzerain," a term discussed at Ps iii 4. Thus the composite title accords with Ps cxv 9, "Helper and Suzerain."

115. *you wicked.* After the three introductory verses this is the only line in which God is not addressed; see the first NOTE on vs. 128.

that I may observe. Seeing the subjunctive mode in the ending of *w^e^'eṣṣ^e^rāh.*

117. *Perpetual One.* Identifying *tāmīd* as one of Yahweh's titles; see the second NOTE on vs. 44.

118. *Make a mound.* Disputed *sālītā* may be derived from *sālāh,* a by-form of *sālal,* "to cast up a highroad, to make a mound"; another instance of this verb is registered at Ps xlvi 4. The imperative mode of the preceding two verses strongly suggests that *sālītā* was intended as precative, that is, as a prayer. For the imagery, cf. Ps cx 6, "He routed nations; he heaped corpses high."

who stray. Those Israelites who give up Yahwism for polytheism.

their idolatry. The third NOTE on Ps v 7 cites evidence for this nuance of *tarmītām;* the psalmist presumably intended more than the *idem per idem* assertion of KJ, "for their deceit is falsehood."

119. *You reject.* Though the reading *ḥšbt,* "you consider," of some manuscripts and ancient versions is now partially supported by 11QPs[a], *ḥšbty,* "I consider," consonantal *hšbt* makes excellent sense when pointed *h^e^šībōtā,* second-person hiphil singular of *šūb,* "to turn back." The meaning "reject, refuse" is witnessed in several texts cited by BDB, p. 999b, for example, Ps cxxxii 10.

as dross. sīgīm and vs. 118 *šōgīm,* "who stray," form a wordplay.

120. *bristles out of awe of you.* Cf. Job iv 15, "A wind passed before my face, a storm made my body bristle," a description of the effect of God's presence; see Dahood, *Biblica* 48 (1967), 544–45.

121. *Defend for me.* Consonantal *'śyty* (MT *'āśītī,* "I made") may conceal a new form, probably to be pointed *'āśītāy.* It would parse as second-person *'āśītā* plus the first-person singular suffix *-y* (instead of *-anī*). The verb, being parallel to jussive "do not leave me," parses as precative, while the suffix *-y* appears to be datival. BH[3] reports six manuscripts reading second-person *'āśītā,* which favors our explanation.

122. *Assure.* The psalmist petitions God to engage to protect or indemnify him against harm by his oppressors. This technical meaning of *'rb,* "to enter in" (cf. Ps civ 34), is frequent in Ugaritic.

O Good One. Analyzing *leṭōb* into vocative *lamedh* and the divine title examined in the second NOTE on Ps civ 28; cf. vs. 68 and Prov xiii 21, "The Evil One will pursue sinners, but the Good One [*ṭōb*] will reward the just." For details, see Dahood in ETL 44 (1968), 53.

lest. For this nuance of *'al,* cf. second NOTE on Ps ix 20 and third NOTE on Ps lxvi 7.

126. *O Yahweh.* As in vs. 122, the *lamedh* before *yhwh* parses as the vocative particle. In one manuscript the *lamedh* is missing, and *Juxta Hebraeos* correctly translates, *tempus est ut facias Domine,* "It is time that you act, O Lord." One may doubt, however, whether Jerome grasped the vocative function of *lamedh* here; in numerous other verses where this particle occurs he evinces no knowledge of its nature.

127. *Most High Honest One.* Taken as the inferential conjunction "therefore," *'al kēn* does not connect with what precedes, but understood as the composite title studied at vs. 104, it makes good sense.

128. *Most High Honest One.* Cf. preceding NOTE. As in vs. 104, this title contrasts Yahweh's truth with "every false way." If this identification of the divine appellative proves correct, then vs. 115 remains the only verse after the three introductory lines in which God is not addressed.

all your precepts. Even conservative commentaries, such as that of Kirkpatrick, consider this verse corrupt, but the consonantal text now proves sound. Instead of MT *piqqūdē kōl,* read *piqqūdekā,* "your precepts," with the remaining *l* to be attached to next word as the emphatic particle.

I consider truly right. Reading *leyiššartī* (see previous NOTE), the emphatic *lamedh* followed by the piel of consideration, *yiššartī,* a function of the piel noticed in vs. 30 and at Ps cxvi 15. The ascription of an intensifying function to *lamedh* serves also to explain the postposition of the verb, a usage recurring in vs. 38. The writer has discussed the variant reading of 11QPs[a] in his review of J. A. Sanders, *Discoveries in the Judaean Desert of Jordan, IV,* in *Biblica* 47 (1966), 142. 11QPs[a] *pqwdy kwl yšrty* indicates rather convincingly that the force of the emphatic *lamedh* was no longer appreciated in the first century B.C. J. H. Eaton, VT 18 (1968), 557–58, has independently reached the same conclusion, and has proposed a translation similar to the one that I suggested in *Biblica* 47 (1966), 142, 408.

129. *are wonderful.* For MT *pelā'ōt,* 11QPs[a] reads, interestingly enough, *palgē nōpet,* "streams of honey," a lection which evokes Job xx 17, "He will not feast on streams of oil, on torrents of honey and cream"; for details, see *Biblica* 48 (1967), 437.

Most High Honest One. Again identifying *'al kēn* as a divine title suspended between two longer colon in a 7:2:6 syllabic pattern; see NOTE on vs. 104.

130. *Unfold.* 11QPs[a] *ptḥ dbrykh wh'r* indicates that the monks of Qumran understood *ptḥ* as an imperative (so in Syr., Targ.), since *wh'r*

is evidently a hiphil imperative. Hence vocalize *p^{e}taḥ* for MT *pētaḥ*, "the unfolding" (RSV).

which illuminate. A relative clause without relative pronoun (see vs. 96). For MT singular *yāʾīr* I read plural *yāʾīrū*, another instance of *scriptio defectiva;* cf. the second NOTE to vs. 103.

give . . . insight. That an imperative is desired in the second colon is clear from Syr. and *Juxta Hebraeos, doce,* "teach," but hiphil participle *mēbīn* need not be emended to *hābēn* (11QPs^a has *mbyn*) since the Psalter witnesses some eight examples of participles in parallelism with imperatives. Cf. fourth NOTE on Ps lxxiv 12, second NOTE on Ps lxxx 2, and for NT usage, A. P. Salom, "The Imperatival Use of the Participle in the New Testament," in *Australian Biblical Review* 11 (1963), 41–49, and *Expository Times* 78 (1966), 87, where Salom discusses Moulton's observation that the imperative served also as a participle in the Hellenistic period.

131. *With gaping mouth.* Literally, "I opened wide my mouth." In Ugaritic *pʿr* denotes "to declaim" (i.e., "open wide") in UT, 68:11, *wypʿr šmthm,* "And he declaimed their names." Cf. Job xxix 23, "They opened wide their mouths as for the spring rains," a fitting commentary on our text since it describes the attention with which Job's listeners absorbed his words.

132. *as you do.* ZLH, p. 486a, commendably handles this meaning of *mišpāṭ,* "custom," which is determined by the suffix of *š^{e}mekā,* "your name." This stylistic observation makes it more difficult to endorse Kirkpatrick's (*Psalms,* p. 726) translation, "as is the right of those that love thy name."

133. *by your word.* The vicissitudes of Hebrew prepositions are illustrated by MT *b^{e}ʾimrātēkā* read as *k^{e}ʾimrāteka,* "according to your word," by sixteen manuscripts and LXX, and now appearing in 11QPs^a as *lʾmrtkh,* "for/to/by your word."

134. *that I may keep.* Heb. *w^{e}ʾešm^{e}rāh* preserves the subjunctive or volitive ending expressing purpose.

136. *Most High.* The syntactic difficulty of the hapax legomenon construction *ʿal lōʾ šām^{e}rū,* usually rendered "because they do not keep," is pointed up further by 11QPs^a which inserts the conjunction *ky* in the second colon: *ʿl ky lwʾ šmrw twrtkh.* Briggs simply deletes *ʿal* as an interpretive gloss, though he does not tell us what this gloss was meant to interpret. If a gloss, it is perfectly obfuscating. The identification of *ʿal,* on the other hand, with the divine title recognized in vss. 104, 127–128, eliminates the syntactic problem.

137. *upright in your judgments.* The widely accepted translation of *yāšār mišpāṭekā,* "right are thy judgments" (RSV) violates elementary rules of Hebrew grammar touching agreement of number between subject and predicate. Joüon, GHB, § 148b, n. 2, was alive to the discord and suggested the singular vocalization *mišpāṭekā* (pausal), "your judgment." 11QPs^a

likewise sensed the difficulty and accordingly made both the subject and the predicate plural: *wyšrym mšpṭykh.* The poet's predilection for composite divine titles (cf. introductory NOTE) suggests that both *ṣaddīq,* "just," and *yāšār,* "upright," are predicated of Yahweh, so that plural *mišpāṭekā,* "your judgments," parses as an accusative of specification or limitation. Compare vs. 75, *ṣaddīq* (MT *ṣedeq*) *mišpāṭēkā,* "Just in your judgments," and Ps lxvi 3, *nōrā' ma'aśekā,* "terrifying by your deeds." Cf. *Biblica* 48 (1967), 438. When predicating *ṣaddīq* and *yāšār* of Yahweh, the psalmist evokes the composite divine title of Ps xi 7 and of Phoenician mythology in which, according to Philo Byblius (Eusebius *Praeparatio evangelica* I. 10, 13), Justice and Rectitude (*sydyk, misor*) were considered divinities. Philo's assertion is confirmed by the divine names *ṣdq mšr* in RŠ 24.271:14, discussed by Astour in JAOS 86 (1966), 282–83.

138. *justly.* Parsing *ṣedeq* as an accusative of manner like Ps lviii 2, *mēšārīm,* "with equity"; cf. GK, § 118q. Contrast KJ "Thy testimonies *that* thou hast commanded *are* righteous and very faithful."

fidelity to you. Suffixless *'emūnāh* shares the suffix of its opposite number *'ēdūtekā,* "your stipulations," but whereas the suffix of "your stipulations" is possessive or subjective, the supplied suffix of *'emūnāh* is objective. Cf. Ps lxxxvi 11, "Yahweh, teach me your way, / that I may walk faithful to you alone [*ba'amittekā*]." This analysis brings out more clearly the vassal treaty terminology of the verse; see following NOTE.

O Grand One. Repointing MT *me'ōd,* "much" (RSV, "in all faithfulness"), to *mā'ēd,* the divine title discussed at Ps cix 30 and identified in vss. 8, 96, 140, and 170 of this psalm. In the treaty terminology of our verse this title of the suzerain is particularly apt, especially since it forms a semantic inclusion with *ṣiwwītā,* "You imposed." See the second NOTE on Ps cxv 9.

139. *My antagonists.* Namely, those who rejected the law of God. The fact that the subject of *ṣāmat* (or quadriliteral *ṣmtt;* NOTE on Ps lxxxviii 17), "to annihilate," in its other twelve occurrences is always a person favors the assumption that the abstract noun *qin'ātī,* usually translated "my zeal," also designates persons. This assumption is borne out by the observation that the second-colon counterpart is concrete *ṣāray,* "my adversaries." Among the numerous examples in the Psalter of abstract nouns parallel to concrete substantives, Ps xxv 19 is perhaps most relevant. In addition to the meanings "to be jealous, zealous," *qānā'* also denotes "to rival, oppose," as observed by W. F. Albright in VT 9 (1959), 344. Isa xxvi 11b takes on a different hue when seen in the light of the abstract // concrete phenomenon: *yeḥezū weyībāšū* (MT *yēbōšū*) *qin'at 'ām 'ap 'ēš ṣārekā tō'kelēm,* "The antagonists of your people (*qin'at 'ām* shares the suffix of parallel and synonymous *ṣārekā*) will look and wither; with your fiery wrath will you devour your adversaries." Contrast RSV, "Let them see thy zeal for thy people, and be ashamed. Let the fire for thy

adversaries consume them." Consult also Isa xi 13a (courtesy of H. J. van Dijk), and the possible repercussions on Ps lxix 10.

ignored your commandments. The psalmist doubtless refers to the apostate Israelites who hated him because of his adherence to Yahweh's law. On *šākaḥ,* "ignore," cf. Ps ix 18; the psalmist's choice of the term *d^ebārekā,* literally "your words," probably designates the Ten Commandments that are sometimes called "the ten words." Consult the second NOTE on vs. 57.

140. *O Grand One.* The central position of consonantal *m'd* prompts its vocalization *mā'ēd* (MT *m^e'ōd,* "much") and the scansion of the verse into a 7:2:7 syllabic sequence. On *mā'ēd,* "Grand One," see third NOTE on vs. 138. This revocalization and new interpretation sharpens the contrast between the psalmist, who calls himself "your servant," and Yahweh, addressed as the "Grand One."

141. *young.* Though most modern versions understand *ṣā'īr* as "small" (*The Grail Psalms* goes a bit far with "weak"), LXX *neōteros,* "young," seems the most accurate version. In vs. 9 the psalmist styles himself a *na'ar,* and it is relevant to notice the parallelism of these two words in RŠ 24.251:rev.:13–14, *tbky km n'r tdm' km ṣġr,* "You weep like a boy, shed tears like a child." See Astour in JNES 27 (1968), 28, 33.

142. *O Eternal One.* Analyzing *l^e'ōlām* (11QPs^a significantly drops the *l^e,* reading mere *'wlm*) into the vocative *lamedh* followed by the divine title. The line, like vs. 144, thus scans into a 6:3:7 pattern; cf. CBQ 29 (1967), 577.

143. *anguish and distress overtook me.* The motif of two messengers discussed at Ps cxvi 3.

144. *O Eternal One.* Like vs. 144, this verse scans as 6:3:7, but instead of expressing two independent ideas, this line reads as enjambment, embodying a prayer and its motive. Consult T. Penar, VD 45 (1967), 40.

145. *that I may observe.* The postposition of *'eṣṣōrāh* to the end of the verse has obscured to many translators the volitive mode of this verb; cf., for example, RSV, "answer me, O Lord! I will keep thy statutes." See next verse.

146. *that I may keep.* As in vs. 145, the verb is in the volitive mode.

147. *I looked toward you.* One of the more puzzling expressions in this hymn, *qiddamtī* yields excellent sense here and in vs. 148 (*qidd^emū*) when it is seen to share the suffix of *d^ebārekā,* "your words." One might also translate "I faced you at dawn," that is, "I faced East at dawn." RSV apparently adopts the emendation of *qiddamtī* to *qamtī,* proposed in BH^3, since it offers, "I rise before dawn and cry for help."

148. *looked toward you.* Failure to recognize the employment of the double-duty suffix (see preceding NOTE) in *qidd^emū* produces a rendition in RSV that requires nimble exegesis: "My eyes are awake before the watches of the night."

149. *Yahweh.* Reading the line as 8:2:8, with vocative *yhwh* suspended

between the longer cola that are arranged in a chiastic pattern. The same syllabic sequence and chiasmus recur in vss. 166, 174; cf. Ps. cix 14.

150. *Pursuers of idols.* The psalmist probably has in mind the apostate Israelites, mentioned in vs. 139, who abandoned Yahwistic monotheism for the worship of idols. In the construct chain *rōdᵉpē zimmāh,* the latter bears the meaning investigated at Ps xxvi 10, while the nuance of the former can be seen in Hos viii 3, *zānaḥ yiśrā'ēl ṭōb 'oyēb yirdᵉpū hēm,* "Israel rejected the Good One, they followed the Foe" (i.e., Baal). On Hos viii 3, see Dahood in ETL 44 (1968), 45.

draw near . . . gone far. An effective employment of chiasmus.

151. *the Near One.* The adjective *qārōb* may be simply understood as "near" (so the versions), or it may be the divine title identified at Ps lxxv 2. The psalmist's predilection for divine epithets favors the second interpretation.

152. *O Primeval One.* Parallel to vs. 151, *qārōb,* "the Near One," *qedem* seems to be the divine appellative recently identified in Prov viii 22. Cf. CBQ 30 (1968), 512–21.

I acknowledge your stipulations. The phrase *yāda'tī-m 'ēdōtekā* (MT *mē'ēdōtekā*) contains an enclitic *mem;* cf. vs. 18, and especially UT, 2060:14, *yd'm l yd't,* "You know perfectly well," a phrase containing both an enclitic *mem* and emphatic *lamedh.* Consult on this text H. B. Huffmon and S. B. Parker in BASOR 184 (1966), 36–38.

your stipulations. For MT *mē'ēdōtēkā* 11QPs[a] read *md'tkh,* "from the knowledge of you."

from eternity. From the context it appears that *lᵉ* in *lᵉ'ōlām* denotes "from." Cf. the related context of Ps xlv 3, and third NOTE on Ps lxxviii 69. Contrast the translation of Jonathan A. Goldstein in JNES 26 (1967), 303, who translates the verse in the light of 11QPs[a] "Long have I known from the knowledge of thee that thou hast founded me forever," and concludes that the verse may express the doctrine that the knowledge of God leads to immortality.

155. *Keep distant . . . your salvation.* To account for the lack of gender agreement between masculine *rāḥōq* and feminine *yᵉšū'āh,* critics cite the purported lack of numerical agreement between singular *yāšār* and plural *mišpāṭekā* in vs. 137. The new solution proposed for the latter text requires a reexamination of the currently accepted anomaly. Gunkel was alert to the problem and proposed reading feminine *rāḥᵃqāh.* The ever-growing number of infinitives absolute in Northwest Semitic permits the parsing of MT *rāḥōq* as an infinitive absolute, precisely as in Ps xxii 2, with the function of an imperative; cf. GK, § 113bb. D. N. Freedman, *apud* McKenzie, AB, vol. 20, § 31, n. *d,* has identified the qal infinitive absolute *rāḥōqī* in Isa liv 14.

The psalmist's harsh prayer accords with his reaction in vs. 158, "I looked at the faithless and was disgusted."

your salvation. Suffixless *yᵉšū'āh* gets determined by the suffix of *ḥuqqekā,* "your statutes," much like the pair in vs. 171, and Ps iii 9 as explained in *Psalms II*, p. XXVI. Cf. also Isa xlvi 13b where the suffix of second-colon *tip'artī*, "my glory," likewise modifies first-colon *t^{e}šū'āh*, "my victory."

158. *because.* Some commentators (e.g., Gunkel) experienced difficulty with *'ašer*, correctly rendered by RSV "because," the meaning proposed in vss. 38–39.

160. *The essence.* Heb. *rō'š* has presented a problem of translation and syntax; KJ, for example, translates "*from* the beginning," but RSV "the sum." The interpretation of second-colon *kl* sustains the definition "essence" or "sum." Cf. Amos vi 6, *rē'šīt š^{e}mānīm*, "finest oils," and Phoen. *r'št nḥšt*, "the finest bronze."

your truth. Second-colon *ṣidqekā*, "your justice," shares its suffix with its first-colon counterpart *'^{e}met*. 11QPs[a] appreciated the strict parallelism between these two nouns, and accordingly left them both suffixless.

O Eternal One. Consult the NOTE on vs. 142. The initial *ū* of *ūl^e'ōlām* may be explained either as emphatic or as a secondary addition once the vocative function of *l^e* was no longer understood.

The content. Distinguishing between the homonyms *kol*, "all, every," from *kll*, and *kl*, "content," from *kw/yl*, "to comprehend, contain." For a recent discussion of this root, see McDaniel in *Biblica* 49 (1968), 213–15.

This noun, probably recurring in vs. 172, makes an apt synonym to *rō'š*, "essence," and brings to light this verse pattern: A+B+C—Vocative—Á+B́+Ć.

your judgment. Absolute *mišpāṭ* (MT *mišpaṭ*) receives its determination from *d^{e}bār^{e}kā*, "your word." The sequence of double-duty suffixes in this verse is matched by UT, 2 Aqht:I:26–27, *wykn bnh bbt šrš bqrb hklh*, "So that a son of his may be in his house, a root of his in his palace," where *bnh//šrš* and *bt//hklh* reveal the same chiastic arrangement of dual-purpose suffixes as biblical *dbrk//mšpṭ* and *'mt//ṣdqk*.

161. *Corrupt men.* See vs. 23.

indeed. Explaining *kī* (see next NOTE) as emphatic.

my pursuers. Reading *m^{e}dabb^{e}ray kī* for MT *midd^{e}bār^{e}ykā*, and assigning to *m^{e}dabb^{e}ray* the meaning studied at Pss ii 5, xxxviii 13, and cxvi 10; cf. HALAT, p. 201a. In a letter dated 9 February 1967, S. Speier of Zurich called to my attention that Joseph Qimḥi (twelfth century A.D.) in his *Sefer ha-shorashim*, col. 134, cites scholars who already explained *dbr* in Ps ii 5 as "drive away."

This reading and translation avoid the harsh sequence encountered in the versions, such as KJ, "But my heart standeth in awe of thy word. I rejoice at thy word." As commentators hasten to point out at this verse, dread is not inconsistent with joy, but a skilled poet would hardly affirm his dread of and his joy in God's word in immediately succeeding cola. Nor is the usual citation of Matt xxviii 8 wholly relevant, since it describes the emotional reaction to quite a different phenomenon.

Of course, the elimination of MT "your words" leaves the verse without a term reflecting or designating the law of Yahweh, such as precepts, stipulations, commands, words, etc. Since the prevailing impression is that every verse contains at least one such term, the proposed translation gives rise to serious misgivings. These misgivings, however, are allayed by a re-examination of the psalm text which reveals that no such term is to be found in the following verses: 37, 90, 121, 122, 132, and 149.

162. *because your utterance.* Revocalizing MT *kᵉmōṣē'*, "like one who finds" (11QPs[a], interestingly enough, reads *mmwṣ'*, "than one who finds") as *kī mōṣā'*, "utterance"; cf. *mōṣā' pī*, "utterance of the mouth" (Deut viii 3) or *mōṣā' śᵉpātāy*, literally, "the utterance of my lips" (Ps lxxxix 35); UT, I Aqht:I:75; *bph rgm lyṣa*, "From his mouth the word had not gone forth." Suffixless *mōṣā'*, "your utterance," participates in the determination supplied by the suffix of *'imrāteka*, "your word." Thus these two synonyms are counterposed to the two synonyms of vs. 161, "Corrupt men" and "my pursuers."

my great boon. With *šālāl rāb* being determined by first-colon *'ānōkī*, "I."

166. *Yahweh.* The double-duty vocative *yhwh* serves the chiastically arranged cola in an 8:2:8 syllabic sequence; similarly in vss. 149 and 174. Cf. also Ps cix 14.

169. *Yahweh.* This line is scanned into 9:2:9, with vocative *yhwh*, the double-duty modifier, linking together the longer cola.

171. *your praise.* Suffixless *tᵉhillāh* receives its determination from second-colon *ḥuqqekā*, "your statutes," exactly as in vs. 155, where the suffix of *ḥuqqekā* serves also to modify *yᵉšū'āh*, "your salvation." 11QPs[a] sensed that *tᵉhillāh* meant more than indeterminate "praise" (cf. RSV, "My lips will pour forth praise") and accordingly inserted *lkh*, "to you." It is pretty clear, then, that this poetic device (significantly absent in the Qumran Hodayot) was no longer current in the first century B.C.

you have taught me. As in Ps xciv 12, *tᵉlammᵉdēnī* is a *tqtl* form expressing activity completed in the past. This interpretation results in a version at odds with RSV, "My lips will pour forth praise that thou dost teach me thy statutes," a fuzzy translation at best.

172. *the content.* Consult the fourth NOTE on vs. 160.

174. *Yahweh.* As in vss. 149 and 166, the psalmist places vocative *yhwh* between two cola arranged in a chiastic or diagonal pattern.

PSALM 120

(cxx 1–7)

1 *A song of ascents.*

To Yahweh when I was besieged,
I called and he answered me.
2 Yahweh, deliver me
from lying lip,
from treacherous tongue.
3 How he will give to you!
How he will add to you!
O treacherous tongue,
4 Like sharpened arrows of a warrior,
like glowing coals of broom.
5 Woe to me, whether I sojourn near Meshech,
or dwell near the tents of Kedar!
6 Too close do I dwell
to the hater of peace.
7 As for me, peace indeed did I talk,
but they, only war.

Notes

cxx. The title *šîr hamma'alōt,* whose precise meaning is disputed (see the next NOTE), is prefixed to fifteen psalms (cxx–cxxxiv), which appear to have formed a separate collection probably composed in the early sixth century or late seventh century B.C. These poems are characterized by the "ascending" structure, in which each verse takes up and repeats a word or clause from the preceding verse. Thus vs. 3 *lāšōn remiyyāh,* "O treacherous tongue," is repeated from vs. 2; vs. 6, *šākenāh,* "have I dwelt," resumes vs. 5, *šākantī,* "dwell," and vs. 7, *šālōm,* "peace," repeats the final word of vs. 6. This stairlike pattern has induced some scholars to propose that *ma'alōt,* "ascents," be interpreted in this technical sense.

Though these poems contain many archaic elements, these elements are preponderantly artistic and archaizing rather than genuinely primitive.

Albright (YGC, pp. 254–55) observes that the repetitive parallelism of these fifteen psalms is so irregular and so different from archaic repetitive parallelism that their authors evidently did not understand the rules of the style they were attempting to imitate. This assessment should not, however, blind us to the poetic talents and inspiration which the NOTES to these psalms will try to make evident.

Though commonly classified as a lament, Ps cxx is unusual: it is an answered lament. After the introductory verse stating that he prayed and was heard, the psalmist in the remaining verses substantiates his complaint. His affliction is caused by a particular individual as well as by a group from whose calumnies the poet prays to be delivered.

1. *A song of ascents.* This title recurs in each of the next fourteen psalms. Of uncertain meaning, the technical term *šîr hammaʿalōt* has been explained by some as a "Pilgrim Song" sung by pilgrims as they "went up" to Jerusalem for the great annual feasts. Cf. Exod xxiii 17; Deut xvi 16; I Kings xii 28; Matt xx 17; Luke ii 41 f. Others hold that these psalms were sung by the returning exiles when they "went up" to Jerusalem from Babylon, or that they were sung by the Levites on the fifteen steps by which they ascended from the court of the women to the court of the Israelites in the temple. Hence these psalms are also termed the "Songs of Degrees" or the "Gradual Psalms." The textual discoveries at Qumran suggest a new possibility. 11QPs[a] Zion, 14, reads, *ʿrbh b'p tšbḥtk ṣywn mʿlh lkwl tbl,* "May your praise, O Zion, enter into his presence, extolment from all the world." Thus *mʿlh,* "extolment" (cf. I Chron xvii 17; Ps cxxxvii 6; 11QPs[a] cli 3[5–6]), makes it possible to propose "song of extolments" as the translation of *šîr hammaʿalōt,* a term which fits most, though not all, of these psalms. For further details on Qumranic *mʿlh,* "extolment," see *Biblica* 47 (1966), 143.

when I was besieged. Commonly translated "in my distress," *baṣṣārātāh lī* is preferably interpreted in the light of the observations made at Ps xx 2. The image of the psalmist beleaguered by maligners has much in common with the metaphor of slanderers in Ps iii 7, "I fear not the shafts of people / deployed against me on every side." This precision brings out the inclusion with vs. 7, *šālōm,* "peace," and *lemilḥāmāh,* "only war," and accords with other military terms in the poem. The unusual form *ṣārātāh* (*ṣārāh* is the normal word) is probably an accusative based on *ṣaratu,* much like *'ēmātāh,* "terror," from original *'ēmatu.* To be sure, after the preposition *ba* one would expect the genitive case ending, but since the psalmist lived in a period when case endings were no longer in regular use, *ṣārātāh* could be explained as a technical misuse by the poet.

I called and he answered me. Many versions take as present the two verbs which MT understood as referring to the past. In the translation adopted here, the psalmist recalls past answers to his prayers as an encouragement to fresh prayer in his present state of siege. This seems a more natural explanation of the verse than to take it as a confident anticipation of a favorable answer: "I call . . . and he will answer me."

2. *me.* Here and in vs. 6 the psalmist employs *napšī,* literally "my soul," as a substitute for the pronominal suffix.

lip . . . tongue. The parallelism between *śepat* and *lāšōn* permits the textual critic to restore UT, 67:II:2–3, *špt lšmm [l]šn lkbkbm,* "a lip to heaven, tongue to the stars." Not availing herself of the mutual bearing of Hebrew and Ugaritic parallelism, A. Herdner, in her critical edition of the Ras Shamra tablets, *Corpus des tablettes en cunéiformes alphabétiques découvertes à Ras Shamra-Ugarit de 1929 à 1939,* I (Paris, 1963), p. 33, reads simply [ ]*šn,* proposing no restoration. Contrast UT, Glossary, No. 1398, and Aistleitner, WuS, No. 1484, which restore *[l]šn.*

treacherous tongue. The MT vocalization *lāšōn remiyyāh* for classical *lešōn remiyyah* has invited the emending hand to set the text to rights, but the recurrence of the phrase in the next verse and in Prov vi 24, *lāšōn nokriyyāh,* "the tongue of the stranger woman," counsels restraint. Pss cxx–cxxxiv teem with dialectal elements still too little understood for emendation.

3. *How . . . How.* Understanding *mah* as an exclamation rather than as interrogative "What?" Cf. Pss iii 2, viii 2, xxi 2, xxxvi 8, etc. This verse still remains unclear in its intent.

he will give. The subject presumably is God who, the psalmist believes, will amply punish the slanderer for the harm he has caused. The elliptical nature of the expression, however, precludes an incontestable explanation of the psalmist's words *mah yīttēn.*

4. *Like . . . like.* The desire to balance the line with eight syllables in each colon may explain the use of the double-duty preposition *'im,* "like," a meaning documented at Pss xxviii and cvi 6. It may be pointed out here that J. J. Greswell in her book, *Grammatical Analysis of the Hebrew Psalter* (Oxford, 1873), p. 241, comments on our verse: "The particle *'im* is sometimes one of similitude, as in Ps cvi 6, 'We have sinned *like* our fathers'" (courtesy of W. Watson). Other instances of double-duty prepositions placed in the second colon are remarked at Pss xxxiii 7, lxxix 6, lxxxix 6, cv 30.

sharpened arrows. For the comparison of the malicious tongue to a bow that shoots arrows of falsehood, see the first NOTE on Ps iii 7, Ps lxiv 4, *'ašer šānenū kaḥereb lešōnām dārekū ḥiṣṣām dābār mār,* "Who sharpen their tongue like a sword, aim their poisonous remark like an arrow," where *ḥiṣṣām,* with an adverbial *mem* ending, balances the preposition of *kaḥereb,* while *dābār mār,* "their poisonous remark," shares the suffix of *lešōnām,* "their tongue." *Psalms II* construed the verse in a slightly different manner. Cf. also Jer ix 2, *wayyadrekū 'et lᵉšōnām qaštām,* "They aimed their tongue like a bow," and Ecclus li 5, *ḥṣy lšwn mrmh,* "the arrows from a treacherous tongue."

By choosing the adjective *šᵉnūnīm,* from the root *šnn,* "tooth," the poet suggests the sequence of "lip," "tongue," and "tooth," that evokes the Ugaritic sequence of *pk,* "your mouth," *šntk,* "your teeth," and *šptk,* "your lips," in UT, 1001:4–5. JB blunts the image by rendering *šᵉnūnīm* as "hardened" instead of "sharpened."

glowing coals. The juxtaposition of two similes comparing the slanderous tongue to sharpened arrows and to glowing coals resembles the image of Ps vii 14, "[O that he would] make his arrows into flaming shafts!" Cf. also Eph vi 16, "with which you will be able to quench all the flaming arrows of the Evil One." Hence the statement of J. Leveen, VT 16 (1966), 443, that "the rendering of [*dōlᵉqīm* in Ps vii 14] *fiery shafts* for arrows seems scarcely appropriate" is difficult to endorse.

of broom. A desert shrub or bush whose roots and foliage were used for fuel. From this shrub the Arabs still manufacture charcoal of the highest quality, which burns hottest and retains heat for the longest time.

5. *Woe.* Recognizing in the hapax legomenon *'ōyāh* (classical *'ōy*) the accusative ending *-āh* (like vs. 1, *ṣārātāh*) and another of the dialectal elements that characterize the "Songs of Ascents."

whether . . . or. The force of conditional *kī* in the phrase *kī gartī* extends to the second colon so that *šākantī,* a synonymous verb, also becomes conditional, "or dwell."

I sojourn near Meshech. The meaning and grammatical analysis of *gartī mešek* have long presented a problem, but I follow a suggestion of D. N. Freedman who makes *gartī mešek* share the preposition of second-colon *šākantī 'im 'ohᵒlē qēdār,* "or dwell near the tents of Kedar!" The first NOTE on vs. 4 comments on the use of the double-duty preposition *'im,* "like." Thus the use of double-duty *kī* and *'im* in this line serves to interlock tightly the parallel cola.

Meshech . . . Kedar. Mentioned in Gen x 2 as a son of Japheth *mešek* was a region between the Black Sea and the Caspian inhabited by barbarous people, while Kedar (cited in Gen xxv 13 as the second son of Ishmael) was one of the nomadic tribes that roamed the desert of the Arabian peninsula. The common element in these odd place names is distance from the psalmist: one is far to the north and east, the other is far to the south and east. Even were he to reside as far away as Meshech or Kedar, the psalmist would still feel too close to the hater of peace.

dwell near the tents. The phrase *šākantī 'im 'ohᵒlē* collocates the Ugaritic roots cited at Ps lxxviii 55.

near. BDB, p. 768a, cites numerous texts in which *'im* equals "near"; cf. Exod xxii 24, etc.

6. *Too close.* Often translated in a temporal sense, "Too long," *rabbat*

yields better sense in the context if understood in a local sense akin to second-colon *'im,* "near."

the hater of peace. Some manuscripts and versions read plural *śōnᵉ'ē,* "haters of," for MT singular *śōnē',* since the psalmist speaks of plural enemies in vss. 5 and 7. But MT singular can be preserved because, as noted at Pss v 10 and lviii 8, the shifting from singular to plural is characteristic of the heated language of laments. Of course, "the hater of peace" is to be identified with singular *lᵉkā,* "to you," and "treacherous tongue" in vs. 3.

7. *peace indeed did I talk.* In the clause *šālōm wᵉkī 'ᵃdabbēr,* C. H. W. Brekelmans, OTS 15 (1969), 173–75, has correctly parsed *wᵉkī* as a double emphatic that causes the verb to be pushed to the end of the clause. Thus emphatic *wᵉkī,* "indeed," is the counterpart of the emphatic *lamedh* in the second colon. On the phrase *šālōm 'ᵃdabber,* "peace did I talk," see Pss xxxv 20 and lxxxv 9, *yhwh kī yᵉdabbēr šālōm,* "Yahweh indeed has promised well-being."

peace . . . war. The antithesis between *šālōm* and *milḥāmāh* can be traced back to the second millennium in UT, 'nt:III:11–14, *qryy barṣ mlḥmt št b'prt ddym sk šlm lkbd arṣ arb dd lkbd šdm,* "Banish war from the earth, put love into the ground. Pour peace into the heart of the earth, rain love into the heart of the fields."

but they. The contrast between *'ᵃnī,* "I," and *hemmāh,* "but they," recalls the parallelism of *'nk,* "I," and *hmt,* "they," in Phoenician Kilamuwa, line 13. This parallelism makes it more difficult to credit LXX *ḥinnām,* "without provocation," instead of MT *hemmāh.*

only war. Ehrlich (*Die Psalmen,* p. 326) has rightly seen that *lᵉmilḥāmāh* should be read for MT *lammilḥāmāh,* and the *lamedh* explained as emphatic. Ehrlich's appeal to the Arabic *lamedh* of reinforcement is confirmed by the frequency of this particle in Northwest Semitic. Cf., for example, Ps lxix 11, *laḥᵃrāpōt,* "abuse itself," and Ecclus xxx 17, *ṭwb lmwt mḥyy šw',* "Death itself is better than a vapid life." Modern versions, such as CCD, JB, RSV (*The Oxford Annotated Apocrypha,* ed. B. M. Metzger [Oxford, 1965]), take no account of this particle in the last text; e.g., RSV, "Death is better than a miserable life."

As noticed at vs. 1, *milḥāmāh,* "war," forms an inclusion with vs. 1, "I was besieged."

PSALM 121
(cxxi 1–8)

1 *A song of ascents.*

I raise my eyes to the Mountain,
    whence will help come to me?
2 My help will come from the home of Yahweh,
    who made heaven and earth.
3 He shall not put your foot in the Quagmire,
    your guardian shall not slumber.
4 Indeed he never slumbers nor sleeps,
    the guardian of Israel.
5 Yahweh is your guardian,
    Yahweh is your shade,
    the Most High is your right hand.
6 By day the sun
    will not strike you
Nor the moon at night.
7 Yahweh will guard you
    from every evil
He will guard your life.
8 Yahweh will guard your going and your coming,
    from now unto eternity.

NOTES

cxxi. In this liturgy of blessing, the psalmist, who seems to be a representative or leader of Israel, asks in vs. 1 a rhetorical question which he answers in vs. 2. In vss. 3–8 divine blessings and promises are pronounced by the priest.

Like Ps cxx, this poem employs the "stairlike" pattern in which successive verses repeat words or ideas expressed in preceding lines. Thus vs. 2, *'ezrī,* "my help," resumes vs. 1, *'ezrī;* vs. 4, *šōmēr yiśrā'ēl,* "the guardian of Israel," is a reprise of vs. 3, *šōmᵉrekā,* a thought upon which the psalmist rings the changes in vss. 5, 7–8.

Though no actual indication exists in the psalm itself, this poem, like the others in the group, probably dates to the sixth century B.C.

1. *A song of ascents.* Commentators have long maintained that the curious reading *šīr lamma'alōt* is a mistake for *šīr hamma'alōt,* a suspicion supported by 11QPs[a] *šyr hm'lwt.* However, MT does remain the more difficult reading and is grammatically viable, given the use of the genitive *lamedh,* say, in Ps cxxii 5. What is more, 11QPs[a] does read *lm'lwt* at Ps cxxiii 1, where MT has *hamma'alōt.*

I raise my eyes. Comparing *'eśśā' 'ēnay* with UT, 76:II:13, *wyšu 'nh aliyn b'l,* "Then Victor Baal raised his eyes."

the Mountain. Probably designating both Yahweh's celestial abode and Yahweh himself, the likely subject of the epithet "the Mountain of Zion" in Ps cxxv 1. Cf. Ps cxxiii 1, where the psalmist states that he raises his eyes to the Enthroned of Heaven, and Albright, YGC, p. 25, who renders Ps xviii 32b, "And who is a Mountain, except our God?" As noted at Ps lxi 3, the plural form *hārīm* parses as a plural of majesty, "Mountain," since it designates the divinity. *The Oxford Annotated Bible* seems to take the wrong tack when commenting, "*The hills* may be the 'high places' where the baals, the local fertility gods, were worshiped (2 Kg. 23.5)." Failure to appreciate the celestial significance of *har,* "mountain," has led Ginsberg, in HWFB, pp. 79–80, into a drastic and inadmissible emendation of Isa xiv 13, *har mō'ēd,* "the (celestial) mountain of the Assembly," into *pḥr mō'ēd,* "Company of the Assembly."

will help come to me. In the phrase *yābō' 'ezrī* the suffix of *'ezrī* serves a dative function, as in Ps xx 3, *yišlaḥ 'ezrekā,* "May he send you help." Cf. also Prov vi 11 (=xxiv 34), *ūbā' kimehallēk rē'šekā,* "And poverty will come upon you like a vagabond," and van Dijk, EPT, pp. 107–8.

2. *will come.* Supplying the verb *yābō'* from the preceding colon as a double-duty verb, a stylistic phenomenon commented upon at Ps xci 9. The formal absence of *yābō'* in this colon has prompted critics to delete it in vs. 1b. The solution proposed here is more respectful of the received text.

from the home. Namely, from his heavenly mountain. In keeping with the observations at Ps xxxvi 10 concerning *'immekā,* "in your house," *mē'im* seems to connote more than "from," as traditionally rendered. French *chez* might be compared with Heb. *'im,* "in the house of."

heaven and earth . . . 3. Quagmire. This tripartite division of the universe resembles the sequence in Ps cxv 16–17, "heaven . . . earth . . . the Fortress."

3. *shall not.* The poet employs *'al* instead of *lō',* "will not," for emphasis.

Quagmire. The evidence for this definition of *mōṭ,* a term describing the slimy nature of the nether world, is given at Pss xiii 5 and lxvi 9. Cf. also Prov xxiv 11. He who never slumbers will not allow the psalmist to fall into the eternal sleep of Sheol. Implicit here is the belief in a blessed afterlife with Yahweh, as in Pss xvi 10, xlix 16, lxxiii 24, etc.

your guardian. In vs. 4, too, the psalmist holds back explicit mention of the subject till the end of the verse. In the comment to Ps cv 17, this stylistic technique has been termed the explicitation of the subject in the second colon.

4. *never slumbers nor sleeps.* Unlike Canaanite Baal, "who perhaps is asleep and must be awakened" (I Kings xviii 28). The parallelism of the roots in *yānūm* and *yīšān* has served to interpret the meaning of UT, Krt:31–32, *bm bkyh wyšn bdmʿh nhmmt,* "As he weeps, there is sleep, as he sheds tears, slumber." See below on Ps cxxxii 4, and Ginsberg, LKK, p. 34.

the guardian of Israel. See the third NOTE on vs. 3 for this second-colon explicitation. This point of style is obliterated in RSV, "Behold, he who keeps Israel will neither slumber nor sleep."

5. *your shade.* Read pausal *ṣillekā* for MT *ṣillᵉkā.* In *Biblica* 44 (1963), 300, and *Mélanges E. Tisserant,* I, p. 94, I have suggested on the strength of the parallelism the participial vocalization *ṣollekā,* "the one who shades you." This reading remains probable. Whichever way it is taken, it is virtually a title of the protecting God.

the Most High is your right hand. A study of the verse structure and parallel elements reveals that *ʿal* should answer to *yhwh* in the preceding cola, and that *yad yᵉmīnekā,* "your right hand," is meant to balance *šōmᵉrekā,* "your guardian," and *ṣillekā,* "your shade." This analysis finds confirmation in Ps cxli 3, where the elements of the composite divine title *yhwh ʿal* are placed in corresponding cola, and in I Sam ii 10, *yhwh yēḥattū mᵉrībāw ʿālū* (with nominative ending *-ū;* MT reads *ʿālāw*) *baššāmayim yarʿēm,* "Yahweh dismayed [*yēḥattū* preserves the singular indicative ending *-ū*] his opponents, the Most High thundered from heaven." It should be noticed that the prayer *niṣṣᵉrāh ʿal,* "Guard, O Most High," in Ps cxli 3 collocates two of the ideas present in our verse. See also second NOTE on Ps lv 23, and Paul Schröder, *Die phönizische Sprache* (Halle, 1869), p. 200, n. 2, who gratuitously assumes that in the Neo-Punic personal name *brkʿl,* "Blessed by the Most High," a *b* has fallen out of an original *brkbʿl,* "Blessed by Baal." Cicero, cited by Schröder, correctly reports the name as Barichal.

6. *By day . . . at night.* Consult the first NOTE on Ps xlii 9 which discusses the stylistic pairing of *yōmām,* "By day," with the adverbial ending *-ām,* with the prepositional phrase *ballaylāh,* "at night," and cites relevant Ugaritic parallels. The English versions efface this grammatical distinction of the Hebrew when rendering the latter "by night." A similar balance between the preposition *bᵉ* and the adverbial ending *-ām* can be seen in Job ix 17, where *biśᵉʿārāh,* "from the storm," stylistically matches *ḥinnām,* "without cause," or better, "secretly."

the sun . . . the moon. Gunkel, among others, expresses surprise that the poet determines *šemeš* with the article *haššemeš*, "the sun," but leaves parallel *yārēaḥ*, "the moon," undetermined by the article. The reason for the difference may not be semantic but prosodic: the poet needed another syllable in the first colon. The article, like other particles, can also serve a dual purpose, as here, modifying both parallel nouns.

will not strike you. Scanning *lō' yakkekkāh* as a dangling verbal phrase predicated of the preceding and following cola that are arranged in a chiastic pattern. The syllable count thus becomes 5:4:6 (or 5 if the *w* is considered a secondary addition), instead of traditional 9:6. Other instances of double-duty modifier in diagonally arranged lines are cited in the third NOTE on Ps cix 14.

the moon. Emending *yārēaḥ* to *qeraḥ*, "the cold," Ehrlich (*Die Psalmen*, p. 327) asserts with more aplomb than address that the moon is a harmless chap (*ein harmloser Geselle*), who never hurts anyone. But the ancients believed otherwise. The notion that the moon beamed harmful influences was widespread in the ancient Near East; cf. Matt xvii 15, where Greek *selēniázetai* literally means "he is moonstruck" (cf. "lunatic"); S. Kirst, "Sin, Yeraḫ und Jahwe: Eine Bemerkung zum vorderasiatischen Mondkult," in *Forschungen und Fortschritte* 32 (1958), 213–21, especially 218, n. 58. Once again, the received text is vindicated (even were there no parallelism with "the sun" to secure the reading). 11QPs[a] *yrḥ*, "moon," further undermines Ehrlich's proposal.

7. *from every evil.* Scanning *mikkol rā'* as a double-duty formula sandwiched between two verbal clauses (see third NOTE on vs. 6), with a resultant 6:3:6 syllable sequence instead of traditional 9:6.

8. *from now unto eternity.* Comparing *mē'attāh we'ad 'ōlām* with UT, 1 Aqht:161, *'nt brḥ p'lmh*, "now, primordially, and to eternity."

PSALM 122

(cxxii 1–9)

1 *A song of ascents. Of David.*

I rejoiced among those who said to me,
"We will enter the house of Yahweh!"
2 My feet were standing
within the gates of Jerusalem,
3 Jerusalem which was built as his city,
which was compacted by him alone,
4 There the tribes go up,
the tribes of Yah.
It is a decree, O Israel,
to give thanks to Yahweh's name,
5 Because there they sat
on thrones of judgment,
on thrones of the House of David.
6 May they pray for your peace, Jerusalem,
may they prosper who love you!
7 Let there be peace within your walls,
prosperity within your citadels!
8 For the sake of my brothers and my friends
I firmly say, "Peace be within you."
9 For the sake of the house of Yahweh our God
I will seek your good.

NOTES

cxxii. A song of Zion (cf. Ps xlviii), probably composed by a pilgrim on his return home, while reflecting upon the happy memories of the pilgrimage to Jerusalem.

The poem is comprised of three stanzas. In the first (vss. 1–4a) the poet describes his joy when arriving at the Holy City, but in the second strophe (vss. 4b–5) he pronounces a brief homily on why one should make a pilgrimage to Jerusalem, the seat of government. In the final stanza (vss. 6–9) he invokes blessings on the Holy City.

As in the other "Songs of Ascents," the poet employs the stairlike pattern in vss. 2b–3, "Jerusalem"; 4, "tribes . . . tribes of Yah"; 4–5, "There . . . there"; 5, "thrones of judgment, thrones"; 6–7, "peace . . . peace," "prosper . . . prosperity"; 8–9, "For the sake of." The psalm contains a surprising number of Northern dialectal forms and constructions that are registered in the following NOTES, and the use of double-duty suffixes in vss. 3 and 6 is particularly effective.

1. *Of David.* Briggs (CECBP, II, p. 448) stoutly affirms that *l^edāwīd* is a late conjecture, due to the gloss in vs. 5, since it is impossible that the psalm could have been in the Psalter of David. His argument is sustained by the absence of *l^edāwīd* in the Targ. and *Juxta Hebraeos,* but weakened by 11QPs^a *ldwyd.* It recurs, moreover, in MT Ps cxxiv 1, unhappily not preserved in 11QPs^a.

"We will enter the house of Yahweh!" Critics correctly object to the cohortative translation of *nēlēk,* "Let us go to the house of the Lord!" (RSV). One would then expect *nēlekā* "Let us go." The syntax of *bēt yhwh nēlēk,* wherein the verb of motion *nēlēk* governs the accusative *bēt yhwh,* reflects older usage documented in UT, 122:9, *lk bty rpim,* "Enter my house, O Rephaim!"

2. *My feet.* The Syriac reads *raglay,* a lection now supported by 11QPs^a *rgly.* To achieve this meaning it may not be required to depart from consonantal *rglynw* (MT *raglēnū,* "our feet"), since it may conceal an unrecognized morpheme first identified in Ugar. *ankn,* "I," that is, *ank* plus an afformative *-n.* Thus *rglynw* may contain the afformative *-n* witnessed in *ankn,* "I," permitting the translation "my feet." In Ps cxli 7, unexplained *ʿ^aṣāmēynū,* which makes sense when emended to *ʿ^aṣāmay,* "my bones," may need no emendation when analyzed in the same manner as *rglynw,* "my feet." Cf. also Ugar. *qšthn,* "his bow," where the singular suffix *-h,* "his," is followed by *-n.*

within. This meaning of *b^e* recurs in vss. 7–8.

the gates of Jerusalem. Since parallel *bēt yhwh,* "the house of Yahweh" (vs. 1), and identical "Jerusalem" (vs. 3) stand in the third person, it seems desirable to maintain the third person in *šʿryk yrwšlym;* this becomes feasible when the putative second-person suffix of *šʿryk* is parsed as the emphatic *kī* in the construct chain, a poetic verbal mechanism cited in the third NOTE on Ps cxvi 19. Several scholars, such as Bickell and Duhm, to preserve the consonance of person in vss. 2–3, have proposed the emendation *šaʿ^arē y^erūšālāim,* "the gates of Jerusalem." See the NOTES on vs. 6, where the same problem recurs.

3. *which.* Recognizing in the article of *habb^enūyāh* the function of a relative pronoun, an analysis sustained by parallelism with second-colon *še,* "which." Cf. Ezek xxvi 17, *hāʿīr hahullālāh,* "O city which had been

praised," where the article *ha* serves as the relative pronoun. Joüon, GHB, § 145d–e, recognizes several examples, but incorrectly concludes that the usage is proper to late biblical books. One of the most ancient poems of the Bible, Gen xlix contains a clear instance of this usage in vs. 21, "Naphtali is a hind let loose, which yields [*hannōtᵉnā*] lovely fawns," as rightly rendered by the JPS Torah. The recurrence of this relative in Ps cxxiii suggests that it was written by the same poet.

as his city. The suffix of *ʿīr* is forthcoming from second-colon *lāhū*, "by him." The same usage is noticed at Ps xlvi 5, "God brings happiness to his city [*ʿīr*, sharing suffix of second-colon *miškᵉnī*], / the Most High sanctifies his habitation." See below on vs. 6. A new text illustrating "God the Builder" motif has been identified in Prov viii 31, *bōnēy* (MT *bᵉnēy*) *'ādām*, "the Builder of Earth"; see Dahood, "Proverbs 8, 22–31: Translation and Commentary," in CBQ 30 (1968), 512–21.

which. Relative pronoun *še* is another of the dialectal elements that mark the Songs of Ascents. As noted by H. Bauer and P. Leander, *Historische Grammatik der hebräischen Sprache* (Halle, 1922), p. 29, *še* was originally at home in North Israel and only later did it find wider extension. For the use of *še* in Ecclesiastes, see Dahood, *Biblica* 33 (1952), 45–46, and Donald Broadribb, *Abr-Naharaim* 3 (1961–62), 31–32, who examines it in the Song of Sol.

by him. 11QPsᵃ clearly grasped the sense, as evidenced by its reading *lw*, "by him." But consonantal *lh* need not yield to *lō*, if it be pointed *lāhū*, "by him," equal to Ugar. *lh*, Phoen. *lh* (Friedrich, PPG, § 22). True, this vocalization and analysis suppose that the Songs of Ascents were composed in a North Israelite dialect closely related to Phoenician, a not unreasonable supposition in view of the dialectal elements uncovered thus far.

With the passive verb *ḥubbᵉrāh*, "compacted," i.e., "compactly built," the *l* of *lāhū* notifies the agent, and the choice of disyllabic *lāhū*, instead of 11QPsᵃ *lw* (*lō*), may have been dictated by metrical considerations; the syllable count becomes 10:9 instead of 10:8. If biblical Jerusalem resembled the Old City of today, "compacted" aptly describes it.

alone. Repointing MT *yaḥdāw*, "together," which is altogether omitted by 11QPsᵃ, to *yāḥīdū*, an adjective preserving, for metrical reasons, the nominative ending. To be sure, one expects the genitive ending, but as noted at Ps cxiv 8, case endings were occasionally confused by the psalmists. Grammatically, *yāḥīdū* stands in apposition with the suffix of *lāhū*, "by him," as in Pss lxxxvi 11, *ba'ᵃmittᵉkā yāḥīd*, "faithful to you alone," and lxxxviii 18, *ʿālay yāḥīd*, "on me alone." In our verse, one may also read *yāḥīd* and attach the final *w* to the next word as the conjunction.

4. *O Israel.* As in Ps lxxiii 1, parsing *lᵉ* of *lᵉyiśrā'ēl* as vocative *lamedh*, a proposal set forth in VT 16 (1966), 308, and *Biblica* 47 (1966), 407, and now partially supported by 11QPsᵃ, which omits it.

Whether this omission is due to a lack of understanding of the nature and function of the vocative particle cannot be made out with certainty because 11QPs[a] reads *'dt yśr'l,* "the congregation of Israel," for MT *'ēdūt l^eyiśrā'ēl,* "It is a decree, O Israel."

In his fervor the psalmist reminds his fellow Israelites of their obligation to journey to Jerusalem publicly to thank Yahweh. The next verse states the reason.

5. *Because. kī* gives the reason for the admonition of vs. 4b. Failing to seize the nexus between vss. 4b and 5, RSV significantly omits *kī* altogether in its translation.

there. šammāh forms a theological wordplay with vs. 4, *šēm,* "name."

they sat. The kings and judges of Israel being the subjects understood.

on thrones. Scanning the line into a 6:6:7 tricolon instead of the traditional 12:7 bicolon. There has been considerable divergence in the grammatical analyses of the sequence *yāš^ebū kiss^e'ōt;* e.g., RSV reads, "There thrones for judgment were set." The margin of discrepancy may be reduced, however, by the admission that *yāšab,* "to sit," can govern the accusative case as in our translation. Cf. UT, 127:37–38, *rd lmlk amlk ldrktk aṯbnn,* "Come down from your royal throne that I might rule, from the seat of your dominion that I may sit thereon" (see UT, § 9.11, p. 73, for syntax of *aṯbnn*); Ezek xxviii 2 and xlvii 6, *wayyōšībēnī* (MT *way^ešībēnī*) *š^epat hannāḥal,* "And he made me sit on the bank of the river" (courtesy H. J. van Dijk). For Phoenician usage, see R. T. O'Callaghan, *Orientalia* 18 (1949), 186, and C. C. Torrey, JAOS 57 (1937), 400.

thrones of judgment. The phrase *kiss^e'ōt l^emišpāṭ* "thrones of/for judgment," echoes the collocation in UT, 49:VI:27–29, *l ys' alt ṯbtk lyhpk ksa mlkk lyṯbr ḥṭ mṯpṭk,* "Surely he will pluck out the supports of your enthronement; he will indeed upset your royal throne; surely he will break the scepter of your authority."

6. *May they pray.* MT imperative *ša'^alū* produces an unwarranted shift from second to third person that obtrudes in RSV's "Pray for the peace of Jerusalem! 'May they prosper who love you!'" This dissonance can be avoided by reading precative perfect *šā'^alū,* which restores the third person desiderated by the parallelism. Cf. Ps cxxxvii 6, where Northwest Semitic grammar similarly restores concord of persons that was lacking.

May they pray for your peace. Biblically attested in this precise form only here and in Jer xv 5, the phrase now appears in UT, 2010:8:12, *šil šlmy,* "the praying for my well-being."

your peace. With *š^elōm* (cf. Ps cxix 26, 59, 109 for construct with double-duty suffix) sharing the suffix of second-colon *'ōh^abāyik,* "who love you," just as in vs. 3. One may of course also read the absolute form *šālōm.* The wordplay on "Jerusalem" and *šālōm,* "peace," has often been noted.

Jerusalem. Referred to in the third person in vss. 2–3, Jerusalem is now directly addressed in the remaining four verses.

may they prosper. Jussive *yišlāyū,* which preserves the third-person radical *-y* (also -w) as in Job xii 6, makes an excellent third-person counterpart to precative *šā^a lū,* "pray," in the first colon. The psalmist creates effective assonance and alliteration with four of the line's five words containing the *sh* sound. A similar sound sequence is noticed at Ps lxix 13.

who love you. The reading *'ōh^o lāyik,* "your tents," found in one Hebrew manuscript and judged "probably correct" by the critical apparatus of BH³, is checkmated by 11QPsᵃ [ ]*whbyk,* "who love you."

7. *peace . . . prosperity.* The Hebrew *šālōm* and *šalweh* is more assonant.

8. *my brothers and my friends.* Who were unable to make the pilgrimage to Jerusalem. As observed in the fifth NOTE on Ps xxxv 13, *'aḥay w^e rē'āy* features the same parallelism as UT, 1019:8, *laḫy lr'y,* "to my brother, to my friend." The number of parallel pairs of words in Ugaritic and in Hebrew has reached 290, as pointed out in the fourth NOTE on Ps cii 20. The phrase "my brothers and my friends" is a form of hendiadys and apparently equals the English cliché "each and every."

I firmly say. The proposal to delete the emphatic ending *-nā',* here rendered "firmly," finds support in 11QPsᵃ *'dbrh šlwm,* but is countered by the current 8:8 syllable count of MT.

9. *the house of Yahweh.* Forms an inclusion with vs. 1, *bēt yhwh.*

PSALM 123

(cxxiii 1–4)

1 *A song of ascents.*

I raise my eyes to you,
    who are enthroned in heaven.
2 Yes, like the eyes of slaves
    on the hand of their master,
Like the eyes of a maid
    on the hand of her mistress,
So our eyes are on Yahweh our God,
    till he have mercy on us.
3 Have pity on us, Yahweh,
Have pity on us, O Master,
    sated as we are with contempt.
4 Too long has our throat been sated
    with the scorn of the nonchalant,
    with the contempt of the presumptuous.

NOTES

cxxiii. A supplication of the people who, through their spokesman (vs. 1), protest their dependence on the Lord (vs. 2), and beseech him to be merciful toward their humiliation.

Like the other "Songs of Ascents," this graceful poem employs repetitive parallelism or the stairlike pattern in vss. 2–4, and shows familiarity with Canaanite motifs (vss. 2–7). The congruency of metaphor, hitherto unrecognized, in vss. 3–4 further bespeaks the poetic gifts of the psalmist. Several dialectal forms and constructions are noticed below.

1. *who.* Parsing *ha,* as in Ps cxxii 3, as the relative pronoun. RSV seems to handle it conflatedly, understanding it both as the vocative particle and as the relative: "O thou who art enthroned." Cf. Ezek xxvii 3, *l*ᵉ*ṣōr hayyōšebtī ʻal m*ᵉ*bō'ōt yām,* "O Tyre, who rule over the gateway to the sea!"

are enthroned. For this nuance of *yōš*ᵉ*bī,* see Pss ii 4 and cii 13.

Unable to account for the genitive ending of *yōšebī* (consult the NOTES on Ps cxiii 5–7), 11QPs[a] simply dropped the genitive ending, reading *ywšb*. This telltale lection reveals the limitations of the monks of Qumran near Jerusalem vis-à-vis the grammar of Hebrew poetry, and at the same time warns us not to expect greater poetic comprehension from the roughly contemporary translators of the LXX in Egypt.

in heaven. The bearing of *baššāmāyim* on the exegesis of Ps cxxi 1, *hārīm*, "the mountain," is noticed there.

2. *like the eyes . . . Like the eyes . . . So our eyes.* The poetic sequence *ke'ēnē . . . ke'ēnē . . . kēn 'ēnēnū* owes much to Canaanite models, as illustrated by a comparison with UT, 49:II:28–30, *klb arḫ l'glh klb ṭat limrh km lb 'nt aṯr b'l*, "Like the heart of a wild cow for her calf, like the heart of a wild ewe for her lamb, so was the heart of Anath for Baal." The lack of an explicit verb in both texts shows the query of BH[3] whether a verb has fallen out after *šipḥāh*, "maid," (cf. Targ.) to be baseless. Consult Dahood, CBQ 22 (1960), 73–74; on Ps lxxxiii 15, the NOTE ad loc.; on Prov x 26, C. I. K. Story, JBL 64 (1945), 322, and Albright, VTS, III, p. 5. This pattern also appears in Isa lxi 11.

the hand. Not the hand that punishes, as interpreted by Baethgen and Ehrlich, but the hand which issues benefactions; cf. Ps civ 27–28.

3. *Have pity on us.* For a similar Ugaritic formula, see first NOTE on Ps lxxxvi 3.

O Master. In the phrase *kī rab* the latter is sometimes deleted as disruptive. If, however, *rab* is understood as a divine title, the line scans as a 5:5:4 tricolon. Cf. Ps cxlv 7, *zēker rab ṭūbekā yabbī'ū*, "They shall pour forth the record, O Master, of your goodness." Construed thus, *rab* in our verse forms a theological wordplay with vs. 4, *rabbat*, "too long," somewhat like Ps cxxii 4–5, *šēm*, "the name," and *šāmmāh*, "there.

This analysis of the word pattern helps secure the MT reading of Ps xxx 11 where some critics propose to delete one *yhwh*. No deletion seems required when the word patterns of the respective verses are set side by side.

sated . . . with contempt. The expression *śāba'nū būz* might be compared with even more figurative UT, 51:III:15–16, *qlt bks ištynh*, "Humiliation from my chalice have I drunk." Cf. Job xxxiv 7, *yišteh la'ag kammāyim*, "He [Job] gulps scorn like water."

4. *our throat.* The consistency of metaphor (see preceding NOTE) is maintained when *napšēnū*, usually translated "our soul," is defined as "our throat," a meaning frequent in the Psalter and not uncommon in the "Songs of Ascents"; cf. for example, Pss cxxiv 4, 7, cxxxi 2. See also Eccles vi 7, *kol 'amal hā'ādām lepīhū wegam hannepeš lō' timmālē'*, "All man's trouble is for his [Death's] mouth, and yet his [Death's] throat is never filled," where *timmālē'*, "filled," a synonym of *śābēa'*, "to be sated," is predicated of *nepeš*, "throat." Cf. Dahood, *Biblica* 49 (1968), 368, and Ps cvii 9, "he satisfied the throbbing throat" (*hiśbīa' nepeš*).

the scorn of the nonchalant. Older commentators agree that the phrase *halla'ag hašša'ᵃnannīm* is syntactically non-viable because of the article with construct *halla'ag*. Thus Briggs terms it "impossible in Hebrew grammar" (CECBP, II, p. 452), Gunkel likewise dismisses it as *grammatisch unmöglich* (*Die Psalmen,* p. 545), and then proceeds to set the text to rights. Advances in Northwest Semitic philology, however, indicate that our phrase needs no emendation. The ever-growing number of Phoenician and Hebrew texts with the article in a construct chain forbids the "improvement" of the present reading; cf. *Psalms II,* p. xx; PNWSP, pp. 35–36; C. H. Gordon, JNES 8 (1949), 114; G. R. Driver, JBL 73 (1954), 130–31.

Who are meant by "the nonchalant" cannot be precisely determined; some identify them as heathen oppressors of Israel, while other commentators see in them insouciant Israelites who disregard the judgments of God and the sufferings of men alike; cf. Amos vi 1. In any case, their attitude is far removed from the devout worshipers who profess their dependence (vs. 2) upon Yahweh. The root *š'n* occurs in Ugaritic tablets published in recent years; see UT, Glossary, No. 2371.

the contempt of the presumptuous. The sequence of article plus noun (*habbūz*) followed by the *l* indicating possession followed by another noun (*ligᵉ'ēyōnīm*) creates a pleasant variation to the preceding construct chain without affecting the meaning.

PSALM 124

(cxxiv 1–8)

1 *A song of ascents. Of David.*

Had it not been Yahweh who was for us,
    let Israel firmly say,
2 Had it not been Yahweh who was for us,
    when men rose up against us—
3 Then they would have swallowed us live,
    when their wrath blazed against us;
4 Then the waters
    would have engulfed us like a torrent,
    sweeping over our neck;
5 Then would have swept over our neck
    the raging waters.
6 Blessed be Yahweh,
    who did not give us
    like prey to their teeth.
7 Our neck has escaped like a bird
    from the snare of the fowlers.
The snare is broken,
    and we have escaped.
8 Our help is in the name of Yahweh,
    who made heaven and earth.

NOTES

cxxiv. A hymn of thanksgiving in which the community acknowledges that the Lord alone delivered them from impending destruction. The reference may be to the fundamental salvation celebrated at the festivals.

The hymn consists of two stanzas. In vss. 1–5 the poet likens the peril brought on by men to the voracious jaws of the nether world and the seething currents of Sheol. Verses 6–8 praise Yahweh for having rescued them from their enemies.

1. *who.* Failing to translate relative *še,* some commentators (e.g., Gunkel) and versions (e.g., CCD) distort somewhat the sense of the condition. Thus CCD's, "Had not the Lord been with us," fails to bring out Yahweh's superiority over heathen deities. The psalmist asserts that if its God had been, say, Baal or Marduk, Israel would have perished in the danger confronting it.

for us. Cf. Ps lvi 10.

firmly say. See the second NOTE on Ps cxxii 8.

2. *against us.* The proposal to delete *'ālēnū,* registered in the apparatus of BH^3, disregards the antithetic parallelism of *lānū,* "for us," and *'ālēnū,* "against us," as well as the Ugaritic balance between *l* and *'l* cited in the first NOTE on Ps ciii 10.

3. *they would have swallowed us.* To portray the peril created by evil men, the poet appropriates mythical language which in an earlier period described the enormous maw of the insatiable monster, Death. Cf. Pss lv 16, lxix 16; Prov i 12, *niblā'ēm kišᵉ'ōl ḥayyīm,* "Let us swallow them live like Sheol," and R. B. Y. Scott, AB, vol. 18, NOTE ad loc.

against us. This use of *bānū* sheds light on RŠ 24.244:61, *b ḥrn pnm trǵn(w),* "Against Ḥoron her fury waxed," in which *pnm* equals Ps xxxiv 17, *pānīm,* "fury," and the new Ugaritic verb *rǵn* is identified with Heb. *rā'an,* "to grow luxuriant." Contrast Astour, JNES 27 (1968), 22, who translates, "To Ḥoron she inclined her face," an inadequate version since the next line states that "She deprived him of his virility."

4. *Then the waters.* Usually read as a bicolon, this verse may also be scanned as a 5:6:6 tricolon; the latter scansion is adopted especially because it helps resolve the grammatical anomalies besetting the current reading and interpretation.

As in Ps lxix 2, 15 and Jon ii 6, *hammayim* designates the waters of the nether world. Cf. also Ps xlii 8.

like a torrent. Customarily explained as a hapax legomenon feminine form of masculine *naḥal,* "torrent," *naḥlāh* ill accords with the following masculine verb *'ābar.* Hence *naḥlāh* should be parsed as masculine *naḥal* with the accusative ending expressing the manner in which the waters would have engulfed Israel. The second colon thus consists of the verb *šᵉṭāpūnū* followed by the accusative of manner *naḥlāh.* This parsing agrees with the style of the Psalms of Ascents, which contain a surprising number of case endings.

sweeping . . . 5. would have swept. Both times repointing MT *'ābar* to infinitive absolute *'ābōr.* The chiastic arrangement of vss. 4–5 resembles the diagonal pattern of vs. 7.

5. *would have swept.* Repointed to infinitive absolute, *'ābōr* serves as predicate of the plural subject in the second colon.

over our neck. RSV "over us" obscures the meaning of *napšēnū* and the imagery suggested by Jon ii 6, *'ᵃpāpūnī mayim 'ad nepeš* (see Isa viii 8), "The waters encircled me up to my neck."

the raging waters. The nominal phrase *hammayim hazzēdōnīm* chiastically balances the nominal expression of vs. 4a, *'ᵃzay hammayim,* "Then the waters."

6. *Blessed be Yahweh.* Scanning the line as a 4:6:6 tricolon with two beats in each colon; hence the proposal of BH[3] to shift the MT *athnach,* or principal pause, should be declined.

give us like prey to their teeth. The psalmist resumes the figure of vs. 4, which likens Israel's enemy to Death represented as a devouring monster. That this is so becomes evident upon comparing biblical *nᵉtānānū ṭerep lᵉšinnēhem* with UT, 51:VIII:15–20, *al tqrb lbn ilm mt al y'dbkm kimr bph klli bṯbr nt'nh tḫtan,* "Do not approach the son of the gods Mot [=Death], lest he put you two like a lamb into his mouth, lest like a lambkin you be crushed by his grinding teeth!" For the reading *nt'nh* in lieu of UT *nqnh,* see M. Dahood, CBQ 17 (1955), 300–3.

7. *Our neck.* Gunkel, following L. Dürr, is probably correct when, as in vs. 4, he translates *napšēnū* by *unser Hals,* "our neck," (contrast RSV's "we"). The juxtaposition of *šinnēhem,* "their teeth," and *napšēnū,* "our neck," recalls the parallelism of Ps lvii 7, "They spread a net for my feet, a noose for my neck."

escaped . . . escaped. The chiastic arrangement of the four cola in vs. 7 resembles the diagonal pattern of vss. 4–5.

the fowlers. The attempt of L. Kopf, VT 8 (1958), 178, to relate Heb. *yōqᵉšīm* to Ar. *wṯq* (*wiṯaq,* "bond") is debarred by Ugar. *yqš,* "fowler," which reveals that the third radical is *š,* not *ṯ* (Kopf also assumes metathesis). What is more, the Arabic root *wṯq* now appears in Ugar. *yṯq,* "he binds," further ruling out an etymological connection with *yqš,* "fowler."

PSALM 125

(cxxv 1–5)

1 *A song of ascents.*

Those who trust in Yahweh
are like the Mountain of Zion;
Never will be upset
the Enthroned of Jerusalem.
2 Like the mountains round about her
is Yahweh round about his people,
from now unto eternity.
3 The scepter of the wicked surely will not rest
over the land allotted to the just,
Provided the just do not extend
their hands into mischief.
4 Show your goodness, Yahweh, to the good,
and to those upright in their hearts.
5 But those tottering for their devious ways—
may Yahweh cause them to pass away
with the evildoers.
Peace upon Israel!

NOTES

cxxv. A supplication of the people for deliverance from national enemies; a group lament. In the first stanza (vss. 1–3) the faithful express their confidence in Yahweh's protection. The second stanza (vss. 4–5) contains the prayer for help and for the destruction of the reign of the wicked. If the proposed translation of vs. 3b *lᵉmaʿan* is sound, we have a conceptual contact with Ezekiel and consequently a reason for dating the psalm in the early sixth century B.C.; cf. the introductory NOTE to Ps cxx 1.

1. *the Mountain of Zion.* From the prosodic analysis of this verse emerges the parallelism of *har ṣiyyōn* and *yōšēb yᵉrūšālaim,* "the Enthroned of Jerusalem." It would seem to follow, then, that in the phrase *har*

ṣiyyōn, har is a divine epithet describing Yahweh. In *From the Stone Age to Christianity,* p. 186, Albright discusses the element *har,* "Mountain-god," in Hyksos personal names; see also the third NOTE on Ps cxxi 1.

Never will be upset. There has been considerable discrepancy among the versions and commentators (see Gunkel) regarding the scansion of this line. I scan it into two bicola (RSV takes it as one bicolon), with a 7:4//6:6 syllable count. The first bicolon states the topic sentence, whereas the second supplies the reason for the stability of Mount Zion. Most versions (including 11QPs[a]) make Mount Zion the subject of *lō' yimmōṭ,* but in the present interpretation the Enthroned of Jerusalem becomes the subject. Unlike the idols of whom *lō' yimmōṭ,* "it will not be overthrown," is asserted by the idol maker in Isa xl 20 and xli 7, the God of Israel will never be vanquished.

the Enthroned of Jerusalem. With the LXX repointing MT *yēšēb* to *yōšēb,* and comparing the divine title *yōšēb yᵉrūšālaim* with Pss ix 12, *yhwh yōšēb ṣiyyōn,* "Yahweh, the King of Zion," xcix 1, *yōšēb kᵉrūbīm,* "Enthroned upon the Cherubim," and cxxxv 21, *šōkēn yᵉrūšālaim,* "the Resident of Jerusalem." The versions which accept MT *yēšēb* render it "abides" (RSV), a meaning for which the evidence is tenuous; the text most frequently cited to sustain this translation, Mic v 3, lends iself to divergent interpretations.

2. *Like the mountains.* With *hārīm* sharing the preposition *kᵉ* of vs. 1, *kᵉhar ṣiyyōn,* "like the Mountain of Zion."

round about her. The girdle of mountains about Jerusalem reminds the psalmist of Yahweh's enfolding protection of his people.

unto eternity. An attempt to reproduce the emphatic *wᵉ* of *wᵉ'ad,* as in Ps cxxi 8.

3. *The scepter of the wicked.* The *šēbeṭ hārešaʿ* will prove ineffectual against the just who are defended by "the Enthroned of Jerusalem." The contrast between *šēbeṭ hārešaʿ* and vs. 1 *yōšēb yᵉrūšālāim* recalls the association of similar concepts in UT, 52:8–9, *mt wšr yṯb bdh ḫṭ ṯkl bdh ḫṭ ulmn,* "Death and Corruption sits enthroned. In his hand is the staff of bereavement, in his hand the staff of widowhood." In the phrase *šēbeṭ hārešaʿ*, abstract *rešaʿ*, "wickedness," assumes a concrete meaning because of its antithetic parallelism with concrete *ṣaddīqīm,* "the just." See the second NOTE on Ps lxxxii 2 and the first NOTE on Ps cvii 42.

surely. Proposals to expunge *kī* are to be rejected on two counts: 11QPs[a] has *ky,* and the numerous new examples of emphatic *kī* supply an alternative to conjunctional "because" which does create a problem.

not rest. LXX causative *yānīḥ* "permit to rest," adopted by some critics in preference to MT qal *yānūᵃḥ,* "will rest," is countered by 11QPs[a] *ynwḥ,* a qal form which makes excellent sense here.

Provided. The security of the heritage of the just is conditional, a thought resembling some passages of Ezekiel who maintains (xviii 24) that if a righteous man commits iniquity, he will die. The similarity of thought thus supports the sixth-century date for the Songs of Ascents proposed in the introductory NOTE to Ps cxx.

For this definition of *lᵉmaʻan,* "provided," see Josh iv 24, which has been considered anomalous when translated "thus" but which reads coherently when understood as "provided."

the just. The presence of *haṣṣaddīqīm* in 11QPsᵃ supplies another reason for rejecting the tentative proposal of BH^3 to delete it. BHS happily omits the proposal to delete of BH^3.

do not extend their hands into mischief. On UT, 127:32, *šqlt bǵlt ydk,* "You have let your hands fall into mischief," Ginsberg LKK, p. 49, correctly comments: "The whole phrase sounds curiously like Ps cxxv 3b, which would seem to favor a combination of Heb. *ʻawlā(ṯā)* with Arab. *ǵwl* and *ǵyl* as well as (hardly to the exclusion of) Arab. *ʻwl.*" The biblical phrase *yišlᵉḥū . . . yᵉdēhem* equals Phoenician Kilamuwa, line 6, *wkl šlḥ yd,* "And every man extended his hand."

mischief. Heb. *ʻawlātāh* equals Ugar. *ǵlt,* quoted in preceding NOTE. The form should be explained in the same manner as Ps cxx 1, *ṣārātāh.* As in Ps cxx 1, one would expect a genitive case ending after the preposition *bᵉ*, instead of accusative *ʻawlātāh.* It would seem that the accusative ending often displaced the other case endings.

4. *in their hearts.* The present 8:8 syllable count renders it difficult to give up *bᵉlibbōtām* in favor of *bᵉlēb,* an ancient reading now supported by 4QPsᵉ and 11QPsᵃ.

5. *those tottering.* Repointing MT *hammaṭṭīm* (from *nāṭāh*) to *hammāṭīm,* from *mwṭ,* "to totter," found in vs. 1. The poet contrasts, by way of inclusion with vs. 1, the worshipers of false gods with the solidity of those who trust in Yahweh, who will never be vanquished. Grammatically, *hammāṭīm* stands as *casus pendens;* see Ps ciii 15.

for their devious ways. Parsing *ʻaqalqallōtām* as an accusative of cause; consult the first NOTE on Ps cxvi 1. The root of "devious ways" appears in the Ugaritic epithet *bṯn ʻqltn,* "the twisting serpent."

The psalmist ascribes the debilitated condition of evildoers to their immoral behavior.

cause them to pass away. The recognition of the nuance of qal *hālak,* "to pass away" discussed at Ps lviii 9, permits one to dispense with the emendation of hiphil *yōlīkēm* to *yᵉkallēm,* "May he make an end of them," proposed by T. K. Cheyne in his commentary on *Psalms.*

the evildoers. The scribe of 11QPsᵃ betrays greater zeal than MT by inserting *kwl,* "all," before *pōʻᵃlē ʼāwen.*

Peace upon Israel! How RSV "Peace be in Israel!" answers to *šālōm ʻal yiśrāʼēl* is not immediately evident.

PSALM 126
(cxxvi 1–6)

1 *A song of ascents.*

When Yahweh restored the fortunes of Zion,
  we became like the sands of the sea.
2 Then our mouth was filled with laughter,
  and our tongue with shouts of joy.
Then even the nations said:
  "Yahweh showed his greatness
  by working with them."
3 Yahweh showed his greatness
  by working with us;
  we grew happy.
4 Yahweh restored our fortunes
  like torrents in the Negeb.
5 Those who sowed in tears,
  amid shouts of joy did reap.
6 Though he went forth weeping,
  bearer of his seed pouch,
He came home amid shouts of joy,
  bearer of his sheaves.

NOTES

cxxvi. A hymn of thanksgiving composed for one of the religious festivals. In the past, scholars have tended to identify the restitution mentioned in the opening line with the liberation from the Babylonian Exile in 539 B.C., but the new interpretation of vs. 1, *šībat*, "the fortunes" (see first NOTE to vs. 1), no longer permits such a precise identification. What specific restoration is celebrated by the hymn cannot be determined from the contents of the poem. At any rate, the date of composition need not be post-Exilic; in fact, the occurrence of *šībat* in an eighth-century Aramaic inscription, and the several archaic forms commented upon in the NOTES point to an earlier period of composition. The hymn consists of two parts: vss. 1–4 comprise the first stanza, and vss. 5–6 are a didactic reflection upon the change of fortunes described in this first stanza. Stylistically, vss. 1 and 4 illustrate a classic example of inclusion, with vs. 4, *šōbāh yhwh,* "Yahweh restored," answering to vs. 1, *bešūb yhwh,* "When Yahweh restored," and vs. 4, *ka'apīqīm bannegeb,* "like torrents in the Negeb," evoking vs. 1, *keḥōl-m yām,* "like the sands of the sea."

Since "tears" symbolize death and "shouts of joy" resurrection (e.g., Ps xxx 6, "In the evening one falls asleep crying, but at dawn there are shouts of joy"), the poet, by contrasting in the second stanza *dim'āh,* "tears," and *bākōh,* "weeping," with *rinnāh,* "shouts of joy," seems to hint at a resurrection which will follow the present sorrow. What lends weight to this interpretation is the hymn's closing word *'alummōtāyw,* denoting "his sheaves," but whose consonants evoke Prov xii 28, *'al-māwet,* "immortality" (which, with the third-person masculine suffix, would read *'al-mōtō* instead).

1. *When Yahweh restored the fortunes.* On the cognate phrase *bešūb šebūt* in Pss xiv 7, lxxxv 2, see the apposite NOTES. Here, however, the text reads *bešūb . . . šībat,* and critics (e.g., Kraus, *Psalmen,* II, p. 853, who terms *šībat* "manifestly a scribal error" for *šebūt* or *šebīt*) have not hesitated to emend *šībat* to *šebūt.* This ill-advised emendation is proposed anew by Bardtke in BHS. But this emendation is now proved unsound by the Aramaic phrase *hšbw 'lhn šybt b*[*yt 'by*], "The gods restored the fortunes of [my father's house]," in the Sefîre Inscription (III:24) of the mid-eighth century B.C. Aram. *šybt* answers to Heb. *šībat,* while Aram. *hšbw šybt* shows that the noun is a cognate accusative and so supports the derivation of biblical *šebūt* (vs. 4) and *šībat* from *šūb,* "to restore" rather than from, *šābāh,* "to take captive." The Aramaic context, which is one of restoration, further shows that the biblical expression in Pss xiv 7 and lxxxv 2 has been correctly understood as referring to restoration of fortunes and not to return from captivity. See A. Dupont-Sommer, *Bulletin du Musée de Beyrouth* 13 (1956), 27; Greenfield, *Acta Orientalia* 29 (1965), 4; Fitzmyer, *The Aramaic Inscriptions of Sefîre,* pp. 119–20.

we became. Commentators point out that the most nettlesome problem in this poem is that of verbal tenses. Since *hāyīnū* here, *'āz yimmālē'* and *higdīl* in vs. 2, apparently describe past events, one treads on safe ground when interpreting the subsequent verbs as also referring to completed action in the past; cf. the NOTE on vs. 4, *restored.*

like the sands of the sea. MT *keḥōlemīm,* "like dreamers," has never been successfully fitted into the context of the verse (J. Strugnell's proposal "then were we as men who had been/were healed" in JTS 7 [1956], 239–43, has correctly been declined by Kraus, *Psalmen,* II, p. 853). The ancient versions also differ sharply in their interpretations. One must accordingly seek a new solution to consonantal *kḥlmym,* which might be read *keḥōl māyim,* literally "like the sands of the waters," where *māyim* stands for "the sea" as in Exod xv 8, 10; Ezek xxvii 26, and Isa xliii 2, *kī ta'abōr bammayim,* "When you passed through the waters," an allusion to the Exodus. D. N. Freedman, *apud* McKenzie, *Second Isaiah,* § 12, Isa xliii 2, n. *a,* would make the allusion even more explicit by reading *bemō yām,* "through the sea," but this seems unnecessary. Or one may read *keḥōl-m yām,* with *-m* explained as an enclitic *mem* in a construct chain (*Psalms II,* Index of Subjects, s.v.). With either reading the sense remains substantially the same. Cf. Gen xxxii 13, "I will make your offspring like the sands of the sea" (*keḥōl hayyām*); I Kings iv 20; Hos ii 1.

But on balance, the reading *ḥōl-m yām* is to be preferred because the standard idiom is *ḥōl yām,* "sands of the sea," and the insertion of the enclitic *mem* within this construct chain will help to explain why later scribes and the Masoretes missed the correct analysis of the text. Compare the discussion of the variant readings at Ps xviii 16, *'apīqē-m yām,* "fountainheads of the sea," where the parallel text in II Sam xxii 16 reads *'apīqē yām,* without the enclitic *mem.*

2. *our mouth . . . our tongue.* On the parallelism of *pīnū,* "our mouth," and *lešōnēnū,* "our tongue," here arranged chiastically, see NOTE on Ps lxxvi 17, *my mouth . . . my tongue. The Grail Psalms* can be faulted for rendering *lešōnēnū,* "our tongue," as "on our lips."

was filled with laughter. The phrase *yimmālē' śeḥōq,* with the niphal vocalization of the verb, may bear on the vocalization of UT, 'nt:II:25–26, *ymlu lbh bšmḫt,* "Her heart was filled with happiness." In other terms, *ymlu* probably parses as a niphal verb form as recognized by Aistleitner, WuS, p. 184, and others.

shouts of joy. The root of *rinnāh* is witnessed in UT, 1001:6, *arnn,* "I shout for joy," and in 1001:5 where Gordon correctly restores the damaged third letter *brnk=ba-runni-kā,* "when you shout for joy."

The A+B+C//Ć+B́ pattern of this line, recognizable also in Ps cv 43, has Canaanite precedents in UT, 51:IV:10–11. Our verse and the Ugaritic text may be juxtaposed, to illustrate the single verb and the chiastic arrangement:

'āz yimmālē' śeḥōq pīnū	*št gpnm dt ksp*
ūlešōnēnū rinnāh	*dt yrq nqbm*
Then was filled with laughter our mouth, and our tongue with shouts of joy.	He put a harness of silver, of gold, trappings.

even the nations. Analyzing *ba* of *baggōyīm* as the emphatic *ba* (or *beth*) discussed at Pss xxix 4 and lv 19. Compare Ps cxv 2, *lammāh yō'merū haggōyīm,* "Lest the nations say." Thus analyzed, *baggōyīm* is no longer subject to the deletion recommended when it was understood as "among the nations" and the verb *yō'm^erū* was parsed impersonally as "They said among the nations." With Gunkel (*Die Psalmen,* p. 550) I read this line as a 7:4:6 tricolon.

showed his greatness. Though modern lexicographers usually define the phrase *higdīl la'^aśōt,* "He did great things," the ancient versions exhibit less sureness. As in Ps cxxxviii 2, *higdīl* may also be parsed as the hiphil elative, treated at Pss li 9 and xcii 14.

by working. The construct infinitive *la'^aśōt* may be categorized as circumstantial, a topic noticed at Ps ci 8.

with them. Though most recent versions translate *'im 'ēlleh,* "for them," one can defend the more common meaning of *'im* to bring out the theological point that the Israelites cooperated in the restoration of their fortunes.

with . . . 3. with us. The pair *'im . . . 'immānū* may be compared with a similar parallelism that recurs in Ugaritic letters; e.g, UT, 1015:14–20, "With us two [*'mny*] there is perfect well-being. Whatever well-being is with [*'m*] my mother—send me a reply."

3. *we grew happy.* The occurrence of *hāyīnū ś^emēḥīm,* "we grew happy," and vs. 1, "we became like the sands of the sea" in the same context evokes the description of Solomonic Palestine in I Kings iv 20, "Judah and Israel were as many as the sand by the sea; they ate and drank and were happy" (*ś^emēḥīm*).

4. *restored.* MT emphatic imperative *šūbāh,* "Restore!" creates the main syntactic and semantic difficulty in this psalm. In vs. 1 Yahweh is said to have restored the prosperity of Zion, but here he is being begged to make Israel prosper. See Ps lxxxv 2–5 for a similar difficulty. Alive to the problem, Briggs and others take vs. 1 as present tense, "When Yahweh restores the prosperity of Zion, we are like dreamers." Briggs, though, does express some uneasiness because of vs. 2, *'āz yimmālē'* "Then was filled," which elsewhere describes past happenings. Hence for MT *šūbāh* read the *qatala* verb *šābāh,* or the Phoenician form *šōbāh* where *ā* becomes *ō,* the archaic form of classical Hebrew *šāb;* for further discussion of *qatala* forms, see NOTE on Ps ciii 19, *he rules.*

The reason for the longer form *šōbāh* would seem to be metrical, as observed by D. N. Freedman. Verse 4, which balances vs. 1 and introduces the second stanza, has a syllable count 9:7, exactly like vs. 1.

like torrents. In view of Ps xviii 16 (=II Sam xxii 16), *'^apīqē-m yām,* "the fountainheads of the sea," and Ugar. *apq thmtm,* "the fountainheads of the two deeps," one may suggest that *'^apīqīm,* "torrents," harks back to vs. 1, *yām,* "the sea."

torrents in the Negeb. The period of the rains is particularly glorious in the Negeb, the arid district to the south of Judah, where the brooks are dried up all summer long. Thus the sand suggested by the term Negeb refers back to *ḥōl,* "sands," of vs. 1. When the winter rains come, the desert rejoices and blossoms like a rose (cf. Isa xxxv 1); see Nelson Glueck, *Rivers in the Desert: The Exploration of the Negev* (London, 1959), pp. 92–94.

5. *in tears, amid shouts of joy*. As in vs. 2a, the Hebrew word order is chiastic or diagonal, and the assonance of *bᵉdim'āh* and *bᵉrinnāh* with identical sequence of vowels is worthy of note.

tears . . . 6. weeping. The concurrence of *dim'āh*, "tears," and *bākōh*, "weeping," recalls the frequent parallelism of these roots in Ugaritic, a parallelism witnessed anew in RŠ 24.251:rev.:11, *tbky km n'r tdm' km ṣġr*, "You weep like a lad, shed tears like a child"; see Astour in JNES 27 (1968), 29, 33.

did reap. Taking the *yqtl* verb *yiqṣōrū* as a punctual form expressing past time, and not as stating a present event or wish, as interpreted by RSV, "May those who sow in tears reap with shouts of joy!"

6. *bearer of his seed pouch*. Though one of the first two words is often deleted, MT *nōśē' mešek hazzāra'* is vouched for by 11QPs[a] and must accordingly be dealt with as it stands. What is more, the 7:7::6:6 syllable count dissuades textual alteration. From comparison with Amos ix 13, *mōšēk hazzāra'*, "the strewer of seed," one may conclude that *nōśē' mešēk* is the semantic equivalent of *mōšēk*, "the strewer." Hence *mešek* must be the seed container carried by the sower. Imperial Aramaic *mšk*, "skin, leather," supplies a ready explanation: the seed container would thus be a leather bag.

his seed pouch. In the expression *mešek hazzāra'*, the article seems to balance the suffix of *'ᵃlummōtāyw*, "his sheaves"; cf. the NOTE on Ps civ 2, *as his garment*.

PSALM 127

(cxxvii 1–5)

1 *A song of ascents. Of Solomon.*

If Yahweh does not build the palace,
in vain do its builders labor on it;
If Yahweh does not guard the city,
in vain does the guard keep vigil.
2 Failure to you who rise early,
who put off going to bed,
who eat the bread of idols—
But the Reliable gives prosperity to his beloved.
3 Indeed, sons are Yahweh's patrimony,
fruit of the womb his reward.
4 Like the arrows in a warrior's hand
are the sons of one's youth.
5 How blest the man who has filled
his quiver with them!
He shall not be humiliated but shall drive back
his foes from the gate.

NOTES

cxxvii. Composed for a king, this Wisdom psalm stresses the truth that without the blessing of the true God—as opposed to the heathen divinities—all human endeavor is futile (vss. 1–2). With God's benediction, here exemplified by numerous sons, a king will overcome his adversaries (vss. 3–5).

Current critical scholarship favors the view that this psalm consists of two independent songs with no connection of thought, but the observable semantic and literary bonds between the opening and closing verses oppose this dissection. Thus Yahweh's protection of the city in vs. 1 is counterbalanced by his beloved's defense of the city in vs. 5; the inclusion begun by vs. 1, *'īr*, "city," is ended by vs. 5, *šā'ār*, "gate" (of the city); the alliteration of "b" sounds in vs. 1a, *yibneh bayit . . . bōnāyw bō* is echoed by vs. 5b, *yēbōšū . . . yᵉdabbᵉrū . . . 'ōyᵉbīm baššā'ar;* and the repetition of "š" (=*sh*) sounds in vs. 1b, *yišmor . . . šāw' šāqad šōmēr* recurs in vs. 5a, *'ašrē . . . 'ᵃšer . . . 'ašpātō.* Surely these interlocking details point to an originally unified composition.

The royal character of the poem as well as the concision of expression and the considerable literary rapport with early non-biblical texts point to a pre-Exilic date of composition. Verses 4–5 are noteworthy because they clearly illustrate congruence of metaphor as a criterion for establishing the meaning of a disputed text.

1. *Of Solomon.* Though missing in LXX, MT's ascription of the psalm to King Solomon is witnessed in the other ancient versions and is now attested in 11QPsᵃ *lšlwmh.* Many commentators (among them Baethgen) claim that this attribution stemmed from the misinterpretation of vs. 1 *bayit* as "temple," and from the use of the term *līdīdō,* "to his beloved," in vs. 2; in II Sam xii 25 it is reported that David gave his son Solomon the secondary name *yᵉdīdyāh,* "the beloved of Yahweh." To go so far afield to find reasons for such attribution seems needless when the sapiential contents of the poem might sufficiently explain this superscription.

in vain . . . in vain . . . 2. *Failure.* The triple repetition of *šāw'* proves effective not only in its primary designation but also in its allusive power because *šāw',* "vanity," is a biblical term for useless pagan idols; cf. third NOTE on xxiv 4 and below on *the bread of idols.*

the city. The concurrence of *'īr,* "city," and vs 5, *ša'ar* "(city-)gate," furnishes an argument for the original unity of the psalm.

guard . . . in vain does the guard keep vigil. The alliteration of *yišmor . . . šāw' šāqad šōmēr* links this line to vs. 5a, which is similarly characterized by alliteration.

2. *Failure to you . . . to his beloved.* D. N. Freedman notes the apparent wordplay and chiasmus in *šāw' lākem* and *līdīdō šēnā'.*

the bread of idols. The daily bread which the pagans believe comes from their gods. Though MT *hā'ᵃṣābīm,* "toils," is followed by most versions (KJ "the bread of sorrows"), Jerome in his *Juxta Hebraeos* read *panem idolorum;* he saw, in my opinion rightly, in consonantal *h'ṣbym* the term *hā'ᵃṣabbīm,* which designates "idols" in Pss cvi 36, 38 and cxxxix 24. Thus by the juxtaposition in the Hebrew text of *hā'ᵃṣabbīm* and much-disputed *kēn,* here understood as "the Reliable," the poet vividly contrasts the precariousness of relying on capricious gods against the dependability of the Reliable One of Israel. Of course, the traditional version "the bread of toil" would still be suggested by the word *ha'ᵃṣabbīm,* "idols."

the Reliable. The divine appellative *kēn* is discussed at royal Ps cx 7; it recurs in Ps cxxviii 4.

prosperity. Perhaps the most discussed single word of the poem, MT *šēnā'* has mostly been taken as the Aramaic spelling of *šēnāh,* "sleep" (cf. GK, § 231), but, in view of the parallel words of the context, identification with Syr. *šaynā'*, "prosperity," Ethiopic *sene'*, "peace," proves more satisfactory. See also Prov xiv 17. The contraction of the diphthong *-ay* in *šaynā'* to *ē* in *šēnā'* would mark the word as Northern Israelite where such contraction was normal; cf. *Psalms II*, Index of Subjects, s.v., and THE GRAMMAR OF THE PSALTER. For another view, see D. Winton Thomas, VT 18 (1968), 268.

3. *sons are Yahweh's patrimony.* A primary concern of a king was the continuity of the dynasty through numerous sons. Note the king's lament in Ps lxxxix 46, "You cut short the days of his youth, / robed his young manhood with sterility." This theme is central to the Ugaritic Legend of Aqht. This phrase sheds light on Prov xiii 22, *ṭōb yanḥīl bᵉnē bānīm wᵉṣāpūn laṣṣaddīq ḥēl ḥōṭē'*, "The Good One bestows children's children as heirs, and reserves for the just man the sinner's wealth."

his reward. The widespread use of double-duty suffixes makes it unnecessary to read *śᵉkārō*, "his reward" (cf. BH[3]), since suffixless *śākār* can share the suffix of vs. 2, *līdīdō*, "to his beloved."

4. *the arrows . . . 5. his quiver.* The parallelism of *ḥiṣṣīm*, "the arrows," and *'ašpātō*, "his quiver," recalls the phrase *uṯpt ḥẓm*, "a quiver of arrows," in UT, 1124:1, 2, 4. The figure begun here bears on the translation and interpretation of vs. 5. Thus both the parallelism and the congruence of metaphor rule out the LXX reading *tēn epithumian autou*, "his desire," where MT reads *'ašpātō*, "his quiver."

the sons of one's youth. Sons born while their parents are young and vigorous (contrast Gen xxxviii 3, *ben zᵉqūnīm*, "the son of old age"). Such children are not only themselves more vigorous, but also grow up in time to be the defense and assistance of their parents' old age. A Canaanite proverb preserved in Akkadian fragments from Ras Shamra wryly observes that "A son born too late is no advantage"; see Jean Nougayrol, *Comptes Rendus de l'Académie des Inscriptions et Belles Lettres*, 1960 (appeared 1961), p. 170, and C. F. A. Schaeffer, *Archiv für Orientforschung* 19 (1959–60), 195. It might also be noted that the phrase *bᵉnē hannᵉ'ūrīm*, "the sons of one's youth," juxtaposes two roots occurring parallel in UT, 2068:25–26, *annmn wṯlṯ n'rh rpan wṯn bnh*, "ANNMN and his three youths, RPAN and his two sons/children." Furnished with such parallels, the modern translator is prevented from perpetrating such howlers as LXX's, "the sons of them who were shaken off," confusing *n'r* I, "youth," with *n'r* II, "to shake off."

5. *How blest . . . who . . . his quiver.* There is good alliteration in the sequence *'ašrē . . . 'ᵃšer . . . 'ašpātō*, which links this line to the alliterative vs. 1c–d.

the man. Proposals to repoint *geber*, "man," to *gibbōr*, "warrior," receive a setback from 4QPs Commentary on Psalms (B), published with A. A. Anderson by John M. Allegro, *Qumrân Cave 4*, I (4Q158–4Q186) (Discoveries in the Judaean Desert of Jordan, V; Oxford, 1968), pp.

51–52, which reads *gbr* (=*geber*), not *gbwr* (=*gibbōr*). In II Sam xxiii 1, King David is called *haggeber,* "the man."

his quiver. The parallelism with *ḥiṣṣīm,* "arrows" (see first NOTE on vs. 4) further points up the unsoundness of LXX's translation of *'ašpātō,* namely, "his desire."

be humiliated. Recognizing that the subject should be the singular "warrior" and "man" of vss. 4–5, many commentators (e.g., Hans Schmidt, *Die Psalmen,* p. 228) emend apparently plural *yēbōšū* to singular *yēbōš.* Given the respectable number of third-person singular masculine verbs ending in *-ū* (see *Psalms II,* Index of Subjects, s.v., and THE GRAMMAR OF THE PSALTER), such an emendation is no longer necessary. The archaic quality of this line supports this analysis, which is also valid for *y^edabb^erū,* "[he] will drive back." Hence the first NOTE on Ps xxxv 4 should be corrected so that both verbs read as singular.

shall drive back. In the versional understanding of this clause (RSV, "when he speaks with his enemies in the gate") the psalmist shifts from a military metaphor in vss. 4–5a to a forensic figure in vs. 5b, since it was in the open space near the city gate that justice was administered. In modern philology, however, one must assume consistency of metaphor, one of the cardinal criteria for determining the sense of a verse. Accordingly, *y^edabb^erū* must be taken in the sense discussed at Pss ii 5, xviii 48, xxxviii 13, xlvii 4, so that the biblical clause *y^edabb^erū 'et 'ōy^ebīm baššā'ar* can scarcely be dissociated from EA 76:38–41, *uššira ṣābē pitāti rabā u tudabir ayābi šarri ištu libbi mātišu,* "Send a large number of archers that they might drive out the king's foes from the midst of his country," and EA 138:68–70, *tidabbiru ṣābē aziri ištu āli,* "They will drive the troops of Aziri from the city"; cf. also EA 279:20–23 for similar terminology. This proposal, set forth in TS 14 (1953), 87, has been adopted by HALAT, p. 201b (its emendation of *y^edabb^erū* to *y^edabbēr* proves needless since the former can also be parsed as singular; cf. preceding NOTE), by Lipiński, RB 75 (1968), 351–52, n. 131, and Hanson, PMS, III, pp. 74, 120.

his foes. With *'ōy^ebīm* sharing the suffix of *'ašpātō,* on the principle of the double-duty suffix, much like Ps lxviii 24, *'ōy^ebīm,* "your foes," and Prov xxvii 23 *ṣō'nekā,* "your sheep," parallel to suffixless *'^adārīm,* "your flocks."

from the gate. Where the enemy would make the most concerted assault. In the phrase *baššā'ar,* the preposition *ba* equals El Amarna *ištu,* "from," in the expression *ištu āli,* "from the city," cited above. The clarification of this line has repercussions on Isa xxviii 6b, *w^elig^ebūrāh m^ešībē milḥāmāh šā'rāh,* "and for the warriors who drive back the troops from the gate," where *šā'rāh,* with the *hē directionis* ending, denotes "from the gate"; cf. GK, § 90e on Jer i 13, xxvii 16; Josh x 36, xv 10; Judg xxi 19; Isa xlv 6.

Of course, the metaphor is most apposite when describing the king, the supreme military commander. Applied to a private citizen, the imagery becomes somewhat forced. It was the king's responsibility to repulse the attackers from the gates of his city.

PSALM 128
(cxxviii 1–6)

1 A *song of ascents.*

How blest each one who fears Yahweh,
who walks in his ways!
2 The fruit of your toil indeed shall you eat,
happiness and prosperity shall be yours.
3 Like a fruitful vine shall be your wife
within your house,
Your children like olive shoots
around your table.
4 See how the Reliable blesses
the man who fears Yahweh.
5 May Yahweh of Zion bless you!
Enjoy the prosperity of Jerusalem
all the days of your life;
6 Enjoy the children of your children,
the peace of Israel's Most High.

NOTES

cxxviii. A Wisdom psalm which teaches that the man who worships the Lord and obeys his commandments is rewarded with a happy and prosperous family. A companion piece to Ps cxxvii, this poem reveals one syntactic phenomenon (vs. 2) and two sets of parallel words (vs. 3) that have counterparts in the much older Ugaritic tablets. The probable occurrence in vs. 4 of the divine appellative *kēn*, "the Reliable," further suggests the common origin of both psalms in the pre-Exilic period.

1. *who fears . . . who walks.* Some recent versions (e.g., *The Grail Psalms*, BJ, JB) incorrectly render singular *yᵉrēʾ* and *hahōlēk* as plurals; thus JB reads, doubtless under the influence of the LXX which took them as plurals, "Happy, all those who fear Yahweh and follow in his paths."

2. *Your toil.* The Hebrew literally reads "your palms."

indeed shall you eat. The unusual word order, with *kī tō'kēl,* "indeed shall you eat," standing at the end of the clause, becomes readily explicable with the identification of *kī* as the emphatic particle which forces the verb to the end of its clause. As noticed at Ps xlix 16, the ancient versions did not appreciate this usage and consequently in their translations this emphatic particle does not appear as such; here LXX simply dropped *kī,* but Ugaritic affirmative *k* with the postposition of the verb exposes the shortcomings of LXX and other ancient versions. Additional examples include Job xxxviii 5, *mī śām m^e^maddehā kī tēdā',* "Who marked its dimensions—surely you know!" and Prov xxx 4, *mah-ššᵉmō ūmah-ššem bᵉnō kī tēdā',* "What is his name, and what is his son's name—surely you know!"

3. *fruitful.* The psalmist employs the archaic feminine participle *pōriyyāh,* which preserves the final *-y* of the root (GK, § 75k), doubtless in order to add two syllables to the colon. Thus the 9:7 syllable count corresponds to the 9:7 count of the following couplet. Had he used the ordinary feminine participle *pōrāh,* his line would have read 7:7.

your wife . . . Your children. For the Ugaritic-Hebrew parallelism between these two nouns, consult the first NOTE on Ps cix 9, and THE GRAMMAR OF THE PSALTER.

within your house. Heb. *bᵉyarkᵉtē bēteka* literally means "within the penetralia of your house," but the balance with *sābīb,* "around," suggests that the original literal meaning had weakened. One senses similar attenuation even earlier in UT, 128:III:14–15, *btk rpi arṣ bpḫr qbṣ dtn,* "Amid the Rephaim of the nether world, among the assembled of Dothan," where *bpḫr,* literally "in the assembly," seems to be no more than a synonym of *btk,* "amid." The noun *yrkt,* "innards," now appears in a liver omen text from Ras Shamra published by O. Loretz and M. Dietrich in the *Festschrift C. F. A. Schaeffer* (Paris, 1970).

your house . . . your table. The uncommon parallelism between *bēteka,* "your house," and *šulḥānekā,* "your table" (cf. Ps xxiii 5–6; Prov ix 1–2), finds a Canaanite counterpart in UT, 'nt:II:29–30, *'d tšb' tmtḫṣ bbt tḫtṣb bn ṯlḥnm,* "Till sated, she smites in the house, battles between the two tables." In the face of 290 such pairs of parallel words common to Hebrew and Ugaritic it becomes difficult to understand the skepticism of Barr, *Comparative Philology and the Text of the Old Testament,* who writes, "If it is true that certain stock parallelisms were held in common with pre-Israelite poetry, it is possible that items which are formally identical with Canaanite or Ugaritic materials may nevertheless have come to be understood and used with another sense in Hebrew" (p. 229). Surely Professor Barr is being hypercritical. Is he ready to maintain that in the present verse the psalmist employs the parallelism "table//house" in senses different from those of the Canaanite poet who paired *ṯlḥn,* "table," with *bt,* "house," or that the Hebrew poet who paralleled "wife" and "children" entertained concepts substantially different from the Ugaritic writer who balanced *i<u>t</u>t*, "wife," with *bnm*, "children"?

4. *how.* Explaining *kī* as the interjection cited and documented at Ps lvi 2–3; see also James Muilenburg, HUCA 32 (1961), 143, who recognized that *kī* often has the meaning "how!" Unable to cope with *kī* here, the ancient versions ignore it and the apparatus of BH^{3} recommends that we too ignore it.

the Reliable. The divine epithet *kēn* is noticed at Ps cxxvii 2, where it is followed by Yahweh, precisely as here.

blesses. Repointing MT pual *y^{e}bōrak*, "is blessed," to piel *y^{e}bārēk*, "blesses."

the man. Reading contextual *geber* for pausal MT *gāber*, and joining it to the second colon to form a 3+3 bicolon with a 7:6 syllable count.

who fears Yahweh. The term *y^{e}rē' yhwh* forms an inclusion with vs. 1, *y^{e}rē' yhwh*, "who fears Yahweh," further showing that the singular reading in vs. 1 is correct against the plural of LXX and some recent versions.

5. *Yahweh of Zion.* Reading *yhwh-m ṣiyyōn*, a construct chain with interposed enclitic *mem*, for MT *yhwh miṣṣiyyōn*, "Yahweh from Zion"; cf. Pss cxxxiv 3, cxxxv 21, where the parallelism is cogent, and Ugar. *b'l ṣpn*, "Baal of Mount Zaphon." In our verse *yhwh-m ṣiyyōn*, "Yahweh of Zion," forms an inclusion with vs. 6d, *'al yiśrā'ēl*, "Israel's Most High."

Enjoy. As noted at Ps cvi 5, the idiom *r^{e}'ēh b^{e}* means "to enjoy." The 9:6 syllable count perfectly matches the 9:6 sequence in synonymous vs. 6.

6. *Enjoy the children.* In the idiom *r^{e}'ēh bānīm* the psalmist forgoes the preposition *b^{e}* (see preceding NOTE) because *bānīm*, "the children," begins with *bā*. The omission of *b^{e}* before *bayit*, "in the houes," affords a good analogy.

the children of your children. In the expression *bānīm l^{e}bānekā* the preposition *l^{e}* may be taken as "from" or as the *lamedh* of property, namely, "the children belonging to your children."

the peace of. Repointing MT absolute *šālōm* "peace," to construct *š^{e}lōm*, "the peace of."

Israel's Most High. Though the traditional rendition of *šālōm 'al yiśrā'ēl* as the blessing "Peace upon Israel!" is in itself meaningful, it cannot be easily pegged into these carefully carpentered lines. Hence *'al yiśrā'ēl* is preferably interpreted as the divine title forming the counterpart of vs. 5a, *yhwh-m ṣiyyōn*, "Yahweh of Zion." On *'al*, "Most High," see the second NOTE on Ps cxxi 5. In the *šīrē hamma'^{a}lōt*, "the Songs of Ascents," the divine title *'al*, "Most High," is very fitting.

PSALM 129

(cxxix 1–8)

1 *A song of ascents.*

"Much have they oppressed me since my youth,"
let Israel say—
2 "Much have they oppressed me since my youth,
but they have not prevailed over me.
3 Upon my back the plowmen plowed,
upon it they made their furrows long."
4 May Yahweh the Just snap
the yoke of the wicked!
5 May they retreat in humiliation,
all those who hate Zion!
6 May they be like grass on the housetops,
which before the plucker's eyes withers away,
7 So that the reaper cannot fill his hand,
the gatherer of sheaves his bosom,
8 Nor those who pass by say,
"Yahweh's blessing be yours;
We bless you in the name of Yahweh!"

NOTES

cxxix. A national lament consisting of two stanzas. Verses 1–3 briefly but graphically describe the oppression to which Israel has been subjected during her long history; despite these sufferings Israel has been preserved by God. The second stanza (vss. 4–8) consists of a prayer for the overthrow of Israel's present enemies. The psalm itself does not furnish enough indication to identify the enemies denounced, nor is it possible to establish the date of composition.

1. *since my youth.* The history of Israel is here, as in some other biblical texts such as Hos 17, xi 1; Jer ii 2, compared to the life of an individual.

Israel's life began in Egypt, and from the period of Egyptian bondage on, it has repeatedly been oppressed by enemies.

let Israel say. Namely, let Israel thankfully recall the lessons of its history; cf. Ps cxxiv 1.

3. *Upon my back.* Comparing UT, 62:4–5, *ṯḥrṯ km gn aplb k'mq ṯlṯ bmt,* "She plows her breast like a garden, like a valley she furrows her back," and Isa li 23, "Who said to you, 'Bow down that we may walk over you'; And you flattened your back like the ground, like a street for them to walk on."

the plowmen. Heb *ḥōrᵉšīm* equals Ugar. *ḥrṯm,* "plowmen."

the plowmen plowed. For MT *ḥārᵉšū ḥōrᵉšīm,* 11QPsᵃ reads *ḥršw rš'ym,* "the wicked plowed," and LXX *hoi hamartōloi,* "the sinners," suggests that their Hebrew master copy also had *rš'ym.* In view of the prevailing agricultural metaphor, MT must be judged the superior reading. The credibility of such a figure has been established in the Ugaritic text cited in the next to the last NOTE, even though the meaning of the metaphor had been blurred by the time of the LXX and 11QPsᵃ, and this obscuration may help to explain how the variant *rš'ym,* "the sinners," originated.

upon it . . . their furrows. This translation emerges when the consonantal cluster *lm'nwtm* is broken up into *lāmō,* "upon it" (examined at Ps lv 20), and *'ᵃnōtām,* "their furrows," a plural noun to be equated with *'nt* in the Ugaritic phrase *'nt mḥrṯt,* "the furrows of the plowland," a phrase collocating two roots concurring in our verse; see *Psalms I,* p. XLII.

4. *May . . . snap.* Though all versions understand *qiṣṣēṣ* as an indicative verb stating a historical fact, the optative or jussive forms in the subsequent verses suggest that *qiṣṣēṣ* should be interpreted as a precative perfect, a mode frequently found in parallelism with jussive verbs. If we translate *qiṣṣēṣ* as historical perfect ("he has cut the cords of the wicked" RSV), then the following prayer becomes rather pointless ("May all who hate Zion be put to shame and turned backward" RSV). In other words, the second stanza, which consists of a prayer, begins at vs. 4, and not in vs. 5, as analyzed by most commentators.

Yahweh the Just. Identifying *yhwh ṣaddīq* as a composite divine title (contrast RSV, "The Lord is righteous") which casts new light on Ps xi 5, *yhwh ṣaddīq yibḥᵉnū rāšā'* (MT *yibḥan wᵉrāšā'*), "Yahweh the Just will assay the wicked" (the verb *yibḥᵉnū* may be explained as a plural of majesty, as in Ps xlvi 5, or as the singular *yaqtulu* form; contrast *Psalms I,* ad loc.), and Ps xi 7, *kī ṣaddīq yhwh ṣᵉdāqōt 'āhēb,* "Because the Just Yahweh loves just actions." The composite divine title *yhwh ṣaddīq,* "Yahweh the Just," may also be recognized in Zeph iii 5, *yhwh ṣaddīq bᵉqirbah lō' ya'ᵃšeh 'awlāh,* "Yahweh the Just is in her midst; he does no wrong." The LXX also read these words as a composite title; contrast RSV, "The Lord within her is righteous, he does no wrong." On the divine title *ṣaddīq* alone, see *Psalms II* on Ps lxxv 11, and the NOTES on Pss cxii

4, cxix 137, 138, and cxli 5, and for the composite title *ṣaddīq 'ātīq,* "the Ancient Just One," consult NOTES on Ps xxxi 19.

By recognizing that the second stanza begins in vs. 4, we recover an inclusion created by *yhwh ṣaddīq,* "Yahweh the Just," and the final words of the psalm in vs. 8, *šēm yhwh,* "the name of Yahweh."

the yoke. Interpreting *'ᵃbōt,* "thongs," as metonymy for "yoke," as observed at Ps ii 3; BJ also understands *'ᵃbōt* as *le joug.* This prayer can be understood in two different ways: if the metaphor of the preceding verse is continued, the sense is that the plowers' harness be broken so that they could no longer continue their plowing. But if the figure has been changed, then Israel may be the ox, and the yoke (or the thongs which fasten it) would be the yoke of servitude. Just what historical subjection the psalmist had in mind cannot be determined from the contents of the lament.

5. *May they retreat in humiliation.* Literally "May they be humiliated and turn backward," *yēbōšū wᵉyissōgū 'āḥōr* is a good instance of hendiadys; cf. Meir Weiss, JBL 86 (1967), 421, who writes, "It has been established that hendiadys is in more frequent use in biblical Hebrew than in any other language."

all those who hate Zion! The poet creates suspense by making the subject explicit only in the second colon; see the first NOTE on Ps cv 17. RSV destroys this suspense by advancing the subject: "May all who hate Zion be put to shame and turned backward!"

6. *grass on the housetops.* Grass or grain springs up quickly on the flat roofs of Palestine which are covered with packed earth; having no depth of soil to take strong root in, (Matt xiii 5 f.) it withers quickly and yields no joyous harvest. Previously unwitnessed in other Semitic languages, Heb. *gāg,* "roof, housetop," plural *gaggōt* appears in Ugaritic both as singular *gg* and as plural *ggt,* thus illustrating the close lexical relationship between these two Canaanite dialects. Cf. UT, Glossary, No. 556.

before . . . eyes. Much-disputed *qadmat,* which numerous scholars identify with Aram. *qadmat,* "before" (temporal), in Ezra v 11; Dan vi 11, can also be interpreted spatially which here makes better sense; see the next NOTE. The unusual prepositional form *qadmat* conforms to the pattern attested in the Phoenician prepositions with the *-t* ending, such as *'lt,* "upon" (cf. also Ugar. *'lt*), *pnt,* "before," and *btkt,* "in the midst of;" cf. Harris, *A Grammar of the Phoenician Language,* pp. 62–63. For *qdmt,* "in the presence of," in Egyptian Aramaic of the Persian period, consult J. T. Milik, *Biblica* 48 (1967), 549.

the plucker's. Repointing MT perfect *šālap* to participial *šōlēp,* which balances nicely the participles *qōṣēr,* "the reaper," and *mᵉ'ammēr,* "the gatherer of sheaves," in vs. 7. The root *šlp,* "to pluck," probably occurs in the Ugaritic name of a musical instrument *ṯlb,* listed in a series with *knr,* "lyre," *tp,* "drum," and *mṣltm,* "cymbals"; cf. UT, Glossary, No. 1274. Hence it would be an instrument activated by plucking the strings.

withers away. The comment of Schmidt, *Die Psalmen,* p. 230, that *yābēš* is an explanatory gloss on the uncommon word *šādap,* "to be blasted," overlooks the wordplay on *yābēš,* "withers away," and vs. 5 *yēbōšū,* "in humiliation." As noticed at Ps lx 5, puns are not infrequent even in laments. Though damaged, 11QPs[a] *yb*[ ] sustains MT *yābēš.*

7. *So that.* Just as the relative pronoun *'ᵃšer* also functions as the conjunction "so that" (BDB, p. 83b), so relative pronoun *š* may well have carried that meaning in our verse. To work *š* into their translations current versions resort to paraphrase, e.g., RSV, "with which [=*š*] the reaper does not fill his hand."

8. *Yahweh's blessing be yours.* Words that would customarily be spoken by passers-by to the harvesters. Cf. Ruth ii 4, "Boaz came from Bethlehem, and said to the reapers, 'Yahweh be with you!' "

We bless you. This greeting seems to be an emphatic repetition of the preceding blessing; cf. Ps cxviii 26.

the name of Yahweh. The second stanza closes with the words *šēm yhwh,* which form an inclusion with the opening words of the stanza in vs. 4, *yhwh ṣaddīq,* "Yahweh the Just."

PSALM 130

(cxxx 1–8)

1 *A song of ascents*

Out of the depths I cry to you, Yahweh,
2 Lord, hear my voice!
Let your ears be alert
to my plea for mercy.
3 If you should keep record of iniquities, Yah,
Lord, who could survive?
4 But with you there is forgiveness,
that you might be revered.
5 I call Yahweh,
my soul calls,
and for his word I am waiting.
6 My soul looks to my Lord
through the watches till morning,
through the watches till morning.
7 Wait, O Israel, for Yahweh,
because with Yahweh there is kindness,
and with him abundant redemption.
8 He himself will redeem Israel
from all iniquities against Him.

NOTES

cxxx. The sixth of the Penitential Psalms, the *De Profundis* is the lament of an individual who, like the author of Ps li, pleads for deliverance from sin that has plunged him into a spiritual abyss which he likens to the depths of the nether world. Some commentators claim that vss. 7–8 stamp the psalm as the lament of the congregation and not of an individual, but the exhortation to Israel in those verses does not necessarily imply that the speaker in vss. 1–6 is Israel personified. In fact, it tends to distinguish the speaker from Israel.

Though the status of the individual is not clearly indicated, the several telling similarities of expression in this lament and in royal Ps lxxxvi warrant the tentative identification of the speaker as the Israelite king. Thus the divine address *'ᵃdōnāy* (vss. 2, 3, 6) corresponds to Ps lxxxvi 3, 5, 8, 12, 15; vs. 2, *qōl taḥᵃnūnāy,* "my plea for mercy," finds a counterpart in Ps lxxxvi 6; the root of the rare noun *sᵉlīḥāh,* "forgiveness" (vs. 4), occurs in the divine attribute *sallaḥ,* "forgiving," a hapax legomenon in Ps lxxxvi 5.

If this correlation does have meaning, the psalm would date to the pre-Exilic period when Israel still had a king. Hence one must dissent from the majority opinion, recently reaffirmed by Kraus, *Psalmen,* II, p. 870, who asserts that for linguistic and formal reasons (which he fails to spell out) Ps cxxx must be assigned to a relatively late (i.e., post-Exilic) period.

The lament is essentially in two parts, with the major break at the end of vs. 4. In the first stanza, the psalmist addresses Yahweh, but in the second (vss. 5–8) he speaks to Israel. From his own nightlong vigils the poet can assure his fellow believers that patience in prayer will unfailingly win divine forgiveness for repentant sinners. Thus in its twofold structure this poem closely resembles Ps cxxxi.

1. *Out of the depths.* The psalmist depicts himself in the nethermost regions of Sheol; similar descriptions are encountered in Pss xviii 6–7, lxi 3; Jon ii 7–8; Lam iii 35; Ecclus li 9. The psalmist's sin has cast him into depths from which only the forgiving God can deliver him.

2. *hear . . . Let your ears be alert.* This sequence of synonymous expressions finds an earlier counterpart in UT, 127:42, *ištmʿ wtqǵ udn,* "Hear and be alert of ear," a phrase collocating the roots of *šimʿāh,* "Hear!" and *'oznekā,* "your ears."

3. *you should keep record.* The verb *tišmor,* usually rendered "If you should mark," means not only to observe iniquities carefully, but also to record them strictly along with their well-deserved punishment. Compare Ps lxxix 8, "Do not record to our debit, O Scribe, the iniquities of our forefathers," and the accompanying NOTE on the motif of the divine bookkeeper, also touched upon at Ps cix 14–15.

Yah, Lord. Some critics believe that for MT *yāh 'ᵃdōnāy* we should read only *yhwh* or only *'ᵃdōnāy,* but the current 7:7 syllable count (consult the second NOTE on vs. 7) and the confirmation of MT by 11QPsᵃ, *yh 'dwny,* are arguments against textual changes here.

Lord. The reading *'ᵃdōnāy* is further (see preceding NOTE) upheld by the observation at Ps lxxxvi (introductory NOTE) that the repeated use of this divine address (see vss. 2, 6) implies that the servant is addressing his master, a usage that falls in with the literary style of Akkadian and Canaanite royal correspondence.

4. *that you might be revered.* The thought of the poet, that forgiveness leads to the worship of God, finds more ample expression in Rom ii 4,

"Or do you think lightly of his wealth of kindness, of tolerance, and of patience, without recognizing that God's kindness is meant to lead you to a change of heart?"

5. *I call Yahweh.* Here the psalmist addresses Israel and describes how with heart and soul he invokes Yahweh until he receives a reply. Though traditionally rendered "I wait," *qiwwītī*, followed by third-person *qiwwᵉtāh* "[my soul] calls," can scarcely be dissociated from Ps xl 2, *qawwōh qiwwītī yhwh*, "Constantly I called Yahweh." This derivation nicely aligns vs. 5, which begins the second stanza, with vs. 1, *qᵉrā'tīkā* "I cry to you." To the bibliography of *qwh*, "to call," should be added Lipiński, RB 75 (1968), 343–44, n. 99.

I call . . . I am waiting. Beginning the verse with a verb followed by accusative Yahweh, and closing with a prepositional phrase and verb, the poet establishes an inclusion along with chiasmus.

6. *My soul looks to my Lord.* In a state of expectation, similar to that described in Ps cxxiii 2, "So our eyes are on Yahweh our God, / till he have mercy on us."

to my Lord. Reading *la'dōnay-mi*, with enclitic *-mi*, for MT *la'dōnāy mi;* see the next NOTE.

through the watches. Once the initial *mem* of MT *miššōmᵉrīm* "than the watchmen," has been attached to the preceding word as the enclitic *mi*, consonantal *šmrym* may be vocalized *šimmūrīm*, "watches, vigils," a noun attested twice in Exod xii 42, *lēl šimmūrīm hū' lᵉyhwh*, "a night of watches for Yahweh." In the later Jewish system there were three watches in the night and four according to the Greco-Roman reckoning. Syntactically, *šimmūrīm* functions as an accusative of duration of time, like Ps xvi 7, *lēlōt*, "during the watches of the night," or UT, 1019:2–5, "May the gods protect you, keep you hale, strengthen you for a thousand days and ten thousand years" (*alp ymm wrbt šnt*).

through the watches till morning. By repeating the phrase *šimmūrīm labbōqer* the poet tries to suggest how the time seemed to drag on while he awaited the divine reply assuring him that he had been forgiven. Hence those critics appear ill-advised to delete the phrase as dittographic, a deletion now countered by 11QPsᵃ.

7. *Wait, O Israel, for Yahweh.* This exhortation, missing in some manuscripts of the LXX, has been treated by some scholars as an intrusion from Ps cxxxi 3, but its presence in 11QPsᵃ counsels caution. To be sure, here it lacks the balancing colon found in Ps cxxxi 3, but its very wording suggests that it was a stereotyped formula employed when a hortatory formula was needed. That it should stand *extra metrum* should not alone brand it as an intruder, especially since it serves here as a good introduction to the psalmist's message.

with him. In order to read vs. 7b–c as a 3+2 bicolon, Gunkel and others delete *'immō*. But this deletion is confuted by the presence of *'mw* in 11QPsᵃ, the current 7:7 syllable count (see second NOTE on vs. 3), and by the consideration that all three cola of vs. 7 can readily be scanned as 3+3 instead of 3+2.

redemption. 8. *He . . . will redeem.* The sequence of noun-verb from the same root, namely *p^e^dūt*, "redemption," and *yipdeh*, "He . . . will redeem," evidently follows a Canaanite pattern witnessed in UT, 68:11–12, *šmk at ygrš ygrš grš ym*, "Your own name is Driver! Driver, drive out Sea!"; 51:IV:41–42, *tḥmk il ḥkm ḥkmt ʿm ʿlm*, "Your message, El, is wise; your wisdom is eternal sagacity." Cf. also Ps cxlvii 10–11; Job xii 2, xxxiv 35; Prov ix 2–3, xiii 21–22, for other instances of this stylistic device.

iniquities against Him. Commonly rendered "his (=Israel's) iniquities," the suffix of *ʿ^a^wōnōtāyw* may also be taken as an objective suffix, namely Israel's iniquities against Yahweh. From this parsing emerges an inclusion, the verse beginning with *w^e^hūʾ*, "He himself," and ending with *-āyw*, "against him" (courtesy of Wilfred Watson). Cf. the NOTE on Ps xviii 24, *mēʿ^a^wōnī*, "not to offend him," and Job xxii 18.

PSALM 131

(cxxxi 1–3)

1 *A song of ascents. Of David.*

Yahweh, my heart is not haughty,
nor my eyes raised high.
I have not meddled with lofty matters,
nor with thoughts too wondrous for me have I been filled.
2 But I have kept my soul level and tranquil,
like an infant with its mother;
like an infant with him is my soul.
3 Wait, Israel, for Yahweh,
from now until eternity.

NOTES

cxxxi. This psalm of trust (cf. Ps xi), whose speaker might well be the king, consists of nine 3-beat cola. In the first four cola the psalmist directly addresses Yahweh (vs. 1), denying that he has been haughty or has behaved arrogantly. In the last four, however, he speaks to the congregation (vss. 2b–3), revealing how he achieved equanimity of soul and exhorting Israel to trust in the Lord. The fifth colon (vs. 2a) serves as a transition and seems to be addressed both to Yahweh and to Israel.

1. *my heart is not haughty*. Cf. royal Ps ci 5b.

my eyes raised high. In the phrase *rāmū ʿēnay* we have the second literary rapprochement with royal psalms; cf. Pss xviii 28 and ci 5b.

I have not meddled. Cf. the warning to Baruch in Jer xlv 5 and the expansion of this thought in Ecclus iii 18 ff. Piel *hillaktī* literally means "go to and fro." The *qtl* form *hillaktī* makes a good chiastic counterpart to the *yqtl* verb *'immālē'* in the second colon. The negative particle *lō'* also negatives the second-colon verb.

lofty matters. Frequently rendered "great matters," *g*ᵉ*dōlōt* seems here to bear the nuance discussed at Pss civ 25 and cviii 4; see below the first NOTE on vs. 2.

have I been filled. Unexplained MT *'im lō'* in vs. 2 fulfills a semantic and metrical function when attached to the end of vs. 1 and vocalized as niphal *'immālē'*. Semantically, it completes the thought of first-colon *hillaktī,* "I have [not] meddled," and metrically restores a needed beat to vs. 1d. With this transposition all nine cola of the psalm possess three beats each.

In addition to being chiastically paired with *lō' hillaktī,* "I have not meddled," *'immālē'* shares its negative particle; other instances of double-duty negatives are listed at Ps lxxv 6, and the recognition of this ellipsis promises to make sense of Job xv 30, xxvii 15, xxxix 17.

The construction *b^eniplā'ōt . . . 'immālē',* "with thoughts too wondrous . . . been filled," besides its biblical analogues, enjoys a good parallel in UT, 'nt:II:25–26, *ymlu lbh bšmḫt,* "Her heart is filled with happiness."

2. *I have kept . . . level.* This literal translation of *šiwwītī* brings out the thought of the psalmist who avows that his mind has not reached up for doctrines too towering for his understanding.

As noted above in the introductory NOTE, this fifth of nine cola serves as a hinge joining the two parts of the psalm.

with him. Repointing MT *'ālay,* "upon me," to *'ālēy;* the suffix of *'alēy* parses as the Phoenician third-person suffix. Thus we can see the interesting parallelism of two different third-person singular suffixes in the balance of *'immō,* "his mother," and *'ālēy,* "with him." This form is recorded in Phoenician Kilamuwa, lines 7–8, *wškr 'nk 'ly,* "And I was drunk (i.e., helpless) before him," and in Isa lii 14, *šām^emū 'ālēy kī* (MT *'āleykā*) *rabbīm,* "Full many were aghast at him." For further details, see the writer's article, "Phoenician Elements in Isaiah 52:13 – 53:12," appearing in the *W. F. Albright Anniversary Volume* (1971).

For a cognate sentiment, cf. Ps xxvii 10, "Though my father and my mother abandon me, / yet Yahweh will receive me."

3. *Wait, Israel.* Filled with the sense of security that comes with trust in Yahweh, the psalmist can exhort his fellow Israelites to await the coming of divine consolation and reassurance.

PSALM 132

(cxxxii 1–18)

1 *A song of ascents.*

"Remember Yahweh, O David,
all his triumphs too.
2 He who swore to Yahweh,
vowed to the Mighty of Jacob,
3 'I will not approach the canopy in my house,
or ascend the couch spread for me.
4 I will not give sleep to my eyes,
to my pupils slumber,
5 Until I find a place for Yahweh,
a dwelling for the Mighty of Jacob.'"
6 "Look! we heard about it in Ephrathah,
we learned about it in the fields of Jaar.
7 Let us go to his dwelling,
let us worship at his footstool."
8 "Arise, Yahweh, to your resting place,
you, and the ark your fortress.
9 May your priests be clothed with justice
and your devoted ones shout for joy.
10 'For the sake of David your servant,
turn not away the face of your anointed.'"
11 "Yahweh has sworn, O David,
truly, he will not swerve from it.
'The fruit of your body
will I set upon your throne,
12 If your sons keep my covenant,
and my stipulation which I shall teach them;
Their sons, too, for ever
will sit upon your throne.
13 For Yahweh has chosen Zion,
he has desired it for his seat.

14 This is my resting place for ever,
here will I sit because I have desired it.
15 Her pilgrims will I abundantly bless,
her needy will I satisfy with food.
16 Her priests will I clothe with salvation,
and her devoted ones will always shout for joy.
17 There I will make a horn glow, O David,
I will trim the lamp, O my anointed!
18 His foes will I clothe with humiliation,
but upon him will sparkle his crown.' "

Notes

cxxxii. The lack of early non-biblical psalms severely limits the contribution of Northwest Semitic philology toward the resolution of problems of literary genre in the Psalter. Here, however, the application of purely philological data afforded by recent textual discoveries markedly clarifies the form of Ps cxxxii. Commentators agree that the structure of this poem is "strange," "peculiar," and "difficult to recognize." Attempts to determine its genre have resulted in at least three classifications: "Song of Zion," a "Royal Psalm," and simply a "liturgy." For fuller discussion, see Kraus, *Psalmen*, II, pp. 878–83, and T. E. Fretheim, "Psalm 132: A Form-Critical Study," in JBL 86 (1967), 289–300.

From the translation proposed here, this royal psalm appears to have been composed in the tenth century as part of the liturgy for the feast when the ark was carried in procession to Jerusalem (vss. 6–10). According to II Sam v 6–12, King David, after he took Jerusalem, built an encircling wall and then a palace for himself and his retinue, but there is no mention of an abode for Yahweh. II Sam vi 10–12 reports that David was unwilling to remove the ark from the house of Obed-edom the Gittite to Jerusalem until "it was told King David that Yahweh had blessed the house of Obed-edom and all that belonged to him, because of the ark of God." We are not informed who it was that informed the king, but we may suppose that it was his confidant the prophet Nathan. In fact, vs. 1 of our psalm may have been spoken by Nathan on this occasion because the king's reaction is immediate. He at once orders the ark to be brought to Jerusalem, and the procession described in II Sam vi 13–19 may serve as commentary on vss. 6–10 of our psalm, as will be indicated in several of the Notes.

The psalm divides into three stanzas: vss. 1–5 contain David's promise to find a home for Yahweh in Jerusalem; vss. 6–10 describe the procession and give the text of prayers asking God to come to Jerusalem, to bless his priests, and his king. The third stanza (vss. 11–18) cites the text of Yahweh's oath to perpetuate both the Davidic dynasty and his own presence in Jerusalem.

As can be seen from the following NOTES, the language of the psalm is extremely archaic. Scholars have long noticed the difference between Ps cxxxii and the other Songs of Ascents; it differs not only in length, but also in rhythm. We miss the rhetorical repetition and the elegiac measure which mark many of them. But no scholar has yet documented the archaic quality of the language. In fact, Delbert R. Hillers, "Ritual Procession of the Ark and Ps 132," in CBQ 30 (1968), 48–55, writes, "Its language displays little or no real archaism of the sort that might be expected to appear in a poem from the early centuries of the monarchy. *šᵉnat* (for **šinat*), v. 4, may be an example of the preservation of an older feminine absolute singular ending, **-at,* but this single example of what might be an archaism is insufficient evidence for calling the whole psalm archaic." True enough, isolated archaic elements do not suffice to mark a poem as early, but the sheer concentration of archaic words, forms, parallelisms, and phrases in this textually well-preserved poem accords with the contents which point to a tenth-century date of composition.

Some of the literary characteristics which may be singled out here include the triple use of the vocative *lamedh* (vss. 1, 11, 17); *lᵉ*, "upon," for *'al,* in vss. 11–12; the uncommon meaning of vs. 15, *ṣydh,* "her pilgrims," vs. 17, *'aṣmīᵃḥ,* "I will make glow," vs. 18, *yāṣīs,* "will sparkle"; chiasmus (vss. 4, 8, 15–16); court style in vss. 1–2, 13–14, 17–18; phrases matched in Ugaritic (vss. 5, 11, 12, 15), and the sequence A+B+C//B́+Ć in vss. 2, 4, 5, 6, a very frequent pattern in the Ras Shamra tablets.

1. *Remember Yahweh, O David.* This radical departure from the traditional "Remember, O Lord, in David's favor" (RSV) derives from parsing *lᵉ* as vocative in *zᵉkōr yhwh lᵉdāwīd;* the vocative *lamedh* presumably recurs in vss. 11 and 17. The only other occurrence of this particular sequence is Ps cxxxvii 7, *zᵉkōr yhwh libnē 'ᵉdōm,* rendered by RSV, "Remember, O Lord, against the Edomites." It does seem a trifle odd that in the same formula *lᵉ* should first be translated "in [David's] favor," and then "against" in Ps cxxxvii 7. But as will be seen below, the structure of Ps cxxxvii favors the translation "Remember Yahweh, O sons of Edom!" so that here too the *lamedh* of *lᵉdāwīd* should be parsed as vocative. Cf. Ps xcviii 3, *zᵉkōr* (MT *zākār*) *ḥasdō we'ᵉmūnātō lᵉbēt yiśrā'ēl,* "Remember his love and his fidelity, O house of Israel!"

To be sure, biblical tradition portrays King David as devout and hence not needing such a reminder, but a careful reading of II Sam v 1–16 suggests that such a reminder may not have been out of place. II Sam vi 11 reports that the ark remained in the house of Obed-edom the Gittite three months and would probably have stayed there longer had not someone (perhaps the prophet Nathan) reminded David that it was time that the ark be brought to Jerusalem.

his triumphs. Repointing MT *'unnōtō*, a vocable of disputed meaning, to *'anwōtāyw*, a defective spelled plural of *'anwāh*, "triumph." Cf. royal Ps xviii 36, "And by your triumph [*'anwātekā*] you made me great." As noticed in the Introduction, the root *'nw*, "to triumph," is a hallmark of royal psalms. As is clear from Ps xviii 36 the victories won by the Israelite king are properly Yahweh's victories since it was only by his help that they were realized.

too. An attempt to reproduce the emphatic nature of the *nota accusativi 'ēt.*

2. *He who swore.* Namely, King David. The shift from the direct (second person) address of vs. 1 to the indirect (third person) address here, illustrates court style which is preserved in some royal psalms, as noticed in the introductory NOTE to Ps lxi. Other instances of court style recur in vss. 13 and 17–18. Penar, in VD 45 (1967), 36, in order to retain the second person in both vss. 1–2, vocalizes the perfect forms *nišba'* and *nādar* as infinitives absolute, and translates, "You who swore . . . you who vowed." It should be pointed out that the problem of shift of person also besets the traditional rendition of these lines which construe Yahweh as second person in vs. 1 and as third person in vs. 2: "Remember, O Lord, in David's favor . . . how he swore to the Lord" (RSV).

the Mighty of Jacob. The recurrence of this title in vs. 5, together with the impressive list of archaic forms and usages registered in these NOTES, suggest that *'abīr ya'aqōb*, "the Mighty of Jacob," is related more closely to the occurrence of this title in the eleventh-century Gen xlix 24 than to the later use in Isa xlix 26 and lx 16. In Ugaritic *ibr*, "mighty," is used to designate things of unusual strength, such as a stallion or an ox.

3. *the canopy in my house.* In the phrase *'ōhēl bētī*, literally "the tent in my house," *'ōhel* probably designates the canopy or baldachin over the bed. Compare Prov vii 17, *naptī miškābī mōr 'ōhālīm* (MT *'ahālīm*) *qinnāmōn* (MT *we*-), "I have sprinkled my bed with myrrh, my canopy with cinnamon," with the suffix of *miškābī*, "my bed," also modifying its plural counterpart *'ōhālīm*, "my canopy," the same stylistic device employed in, say, Prov xxvii 23.

ascend the couch. The phrase *'e'eleh 'al 'ereś* recalls UT, 2 Aqht:I:39, *l'ršh y'l*, "He ascends his couch."

4. *sleep.* MT's pointing *šenat* rather convincingly indicates that the Masoretes did not understand the form *šnt*, which they vocalized anomalously. Scholars agree that the correct vocalization should be *šēnāt*, an archaic form with the feminine ending *-āt;* cf. Ugar. *šnt*, "sleep," and the pairing of *šēnāh*, "sleep," with *tenūmāh*, "slumber," in the ancient proverb in Prov vi 4.

sleep . . . slumber. The Hebrew balance of *šēnāt* with *tenūmāh* answers to the Ugaritic parallelism of these roots cited at Ps cxxi 4. Cf. UT, Krt:33–35, *šnt tluan wyškb nhmmt wyqmṣ*, "Sleep overcomes him and he reclines, slumber and he curls up." To forgo sleep and bed until he accomplishes his purpose is a strong oath indeed, but one which harmonizes with the ardent temperament of David. For example, the external display of emotion on the removal of the ark to Jerusalem, which disgusted Michal (II Sam vi 16), is indicative of his personal devotion and furnishes an insight into the psychological aspects of his personality.

to my eyes, to my pupils. Preserving the chiastic order of the Hebrew; the psalmist employs chiastic word order also in vss. 8, 15–16.

my pupils. The comments at Ps xi 4 that "eyelids" (RSV) is an incorrect translation of *'ap'appay* is sustained not only by Ugar. *'p'p,* "pupils," but also by 4Q 184:13, *w'p'pyh bpḥz trym lr'wt,* "And she wantonly raises her pupils to see." One does not see with the eyelids. Cf. also Jer ix 17 and Brekelmans, BO 23 (1966), 308, who observes that "Neither in Ugaritic nor in Hebrew does this word [*'p'p*] signify the eyelash, but rather the eye itself."

5. *a place.* This use of the word *māqōm,* "a place," recalls the narrative describing the procession of the ark to Jerusalem in II Sam vi 17, "And they brought in the ark of Yahweh, and set it in its place (*mᵉqōmō*) inside the tent which David had pitched for it."

a dwelling. Where II Sam vi 17 uses *'ōhel,* "tent," the psalmist employs *miškānōt,* "a dwelling." Since, however, *'ōhel,* "tent," and *miškānōt,* "dwelling," occur frequently in Ugaritic-Hebrew parallelism, the two words may be considered synonymous and even interchangeable.

As observed in the sixth NOTE on Ps xliii 3, plural *miškānōt* with singular meaning "dwelling," conforms to the Ugaritic-Hebrew pattern characteristic of names for habitations. Cf. R. de Vaux, RB 73 (1966), 448, 487, who also recognizes that biblical nouns such as *'ōhel,* "tent," *hēkāl,* "temple," *bayit,* "house," were borrowed from the sedentary Canaanites in Palestine, so that theorizing about the nomadic origins of these and similar terms in Hebrew loses much of its relevance.

6. *Look!* The interjection *hinnēh* introduces the words of the Israelites about to set out in procession with the ark toward Jerusalem.

we heard about it. The famous "it" problem created by the feminine suffixes of *šᵉmaʿᵃnūhā* and *mᵉṣā'nūhā* has "never been satisfactorily explained," as recently stated by Hillers, CBQ 30 (1968), 52, n. 15. The problem does not seem to be insoluble; one may easily assume that the suffixes refer to the oath sworn by David in vs. 2. The Hebrew word for "oath" is feminine *šᵉbū'āh.* Once they heard of the king's decision to bring the ark to Jerusalem, the Israelites in the environs of Jerusalem made plans to participate in the procession.

Ephrathah . . . the fields of Jaar. Place names which have not been certainly identified, though some equate the former with Bethlehem, David's city (though the ark never had any known connection with Bethlehem), and the latter with Kiriath-jearim, where the ark had been kept from Samuel's time until David became king in Jerusalem (I Sam vii 1–2; II Chron i 4).

we learned about it. For this nuance of *meṣā'nūhā*, cf. Eccles vii 14, 27, 29; Job xxxvii 23; see BDB, p. 593a.

7. *Let us go*. The cohortative verb *nābō'āh* expresses the mutual exhortation of the Israelites to go to Jerusalem where the ark will be placed.

his footstool. Referring either to the sanctuary where the ark will be temporarily placed, or to the ark itself. For a full discussion of *hdm*, "footstool," in the Ras Shamra texts, see Gössmann, "Scabellum pedum tuorum," *Divinitas* 11 (1967), 36–44, and pp. 45–52 for the footstool in Near Eastern archaeology. Its use here may chronologically link our psalm to tenth-century Ps cx 1. Though Yahweh is not explicitly mentioned in this line, the suffixes of *miškenōtāyw*, "his dwelling place," and *hadōm raglāyw*, "his footstool," do refer to him. He is, however, directly addressed in the next verse, so perhaps we have here an instance of delayed explicitation, a topic treated at Ps cv 17.

8. *Arise, Yahweh*. This prayer inviting God to occupy the resting place prepared for him in Jerusalem was probably uttered by the priests. It is quoted in II Chron vi 41 at the end of Solomon's prayer at the dedication of the temple. Some commentators suppose that in vss. 8 ff. the psalmist brings us into the Solomonic age, but it is more natural to assume that he is still describing David's transfer of the ark to Mount Zion.

your resting place. Namely within the tent pitched by David in Jerusalem, as described in II Sam vi 17. The choice of the term "resting place" suggests that it will be but a temporary dwelling, until the temple is built. F. M. Cross, Jr., in *Biblical Motifs: Origins and Transformations*, ed. Alexander Altmann (Cambridge, Mass., 1966), p. 22, prefers to read with II Chron vi 46, *lenūḥekā*, "to your rest," especially since Ugar. *nḫt* is used precisely of a royal throne. He explains the present reading as an anticipation of vs. 14, *menūḥātī*, "my resting place." Hillers, CBQ 30 (1968), 50–51, proposes the translation "Arise, O Yahweh, from your resting-place, You and your mighty ark," but this destroys the parallelism between vs. 7, "Let us go to his dwelling [*lemiškenōtāyw*]," and "Arise, Yahweh, to your resting place [*limenūḥātekā*]."

the ark your fortress. On *'arōn 'uzzekā*, see the comments at Ps lxxviii 61, and G. Henton Davies, "The Ark in the Psalms," in *Promise and Fulfilment: Essays Presented to Professor S. H. Hooke*, ed. F. F. Bruce (Edinburgh, 1963), pp. 51–61. This is the only explicit reference to *'arōn*, "ark," in the Psalter, but its connection with *'uzzekā*, "your fortress," permits the exegete to recognize other allusions to the ark in the Psalter. Heb. *'arōn* equals Ugar. *arn*, which denotes "box," and Phoen. *'rn*, "sarcophagus."

9. *your priests . . . your devoted ones*. These parallel nouns may be interpreted as an instance of hendiadys, namely, "your devoted priests."

with justice. II Chron vi 41 reads trisyllabic *tešū'āh*, "salvation," for our disyllabic *ṣedeq,* "justice," but the present 9:9 syllable count sustains the psalm text against II Chron vi 41.

shout for joy. The current 9:9 syllable count also discountenances the insertion of absolute infinitive *rannēn* before *y^{e}rannēnū,* "shout for joy," as proposed by some commentators on the basis of vs. 16.

10. *For the sake of David . . . turn not away.* Understanding this line as a prayer sung by the priests during the procession of the ark.

David . . . your anointed. As in vs. 17, where *m^{e}šīḥī,* "my anointed," parallel to David, is David himself, so here *m^{e}šīḥekā* again parallel to David, refers to David himself, and not to one of his successors.

11. *O David.* As in vs. 1, the *l^e* of *l^{e}dāwīd* preferably parses as the vocative *lamedh.* Yahweh's oath corresponds to David's oath in vs. 2.

truly. The NOTE on Ps xxxi 7 cites the evidence for this interpretation of *'^{e}met.* RSV, however, joins *'^{e}met* to the first colon, "The Lord swore to David a sure oath (='^{e}met), but the resulting syllabic and accentual imbalance (9:6 syllable count and 4+2 beat) argues against this translation. When *'^{e}met,* "truly," is construed with the second colon as an emphatic substantive, the syllable count becomes a better balanced 7:8 with a 3+3 beat.

from it. The antecedent of the suffix in *mimmennāh* being feminine *š^{e}bū'āh,* "oath," the implied object of first-colon *nišbā',* "has sworn." This explanation tends to confirm the interpretation given the feminine suffixes in vs. 6.

The fruit of your body. The construction *mipp^{e}rī biṭn^{e}kā* recalls UT, 49:I:17–18, *tn aḥd b bnk wamlkn,* "Give one of your sons that I might make him king."

The widely shared suspicion is that the current 2+2 beat of vs. 11b has resulted from the falling out of a word; the prevailing measure is 3+3. But the present 6:6 syllable count and the scansion of vs. 8 into 2+2+2 make it difficult to believe that the text is here defective.

will I set upon your throne. The 11QPs^a variant *'šyt 'l* (MT *l^e*) *ks'* points up the antiquity of the construction *'āšīt l^e,* which is now seen to be identical with UT, 62:14–15, *lktp 'nt ktšth,* "Upon the shoulder of Anath indeed she put him." Had this usage been current in post-Exilic times, to which numerous commentators assign this psalm, the monks of Qumran would in all likelihood have maintained the MT reading; see below on vs. 12b, *yēš^{e}bū l^{e}kissē',* where 11QPs^a reads *y'lw lks'.* The only other biblical occurrence of the construction *šīt l^e,* "to put upon," is in the ancient Ps xxi 4.

12. *my stipulation.* MT *'ēdōtī* is anomalous in that it appends the singular form of the first-person suffix, i.e., *ī,* to a noun which appears to be plural, namely, *'ēdōt.* Perhaps *'ēdōt* might be explained as the Phoenician feminine singular form which ends in *-ōt;* hence the affixing of the suffix *-ī* would be correct; see the second NOTE on Ps liii 7.

which. The relative pronoun *zō,* occurring elsewhere only in the North-

Israelite Hos vii 16, answers to the Ugaritic relative pronoun *d*, pronounced *dū*.

I shall teach them. Heb. *'ᵃlammᵉdēm* may be compared with Ugar. *almdk*, predicated of the goddess Anath in the damaged text 3 Aqht: 'rev.':29.

will sit upon your throne. On the Canaanite background of the uncommon (three occurrences against seventeen of *yāšab 'al* in Psalms) expression *yēšᵉbū lᵉkissē'* (instead of *'al kissē'*), see the comments at Ps ix 5. No longer familiar with the idiom *yāšab lᵉ*, "to sit upon," the scribes of 11QPsᵃ read instead *y'lw lks'*, "they will mount the throne."

13. *Yahweh has chosen . . .* 14. *will I sit*. This shift from the third to the first person exemplifies the court style commented upon at vss. 1–2 and 17–18.

his seat. Heb. *mōšāb* equals Ugar. *mṯb*, a frequent designation of divine abodes.

14. *my resting place . . . will I sit*. In *mᵉnūḥātī*, "my resting place," and *'ēšēb*, "will I dwell," one sees the two roots occurring in tandem in UT, 49:III:18, *aṯbn ank wanḫn*, "I will sit and rest," and in Phoenician Karatepe II:7–8, *šbt n'mt wnḥt lb*, "pleasant dwelling and peace of mind." On the bearing of this parallel pair for Isa xxx 15, *bᵉšūbāh wānaḥat*, "by sitting still and keeping quiet," see M. Dahood, CBQ 20 (1958), 41–43, and second NOTE on Ps xxiii 6.

here. A hapax legomenon in the Psalter, *pōh* equals Ugar. *p*, "here," El Amarna *pū*, Amorite *pā*, and Punic *pho* in the *Poenulus* of Plautus.

15. *Her pilgrims*. The apparently chiastic pattern of vss. 15–16 suggests that consonantal *ṣydh* (MT *ṣēdāh*, "her provisions") is the opposite number of vs. 16b, *ḥᵃsīdehā*, "her devoted ones." In fact, two ancient Greek manuscripts, the Sinaiticus and Alexandrinus, read *chēran*, "widow[s]," and the Vulg. offers *viduam eius*, "her widow." Hence vocalize either *ṣayyᵉdehā* (cf. Jer xvi 16, *ṣayyādīm*, "hunters") or participial *ṣādehā*, literally, "those who travel to her," from the root *ṣw/yd* which means "to hunt," but also, as is clear from Ugaritic usage, "to travel, range." Consult the discussion at Ps lxvi 11. With the reading *ṣādēhā* the syllable count of vs. 15 evens at 8:8.

will I abundantly bless. Heb. *bārēk 'ᵃbārēk*, which balances vs. 16b, *rannēn yᵉrannēnū*, "will ever shout for joy," may be compared with UT, 128:II:18–19, *brkm brk* [*il*], "El repeatedly blessed him."

will I satisfy with food. The syntax of *'aśbīᵃ' lāḥem*, with *lāḥem* an accusative of means, is identical with that of vs. 16a, *'albīš yeša'*, "will I clothe with salvation," and resembles that of UT, Aqht:II:20, *kšb't yn*, "When I am sated with wine."

16. *always*. An attempt to reproduce the emphasis intended by the piel infinitive absolute *rannēn*, whose root, as noted at Ps cxxvi 2, now occurs in Ugaritic.

17. *There*. In Jerusalem. The sequence in vs. 14, *pōh*, "here," and

vs. 17, *šām*, "There," resembles the sequence in UT, 54:11–12, *yd ilm p kmtm*, "The hand of the god here is like Death," and 16–18, *w mnm rgm d tšm' ṯmt*, "And whatever report that you hear there."

I will make a horn glow. There is no agreement concerning the meaning of the traditional version, "I will make a horn sprout for David." The figure may mean simply that Yahweh will restore the prosperity of the house of David, or it may refer to the prophecies of Jer xxiii 5, xxxiii 15; Zech iii 8, vi 12, where *ṣemaḥ*, "sprout," is used as the title of the messianic king. The clear metaphor, however, of the second colon (see II Sam xxi 17 where David is styled *nēr yiśrā'ēl*, "the lamp of Israel") suggests that first-colon *'aṣmīaḥ*, bears the primary sense of this verb in Syriac, "to shine brightly"; cf. J. C. Greenfield in HUCA 30 (1959), 149, n. 41, 151. In other words, the psalmist did not mix his metaphors. In vs. 18, it should be remarked, *yāṣīṣ*, "will sparkle," elsewhere always denotes "to blossom," so that in two successive verses occur two commonly attested verbs in meanings unwitnessed beyond these verses. Cf. likewise Ezek xxix 21.

In parallelism with *nēr*, "lamp," *qeren* would signify a lamp in the shape of an animal. Compare Akk. *qarnu*, a drinking horn made of pottery or bronze, having a base in the form of an animal, and consult Armas Salonen, *Die Hausgeräte der alten Mesopotamier* (Helsinki, 1966), II, pp. 239–42. We need not enter the discussion concerning the possible meaning of **qāran*, "to radiate light," in Exod xxxiv 24; Hab iii 4, since it has been recently studied by Jack M. Sasson in VT 18 (1968), 385–86. It is well known that the *qeren*, "horn," was used as a flask for oil (I Sam xvi 1, 13; I Kings i 39), so its use as a lamp may be supposed.

O David . . . O my anointed! Parsing both *lamedhs* as vocative particles, as in vss. 1 and 11.

I will trim. Practically all versions take the *qtl* form *'āraktī* as expressing past time (RSV, "I have prepared a lamp for my anointed"), but its balance with future *'aṣmīaḥ*, "I will make glow," indicates that it is merely a stylistic *qtl* variant of the future *yqtl* form.

The burning lamp is a natural metaphor for the preservation of the dynasty; when a man died without offspring, his lamp was said to be put out. Cf. I Kings xi 36, xv 4; II Kings viii 19; and Prov xiii 9, *'ōr ṣaddīqīm yiśmaḥ* (related to *yaṣmīaḥ*) *wenēr rešā'īm yid'āk*, "The light of the just burns bright, but the lamp of the wicked will go out"; cf. HWFB, pp. 40–41. For a possible Ugaritic parallel, see T. H. Gaster, *Thespis* (Anchor Books, 1961), pp. 335–36, who also cites many relevant biblical texts.

18. *His foes.* The sudden change from the direct address of vs. 17 to the third person coincides with the court style noticed in vss. 1–2.

will I clothe with humiliation. The wordplay in the phrase *'albīš bōšet* is noticed at Ps cix 29.

upon him. Namely, David, and not upon David in the person of his representative, as maintained by some expositors.

will sparkle. Like vs. 17, *'aṣmīᵃḥ,* "will I make glow," which bears a unique sense, *yāṣīṣ,* elsewhere always denoting "to blossom," here alone means "will sparkle." This root, not found in other Semitic languages, is witnessed in Ugar. *ṣṣ,* "salt mine."

PSALM 133
(cxxxiii 1–3)

1 *A song of ascents. Of David.*

Indeed how good and how pleasant
the dwelling of brothers together!
2 Like the precious oil upon the head,
running down upon the beard,
the beard of Aaron,
Which flows over the collar of his robes;
3 Like the dew of Hermon,
which descends upon the mountains of Zion.
For there Yahweh confers
the blessing—
life for evermore!

NOTES

cxxxiii. A Wisdom psalm comparing the joys of fraternal harmony to the oil used in the consecration of the high priest Aaron and to the copious dew that descends upon Mount Hermon in Lebanon. It assures that the reward of fraternal harmony will be everlasting life. Exegetes have long puzzled over the semantic connection between brotherly unity, the fragrant oil upon Aaron's beard, and the dew on Hermon's slopes. One cannot pinpoint the connection which the psalmist saw when drawing these comparisons, but the Ugaritic-Hebrew parallelism, *ṭl šmm šmn arṣ*, "the dew of heaven, the oil of earth" (see the second NOTE to vs. 2), may supply a literary clue.

Gunkel (*Die Psalmen*, p. 571) has recognized the North-Israelite provenance of the psalm, and the following NOTES bear out his observation. Being didactic, with strong resemblances to Pss cxxvii–cxxviii, the psalm does not readily lend itself to precise dating. The philological comments which follow point, though, to a pre-Exilic date of composition.

1. *Of David.* Though wanting in the Targum and in some manuscripts of the LXX, the attribution to David is sustained by 11QPs[a] *ldwd*.

good . . . pleasant. The parallelism of *ṭōb,* "good," and *nāʿīm,* "pleasant," recalls the collocation of these roots in UT, ʿnt:I:19–20, *mṣltm bd nʿm yšr ǵzr ṭb ql,* "With cymbals in the hands of the Pleasant One, the good/sweet-voiced youth sang"; cf. also Ps cxxxv 3.

pleasant the dwelling. The juxtaposition *nāʿīm šebet* resembles the expression *šbt nʿmt,* "pleasant dwelling," in Phoenician Karatepe II:13.

together. In full harmony, as indicated by the emphasis intended by *gam* in the phrase *gam yāḥad.*

2. *Like the precious oil.* Or, "Like the sweet oil," since *haṭṭōb* can bear the meaning "sweet," as noted at Ps xxxiv 9; the LXX translates *myron,* "sweet oil." Anointing with consecrated oil was part of the ordination ceremony; Exod xxix 7.

Like the precious oil . . . 3. Like the dew. The comparison with *šemen,* "oil," and *ṭal,* "dew," echoes the Late Bronze Age parallelism found in UT, ʿnt:IV:87, *ṭl šmm šmn arṣ,* "the dew of heaven, the oil of earth" (=the rain), and early biblical usage in Gen xxvii 28 (also vs. 39), *wᵉyitten lᵉkā hāʾᵉlōhīm miṭṭal haššāmayim ūmiššamnī* (with the genitive ending; MT *mišmannē,* which has never been satisfactorily explained) *hāʾāreṣ,* "And may God give you of heaven's dew and of earth's oil" (=rain). From this uncommon parallelism one may argue for an early date of composition; the poem is surely not post-Exilic, as maintained by some recent commentators.

running down. The lack of the article with *yōrēd* has induced some critics to eliminate the article with *kaššemen,* "like the oil," and to explain *haṭṭōb,* "the precious," as a noun instead of an adjective modifying "the oil." But the presence of the article with vs. 3, *habbᵉrākāh,* "the blessing," and its absence with appositional *ḥayyīm,* "life," bespeak a dialectal syntax of the article which accords with Phoenician rather than with classical Hebrew usage; consult Harris, *A Grammar of the Phoenician Language,* p. 66. However, those who want to read *šeyyōrēd,* "which runs down," need not assume the haplography of an *š,* since the preceding word (*rōʾš,* "head") ends in this letter; as noticed at Ps lx 11, the single writing of a consonant where morphology requires two is well attested.

the beard of Aaron. Though Aaron was the ancestor and the prototype of the priests in Israel, it is doubtful that Aaron here might denote any high priest. By the use of the present participles the psalmist apparently wishes to recall the scene of the consecration of Aaron himself, described in Lev viii.

Which. The lexicons describe *še* as a relative pronoun limited to late Hebrew and passages with North Palestinian coloring; the latter half of the statement can be readily accepted, but the occurrence of *še* in the very early Canticle of Deborah (Judg v) calls for a modification of the former half regarding the lateness of this usage. The Ugaritic personal name *šbʿl,* syllabically written *šu-baʿal* or *šubaʿla,* can well be interpreted "the One of Baal," in which *šu* is the relative pronoun; see A. Caquot, *Syria* 39 (1962), 238, n. 2.

Which flows over. There is question whether this clause refers to the oil or to Aaron's beard. The Masoretic accentuation relates it to Aaron's beard; the ancient versions understood it as referring to the oil. The "oil" interpretation is adopted here, since the two bases of comparison are the "oil" and the "dew"; the "flowing beard" is not to the point.

the collar. Literally "mouth" or "opening," *pī* denotes the hole through which the head passed; cf. Exod xxxix 23; Job xxx 18, *pī kuttontī,* "the collar of my coat."

of his robes. The long-standing emendation of the hapax legomenon feminine plural form *middōtāyw* to masculine plural *middāyw* finds new support in 11QPs[a] *mdyw* and 11QPs[b], which also reads *mdyw;* see J. van der Ploeg, "Fragments d'un manuscrit de psaumes de Qumran (11QPs[b])," in RB 74 (1967), 408–12. This new evidence is neutralized, however, by Ugar. *md,* "robe," but with feminine plural *mdt,* "robes," occurring in a text published in 1957; cf. C. Virolleaud, *Palais royal d'Ugarit,* II (Paris, 1957), p. 141. Cf. also Qumranic *mdt hdr* in 1QS IV:8, usually rendered "resplendent attire."

3. *the dew of Hermon.* Hermon is the majestic, snow-capped mountain to the north of the Holy Land in Lebanon, but visible in many parts of Palestine. G. A. Smith, *The Historical Geography of the Holy Land* (25th ed.; London, 1931), p. 65, observes that "The dews of Syrian nights are excessive; on many mornings it looks as if there had been heavy rain." The dew that falls on the slopes of Mount Hermon (cf. Ps lxxxix 13) is particularly abundant. In some texts dew is a symbol of what is refreshing and invigorating, but in Isa xxvi 19 it symbolizes the resurrection and immortality. The mention of "life for evermore" at the end of our verse suggests some allusion to immortality in "the dew of Hermon."

the mountains of Zion. One need not suppose that the psalmist imagined that the dew which fell upon the mountains of Zion was physically influenced by Mount Hermon. What he probably meant is that the life-producing effect of harmonious living is as though the most copious dew fell upon the arid mountains of Zion. Both stimulate life and fertility, and that seems to be the point of the comparison.

For there. In Zion, where brothers dwell in concord. Scholars have long felt that the final line is overloaded, but its scansion as a 2+2+2 line (with Gunkel) with a 6:5:6 syllable count should forestall deletions. In fact, the 6:5:6 count may serve to neutralize the proposed alteration of *šām,* "there," to the longer form *šāmmāh,* now supported by 11QPs[a] *šmh.* The latter reading would produce a 7:5:6 line.

confers. For this nuance of *ṣiwwāh,* which RSV renders "has commanded," see second NOTE on Ps xlii 9, and *La Bible de la Pléiade,* II, p. 1192, which renders *ṣiwwāh* by "a conféré."

the blessing. Namely, the blessing par excellence, specified by the following phrase.

life for evermore. Another affirmation of the Israelite belief in eternal life. Though missing in 11QPs[a], *ḥayyīm,* "life," is proved authentic both by the 6:5:6 syllable count and by its association with *ṭal,* "dew," a connection witnessed in Isa xxvi 19. D. N. Freedman makes the interesting observation that by omitting *ḥayyīm,* "life," and substituting *šlwm 'l yśr'l,* "peace upon Israel," the Qumranic sect may have wished to get rid of this obvious reference to eternal life. He further notes that MT *ḥayyīm,* "life," is secured by the paronomasia between *ḥayyīm* and vs. 1, *'aḥīm,* "brothers."

The LXX can be taxed with similar tendentiousness in Prov xiv 32, "For his evil the wicked will be flung headlong, but at his death the just will find refuge." Since this verse affirms the belief in an afterlife, it appears that LXX changed MT *b*[e]*mōtō,* "at his death," to *b*[e]*tummō,* "because of his integrity," to avoid such an affirmation. The CCD version glosses thus: "The *life forever* was understood in the first place as the preservation of earthly life; it is capable of a fuller application in the light of the Gospel." The numerous texts of the Psalter and other biblical books which state or imply this belief (see the Introduction) show that the phrase *ḥayyīm 'ad hā'ōlām* was capable of a fuller application many centuries before the Gospel.

PSALM 134

(cxxxiv 1–3)

1 *A song of ascents.*

Come, bless Yahweh,
all the works of Yahweh,
You who stand in the house
of Yahweh through the watches of the night,
2 Lift up your hands toward the sanctuary,
and bless Yahweh.
3 May he bless you, Yahweh of Zion,
who made heaven and earth!

NOTES

cxxxiv. A short liturgical hymn, probably sung in the temple, summoning priests and Levites to praise the Lord and his works (vss 1–2); they respond by blessing the congregation (vs. 3). Some recent versions (*La Bible de la Pléiade*, BJ) follow the LXX in restoring an entire colon to vs. 1b, but 11QPs[a] sides with MT, which is followed here.

1. *all the works of Yahweh.* Repointing *'abdē*, "servants of," to *'ᵃbādē*, "the works of," a substantive studied at Pss cxiii 1 and cxxxv 1. From this reading emerges in vs. 1 a the material pattern A+B+C//Ć, wherein Ć is an extension of first-colon C, "Yahweh." Semantically and stylistically, *kōl 'ᵃbādē yhwh*, "all the works of Yahweh," is the chiastic counterpart of vs. 3, *'ōśēh šāmayim wā'āreṣ*, "who made heaven and earth," since "all the works" equals the merismic or twofold inclusive expression "heaven and earth." Yahweh is of course identical with *'ōśēh*, "who made" or "the Maker of."

You who stand. Parsing *hā'ōmᵉdīm* as the vocative addressed by the preceding imperative *bārᵃkū*, "bless," as well as by the following (vs. 2) imperative *śᵉ'ū yᵉdēkem*, "Lift up your hands!" The same pattern is discernible in Ps cxxxv 1–3.

in the house of Yahweh. Since MT is sustained by 11QPs[a], one hesitates to insert with LXX "in the courts of the house of our God" (Ps cxxxv 2).

Metrically, the eleven-syllable line can be read as 2+2, with a 6:5 syllable count, when the construct chain *bᵉbēt yhwh* is broken up and distributed over two cola. This breakup of a composite phrase entitles its two components to an accent apiece instead of the one accent in MT.

the watches of the night. This meaning of plural *lēlōt* is noted at Pss xvi 7 and xcii 3.

2. *Lift up your hands*. In a gesture of supplication, already customary among the Canaanites as is clear from UT, Krt:75–76, *ša ydk šmm*, "Lift up your hands toward heaven."

your hands. The archaic spelling *ydkm* (11QPs[a] has the normal spelling *ydykm*) is noteworthy, reflecting an early date or Northern provenance (courtesy of D. N. Freedman). Cf. the Northern spelling in Ps xvi 4, *mdm*, "from my hands," and in Ps cxxxix 5, *kappekā* (*kpk*), "your palms." See the Ugaritic text cited in the next NOTE.

toward the sanctuary. MT *qōdeš* is capable of at least two probable analyses. It might be parsed as an accusative of place toward which, a usage discussed at Ps cv 25. Compare the construction at Ps xxviii 2, "When I lift up my hands/toward [*'el*] your sacred shrine." But the most pertinent parallel comes from UT, Krt:75–76, *ša ydk šmm*, "Lift up your hands toward heaven," where *šmm* is an accusative of direction, exactly like biblical *qōdeš* in the proposed translation. In the doublet of Krt:167–168, *nša ydh šmmh*, "He lifted his hands heavenward," the poet employs the alternate construction with *he directionis* of *šmmh*. The defective spelling of *yᵉdēkem*, "your hands," noticed in the preceding NOTE, strengthens the relevance of the Ugaritic parallel. Since the priests and Levites already stand in the temple, the sanctuary toward which they lift their hands would be the heavenly one; see the discussion of *qōdeš*, "sanctuary," at Pss liii 7, lx 8, and cl 1.

On the other hand, *qōdeš* might also be taken collectively as "holy ones," a meaning examined at Ps lxxvii 14. The command would thus read, "Lift up your hands, you holy ones!"

the sanctuary . . . 3. Yahweh of Zion. Compare the revised interpretation of Ps xx 3, "May he send you help from the sanctuary, / from Zion sustain you," where both the sanctuary and Zion are to be interpreted celestially, as proposed in *Psalms* II on Ps liii 7.

and bless Yahweh. The current 7:7 syllable may be cited as an argument, albeit minor, against 11QPs[a], which inserts *šm*, "the name of," before Yahweh, thus producing a 7:8 line.

3. *May he bless you*. In this supplication made by the priests, the singular suffix *-kā*, "you," probably refers to the congregation conceived as a single entity.

Yahweh of Zion, who made heaven. The fact that it balances the construct chain *'ōśēh šāmayim* suggests that *yhwh miṣṣiyyōn* should likewise be parsed as a construct chain; cf. the discussion at Pss cx 2 and cxxxv 21, where this divine title balances the construct chain *šōkēn yerûšālāim,* "the Resident of Jerusalem."

who made heaven and earth! The stylistic function of this phrase is exposed in the first NOTE on vs. 1. With this solemn affirmation of faith the Songs of Ascents (cxx–cxxxiv) close. For the bearing of *'ōśēh šāmayim wā'āreṣ,* "who made heaven and earth," on the interpretation of Karatepe *'l qn 'rṣ,* "El, the Creator of Earth," see W. F. Albright, *Norsk Teologisk Tidsskrift* 56 (1955), 8.

PSALM 135

(cxxxv 1–21)

1 Praise Yah!
Praise the name of Yahweh!
Praise the works of Yahweh!
2 You who stand in the house of Yahweh,
in the courts of the house of our God.
3 Praise Yah, for Yahweh is good,
chant to his Name, truly pleasant.
4 For Yah chose Jacob for himself,
Israel as his private possession.
5 Indeed I acknowledge
that Yahweh is great,
and that our Lord is greater than all gods.
6 Whatever he wills, Yahweh does,
in heaven and on earth,
in the seas and in all the deeps.
7 He brings up clouds from the end of the earth,
makes lightning for the rain,
leads forth the wind from his storehouses.
8 It was he who smote the first-born of Egypt,
man as well as beast.
9 He sent signs and wonders
into the midst of Egypt,
Against Pharaoh and against all his servants.
10 It was he who smote great nations,
and who slew mighty kings;
11 Even Sihon, king of the Amorites,
and Og himself, king of Bashan,
yes, all the kings of Canaan.
12 And he gave their land as patrimony,
patrimony for Israel his people.
13 Yahweh—your name is eternal,
Yahweh—your title is for all generations.

14 Indeed Yahweh defends his people,
and toward his servants shows himself compassionate.
15 The idols of the nations are silver and gold,
the work of men's hands.
16 Mouths have they,
but they do not speak;
Eyes have they,
but do not see.
17 They have ears,
but do not hear,
Nor is there any breath in their mouths.
18 Like them shall their makers become,
everyone who trusts in them.
19 House of Israel, bless Yahweh,
house of Aaron, bless Yahweh;
20 House of Levi, bless Yahweh,
you who fear Yahweh, bless Yahweh.
21 Blessed be Yahweh of Zion,
the Resident of Jerusalem.
Praise Yah!

NOTES

cxxxv. This hymn begins (vss. 1–4) with a call to glorify God, who chose Israel to be his own treasure, and ends (vss. 19–21) with a similar exhortation. His omnipotence is manifested in nature (vss. 5–7) and in history (vss. 8–12). He is the defender of his people, while the pagan gods are lifeless idols who cannot save their worshipers (vss. 13–18).

Though many of its verses were borrowed from other psalms, this hymn possesses real vigor of rhythm and spirit. Especially noteworthy are the A+B//B́ pattern in vs. 2, the A+B+C//C+D sequence of vs. 12, and the A+B+C//B́+Ć pattern in vs. 4. Conceptually significant are vss. 4–5 with their treaty terminology, and vs. 21 with its two divine titles, "Yahweh of Zion," and "the Resident of Jerusalem."

1. *Praise Yah . . .* 21. *Praise Yah.* The inclusion formed by this exhortation, as well as the 11QPs^{a} reading (see below on vs. 21), tells against the LXX transfer of vs. 21 *hal^{e}lū yāh,* "Praise Yah!" to the beginning of Ps cxxxvi.

It should be noted, however, that the A+B+C pattern of the three *hal^{e}lū,* "Praise!" cola in vs. 1 is curiously inverted into a C+B+A sequence by 11QPs^{a}. In Ps cxiii 1 these three cola appear in an A+C+B formation.

the works of Yahweh. The problems attendant upon translating *'abdē* as "servants of" in the summons *hal^e^lū 'abdē yhwh* evaporate when *'abdē* is repointed *'^a^bādē* and defined as "the works of," precisely as in Pss cxiii 1 and cxxxiv 1. Consult the discussion at Ps cxiii 1. In the present poem the works to be praised are catalogued in vss. 4–12. The theological doctrine of praising Yahweh himself first, then his name, and finally his works, is couched somewhat differently in Ps cxiii 1, where the objects of praise are Yahweh himself, then his works, and finally his name. In 11QPs^a^, however, the order is completely reversed, beginning with his works, continuing with his name, and concluding with Yahweh himself: *hllw 'bdy yhwh hllw šm yhwh hllw yh,* "Praise the works of Yahweh! Praise the name of Yahweh! Praise Yah!"

The fact that *'^a^bādēhem,* "their works," occurs in Eccles ix 1, and that Ecclesiastes frequently employs the relative pronoun *š* and attests *s^e^gullāh,* "private possession" (ii 8) affords a chronological correlation which may help to fix the psalm's date of composition. On the probable fifth-century B.C. date of Ecclesiastes, see Albright, YGC, p. 258.

2. *You who stand.* Syntactically, *še'ōm^e^dīm* stands as the vocative dependent upon triple *hal^e^lū,* "Praise!" in vs. 1, as well upon the two imperatives of vs. 3.

Yahweh . . . our God. The breakup of the composite divine name *yhwh '^e^lōhēnū* may be compared with the distribution over succeeding cola in vs. 5 of the divine name *yhwh '^a^dōnēnū,* "Yahweh our Lord."

house . . . courts. For the Canaanite parallelism between these two terms, see the discussions at Pss lxxxiv 11 and cxvi 19. The biblical parallelism between *bēt* and *ḥāṣēr* could have served C. Virolleaud well when interpreting (*Ugaritica,* V, p. 550) RŠ 24.258:17–18, *il hlk lbth yštql lḥṭrh,* "El went to his house, he reached his court." From the balance with *bt* it seems clear that *ḥṭr* is a dialectal form of *ḥẓr,* "court." Virolleaud explains *ḥṭr* as dialectal for *ḥdr,* "room," but this identification slights the frequent Ugaritic-Hebrew parallelism between *bt* and *ḥẓr.* The pairing between *bt,* "house," and *ḥdr,* "room," has not turned up yet in published tablets.

3. *truly pleasant.* Ascribing *kī nā'īm* to the divine Name as in Ps liv 8, though some versions predicate this attribute of Yahweh himself; CCD skirts the problem by rendering *kī nā'īm,* "which we love," though on what philological basis is not explained in the accompanying notes.

4. *chose . . . for himself.* The construction *bāḥar lō* is cited to justify the reading and translation of Ps xlvii 5, *yibḥar lannū* (MT *lānū*), "He chose for himself."

his private possession. In recent years *s^e^gullātō,* "his private possession," has received considerable attention from Assyriologists, who identified it with Akk. *sikiltu,* "private accumulation or hoard, private purse"; cf. E. A. Speiser, *Orientalia* 25 (1956), 1–4; M. Greenberg, JAOS 71 (1951), 172–74; M. Held, JCS 15 (1961), 11, who examines the problems which must be solved if Akk. *sikultu,* which often means "embezzled goods," is to be identified with Heb. *s^egullāh*. For the provenance of the biblical term the scholar need no longer go so far afield, thanks to a Ugaritic letter published in 1965 by C. Virolleaud, *Palais royal d'Ugarit*, V (Paris, 1965), pp. 84–86. In this letter couched in treaty terminology (UT, 2060) the Hittite suzerain reminds Hammurapi, the last king of Ugarit, that he, Hammurapi, is his servant (*'bdh*) and his "private possession" (lines 7, 12, *sglth*=Heb. *s^egullātō*). Consult further Dahood, *Orientalia* 34 (1965), 483; *Biblica* 50 (1969), 341; Huffmon and Parker, BASOR 184 (1966), 37, n. 12. This word is familiar in the context of Israel's election, e.g., Exod xix 5; Deut xxvi 17–18.

5. *Indeed.* Taking *kī* as emphatic rather than as conjunctive "Because."

I acknowledge. Interpreting *'^anī yāda'tī* in the precise sense it bears in the Ugaritic letter cited at vs. 4. UT, 2060:12–14 reads *'[bdh w] sglth at ht* [ ] *špš b'lk yd'm l yd't*, "His servant and private possession are you. Now [how is it] that you no longer acknowledge the Sun as your master?" Consult Herbert B. Huffmon, "The Treaty Background of Hebrew YADA'," BASOR 181 (1966), 31–37; Huffmon and Parker, "A Further Note on the Treaty Background of Hebrew YADA'," BASOR 184 (1966), 36–38, who show that in covenantal contexts *yāda'* means "to recognize as the legitimate suzerain." That we are dealing in this psalm with a similar context appears from such terms as vs. 4, *s^egullātō*, "his private possession," and vs. 5, *'^adōnēnū*, "our Lord"; see the next NOTE.

our Lord. The treaty terms cited in the preceding NOTE support MT *'^adōnēnū*, "our Lord," against 11QPs^a *'lwhynw*, "our God." In the Ugaritic letter the Hittite overlord twice employs the term *adn*, "lord" (2060:6, 9).

is greater. The syntax of *'^adōnēnū mikkol '^elōhīm* grows clearer if second-colon *gādōl*, "great," is also understood with the third colon; cf. Exod xviii 11.

6. *Whatever he wills, Yahweh does.* One may, to be sure, also translate with CCD, "All that the Lord wills he does," but this version obscures a nicety of Hebrew style which may be called explicitation in the second colon whereby the poet defers explicit mention of the subject; cf. the first NOTE on Ps cv 17. This is admittedly a minor point of style, but nonetheless deserves comment.

he wills . . . does. The poet balances the two first-colon verbs *ḥāpēṣ*, "he wills," and *'āśāh*, "does," by two prepositional phrases in the following cola.

seas . . . deeps. Comparing the parallelism of *yammīm*, "seas," and *t^ehōmōt*, "deeps," with UT 52:30, *gp ym . . . gp thm*, "the shore of the sea . . . the shore of the deep." Cf. also Ps xxxiii 7; Job xxviii 14, xxxviii 16; Prov viii 28–29.

and in all. 11QPs^a supports some manuscripts which read *wbkwl* for MT *w^ekol*, but the latter need not be abandoned since it can be explained on the principle of the double-duty preposition, sharing the preposition of *bayyammīm*, "in the seas." Consult the NOTE on Ps cxix 55, *and during the watch*. In fact, we could use a study of prepositions omitted (probably to avoid cacophony) after the conjunction *w*ᵉ, "and"; cf. provisionally Amos ii 7 (D. N. Freedman, CBQ 30 [1968], 226, n. 3); Job xix 24, xxviii 2; Prov iii 18 (Dahood, *Biblica* 47 [1966], 413). See below on Ps cxxxviii 6.

the deeps. Just as Ugar. *sglt*, "private possession," is more immediately relevant to the exegesis of vs. 4 than is Akk. *sikiltu*, "embezzled goods, private hoard," so Ugar. *thm*, dual *thmtm*, plural *thmt*, "deep[s]," replaces Akk. *tiāmātu*, "deeps," as the direct ancestor of the biblical term. Published in 1959 (thirty years after the Ras Shamra discoveries), *La Bible de la Pléiade*, II, p. 1194, annotates this verse: "Les Abîmes, *tehômôth*, assyro-babylonien *tiâmâtu*, 'mer,'" omitting mention of the more relevant Canaanite parallel. On the need for a new orientation in biblical studies, see *Psalms I*, pp. XXVI–XXIX, and Frank M. Cross, Jr., "The Song of the Sea and Canaanite Myth," *in God and Christ: Existence and Province*, ed. Robert W. Funk (*Journal for Theology and the Church* 5; Harper Torchbook, 1968), p. 2, n. 3, who writes, "Thorkild Jacobsen has argued convincingly in a recent paper that *Enuma eliš* is ultimately dependent on West Semitic sources for its motif of the battle with Sea."

7. *clouds . . . lightning . . . rain . . . wind*. These four components of a Palestinian storm (usually accompanied by lightning bolts) bear on the interpretation of *mdl*, a disputed word in UT, 67:v:6–8, *wat qḥ ʿrptk rḥk mdlk mṭrtk*, "But you take your clouds, your wind, your *mdl*, your rains." UT, Glossary, No. 1430, partially followed by J. C. de Moor, ZAW 78 (1966) 69–71, suggests that *mdl* means "lightning," but Werner H. Schmidt, *Königtum Gottes in Ugarit and Israel* (2d ed.; Berlin, 1966), pp. 15, 61, and the present writer, *Biblica* 47 (1966), 414–16, have favored "rain-clouds" as the definition of *mdl*. From a comparison of our verse with the Ugaritic text it becomes solidly probable that *mdl* is the equivalent of Heb. *b*ᵉ*rāqīm*, "lightning." No convincing etymology presents itself.

lightning. 11QPsᵃ *brqym* and the Hebrew-Ugaritic correspondence, cited in the preceding NOTE, virtually rule out the emendation of *b*ᵉ*rāqīm*, "lightning," to *b*ᵉ*dāqīm*, "fissures" ("He makes fissures for the rain"), favored by T. H. Gaster, IDB, II, pp. 551–52.

the wind from his storehouses. The motif of the divine storehouses (cf. Ps xxxiii 7; Job xxxviii 22) finds a cognate theme in the new version of Ps lxxviii 26, "He let loose the east wind from heaven and led forth the south wind from his fortress"; see below on Ps cxlvii 18.

9. *into the midst of Egypt*. Not "in thy midst, O Egypt" (RSV), with the disconcerting shift from third-person Egypt in vs. 8 and a reversion to third-person Pharaoh in vs. 9b. On the form *b*ᵉ*tōkēkī*, "into the midst of," see the third NOTE to Ps cxvi 19, *b*ᵉ*tōkēkī y*ᵉ*rūšālāim*, "in the midst of Jerusalem."

10. *and who slew*. Reading infinitive absolute *w*ᵉ*hārōg* for MT perfect

w^e hārāg, as proposed by John Huesman, "The Infinitive Absolute and the WAW + Perfect Problem," in *Biblica* 37 (1956), 410–34, especially 434. See below on vs. 12, *And he gave.*

slew. The contention of C. Brockelmann, *Orientalistische Literaturzeitung* 48 (1953), col. 257, that in the Zincirli inscriptions *hrg*, "to slay," is a Canaanism is probably corroborated by Ugar. *hrg* in UT, 6:5, a text that unfortunately is not very clear.

11. *Even Sihon . . . Og himself . . . yes, all.* The *lamedh* of *l^e sīḥōn, l^e 'ōg*, and *l^e kol* has usually been parsed as the preposition introducing the direct object, as in Aramaic. It may, however, be parsed as the emphasizing particle, underlining the magnitude of Yahweh's achievement. Other instances of emphatic *lamedh* with *kol*, "all," are listed in the second NOTE on Ps cix 11.

The psalmist here cites historical events described in detail in Num xxi 21–35 and Deut ii 26 – iii 11.

the kings. Among recent versions CCD recognizes that *maml^e kōt* here bears the Phoenician sense documented at Ps lxviii 33.

12. *And he gave.* Reading infinitive absolute *w^e nātōn* for MT *w^e nātan*, as proposed by Huesman, *Biblica* 37 (1956), 434; see NOTE at vs. 10, *and who slew.*

he gave their land as patrimony. The syntax of the clause *w^e nātōn 'arṣām naḥ^a lāh* is reminiscent of the double accusatives used with this verb in UT, 77:22, *atn šdh krmm*, "I will make her fields vineyards."

13. *Yahweh—your name . . . Yahweh—your title.* This nominal sentence, with Yahweh as *casus pendens* and arranged in an A+B+C//A+B́+Ć sequence has an identical counterpart in Ps xi 4a, as scanned and translated in *Psalms I*, ad loc.: *yhwh b^e hēkāl qodšō yhwh baššāmāyim kiss^e ō*, "Yahweh—in the temple is his holy seat, / Yahweh—in the heavens is his throne." The sequence here is likewise A+B+C//A+B́+Ć.

eternal . . . for all generations. The NOTE on Ps lxxxv 6 deals with the frequent Ugaritic-Hebrew pairing of *'ōlām* with *dōr wādōr.*

14. *his people, and toward his servants.* Preserving the chiastic word order of the original.

15. *The idols . . .* 18. *in them.* These verses are almost identical with Ps cxv 4–8.

the nations. The Hebrew term *haggōyīm* consistently designates the nations other than Israel.

the work of men's hands. Other examples of this A+B+C//Ć sequence are listed at Ps cxlii 6. In our verse the entire second colon (Ć) is but a development of first-colon "silver and gold" (C).

17. *Nor is there any.* Nahum Sarna, quoted by UT, Glossary, No. 466, compares the odd pleonastic expression *'ēn yeš* (also in I Sam xxi 9) with Ugar. *bl iṯ bn lh*, "He surely has no son," where negative particle *bl* negates *iṯ*, "there is."

21. *Yahweh of Zion.* Reading *yhwh-m* (with enclitic *mem*) *ṣiyyōn* for

MT *yhwh miṣṣiyyōn*, "Yahweh from Zion." Kraus and others emend the text to *yhwh b^eṣiyyōn*, "Yahweh in Zion," an inadmissible change in the face of 11QPs^a *ybrkkh yhwh mṣywn*, "May Yahweh bless you from Zion!" Though it altered *bārūk*, "Blessed," 11QPs^a does vouch for MT, whose consonants are sound but whose distribution can be improved upon. In the Ugaritic texts the enclitic *mem* is quite frequent with divine names such as *bʿl-m*, "Baal," in 68:9. What is more, the parallelism with the construct chain *šōkēn y^erūšālāim*, "the Resident of Jerusalem," suggests that the first colon contains a construct-chain counterpart. Cf. Ps cxxviii 5.

the Resident of Jerusalem. The divine epithet *šōkēn y^erūšālāim* may be compared with Deut xxxiii 16, *šōk^enī s^eneh*, "the Resident of the Bush," and Ps ix 12, *yōšēb ṣiyyōn*, "King of Zion," literally "the Enthroned of Zion." The proposal to insert *bārūk*, "blessed," at the beginning of the second colon (BH^3 apparatus) is discountenanced by the 6:6 syllable count of the new reading.

Praise Yah! Forms an inclusion with vs. 1, "Praise Yah!" which shows that it should not be transferred to next psalm, as in LXX.

PSALM 136

(cxxxvi 1–26)

1 Give thanks to Yahweh, for he is good,
for his kindness is eternal;
2 Give thanks to the God of gods,
for his kindness is eternal;
3 Give thanks to the Lord of lords,
for his kindness is eternal;
4 To him who alone works great wonders,
for his kindness is eternal;
5 To him who with Understanding made the heavens,
for his kindness is eternal;
6 To him who spread out the earth upon the waters,
for his kindness is eternal;
7 To him who made the great lights,
for his kindness is eternal;
8 The sun as ruler over the day,
for his kindness is eternal;
9 The moon and stars as rulers over the night,
for his kindness is eternal;
10 To him who smote the first-born of Egypt,
for his kindness is eternal;
11 And brought out Israel from their midst,
for his kindness is eternal;
12 With a strong hand and arm outstretched,
for his kindness is eternal;
13 To him who divided the Reed Sea in half,
for his kindness is eternal;
14 And showed Israel through the middle of it,
for his kindness is eternal;
15 But shook off Pharaoh and his host into the Reed Sea,
for his kindness is eternal;
16 To him who marched his people across the desert,
for his kindness is eternal;

17 To him who smote great kingdoms,
for his kindness is eternal;
18 And slew famous kings,
for his kindness is eternal;
19 Even Sihon, king of the Amorites,
for his kindness is eternal;
20 And Og himself, king of Bashan,
for his kindness is eternal;
21 And he gave their land as patrimony,
for his kindness is eternal;
22 Patrimony for Israel his servant,
for his kindness is eternal;
23 Who remembered us in our low estate,
for his kindness is eternal;
24 And snatched us from our adversaries,
for his kindness is eternal;
25 Who gives food to all flesh,
for his kindness is eternal;
26 Give thanks to the God of heaven,
for his kindness is eternal.

NOTES

cxxxvi. Known in the liturgical language of the Jews as "the Great Hallel," this hymn of praise has the form of a litany. Each half-verse is followed by a refrain, the former probably sung by a choir of priests and Levites and the latter by the congregation.

After the introductory invitation (vss. 1–3), this hymn extols Yahweh's greatness in creating the universe (vss. 4–9) as well as his goodness in bringing Israel to the Promised Land (vss. 10–22) and his providence in caring for his people when humiliated. The hymn closes with an inclusion (vs. 26), repeating the introductory summons to thank the Lord.

1. *good.* Heb. *ṭōb* has been correctly reproduced by LXX *chrēstos,* "propitious"; what the psalmist intends is not so much Yahweh's intrinsic essential goodness as his kindness and graciousness toward Israel.

2. *the God of gods.* Borrowed from Deut x 17, the expression *'ᵉlōhē 'ᵉlōhīm* serves to dispel the lingering doubts attending the interpretation of Ps l 1, *'ēl 'ᵉlōhīm,* "the God of Gods."

4. *great wonders.* Though the current MT reading *niplā'ōt* is not metrically disruptive—other 4+3 verses recur in this psalm—the long-standing suspicion of certain critics that of the brace *niplā'ōt gᵉdōlōt,* "great wonders," one is superfluous has been confirmed by 11QPs[a], which omits

g^e^dōlōt, "great." So the version "who alone works wonders" acquires respectability. It would thus seem that with three syllables each, *niplāʾōt,* "wonders," and *g^e^dōlōt,* "great," are metrically interchangeable and may be considered doublets or variant readings. When one of the words is omitted, the syllable count is reduced to nine; the nine-syllable colon is dominant throughout this hymn. This is the only colon with twelve syllables.

5. *with Understanding.* Parsing *bi* of *bit^e^būnāh* as the *beth* of accompaniment, discussed at Ps civ 24, and taking *t^e^būnāh* as personified Understanding, as in Prov viii 1. This motif of Understanding (or Wisdom) at Yahweh's side during the Creation is documented at Ps civ 24. For present purposes the most relevant texts are Prov iii 19 and Job xxxviii 4, *ʾēpōh hāyītā b^e^yosdī ʾāreṣ haggēd ʾim yādaʿtā bīnāh,* "Where were you when I founded the earth? Tell if you are acquainted with Understanding." These questions imply that *bīnāh,* a synonym of *t^e^būnāh,* was present with God when the earth was created.

6. *who spread out the earth.* Cf. Isa xlii 5, xliv 24, and 11QPs[a] *rwqʿ hʾrṣ,* all of which establish the MT reading against doubts raised by some critics (e.g., Briggs), who suspect that the participles in vss. 5–6 were transposed by a copyist's mistake.

upon the waters. The earth was thought to rest upon the subterranean abyss of waters; cf. Ps xxiv 2, "For he based it upon the seas, / established it upon the ocean currents."

7. *lights.* MT plural *ʾōrīm* is a hapax legomenon; 11QPs[a] reads *mʾwrwt,* doubtless under the influence of Gen i 16.

8. *ruler . . .* 9. *rulers.* In vs. 8 we have singular *memšelet* but in vs. 9. the plural form *memš^e^lōt;* ancient versions and modern critics seek harmony by reading singular *memšelet* both times, but 11QPs[a] twice reads the plural *mmšlwt.* MT proves sound when the abstract noun *memšelet,* "rule," is understood as another instance of an abstract noun with a concrete designation, much like abstract *mamlākāh,* "sovereignty, dominion," but often concretely "king" in Phoenician and Hebrew. Thus the hapax legomenon plural form in vs. 9, *memšālōt* (MT construct *memš^e^lōt*) finds its explanation in its plural antecedents "the moon and stars." Hence it becomes impossible to endorse the note in the apparatus of BH[3] recommending the deletion of *kōkābīm,* "stars." In Gen i 16 singular *memšelet,* "ruler," occurs twice to describe the role of the sun and the moon.

12. *arm.* MT *z^e^rōaʿ,* appears with prothetic *aleph* (third NOTE on Ps li 9) in 11QPs[a] *ʾzrwʿ.*

13. *who divided the . . . Sea.* One should note the material similarity of *gōzēr yam* and UT, 52:58, *agzrym,* whose interpretation, unfortunately, is uncertain.

in half. Repointing MT plural *g^e^zārīm,* "parts," to dual *gizrayim,* as suggested by vs. 14, *b^e^tōkō,* "through the middle of it."

17. *kingdoms.* The proposal, inspired by Ps cxxxv 10, to emend *m^e^lākīm* to *gōyīm,* "nations," or to *l^e^ʾummīm,* "peoples," may prove needless in

the presence of *mōlek,* "kingdom." In JBL 56 (1937), 142, and *American Journal of Semitic Languages and Literatures* 57 (1940), 71–74, H. L. Ginsberg showed that the Phoenician title *'dn mlkm* equals Greek *kyrios basileiōn* "lord of kingdoms," and W. F. Albright, JBL 63 (1944), 218, n. 70, availed himself of this insight to translate Num xxiv 7, *mulkō* (MT *malkō*) by "his kingdom"; cf. also Albright in BASOR 87 (1942), 35, n. 20, on *šu-uṭ mu-ul-ka,* "disloyalty to the crown," in an Akkadian tablet of the pre-Israelite period found at Tell el Ḥesī in southwest Palestine.

18. *famous kings.* G. A. Cooke, *A Text-Book of North-Semitic Inscriptions* (Oxford, 1903), p. 35, rightly compares *m*e*lākīm 'addīrīm,* "famous kings," with Phoen. *mmlk*[*t*] *'dr,* "the famous king."

19. *Even Sihon . . .* 20. *Og himself.* Consult the NOTES on Ps cxxxv 10.

21. *And he gave.* Repointing MT preterit *w*e*nātan* to infinitive absolute *w*e*nātōn,* as proposed at Ps cxxxv 12.

23. *in our low estate.* The dispute whether the root of *šiplēnū* occurs in UT, 52:32, *hlh* [*t*]*špl hlh trm,* "See how it subsides, see how it rises!" must not overlook the parallelism in Ps lxxv 8, *zeh yašpīl w*e*zeh yārīm,* "the one who brings down, and the one who raises up."

26. *the God of heaven.* The title *'ēl haššāmāyim* forms an inclusion with vs. 2, "the God of gods," and vs. 3, "the Lord of lords," an inclusion that would be obscured were one to adopt the translation of *Juxta Hebraeos, confitemini Deo caeli,* "confess to God, O heavens."

With its seven syllables this colon forms a metrical inclusion with vs. 1a; in fact, these are the only two cola in the psalm with seven syllables.

PSALM 137

(cxxxvii 1–9)

1 Beside the rivers in Babylon,
there we sat;
loudly we wept,
When we remembered you, O Zion!
2 Beside the poplars in her midst
we hung up our lyres.
3 For there our captors demanded of us
words of song,
and our mockers songs of gladness:
"Sing for us a song of Zion!"
4 O how could we sing Yahweh's song
upon alien soil?
5 Should I forget you,
O Jerusalem,
Let my right hand wither!
6 Let my tongue stick to my palate,
should I remember you not!
If I do not raise you,
O Jerusalem,
Upon my head in celebration!
7 Remember Yahweh, O sons of Edom,
the day of Jerusalem!
You who said, "Strip her, strip her,
to her foundation!"
8 O Daughter Babylon, you devastator,
blest he who repays you
the evil you have done us!
9 Blest he who seizes and dashes
your infants against the rock!

NOTES

cxxxvii. In this lament the psalmist, recently returned from Babylon, prays for vengeance on Israel's enemies—the Babylonians and the Edomites —who destroyed Jerusalem in 587/6 B.C.

In the opening stanza the poet recalls how the Israelites refused to sing their sacred songs on foreign soil for the amusement of their conquerors. Then in three short stanzas he directly addresses Jerusalem (vss. 5–6), the Edomites (vs. 7), and Babylon (vss. 8–9).

The poem is remarkable for the contrast between the tender poignancy of the first six verses and the bitter imprecations of the last three. But unyielding hatred of her foes was the correlate of intense love for Zion. To the psalmist the law of retaliation for cruelty seems only just, and the shocking form in which he expresses his desire for the extermination of his country's destroyer must be judged in the light of customs prevailing in his age. Thus those exegetes who interpret vs. 9, "your infants," as the adult citizens depicted as the children of Mother Babylon will scarcely convince the critics conversant with the curses of the eighth-century B.C. Sefîre Inscriptions in Aramaic.

The language of this sixth-century lament is marked by originality and vividness. One encounters assonance (vss. 1–6), alliteration (vss. 3, 8), two wordplays (vss. 5, 9), vocative *lamedh* (vs. 7), double-duty suffix (vs. 7), the use of the independent personal pronoun as the direct object (vss. 1, 6), and a word with double entendre (vs. 7b).

1. *Beside.* For this nuance of *'al,* see the second NOTE on Ps xxiii 2.

the rivers. Not only the Tigris and Euphrates, with their tributaries such as the Chebar (Ezek i 1, iii 15), but also the numerous canals and irrigation ditches which intersected the country.

in Babylon. Since the opening phrase of vs. 1, *'al nahᵃrōt bābel,* "Beside the rivers in Babylon," balances the first phrase of vs. 2, *'al ʿᵃrābīm bᵉtōkāh,* "Beside the poplars in her midst," it may be argued that *bābel* shares the preposition of *bᵉtōkāh,* "in her midst"; hence translate "in Babylon" rather than traditional "of Babylon." On the other hand, 11QPsᵃ reads *bbbl,* "in Babylon." Since a scribe would more likely omit a *b* than add an extra one, and since the Qumran lection results in a seven-syllable colon that matches vs. 2a, it may be adopted. The syllable count of vs. 1 becomes 7:4::4:7.

we sat. Namely, upon the ground. It was a widespread custom among Semitic peoples to mourn seated upon the ground; e.g., UT, 67:VI:13–16, "He [El] sat upon the ground. He poured ashes of grief upon his head, dust of wallowing upon his skull"; Num xi 4 (D. Beirne, *Biblica* 44 [1963], 201–3); Deut i 45; Jon iii 6; Job ii 12–13; Lam ii 10; Neh i 4.

loudly. Just as *šām,* "there," describes the place, adverbial *gam* describes the manner of weeping. A full discussion of *gam*, "aloud, loudly," is given (with bibliography) in the first NOTE on Ps lii 7; cf. also UT, Glossary, No. 547, and McDaniel, *Biblica* 49 (1968), 31–32. The *šām . . . gam* assonance should be noted, and the collocation *gam bākīnū*, "loudly we wept," compared with the juxtaposition of these roots in UT, 125:13–14, *ytn gh* (the root of *gam*, "loudly," is *g*, "voice") *bky*, "He gave forth his voice weeping."

When we remembered you, O Zion! This seven-syllabled prepositional phrase balances the opening prepositional phrase, also with seven syllables, while the two verbal clauses are sandwiched in the middle to form a 7:4::4:7 pattern with a 3+2+2+3 metrical beat. Hence the proposal to delete this clause (cf. BH^3 apparatus) must be scouted; 11QPs^a preserves it. The prosaic ring of MT *b*^{e}*zokrēnū 'et ṣiyyōn*, "When we remembered Zion," which is one of the reasons for its proposed deletion, can be eliminated if the *nota accusativi 'et* is repointed as feminine personal pronoun *'att*, here functioning as the direct object of *b*^{e}*zokrēnū*, "When we remembered." Thus the poet directly addresses Zion, Jerusalem (vs. 5), the Edomites (vs. 7), and Babylon (vs. 8). This grammatical analysis is supported by the reading of the fourth-century Roman Psalter, "dum recordaremur tui Sion" ("while we remembered you, Sion"). Cf. Robert Weber, *Le Psautier Romain: Et les autres anciens Psautiers Latins* (Vatican City, 1953), p. 331. In vs. 6, too, its reading confirms the proposed parsing. The same grammatical analysis is proposed for vs. 6, "If I do not raise you, O Jerusalem." This usage, discussed at Ps lxiii 2, finds its closest counterpart in Jon ii 8, *'attā* (MT *'et*) *yhwh zākartī*, "You, Yahweh, I remembered," a reading and analysis which retain the second-person address that marks the immediately preceding and following clauses; cf. ETL 44 (1968), 37–38. There it is also noted that the identification of this usage recovers a neat A+B+C//Ć+B́+Á chiastic pattern in Prov viii 21, *l*^{e}*hanḥīl 'ōh*^{e}*bay yēš w*^{e}*'ōṣ*^{e}*rōtay hēm* (MT *w*^{e}*'ōṣ*^{e}*rōtēyhem*) *'*^{a}*mallē'*, "Endowing my friends with my wealth, and with my treasures I satisfy them."

2. *Beside.* Assigning to *'al* the meaning it carries in vs. 1. It is improbable that the lyres were hung "upon" the trees, as most versions have it.

the poplars. Or "the aspens."

we hung up. Since we had no further use for them. The moral inability of the Israelites to sing hymns of praise in Babylonia put them in a class with the denizens of the nether world whose keenest sorrow was their inability to sing Yahweh's praises.

3. *there our captors demanded of us.* Noteworthy is the alliteration of *šām š*^{e}*'ēlūnū šōbēnū*, which has an alliterative counterpart in vs. 8.

our mockers. One of the most recalcitrant hapax legomena of the Psalter (Duhm, *Die Psalmen*, p. 283, terms it "a completely unknown and inexplicable word"), *tōlālēnū* is structurally parallel to *šōbēnū*, "our captors," and hence must be synonymous with it. Etymologically, *tōlālēnū*, "our mockers," can derive from *hll* which in the poel conjugation specifically signifies "to make a fool of, to mock," as observed at Ps cii 9, *mᵉhōlālay*, "my Mocker," an epithet of Death. The initial *t-* of *tōlālēnū* would be the participial preformative comparable to Ps cxxxix 21, *tᵉqōmᵉmekā*, "your challengers," while the disappearance of radical *h* (*thll*>*tll*) enjoys an early analogy in Ugar. *hlm*, "to strike," but whose imperfect tense form is *ylm* instead of *yhlm*.

songs of gladness. This meaning of *śimḥāh*, literally "gladness," is documented at Ps li 10. Just as "our mockers" complements first-colon "our captors," so "song of gladness" fills out the thought of *dibrē šīr*, "words of song."

for us a song. Hummel, JBL 76 (1957), 105, proposes reading *lānū-m šīr*, with enclitic *mem*, but MT *lānū miššīr* can be retained as an example of the partitive *min* construction, much like Ps cxxxii 11, *mippᵉrī biṭnᵉkā*, literally "one of the fruit of your body." Cf. likewise Ps cxxxviii 5. Since the poet is obviously making extensive use of the suffix ending *-nū* (a total of nine in the first three verses), it seems unlikely that he would obscure the effect by adding an enclitic *mem* to one of them.

5. *Should I forget you . . . 6. should I remember you not!* The four cola of this protestation are arranged in a chiastic or diagonal pattern. The chiasmus comes out even more clearly if MT *'eškāḥēk* "I forget you," is repointed *'eškāḥēkī* whose ending *-ēkī* would rhyme with *'ezkᵉrēkī*, "I remember you." This reading does not assume the haplography of a *yod* since the next word (*yᵉrušālaim*) begins with this letter; it would be another instance of shared consonants.

Should I forget you . . . wither. The wordplay on *'eškāḥēkī* and *tiškāḥ* evokes the pun in Isa xxiii 16, "Take your lyre, walk the town, forgotten / haggard whore (*zōnāh niškāḥāh*). Sing sweetly, repeat your songs, that you may be remembered." The frequency of puns in laments receives comment at Ps lx 5; another pun recurs in vs. 9.

O Jerusalem. Heb. *yᵉrūšālaim* is metrically read as a double-duty vocative, suspended between the two parallel clauses and addressed by both. The line now syllabically scans as 5:4:5, very similar to vs. 6c–d, where vocative "O Jerusalem" forms the center piece of a 6:4:5 line. For other instances of double-duty vocatives, consult THE GRAMMAR OF THE PSALTER.

wither. To the documentation of this meaning of *tiškaḥ* given at Pss xxxi 13, lix 12, lxxvii 10, cii 5, may be added M. H. Pope, JSS 11 (1966), 240; Hanson, PMS, III, p. 88.

Other texts mentioning withered hands or arms include I Kings xiii 4; Zech xi 17; Matt xii 10; Mark iii 1, 3; Luke vi 6, and CIS, I, 5510:3, *y'ml yd*, literally, "May he wither as to his hand," where *yd* is the accusative of specification; contrast Charles F. Jean and Jacob Hoftijzer, *Dictionnaire des inscriptions semitiques de l'ouest* (Leiden, 1960), p. 17, lines 1–2.

6. *should I remember you not!* Usually labeled an Aramaism, the

feminine suffix *-kī* of *'ezkerēkī* may well be taken as the archaic Canaanite suffix (discussed in the second NOTE on Ps ciii 3), here preserved for the sake of assonance with first-colon *leḥikkī,* "to my palate," and especially with its inclusion-forming partner *'eškāḥēkī,* "Should I forget you," in vs. 5a. The same assonance is present in Gen xvi 11, as read and interpreted by me in *Biblica* 49 (1968), 87–88.

raise you. Reading *'a'aleh 'att* (MT *'et*) and parsing *'att* as the feminine singular independent pronoun functioning as the direct object, as in vs. 1d. In vss. 5a and 6b Jerusalem is directly addressed in the second person, so there is good reason to believe that she is still being directly spoken to here. The relative frequency in Ugaritic of the personal pronoun in the oblique—here accusative—case and the growing number of biblical examples afford a feasible solution here. As in vs. 1, the reading of the Roman Psalter sustains this grammatical analysis, "si non proposuero tui Hierusalem" ("if I shall not have set you, Jerusalem").

O Jerusalem. As in vs. 5, *yerūšālaim* is scanned as a double-duty vocative; the syllable count is now 6:4:5.

Upon my head in celebration! The picture drawn by the psalmist has not been identified by commentators, but he may be referring to mural or turreted crowns, representing Jerusalem, worn by Israelites on festive occasions. The Mishnah (*Shabbath* vi 1) speaks of "the city of gold," and an Akkadian text from Ras Shamra (cited in the Introduction) mentions a piece of jewelry called *âlu ḫurāṣu,* "a city of gold." There are also coins from Sidon and elsewhere showing a goddess with a mural crown upon her head; cf. S. A. Cook, *The Religion of Ancient Palestine in the Light of Archaeology* (London, 1930), pp. 190–92, and McKenzie, *Second Isaiah,* who in a NOTE *ad locum* explains Isa xxxv 10, *śimḥat 'ōlām 'al rō'šām,* "eternal joy upon their heads," as a metaphor "which may have a basis in a cultic or festive practice of wearing wreaths or garlands to symbolize rejoicing."

7. *Remember Yahweh, O sons of Edom.* With Jerusalem addressed directly in vss. 5–6 and Babylon cursed in the second person in vss. 8–9, the critic looks for a second-person imprecation of Edom in our verse. Such emerges with the analysis of the *lamedh of libnē 'edōm,* "O sons of Edom!" as the vocative *lamedh.* Compare Ps cxxxii 1, *zekōr yhwh ledāwīd,* "Remember Yahweh, O David!" and Ps xcviii 3, *zekōr* (MT *zākar*) *ḥasdō we'emūnātō lebēt yiśrā'ēl,* "Remember his love and his fidelity, O house of Israel!" In our verse singular imperative *zekōr* may be retained, though the persons addressed are plural "O sons of Edom!" since the imperative precedes. Cf. GK, § 145o. One may also read the infinitive absolute *zākōr,* since the infinitive absolute often serves as a surrogate for the imperative.

The Edomites, who helped the Babylonians sack Jerusalem in 587/6 B.C., figure in a letter found at Tell Arad in southern Palestine dating to ca. 600 B.C. This letter deals with the urgent dispatch of men from Arad to a certain Elisha at Ramath-Negeb, against a threatening attack by the Edomites. For further details see Yohanan Aharoni, "Arad: Its Inscriptions and Temple," *The Biblical Archaeologist* 31 (1968), 2–32, especially 17–18.

the day. When Jerusalem was captured and destroyed by the Babylonians. For a similar nuance of *yōm,* compare Ps xxxvii 13; Obad 12–14; Job xviii 20, and Hittite *ḫali,* "day," but also "day of death"; H. Th. Bossert in *Archiv für Orientforschung* 18 (1956), 366; in Ps lxxxi 16, *'ittām,* literally "their time," is rendered "their doom."

Strip her, strip her. The repeated imperative *'ārū* shares the feminine suffix of *bāh,* "her." Here Jerusalem is depicted as a woman being despoiled of her clothing; compare Isa xlvii 2–3; Ezek xvi 37; Lam i 8. The traditional version of *'ārū 'ārū,* "Rase it, rase it!" (RSV) is not sustained by collateral texts.

to her foundation! Here *y^esōd* has a double sense, namely "buttocks," and "foundation." For a related sense of *y^esōd,* "foundation," compare Hab iii 13, *'ārōt y^esōd 'ad ṣawwā'r,* "Stripping him tail-end to neck"; cf. W. F. Albright, in *Studies in Old Testament Prophecy* (the T. H. Robinson sixty-fifth anniversary volume), ed. H. H. Rowley (Edinburgh, 1950), p. 13. The law of retaliation remains operative when Edom, depicted as a drunken woman, is described in Lam iv 21, *tišk^erī w^etit'ārī,* "You will get drunk [on the cup of Yahweh's wrath] and strip yourself." The Hebrew poet employs the same verb of Edom that the Edomites used when they clamored for the spoliation of Jerusalem.

8. *O Daughter Babylon.* Not "O daughter of Babylon" (RSV); see Ps ix 15 on the expression *bat ṣiyyōn,* "Daughter Zion." The "genitives" which follow the construct *bat,* "daughter," are explanatory or appositional; cf. GK, § 128k; W. F. Stinespring, "No Daughter of Zion," *Encounter* 26 (Indianapolis, 1965), 133–41, and Alexander A. Di Lella, CBQ 30 (1968), 628.

In our verse, "Daughter Babylon" is a personification of the Babylonian empire.

you devastator. Repointing MT *hašš^edūdāh* to *haššādōdāh* and comparing the form with Jer iii 7, 10, *bāgōdāh,* "treacherous," as recommended by some scholars. Of course, the *ū* vowel of *š^edūdāh* may well be another instance of the shift of *ō* to *ū* in the Phoenician dialect; see the discussion at Ps ciii 14.

you devastator, blest he who repays you. The alliteration of *shin* sounds in *hašš^edōdāh 'ašrē šey^ešallem lāk* resembles the alliteration of vs. 3.

9. *seizes and dashes.* The poet balances these two first-colon verbs with the two nouns "your infants" and "the rock" in the second colon.

your infants. The practice of Oriental warfare spared neither women nor children in a war of extermination; cf. Isa xiii 16; Hos x 14; Nah iii 10.

the rock. Just as the psalmist played on words in vs. 5, so here he resorts to punning on *sela'*, "rock," but also a place name in Edom (some identify *sela'* with Petra), and vs. 8, "Edom." This wordplay, it might be remarked, secures vs. 8 *'ᵉdōm* against the emendation to *'ᵃrām*, "Aram," that is occasionally proposed.

PSALM 138

(cxxxviii 1–8)

1 *Of David.*

I thank you with all my heart,
before the gods I sing to you.
2 I prostrate myself toward your holy temple,
and I thank your Name.
Through your kindness and through your fidelity
you surely glorified
Before all your Name, your promise.
3 When I called you granted me triumph,
you helped me storm with my ardor strong.
4 All the kings of the earth will praise you, Yahweh,
when they hear the words of your mouth.
5 And they will sing of Yahweh's dominion:
"How great is the glory of Yahweh!"
6 Though Yahweh is the Exalted, he regards the lowly one,
and though the Lofty, he heeds even from a distance.
7 When I march amid my adversaries,
keep me alive before the fury of my foes.
Stretch forth your left hand,
and give me victory with your right hand.
8 May Yahweh avenge me so long as I live!
Yahweh, your kindness is eternal,
the special work of your hands do not forsake!

NOTES

cxxxviii. This poem affords a paradigmatic example of the effects which can be produced by the application of Northwest Semitic philological principles to the biblical text. From his traditional (*videlicet* pre-Ugaritic) approach to the text, Kraus (*Psalmen,* II, p. 910) concludes that the psalm is decidedly not the song of a king, that its language is relatively late and probably post-Exilic, and, finally, that its contents presuppose the message of Second Isaiah. Results just the contrary emerge, however, when we take cognizance of epigraphic discoveries during the past forty years. These reveal that the poem is a royal song of thanksgiving, and accordingly to be classified with Pss xviii, xcii, cxliv. Its words, parallelisms, and poetic devices find their closest counterparts in the Ugaritic tablets and in some tenth-century psalms, so a date in the Davidic period seems reasonable.

This royal song of thanksgiving divides into three stanzas. In vss. 1–3 the king expresses his thanks and states the motive (vs. 3) for his solemn thanksgiving. In vss. 4–5 he records what will be the reaction of heathen kings to the divine message that the Israelite king plans to publish abroad. The psalmist closes the hymn with a reflection upon divine Providence (vs. 6), and implores God to protect him during future military encounters.

1. *Of David.* Some manuscripts of the LXX add "of Haggai and Zechariah," possibly preserving a tradition that the psalm belonged to the period of the Restoration, but of this tradition there is no trace in 11QPs[a].

I thank you. Heb. *'ōdᵉkā,* which forms an inclusion with vs. 2, *'ōdeh 'et šᵉmekā,* "I thank your Name," sounds the keynote of the poem. The ancient versions, and now 11QPs[a], insert the divine name *yhwh* after *'ōdᵉkā,* "I thank you," but the semantic and syllabic chiasmus of the first four cola with a 7:10::10:7 syllable count discountenances the insertion of *yhwh,* which would upset the syllabic chiasmus. This insertion would moreover disturb the chiastic grammatical sequence of verb+suffix+prepositional phrase//prepositional phrase+verb+suffix. Other instances of syllabic chiasmus are cited at Ps civ 28.

with all my heart. Compare royal Ps lxxxvi 12. LXX, followed by some modern versions such as BJ, *La Bible de la Pléiade, The Grail Psalms,* inserts the clause "because you heard the words of my mouth," but its absence in 11QPs[a] and its disturbance of the chiastic pattern argue against its acceptance as the original reading.

with all my heart, before the gods. The apparent A+B//B́+Á indicates that *neged 'ᵉlōhīm* expresses a prepositional idea that balances the prepositional phrase *bᵉkol libbī,* "with all my heart." In the light of this structure, the translation of *neged 'ᵉlōhīm* proposed in the second NOTE on Ps liv 5 becomes less probable.

Exegetes disagree in their translation and explanation of *'ᵉlōhīm;* one modern version, in fact, renders it by "the mighty" (JPS), but the solution most consonant with the context identifies the gods with the deities of the heathen kings mentioned in vs. 4, "All the kings of the earth." Before these gods and their worshipers the Israelite king proclaims his faith in Yahweh. In fact, vs. 2, "I prostrate myself toward your holy temple," suggests that the Israelite king finds himself abroad where heathen deities are worshiped. In such circumstances his statement becomes much more intelligible. Cf. royal Ps lvii 10, "I will thank you among peoples, / O Lord / I will sing to you among nations."

I sing to you. Parsing as datival the suffix of *'ᵃzammᵉrekkā,* as in royal Ps lvii 10 where this verb is likewise balanced by *'ōdᵉkā,* "I will thank you."

2. *toward.* For this nuance of *'el* see Ps xxviii 2, "When I lift up my hands toward your sacred shrine" (*'el dᵉbīr qodšekā*), and Ps v 8b, which is identical in wording to our clause and should be rephrased in *Psalms I* accordingly, i.e., "I will worship toward (facing) your holy temple." Briggs in fact believes that Ps v 8b has been transferred to our text where it has no place, but the 7:10::10:7 syllable count overrules his contention. If "toward" is the intended meaning of *'el,* then the king must have been absent from Jerusalem on a military expedition. Had he been in Jerusalem, he would doubtless have gone directly to the temple to give thanks.

and I thank your Name. Because the psalmist, as in royal Ps liv 8–9, ascribes his deliverance from military enemies to the hypostatized Name of Yahweh. By construing this clause as the end of an inclusion begun by vs. 1, *'ōdēkā,* "I thank you," the critic has a point of departure for the stichometric analysis of the next line, which is generally considered corrupt.

your kindness . . . your fidelity . . . your Name, your promise. The prevailing critical view that this line is corrupt is belied by D. N. Freedman's observation that its four words ending with the suffix *-kā,* "your," correspond to the four words in vss. 1–2a which also end in *-kā.* Its integrity is further vouched for by 11QPsᵃ.

your kindness . . . your fidelity. The occurrence of the pair *ḥesed* and *'ᵉmet* in royal Pss lvii 11, lxi 8, lxxvi 15, lxxxix 2, 15, xcii 3, cviii 5, affords another phrasal criterion for the classification of the present hymn.

you surely glorified. By scanning *kī higdaltā* as a double-duty verb predicated of both the preceding and the following prepositional phrases we recover a meaningful line with the metrical count 10:4:9. Failure to recognize the emphatic character of *kī,* "surely," hitherto taken as causal "because," seems to have impeded the correct translation and scansion of this line.

Before all. Repointing MT construct *kol,* "all of," to absolute *kōl,* "all." Though *'al* in the first colon means "through," here it seems to bear the meaning found in vs. 7, *'al 'ap,* "before the fury." The use of the same preposition in the same verse with different senses is not uncommon; cf. the first NOTE on Ps ci 6 and below on Ps cxlviii 6. In vs. 1 the king thanks Yahweh "before the gods," and here he asserts that Yahweh showed the greatness of his Name and his promise "before all."

your Name. This second mention of the divine Name supplies another clue to the identification of the psalmist; the *šēm,* "Name" of Yahweh figures prominently in royal Pss xviii 50, xx 2, 6, 8, liv 8–9, lxxxvi 9, 12.

your promise. Or "your word." For this nuance of *'imrāteká,* whose similarity with its first-colon counterpart *'ᵃmittᵉkā,* "your fidelity," might be noted, see first NOTE on Ps xii 7 and Ps cv 19.

3. *When.* For this translation of *bᵉyōm,* consult NOTE on Ps lxxvii 3, and W. F. Albright, in *Mélanges . . . André Robert* (Paris, 1957), p. 23, n. 3.

you granted me triumph. For this definition of *ta'ᵃnēnī,* cf. the second NOTE on Ps xviii 36. Since it occurs in royal Pss xviii 36, xx 2, 7, lx 7, lxxxix 23, cii 24, cxxxii 1, this verb may be considered characteristic of royal psalms. In fact, it was the appearance of this verb in the royal Phoenician Inscriptions of Karatepe which triggered its recognition in biblical passages.

4. *the kings of the earth . . .* 5. *Yahweh's dominion.* The Ugaritic parallelism *mlk//drk* reflected in the phrases *malkē 'āreṣ,* "the kings of the earth," and *darkē yhwh,* "Yahweh's dominion," is noticed at Ps cii 24. See below on Ps cxlvi 9–10.

will praise you, Yahweh. When the kings of the nations learn of Yahweh's intervention on behalf of the Israelite king, they will join in the royal psalmist's thanksgiving. This interesting touch of universalism falls in with the exegesis proposed for royal Ps lxxxvi 9, "If you act, all the pagans will come to prostrate themselves before you, my Lord," and with the royal universalistic aspirations discussed in the introductory NOTE to Ps cii.

they hear. In tandem with the *yqtl* verb *yōdūkā,* "will praise you," the *qtl* form *šāmᵉ'ū* is a stylistic variant expressing a present-future action.

5. *And they will sing of.* The hapax legomenon construction *wᵉyāšīrū bᵉ* has invited emendation to *wᵉyāśīḥū bᵉ,* "And they will meditate on," but this alteration finds no support in 11QPs[a] *wyšyrw.* What is possibly involved here is a partitive construction, to be compared with Ps cxxxvii 3, *šīrū . . . miššīr,* suggesting that mere mortals can retail only a fragment of God's power; cf. Job xxvi 14, *hen 'ēlleh qᵉṣōt darkō,* "Lo, these are but bits of his power" (Pope, *Job,* and NOTE thereon). The reading *yāšīrū* is further secured by its parallelism with vs. 4, *yōdūkā,* "will praise you," a parallelism which corresponds to the two verbs the poet predicates of himself in vs. 1, *'ōdᵉkā,* "I thank you," and *'ᵃzammᵉrekā,* "I sing to you." In numerous verses the verbs *šīr* and *zimmēr* form a pair.

dominion. For this definition of *darkē* see TS 15 (1954), 629–31, where Baethgen's (*Die Psalmen,* p. 407) pre-Ugaritic translation *das Walten Jahves,* "the dominion of Yahweh," is shown by subsequent discoveries of extrabiblical texts to have been uncannily correct.

How great. Taking the phrase *kī gādōl* as the opening words of their song and parsing *kī* as the interjection "How!" best known from Gen i 12, *kī ṭōb,* "How good" (first NOTE on Ps xxxii 10). The concurrence in this verse of *darkē,* "dominion," and *gādōl,* "great," is reminiscent of their collocation in Ps lxxvii 14, "O God, your dominion is over the holy ones: / What god is greater than you, O God?"

the glory of Yahweh. Some critics (e.g., Briggs) have resorted to emendation in order to remedy the jarring shift from the double mention of Yahweh in the second person in vs. 4 to the third person of "Yahweh's dominion" and "the glory of Yahweh" in our verse. 11QPs^a supports MT, so emendation must be scouted. One could urge that *darkē yhwh* receives its determination from vs. 4a, *yōdūkā,* "will praise you," and that *k^{e}bōd yhwh* shares the suffix of vs. 4b, *'imrē' pīkā,* "the words of your mouth," but a similar shift in vss. 7–8, which will not permit such an explication, argues that the psalmist is employing court style which is distinguished by such sudden transitions from second to third person.

6. *Though.* 11QPs^a *ky* rebuts the proposal of BH^3 to delete *kī.* This particle introduces the psalmist's reason.

the Exalted. As a direct appellation of Yahweh, *rām* appears in Isa vi 1, lvii 15; cf. Albright in *Studies in Old Testament Prophecy,* p. 16, on Hab iii 10, and Dewey M. Beegle, BASOR 123 (1951), 28, on the personal names *'ădōn-lā-rām,* "the Lord is truly exalted," and *rūmlāyāhū* "Be exalted, O Yahu!"

the lowly one. Though current psalms scholarship understands *šāpāl* in a collective sense denoting an entire class, I suspect that the king here refers to himself, employing a term which recalls the use of *'ebed,* "servant," a designation of the king in royal Ps lxxxix 40, 51. There is a similar usage in the Aramaic Inscription of King ZKR (KAI, 202:2), who states *'š 'nh 'nh,* "I am a humble man," namely, before his god. Cf. also Zech ix 9 and D. R. Hillers, CBQ 30 (1968), 53, n. 20.

The contrast between *rām,* "the Exalted," and *šāpāl,* "the lowly one," has a predecessor in UT, 52:32, *hlh tšpl hlh trm,* "See how it subsides, see how it rises!" Cf. also Ps lxxv 8 and Eccles x 6.

and though. With first-colon *kī* extending its adversative force to the second colon. The NOTE on Ps cxxxv 6, *and in all,* observes that prepositions are sometimes omitted after the conjunction *w^e;* perhaps the same obtains with particles like *kī.*

In our text the sound sequence *w^{e}kī gābō^{a}h* might be considered harsh.

the Lofty. The contrast between this rendering and traditional "but the haughty he knows from afar" (RSV) stems from understanding *gābō^{a}h,* not as the antithesis of *šāpāl,* "the lowly one," but as synonymous with *rām,* "the Exalted," and hence another appellation of Yahweh. For a discussion of this title, very frequent in rabbinic literature, consult the NOTE on Ps x 4, *Since the Lofty One,* and Robert Gordis, *The Book of God and Man: A Study of Job* (Chicago, 1965), p. 329.

he heeds. The unexplained (Joüon, GHB, p. 147, n. 1) MT form *y^eyēdā'* loses its anomalous character when its initial y- is attached to the preceding word as the genitive ending; see the next NOTE. On *yāda'*, "to care for, heed" see first NOTES on Pss i 6 and ix 11.

from a distance. For MT *mimmerḥāq,* reading *mimmerḥāqī,* with the final -*ī* coming from the following word *y^eyēdā'*. The ending of *merḥāqī* is the genitive, here preserved to add another syllable to the second colon; the syllable count is now 9:9. In a Ugaritic omen text published by Loretz and Dietrich in *Festschrift C. F. A. Schaeffer* occurs the expression *yḥdy mrḥqm,* "He inspects from a distance."

The psalmist's assertion gains in appositeness when interpreted in view of vss. 1–2, which seem to indicate that he is far from Jerusalem. Though Yahweh has his principal abode in Jerusalem, he knows what occurs in distant lands and looks after his worshipers abroad.

7. *I march.* Since the context appears to be military, *'ēlēk* assumes the nuance witnessed in such texts as Ps lxviii 25; Judg i 10, ix 1; Nah ii 6; Hab i 6; Prov xxiv 6; UT, Krt:92, *hlk lalpm,* "They marched by thousands," in a description of a military campaign, and Mesha:14–15, *w'hlk bllh w'ltḥm bh,* "And I marched by night and fought against it."

Having thanked God for a military victory, the psalmist ends his hymn with a prayer for protection on future expeditions.

amid. The 11QPs^a variant *btwk* for MT *b^eqereb* is of no semantic consequence, but is nonetheless to be ruled out because three of the words in our verse—*b^eqereb,* "amid," *yādekā,* "your left hand," and *y^emīnekā,* "your right hand"—occur in three successive cola of UT, 76:II:5–7, *il hd bqrb hklh qšthn aḫd bydh wqṣ'th bm ymnh,* "The god Hadd [is not] inside his palace. His bow he took in his left hand, and his arrows in his right hand."

my adversaries . . . my foes. The customary rendition of *ṣārāh* by "trouble" (RSV) must be reexamined in the light of the abstract//concrete poetic device whereby the abstract noun acquires a concrete denotation. In the present instance, abstract *ṣārāh,* "adversity," signifies "adversaries" by virtue of its parallelism with concrete *'ōy^ebāy,* "my foes," precisely as in royal Ps liv 9 where the Ugaritic balance between abstract *ṣrt,* "adversary," and concrete *ib,* "foe," is cited. See below on Ps cxliii 11, and M. Tsevat, *A Study of the Language of the Biblical Psalms* (Philadelphia, 1955), p. 133, n. 40, where his comment on Ugar. *ṣrt* reads, "The constant parallel to *'ib,* "enemy," makes the meaning, *abstractum pro concreto,* certain." Cf. also Georg Fohrer in *Words and Meanings: Essays Presented to David Winton Thomas,* eds. Peter R. Ackroyd and Barnabas Lindars (Cambridge, 1968), pp. 98–99.

my adversaries. In addition to its concrete meaning, undetermined abstract *ṣārāh* receives its determination from its counterpart *'ōy^ebāy,* "my foes," on the principle of the double-duty suffix; another instance recurs in vs. 8. The extremely close nexus between these two words also supplies a valuable clue regarding the stichic division of this long line. Taking each synonym as the last word of its respective colon, we may scan the line as a quadricolon with an 8:9:5:9 syllable count, instead of the current versional division into three cola.

keep me alive . . . Stretch forth . . . give me. In his prayer the psalmist employs the more polite jussive forms instead of direct imperatives; this may be characteristic of court style. For the sake of brevity I render all three jussives as imperatives.

before. Parallel to *b^{e}qereb,* "amid," *'al* bears the same meaning as vs. 2, *'al.*

your left hand . . . your right hand. Just as second-colon "my foes" conditioned the meaning of first-colon "my adversaries," so the pairing with *y^{e}mīnekā,* "your right hand," affects the signification of neutral *yādekā* and gives it the more specific sense "left hand," as in royal Ps xxi 9. To the bibliography cited in first NOTE on Ps xxvi 10 and second NOTE on Ps lxxiv 11 should be added Stuhlmueller, CBQ 29 (1967), 196 [502], who renders Isa xlviii 12–13, "I am First (*rī'šōn*) / just as I am Last (*'aḥ^{a}rōn*). / Yes, my left hand (*yādī*) laid the foundation of the earth / my right hand (*y^{e}mīnī*) spread out the heavens." Just as First is the antithesis of Last, so *yādī* is the antithesis of *y^{e}mīnī,* "my right hand," not its complement as maintained by B. Couroyer in RB 73 (1966), 519, n. 38.

Paul Humbert, "Etendre la main," VT 12 (1962), 383–95, has shown that the expression *šālaḥ yād* is generally used in a hostile sense, so that from the psalmist's description we may picture Yahweh as destroying the psalmist's enemies with his left hand, and making him victorious with his right. That Yahweh employed both hands may also be inferred from vs. 8 where the poet prays God not to forsake the special work of his hands. Since Yahweh used both hands to create him, the psalmist argues, he should also use both hands to defend him.

give me victory. Ancient and modern versions make "your right hand" the subject of the clause (RSV, "and thy right hand delivers me"), but *tōšī'ēnī* may also be parsed as the second-person masculine singular; in other terms, the subject of *tišlaḥ,* "Stretch forth," remains the subject of *tōšī'ēnī,* "give me victory." In military contexts this verb often has the meaning "to give victory," as noted at Ps xx 7.

with your right hand. As in royal Pss xviii 36, xx 7b, *yōšī^{a}' y^{e}mīnō,* "[He] has given victory with his right hand," lx 7, *hōšī'āh y^{e}mīn^{e}kā,* "Give us victory with your right hand," *y^{e}mīnekā* parses as the accusative of means; cf. Exod xv 6–7, *y^{e}mīn^{e}kā yhwh tir'aṣ 'ōyēb ūb^{e}rōb g^{e}'ōn^{e}kā tah^{a}rōs qāmekā,* "With your right hand, Yahweh, you shattered your foes, and by your great majesty you felled your assailants," where the accusative of means *y^{e}mīn^{e}kā,* "with your right hand," is stylistically balanced by the preposition of means in *b^{e}rōb g^{e}'ōn^{e}kā* "by your great majesty."

8. *May Yahweh avenge me.* As in vss. 4–5, here the poet shifts from a direct second-person address of Yahweh in vs. 7 to the third person,

and then reverts to the second person in the following two cola. For this meaning of *yigmōr* (or *yigmor*) "May [Yahweh] avenge me," see the first NOTE on Ps vii 10, and HALAT, p. 190a. The verb shares the suffix of *beʿōdī*, "so long as I live"; another instance of double-duty suffix is annotated at vs. 7.

so long as I live. Repointing MT *baʿadī* (the phrase *yigmōr baʿadī* is hapax legomenon) to *beʿōdī*, precisely as in Ps iii 4, *māgān beʿōdī* (MT *māgēn baʿadī*), "my Suzerain as [so] long as I live." Cf. also Ps cxii 8 and Jer xi 14, *beʿōd* (MT *beʿad*) *rāʿātām*, "so long as their wickedness perdures." In our verse *beʿōdī* makes a neat parallel to second-colon *leʿōlām*, "eternal," and reveals the poetic figure of the breakup of the composite phrase *beʿōd ʿōlām*, literally "so long as eternity perdures."

What further sustains this reading and analysis of *beʿōdī . . . leʿōlām* is the appearance of a cognate expression in the Ugaritic prayer, UT, 1019:2–6, *ilm tǵrk tšlmk tʿzzk alp ymm wrbt šnt bʿd ʿlm*, "May the gods protect you, keep you hale, strengthen you, for a thousand days, ten thousand years, so long as eternity perdures"; cf. Virolleaud, *Palais royal d'Ugarit*, II, p. 40. Our verse, too, expresses a prayer.

The interesting chiastic metrical structure of the opening four cola is matched by this closing tricolon with a 3+3+3 beat and an ascending syllable count of 7:8:9.

the special work. Many manuscripts read singular *maʿaśeh*, "work," for MT plural *maʿaśē*, "work"; though modern critics often prefer the former reading, 11QPsᵃ *mʿśy* suggests that we retain plural *maʿaśē*, which can be explained as a plural of majesty referring to the king. A similar phenomenon can be seen in plural *yedīdekā*, "your beloved," a plural of majesty designating the king in Ps lx 7, and in Ps lxxxix 51, *ʿabādekā*, "your servant," another plural term for the king.

We may note further that four manuscripts (cf. BH³) and the Syriac version disrupt the present ascending 7:8:9 syllable count by prefixing the conjunction *ū* to *maʿaśē;* MT must thus be preferred.

PSALM 139

(cxxxix 1–24)

1 *For the director. A psalm of David.*

Yahweh, examine me,
        and know me yourself!
2 You know my sitting and my standing,
        you discern my thoughts from a distance.
3 My departure and my arrival you survey,
        and all my travels superintend.
4 The word is not even off my tongue,
        yet, Yahweh, you know all of it.
5 Behind and before you encompass me,
        and you lay your palms upon me.
6 Too overpowering for me is your knowledge,
        too towering, I cannot master it.
7 Where can I go from your spirit?
        Oh where from your face can I flee?
8 If I climb the heavens, you are there!
        If I make Sheol my bed, you are here!
9 Should I raise my wings in the Orient,
        that I might settle in the westernmost sea,
10 Even there your left hand you would lower upon me,
        and seize me with your right hand.
11 Then I realized,
        Even in the Darkness he observes me,
        and in the Night daylight is all round me.
12 Even the Darkness is not very dark for you,
        since the Night shines for you like the day,
        the Darkness like light.
13 Yes, you created my inmost self,
        have sheltered me from the womb of my mother.
14 I praise you, Most High,
        because you are awesome;

I fall in adoration before you,
so dreadful in your deeds.
My soul itself you have known of old,
15 my bones were never hidden from you,
Since I was nipped off in the Secret Place,
kneaded in the depths of the nether world.
16 Your eyes beheld my life stages,
upon your scroll all of them were inscribed;
My days were shaped,
when I was not yet seen by them.
17 But for me, how weighty are your thoughts,
O El, how powerful their essence!
18 Could I count them—more numerous than sand!
May I rise and my continuance be with you!
19 Oh that you, O God, would slay the wicked!
O men of idols, turn away from me!
20 Because they gaze upon every figurine,
raise their eyes to vanities arrayed.
21 Look! those who hate you, Yahweh, have I hated,
and your challengers held in loathing.
22 With perfect hatred have I hated them,
they have been my foes.
23 Examine me, El,
and know my heart;
Test me,
and know my cares.
24 Then see if an idol has held sway over me,
and lead me into the eternal dominion!

NOTES

cxxxix. A psalm of innocence composed by a religious leader (cf. vs. 21) who was accused of idol worship. Creating an inclusion, the psalmist begins (vs. 1) and ends (vss. 23–24) the poem with an appeal to Yahweh to investigate personally, on the basis of his omniscience and universal presence, the charges of idolatry brought against him. Verses 2–6 contain a description of God's knowledge as well as his foreknowledge; vs. 2, *yāda'tā*, "You know," and vs. 6, *da'at*, "your knowledge," and *lāh*, "it" (your knowledge) neatly indicate the limits of the stanza describing the divine omniscience. In the following stanza (vss. 7–12) the poet portrays the cosmic presence of Yahweh in heaven (vs. 8a), in the nether world (vss. 8b and 11–12), and upon the surface of the earth (vss. 9–10). In this description the poet skillfully appropriates two motifs: the tripartite division of the cosmos (first NOTES on Pss lxi 3 and lxxvii 19) and the four cardinal points (sixth NOTE on Ps lxxiv 12 and third NOTE on Ps lxxv 7). When describing God as the Creator and Provider in the next stanza (vss. 13–16), the poet implicitly resumes the thought of vss. 2–6, since these divine attributes imply universal knowledge, especially since the creation of man took place in the nether world (vs. 15b–c). In the final stanza (vss. 17–22), which begins with *welī*, "But for me," and ends with vs. 22, *lī*, "my," the psalmist professes his faith in God's omniscience (vss. 17–18a), then avows his innocence and repudiates idolaters and idol worship. Thus the psalm is a carefully structured unity whose parts are bound by numerous verbal and conceptual links pointed out in the following NOTES.

Though some ambiguities inherent in the consonantal system of writing remain, the application of Northwest Semitic philological principles to the MT (greatly superior to 11QPs[a] which preserves vss. 8–24) makes it difficult to endorse the view, lately maintained by CCD, that the current Hebrew text is rather poorly preserved. This application also uncovers new literary and semantic rapprochements with the Book of Job, thus lending substance to the view that ascribes the psalm to the same literary ambience as Job. In fact, the dating of the psalm, wrongly dated in the post-Exilic period by many scholars, will depend to a considerable degree on the date of Job, now correctly being ascribed to the seventh century B.C. by Pope in his introduction to *Job;* Albright, YGC, p. 258, and Hans Bardtke in *Das Ferne und Nahe Wort: Festschrift Leonhard Rost,* ed. Fritz Maass (Berlin, 1967), pp. 1–10.

This translation and the NOTES owe much to the dissertation of Jan C. M. Holman, "Psalm 139: Basic Exegesis," appearing in *Biblische Zeitschrift* 14 (1970).

1. *examine me.* Since he has been accused of worshiping idols, the psalmist asks Yahweh to examine him concerning the accuracy of the charge. The traditional rendering of perfect *ḥaqartanī* as preterit "thou hast searched me" (RSV) is inexplicable in view of the ending of the poem (vs. 23), *ḥoqrēnī 'ēl weda' lebābī,* "Examine me, El, and know my heart." From the two imperatives of vs. 23 it seems reasonably clear that the beginning of the inclusion must also be understood as an imperative; the closing request is meaningless if the opening verbs state facts rather than express requests. Hence *ḥaqartanī* must be parsed as a precative perfect, much like the precative perfects in Ps ix 5–6 that are balanced by imperatives in vss. 20–21. Note too that the psalm of innocence Ps xxvi begins with a series of imperatives (vss. 1–2).

and know me. Repointing MT *wattēdā',* with consecutive *waw,* to *wetēda',* with conjunctive *waw.* It parses as a jussive following the precative perfect *ḥaqartanī,* "examine me," whose pronominal suffix it shares. This jussive has its counterpart in imperative *weda',* "and know," in vs. 23.

A precative-jussive sequence may be seen in UT, 77:38–39, *ar yrḫ wyrḫ yark,* "Let shine the moon, and may the moon shine upon you!"

yourself. Following the long-standing recommendation to transfer vs. 2, *'attāh,* "you," to the end of vs. 1. Both verses profit metrically from this transfer, and vs. 1 acquires a chiastic structure, the verse now beginning with *yhwh* and ending with *'attāh,* "yourself." The psalmist will not settle for an inquiry conducted by one of Yahweh's messengers or interpreters, but demands an investigation of the charges by Yahweh in person.

2. *You know.* In vss. 2–4 the psalmist describes the omniscience of Yahweh. Knowing every detail of the psalmist's daily routine, God should be able to pass judgment on his guilt or innocence.

You know . . . you discern. For the Ugaritic parallelism *yd'//bn* see the first NOTE on Ps lxxxii 5.

my sitting and my standing. The phrase *šibtī wᵉqūmī* is an instance of merismus or antithetic parallelism embracing the whole outward life of the psalmist. The following colon describes God's knowledge of his inner life.

you discern my thoughts. The identification of this same phrase in Job xvi 21 requires modification of the current view that *rē'ī,* "my thoughts," is an Aramaism occurring only in this psalm (see also vs. 17). Job xvi 21 reads, *wᵉyōhaḥ lᵉgeber 'im 'ᵉlōᵃh ūbīn* (MT *ūben*) *'ādām lᵉrē'ēhū,* "Can mere man argue with God, or mortal discern his thoughts?" For details, cf. Dahood in *The Role of the Phoenicians in the Interaction of Mediterranean Civilizations,* p. 124. The identification of the phrase in Job further secures the reading *lᵉrē'ī,* "my thoughts," against those manuscripts and versions (LXX, Syr.) which read *lᵉdē'ī,* "my knowledge." In 11QPsᵃ the first seven verses of this psalm are missing. This striking rapprochement with the Book of Job affords invaluable insight into the literary ambience of our poet.

my thoughts. The use of singular *rē'ī* with a collective meaning, whereas in vs. 17 the poet employs plural *rē'ekā,* "your thoughts," may have been inspired by the desire for assonance with first-colon *šibtī* and *qūmī.* In vs. 15a he uses collective singular *'aṣmī,* "my bones," to effect assonance with vs. 14, *napšī,* "my soul." The counterweight of *rē'ī,* "my thoughts," is found in vs. 23, *śar'appāy,* "my cares," with which it forms an inclusion.

from a distance. The keenness of God's vision is set forth in terms recalling the sight of an eagle in Job xxxix 29, *lᵉmērāḥōq 'ēnāyw yabbīṭū,* "His eyes view from a distance."

3. *My departure.* With Zorell, ZLH, p. 79b, *'orḥī* is preferably parsed as an infinitive construct of *'āraḥ,* "to depart, make a journey," since its opposite number in vs. 2 is the infinitive construct *qūmī,* "my standing." Contrast RSV "my path," a poor parallel to *rib'ī,* which it renders "my lying down."

my arrival. The working hypothesis that *'orḥī wᵉrib'ī* represents the meristic equivalent of vs. 2, *šibtī weqûmī,* finds support in UT, 2 Aqht:v: 12–13, *hlk qšt ybln hl yšrb' qṣ't,* "Look, he brings a bow; look, he fetches arrows," where causative *yšrb',* "he fetches," stems from *rb',* signifying "to come, arrive," in the simple conjugation. Compare *bō',* "to come," but "to bring" in hiphil.

you survey. Jacob Barth, *Zeitschrift der deutschen morgenländischen Gesellschaft* 41 (1887), 607, proposed what remains the most viable etymology of *zērītā,* "you survey," when relating it to *zeret,* "span," i.e., something measured. On Ugar. *dry,* "to cut into pieces," cf. M. Dahood, *Biblica* 38 (1957), 62–64, and on Ugar. *drt,* "span, measure," UHP, pp. 7–8.

my travels. Within the context this seems to be the sense of *derākay,* literally "my ways."

superintend. The root of *hiskantāh* is well attested in Ugar. *skn,* "governor," and *skn bt* (=Isa xxii 15), "superintendent of the palace."

4. *The word.* Supposedly an Aramaism in our poem and commonly accepted as such elsewhere in the Bible (cf. Wagner, *Aramäismen,* pp. 77–78), *millāh* is more accurately classified as part of the Northwest Semitic vocabulary which gained wide currency in Aramaic dialects. As noticed in *Biblica* 44 (1963), 71–72, the verb *mll,* "to speak," occurs in Karatepe II:16–17, *wbl kn mtmll bymty ldnnym,* "But there was no one speaking against the Danunians in my days." The noun *mlh,* "word," occurs already in the Aramaic Sefîre Inscriptions of ca. 740 B.C.

even. Understanding *kī,* as in vs. 13, as the asservative particle balancing second-colon *hinnēh,* which is also emphatic. Since this verse climaxes the poet's disquisition on God's omniscience (vs. 5 begins a new topic), the use of two emphatic particles is apposite.

off my tongue. Better than RSV "on my tongue." See C. H. Gordon, *Introduction to Old Testament Times* (Ventnor, N.J., 1953), pp. 92–93, who compares the *Iliad* x 540, "Not yet was his whole word spoken," and UT, 1 Aqht:113, *bph rgm lyṣa,* "From his mouth the word had not gone forth."

you know. yāda'tā forms an inclusion with vs. 2, *yāda'tā* and closes the first stanza (vss. 2–4) describing Yahweh's omniscience.

all of it. The concept of *kullāh* will be evoked by vs. 16, *kullām,* "all of them," referring to the stages of the psalmist's life known by God even before they transpire.

5. *Behind and before.* Another case of merismus, *'āḥōr wāqedem* secondarily suggests "west and east" (the four cardinal points are found in vss. 9–10). Compare Isa ix 11; Job xviii 20 where "westerners" (*'aḥarōnīm*) and "easterners" (*qadmōnīm*) are said to be astounded, another instance of merismus designating the whole earth from one end to the other, and Job xxiii 8, where *qedem,* "east," contrasts with *'āḥōr,* "west." Cf. Fohrer in *Words and Meanings,* p. 96.

you encompass me. An attempt to preserve the metaphor suggested by *'āḥōr wāqedem* (see preceding NOTE). Most ancient versions derived *ṣartānī* from *ṣūr*, a by-form of *yāṣar*, "to form, fashion," but this derivation ill suits the context. More consonant with the theme of the second stanza is the derivation from *ṣūr*, "to shut in, besiege," favored by BDB, p. 848b.

and you lay. One suspects that the consecutive *waw* of *wattāšet* should be read as the conjunctive *waw*, so that the form would read *wᵉtāšīt;* both *ṣartanī* and *tāšīt* express present activity and the *qtl//yqtl* is a stylistic variation of verb forms. Expositors offer contrasting interpretations of the action depicted here, but Yahweh's absolute control of the psalmist's movements seems uppermost in the psalmist's mind. Cf. Job xiii 21, "Your palm remove far from me, and with your arm do not terrify me!" In our verse the word order is chiastic.

your palms. Since in vs. 10 "left hand" connotes north, and "right hand" south, the poet virtually alludes to the four cardinal points. The remarkable defective spelling *kpkh* for standard *kpykh* points to the Northern Israelite origin of the psalm. A similar instance of defective spelling is witnessed in Prov xxxi 20, *kappehā* (MT *kappāh*) *pārᵉśāh le'ānī wᵉyādehā šillᵉḥāh lā'ebyōn,* "Her palms she stretches out to the poor, and her hands she extends to the needy." Here the A+B+C//Á+B́+Ć pattern requires that consonantal *kph* be vocalized dual *kappehā,* "her palms," instead of MT singular *kappāh,* "her palm." It is now widely admitted that Prov xxxi 10–31 is an Israelite adaptation of a Canaanite-Phoenician poem that would have been written without vowel letters; on this assumption the Masoretic mispointing becomes explicable.

6. *Too overpowering.* The unexplained morphology of consonantal *pl'yh* grows clearer with the analysis into *p,* "and, for" and *l'yh,* "to be strong," discussed at Ps vii 13. What lends this analysis conviction is the parallelism with second-colon *'ūkal,* "I can [not] attain," the same parallelism as in Prov xxx 1, *lᵉ'ītī'ēl wᵉ'ūkal,* two personal names which may be interpreted "I am strong, O El," and "I am able," as proposed in PNWSP, p. 57, and followed by Fritsch, *Journal of Religion* 46 (1966), 71, and E. Lipiński, VT 17 (1967), 68–75, especially 74–75. Hence vocalize *lā'ᵉyāh,* with the preservation of the third radical *-y* as, for instance, in Ps lvii 2, *ḥāsāyāh.*

for me. The poet effectively contrasts *mimmennī,* "for me," with vs. 12, *mimmekā,* "for you," and vs. 15, *mimmekkā,* "from you."

your knowledge. Heb. *da'at* need not be furnished with its own suffix since it can share that of vs. 5, *kappekāh,* "your palms." The LXX also reads "your knowledge."

Relevant to this discussion is the reading of Symmachus, *hyperbállei me hē gnōsis sou,* "Your knowledge overpowers me."

7. *Where . . . Oh where.* The sequence *'ānāh . . . wᵉ'ānāh* may be compared with UT, 49:IV:46, *an lan yšpš,* "Where, Oh where, O sun goddess?"

from your spirit . . . from your face. Signifying Yahweh's presence everywhere. This psalm has been fittingly entitled "The Hound of Heaven" by *The Grail Psalms.*

can I flee? By his question the poet does not imply that he wishes to escape God, but that escape would be impossible even if he wished it. The alliteration of the words is interesting; in the first colon the first two words begin with *aleph* and the third begins with *mem,* while in the second colon (prescinding from emphatic *waw* of *wᵉʼānāh,* "Oh where?") the first and third words begin with *aleph* and the middle vocable with *mem.* Again the word order is chiastic; after the particle *ʼānāh,* "Where?" with which each colon begins, we have in vs. 7a verb plus prepositional phrase but prepositional phrase plus verb in vs. 7b.

8. *If I climb the heavens.* Grammatically, *šāmayim,* "the heavens," is an accusative of place, a construction present in UT, Krt:75–76, *ša ydk šmm,* "Raise your hands toward heaven."

If I climb the heavens . . . If I make Sheol my bed. Commentators have correctly directed attention to the similar sentiment in EA 264:15–19, *šumma nitilli ana šamē/šamema šumma nurad ina irzite ù rēšunu/rušunu ina qateka,* "If we ascend to heaven, if we descend to the nether world, our head is in your hands." Cf. Amos ix 2, "If they burrow into Sheol, from there will my hand take them; if they mount the heavens, from there I will make them descend."

there . . . you are here. The rare parallelism between *šām,* "there," and *hinnekā,* "you are here," might be compared with UT, 95:10, *hnny ʻmny,* "here with us two," and 14–15, *ṯmny ʻm adtny,* "there with our lady."

if I make Sheol my bed. The psalmist uses an explicitly subjunctive verb form *ʼaṣṣīʻāh* to express condition, whereas in the first colon he employed the conditional particle *ʼim* followed by an ordinary imperfect form *ʼessaq.*

The motif of Sheol as a place of beds is documented at Ps lxxxviii 6. To the texts cited there should be added 4Q (Discoveries in the Judaean Desert, V) Text 184:5–6, *yṣwʻyh yṣwʻy šḥt* [. . .] *mʻmqy bwr mlwnwtyh mškby ḥwšk,* "Her [the harlot's] beds are beds of the Pit, [. . .] the depths of the Shaft, her lodgings are the couches of Darkness."

Though one tradition, represented by such texts as Ps lxxxviii 6 and Jon ii 5, holds that God is absent from Sheol, another school of thought confesses Yahweh's presence even in the realm of the dead; cf. Pss xxiii 4, xcv 4; Hos iv 16; Amos ix 2; Job xxvi 6; Prov xv 11. Hence one must modify the comment of *The Oxford Annotated Bible* to this verse, "It is a new thought that God is in Sheol as well as in heaven."

9. *my wings.* Repointing after LXX, Syr. *kᵉnāpay* for MT construct *kanpē,* "the wings of." The biblical phrase *ʼeśśāʼ kᵉnāpay* has a close cognate in UT, 76:II:10, *tšu knp btlt ʻnt,* "Virgin Anath raised her wings."

in the Orient. The psalmist pictures a flight from the extreme east to the farthest west. Like vs. 8, *šāmayim,* "the heavens," and vs. 11, *ḥōšek,* "in the Darkness," both accusatives of place, *šaḥar*, "in the Orient," parses as an accusative of place in balance with the prepositional phrase in the second colon, *b*ᵉ'*aḥ*ᵃ*rīt yām*, "in the westernmost sea." Through this grammatical analysis we rediscover the first of the four cardinal points poetically expressed in vss. 9–10. Thus *šāḥar* here answers to vs. 5, *qedem*, which connotes "east," and is reminiscent of the parallelism in UT, 75:I:7–8, *km šḥr . . . km qdm*, "like the dawn/Orient . . . like the daybreak/east." Cf. second NOTE on Ps lxxxviii 14. As a corollary, 11QPsᵃ *šḥr* further excludes the emendation to *knšr*, "like an eagle," based upon the Syriac version.

that I might settle. Parsing *'eškᵉnāh* as a subjunctive or volitive form ending in *-āh* to express purpose. Cf. Jon iv 2, *qiddamtī librōᵃḥ taršīšāh*, "I rose at dawn/in the east to flee to Tarshish," where the denominative verb from *qedem*, "dawn, east," is subtly contrasted with Tarshish which stood in the extreme west.

in the westernmost sea. In the prepositional phrase *b*ᵉ'*aḥ*ᵃ*rīt yām*, which the psalmist employs as a stylistic variant to the first-colon accusative of place (cf. Exod xv 6–7 for balance between accusative of means and prepositional phrase), the concept "west" is expressed twice; cf. vs. 5, *'āḥōr*, "behind," but connoting west, and *yām*, "west," in Ezek x 19 and elsewhere.

10. *your left hand.* Primarily denoting "left hand" in this context (see the fifth NOTE on Ps cxxxviii 7), *yādᵉkā* secondarily connotes the north, thus giving the third cardinal point in this description of divine omnipresence. Cf. L. Alonso Schökel, *Salmos* (Madrid, 1966), p. 364, who renders *yādᵉkā* by *tu izquierda*, "your left hand."

you would lower upon me, and seize me. Preserving the chiastic word order of the original. MT *tanḥēnī*, "you would lead me," has a beneficent meaning that wherever the psalmist goes God's providential care accompanies him, but such is not the tenor of the passage. As in vs. 5, the burden of these verses is that there is no place in the universe where the poet can escape Yahweh's control and dominion. Hence one should repoint to *tᵉnīḥēnī*, the hiphil of *nwḥ*, "to rest." Cf. Eccles xi 6, "From morning sow your seed, and till evening lower not [*'al tānaḥ*] your hand," and Isa lxiii 14, *rūᵃḥ yhwh tᵉnīḥennū kēn nihagtā 'ammᵉkā*, "Your spirit, Yahweh, you lowered upon him [Moses]; thus did you guide your people." As in the Isaiah text, the suffix of *tᵉnīḥēnī* in our verse is datival. Though 11QPsᵃ *tnḥny* seems to sustain MT, it excludes the emendation to *tiqqāḥēnī*, "will you take me," inspired by the LXX and Syriac versions.

and seize me. Retaining Yahweh as the subject of *tō'ḥᵃzēnī* and comparing the NOTE on Ps cxxxviii 7, *give me victory.* The versions understand the verb in a friendly sense, but the context requires a hostile meaning, as in Job xvi 12, "I was at ease and he crushed me, / Seized [*'āḥaz*] me by the neck and mangled me." This semantic rapprochement between the psalm and Job furnishes another indication of the literary provenance of the psalm.

with your right hand. As in Ps cxxxviii 7, *yᵉmīnekā* parses as the accusative of means. The Canaanite poet expresses a similar idea by the use of a prepositional phrase in UT, 76:II:6–7, *qšthn aḫd bydh wqṣ'th bm ymnh,* "His bow he took in his left hand, and his arrows in his right hand." Since it also means "the south," *yᵉmīnekā,* "your right hand," refers to the fourth cardinal point in this description of God's omnipresence. The motif of the four cardinal points is documented in second NOTE on Ps xlviii 8 and sixth NOTE on Ps lxxiv 12. This grammatical analysis discloses that the psalmist repeats the thought of vs. 5, only altering the directional allusions; here he refers to the north and the south, while alluding to the west and the east in vs. 5.

11. *in the Darkness . . . the Night . . .* 15. *the Secret Place . . . the nether world* These four terms for the underworld may profitably be compared with Ps lxxxviii 12–13, which list the four epithets "the Grave . . . Abaddon . . . the darkness . . . the Land of Forgetfulness."

in the Darkness. Like vs. 8, *šāmayim,* "the heavens," and vs. 9, *šaḥar,* "in the Orient," *ḥōšek* parses as an accusative of place. The close literary ties between the psalm and Job are further underscored by the specific use of *ḥōšek* in Job xvii 13, "When I called Sheol my house, in the Darkness (*baḥōšek*) spread out my couch," and in xviii 18, "They will chase him from daylight into the Darkness, and from the world they will drive him." A full discussion can be found in Tromp, *Primitive Conceptions,* pp. 95–98.

he observes me. A viable solution of disputed *yᵉšūpēnī* (11QPsᵃ *yšwpny* dissuades emendation) is supplied by Job ix 17, *'ᵃšer biśᵉ'ārāh yᵉšūpēnī wᵉhirbāh pᵉṣā'ay ḥinnām,* "Who observes me from the storm cloud, and stealthily multiplies my bruises" (on *ḥinnām,* "stealthily," see discussion at Ps xxxv 7). The verb *šāfa,* "he watches, looks," is very common in Arabic. Accordingly one must decline the long-standing emendation of *yᵉšūpēnī,* "he observes me," to *yᵉśūkkēnī,* "he hedges me in," recommended anew by Bardtke, *Liber Psalmorum,* in the new edition of the Hebrew Bible, BHS.

in the Night. Like its opposite number *ḥōšek,* "in the Darkness," *laylah* is an accusative of place. Again Job provides the desired nuance: xxvii 20, *taśśīgēhū kammayim ballāhōt laylah gᵉnābattū sūpāh,* "Terrors will overtake him like a flood, / Night will kidnap him like a tempest." For details, see fourth NOTE on Ps lxix 25, and compare also Job xxxiv 25 and UT, 137:14, *ǵr ll,* "The Mountain of Night," probably an epithet of the abode of the dead. The parallel pair *ḥšk//ll* occurs in the Phoenician Inscription of Arslan Tash (lines 19–20).

daylight. Cf. Job xviii 18, cited in the second NOTE on this verse, where *'ōr,* "daylight," is synonymous with *tēbēl,* "the world." 11QPsᵃ reads *'zr* (MT *'wr*) *b'dy,* "He encircles round me," a reading whose tautology tells against its originality, since our poet is very economical with words.

all round me. The hapax legomenon *ba'ᵃdēnī* (11QPsᵃ eliminates it, reading the common form *b'dy;* cf. *Biblica* 47 [1966], 142) has been explained as the preposition *ba'ad* followed by the verbal suffix *-ēnī,* which would be anomalous here. Ugaritic and South Arabic *b'dn,* "around," argue that the preposition here is also *b'dn* followed by the correct nominal suffix *-ī;* see the discussion of *taḥtēnī* at Ps xviii 40, *beneath me*. The choice of this alternate form *ba'ᵃdēnī* is perhaps motivated by the desire for assonance with the corresponding first-colon word *yᵉšūpēnī,* "he observes me."

12. *Even the Darkness*. As in vs. 11, *ḥōšek,* "the Darkness," designates the underworld. Though many critics consider the line overloaded, and accordingly delete as an Aramaic gloss the last two words, which however are present in 11QPsᵃ, the verse can be scanned as a tricolon with a 9:9:6 syllable count.

is (not) very dark. Hiphil *yaḥšīk* with intransitive force is a hapax legomenon which BDB, p. 365a, defines "hide, conceal," and which 11QPsᵃ prefers to read as qal *yḥšk*. What is perhaps involved here is the elative use of the hiphil, to be compared with Ps li 9, *'albīn,* "I'll be much whiter" (fourth NOTE on Ps li 9 and THE GRAMMAR OF THE PSALTER).

the Night. As in vs. 11, *laylāh,* "the Night," is the nether world.

shines for you. Reading *yᵉ'īrekā* (for MT *yā'īr ka-*), whose dative suffix *-kā* expresses the dative of advantage. Cf. UT, 77:39, *wyrḫ yark,* "And may the moon shine upon you!" and Isa lx 19, *lō' yā'īr lāk,* "[The moon] will not shine for you." Prosodically, the reading *yᵉ'īrekā* creates fine assonance with *mimmekā,* "for you," and serves as the predicate of both the preceding and following similes.

13. *Yes*. With Briggs (CECBP, II, p. 496), interpreting *kī* as the asseverative particle, and not causal with many versions. The point of the affirmation seems to be that creation implies full knowledge of the person created. Hence Yahweh should know the inmost thoughts of the psalmist. Other texts illustrating the "creation connotes cognition" motif include Ps xxxiii 15, "The Creator inspects their intention, / the Observer all their works."

my inmost self. Heb. *kilyōtāy* literally denotes "my reins."

have sheltered me. One encounters various translations and derivations of MT *tᵉsukkēnī* (11QPsᵃ *tswkny*), but the recognition that the preposition *bᵉ* of the following word *bᵉbeṭen* might well mean "from" (cf. LXX *ek gastròs,* Syr. *min karsēh,* "from the womb") should enter into the discussion of the etymology of *tᵉsukkēnī*. Witnessed in Pss v 12, cxl 8, and Job i 10, *sākak,* "to screen, shelter," makes an unexceptionable parallel to *qānītā,* "you created," and turns the verse into an affirmation of the two doctrines of Creation and Providence. The pairing of *qtl* and *yqtl* verb forms accords with the canons of pre-Exilic poetry, and renders a late dating of the psalm highly improbable.

from the womb. Consult the preceding NOTE and *Biblica* 44 (1963), 301, on b^e, "from," in the phrase b^e*beṭen.* The psalmist may be adumbrating here the motif explicitly mentioned in vs. 15 and in Job i 21.

14. *I praise you, Most High.* This much-disputed verse may be scanned as a tetracolon with a 4:5:5:6 syllable count. Since the expression *'ōdeh 'al* does not recur elsewhere with *'al* as the preposition, it seems indicated that *'al* (or *'ēl*) be identified as the divine epithet, and the phrase be compared with Ps xxxii 5, *'ōdeh 'ēlī* p^e*šā'ay* l^e*yhwh,* "I shall confess, O Most High, / my transgressions, O Yahweh!" The collocation with vs. 13a, *qānītā,* "you created," seems designed to evoke Gen xiv 19, *'ēl 'elyōn qōnēh šāmayim wā'āreṣ,* "El Most High, the Creator of Heaven and Earth," while the connection with the concept of Providence in vs. 13b echoes Ps lv 23, "Your Provider is the Most High Yahweh, / your Benefactor who will sustain you."

you are awesome. With its reading *nwr' 'th,* "you are awesome," 11QPs[a] opens an exit from the impasse created by MT *nōrā'ōt,* "awesome things." But it is not necessary to supply an extra *aleph* with 11QPs[a], since the evidence quoted at Ps lx 11 proves that when the same consonant (especially *aleph*) ended one word and began the next, it was often written but once; thus consonantal *nwr't* can be vocalized *nōrā' 'attā,* as observed in *Biblica* 47 (1966), 141.

I fall in adoration before you. Redividing and repointing MT *niplētī niplā'īm* to *nāpaltī nāpōl ('āyōm),* a finite verb (modified by the suffix of *ma'*^{a}*śekā,* "your works,"—hence "I fall . . . before you") followed by the infinitive absolute. Compare Job xxxvii 2, *šim'ū šāmō*^{a}*',* "Listen carefully!" This unusual position of the infinitive absolute after the finite verb argues another stylistic connection between the psalm and Job. Cf. also UT, 121:II:10, *yspi spu,* and contrast Esth vi 13, *nāpōl tippōl,* "She fell in adoration." The third colon thus corresponds conceptually to the first colon, and the fourth colon answers to the second.

so dreadful in your deeds. When the final three consonants of MT *niplā'īm* are repointed *'āyōm,* "dreadful," there emerges the parallelism with second-colon *nōrā',* "awesome," which recalls Hab i 7, *'āyōm* w^e*nōrā',* "dreadful and awesome."

in your deeds. The syntax of the phrase *'āyōm ma'*^{a}*śekā,* "so dreadful in your deeds," has been elucidated by a comparison with Ps lxvi 3, *mah nnōrā' ma'*^{a}*śekā,* "so terrifying by your deeds." In other contexts the works of God often refer to Creation and Salvation; in this passage the psalmist intends Creation and Providence.

My soul itself. The w^e of w^e*napšī* evidently serves the role of emphasis.

you have known. Repointing MT *yōda'at* (participle) to preterit *yāda'tā;* thus the pairing with *nikḥad,* "hidden," equals that of Ps lxix 6, "O God, you know [*yāda'tā*] my folly, / and my faults are not hidden [*nikḥādū*] from you."

of old. Given the large number of dialectal forms in the Psalter, the proposed emendation of consonantal *m'd* to *mē'āz* may prove needless; suffice it to read *mē'ād,* "of old," discussed at Ps xciii 5, for MT *m^{e}'ōd,* "much." Another dialectal form receives comment at vs. 16.

15. *my bones.* MT *'oṣmī* is a hapax legomenon in this sense, and GB, p. 611b, correctly suspects that consonantal *'ṣm* relates to *'eṣem,* "bone," rather than to *'ōṣem,* "might"; one may dissent, however, from his proposed plural vocalization *'^{a}ṣāmay,* "my bones." 11QPs[a] reads differently, *'ṣby,* "my pain[s]." Since the psalmist gives evidence of seeking prosodic effects such as rhyme and assonance (cf. vss. 11–12, 23), the preferable reading seems to be *'aṣmī,* understood collectively, a disyllabic counterpart to *napšī,* "my soul"; the 8:8 syllable count would become 8:9 with the trisyllabic plural form *'^{a}ṣāmay,* "my bones." Consult the NOTE to collective singular *rē'ī,* "my thoughts," in vs. 2, and the third NOTE on Ps ciii 1.

Since. With its temporal as well as causal meanings, English "Since" well reproduces Heb. *'^{a}šer,* which also carries these two senses. Which is intended here cannot be determined with certainty.

I was nipped off. The pual hapax legomenon *'uśśētī* may tentatively be derived from *'iśśāh,* "to squeeze, press," recognized by most lexicons in Ezek xxiii 3, 8, 21, and by some dictionaries also here. On the occurrence of this verb in Prov vi 32, see Dahood, PNWSP, pp. 13–14; Scott, *Proverbs • Ecclesiastes,* ad loc.; Barucq, *Le livre des Proverbes,* p. 80.

The metaphor would be that drawn by Job xxxiii 6, "Indeed I am like a juglet from God; from clay I, too, was nipped off [*qōraṣtī*]." This motif neatly accords with the description of Sheol, the place of man's creation, as a land of slime and mud; cf. first NOTE on Ps v 10, fourth NOTE on Ps vii 6, third NOTE on Ps xxii 16, second NOTE on Ps xxx 10, and the comments on Ps xc 3.

in the Secret Place. From the apparent synonymous parallelism with "the depths of the nether world," one may infer that *sēter* is another poetic name for Sheol. This inference is borne out by Job xiv 13, "Oh that you would hide me in Sheol / put me into the Secret Place [*tastīrēnī*] till your anger pass"; Isa xlv 19, *lō' bassēter dibbartī bim^{e}qōm 'ereṣ ḥōšek lō' 'āmartī l^{e}zera' ya'^{a}qōb tōhū baqq^{e}šūnī,* "I did not speak in the Secret Place, in the tomb of the nether world of darkness. I did not say, 'O offspring of Jacob, seek me in chaos'"; Job xl 13, "Bury them in the dust together; / swathe their faces in the Hidden Place [*ṭāmūn*]"; Job iii 21, "Who await Death and annihilation by him, that the Hidden Place [*maṭmūnīm*] might engorge them." Tromp, *Primitive Conceptions,* ad loc., discusses all these texts.

kneaded. Another hapax legomenon in the pual conjugation, *ruqqamtī* is often defined, "I was skilfully wrought" (BDB, p. 955b), and the underlying metaphor understood as cloth of variegated colors, since *rōqēm* does signify "a variegator, a weaver in colors." However, commentators who adopt this translation (the ancient versions seem unfamiliar with the idea) cannot explain satisfactorily the comparison of the human body with multicolored cloth. Gunkel, for example, suggests (*Psalmen*, p. 591) that the poet is thinking of the bright colors inside the human body. If the figure is that of the potter (see NOTES on vs. 16), *ruqqamtī* would describe the action of working the clay into a uniform mixture by pressing, folding, and stretching.

the depths of the nether world. The fifth NOTE on Ps lxiii 10 examines this translation of *taḥtīyyōt 'āreṣ,* which effectively rules out the exegesis of this expression as "figurative language for the 'womb'" (CCD). This definition and the identification of *'al,* "Most High," in vs. 14, relate this passage to Ps lxxxvi 13, "Since your love is great, O Most High, you will rescue me from deepest Sheol."

Certain commentators (cf. Briggs, CECBP, II, p. 497) deny the concept of the creation of the substance of the human body in Sheol, the abode of the dead, beneath the earth. Such a concept would imply pre-existence, a thought elsewhere unknown to the Old Testament, according to these same expositors, and improbable in itself. But an impressive number of texts take for granted that man originated and pre-existed in the nether world; cf., e.g., Gen ii 7, iii 19; Ps xc 3; Eccles iii 20, v 14, xii 7; Ecclus xl 1; Job i 21.

16. *my life stages.* As proposed in *Biblica* 40 (1959), 168–69, the hapax legomenon *golmī* (MT) can be rendered meaningfully when repointed to *gīlay-mī* (with enclitic *mī*) and *gīl* identified with the substantive in Ps xliii 4 and Dan i 10. Also see P. Bonnard, *Le psautier selon Jérémie* (Paris, 1960), p. 226, and Wagner, *Aramäismen,* p. 41.

upon your scroll. Upon which are written God's decrees regarding the psalmist's destiny; cf. Ps xl 8, "In the inscribed scroll it is written to my debit"; Rev v 1–5; and Exod xxxii 32.

your scroll . . . were inscribed. Consult the third NOTE on Ps lxix 29 for the Ugaritic-Hebrew collocation of the roots *spr* and *ktb.*

all of them. The plural suffix of *kullām* finds its plural antecedent in revocalized *gīlay-mī,* "my life stages," and harks back to vs. 4, *kullāh,* "all of it."

My days. Plural *yāmīm* is modified by the suffix of "my life stages"; cf. Pss xviii 15, lxxvii 19; Prov xxvii 23, etc.

were inscribed. The texts cited at Ps lxix 29 point to the conclusion that *kātab,* "to write, inscribe," was used as a *terminus technicus* for determining the fate of a man.

I was not yet seen. One of the more baffling phrases, MT *lō' 'eḥad* yields good sense when vocalized *lō' 'eḥāde* and the latter parsed as the dialectal niphal form for classical *'eḥāze,* "I was seen"; another instance of Canaanite *d* for Heb. *z* is remarked upon in vs. 14, *mē'ād,* "of old," for classical Heb. *mē'āz,* while the other biblical occurrences of Ugar. *ḥdy,* "to gaze, perceive," are treated in NOTES on Pss iv 9, xxi 7, xxxiii 15, and xlix 11. Like the Servant (Isa xlix 1, 5), Jeremiah (i 5), and the

Apostle Paul (Gal i 15), the psalmist was predestined; his life stages and his days were decided and counted even before he was seen by them.

by them. In *Biblica* 40 (1959), 34, *bāhem* was rendered "among them," but 11QPs[a] *mhmh* and the reading *mhm* of three manuscripts suggest that *bāhem* expresses the agent with the passive verb *'eḥāde,* "I was seen." This analysis obtains for Gen xlix 6, "Into their council let my soul not enter, by their assembly let my liver not be inspected [*biqᵉhālām 'al tēḥāde*]." Cf. also Judg vii 7; I sam xiv 6, and Ezek xxvii 34, *'attā nišbart* (MT *'ēt nišberet*) *miyyammīm bᵉmaʿᵃmaqqē māyīm,* "Now you are wrecked by the sea, by the depths of the sea." Though the divine eyes beheld the psalmist's career even before he was created, the days had to await his conception before they could perceive him. Compare Job iii 3, "Perish the day I was born, and the night that saw the conception of a man."

17. *But for me.* With *lī* begins a new stanza that also closes with *lī* in vs. 22.

how weighty . . . O El. The concurrence of *yāqᵉrū* and *'ēl* in the same colon can scarcely be dissociated from RŠ 24.252:2 where *gṯr w yqr,* "massive and weighty," are epithets of El; cf. UT, Glossary, No. 1144a.

your thoughts. Though the ancient versions took *rēʿekā* as "your friends," the modern translations which offer "your thoughts," can cite the resultant linkage with vs. 2, *rēʿī,* "my thoughts," and the contrast between the weighty thoughts of El and the poet's superficial ones.

their essence. "Their principalities" (LXX) and "their poor" (*Juxta Hebraeos*) illustrate the interpretations to which Heb. *rā'šēhem* has lent itself, but the improved translation of Ps cxix 160, "The essence [*rō'š*] of your word is your truth, / O Eternal One, / The content of your judgment is your justice," argues the appositeness of predicating *rā'šēhem,* "their essence," of God's thoughts.

18. *more numerous.* Contrary to most versions, I consider *yirbūn* the last word of the triplet begun in vs. 17, which is characterized by a decreasing 9:8:7 syllable count; cf. first NOTE on Ps cxliv 12.

May I rise. In tandem with jussive *'im tiqṭōl,* "Oh that you would slay!" perfect *hᵉqīṣōtī* parses as precative; the psalmist pleads to be enrolled among the just who will enjoy the gift of resurrection and everlasting existence with God. For the documentation of this eschatological sense of the verb, see discussion at Ps xvii 15. In vs. 24 he asks to be led into the eternal kingdom, thus reiterating the desire expressed here.

The three prayers uttered in this triplet (with a 9:8:9 syllable count) are stylistically interesting. The first prayer is couched in the first-person singular precative perfect *hᵃqīṣōtī,* "May I rise"; the second is addressed to God in the second person, *'im tiqṭōl,* "Oh that you would slay!" and for the third request the poet employs the plural imperative *sūrū,* "turn away!" Using the precative perfect, the jussive, and the imperative forms, the poet rings all the changes that the Hebrew language puts at his disposal for the expression of wishes.

my continuance. As in Pss ciii 5 and cxxxviii 8, *'ōdī* is invested with eschatological meaning, denoting the psalmist's perpetual existence with God after his resurrection. The poet sets off his envisioned eternity with Yahweh against the death he invokes—and is sure will be meted out—upon the wicked.

19. *Oh that you . . . would slay.* Critics correctly compare the optative use of *'im* in this verse with that in Ps lxxxi 9, but are less felicitous when labeling *tiqṭōl* an Aramaism and an argument for the post-Exilic dating of the psalm. The occurrence of *qāṭal* "to slay," in Job xiii 15 and xxiv 14—another lexical link between the psalm and Job—and in the eighth-century Inscription of Panamuwa in a mixed Phoenician-Aramaic dialect, as well as in the contemporary Aramaic Sefîre Inscriptions, shows that this root belonged to the vocabulary of Northwest Semitic. Hence it is not specifically an Aramaism, and its appearance in the psalm does not necessarily betoken a late date of composition.

O men of idols. Since the psalmist has been accused of worshiping idols, he must prove his loyalty to Yahweh by repudiating and imprecating idolaters. The expression *'anšē dāmīm* is examined at Pss v 7 and xxvi 9, both of which are psalms of innocence. The *waw* of MT *wᵉ'anšē,* significantly omitted in LXX, Symm., *Juxta Hebraeos,* and 11QPsᵃ, may be parsed as the vocative particle documented in the second NOTES on Pss lxxiv 12 and lxxxvi 10. Another instance occurs in Ps cxlv 6.

20. *Because they gaze upon.* The grammatical subject of third-person *'ᵃšer yō'mᵉrū* is third-person *rāšā',* "the wicked," in vs. 19a, though conceptually second-person "O men of idols" in vs. 19b is also included.

gaze upon every figurine. The defective spelling of the original may account for MT *yō'mᵉrūkā* (11QPsᵃ *y'mrwk*) *limᵉzimmāh,* which yields better sense when read *yō'mᵉrū kol mᵉzimmāh.* The fact that *mᵉzimmāh,* "figurine," is preceded by vs. 19 *dāmīm,* "idols," and followed by *šāw',* "vanities," relates this psalm closely to Ps xxvi, also a psalm of innocence, which contains these terms in vss. 4, 9, and 10.

Since the verb *'āmar,* "to say," is normally followed by a preposition instead of a direct object, it appears likely that *yō'mᵉrū* refers to visual activity, a meaning discussed at Ps cv 28.

raise their eyes. Though 11QPsᵃ reads preterit plural *nś'w,* MT *nāśū'* can be explained as an infinitive absolute of the Phoenician type whereby *nāśō'* becomes *nāśū'* through a normal sound change of *ō* to *ū;* consult the second NOTE on Ps ciii 14. To be sure, *nāśū'* is elliptical and its object must be sought in terms of the parallelism, which suggests that "their eyes" is the object to be supplied. For the thought, cf. Ps ci 3.

arrayed. Much-contested MT *'ārekā,* "your cities," yields considerable sense when revocalized *'ārīk,* an adjective or passive participle of *'ārak,* "to arrange, array." Cf. Bauer and Leander, *Historische Grammatik*, p. 470, on the passive meanings conveyed by adjectives of this formation.

21. *Look!* For this interjectional translation of *h^a^lō'*, commonly rendered as an interrogative particle (RSV, "Do I not hate them . . . ?"), see second NOTE on Ps liv 2. The psalmist's impatience is captured better by "Look."

Yahweh. Proposals to delete *yhwh* are countered by 11QPs[a], which reads the Tetragrammaton.

have I hated. The verb *'eśnā'* is a *terminus technicus* in oaths abjuring idol worship, as noted at Ps v 6. The two *yqtl* verbs in this verse seem to express the same past time as the two *qtl* forms of the next line.

your challengers. MT *bit^e^qōm^e^mekā* now appears in 11QPs[a] as *mtqwm-mykh,* whereas the preceding preposition *b* of MT has been changed to *m,* "from." Heb. *t^e^qōm^e^mekā,* "your challengers," remains morphologically difficult, but not to be emended on that account; cf. Ugar. *tgrš,* the name of a magic club, with preformative *t-*, and Ps cxxxvii 3, *tōlālēnū,* "our mockers."

These "challengers" seem to be the false gods worshiped by "those who hate you."

22. *my (foes).* Heb. *lī* forms an inclusion with vs. 17, *w^e^lī,* "But for me," and closes the stanza begun in vs. 17.

23. *Examine me, El.* Imperative *ḥoqrēnī,* "Examine me," forms an inclusion with vs. 1, *ḥ^a^qartānī,* and proves that the latter is correctly parsed as the precative perfect "Examine me," a stylistic surrogate for the imperative form. In his plea in vs. 1, the psalmist uses the divine name Yahweh, but here he addresses him as El; in other words, he divides the composite divine name *yhwh 'ēl,* a stylistic characteristic of Ps cxliii, to be examined below. See the list of composite divine names in the Introduction to this volume.

and know. Imperative *w^e^da'* responds to jussive *w^e^tēda',* "and know," in vs. 1.

my heart. Briggs (CECBP, II, p. 502) rightly comments that the full form *l^e^bābī* is employed for euphony. With it the quadricolon evinces an ascending syllable count of 4:5::4:5, which is upset in 11QPs[a] *lby,* a reading which shows that by the first century B.C. at least (since the monks of Qumran copied from earlier master copies) such metrical niceties were no longer appreciated. With the Qumranic reading *lby* the resultant syllable count is 4:4::4:5; that the psalmist sought to end the poem with syllabically balanced verses may be inferred from the 7:7 balance in vs. 22, the 4:5::4:5 sequence here, and from the 9:9 syllable count in vs. 24.

my cares. Or "my anxious thoughts," resuming vs. 1, *rē'ī,* "my thoughts." The poet's anxieties may have been due to his constant efforts to avoid idolatry, mentioned in the next verse. Recurring only in Ps xciv 19, *śar'appāy,* spelled *sr'py* in 11QPs[a], is an alternate form, with epenthetic or secondary *r,* of *ś^e^'ippīm,* "cares, anxious thoughts," which occurs only in Job iv 13 and xx 2. Consult the first NOTE to Ps xciv 19. Here then is another significant bond between this psalm and Job.

24. *an idol.* Identifying MT *'ōṣeb* with Isa xlviii 5, *'oṣbī,* "my idol"; this too is how the Targum construed the word, the fourth synonym in this poem designating pagan idols. 11QPs[a] *'ṣb* supposes *'āṣāb,* "idol," rather than *'ōṣeb,* which would probably be written fully *'wṣb;* cf. R. Tournay, RB 73 (1966), 261. In Biblical Hebrew *'āṣāb,* "idol," appears only in the plural form, but that fact does not firmly preclude the cropping up of the singular form *'āṣāb;* either *'ōṣeb* or *'āṣāb* would produce the same sense in our verse.

has held sway over me. One can appreciate the motives of critics who delete MT *derek* as contributing little to the thought, but 11QPs[a] *drk* and the 9:9 syllable count dissuade deletion. The consonants, however, become charged with meaning when vocalized as the verb *dārak,* studied at Ps xlv 4. Compare Ps lxxvii 14, "O God, your dominion is over the holy ones [*baqqōdeš darkekā*]: / What god is greater than you, O God?"

and lead me. The psalmist, convinced that the divine inquiry will find him innocent of the charges of idolatry preferred against him, requests to be conducted into Paradise when his time comes. It may be observed that Ps xvii, a psalm of innocence, closes with the affirmation, "At the vindication / I will gaze upon your face; / At the resurrection / I will be saturated with your being." This request is thus a reprise of vs. 18, "May I rise and my continuance be with you!"

As pointed out at Pss v 9 and lxxiii 24, *n*ᵉ*ḥēnī,* "lead me," is here a *terminus technicus* connoting "to lead into Paradise."

into the eternal dominion. Gunkel's comment is revealing: "*derek 'ōlām* does not, in any case, mean the way to eternal blessedness." He himself opts for "the ancient, i.e., the good old way," and then cites three other opinions, all equally questionable. From the same root as *dārak,* "to hold sway," *derek* equals Ugar. *drkt,* "dominion, kingdom." Cf. Amos iv 10, where this definition renders gratuitous the emendation of *b*ᵉ*derek* to *k*ᵉ*deber,* "like the pestilence." Hence translate, "I sent among you a pestilence from the dominion of Egypt (*b*ᵉ*derek miṣrayim*)." Cf. Isa x 26, "And his rod will be against the sea, and he will lift it against the dominion of Egypt [*b*ᵉ*derek miṣrayim*]."

PSALM 140
(cxl 1–14)

1 *For the director. A psalm of David.*

2 Rescue me, Yahweh, from the evil man,
from the man of violence protect me,
3 Because they plan evil things in their heart,
the day long conspire warfare.
4 They sharpen their tongue like a serpent,
viper's venom is under their lips. *Selah*
5 Guard me, Yahweh, from the hands of the wicked,
from the man of violence protect me.
Because they plan to trip my feet,
6 the presumptuous have hidden a trap for me;
The villains have spread out a net,
at path's edge have set lures for me. *Selah*
7 I said, "O Yahweh, you are my God,
give ear, Yahweh, to my plea for mercy.
8 Yahweh, my Lord, my fortress of safety,
shelter my head in the day of arms!
9 Grant not, Yahweh, the wishes of the wicked,
his evil design do not promote, O Exalted!" *Selah*
10 The mischief-makers who surround me—
may the poison of their lips drown them!
11 May he heap upon them hot coals,
into the Fire may he plunge them!
From the Miry Bog let them not rise!
12 The man of tongue—
let him not be established in the land;
The man of violence—
may the Evil One hunt him into Exile!
13 I know that Yahweh will maintain
the cause of the persecuted, the rights of the poor.
14 Indeed, the just shall give praise to your Name,
the upright shall dwell before your face.

NOTES

cxl. A lament in which the psalmist prays for deliverance from personal enemies. The lament consists of five stanzas of approximately equal length, the ends of the first three stanzas being indicated by the musical notation *Selah* (vss. 4, 6, 9). In the first stanza (vss. 2–4), the poet prays to be delivered from slanderers whom he compares to serpents, and in the second strophe (vss. 5–6) he likens his treacherous foes to hunters in search of prey. The third stanza (vss. 7–9) gives the text of his plea to Yahweh, while the fourth (vss. 10–12) contains the imprecations uttered against his foes. Praying that the evil plans of his adversaries recoil upon themselves, the psalmist resumes the metaphor of the serpents (vs. 10) and of the hunter (vs. 12). In the final strophe (vss. 13–14) the poet expresses his confidence that Yahweh will uphold the cause of justice by rewarding the persecuted and the poor in the future life.

This lament is linguistically noteworthy for the surprisingly large number of hapax legomena and archaic forms that are commented upon in the NOTES. These in turn point to an early date of composition. The poet was particularly fond of chiasmus (vss. 2, 5, 6, 9, 11, 14) and twice employed the *casus pendens* construction (vss. 10, 12).

2. *Rescue me . . . protect me.* Imperative *ḥalleṣēnī*, "Rescue me," is balanced by jussive *tinṣerēnī*, "protect me," in this chiastically arranged verse. For the Canaanite antecedents of this imperative-jussive sequence, see the discussion at Ps v 4. In vss. 7–8 the psalmist pairs the imperative with the precative perfect.

3. *Because.* Usually translated as relative pronoun "Who," *'ašer* may also be interpreted as causal "Because," a usage frequently recognized by the lexicons; cf. Ps cxxxix 15.

they plan . . . conspire. The pairing of the *qtl* verb *ḥāšebū*, "they plan," with the *yqtl* form *yāgūrū*, "(they) conspire," is a stylistic practice of Canaanite parentage, as noted at Ps iv 4 and elsewhere.

in their heart. With names of parts of the body the poet was free to use or to dispense with the suffix. In vs. 4 the psalmist uses *lešōnām*, "their tongue," but for syllabic (9:9) reasons he forgoes the suffix in *belēb*, "in their heart," exactly as in UT, 1 Aqht:34, *tbky pġt bm lb*, "Pughat wept from her heart." See the first NOTE to Ps cxi 1.

conspire. For this definition of *yāgūrū*, see first NOTE on Ps lvi 7.

4. *They sharpen.* Since *šānanū* contains the root of *šēn*, "tooth" (cf. Ugar. *yšnn*, "he gnashes his teeth"), the psalmist manages to mention or allude to six parts of the body in vss. 3–6: heart, teeth, tongue, lips, hands, and feet. Cf. Pss cvii 9 and cxx 2–4. The psalmist succeeds in imitating the hissing sounds of serpents: *šānanū lešōnām kemō nāḥāš.*

their tongue . . . their lips. The second NOTE on Ps cxx 2 cites the restored Ugaritic text with the parallelism of *lšn,* "tongue," and *špt,* "lip."

a serpent. Hitherto witnessed in other Semitic languages only in the Arabic metathetic form *ḥanašu,* "serpent," *nāḥāš* now finds its exact counterpart in RŠ 24.244, *ytt nḥšm mhrk bn bṯnm itnnk,* "A present of serpents is your dowry, snakes are your gift"; cf. *Biblica* 49 (1968), 359.

serpent . . . venom. The origin of this parallelism between *nāḥāš,* "serpent," and *ḥamat,* "venom," can now be traced to the Late Bronze Age (1500–1200 B.C.) in RŠ 24.244:11–12, *lnh ydy ḥmt hlm ytq nḥš,* "From him he shall extirpate the venom. Straightway let him bind the serpent." Cf. Astour in JNES 27 (1968), 14–16.

viper's venom. At Ps xc 9 is cited an article of Ely E. Pilchik, who assures us that "In 40 years of Old Testament study I have never come across a spider in the Psalms" (p. 404), but here the Mishna understands MT *'akšūb* as "spider," an interpretation now sustained by 11QPs[a] *'kbyš,* "spider," and pointing to the conclusion that the Mishnah worked from a manuscript preserving the same tradition as 11QPs[a]. These readings do not, however, warrant the alteration of the hapax legomenon in MT *'akšūb,* a type of horned viper. The morphological resemblance of *'akšūb,* "viper," to *'akbūr,* "mouse," argues the authenticity of the former.

5. *Guard me . . . protect me.* As in vs. 2, the psalmist balances an imperative with a jussive form, both of which are rendered as imperatives in English. Again the word order is chiastic or diagonal.

Because. Cf. the first NOTE on vs. 3. This causal adverb introduces the third colon in vs. 5c.

6. *the presumptuous.* For this nuance of *gē'īm,* see the discussion at Ps xciv 2. The mistake of the presumptuous is their assumption that Yahweh will not intervene on behalf of his own.

villains. With Driver, JBL 73 (1954), 136, repointing MT *ḥabālīm,* "ropes," to *ḥabbālīm,* "villains," from *ḥābal,* "to deal corruptly." This derivation recovers the synonymy with *gē'īm,* "the presumptuous," and the chiastic structure of the first two cola of vs. 6. Since chiasmus marks the style of our poet (vss. 2, 5, 9, 11), the argument from chiasmus carries conviction here. Cf. also Job xxi 17, "How often is the lamp of the wicked [*rešā'īm*] snuffed out, / or destruction come upon them? / *ḥabbālīm* [MT *ḥabālīm,* "pains"] *yeḥallēq be'appō,* or has he destroyed villains in his anger?"

a net. For the Canaanite equivalent of *rešet,* see first NOTE on Ps lvii 7.

7. *O Yahweh.* As proposed in second NOTE on Ps xvi 2 and VT 16 (1966), 309, the *lamedh* of *layhwh* parses as the vocative particle, a proposal endorsed by Hanson, PMS, III, p. 93.

give ear, Yahweh. On the basis of the Syriac, some commentators delete the Tetragrammaton *yhwh* which stands in the vocative case, but when first-colon *layhwh* is parsed as vocative, the deletion becomes inadmissible. The line currently scans into 2+2//2+2 with a 10:11 syllable count.

8. *my Lord.* The current 10:10 syllable count rules out the deletion of *'ᵃdōnāy,* "my Lord," recently proposed by Hanson, PMS, III, p. 122.

shelter. Parsing *sakkōtāh* as a precative perfect balancing imperative *ha'ᵃzīnāh,* "give ear," in vs. 7. In vss. 2 and 5 the poet achieves variety by pairing imperatives and jussives. The full spelling of precative perfect *sakkōtāh* accords with the examples cited in the first NOTE on Ps iv 8.

my head. Or simply "over me," since *lᵉrō'šī* may be only a ballast variant of *l,* "upon," just as Ugar. *lriš,* literally "upon the head," is but a synonym of *l,* "upon."

arms. Heb. *nāšeq* equals Ugar. *nṯq,* the name of a ballistic weapon in 1123:1–3, *arb'm qšt alp ḥẓm walp nṯq,* "Forty bows, a thousand arrows, and a thousand darts." Cf. also UT, 51:VII:39, *nṯq dmrn.*

9. *Grant not . . . do not promote.* A recognition of the chiastic sentence structure helps elucidate the obscure elements of this verse.

the wishes. The hapax legomenon *ma'ᵃwayyēy* is an interesting form, preserving the original third radical *-y* of the verb *'āwāh,* "to desire," and may be listed among the archaic elements of this lament.

do not promote. Literally "do not make him obtain," hiphil *tāpēq* derives from *pūq,* "to obtain," a root witnessed in UT, Krt:12, *aṯt ṣdqh lypq,* "His legitimate wife he obtained," as well as in Phoenician.

O Exalted! Parallel to first-colon vocative Yahweh, *yārūmū* also parses as a vocative from the root *yrm,* examined at Ps xviii 47. Cf. Isa xxx 18, *wᵉlākēn yᵉḥakkeh yhwh laḥᵃnanᵉkem wᵉlākēn yārūm lᵉraḥemᵉkem,* "But Yahweh is waiting to take pity on you, the Exalted to be gracious to you," and Isa lii 13, *hinnēh yaśkīl 'abdī yārūm,* "Behold the Exalted will prosper his servant!" In our verse the ending of *yārūmū* is the nominative ending. In Arabic the vocative case takes either the nominative or the accusative ending; in Ugaritic the evidence is ambiguous. Cf. also I Sam ii 10 where *'ālū,* "Most High," with the nominative ending, balances first-colon Yahweh, just as *yārūmū* comprises the second element of an originally composite title *yahweh yārūmū,* to be compared with Ugar. *yrm b'l,* "Baal is the Exalted."

From this analysis it appears that each element of the first colon has a synonymous counterpart in the second colon in an A+B+C//Ć+Á+B́ pattern with an 11:9 syllable count. Hence one may dissent from the judgment of Hanson, PMS, III, p. 122, "The Hebrew is unclear and perhaps corrupt."

10. *The mischief-makers who surround me—the poison of their lips.* D. N. Freedman has noticed from the principle of congruent metaphors that the four Hebrew words *rō'š mᵉsibbay 'āmāl* (MT *mᵉsibbāy 'ᵃmal*) *śᵉpātēmō* comprise two construct chains, one inside the other. Thus *rō'š śᵉpātēmō,* "the poison of their lips," is an envelope figure enclosing the other construct chain. Since congruence of metaphors demands the union of *rō'š,* "poison," and *śᵉpātēmō,* "their lips," *mᵉsibbay 'āmāl* (MT *'ᵃmal*)

must be parsed as a construct chain, literally "my surrounders of mischief," of the type documented at Ps xviii 18. Of the examples cited there the most relevant is perhaps Ps xxxv 16, *lō'ᵉgay mā'ōg*, "my encircling mockers." In view of all the instances of interposition in construct chains cited in THE GRAMMAR OF THE PSALTER, such a word order no longer seems bizarre. Thus Ugaritic witnesses interesting examples of verbs intervening in construct chains: UT, 49:II:17–19, *npš ḫsrt bn nšm npš hmlt arṣ*, "The appetite of men was lacking, the appetite of earth's multitudes." Here the verb *ḫsrt*, "was lacking," is interposed between construct *npš*, "appetite," and *bn nšm*, "men"; since *npš hmlt arṣ*, "the appetite of earth's multitudes," is a construct chain, it follows that *npš bn nšm* is also a construct chain literally meaning "the appetite of the sons of men." Cf. likewise UT, 'nt: II:40–41, *ṭl šmm tskh rbb tskh kbkbm*, "The dew of heaven she poured upon herself, the spray of the stars she poured upon herself." Parallelism with *ṭl šmm*, "The dew of heaven," shows that *rbb kbkbm*, "the spray of the stars," is also a construct chain interrupted by the verb *tskh*, "she poured upon herself." See the second NOTE on Ps cxlv 7.

the poison. Once *rō'š* is related to vs. 4, *ḥᵃmat*, "venom," and to "their lips" here, it becomes clear that it must be identified with Ps lxix 22, *rō'š*, "poison," and not with its homonym signifying "head."

drown them. Either the Ketiv *yᵉkassūmō* or Qere *yᵉkassēmō* is syntactically viable, since the former can also be explained as a singular imperfect verb ending in *-ū*. The suffix ending *-mō*, recurring thrice in this poem, is another sign of early composition, since this ending recurs repeatedly in the ancient poem in Exod xv.

The law of retaliation requires that the evildoers be done in by the same means they use to harm others; hence the psalmist prays that the viper's poison beneath their lips (vs. 4) submerge them. In vs. 12 he asks that Death hunt down his adversaries just as they hunted him with snares and lures (vs. 6). Ps lix 13 expresses a similar sentiment.

11. *May he heap.* Again following the Ketiv in pointing *yāmīṭū* as against Qere *yimmōṭū;* for this sense of the hiphil, cf. Ps lv 4, *kī yāmīṭū 'ālay 'āwen*, "For they heap invective upon me." A comparison of these two texts suffices to discountenance the frequent emendation of *yāmīṭū* to *yamṭēr*, "May he rain down," lately endorsed by PMS, III, p. 122. The subject of *yāmīṭū* with the archaic *yaqtulu* ending, would be Yahweh, also the subject of second-colon *yappīlēm*, "may he plunge them!" As in vss. 2, 5, 6, 9, the word order of the first two cola is chiastic.

into the Fire. Namely, of hell. The psalmist first asks God to punish his maligners upon earth with glowing embers, after the manner of the destruction of Sodom and Gomorrah, and then he requests that they be hurled into hellfire. That this is not exclusively a New Testament (Mark ix 43; Luke xvi 24) concept emerges from a clearer understanding of Ecclus ix 8, *b'd 'šh [h]šḥtw rbym wkn 'hbyh b'š tlhṭ*, "Because of a woman many have been pitted, and thus her lovers are consumed by fire"; Job xv 30, *lō' yāsūr mīnnī ḥōšek yōnaqtō tᵉyabbēš šalhābet wᵉyāsūr bᵉrewaḥ* (MT *bᵉrūᵃḥ*) *pīū*, "He will not escape from Darkness, his offshoot Flame will wither, nor [double-duty negative *lō'*] will he escape from its massive mouth." Since *'āreṣ* in the preceding verse (Job xv 29) designates the nether world, darkness, flame, and mouth are also attributes of hell. Cf. Job xx 26 for a further collocation of *ḥōšek*, "Darkness=Sheol," and *'ēš*, "fire." One may accordingly hesitate to accept the conclusion of David Winston, "The Iranian Component in the Bible, Apocrypha, and Qumran: A Review of the Evidence," in *History of Religions* 5, No. 2 (Winter 1966), 183–217, that "The [biblical] notion of an eschatological judgment by fire is of Iranian origin" (p. 206). Our psalm probably antedates the Persian period by several centuries.

may he plunge them. The problem of stichometry is perhaps the most serious bedeviling this line, but if *yappīlēm*, "may he plunge them," is construed as the chiastic counterpart of first-colon *yāmīṭū*, "May he heap," then the line breaks up into a neatly arranged 3+2+3 tricolon with a 9:5:9 syllable count that counterbalances the 2+3+2 tricolon in vs. 10.

From the Miry Bog. "From" is one of the frequent meanings of *bᵉ*, while the hapax legomenon *mahᵃmōrōt* (cf. Ecclus xii 16), whose ending *-ōt* may well be the Phoenician singular feminine ending as in vs. 12, *madḥēpōt*, "Exile," Ps lxxiii 18, *ḥᵃlāqōt*, "Perdition," and *maššū'ōt* "Desolation," all designations of the nether world, equals Ugar. *mhmrt*.

R. Dussaud in *Revue de l'histoire des religions* 111 (1935), 33, n. 4, was perhaps the first to identify biblical *mahᵃmōrōt* with *hmry*, the name of Death's city in Ugaritic texts, and *mhmrt//npš*, "throat." Though this equation is now widely accepted (cf. UHP, p. 56; *Biblica* 40 [1959], 167–68; Brekelmans BO 23 [1966], 308; G. Widengren, VT 4 [1954], 98–99), there is still some variation in the definition assigned it. Some prefer "gullet," others "deep pits," and many opt for "watery pits"; cf. second NOTE on Ps xlvi 3. On the Canaanite provenance of this biblical hapax legomenon there is, however, no dispute.

Nor need there be any conflict between the juxtaposed concepts of hellfire and Miry Bog since the impassioned curse aims to accumulate various types of punishment upon the wicked. In Job xv 30 and xx 26, cited above, the author describes the nether world as a place both of darkness and of flame.

let them not rise! As Briggs, CECBP, II, p. 506, correctly observes, this phrase means "May they have no resurrection," as in Isa xxvi 14, *rᵉpā'īm bal yāqūmū*, "The Shades shall not rise." The psalmist reiterates the statement of Pss i 5 and xxxvi 13 which deny the resurrection of the wicked. In other words, he contrasts the fate of the wicked with that of the just, who in vs. 14 are promised eternal beatitude in Yahweh's presence.

12. *The man of tongue.* A graphic phrase for slanderer. Like second-

colon *'îš ḥāmās,* "The man of violence," and Ps ciii 15, *'enôš,* "Man," *'îš lāšōn,* "The man of tongue," stands in the *casus pendens,* "the hanging case," awaiting its predicate.

not be established. May he never gain a fixed residence. Cf. Prov xxi 28, "The false witness will be a wanderer, and the eavesdropper will ever be pursued."

the Evil One. An epithet of personified Death, *ra'* (the *athnach* of MT *rā'* should revert to the preceding word) is synonymous with *rāšā',* "the Wicked One," a title of Death documented at Ps lxxxiv 11. The Targum correctly grasped the burden of the curse: "The angel of death will drive him down to hell." In the Introduction to this volume Ps xxiii 4, *lō' 'îrā' rā'* is rendered "I will not fear the Evil One," where *rā'* forms a theological wordplay with vs. 1, *rō'î,* "my shepherd."

hunt him. As in vs. 10, the *lex talionis* is also operative here. Just as the psalmist's detractors used the tools of a hunter to try to capture him, so may Death the Hunter pursue them into hell. The motif of Death the Hunter stands forth clearly in Pss xviii 6, "The cords of Sheol surrounded me, / the traps of Death confronted me," xlii 7, and ambivalently in cxvi 3, "The bands/cords of Death encompassed me." Cf. Tromp, *Primitive Conceptions,* pp. 164, 174. See below on Pss cxli 10, cxlii 7, and cxliii 3. This motif recurs several times in the Qumran Scrolls; 1QH (Hodayot) 2:21; 3:9.26; CD (Covenant of Damascus) 14:2.

Exile. Another of this poem's numerous hapax legomena, *madḥēpōt* can meaningfully be derived from *dāḥap,* "to drive out, thrust," and explained as a place name morphologically similar to vs. 11, *mahamōrōt,* "the Miry Bog," also a term for Sheol. Its *-ōt* ending may reflect the feminine singular termination of Phoenician. For the thought, cf. Ps xxxv 6, "Let their destiny be Darkness and Destruction, / with the angel of Yahweh pursuing them." In Ps lvi 14 the nether world is called *deḥî,* "Banishment," a term synonymous with *madḥēpōt,* "Exile."

13. *I know.* Note the defective spelling of *yāda'tî* "I know," which recalls the *scriptio defectiva* of Ps xvi 2, *'āmartî,* "I said."

will maintain. Not only during this life but especially in the afterlife, as may be deduced from the next verse.

14. *the just.* As in Pss lxix 29 and cxlii 8, *ṣaddîqîm* designates the just in heaven. Thus the contrast between "the just" here and vs. 12 "Exile" is substantially identical with that in Ps cxlii 8, where the psalmist opposes "the just" and "the Prison," an epithet of Sheol.

the just . . . the upright. For Ugaritic and Phoenician texts balancing the roots of *ṣaddîqîm,* "the just," and *yešārîm,* "the upright," see NOTE on Ps ix 9.

shall give praise. The poet contrasts the just in heaven with the wicked in Exile or Sheol, where there is no praise of Yahweh; cf. especially Ps cxlii 8.

shall dwell. Cf. Pss xxiii 6, "And I shall dwell in the house of Yahweh / for days without end," and lxi 8, "Let him sit enthroned before God forever," texts which describe eternal union with God in the afterlife.

before your face. Consult the discussion of *'et pānekā* in Ps xvi 11, which also depicts the beatific vision.

PSALM 141

(cxli 1–10)

1 *A psalm of David.*

Yahweh, I call you,
hasten to me!
Give ear to my voice,
as I call to you!
2 May my prayer be ever set
as incense before you,
The uplifting of my palms
as an evening sacrifice.
3 Put, O Yahweh, a muzzle on my mouth,
guard, O Most High, the door of my lips.
4 Incline not my heart to an evil word,
to perform wanton deeds with the wicked.
With men who are evildoers—
never will I dine on their delicacies.
5 May the Just One strike me,
the Kind One chastise me:
With fine oil never let my head glisten,
nay, my constant prayer will be against their evil customs!
6 Let their judges drop into the clutches of the Crag,
and let them hear how dulcet are his words!
7 Like one rent and riven in the nether world,
my bones are strewn at the mouth of Sheol.
8 But on you, Yahweh,
are my eyes, O Lord;
In you I seek refuge, El,
protect my life!
9 Keep me from the clutches of the snare they spread for me,
and from the bows of evildoers.
10 May they fall into his nets
the wicked—one and all,
While I myself escape.

NOTES

cxli. The lament of an Israelite living in the North Israelite dispersion after the fall of Samaria in 721 B.C. Brought to trial for having refused to participate in pagan rites (vs. 4b) and banquets (vss. 4d and 5c), the psalmist, in the first stanza (vss. 2–5) prays God to guard his lips lest he abjure his Yahwist faith and to punish him severely should he partake of heathen banquets. The second stanza (vss. 6–10) opens and closes with imprecations against his judges (vss. 6 and 10); in the middle verses (7–9) the psalmist likens his desperate situation to that of one who has been dismembered, whose bones have been scattered at the entrance to Sheol from where, however, he still manages to fix his gaze on Yahweh and to await deliverance.

From vs. 2 earlier commentators have correctly inferred that the psalmist lived some distance from Jerusalem. Advances in our knowledge of the Phoenician language makes it possible to specify the Phoenician territory as the probable place of this poem's composition. The NOTES detail the linguistic evidence, but here may be singled out the three hapax legomena *dāl*, "door" (=Phoen. *dl*), *'īšīm pō'alē 'āwen*, "men who are evildoers" (=Phoen. *'šm r'm*, "evil men"), *man'ammēhem*, "their delicacies" (=Phoen. *mn'm*).

Though R. Tournay, "Le Psaume CXLI," in VT 9 (1959), 58–64, argues for a third-century B.C. date on the basis of the Phoenician parallels (p. 63), the fact that the most striking Phoenician correspondences appear only in the eighth-century Karatepe Inscriptions urges a pre-Exilic date of composition.

1. *I call you . . . as I call to you!* This verse is marked by chiasmus as well as by the inclusion created by *qerā'tīkā*, "I call you," and *beqor'ī lāk*, "as I call to you!"

hasten to me! Give ear to my voice. Assonance characterizes the prayers *ḥūšāh lī ha'azīnāh qōlī*.

2. *be ever set . . . before you.* The psalmist evidently lived far from Jerusalem; hence he asks God to consider his prayer as if he spoke it while assisting at the daily sacrifice in the temple of Jerusalem. Compare Mal i 11.

incense . . . uplifting . . . sacrifice. It is interesting that all three words have their correspondences in Phoen. *qṭrt*, "incense," *mš't*, "payment," and *mnḥt*, "sacrifice."

the uplifting of my palms. The outward symbol of an uplifted heart, this gesture of prayer carries on a Canaanite custom known to us from the description of a sacrifice and its accompanying gestures in UT, Krt: 75–78, *ša ydk šmm dbḥ lṯr abk il šrd b'l bdbḥk*, "Lift up your hands toward heaven. Sacrifice to Bull, your father El; with your sacrifice make Baal come down." By his prayer alone the psalmist hopes to achieve the effect normally produced by the burning of incense and the sacrifice of animals.

3. *Put . . . guard.* The psalmist begs Yahweh to muzzle his lips lest under duress he should profess belief in pagan gods.

Yahweh . . . Most High. The composite divine name *yhwh . . . 'al* is discussed at Ps cxxi 5.

a muzzle. For this definition of *šomrāh,* see JBL 80 (1961), 270, and the NOTES on Ps xxxix 2.

muzzle . . . guard. The concurrence of the roots of *šomrāh,* "muzzle," and *niṣṣ^erāh,* "guard!" may bear on the interpretation of the expression *šmr wnṣr* found on Punic talismans, and studied (inconclusively) by Lidzbarski, *Ephemeris für semitische Epigraphik,* I (Giessen, 1902), p. 172.

my mouth . . . my lips. For the Ugaritic parallelism of these two words, cf. the second NOTE on Ps lix 8.

guard. The energic imperative *niṣ^er^ah* balances the energic imperative *šītāh,* "Put," of the first colon; the proposal to read qal passive participle *n^eṣūrāh* (BH^3) must therefore be declined since it would upset the present A+B+C//Á+B́+Ć pattern. The unique form *niṣ^erāh,* with the *dagesh dirimens* (for the vocalization see Bauer and Leander, *Historische Grammatik,* p. 368t), may owe its existence to the need for another syllable to even the syllable count at 8:8. Cf. Prov v 2, "By heeding my reflections and knowledge your lips will be safeguarded [*yinnāṣērū;* MT *yinṣōrū*]." The niphal reading recovers a syllabically balanced 8:8 line in Prov v 2.

Most High. When proposing to read *'elyōn,* "Most High," for MT *'al,* because another beat was needed in the second colon, Briggs displayed sound prosodic instinct. He also saw that the expression *niṣ^erāh 'al* was unexampled, the verb *nāṣar* elsewhere governing a direct object. Gunkel, *Psalmen,* p. 597, was also alert to the difficulty created by this unparalleled expression. But the identification of *'al* as the second component of the composite name *yhwh 'al,* "Yahweh Most High," gives *'al* its own accent so that the line scans as 4+4 with an 8:8 syllable count. Hence the emendation to *'elyōn* is unnecessary.

the door. A hapax legomenon in the Bible, *dāl* (the common form being *delet,* "door," Ugar. *dlt*) occurs in Phoenician and Punic as *dl.* The coincidence is further indication that this lament was composed in Phoenician circles. For the thought, compare Mic vii 5, *pitḥē pīkā,* "the gates of your mouth," and Ecclus xxii 27, "Who will set a guard over my mouth, a skillful seal upon my lips?"

4. *wanton deeds.* The poet doubtless refers to the heathen religious rites in which he was invited to participate. In vs. 5 he terms them "evil customs."

with the wicked. That *b^e* of *b^erešaʿ* is the *beth* of accompaniment follows from its pairing with *'et,* "with," in the next colon.

the wicked. In harness with concrete *'īšīm pōʿalē 'āwēn,* "men who are evildoers," the abstract noun *rešaʿ,* "wickedness," assumes a concrete meaning; see the second NOTE on Ps cix 2. In vs. 10 they reappear in the concrete plural form *rešāʿīm,* "the wicked." There is a similar usage in the Phoenician phrase *śbʿ wtrš,* "grain and wine," but literally "satiety and wine"; cf. Prov iii 10.

men. Found only here, in Isa liii 3, and Prov viii 4, *'īšīm* is the normal plural of *'īš* in Phoenician; here, then, is another clue to the origin of the poem.

men who are evildoers. The phrase *'īšīm pōʿalē 'āwen* is semantically close to Phoenician Karatepe, I:15, *'šm rʿm,* "evil men." Functionally, the first colon stands in the *casus pendens,* a construction noted at Ps cxl 10, 12.

never. Parsing *ū* of *ūbal* as the emphatic *waw;* another instance recurs in vs. 5. In the Phoenician dialect *bl* is the ordinary negative particle; Heb. *lō',* "not," remains to be certainly identified in Phoenician texts.

will I dine on their delicacies. The phrase *'elḥam bemanʿammēhem* is syntactically and lexically Canaanite-Phoenician. The partitive construction *'elḥam be,* witnessed in Phoenicianizing Prov ix 5 and in Judg xiii 16, occurs in UT, 52:6, *lḥm blḥm,* "Dine on the food." We have a new Ugaritic instance of the partitive use of *b* in *Ugaritica,* V, text 1:20–21 (pp. 544–51), where the gross description of the god El in a state of delirium tremens reads, *ylšn bḫrih wṯnth,* "He licks his excrement and his urine." The verb *ylšn,* a denominative verb from *lšn,* "tongue," is here followed by the preposition *b* with a partitive function. The hapax legomenon *manʿammēhem,* "their delicacies," occurs four times as *mnʿm* in the Karatepe Inscriptions. Thus the genuineness of the biblical hapax legomenon, impugned by those who emend it to *maṭʿammēhem,* "their dainties," has been solidly vindicated and the provenance of the entire expression notably elucidated.

The psalmist here denounces the pagan religious banquets whose details are now coming to light in recently published Ugaritic tablets. Cf. Virolleaud in *Ugaritica,* V, pp. 544–51.

5. *the Just One.* An appellative of Yahweh discussed at Ps cxii 4; Hanson, PMS, III, p. 94, also makes this identification. Cf. further Baethgen, *Die Psalmen,* p. 416. The chiastic order of the first two cola can scarcely be reproduced in translation.

strike me. In vigorous, staccato language the psalmist calls upon the Just One to strike him (dead?) if he fails to keep his oath. Unwitnessed in other Semitic languages except Ethiopic, the verb *hlm,* "to strike," appears seven times in Ugaritic, and its subject is always a god or his emissary, so that its predication here of Yahweh conforms to Canaanite usage.

the Kind One. Repointing MT *ḥesed,* "kindness," to *ḥāsīd.* This repointing involves no consonantal changes because in Phoenician defective spelling both nouns would be written *ḥsd;* cf. Ps cxlv 17 where both *ṣaddīq*, "just," and *ḥāsīd*, "kind," are predicated of Yahweh, and Jer iii 12, where God calls himself *ḥāsīd*, "the Kind One." It should be noted, though, that MT abstract *ḥesed*, "kindness," can be retained and acquire the concrete meaning "the Kind One," by reason of its matching concrete *ṣaddīq*, "the Just One."

chastise me. The poet asks the Kind One to punish him cruelly should he ever falter. The initial *waw* of *wᵉyōkīḥēnī* might be explained either as the emphasizing *waw*, as in vs. 4, or it might be attached to the preceding word; thus *ḥāsīdū*, "the Kind One," with the nominative ending, would be comparable to Ps cxl 9, *yārūmū*, "O Exalted!"

With fine oil. Parsing *šemen rō'š* as an accusative of material preceding its verse; cf. THE GRAMMAR OF THE PSALTER, especially examples from Ps civ 15.

fine oil. With which the head was anointed for banquets; cf. Ps xxiii 5; Amos vi 6; Eccles ix 8; Luke vii 46. 11QPsᵃ *šmn rw'š* shows that the emendation to *šemen rāšā'*, "the oil of the wicked," based on the LXX and Syr., need no longer enlist our attention. Rather we must compare *šemen rō'š*, literally "the oil of essence" (cf. Ps cxix 160, *rō'š*, "essence"), with Exod xxx 23, *bᵉśāmīm rō'š*, "fine spices"; Amos vi 6, *rē'šīt šᵉmānīm*, "the finest oils," and Phoen. *r'št nḥšt*, "choice copper." The wordplay on the two meanings of *rō'š*, namely "essence" and "head," is characteristic of Hebrew laments.

never let my head glisten. Unintelligible MT *'al yānī rō'šī* yields good sense when read *'al yānīr rō'šī*, an instance of shared consonants. Thus consonantal *ynyr'šy* may be read *yānīr rō'šī;* consult the second NOTE on Ps cxxxix 14. The verb *yānīr* would be the qal imperfect of *nyr*, "to shine," present in the nouns *nēr* and *nīr*, "lamp." Though this root has heretofore not been attested in Hebrew verbs, its use as a verb in UT, 1015:9–10, *pn špš nr by mid*, "The face of the Sun [=king] shone much upon me," warrants its identification as a verb in Hebrew.

nay. Parsing *kī* as the emphatic particle instead of as the causal conjunction "because."

my constant prayer. Though somewhat sticky, the phrase *'ōd ūtᵉpillātī* produces sense when taken as hendiadys, literally "always and my prayer." Though generally considered corrupt, this colon's integrity is vouched for by 11QPsᵃ and by the stylistic observation that "my constant prayer" forms an inclusion with vs. 2, *tikkōn tᵉpillātī*, "Let my prayer be ever set." The second stanza, too, is marked by inclusion (vs. 6, *nišmᵉṭū*, "Let . . . drop," and vs. 10, *yippᵉlū*, "May they fall").

against. For this nuance of *bᵉ*, see the second NOTE on Ps cxxiv 3.

6. *Let . . . drop.* 10. *May they fall.* Precative perfect *nišmᵉṭū* "Let . . . drop," begins an inclusion that closes with the jussive verb in vs 10, *yippᵉlū*, "May they fall." To be sure, most commentators consider vs. 6 corrupt (so most recently Bardtke, *Liber Psalmorum*, in BHS), but the

current 11:11 syllable count bespeaks a sound, albeit difficult text in which sense can be found.

their judges. Or "their rulers." In Phoenician texts *špṭ* designates an official whose precise functions are hard to establish, but in the Punic texts from Carthage in North Africa *špṭ* denotes the highest magistrate, the *suffete,* whose office was comparable to that of a Roman consul.

Like the lamenting psalmist in Ps cix 6, our psalmist invokes upon the heathen judges condign punishment for their unjust decision.

drop into the clutches of the Crag. Compare Heb x 30–31, "'The Lord will judge his people.' It is a terrible thing to fall into the hands of the living God." While he prays that his enemies fall "into the clutches of the Crag" (*bīdē sela'*), the psalmist pleads in vs. 9 to be protected "from the clutches of the snare" (*mīdē paḥ*).

the Crag. Or "the Rock." As a designation of Yahweh, *sela'* recurs in Pss xviii 3, xxxi 4, xlii 10, lxxi 3.

let them hear. Parallel to precative *nišmᵉṭū,* "Let drop," *šāmᵉ'ū,* "let them hear," also parses as precative perfect.

dulcet are. The psalmist is ironic. The second occurrence in this psalm (cf. vs. 4) of the root *n'm* in the verb *nā'ēmū,* "dulcet are," is significant in determining the cultural background of this psalm for, as Gordon, UT, Glossary, No. 1665, observes, "Only in Ugaritic and Phoenician is *n'm* the normal word for 'good.'"

his words! Repointing MT *'ᵃmāray,* "my words," to *'ᵃmārēy,* with the Phoenician third-person suffix *-y,* and identifying these words with the sentence Yahweh will pass on the judges imprecated by the psalmist.

7. *Like one rent and riven.* MT *kᵉmō pōlēᵃḥ ūbōqēᵃ',* "Like one rending and riving," can be coaxed into meaning when repointed *kᵉmō pūlaḥ ūbūqa'* and parsed as a relative clause without the relative pronoun formally expressed, as in vs. 9; see the last NOTE on Ps lxxxv 9 and the second NOTE on Ps cxix 96. Vocalized as qal passives, *pūlaḥ,* "rent," and *būqa',* "riven," make fine parallels to second-colon niphal *nipzᵉrū,* "are strewn."

riven . . . strewn. These two concepts are collocated in UT, 49:II:31–35.

the nether world. Since its counterpart is evidently *pī šᵉ'ōl,* "the mouth of Sheol," *'āreṣ* refers, as in many other passages, to the underworld. The psalmist's condition is so desperate that it must be painted (hyperbolically, of course) in terms of one who has been drawn and quartered in hell. Cf. Ps xxii 16–18 (in revised translation), "And they put me upon the mud of Death. / For jackals have surrounded me, / a pack of evildoers encircles me. / Because they have picked clean my hands and my feet, / I can number all my bones."

my bones. Though 11QPsᵃ reads *'ṣmy,* "my bones," there may be no need, in view of the first NOTE on Ps cxxii 2, to emend consonantal *'ṣmynw.*

my bones are strewn at the mouth of Sheol. A closely related description appears in Jer xv 7, *wā'ezrēm bᵉmizreh bᵉša'ᵃrē hā'āreṣ* "And I winnowed them with a pitchfork at the gates of the nether city." Consult Tromp, *Primitive Conceptions*, p. 30.

at the mouth of Sheol. Compare Ps xxii 16–18, cited three NOTES above; Ps ix 14, "Raise me up from the gates of Death," and Ps xlii 7. Similar imagery recurs in Eccles vi 7 (*Biblica* 49 [1968], 368) and Job xv 30 as translated at Ps cxl 11.

8. *on you, Yahweh, are my eyes.* The same expression recurs in Ps cxxiii 2. Though dismembered and his bones scattered at the entrance to Sheol, the psalmist keeps his gaze fixed on Yahweh. Cf. Ps lxix 3–4, "I have sunk into the abysmal mire / where there is no footing. . . . My eyes grow bleary / as I wait, O my God!"

Verse 8 is here scanned as a quadricolon with a 3+2//3+2 beat and a 6:5::6:4 syllable count.

El. Repointing MT *'al,* "not," to the divine name *'ēl,* which balances first-colon Yahweh. From this revocalization emerges the composite divine name Yahweh El that in Ps cxliii recurs three times.

protect. MT *t*^{e}*'ar,* usually derived from *'ārāh,* "be naked, bare," yields better sense (the following verb is *šomrēnī,* "Keep me") when vocalized *tā'īr* and derived from *'yr,* Ugar. *ġyr,* "to protect" (second NOTE on Ps ix 7). The sound of repointed *tā'īr evokes* vs. 5, *yānīr,* "(never) glisten." For a recent discussion of this verb and the discovery of a new attestation in Mal ii 12, see Benedikt Hartmann, "Mögen die Götter dich behüten und unversehrt bewahren," in HWFB, pp. 102–5.

9. *from the clutches of the snare.* The phrase *mīdē paḥ* may be and Ecclus li 3, where *yd,* "clutch," parallels *mwqš,* "lure."
compared with Prov vi 5, *miyyad yāqūš,* "from the fowler's clutch,"

the snare they spread. In the phrase *paḥ yāq*^{e}*šū* the poet omits the relative pronoun as in vs. 7. Ugar. *yqš,* "fowler," reveals that the third radical of this root is *-š,* so that attempts to combine Heb. *yqš* with Ar. *wqṣ,* "to break, devour the prey," (cf. GB, p. 315a) should be abandoned.

and from the bows. MT *ūmōq*^{e}*šōt,* "and the lures," labors under two difficulties. The first is the lack of the preposition *min,* "from" (BH^{3} recommends, with the LXX, *ūmimmōq*^{e}*šōt,* "and from the lures"), but this obstacle is not insurmountable because the phrase can share the preposition of first-colon *mīdē,* "from the clutches of." The second difficulty appears more serious; elsewhere the plural of *mōqēš,* "lure," is always masculine *mōq*^{e}*šīm,* as, for instance, in Ps cxl 6. Both these difficulties can be overcome by repointing to *ūmiqq*^{e}*šōt,* "and from the bows"; this plural form of *qešet,* "bow," thus coincides with Ugaritic plural *qšt,* "bows," as pointed out at Ps xxxvii 14 and in UHP, p. 15.

In the ancient Near East birds were hunted with nets and with bows. Thus an Egyptian relief from the tomb of Ka-gemmi at Sakkarah represents fowling by means of a cagelike net spread in the marches and filled with birds. Hidden from the birds by a blind stands the fowler, who holds a rope in one hand and with the other signals his three companions to close the trap by pulling the rope. A relief from the palace of Sargon II at Khorsabad shows Assyrian hunters in a wood shooting birds and other game. It depicts a beardless hunter drawing a bow, obviously aimed at one of the birds represented near the tops of the trees. Consult Pritchard, *The Ancient Near East in Pictures,* figs. 185 and 189.

10. *May they fall.* Jussive *yippᵉlū* forms an inclusion with vs. 6 precative perfect *nišmᵉṭū,* "Let them drop." Customarily read as a 4+3 bicolon (so Gunkel), this verse is preferably scanned as a 2+2+2 tricolon, with a 7:5:7 syllable count.

his nets. The antecedent of the unexplained suffix of *makmōrāyw* being vs. 6, *sela',* "the Crag," an epithet of Yahweh. This imprecation of exact retribution conforms to similar curses in Pss vii 16, 17, ix 16, 17 and cxl 10, 12.

the wicked. Concrete plural *rᵉšā'īm* harks back to the abstract noun *reša'* in vs. 4 which, because it parallels concrete "evildoers," is endowed with the concrete signification "the wicked."

the wicked—one and all. Reading *rᵉšā'īm yāḥad* (pausal, MT *yaḥad*) as a separate 2-beat colon; hence the MT *athnach* under *rᵉšā'īm,* "the wicked," should be deleted. Though some versions read MT *yaḥad,* "one and all," as *yāḥīd,* "alone," 11QPsᵃ *yḥd* (=*yaḥad,* not *yāḥīd*) upholds MT.

PSALM 142

(cxlii 1–8)

1 *A maskil of David. A prayer when he was in the cave.*

2 With my voice I cry to Yahweh,
with my voice I beg Yahweh for mercy.
3 I pour out before him my plaint,
my agony before him I describe:
4 "As my spirit ebbs from me,
yes, you know my path.
Along the road which I must walk
they have hidden snares for me.
5 Look to the right and see,
not one is there who recognizes me;
Flight has fled from me,
no one cares for me.
6 I cry to you, Yahweh,
I say, you are my refuge,
my portion in the land of life eternal!
7 Heed, O El, my cry,
for I am brought low, O Grand One!
Rescue me from my hunters,
since they are mightier than I.
8 Lead my life out from the Prison
that I might praise your name.
Round me let the just form a circle,
for you are my benefactor, Most High."

Notes

cxlii. The lament of an Israelite on his deathbed. Attempts to group the disparate details of this psalm into a unified composition have always fallen short, but a reasonable coherence emerges with the identification of the poem as the prayer of one dying who, totally abandoned by his fellow men, implores Yahweh to be his refuge at death, and to lead him after death from the dungeon of Sheol into the land of life eternal. This reconstruction follows from the identification of the psalmist's foes as Death and his emissaries, and of *masgēr*, "Prison," in vs. 8 as a name of the underworld. Cf. Tromp, *Primitive Conceptions*, p. 156.

This lament consists of an introduction (vss. 2–3), followed by the text of the psalmist's prayer (vss. 4–8), which is placed in quotation marks. The interpretation of individual words and phrases is considerably facilitated by comparison with other prayers which seem to have originated in similar circumstances, namely, Pss xiii, cxvi, and Jon ii.

Precise dating of the poem, on the basis of language and contents, is beyond the reach of current psalms scholarship, though the recovery of divine names and epithets in vss. 5, 7, 8 works with other considerations (such as the ascription of the psalm to David) to favor a pre-Exilic date of composition.

1. *maskil.* Occurring only here in the fifth book of the Psalter, this descriptive psalm title, discussed at Ps xxxii 1, is further elucidated by the observations on Ps ci 2, *'aśkīlāh*, "I will rhapsodize."

2. *With my voice.* Or "Aloud"; see the first NOTE on Ps lxxvii 2.

I cry to Yahweh. The recurrence in vs. 6 of the construction *zā'aq 'el* discountenances the translation of our verse proposed in the last NOTE on Ps lxxvii 2.

Yahweh . . . Yahweh. The repetition of the Tetragrammaton in each colon is matched by the repetition of *l^epānāyw*, "before him," in each colon of vs. 3.

3. *I pour out . . . I describe.* Preserving the chiastic A+B+C//Ć+B+Á pattern of the Hebrew.

I pour out . . . my plaint. This phrase interestingly recurs in the heading of Ps cii 1, which introduces the description of the psalmist's death agony.

before him . . . before him. The repetition of the same prepositional phrase *l^epānāyw*, "before him," which some critics find oppressive and accordingly scratch the second, follows Canaanite usage in UT, 49:II: 16–17, *lkbd arṣ . . . lkbd šdm*, "to the heart of the earth . . . to the heart of the fields."

my agony. As noted at Pss xci 15 and cii 3, *ṣārātī* refers to the agony of death; the psalmist is on his deathbed.

4. *ebbs from me.* The expression *hit'aṭṭēp 'ālay*, found here, in Ps cxliii 4, and in Jon ii 8, appears to be the semantic equivalent of Ps cvii 5, (*napšām*) *bāhem tit'aṭṭēp*, "[Their life] ebbed from them." In other words, both *'ālay* and *b^e* denote "from," an inference sustained by LXX's rendition of Jon ii 8, *en tō ekleípein ap'emoū tēn psychēn mou*, "when my soul was departing from me." On *'al*, "from," consult third NOTE on Ps iv 7 and second NOTE on Ps lxxxi 6.

yes, you. Interpreting *w*^{e} of *w*^{e}*'attāh* as the emphatic *waw.* Yahweh knows full well the path of death which the psalmist must walk. In Ps cxliii 8 the poet entreats God to show him the road he must travel after handing over his soul to God.

they have hidden. The subject of *ṭām*^{e}*nū* being Death and his henchmen, who set traps for the living; cf., e.g., Pss xviii 6, cxvi 3; Prov xiii 14.

5. *not one.* Assigning to *w*^{e} of *w*^{e}*'ēn* an emphasizing rather than a merely conjunctive function.

who recognizes me . . . cares for me. The chiastic order of *lī makkīr* and *dōrēš l*^{e}*napšī* and the semantic equivalence of *lī,* "me," and *l*^{e}*napšī,* "for me," might be noted.

Flight has fled. Escape from oncoming death is impossible. In the phrase *'ābad mānōs* (also in Job xi 20), which is generally rendered by paraphrase rather than by translation, lies a play on words (not unusual in laments) which comes to light when *'ābad* is identified with Akk. *abātu,* "to flee," rather than with Akk. *abātu,* "to destroy." Cf. CAD, I, pp. 45–47. This sense of *'ābad* recurs in Ezek xxi 22 (cf. Job xx 8); Job xxx 2; Prov xxi 28, while *mānōs,* "flight," derives from *nūs,* "to flee, escape." Cf. Ps xl 13, "My iniquities have overtaken me, / and I am unable to escape."

6. *I cry to you.* Abandoned by men, the psalmist turns to his only refuge.

Yahweh . . . my refuge. Placing *yhwh* in the first colon and *maḥsī,* "my refuge," in the second, the psalmist employs the poetic device known as the breakup of composite phrases; cf. Pss xiv 6, xci 9, where the two elements are juxtaposed.

the land of life eternal. As in Pss xxvii 13, cxvi 9, *'ereṣ haḥayyīm* is taken to designate Paradise. The psalmist thus opposes "the land of life eternal" to vs. 8, *masgēr,* "the Prison," his term for the realm of death.

7. *O El.* Comparison with Ps xvii 1, *haqšībāh rinnātī,* "heed my cry" (revised translation), suggests that MT *haqšībāh 'el rinnātī* becomes more freighted with meaning when the otiose preposition *'el,* "to," is repointed to *'ēl,* "El," the first element of the composite divine name *'ēl mā'ēd,* "El the Grand One."

I am brought low. As in Ps cxvi 6, *dallōtī* connotes to be brought down to the gates of Sheol. Since, however, *dallōtī* stems from a root meaning "to be weak," it might also resume the thought of vs. 4, "my spirit ebbs from me," and be rendered "I am weak," which would contrast with the might of the psalmist's enemies stressed in vs. 7d.

O Grand One! By repointing MT *m*^{e}*'ōd,* "much," to adjectival *mā'ēd,* we recover the second example of the breakup of a composite term (see vs. 6) *'ēl mā'ēd,* which compares with *yhwh mā'ēd,* "Yahweh the Grand," documented at Ps cix 30. This identification requires a revised translation and stylistic analysis of Ps xlvi 2, *'*^{e}*lōhīm lānū maḥseh wā'ōz 'ezrāh b*^{e}*ṣārōt nimṣā' mā'ēd* (MT *m*^{e}*'ōd*), "God for us is refuge and stronghold, / the liberator from sieges have we found the Grand One." This repointing of *mā'ēd* discloses a clear chiastic pattern, which may be represented as A+B+C//Ć+B́+Á, as well as the composite divine name. Cf. Prov iii 10, viii 21 (ETL 44 [1968], 38), xiii 6. In Ps cxlv 3 we encounter the composite divine name *yhwh mā'ēd,* "Yahweh the Grand," distributed over succeeding cola.

One can detect in the next line a motive for the psalmist's choice of this divine epithet: the pursuers are mightier than the psalmist, who accordingly appeals to El's massive might.

my hunters. Though *rōdᵉpāy* is commonly rendered "my pursuers," the consistency of metaphor (vs. 4, "they have hidden snares for me") suggests the more precise nuance borne by *rādap* in Ps vii 6; Exod xv 20; I Sam xxvi 20. As in vs. 4d, those hunting down the psalmist are Death and his minions; cf. Pss cxl 12, cxliii 3.

they are mightier. The strength of Death is perhaps best known from the simile in Song of Sol viii 6, "For strong as Death is love, / enduring as Sheol is passion." Cf. also UT 49:VI:17; 54:11–13 and Ps xiii 5, "Lest my Foe [=Death] should boast, 'I overcame him.'"

The identification of Death and his troops as the subject of *'āmᵉṣū,* "they are mightier," sustains the exegesis of Ps xviii 18, "He rescued me from my powerful Foe, / and from my Enemy though stronger than I," where "Foe" and "Enemy" were identified as epithets of Death.

8. *Lead . . . out.* Though the psalmist knows that he must die and enter the nether world, he entreats Yahweh to lead him from this dungeon to "the land of life eternal" (vs. 6).

the Prison. The dispute whether *masgēr* denotes an earthly prison literally or only metaphorically overlooks the import of the following colon, "that I might praise your name." In an earthly prison one could still praise the name of Yahweh. Since a common motif makes Sheol the place where there is no praise of Yahweh, the exegete must conclude that by "the Prison" the poet intends the nether world. The NOTES on Ps lxxxviii 9 document the motif of Sheol the prison. Cf. also the prayer of the Latin Church recited on 20 December as part of the Advent Liturgy: *"O clavis David, et sceptrum domus Israel, qui aperis, et nemo claudit, claudis et nemo aperit: veni, et educ vinctum de domo carceris, sedentem in tenebris et umbra mortis"* ("O Key of David, and Scepter of the house of Israel, you who open and no one closes, who close and no one opens: come, and lead forth the one bound from the prison house, the one sitting in darkness and the shadow of death"). On the Phoenician verb *ysgrnm,* "[lest] they imprison them (namely, in the dungeon of the nether world)," see the first NOTE on Ps lxxix 10; this same nuance recurs in Job xii 14.

that I might praise your name. Namely in Paradise; this seems to follow from the use in the next colon of the term *ṣaddīqīm,* "the just," which designates the blessed in heaven. Cf. Ps cxl 14.

Round me. May the blessed in Paradise gather around the poet to share in his thanksgiving for deliverance from Sheol and admittance to heaven.

let . . . form a circle. MT hiphil indicative *yaktīrū* should perhaps be read as hiphil jussive *yaktērū;* this would afford a better sequel to imperative *hōṣī'āh,* "Bring forth." 11QPs[a] likewise seemed to doubt the desirability of the indicative mode, since it reads *ykt rw,* with the erasure of the *-y-* after *t-*.

the just. Interpreting *ṣaddīqīm* as the righteous in heaven, precisely as in Pss lxix 29 and cxl 14. Critics tax the poet with inconsistency for describing himself in vs. 4 as absolutely isolated and here assuming the presence of just people whom he invites to share his happiness. The psalmist escapes this charge of exaggerating his abandonment when it is recognized that "the just" are not dwellers of this earth.

Most High. Repointing MT *'ālāy* to *'ēlī,* and consulting the two NOTES on Ps xiii 6, which contains the same phrase in a similar context dealing with death and life.

PSALM 143

(cxliii 1–12)

1 *A psalm of David.*

Yahweh, hear my prayer,
give ear, O El, to my plea for mercy.
In your fidelity
answer me
In your justice.
2 But do not bring your servant into court,
since no one alive can be justified before you.
3 For the Foe hunted my soul,
ground my life into the nether world;
He made me dwell in the dark regions,
like the men of the eternal home.
4 My spirit ebbed from me,
within me my heart was desolate.
5 I remembered the days primeval,
numbered your deeds completely,
on the works of your hands I meditated.
6 I stretch out my hands toward you;
in the nether world my throat is parched with thirst for you. *Selah*

7 Hasten to answer me, Yahweh!
my spirit fails, O El!
Should you turn your face from me,
I would resemble those who have descended the Pit.
8 Cause me to hear your kindness at the dawn,
because in you have I trusted.
Show me the road which I must travel,
because to you have I raised my mind.
9 Rescue me from my foes, Yahweh,
my God, truly am I being submerged.

10 Teach me to do your will,
because you are my God.
With your good spirit
lead me
Into the level land.
11 For the sake of your Name, Yahweh, grant me life,
in your justice deliver my life from my adversaries.
12 In your kindness annihilate my foes,
and destroy all who harass me,
For I am your servant.

NOTES

cxliii. The last of the Penitential Psalms, this psalm, like Ps xl, is composite; it consists of two distinct laments of equal length. Closely related in language and thought, the two laments apparently come from the same hand. In the first (vss. 1–6), whose limits are indicated by an inclusion and by the musical notation *Selah,* the poet places himself in the nether world, from which he pleads for mercy. In the second lament (vss. 7–12), the poet is on the verge of death, and asks God to rescue him from Death's grasp and to lead him into celestial happiness.

No clear evidence permits the identification of the psalmist, but some half dozen verbal clues point to his royal character. Thus the double reference to himself as *'abdekā,* "your servant" (vss. 2, 12), the stress on God's "fidelity" (vs. 1) and "kindness" (vss. 8, 12), the appeal to the divine Name (vs. 11), and the balance in vss. 11–12 between abstract *ṣārāh,* "my adversaries," and *'ōyebāy,* "my foes," a pair recurring only in royal Pss liv 9 and cxxxviii 7, have their closest counterparts in royal psalms such as xx, liv, lxxxvi, lxxxix, cxxxviii. The ascription to David and its juxtaposition to royal Ps cxliv sustain the linguistic arguments. On this hypothesis, the two laments date to the pre-Exilic period.

Noteworthy is the triple identification of the composite divine name *yhwh 'ēl,* "Yahweh El," in vss. 1, 7, 9, but always separated over the parallel cola.

1. *Yahweh . . . El.* As in Ps cxli 8, the composite divine name *yhwh 'ēl* is distributed over the parallel cola. The two further recurrences in vss. 7 and 9 make this psalm the best witness to this composite name.

Yahweh . . . 6. for you. Yahweh and vs. 6, *lekā,* "for you," form an inclusion.

give ear, O El. Comparison with Ps lxxxvi 6, *ha'azīnāh yhwh tepillātī,* "Give ear to my prayer, Yahweh," and similar constructions in Pss v 2, xvii 1, xxxix 13, lv 2, lxxviii 1, strongly suggests that MT *'el,* "to," should be repointed *'ēl,* "O El," so that *ha'azīnāh,* "give ear," governs a direct object, as in the six texts cited from the Psalter. Cf. Ecclus li 11. This new vocalization recovers the composite divine name examined in the first NOTE on this verse.

In your fidelity. The feeling that this verse is overloaded has led scholars to propose the deletion of either *be'emūnātekā*, "In your fidelity," or of its opposite number "In your justice," but a solution can be found by taking imperative *'anēnī*, "answer me," as a double-duty imperative set between the two prepositional phrases in a 6:3:5 syllabic sequence. The same solution promises to improve both sense and scansion in Ps lxix 14, *berob ḥasdekā/'anēnī/be'emet yiš'ekā,* "In your great kindness/answer me/with your faithful help." Here the syllable count is 5:3:6; cf. N. Airoldi, *Rivista Biblica Italiana* 16 (1968), 461, n. 16.

2. *bring.* 11QPs[a] *tbw'* and the well-documented (fifth NOTE on Ps xliii 3) meaning "bring" of the qal form undermine the proposal to repoint qal *tābō'* to causative *tābī'*.

court. This meaning of *mišpāṭ* is found in the texts listed in the second NOTE on Ps i 5. The psalmist pleads not to be put on trial and sentenced according to his deserts, since no man can be found just before God.

3. *the Foe.* As in Pss xiii 5, xxxi 9, etc., *'ōyēb* designates Death. Cf. Tromp, *Primitive Conceptions,* pp. 110–18.

hunted. For this nuance of *rādap,* "to pursue," see the fourth NOTE on Ps cxlii 7, and for the motif of Death the Hunter, the fourth NOTE on Ps cxl 12. The similarity between this verse and Ps vii 6 has often been noted, and shows that the "foe" mentioned there is likewise Death. This amounts to saying that the author of Ps vii invokes death upon himself if he has ever been disloyal to friends.

ground. Consult the discussion of *dakkā'*, "Slime," at Ps xc 3.

nether world . . . dark regions. The pair *'āreṣ,* "nether world," and *maḥašakkīm,* "dark regions," balance ideas that are united in the construct chain of Job x 21, *'ereṣ ḥōšek,* "the land of darkness," a description of the underworld.

He made me dwell. Where our poet uses the verb *hōšībānī,* "He made me dwell," the author of Ps vii used *yaškēn,* "Let him cause [my liver] to dwell" (vs. 6), in a very similar context. The last two cola of this verse recur in Lam iii 6, which may be indebted to the psalm that is pre-Exilic in origin.

the men of the eternal home. MT *mētē 'ōlām,* "the dead of eternity," becomes more meaningful when *mētē* is repointed *metē,* "the men of," and *'ōlām* explained as the elliptical equivalent (the clear parallelism obviates ambiguity) of *bēt 'ōlām,* "the house of eternity," a term for the nether world in Eccles xii 5 and in Phoenician. In fact, no ellipsis may be involved here because *'lm* alone means "eternal home" or "sarcophagus" in the tenth-century Phoenician Inscription of Aḥiram, line 1, *kšth b'lm,* "when he put him in the eternal home"; cf. KAI, II, p. 2. Thus *metē 'ōlām,* "the men of the eternal home," may be compared with

Ps ii 12, *nᵉšē qeber,* "mortal men," and Isa xiv 19 *'abnē bōr,* "sons of the Pit" (as in Job v 23 and in Phoenician, *'abnē* is *bᵉnē,* "sons of," with prothetic *aleph*), and Isa v 13, *mᵉtē rā'āb,* "men of the Hungry One" (NOTE on Ps xxxiii 19).

4. *ebbed from me.* The poet had become like "the strengthless dead"; cf. the NOTES on Ps lxxxviii 5. For the construction *tit'aṭṭēp 'ālay,* cf. Ps cxlii 4.

5. *I remembered . . . numbered . . . I meditated.* A similar *qtl-qtl-yqtl* verbal sequence can be seen in Pss lxxvii 17–18 and xciii 3, both of which are modeled on mythological texts. Compare the fourth NOTE on Ps cxlvi 4.

the days primeval. When Yahweh vanquished the forces of chaos and death; cf. Isa li 9–10 and Hab i 12, *hᵃlō' 'attāh miqqedem yhwh 'ᵉlōhē qodšī lē'ōn māwet* (MT *lō' nāmūt,* "We shall not die"), "Surely you, Yahweh, are from primeval times, / my holy God, the Victor over Death!"

numbered . . . completely. Cf. the first two NOTES on Ps lxxvii 13.

numbered . . . I meditated. Preserving the chiastic order of the original.

6. *I stretch out.* In a gesture of prayer the psalmist reaches out from the Stygian gloom toward heaven. In similar conditions the author of Ps cxli 7–8 raised his eyes toward God.

I stretch out . . . for you. In this final line of the first lament the psalmist establishes a double inclusion: with *pēraśtī yāday,* "I stretch out my hands," a gesture of prayer, he resumes the thought of vs. 1, "my prayer," while *lᵉkā,* "for you," harks back to vs. 1, "Yahweh."

in the nether world. With 11QPs[a] and many manuscripts we read *b'rṣ* for MT *kᵉ'ereṣ,* "like the nether world." Here the psalmist elicits the motif (documented at Ps lxviii 7) that depicts the realm of the dead as the land of perpetual thirst, and at the same time ties up the closing line with vs. 3, *lā'āreṣ,* "into the nether world."

my throat. Parallel to *yāday,* "my hands," *napšī* preserves here its original force. For the imagery, cf. Ps xxxiv 9, "Taste and drink deeply, / for Yahweh is sweet."

is parched with thirst. The MT adjective *'ᵃyēpāh,* "parched," modifies *'ereṣ,* "land," but what is needed in this colon is a verb to keep the verse alive. Alert to the problem, RSV renders, "My soul thirsts for thee like a parched land," but the absence of a note precludes our knowing what expedient was employed to recover the verb lacking in MT. Jer iv 31, *'āyᵉpāh napšī,* "My throat is parched," suggests that the verb *'āyᵉpāh* be read also here instead of the adjective. The description in Ps lxix 4 of the psalmist's conditions in Sheol may serve as commentary to our verse: "I am wearied by my crying, / my throat is parched."

Selah. This musical notation marks the end of the first lament.

7. *Yahweh . . . El.* Like the first lament, the second begins with the composite divine name in the vocative case and separated in the parallel cola.

O El! Repointing MT *'al,* "not," which creates a grammatically non-viable verse, to *'ēl,* and attaching it to the second colon of our verse, where it balances vocative Yahweh of the first colon; cf. *Psalms II,* p. XXI. Once transferred to the second colon, *'ēl* supplies the third word needed to counterpoise the three words of the first colon.

Should you turn. In a gesture indicating refusal of request. As noted at Ps civ 29, *tastēr,* an infixed *-t-* form of *sūr,* "to turn," introduces a conditional sentence without a morphological indicator; cf. Joüon, GHB, § 167a.

I would resemble. In *w^enimšaltī* the *w^e* introduces the apodosis or conclusion of the condition stated in the first colon. On the verge of death, the psalmist is doomed to join those in the Pit unless Yahweh swiftly intervenes.

The phrase *nimšaltī 'im,* "I would resemble," semantically and grammatically relates to Ps lxxxviii 5, *neḥšabtī 'im,* "I am reckoned as." In both phrases *'im* denotes "like," a meaning also witnessed in Ugaritic, as observed in the fourth NOTE on Ps lxi 7.

8. *at the dawn.* As in Pss xxvii 5 and xxx 6, dawn symbolizes resurrection and immortality. The dying poet boldly requests eternal life with God. Instead of the *bōr,* "the Pit" (vs. 7), the psalmist demands the *bōqer,* "the dawn," of resurrection and immortality.

which I must travel. In the journey from this life to the next; see Ps cxlii 4.

raised my mind. To Yahweh alone has the psalmist prayed during his lifetime. Compare Ps xxiv 4, "who has not raised his mind to an idol."

9. *Rescue me.* Since he already feels himself to be in the clutches of Death.

from my foes. Namely, Death and his minions; cf. Ps cxlii 4, 7b.

Yahweh, my God. The reading *yhwh 'ēlī* (see next NOTE) recovers the third instance in Ps cxliii of the composite divine name.

my God, truly am I being submerged. Unexplained MT *'ēlekā kissītī* is here read, with no consonantal changes, *'ēlī,* "my El," or "my God," *kī,* the emphatic particle, and pual passive *kussētī,* "am I being submerged." Other texts predicating *kissāh,* "to cover over, submerge," of the nether waters include Job xxii 11, *'ō ḥōšek lō' tir'eh w^ešip'at mayim t^ekassekkā,* "Or will you not see the Darkness, or the flood of waters not submerge you?" Cf. also Ps cxl 10, which alludes to this theme, Exod xv 5, and Tromp, *Primitive Conceptions,* p. 39, n. 88. By his use of this imagery the psalmist evokes the phrase in vs. 7, *yōr^edē bōr,* "those who have descended the Pit."

10. *With your good spirit.* Like Ps li 14, *rūaḥ n^edībāh,* "by your generous spirit," *rūḥ^akā ṭōbāh* parses as an accusative of means preceding its verb. Contrast RSV, "Let thy good spirit lead me," and KJ, "Thy spirit *is* good; lead me." Grammarians (cf. Joüon, GHB, § 138 f.) take

cognizance of the lack of article with *ṭōbāh*, "good," but can offer no satisfactory explanation. Perhaps the reason is syllabic: the present syllable count is 5:3:5, which would be upset by the addition of an article.

lead me. In vss. 7–10 the poet employs six imperative forms which he partially balances in vss. 10b–12 by the use of four jussive forms and one precative perfect, thus achieving considerable variety in the expression of his prayers.

A technical term connoting "to lead into Paradise," *tanḥēnī*, "lead me," opens his closing prayer for a blessed afterlife. Metrically it stands in the middle of an accusative of means and a prepositional phrase in a 5:3:5 syllabic sequence that resembles the 6:3:5 count in vs. 1.

the level land. As noted at Ps lxvii 5, *'ereṣ mīšōr* describes the celestial abode of the just.

11. *For the sake of your Name*. The reason for introducing this motive becomes clearer with the knowledge that the just in heaven continually praised Yahweh's Name; cf., for example, Pss xxiii 2, cxl 14, and cxlii 8.

in your justice. The psalmist harks back to vs. 1, "answer me / In your justice."

deliver. Jussive *tōṣī'* has essentially the same force as imperative *hōṣī'āh*, "Lead out!" in cognate Ps cxlii 8. The poet repeats in other words the request of vs. 9.

my adversaries . . . 12. *my foes*. Namely, the infernal powers who threaten the psalmist's life. As in Pss liv 9 (where the Ugaritic parallelism between *ib*, "foe," and *ṣrt*, "adversary," is cited), and cxxxviii 7, abstract *ṣārāh*, "adversity," acquires a concrete denotation by reason of its parallelism with concrete *'ōyᵉbāy*, "my foes," and also shares its suffix.

12. *In your kindness annihilate*. Comparing Ps liv 7, "in his fidelity he annihilated them completely."

annihilate my foes. The phrase *taṣmīt 'ōyᵉbāy* closely resembles the phraseology of UT, 68:9, where the god Baal is instructed to vanquish his rivals: *ht ibk tmḫṣ ht tṣmt ṣrtk*, "Now your foes must you smite, now must you annihilate your adversaries."

destroy. Following a series of four jussives, perfect *ha'ᵃbadtā* parses as precative, and forms an inclusion with the imperatives with which the second lament opens.

who harass me. Cf. Ps xliii 2, "harassment by the Foe."

For I am your servant. The psalmist is the servant of the living God of Israel. The expression *'ᵃnī 'abdekā* may be compared with the same phrase in UT, 67:II:11–12, where Baal professes his subjection to Death: *bhṯ lbn ilm mt 'bdk an wd'lmk*, "Hail, O divine Mot [=Death], your servant am I and yours for eternity!"

PSALM 144

(cxliv 1–15)

1 *Of David.*

Blessed be Yahweh my mountain,
who trained my hands for warfare,
my arms for battle.
2 My rampart and my fastness,
my bulwark and my haven,
He is my Suzerain, and in him I trust,
the one who prostrated the peoples at my feet.
3 Yahweh, what is man, that you should care about him?
the son of man, that you should think about him?
4 Man is like the vapor,
his days are like a passing shadow.
5 Yahweh, bow your heavens and descend,
touch the mountains that they smoke!
6 Flash your shafts and scatter them,
forge your arrows and disperse them.
7 Stretch forth your hands from high;
snatch me and rescue me
from the waters deep,
from the hand of foreigners,
8 Whose mouth speaks lies,
and whose right hand is a perjured hand.
9 O God, a new song let me sing to you,
on the ten-stringed lyre let me play to you,
10 Who gave victory to his king,
who rescued David his servant.
From the sword of the Evil One snatch me,
11 and rescue me from the hand of foreigners,
Whose mouth speaks lies,
and whose right hand is a perjured right hand.
12 May he bless our sons like plants,
carefully trained from their youth;

Our daughters like pillars,
carved for the structure of a palace.
13 May our garners be filled,
reaching from end to end.
May our sheep bring forth thousands,
be multiplied by myriads in our open spaces;
14 may our cattle be well fed.
Let there be no invasion,
and let there be no exile,
nor outcry in our squares.
15 How blest the people of whom this is so,
how blest the people whose God is Yahweh!

Notes

cxliv. This poem actually consists of two distinct psalms; in this respect it resembles the preceding psalm. The first psalm (vss. 1–11) is in turn a composite work which cannot be placed in a single category (cf. Ps xxxvi), since it contains elements of three different genres: royal hymn of thanksgiving (vss. 1–2), Wisdom (vss. 3–4), and a prayer for victory over human and infernal foes (vss. 5–8), followed by a vow to give formal thanks (vss. 9–11). The second psalm (vss. 12–15) is a king's prayer for the prosperity of his people, asking the blessing of children (vs. 12), crops (vs. 13a), cattle (vss. 13b–14a), and for concord (vs. 14b–d), followed by a sapiential reflection (vs. 15).

Critics tend to describe Ps cxliv as a mosaic of verses culled from other psalms, especially from Ps xviii, and credit its author with limited originality. The recognition, though, of six parallel pairs of words—three of which are braces of infrequent occurrence—that have counterparts in the Ugaritic tablets, of the hapax legomenon phrase *ḥereb rā'āh,* "the sword of the Evil One" (vs. 10) as a designation of Death, and the appreciation of the remarkable word order in vs. 7 and of the unexampled plays on roots in vss. 6–7, permit one to dissent from the majority view regarding the poet's inventiveness. In our present state of knowledge the more prudent conclusion would be that since our poet and the psalmists with whom he shows a close affinity are all indebted to an older literary tradition, it is difficult to establish that our psalm is literarily dependent upon other canonical psalms. Compare, for example, the syntax of vs. 3 with that of Ps viii 5, which expresses the same sentiment.

A royal psalm that mentions David in vs. 10 and whose closest conceptual and linguistic ties are with tenth-century Ps xviii, this composite work may tentatively be ascribed to the tenth century B.C.

1. *my mountain.* Agreeing with MT, 11QPs^{a} lends no support to the suspicion of critics that some words have fallen out after *ṣūrī,* "my mountain."

who trained. In his comment on UT, 3 Aqht:rev.:29, *almdk,* "I will teach you," in a damaged context dealing with the attempts of the goddess Anath to wheedle the bow from Aqhat, T. H. Gaster, *Thespis* (New York, 1950), p. 452, makes the interesting observation that *almdk* is evidently to be taken in the specific sense of Heb. *lammed qāšet,* "to teach archery."

my hands . . . my arms. The parallelism between *yāday,* "my hands," and *'eṣb^{e}'ōtay,* "my arms," has Canaanite antecedents in the Ugaritic text cited in the next NOTE. To date more than 290 pairs of words in Ugaritic have found their counterparts in Biblical Hebrew, and the Psalter witnesses 157 of these parallel pairs.

my arms. Though universally rendered "my fingers," *'eṣb^{e}'ōtay* bears, by reason of the parallelism and through metonymy, the meaning found in UT, Krt:157–58, *yrḥṣ ydh amth uṣb'th 'd ṯkm,* "He washed his hands to the elbow, his arms up to the shoulder." This conditioned meaning is thus analogous to the conditioned meaning of *yād,* "hand," which sometimes signifies "the left hand," when placed in poetic parallelism with *yāmīn,* "right hand." It may further be observed that in the parallel text of Ps xviii 35, *yāday,* "my hands," is paired with *z^{e}rō'ōtay,* the normal word for "my arms." Cf. *Biblica* 44 (1963), 296–97, and UHP, pp. 30–31.

2. *My rampart.* 11QPs^{a} *ḥsdy* (=MT *ḥasdī*) supports none of the four emendations listed by BH^{3} to find a synonym more consonant with the pervading metaphor. Nor does any emendation seem necessary, given the evidence for *ḥesed,* "rampart," exposed at Ps lix 11; see also below on Ps cxlvii 11.

my haven. Repointing MT *m^{e}pal^{e}ṭī,* "my rescuer," to pausal *miplāṭī,* as in Ps lv 9; see the discussion there. From the preceding synonyms it seems clear that a noun of place is called for rather than a participle. Prepositional *lī* "to me," which adds little to the suffix of *miplāṭī,* "my haven," fulfills a grammatical function if advanced to the next colon.

He is my Suzerain. With the transfer of *lī,* "to me," from the preceding colon we recover the nominal sentence *lī m^{e}gānī* which nicely couples with *ūbō ḥāsītī,* "and in him I trust." Though MT *māginnī,* "my shield," is compatible with "I trust," it can scarcely be the proper subject of *hārōdēd,* "the one who prostrated." Thus the vocalization *m^{e}gānī* and the definition proposed at Pss iii 4 and xviii 31, "The Suzerain is he to all who trust in him," commend themselves here.

the one who prostrated. 11QPs^{a} secures MT *hārōdēd* against emendation to *hārōdeh,* a reading found in one manuscript, while comparison with Ps xviii 48, *wayyadbēr 'ammīm taḥtāy,* "and [who] made peoples supine at my feet" (revised translation; see also Ps xlvii 4), and Isa xlv 1, *l^{e}rad l^{e}pānay gōyīm,* "to prostrate nations before him," serves to bring out the meaning of *rōdēd,* from *rādad,* "to hammer, beat down."

the peoples at my feet. 11QPs[a] reads plural absolute *'mym tḥty,* "the peoples at my feet" (=Ps xviii 48), which is semantically easier than MT *'ammī taḥtāy,* "my people at my feet." I adopt the suggestion of D. N. Freedman that consonantal *'my* be read as plural construct *'ammē,* "the peoples," dependent upon the genitive *taḥtāy,* "at my feet." For other instances of a construct before a preposition, see the NOTE on Ps lxxxiv 7, *'ibrē be'ēmeq,* "brooks in the valley," with bibliography.

at my feet. The NOTES on Pss viii 7 and xlv 6 discuss this meaning of *taḥtāy.* New instances include Ps xviii 48; II Sam ii 23; Job ix 13, discussed by me in *The Role of the Phoenicians in the Interaction of Mediterranean Civilizations,* pp. 123–52, especially 139–40.

3. *Yahweh, what is man?* With this variation on Ps viii 5 the psalmist turns from his contemplation of Yahweh's goodness to reflect upon the insignificance and the transitory character of the object of God's munificence.

the son of man. Heb. *ben 'enōš* equals Ugar. *bnš,* spelled *bu-nu-šu,* as pointed out by UT, Glossary, No. 486. Cf. also *Ugaritica,* V, p. 351.

4. *Man . . . his days.* Cf. Pss xxxix 6, 11 and cii 12.

5. *bow your heavens . . . touch the mountains.* The descriptions of Pss xviii 10 and civ 32 are turned into prayers for a theophany.

that they smoke. As in Pss civ 32 and cxlviii 8, the psalmist doubtless describes volcanic activity.

6. *Flash your shafts.* In the phrase *berōq bārāq,* the collective singular *bārāq,* "your shafts," shares the suffix of second-colon *ḥiṣṣekā* "your arrows."

scatter them . . . disperse them. Namely, the lightning bolts, and not the enemies of Yahweh, as commonly held; see the NOTES on Ps xviii 15. Thus Kirkpatrick, *Psalms,* p. 809, comments, "*Them* must refer to the enemies who are in the Psalmist's mind, though he has not expressly mentioned them."

scatter them . . . 7. snatch me. In *tepīṣēm,* "scatter them," and *peṣēnī* "snatch me," the psalmist realizes an effective play on two different roots. The next NOTE registers another rootplay.

forge your arrows . . . 7. Stretch forth. As noted at Ps xviii 15, the first *šelaḥ,* "forge," is a different root from *šelaḥ,* "Stretch forth."

7. *Stretch forth your hands.* Comparing *šelaḥ yādekā* (11QPs[a] is here unfortunately damaged and unable to furnish an argument in favor either of MT dual "your hands" or of the ancient versions which all read singular "your hand") with UT, 128:IV:24, *yd bṣ' tšlḥ,* "She stretched forth her hand into the bowl."

The style of vs. 7 is noteworthy. The first colon consists of imperative + object + prepositional phrase; the second is comprised of two imperatives, each followed by the suffixed object, while the third and forth cola are made up of prepositional phrases modifying the second-colon imperatives.

snatch me and rescue me. The psalmist juxtaposes the two imperatives *peṣēnī wehaṣṣīlēnī,* and then follows with the two prepositional phrases that modify respectively the two imperatives. Cf. the first NOTE on Ps lxxvi 12 which cites other texts with similar word arrangements.

Proposals to emend away *pᵉṣēnī*, "snatch me," founder on the observation that it forms a wordplay with vs. 6, *tᵉpīṣēm*, "scatter them." Nor can one accept, *tout court*, the opinion that *pᵉṣēnī* is here an Aramaism, since Ugaritic witnesses the personal name *bn pṣn*.

the waters deep. As noted at Ps xviii 17, *mayim rabbīm* refers to the waters of the nether world; the psalmist prays for deliverance from death.

the hand of foreigners. The double request—to be snatched from the dangers of Sheol and to be delivered from human foes—sustains the summary description of Ps xviii (introductory NOTE) as a prayer for rescue from the grasp of human enemies and from the clutches of Sheol.

8. *mouth . . . right hand*. These two nouns are collocated in the mythological text, UT, 52:63–64, *y'db uymn ušmal bphm*, "With both right and left hands they are put into their mouths."

whose right hand. Hardly "whose help," as rendered by Hanson, PMS, III, p. 98, with the note (p. 123), "Literally, 'right arm.'" The right hand was uplifted when a solemn oath was sworn (cf. the NOTE on Ps cvi 26) and probably when a pact was made between nations; see George Mendenhall, "Covenant," in IDB, I, especially p. 715a. In our context the foreigners would more likely be accused of violating their covenant with the Israelite king.

a perjured right hand. Literally "a right hand of perjury"; cf. Pss xliv 18 and lxxxix 34 where the verb *šiqqēr*, "to be false," is used in covenant contexts.

9. *sing . . . play*. The frequent Ugaritic-Hebrew parallelism between *šīr* and *zāmar* is noted at Pss lvii 8 and ci 1.

to you . . . 10. *to his king*. The shift from the second person to the third is characteristic of court style; cf., for example, Ps lxxxix 4–5.

10. *to his king . . . his servant*. Comparison with Pss xviii 51–52, cxxxii 10, and I Sam ii 10 reveals that MT *mᵉlākīm*, "kings," should be synonymous with *'abdō*, "his servant." This becomes feasible when consonantal *mlkym* is read *malkī-m*, the singular form with the third-person suffix *-ī*, followed by enclitic *mem*. As in vs. 2, stylistic variation would account for the choice of two different forms of the third-person suffix. One must also reckon with the possibility that MT plural *mᵉlākīm* is a plural of majesty, comparable with Ps lxxxix 51, *'ᵃbādekā*, "your servant," or II Chron vi 42, *mᵉšīḥekā*, "your anointed one"; see also the third NOTE on Ps cxxxviii 8. In this case, plural of majesty *mᵉlākīm*, "king," would share the suffix of its second-colon synonym *'abdō*, "his servant." But the second hypothesis appears less probable.

the sword of the Evil One . . . 11. *the hand of foreigners*. In vs. 7 the psalmist asks liberation from infernal foes (*mayim rabbīm*) and from human adversaries (*yad bᵉnē nēkār*). Here he repeats his prayer, but the infernal foe appears under a different guise; here he is called *rā'āh,* "Evil," an abstract designation acquiring concrete force by reason of being paired with concrete *b^e^nē nēkār,* "foreigners"; compare abstract *rā'āb,* "Hunger," but concretely signifying "the Hungry One" in Ps xxxiii 19 and Isa v 13. Cf. Prov xiii 21, *ḥaṭṭā'īm t^e^raddēp rā'āh w^e^'et ṣaddīqīm y^e^šallēm ṭōb,* "The Evil One will pursue sinners, but the Good One will reward the just," and Ps lxxxiv 11, "the Tent of the Wicked One," where the abstract vocalization of MT *reša',* "Evil," may be retained without its concrete sense being changed.

That Death possessed a sword (the phrase *ḥereb rā'āh,* "the sword of the Evil One," is hapax legomenon) may be inferred from the effects so graphically described in Ps cxli 7, "Like one rent and riven in the nether world, / my bones are strewn at the mouth of Sheol." Cf. the Aramaic text, CIS, II, 212:6, *wyhw' bh ḥlp mwt,* "And the knife of Death will fall upon him." On *ḥlp,* "knife," see N. J. Tromp, "De radice *ḥlp* in lingua hebraica," VD 41 (1963), 299–304, and UT, Glossary, No. 968.

the sword . . . 11. *the hand.* The pairing of *ḥereb,* "sword," and *yād,* "the hand," answers to the parallelism of UT, 128:IV:24–25, *yd bṣ' tšlḥ ḥrb bbšr tštn,* "She stretched forth her hand into the bowl, she put a large knife into the meat." The same brace recurs in the very ancient poem Exod xv 9.

snatch me, 11. *and rescue me.* The word order of the Hebrew is also chiastic.

12. *May he bless.* Usually deleted as dittographic, consonantal *'šr* forms an inclusion with vs. 15, *'ašrē,* "How blest," when vocalized as piel *'iššēr,* just as in Ps xxxiii 12, and parsed as precative perfect. In vs. 14, it may be noted, the psalmist twice employs the precative mode. Of course, one may also defend the imperative piel *'aššēr,* "Bless!" but in this prayer for prosperity God is nowhere addressed in the second person, whereas in vs. 15 he is referred to in the third person, so that the precative expression seems preferable.

Noteworthy is the descending syllable count of the first six cola: 9:9::8:8::7:7; cf. the first NOTE on Ps cxxxix 18. The 9:9 syllable count in the first colon would obviously be upset by the deletion of *'šr.*

carefully trained from their youth. Referring primarily to the plants and secondarily to the sons, though the Hebrew and the English translation are ambiguous. In the phrase *m^e^guddālīm bin^e^'ūrēhēm* the preposition *bi* bears its frequent meaning "from." Contrast RSV, "May our sons in their youth be like plants full grown." This means that our phrase grammatically equals Lam iii 27, "It is good for a man that he bear the yoke from his youth (*bin^e^'ūrāyw*)," and is the semantic equivalent of Job xxxi 18, "*kī minn^e^'ūrēy* (MT *minn^e^'ūray,* "my youth") *gudd^e^lēnī* (MT *g^e^dēlanī*), "For from his youth he was reared by me," and Phoen. *lmn'ry,* "from his youth."

carved. Pual participle *m^e^ḥuṭṭābōt* may well be a dialectal form of *m^e^ḥūṣṣābōt,* given the increasing number of roots with interchangeable *ṭ* and *ṣ*. Already in Ugaritic this interchange is witnessed in such forms as *ḥṭr* and *ḥẓr*, "court"; *ṭhr* and *ẓhr*, "pure"; *lṭpn* and *lẓpn*, a divine epithet. Thus the concurrence of the roots *ḥāṭab*, "to carve," and *bānāh*, "to build" (in *tabnīt*, "structure") relates our verse to mythologically couched Prov ix 1, "Wisdom built (*bānᵉtāh*) her house, she carved (*ḥāṣᵉbāh*) her seven pillars."

palace. The present 8:8 syllable count discountenances the deletion of *hēkāl*, "palace," proposed by BH³.

13. *reaching*. "To reach, attain" seems to be the basic meaning of the root *pwq* in Ugaritic and Hebrew. The common rendition "affording" assumes a connection with Aram. *nᵉpaq*, "to go forth," and "to produce" in the causative conjugation, but this meaning does not fit all the texts witnessing this verb.

from end to end. A tentative translation (following some ancient versions) of the hapax legomenon phrase *mizzan 'el zan*, which KJ renders "all manner of store."

our sheep . . . our cattle. As in Ps viii 8, the pair *ṣō'nēnū* (MT *ṣō'wnēnū*) and *'alpēnū* (MT *'allūpēnū*) seem to form a merismus, denoting all types of domestic cattle. The Ugaritic text balancing these two nouns is quoted at Ps viii 8.

bring forth thousands, be multiplied by myriads. The expression *ma'ᵃlīpōt mᵉrubbābōt* juxtaposes two roots that appear in parallelism in UT, 1019:4–5, *alp ymm wrbt šnt*, "a thousand days and ten thousand years."

14. *well fed*. This definition of *mᵉsubbālīm*, which is supported by LXX, Aquila, Symm., and *Juxta Hebraeos*, seems also to elucidate Eccles xii 5 and Nah iii 15. For another opinion, see JAOS 88 (1968), 92, n. 49, where Moshe Held proposes "Our cattle are well cared for; there is none that breaks out, and none that stampedes, and there is no alarm on our ranges."

Let there be no invasion . . . no exile, nor outcry. Interpreting the triple *'ēn* as precative perfect; cf. vs. 12.

invasion . . . exile. Assigning to *pereṣ*, "invasion" (literally "breach"), and *yōṣē't*, "exile," the frequent military nuance (contrast Held's improbable version cited in next to last NOTE) that is witnessed, for instance, in Amos iv 3, *pᵉrāṣīm tēṣe'nāh*, "Through the breaches you shall go into exile."

15. *How blest*. Heb. *'ašrē* forms an inclusion with vs. 12, *'iššēr*, "May he bless."

PSALM 145

(cxlv 1–21)

1 *A psalm of praise. Of David.*

I will exalt you, my God, O King!
and I will bless your name, O Eternal and Everlasting!
2 Every day I will bless you,
and praise your name to everlasting eternity.
3 Great is Yahweh,
and worthy of praise the Grand,
Since to his greatness there is no limit.
4 Generation shall laud your works to generation,
and shall proclaim your exploits.
5 O Majesty, your glorious splendor shall they describe,
about your wonders will I compose my songs.
6 O Strong One, they shall announce your awesome acts,
and I will number your great deeds.
7 They shall pour forth the record, O Master, of your goodness,
and ring out your justice.
8 Merciful and compassionate is Yahweh,
slow to anger and abounding in kindness.
9 Yahweh's goodness is for all,
and his compassion is upon all his works.
10 All your works shall praise you, Yahweh,
and your devoted ones shall bless you.
11 They shall announce your glorious kingship,
and tell of your power,
12 Making known to the sons of men his exploits,
and the glorious splendor of his kingship.
13 Your kingdom is an eternal kingdom,
and your dominion endures throughout all generations.
14 Yahweh is the sustainer of all who fall,
and the uplifter of all bent double.

15 The eyes of all wait for you,
for it is you who give them
their food in its season,
16 You who open your hand,
and satisfy every living thing with your favor.
17 Just is Yahweh in all his ways,
and kind in all his works.
18 Near is Yahweh to all who call him,
to all who call him in truth.
19 He performs the will of those who fear him,
he hears their cry and saves them.
20 The protector of all who love him is Yahweh,
but all the wicked will he destroy!
21 The praise of Yahweh shall my mouth speak,
and all flesh shall bless his holy name,
to everlasting eternity!

NOTES

cxlv. A hymn celebrating the attributes of Yahweh, especially his kingship. The acrostic arrangement of the psalm means that each new verse begins with the next in order of the Hebrew alphabet; the verse which begins with the letter *nun* is missing in MT, though it is found in one Hebrew manuscript, in the LXX, and Syriac. RSV supplies this verse from these sources: "The Lord is faithful in all his words, and gracious in all his deeds." 11QPs[a] likewise preserves the *nun* verse, reading *n'mn 'lwhym bdbryw wḥsyd bkwl m'śyw*, "God is faithful in his words, and gracious in all his deeds." After each verse 11QPs[a] also preserves a congregational response, "Blessed be Yahweh, and blessed be his name forever!" which is not found in MT. Should the *nun* verse be inserted after vs. 13 in MT and in our translation? It would seem that this problem should not be considered apart from similar problems in the acrostic Pss xxv and xxxiv. In Ps xxv the *waw* and *qoph* verses are wanting, the latter being replaced by a second *resh* verse; moreover, a supernumerary *pe* verse is added at the end. In Ps xxxiv the *waw* verse is missing and a supplementary verse beginning with *pe* is added at the end. All these things considered, I have followed MT in not including the *nun* verse in the present translation.

The acrostic pattern seems not to have obstructed the lyricism of the psalmist, for the hymn effuses originality and warmth. It is remarkable for the number of divine names and appellatives; it may fairly be described as a litany of sacred names. The NOTES below identify new names and titles in vss. 1, 3, 5, 6, 7. Stylistically significant are the word order in vss. 1, 12, 18, the chiasmus in vss. 2, 10, 11, 20, 21, the interlocking inclusions between vss. 1–2 and 21, and the stylistic variation in vs. 4.

Neither content nor style afford a solid basis for determining the date of composition. The acrostic pattern, commonly taken as a sign of lateness, appears in Pss ix–x, which can scarcely be termed late poems, and the several Ugaritic tablets with the letters arranged in alphabetical order suggest that the acrostic pattern may have been used in the Late Bronze Age.

1. *A psalm of praise.* This is the only psalm which bears the title *t^{e}hillāh,* literally "a praise"; from the plural of this word comes the Hebrew title of the whole Psalter, *t^{e}hillīm,* "praises." It is interesting to note that 11QPs^{a} reads *tplh,* "a prayer," suggesting that in their Psalter no psalm bore the heading *t^{e}hillāh,* "a psalm of praise." That MT *t^{e}hillāh* is correct may also be inferred from the inclusion it forms with vs. 21, *t^{e}hillat yhwh,* "The praise of Yahweh."

my God, O King . . . O Eternal and Everlasting! If we assume that the first-colon sequence of verb+object+two vocatives is counterpoised by the second-colon components, we may infer that *l^{e}'ōlām* answers to the vocative particle and divine title *hammelek,* "O King," and parses as vocative *lamedh* plus the divine title *'ōlām,* "Eternal," described at Ps lii 10. The psalmist distributes over the parallel cola the composite divine title *melek 'ōlām,* "the King of Eternity," discussed at Ps x 16. Cf. also Jer x 10 and the title of the Pharaoh in UT, 2008:9, *mlk 'lm.* That we can assume such careful literary carpentry follows from the analysis of the next verse.

2. *Every day . . . everlasting eternity.* As in vs. 1, the elements of both cola are perfectly balanced. Here, however, the sequence of the chiastic verse is prepositional phrase+verb+object//verb+object+prepositional phrase. Thus *l^{e}'ōlām wā'ed* must be interpreted in the light of its opposite number, *b^{e}kol yōm,* "Every day," whereas in vs. 1 *l^{e}'ōlām wā'ed,* by reason of the parallelism, received a different interpretation with a resultant play on words.

3. *Yahweh . . . the Grand.* When MT *m^{e}'ōd,* "much," is revocalized *mā'ēd,* the composite divine name *yhwh mā'ēd,* "Yahweh the Grand," studied at Ps cix 30, becomes clear. Cf. the revised translation of Ps xcvi 4, proposed at Ps cix 30, and I Chron xvi 25. This would then be the second example in this psalm (see vs. 1) of a composite divine name distributed over succeeding cola.

4. *Generation . . . generation.* Ps xxii 31–32 expresses a similar sentiment.

shall laud . . . shall proclaim. Though the subject of the two cola is the same, the poet employs the singular verb *y^{e}šabbaḥ,* "shall laud," in the first colon, (11QPs^{a} reads plural *yšbḥw*), and the plural form *yaggīdū,* "shall proclaim," in the second. With the plural verb form the poet could add one syllable to the second colon to produce a syllabically better balanced (10:9) verse. In vs. 6 the psalmist resorts to an energic form to create syllabic equilibrium, so the metrical argument carries conviction.

This stylistic subtlety was lost on 1QIsª in Isa xliii 9b, *mī bāhem yaggīd zō't wᵉrī'šōnōt yašmī'ūnū,* "Who among them has proclaimed this? And who predicted to us past events?" Here the prophet employs singular *yaggīd,* "has proclaimed," and plural *yašmī'ū,* "predicted," with the same subject, but 1QIsª equalizes both verbs, reading them as plural forms *ygydw* and *yšmy'w,* respectively. Other examples are given in the second NOTE on Ps cv 11, but cf. especially Isa liv 3.

5. *O Majesty.* Since this psalm is a litany of divine titles, MT construct *hᵃdar* gains force when pointed as absolute *hādār* and identified as a divine title in the vocative case.

shall they describe. 11QPsª *ydbrw,* "shall they describe," supports the LXX and Syr., and is tentatively adopted here against MT *didrēy,* "words of."

6. *O Strong One.* Repointing MT *'ᵉzūz,* "strength of," to adjectival *'izzūz* (cf. Ps xxiv 8, *yhwh 'izzūz wᵉgibbōr,* "Yahweh strong and mighty"), and explaining initial *we* as the vocative particle discussed at Ps cxxxix 19.

I will number. Though MT *'ᵃsappᵉrennāh* can be explained as employing the resumptive pronominal suffix, the fact that 11QPsª reads *'spr* suggests that consonantal *'sprnh* expresses the energic form to be pointed *'ᵃsappᵉrannāh.* What is more, the resumptive pronoun construction proves improbable if the antecedent should turn out to be plural; see the next NOTE and UHP, p. 21.

your great deeds. With Ketiv, *Juxta Hebraeos,* and 11QPsª *gdwlwtykh,* reading plural *gᵉdūlōtekā* as against the Qere singular form which is also found in several ancient versions. Parallelism with plural *nō'rōtekā,* "your awesome acts," likewise sustains the plural lection.

7. *They shall pour forth.* An attempt to reproduce the Hebraic idea underlying the verb *yabbī'ū;* from the root *nb'* also derives the noun *mabbūᵃ',* "bubbling spring."

the record, O Master, of your goodness. Heb. *zēker rab ṭūbᵉkā* may well be parsed as a construct chain with vocative *rab,* "O Master" (see Ps cxxiii 3), interposed between the construct and its genitive. Cf. Isa xxvi 7, where *'ōraḥ laṣṣaddīq mēšārīm,* "the path, O Just One, of uprightness," is balanced by vs. 8, *'ōraḥ mišpāṭekā,* "the path of your judgments." Evidence that any part of speech can intervene in a construct chain in poetry continues to mount; see the first NOTE on Ps cxl 10, and THE GRAMMAR OF THE PSALTER.

9. *Yahweh's goodness.* Construing *ṭōb-yhwh* as a construct chain rather than as a nominal sentence with RSV, "The Lord is good." This analysis accords with MT's use of the *makkeph* or hyphen between the two words.

for . . . upon. This balance between *l* and *'l* corresponds to the Ugaritic parallelism noted at Ps ciii 10.

his compassion. Plural *raḥᵃmāyw* may also be rendered "his acts of compassion."

12. *Making known.* Though some versions (e.g., RSV) take the infinitive *lᵉhōdîᵃʻ* as expressing purpose "to make known," it may also be parsed as the circumstantial infinitive discussed in the third NOTE on Ps ci 8. For the thought, cf. Ps lxvii 3.

his exploits. To avoid the jarring shift from the second person hitherto used to the third person of *gᵉbûrōtāyw*, "his exploits," and *malkûtō*, "his kingship," many versions retain the second person also here; thus RSV reads, "to make known . . . thy mighty deeds," with the note that "Hebrew reads *his*." This concession to modern ears does, it would seem, obliterate a device of court style, namely the unexpected shift from second to third person. It should be noted further that Yahweh's kingship is explicitly mentioned in this verse, thus pointing up the appositeness of court style.

the glorious splendor. By which Yahweh struck fear into his rivals, thus enabling him to achieve his mighty deeds. Documented at Pss xxi 6, xlv 4, lxxxix 45, and in *Biblica* 47 (1966), 417, this motif may also be recognized in Exod xv 7; Ecclus x 5; and Job xl 12, where God twits Job in these terms: *wᵉhōdᵉkā* (MT *wahᵃdōk*) *rᵉšāʻîm tᵉḥittēm* (*taḥtām*), "And by your splendor terrify the wicked," as proposed in *Biblica* 49 (1968), 509–10.

and the glorious splendor of his kingship. Since the entire second colon balances only the last component of the first colon, the whole verse may be symbolically represented as A+B+C//Ć, the sequence of vs. 18 and of Ps cxlii 6.

13. *an eternal kingdom.* Comparing *malkût kol ʻōlāmîm* with UT, 68:10, *tqḥ mlk ʻlmk*, "You shall receive your eternal kingdom/kingship."

eternal . . . all generations. This rather frequent pairing of *ʻōlām* "eternal," and *dōr wādōr*, "all generations," is commented upon at Ps cxxxv 13. Containing several ideas echoed in our verse, UT, 68:10 affords an instructive comparison: *tqḥ mlk ʻlmk drkt drdrk*, "You shall receive your eternal kingdom/kingship, your dominion of all generations."

16. *You who open.* Meter is better served when MT *pōtēᵃḥ 'et*, with one beat, is read with LXX *pōtēᵃḥ 'attā*, with two beats; the resultant syllable count is 8:9. 11QPsᵃ *pwtḥ 'th 't ydkh*, with nine syllables, proves syllabically even more satisfactory (9:9) and may be the preferred reading. The sense remains the same whatever lection is adopted.

your favor. As in Ps xix 15, where its shares the suffix of *lᵉpānekā*, "according to your will," *rāṣōn*, "your favor," here shares the suffix of first-colon *yādekā*, "your hand."

17. *Just . . . kind.* This verse clarifies the reading and translation of Ps cxli 5a.

18. *to all who call him in truth.* The psalmist repeats the A+B+C//Ć pattern of vs 12.

19. *He performs the will.* Inasmuch as it is a fixed idiom denoting "to perform the will" in Pss xl 9, ciii 21, cxliii 10, there is no sound reason why *r^eṣōn (y^erē'āyw) ya'^aśeh* should not be translated in the same way here. Contrast the attenuated version of RSV, "He fulfils the desire of all [*sic!*] who fear him." Those who truly worship Yahweh have a right to be answered, and the second colon affirms that he does answer their prayers.

he hears their cry and saves them. The Hebrew is characterized by the alliteration of *š* (=*sh*) sounds, and by verbal roots ending in ' (*'ayin*): *šaw'ātām yišma' w^eyōšī'ēm.* Cf. Ps cxxvii 1, 5.

20. *The protector . . . will he destroy.* Chiasmus and assonance mark this line beginning with *šōmēr,* "The protector," and ending with *yašmīd,* "will he destroy."

21. *The praise of Yahweh.* Forming an inclusion with the psalm title *t^ehillāh,* the phrase *t^ehillat yhwh,* "The praise of Yahweh," fittingly begins the last verse of this hymn of praise.

The praise of Yahweh . . . his holy name. Arranged chiastically, the phrases *t^ehillat yhwh* and *šēm qodšō* form an inclusion with and are an expansion of vs. 2, *'^ahal^elāh šim^ekā,* "praise your name."

to everlasting eternity! This closing phrase evokes the same expression in vss. 1–2, with which it establishes an inclusion.

PSALM 146

(cxlvi 1–10)

1 Praise Yah!
Praise Yahweh, O my soul!
2 May I praise Yahweh my life long,
sing to my God while I have being.
3 Trust not in princes,
in a son of man, in whom there is no security.
4 When his breath departs, he returns to his land;
on that day his projects perish.
5 Blest he whose help is the God of Jacob,
whose hope is Most High Yahweh, his God,
6 Who made heaven and earth,
the sea and all that is in them.
Who keeps faith with the wronged,
7 who defends the cause of the oppressed,
who gives food to the hungry.
Yahweh sets prisoners free,
8 Yahweh opens the eyes of the blind,
Yahweh uplifts those bent double.
Yahweh loves the just,
9 Yahweh protects the strangers.
The fatherless and the widow he reassures,
but the domination of the wicked he overturns.
10 Yahweh shall reign for ever,
your God, O Zion, for all generations.

Praise Yah!

NOTES

cxlvi. The first of the five "Halleluyah Psalms" with which the Psalter ends, this simple hymn celebrates the power and beneficence of God, which it contrasts with the frailty and transitoriness of men. Though this hymn employs two Aramaisms (vss. 4–5) which might be cited as signs of late composition, it still preserves a proportionately high number of parallel pairs of synonyms that appear in the Late Bronze Age texts of Ras Shamra.

2. *May I praise Yahweh . . . sing to my God.* The syntax of *'ahalelāh yhwh* (verb+object) and *'azammerāh le'lōhay* (verb+prepositional phrase) may be cited in support of the reading and translation submitted for Ps lxxv 10, *'aggaddēl 'ōlām* (verb+object), "I shall extol the Eternal," parallel to *'azammerāh lē'lōhē ya'aqōb* (verb+prepositional phrase), "I shall sing to the God of Jacob."

my life long . . . while I have being. Cf. Ps civ 33.

3. *princes . . . son of man.* Heb. *nedībim . . . ben 'ādām* is taken as a meristic expression designating all men; cf. NOTE on Ps cxviii 8–9.

no security. Cf. Ps lx 13 (=cviii 13). The poet contrasts the futility of human resources with the help of Jacob's God (vs. 5).

4. *When his breath departs.* The phrase *tēṣē' rūḥō* may be compared with UT, 3 Aqht:'obv.':24–25, *tṣi km rḥ npšh,* "Let his life depart like breath."

to his land. Namely, to the nether world whence he came; cf. Pss civ 29, cxxxix 15; Eccles xii 7. The psalmist evokes the motif of Sheol as the land to which all mortals must return; Job i 21.

his projects. A hapax legomenon, *'eštōnōtāyw* is an Aramaism, already witnessed in the eighth-century Sefîre Inscriptions. The gradual chronological extension of Aramaic Inscriptions coming to light no longer permits the automatic dating of psalms which contain Aramaisms to the Exilic or post-Exilic period.

perish. To gain stylistic variety, the poet counterbalances two *yqtl* verbs of the first colon with the second-colon *qtl* form *'abedū,* "perish." Compare the first NOTE to Ps cxliii 5.

5. *whose help.* The *beth* of *be'ezrō* may parse either as the emphatic *beth* (see second NOTE on Ps liv 6) or as the *beth essentiae.* It should be noted that its second-colon counterpart is *śibrō,* "whose hope," which is not preceded by *beth.* The chiasmus of *be'ezrō* and *śibrō* further argues equivalence of function in the related terms.

whose hope is Most High Yahweh. Considerations of parallelism, and the fact that the verb *śābar,* "to hope," is used with *le* or *'el,* never with *'al* (the noun *śēber* occurs only here and in Ps cxix 116) indicate that *'al* is not the preposition "upon," but rather the first component of the composite name *'al yhwh,* "Most High Yahweh," identified in Ps xviii 42 (courtesy Giovanni Boggio). Cf. *yhwh 'al* in Ps cxli 3 and *'al 'elōhīm* in Ps vii 11.

6. *heaven and earth, the sea.* These three nouns are collocated in Job xii 7–8 and in UT, 52:61–63, *št špt larṣ špt lšmm wl'rb bphm 'ṣr šmm wdg bym,* "They set a lip against the [nether] world, a lip against heaven. Then entered their mouth the birds of heaven and the fish of the sea."

Who keeps faith. Yahweh never goes back on his pledge to defend the unprivileged.

the wronged. MT *'ōlām,* "eternity," poorly matches the evidently parallel passive participle *'ašūqīm,* "the oppressed." Hence one may, with no consonantal changes, proffer the passive participle vocalization *'awūlīm,* "the wronged," from the root *'wl,* "wrong," and from which derives the denominative piel participle *me'awwēl,* "the criminal," in Ps lxxi 4. That such a root belongs in such a context may further be argued from UT, 127:44–47, *šqlt bǵlt ydk ltdn dn almnt lttpṭ ṭpṭ qṣr npš,* "You have let your hands fall into wrongdoing; you do not judge the case of the widow or defend the cause of the downtrodden." The concurrence in these lines of *ǵlt,* "wrongdoing," and *ṭpṭ,* "cause," compares with the collocation of *'awūlīm,* "the wronged," and *mišpāṭ,* "cause," in our couplet.

9. *the strangers.* The resident aliens in Israel who did not enjoy the rights of citizenship.

The fatherless and the widow. For the parallel pair *yātōm//'almānāh,* compare the second NOTE on Ps cix 9 and UT, 127:48–50, *lpnk ltšlḥm ytm b'd kslk almnt,* "You do not feed the fatherless before you, the widow behind your back."

he reassures. The polel form *ye'ōdēd* has been correctly related (UT, Glossary, No. 1947) to *ǵdd,* "to swell," in 'nt:II:25–27, *tǵdd kbdh bṣḥq ymlu lbh bšmḫt kbd 'nt tšyt,* "Her liver swells with laughter, her heart is filled with joy, Anath's liver with victory."

the domination. Assigning to *derek* the meaning found in Ugar. *drk//mlk,* a parallelism examined at Ps cii 24. Verse 10 begins, it will be noted, with *yimlōk,* "shall reign," thus producing the same sequence of roots as the Ugaritic brace. Some 290 pairs of words in Ugaritic have been identified in Biblical Hebrew, affording a valuable criterion for assessing the literary relationships between these two Canaanite dialects.

he overturns. Or "he turneth upside down" (KJ). Cf. Job viii 3, *ha'ēl ye'awwēt mišpāṭ,* "Does God subvert justice?" and UT, 49:VI:28, *lyhpk ksa mlkk,* "He shall indeed upset your royal throne."

10. *shall reign for ever . . . for all generations.* The phrases *yimlōk . . . le'ōlām* and *ledōr wādōr* are reminiscent of oft-cited UT, 68:10, *tqḥ mlk 'lmk drkt dt drdrk,* "You will receive your eternal kingdom/kingship, your dominion of all generations."

Praise Yah! This command forms an inclusion with vs. 1, "Praise Yah!"

PSALM 147
(cxlvii 1–20)

1 Praise Yah!
How good to hymn our God!
How pleasant to laud our Glorious One!
2 Rebuilder of Jerusalem is Yahweh,
he gathers the outcasts of Israel;
3 The healer of the brokenhearted,
and binder of their wounds.
4 Who assigns a number to the stars,
to them all he gives names.
5 Great is our Lord, surpassing in power,
none can describe his skill.
6 He who reassures the humble is Yahweh,
who reduces the wicked even to the nether world.
7 Sing to Yahweh with thanksgiving,
make music to our God with the lyre.
8 Who covers the heaven with clouds,
who prepares rain for the earth,
who makes the mountains sprout grass.
9 Who gives to the cattle their grain,
to the crows that which they gather.
10 Not in the steed's power does he delight,
not in man's thighs is he pleased,
11 But pleased is Yahweh with those who fear him,
with those who rely on his strength.
12 Laud, O Jerusalem, Yahweh,
praise your God, O Zion!
13 For he strengthened the bars of your gates,
he blessed your sons within you.
14 He grants your limits peace,
with the finest wheat he sates you.
15 He sends his word to the earth,
toward the mountain speeds his thunder.

16 He spreads snow like wool,
frost he strews like ashes.
17 He casts his hail like crumbs,
before his cold—who can stand?
18 He sends his message and melts them,
makes his wind blow, and the waters stream.
19 He declares his words to Jacob,
his statutes and ordinances to Israel.
20 He has not dealt thus with any other nation,
and has never taught them his ordinances.
Praise Yah!

NOTES

cxlvii. Though a certain unity of thought and expression pervade this psalm, the Greek and Latin versions treat the text as two separate hymns. In these versions the first hymn runs from vss. 1–11, and the second from vss. 12–20. The translation and exegesis of vs. 15 submitted here furnish a new argument in favor of the versions, and the concentration of instances of subtle wordplay, alliteration, and assonance in the second hymn may also be cited in their support.

The translation appears improved in vss. 11, 14, 15, 18 by a more rigorous application of the criterion of metaphorical consistency. These two hymns, as the NOTES attempt to bring out, are noteworthy for certain features of syntax (vss. 8c, 9, 14, 20), style (vss. 8, 20), and prosody (vss. 4, 11, 16).

The text provides no clear data for establishing the time of composition, though a sixth-century date may be tentatively suggested on the basis of certain reminiscences of Second Isaiah (vss. 2–3, 5, 15–16).

1. *How good . . . ! How pleasant . . . !* For the exclamatory use of *kī* in *kī ṭōb,* "How good!" and *kī nā'īm,* "How pleasant!" see the NOTES at Pss xxxii 10 and lvi 3, while the second NOTE on Ps cxxxiii 1 comments on the parallelism of *ṭōb* and *nā'īm*. Thus one need not subscribe to the older view that the text of this verse is in some confusion, especially since a clear A+B+C//Á+B́+Ć pattern is discernible.

to hymn . . . to laud. The first NOTE to Ps xxxiii 1 analyzes as piel infinitives *zammerāh* and *nā'wāh;* cf. Ps lxxxvi 11, *leyir'āh,* "to revere."

our Glorious One! If this verse scores into an A+B+C//Á+B́+Ć pattern, then *tehillāh* shares the suffix of *'elōhēnū,* "our God," and becomes identical with the divine title discussed at Ps xxii 4, to be compared with Ps cxlv 5, *hādār,* "Majesty," also a divine title. Verse 20 witnesses another instance of double-duty suffix.

2. *Rebuilder of Jerusalem.* Comparing *bōnēh yerûšālaim* with Ps li 20 "rebuild the walls of Jerusalem."

4. *Who assigns a number.* Namely when he created the stars. Some uncertainty attaches to the translation and interpretation of the hapax legomenon phrase *mōneh mispār* (KJ, "He telleth the number"), but the parallelism here and comparison with the syntax of Isa lxv 12, *ūmānītī 'etkem laḥereb,* "I will destine you for the sword," removes much of the uncertainty. To each star Yahweh gives a number and a name, a theme which underlies Isa xl 26b, *hammōṣī' bemispār ṣebā'ām lekullām bešēm yiqrā'ām* (MT *yiqrā' mērōb;* see the first NOTE on vs. 5), "He who brings forth their host by number, he calls them all by name." In the phrase *mōneh mispār* are juxtaposed the roots which appear in parallelism in UT, 77:45–47 *hn bpy sprhn bšpty mnthn,* "Behold, in my mouth is their number, on my lips their count"; cf. McDaniel, *Biblica* 49 (1968), 214, for the bearing of this poetic parallelism on the translation of Lam iii 22.

to the stars, to them all. The chiastic arrangement of the Hebrew verse may be represented by the symbols A+B+C//Ć+B́+Á, a rather infrequent sequence identifiable in Pss xlvi 2 (see *Biblica* 50 [1969], 79), lviii 7, lxv 12a–13b; Prov iii 10, vii 16, viii 21, xiii 6.

5. *surpassing in power.* The phrase *rab kōaḥ* helps establish both the reading and meaning of cognate Isa xl 26c, *rab* (the *m* of MT *mērōb* should be joined to preceding *yiqrā'* where it would function as the resumptive suffix so frequent in Second Isaiah) *'ōnīm we'ammīṣ kōaḥ,* "surpassing in strength [compare Ugar. *dq anm,* "of slender strength"], and strong in power."

none can describe. Reading *'ēn mesappēr,* for MT *'ēn mispār* "there is no number." Cf. Ps xix 2 where the heavens are said to be *mesapperīm,* "proclaiming," the glory of God. For other instances of MT *mispār,* "number," as a mispointing of another form, see Dahood, *Biblica* 48 (1967), 428–29, and Pope, *Job* (3d ed.), on Job xvi 22a and xxxvi 26b.

his skill. Usually rendered "understanding," *tebūnāh* seems rather to bear the nuance found, say, in Ps lxxviii 72 and Job xxvi 12, where it is coupled, as here, with *kōaḥ,* "power": "By his power he annihilated Sea, and with his skill he smote Rahab." In Ugaritic mythology skill characterizes the god Kothar, whose standing epithet *kṯr wḫss* means "Skillful and Cunning." Cf. Pope, *Job,* on Job xxvi 12b.

6. *He who reassures.* Cf. Ps cxlvi 9. One detects a subtle wordplay on *me'ōdēd,* "He who reassures," and second-colon *'adē,* "to."

who reduces. For this interpretation of *mašpīl,* see the texts cited at Ps lxxv 8 and cf. Isa lvii 9. Like the authors of Pss lxxiii 24, cxix 112; Prov xi 31, xxvi 26, etc., the psalmist evidently believed in rewards and punishment beyond the grave.

the nether world. The recent note of W. L. Holladay in VT 19 (1969), 123–24, validly applies this definition of *'āreṣ* in Hos ii 2 and Exod i 10. The different sense of *'āreṣ* in our vs. 8 is noted in the third NOTE thereon.

7. *Sing*. Cf. the first NOTE on Ps xxii 25 for Ugaritic-Hebrew *'ny*, "to sing an antiphonal song," and F. I. Andersen, VT 16 (1966), 108–12, on Exod xxxii 18. The poet arranges this verse in an A+B+C//Á+B́+Ć sequence, just as in vs. 10.

make music . . . with the lyre. Comparing *zammᵉrū . . . bᵉkinnōr* with Ps xcviii 5 and RŠ 24.252:4 *wyḏmr bknr*, "And he makes music with the lyre."

8. *the heaven . . . the earth*. See the first NOTE on Ps xcvi 11 for the Ugaritic parallelism *šmn//arṣ*.

the heaven with clouds . . . rain for the earth . . . the mountains (sprout) grass. Though each of the three cola begins with a participle, the psalmist varies their structure with an accusative plus prepositional phrase (*šāmayim bᵉ'ābīm*) in the first colon, but in the second he resorts to chiasmus, with prepositional phrase plus accusative (*lā'āreṣ māṭār*). In the third colon, however, he drops the prepositional phrase and employs two accusatives instead (*hārīm ḥāṣīr*).

rain for the earth. The expression *lā'āreṣ māṭār* may be compared with UT, 126:III:7, *n'm larṣ mṭr b'l*, "Sweet to the earth was the rain of Baal." It should be noted that in our verse *'āreṣ* denotes "earth," but in vs. 6 *'āreṣ* means "nether world." This double signification follows Canaanite practice because UT, 67:VI:8–10 uses *arṣ* in the same two senses: *mǵny lb'l npl larṣ mt aliyn b'l ḫlq zbl b'l arṣ*, "We came upon Baal fallen into the nether world. Dead is Victor Baal, perished is the Prince, Lord of Earth!"

the earth . . . the mountains. For the Ugaritic pair *arṣ//hrm*, see the fourth NOTE on Ps lxxii 16. This parallelism recurs in vs. 15, as restored there.

who makes the mountains sprout grass. Good assonance characterizes *hammaṣmīaḥ hārīm ḥāṣīr*, and the double-accusative construction has close analogues in Ugaritic; cf., e.g., the texts cited at Ps cv 30 and in UT, § 13.10–11. The psalmist repeats this construction in vs. 14.

9. *their grain . . . they gather* These meanings of *laḥmāh* and *yiqrā'ū* are examined at Ps xiv 4

that which they gather. If the line is scanned as A+B+C//B́+Ć, *'ašer yiqrā'ū* answers to *laḥmāh*, "their grain," so that *'ašer* parses as the composite relative "that which" and *yiqrā'ū* bears the meaning discussed at Ps xiv 4.

10. *Not . . . not*. A carefully constructed line with an A+B+C//Á+B́+Ć pattern, the pattern recognized in vs. 7.

thighs. A hapax legomenon in the Psalter, *šōqē* now appears in the Ugaritic phrase *šq ymn* (=Exod xxix 22), "the right thigh," whose spelling with *š* reveals the quality of the initial consonant.

is he pleased. 11. *But pleased*. Ending vs. 10 with *yirṣeh*, "is he pleased," and beginning vs. 11 with *rōṣeh*, "But pleased," a participle of the same root, the poet employs the stylistic device commented upon at Ps cxxx 7.

11. *with those who rely on his strength.* Since the entire second colon is but a ballast variant of the C element in the first colon, the verse may be symbolically represented as A+B+C//Ć. Compare Pss cxlii 6 and cxlv 12.

his strength. Better than "his steadfast love" (RSV). In a context stressing the futility of a horse's might and a man's physical prowess, *ḥasdō* should bear the meaning noticed at Ps cxliv 2 (courtesy of Werner Quintens). This psalmist thus voices the same belief as Ps xx 8, "Some through chariots, / and others through horses, / But we through the Name of our God are strong." The same obtains for the identical expression in Ps xxxiii 18, likewise occurring in a context dismissing the efficacy of physical resources. In both contexts consistency of metaphor favors the translation of *ḥasdō* as "his strength"; see below on vs. 14, *your limits.* Translated thus, *ḥasdō,* the last word of the first hymn, forms an inclusion with vs. 5, "Great is our Lord, surpassing in power."

12. *Laud . . . praise.* The Hebrew employs two different verbs—*šabbeḥī* and *halelī*—and our translation attempts to reflect this difference. RSV, on the other hand, obliterates the difference by rendering both imperatives alike, "Praise!"

Yahweh . . . your God. Here the psalmist breaks up perhaps the most common of all literary and liturgical expressions in the Bible, *yhwh 'elōhayik.* D. N. Freedman also calls attention to the partial chiasmus in this line.

13. *he strengthened . . . he blessed.* For a similar collocation of ideas, cf. UT, 1 Aqht:194–95, *ltbrkn alk brkt tmrn alkn mrrt,* "Bless me that I may go blessed; fortify me that I may go fortified."

the bars of . . . he blessed. That the psalmist seeks assonance in his choice of the words *berīḥē,* "the bars of," and *bērak,* "he blessed," may be inferred from the next NOTE.

he blessed your sons within you. Each of the three words in the second colon ends in *-k,* but the poet eschews monotony by having each *-k* preceded by a different vowel: *bērak bānayik beqirbēk.* Of course, there is also the alliteration of *b,* each word beginning with this letter. In the first colon one word ends with *k* and only one begins with *b.*

your sons. The sons of the city, namely, the citizens.

14. *He grants your limits peace.* Though often rendered "He makes peace in your borders" (RSV), the double accusative construction in the second colon (as well as in vs. 8c) suggests that *haśśām gebūlēk šālōm* should be parsed in the same way. Cf. the Aramaic Inscription of Nerab 2, line 3, *śmny šm ṭb,* "He gave me a good name"; Job xxxiv 13, *mī pāqad 'ālāyw 'arṣāh ūmī śāmō* (MT *śām*) *tēbēl kullah,* "Who entrusted the earth to him? Who gave him [the reading *śāmō* evens the syllable count at 8:8] the whole world?" The same usage appears in Isa lx 17, "I will make/grant your overseers peace and your taskmasters justice,"

and in I Sam xxii 7, *lᵉkullᵉkem yāśīm śārē ʾᵃlāpīm,* "Will he make each and every one of you [*lᵉ* of *lᵉkullᵉkem* being the emphatic *lamedh*] commanders of thousands?" (courtesy of W. Kuhnigk).

your limits. Since the psalmist is addressing Jerusalem-Zion and describing the bolts of the city's gates, *gᵉbūlēk,* usually rendered "your borders," more precisely designates the city limits. Cf. Mic v 5, as explained by Kevin Cathcart in *Biblica* 49 (1968), 513–14. As in vs. 11, the application of the principle of metaphorical coherency relieves the textual ambiguity.

the finest wheat. Here functioning as an accusative of material, *ḥēleb ḥiṭṭim,* literally "the kidney fat of wheat," recurs in the very similar context of Ps lxxxi 17, in a prepositional phrase.

he sates you. Like cognate Ps lxxxi 17, our verse is marked by fine chiasmus; the line opens with a participle, closes with a verb, and in between succeed four consecutive nouns in the accusative case.

The use of the verb *yaśbīʿēk,* "he sates you," may cast some light on the Phoenician phrase *śbʿ wtrš* "wheat and wine," that also appears in Prov iii 10. In this phrase, abstract *śbʿ,* "satiety," assumes the concrete meaning "wheat" by reason of being coupled with the concrete substantive *trš,* "wine." Since for both the Phoenicians and the Israelites *śbʿ,* "satiety," connotes "wheat," it could also under certain conditions designate the wheat itself.

15. *He sends . . .* 16. *He spreads.* On the Ugaritic-Hebrew parallelism of *šlḥ//ntn,* consult the first NOTE on Ps lxxviii 24. In fact, the biblical pairing and synonymy should suffice to settle the doubts of Gordon, Glossary, No. 2419, who writes, "*šlḥ* 'to give to, endow with' (2 Aqht:VI: 18, 28)//*ytn* is conceivably, but not necessarily, of different origin."

his word . . . his thunder. Customarily interpreted, in the light of Isa lv 10, 11, to designate God's commandments and laws, *ʾimrātō,* "his word," and *dᵉbārō,* literally "his word," more probably refer to the thunder that accompanies the rain. Again, consistency of metaphor points to this interpretation. The wheat and well-being of the preceding verse and the snow and frost of the next line show the need for rain in our verse. To be sure, vs. 8 describes the preparation of rain and the effects of rainfall on the hillsides, but that verse belongs to the first hymn. The interpretation of *ʾimrātō,* "his word," as thunder thus tends to confirm both the reading and exegesis of Ps lxviii 12, "Let the Lord send forth the word rejoicing a numerous host." The identification of *dᵉbārō,* "his word," with the divine thunder bids fair to upend the current explication of *dābār* in Job xxvi 14, where it is parallel to *raʿam gᵉbūrōtō,* "his mighty thunder."

to the earth. Syntactically *ʾāreṣ* can be parsed as an accusative of place or, and preferably, as sharing the *hē directionis* of *hērāh,* "toward the mountain."

earth . . . mountain. Cf. the first NOTE on vs. 8.

toward the mountain. Often emended to *ʿal,* "upon," or simply deleted,

MT *'ad* receives a *raison d'être* when MT *'ad mᵉhērāh*, "very swiftly," is read *'ad-m hērāh* (cf. Gen xiv 10), "toward the mountain." Thus *'ad* plus enclitic *mem* may be identified with Ugar. *'dm* in 128:VI:2; EA 251:8, *adi-mi*, and *a-di-mi* in the Akkadian letter from Tell el Hesi studied by Albright in BASOR 87 (1942), 35, who describes *a-di-mi* as probably a Canaanitism. The double expression of direction in *'ad-m hērāh* may be compared with such phrases as *'ad 'ᵃpēkāh*, "unto Aphek," *'el haṣṣāpōnāh*, "toward the north," discussed by GK, § 90e, and *'ad rᵉḥōbāh*, "unto Rehob," examined by Albright in YGC, p. 70, n. 40, who too comments upon the numerous examples witnessing the use of both preposition and directive *he* in the same phrase. By the same token one can defend MT at Isa xlv 6, *mimmizraḥ šemeš ūmimma'ᵃrābāh*, "from the rising of the sun and from the west," against 1QIsᵃ which simply dropped the *-āh* ending with the final word: *mmzrḥ šmš wmm'rb*. Of course, the *-āh* ending stands for the *hē* of direction, and is not the feminine suffix as explained by GK, § 91e, and GB, p. 447b. 1QIsᵃ *mm'rb* shows that the *-āh* ending of MT is not the suffix.

speeds. Since his thunder is swifter (*yārūṣ*) than man, Yahweh need not be pleased (vs. 10, *yirṣeh*) with man's limited swiftness, a clever play on words that evokes the pun on *yārūṣ* and *rāṣūṣ* in Isa xlii 3–4.

16. *He spreads . . . he strews*. In Hebrew the word order is chiastic.

frost he strews like ashes. There is good alliteration in Heb. *kᵉpōr kā'ēper yᵉpazzēr*.

17. *He casts . . .* 18. *He sends*. In *mašlīk* and *yišlaḥ* one recognizes another play on roots with which the second hymn abounds.

his hail . . . his cold. Good assonance marks the brace *qarḥō//qārātō*.

his cold. Or "his thunder," if MT *qārātō* derives from the root *qwr*, "to call," as suggested at Ps lxviii 27. Commentators point out that snow must have always been rare in Central and Southern Palestine, and frost is very rare in Jerusalem. Some consequently suggest that this psalm was composed in or after an exceptionally severe winter. This line of reasoning loses much of its cogency with the knowledge that biblical poets often appropriated phrases and metaphors coined by their Phoenician and Canaanite colleagues further north where snow and frost were quite common.

18. *his message*. In tandem with *rūḥō*, "his wind," *dᵉbārō* should have a physical rather than a moral meaning; perhaps the sense proposed in vs. 15 is valid here. By sending a pouring rain accompanied by thunder, Yahweh melts the ice and frost.

19. *his words*. Namely, the Ten Commandments. Parallelism and assonance with second-colon *ḥuqqāyw ūmišpāṭāyw*, "his statutes and ordinances," supports the Qere plural *dᵉbārāyw* against singular Ketiv *dᵉbārō*, "his word." This use of the same word in two different senses falls in with the comments on the two meanings of *'āreṣ* "earth," in vss. 6 and 8.

20. *dealt . . . taught them*. The *qtl–yqtl* verbal sequence is of stylistic interest.

never. A more emphatic synonym of first-colon *lō'*, "not," *bal* is the standard negative particle in Phoenician.

taught them his ordinances. In *mišpāṭīm yōdī'ūm* we have the fourth instance of the double-accusative construction; cf. vss. 8c, 14.

taught them. Repointing qal MT *yᵉdā'ūm* to causative *yōdī'ūm;* LXX, Syr., Targ. read *yōdī'ēm,* "he taught them," and 11QPsª frag. E reads *hwdy'm*. The lection *yōdī'ūm* parses as the *yqtl* plural form balancing singular *qtl* verb *'āśāh,* "dealt," with Yahweh the subject of both verbs! Identical stylistic variation appears in Ps xlvi 5 with God the subject of both verbs: *yᵉśammᵉḥū 'īr 'ᵉlōhīm qiddēš miškᵉnēy 'elyōn,* "God brings happiness to his city, / the Most High sanctifies his habitation." Other examples are listed in the second NOTE on Ps cxlv 4. To be sure, *yōdī'ūm* can also be explained as the archaic singular ending in *-ū;* in the following texts the *yaqtulū* forms with Yahweh as subject can be explained either as archaic singular or as plural of majesty: Pss ix 11, xviii 19, xlvi 5, cxl 11; Prov ix 11.

his ordinances. Suffixless *mišpāṭīm* shares the suffix of vs. 19 *mišpāṭāyw,* "his ordinances"; note similar usage in vs. 1 (third NOTE ad loc.). For the psalmist, God's most laudable act is the revelation of his laws to Israel. This thought forms the climax of the hymn.

Praise Yah! With its opposite number in vs. 1 this command encloses both hymns comprising this psalm.

PSALM 148
(cxlviii 1–14)

1 Praise Yah!
Praise Yahweh from the heavens,
praise him from the heights.
2 Praise him, all his angels,
praise him, all his soldiers!
3 Praise him, sun and moon,
praise him, all stars of morning!
4 Praise him, heaven of heavens,
you waters above the heavens!
5 Let them praise the name of Yahweh,
he alone commanded, and they were created.
6 He stationed them from all time to eternity;
he issued a decree, and it shall never pass away.
7 Praise Yahweh from the nether world,
you sea monsters and all you depths!
8 Fire and hail, snow and smoke,
storm wind executing his command;
9 Mountains and all hills,
fruit trees and all cedars;
10 Wild beasts and all cattle,
reptiles and winging birds;
11 Kings of earth and all peoples,
princes and all tribes of earth;
12 Chosen lads and maidens too,
old men and youngsters alike;
13 Let them praise the name of Yahweh,
for his name alone is exalted.
Though his splendor is above earth and heaven,
14 he raised the horn of his people.
Praise from all his devoted ones,
from the children of Israel, the people close to him!
Praise Yah!

NOTES

cxlviii. A hymn inviting all created beings to praise Yahweh. It is remarkable for its tripartite structure, evidently modeled on the motif distinguishing three categories of beings. In vss. 1–6 the poet directly addresses celestial beings, opening with the imperative *hal^{e}lū 'et yhwh,* "Praise Yahweh," followed by six repetitions of the imperative *hal^{e}lūhū,* "Praise him," and concluding with the single jussive *y^{e}hal^{e}lū,* "Let them praise" (vs. 5). In vs. 7 he directly addresses the nether world and the abysses with the same formula as in vs. 1a, *hal^{e}lū 'et yhwh,* "Praise Yahweh." When, however, he turns to terrestrial creatures in vss. 8–13, he uses no imperative at all but only the third-person jussive in vs. 13a, *y^{e}hal^{e}lū,* "Let them praise," exactly as in vs. 5. The psalmist closes the hymn with a historical reflection in vss. 13c–14 on the relationship between the Lord of the universe and his people Israel.

1. *Praise Yahweh from the heavens.* MT *hal^{e}lū 'et yhwh min haššāmayim,* with its apparently needless *nota accusativi 'et* and full form of *min,* "from," followed by the article in *haššāmayim,* adds up to ten syllables, while the parallel colon numbers only eight. Hence one might incline toward the crisper reading of 11QPs^{a}, *hllw yhwh mšmym,* whose eight syllables perfectly match the eight in the opposite colon. What is more, the Qumranic lection does not alter the sense of MT. Comparison with vs. 7a, though, precludes the adoption of this new reading. Verse 7a, reads *hal^{e}lū 'et yhwh min hā'āreṣ,* "Praise Yahweh from the nether world," and its ten syllables are matched by only eight in the second colon, precisely as in vs. 1. In addition, 11QPs^{a} undermines its own authority by reading in vs. 7a, *hllw 't yhwh m*[. Though fragmentary, this reading is sufficiently telltale, since its *nota accusativi 't,* absent in its text of vs. 1, shows that it probably preserved the same reading as MT in the missing part. Were it consistent, 11QPs^{a} would have read *hllw yhwh,* as in vs. 1a. This case points out the caution that should be exercised before a Qumranic reading is adopted.

from the heavens . . . from the heights. The psalmist diversifies his expression when pairing *min,* "from," with poetic *ba,* "from," in *bamm^{e}rōmīm,* "from the heights," and at the same time avoids a difficult sequence of sounds in the latter phrase. Cf. N. Sarna, JBL 78 (1959), 313. In the parallel nouns *šāmayim* and *m^{e}rōmīm* one can recognize the two roots of the goddess Anath's title *b'lt šmm rmm,* "Mistress of High Heavens," and of the Phoenician phrase *šmm rmm,* "high heavens." Cf. Job xvi 19, xxii 12, and xxv 2.

2. *angels . . . soldiers.* Consult the first NOTE on Ps ciii 21.

3. *sun and moon.* The first NOTE on Ps civ 19 cites the Ugaritic equivalent of this pair.

stars of morning. Frequently rendered "shining stars," or "stars of light," *kōkᵉbē 'ōr* is a hapax legomenon which the LXX translated, "stars and light." Since *'ōr* means "morning" in Job xxiv 14 and Neh viii 3, our phrase could be synonymous with Job xxxviii 7, *kōkᵉbē bōqer,* "the morning stars," namely, those stars still visible at dawn—the planets.

4. *heaven of heavens.* See the first NOTE on Ps cxv 16.

you waters. Above the visible vault of heaven there was believed to be a reservoir, the source of rain; cf. the new translation of Ps civ 3; Gen i 6–7.

above the heavens. There is wonderful assonance and alliteration in Heb. *šᵉmē haššāmayim wᵉhammayim 'ᵃšer mē'al haššāmāyim.*

5. *he alone.* As in Ps xci 3, *kī* seems to emphasize *hū'* "he," rather than introduce a causal sentence. Cf. also Job xii 2, *kī 'attēm,* "you alone." The psalmist rejects the tenets of neighboring religions concerning the origin of the universe.

6. *He stationed them.* Yahweh fixed the heavens, the sun, moon, and planets in their stations, which they have maintained from eternity and will eternally keep.

from all time to eternity. In the phrase *lā'ad lᵉ'ōlām,* traditionally rendered "for ever and ever," the first preposition seems to denote "from" and the second "to," much like UT, 49:II:26–27, *lymm lyrḫm,* "from days to months," and 1 Aqht:167–68, *lht w'lmh,* "from now even to eternity." In vs. 14 the psalmist again uses *lᵉ,* "from." For the meaning of *lā'ad,* "from all time," Job xx 4, *minnī 'ad,* "from all time"; the first NOTE on Ps xxix 10, and Rafael M. Serra, "Algunos posibles ejemplos de interferencias de preposiciones en el hebreo biblico," *Claretianum* 7 (1967), 293–317, especially 301.

it shall (never) pass away. 11QPsᵃ *y'bwr* sustains MT singular *ya'ᵃbōr* against the proposed plural reading; thus RSV translates, "he fixed their bounds which cannot be passed." The subject is singular *ḥoq,* understood in its common signification "decree," here designating the divine decree establishing the eternal orbits of the heavenly bodies. Cf. Ps xxxiii 11 and Matt v 18, xxiv 35.

7. *from the nether world.* In vs. 1 the psalmist invites praise of Yahweh from heaven, and here he employs the same formula to summon praise from the opposite extreme, the nether world. See the next NOTE.

the nether world. Briggs, CECBP, II, p. 540, acutely observes that "the mention of dragons here [in the second colon] with the elements of nature and apart from the other animals of vs. 10 is singular," but the singularity is virtually eliminated with the recognition that first-colon *hā'āreṣ* signifies "the nether world" as pointed out by F. M. Cross, Jr., and D. N. Freedman in JNES 14 (1955), 247–48. Thus the marine dragons find their counterpart in the nether world. What does appear singular is the fact that the psalmist dedicates only one verse to the subterranean beings, after having given six verses to celestial bodies, and reserving the next seven for terrestrial creatures.

the nether world . . . depths. Comparison with Ps lxxi 20, *tᵉhōmōt hā'āreṣ,* "the depths of the nether world," suggests that in our verse the poet is using the device of breakup of composite phrases.

sea monsters. Cf. the discussion of *tannīn* at Ps lxxiv 13.

8. *Fire.* Namely lightning, as in Ps xviii 9.

Fire . . . smoke. Just as hail and snow clearly go together in the presumably chiastic colon, so fire should have smoke as its concomitant. The dispute regarding the correct reading of the second word can be partially resolved in favor of MT when stylistic criteria are applied. MT has *qīṭōr,* "smoke," but the ancient versions, followed by RSV, seem to have read *qeraḥ,* "frost." To the exasperation of textual critics, 11QPs[a] breaks off after *q.* If we assume chiasmus, *qīṭōr,* "smoke," becomes the natural partner of *'ēš,* "fire," and doubtless refers to volcanic smoke, hardly the mists which drift like smoke over the mountains, as put forth by Kirkpatrick and others. At Pss civ 32 and cxliv 5 probable allusions to volcanic activity have been noted. Thus the chiastic parallelism between *'ēš,* "fire," and *qīṭōr,* "smoke," corresponds to the straight parallelism between *'āšān,* "smoke," and *'ēš,* "fire," in the cognate description of Ps xviii 9.

storm wind. Consult the first NOTE on Ps cvii 25, where the compound expression *rūᵃḥ sᵉ'ārāh* is distributed over two parallel cola.

9. *fruit trees.* Biblical *'ēṣ pᵉrī,* literally "the tree of fruit," may be compared with Ugar. *pr 'ṣm,* "the fruit of trees."

fruit trees . . . cedars. For the Ugaritic parallelism *'ṣ//arz* see Ps civ 16. Here the phrase seems to be a merismus, including all cultivated and uncultivated trees.

11. *all tribes of earth.* Some scholars have recognized that if suitable parallelism is to be achieved, *lᵉ'ummīm,* "peoples," must be a homonym of another word which denotes "rulers." Thus G. R. Driver, CML, p. 158, believes to have found this meaning of *l'm* in several Ugaritic passages, and has been followed by J. Gray, *The Legacy of Canaan* (VTS, V, 2d ed.; Leiden, 1965), p. 271. D. N. Freedman proposes to find the solution to the problem of parallelism in MT *šōpᵉṭē,* "rulers of," whose consonants may well be explained as an alternate spelling of *šbṭy,* to be pointed *šibṭē,* "tribes of." Given the number of texts witnessing the alternation *špṭ/šbṭ* (consult PNWSP, p. 43, n. 1, which discusses Prov xix 29; Gen xlix 10; Isa xxxiii 22; II Sam vii 7; I Chron xvii 6), Freedman's proposal appears more convincing. Cf. also Z. Falk, *Leshonenu* 30 (1966), 243–47.

14. *he raised.* Parsing *wa* of *wayyārem* as the *waw* of apodosis; though his glory fills the cosmos, Yahweh deigned to show interest in an insignificant people, described in this same verse as "a people near him." Cf. Ps cxxxviii 6.

he raised the horn. Figurative for granting victory or bestowing prosperity.

Praise from all his devoted ones. CCD has recognized that in the phrase *t*^{e}*hillāh l*^{e}*kol ḥ*^{a}*sīdāyw,* the preposition *l*^{e} means "from": "Be this his praise from all his faithful ones." To be sure, suffixless *t*^{e}*hillāh* may well share the suffix of vs. 13, *hōdō,* "his splendor," but what is meant remains clear even without the suffix translated. Another instance of *l*^{e}, "from," is noted at vs. 6. Stylistically, this clause forms an inclusion with vs. 1, "Praise Yahweh from the heavens," and with vs. 7, "Praise Yahweh from the nether world." This tripartite praise will ascend simultaneously in response to the divine splendor that suffuses heaven and earth (vs. 13c).

The sentiment expressed by this colon is reflected in 11QPs^{a} Zion, lines 11–12, *ʿrbh b'p tšbḥtk ṣywn mʿlh lkwl tbl,* "May your praise, O Zion, enter into his presence, extolment from all the world," as proposed in *Biblica* 47 (1966), 143.

close to him. Cf. Ps cxlv 18. The dative suffix of *q*^{e}*rōbō,* which has occasioned considerable discussion, may instructively be compared with the dative suffix of Ps lxxiii 27, *r*^{e}*ḥēqekā,* "those who go far from you."

Praise Yah! Forms an inclusion with vs. 1, "Praise Yah!"

PSALM 149

(cxlix 1–9)

1 Praise Yah!
Sing to Yahweh a new song,
his praise in the assembly of the devoted.
2 Let Israel rejoice in his Supreme Maker,
the children of Zion be glad with their King.
3 Let them praise his name with dancing,
with tambour and lyre make music to him.
4 Because Yahweh delights in his people,
he will adorn the lowly with victory.
5 Let the devoted exult in their Glorious One,
let them sing for joy on their couches.
6 High praises of God from their throat,
but a two-edged sword in their hand,
7 To wreak vengeance on the nations,
reprisals against the peoples;
8 To bind their kings with chains,
and their nobles with iron shackles;
9 To inflict on them the verdict written—
let that be honor for all his devoted!
Praise Yah!

NOTES

cxlix. Weiser (*The Psalms*, p. 839) observes of this psalm that "from the fifth century A.D. up to the present day the psalm has constantly been interpreted as referring to Maccabean times, though the composition itself does not go beyond very general allusions which fit into every age," and Gunkel (*Die Psalmen*, p. 619) writes that this psalm, which at first sight looks so simple, lends itself to no simple interpretation. Attempts to fix the *Sitz im Leben* break down at one or more points. From the translation proposed here what emerges is a hymn sung and performed in the religious assembly on the eve of a battle against the heathen nations;

cf. Ps xx. Weiser thus appears to be correct when suggesting that "the verdict written" (vs. 9) alludes to the destruction of the pagan nations of Canaan, the accomplishment of which had continually been made the religious duty of the people of Israel (cf. Deut vii 1 ff., xx 13). In this interpretation the psalm would be of pre-Exilic origin, and while the psalm contains two interesting linguistic rapprochements with Second Isaiah, one cannot determine the direction of the purported influence.

1. *the devoted.* With vs. 9, "his devoted," *ḥ*ᵃ*sīdīm* forms an inclusion.

2. *rejoice . . . be glad.* The second NOTE on Ps cxviii 24 cites the Ugaritic text pairing these two verbs.

his Supreme Maker. An attempt to reproduce the plural of excellence *'ōśāyw,* often emended to singular *'ōśō* or *'ōśēhū,* and usually rendered simply "his Maker." This plural of excellence recurs in Isa liv 5 and Job xxxv 10.

their King. The psalmist contrasts the King of Israel with vs. 8, *malkēhem,* "their kings," just as in vs. 5 he opposes "their Glorious One" to vs. 8, *nikb*ᵉ*dēhem,* "their nobles."

3. *with dancing, with tambour and lyre.* Preserving the chiastic word order of the Hebrew. The antiquity of the dance accompanied by tambour and lyre is now attested by RŠ 24.252, which describes *mrqdm,* "the dancers," with *knr,* "lyre," and *tp,* "tambour." Cf. also Exod xv 20.

4. *he will adorn.* Customarily taken as expressing a general truth "he adorns," *y*ᵉ*pā'ēr* is here understood as predicting victory in the forthcoming battle. The fact that *y*ᵉ*pā'ēr* is a hapax legomenon in the Psalter but a favorite verb of Second Isaiah does not necessarily imply literary dependence of the psalmist upon the prophet.

with victory. Or "his victory," since *t*ᵉ*šū'āh* can well share the suffix of first-colon *'ammō,* "his people."

5. *their Glorious One.* As Yahweh delights in his people (vs. 4), so should the Israelites exult in their Glorious One, who is here contrasted with vs. 8, *nikb*ᵉ*dēhem,* "their nobles." The divine appellative *kābōd,* which shares the suffix of second-colon *miškᵉbōtām,* "their couches," thus maintaining a 9:9 syllable count, is documented at Ps iii 4. This colon thus repeats the invitation of vs. 2, and Hos vii 14 can be cited for the exegesis of the entire verse, "They do not cry to me from their heart, but they wail upon their couches."

sing for joy on their couches. The true purport of this clause becomes clearer upon comparison with such texts as Pss iv 5 (see comments there), vi 7, lxiii 7; Hos vii 14 (cited in preceding NOTE); UT, Krt:27–29, which reveal that the bedroom was a proper place for the expression of emotions most deeply felt.

6. *High praises.* Comparing plural *rōm*ᵉ*mōt* with singular *rōmām,* "sound of music," discussed at Ps lxvi 17.

from their throat. Or "in their throat." Cf. Ps cxv 7, *lō' yehgū big*ᵉ*rōnām,* "They emit no sound from their throats."

a two-edged sword. While shouting the praises of God, the dancers brandished swords in a type of sword dance known from Song of Sol vii 1, *meḥōlet hammaḥanāyīm,* "the dance between the two camps," and perhaps recognizable in Job xxi 12, *yiśśe'ū ketōp wekīnnōr weyiśmeḥū leqōl 'ūgāb,* "They take up the scimitar [cf. Ugar. *ktp//ṣmd*] and lyre; they make joyful dance to the sound of the pipe."

sword . . . hand. The third NOTE on Ps cxliv 10 quotes the Ugaritic text collocating *ḥrb,* "sword, knife," with *yd,* "hand."

7\. *the nations . . . the peoples.* The contents of this hymn do not permit certain identification of the adversaries intended. Cf., however, the next NOTE.

8\. *their nobles.* Literally "their honored ones," the nobles bound by chains cut a sorry figure in front of the Glorious One of Israel. In Isa xxiii 8 the merchants of Tyre are termed *nikbaddē 'āreṣ,* "the honored ones of the city." It is possible that in the psalmist's term there is a clue toward the identification of the enemy nations.

iron shackles. The construct chain *kablē barzel* helps identify the literary figure examined in the last NOTE on Ps cv 18.

9\. *on them.* 11QPs[a] *bhm* serves to safeguard MT *bāhem* against its proposed deletion by BH[3]. BHS correctly drops mention of proposed deletion.

the verdict written. Consult the introductory NOTE for one possible interpretation of a much-disputed phrase. Some argue that it refers to the judgment pronounced by Yahweh and recorded in his book for execution at the proper time, while others see here an allusion to the prophetic oracles against the nations.

honor for all his devoted. Resuming the thought of vs. 4b, the poet reminds Israel that its true glory lies in executing Yahweh's decrees regarding the heathen nations.

his devoted. With this term the psalmist binds the last line to the first.

Praise Yah! This summons, missing in LXX but confirmed by 11QPs[a], serves, with vs. 1, "Praise Yah!" to frame the psalm.

PSALM 150
(cl 1–6)

1 Praise Yah!
Praise El in his sanctuary,
praise him in his vaulted fortress.
2 Praise him for his might,
praise him according to his exceeding greatness.
3 Praise him by blowing the trumpet,
praise him with harp and lyre.
4 Praise him with tambour and dance,
praise him with strings and pipe.
5 Praise him with clashing cymbals,
praise him with clanging cymbals.
6 Let everything that breathes praise Yah!
Praise Yah!

NOTES

cl. Since it serves as a doxology to the entire Psalter, this hymn is more elaborate than those doxologies concluding the first four books of the Psalter: xli 14, lxxii 18–20, lxxxix 53, and cvi 48. In this hymn the psalmist invites every living being to praise Yahweh with every musical instrument. Like the other Hallel psalms at the end of the Psalter (cxlv–cxlix), this one seems to have been intended originally for liturgical use, and to have been chosen as the final doxology because of its evident fitness. In 11QPs[a], fully preserved Ps cl is immediately followed by a non-canonical composition called "Hymn to the Creator."

1. *El.* 11QPs[a] *'l* sustains MT *'ēl* against Syr. and *Juxta Hebraeos* which read *yāh.*

his sanctuary. As argued at Ps lx 8, *qodšō* designates God's celestial dwelling, scarcely "his Temple on earth," as unwarrantedly translated by JB. BJ more prudently renders it "son sanctuaire," but without a note explaining which sanctuary is meant. The strict synonymous parallelism, not only of vs. 2 which speaks of God, but also of the entire hymn, strongly urges the recognition of synonymous parallelism in vs. 1 as well.

Thus the balance between *qodšō*, "his sanctuary," and *r^eqīa^' 'uzzō*, "his vaulted fortress," is similar to the pairing of "heavens" and "heights" in the related summons of Ps cxlviii 1.

his vaulted fortress. The first NOTE on Ps viii 3 studies this definition of *r^eqīa^' 'uzzō*, which has been adopted by J. A. Soggin, *Biblica* 47 (1966), 423. The difficulties inherent in this phrase can be appreciated by comparison with the version of Briggs, "[Praise Him for] the spreading out of His strength."

2. *his might.* In vs. 1 there is assonance in the endings of *qodšō*, "his sanctuary," and *'uzzō*, "his . . . fortress," and the same assonance can be maintained in our verse by reading Phoenician feminine singular *g^ebūrōtō*, "his might"//*gudlō*, "his greatness." Both MT and 11QPs^a read plural *g^ebūrōtāyw*, "his mighty deeds," but Syr. has the singular form. Consult the second NOTE on Ps cvi 2.

according to (his) exceeding. 11QPs^a *krwb* supports MT *k^erōb* against seven manuscripts and Syr., which read *b^erōb* "because of (his) exceeding."

3. *by blowing the trumpet.* 11QPs^a seems to preserve the preferable reading in *btqw' šwpr*, an infinitive construct followed by its object, whereas MT *b^etēqa' šōpār* creates the noun *tēqa'*, "blast," that is elsewhere unattested. The Qumranic reading thus recovers a phrase identical with Isa xviii 3, *t^eqōa^' šōpar*, "the blowing of the trumpet."

6. *Praise Yah!* Like Pss cxlvi–cxlix, this hymn opens and closes with the invitation *hal^elū yāh*, thus establishing an inclusion.

The Grammar of the Psalter

By Mitchell Dahood, S.J., and Tadeusz Penar

The third edition of Rudolph Meyer's *Hebräische Grammatik* (Berlin: Band I, 1966; Band II, 1969) is the first Hebrew grammar which attempts systematically to incorporate the results of Ugaritic and Phoenician studies. One of the principal differences between this and the two earlier editions is the sharp increase in the number of references to Gordon's *Ugaritic Manual* (Rome, 1955) and *Ugaritic Textbook* (Rome, 1965, with supp. 1967) and to J. Friedrich's *Phönizisch-punische Grammatik* (Rome, 1951). A Northwest Semitic orientation thus characterizes Meyer's third edition, just as it marks the third edition of W. Baumgartner's *Hebräisches und aramäisches Lexikon zum Alten Testament* (fasc. 1; Leiden, 1967). To make the grammatical and stylistic data acquired by the Northwest Semitic approach to the Psalter more accessible to Hebraists, my research assistant, Tadeusz Penar, and I have prepared this Grammar of the Psalter. It should be a good companion to four recent studies which have systematically examined the biblical text in the light of Northwest Semitic grammar: H. J. van Dijk, *Ezekiel's Prophecy on Tyre* (*Ez. 26, 1–28, 19*): *A New Approach* (Rome, 1968); N. J. Tromp, *Primitive Conceptions of Death and the Nether World in the Old Testament* (Rome, 1969); A. C. M. Blommerde, *Northwest Semitic Grammar and Job* (Rome, 1969); and W. A. van der Weiden, *Le Livre des Proverbes: Notes philologiques* (Rome, 1970). This Grammar should also go far toward meeting the needs listed by F. I. Andersen in his review of *Psalms II* in JBL 88 (1969), 210: "Things to be done include: systematic testing of the Hebrew lexicon in the light of NW Semitic linguistics and comparative literature; systematic rewriting of Hebrew grammar, especially syntax, since Dahood's scattered remarks open up many new questions: especially the importance of syntax in poetic structure; thorough re-evaluation of literary art in Israel (rhetorical criticism and transmission history) in the light of new meanings."

We have chosen to list only those grammatical and stylistic phenomena which, to some degree, have been elucidated by the study of the Psalter within the Northwest Semitic purview. Since this appendix was put together after AB volumes *PSALMS I* and *II* were already in print, it offers the opportunity to include revised translations of some dozen verses or cola differing from the translations found there. In these instances, we have indicated that the translations are revisions.

CONTENTS

I. ORTHOGRAPHY

Defective spelling
of the first person singular in *qtl* forms

Ps v 6 *śn't* (MT *śānē'tā*) for *śn'ty* "I hate"
xvi 2 *'mrt* (MT *'āmart*) for *'mrty* "I said"
xxxviii 9 *nhmt* (MT *minnah*^{a}*mat*) for *nhmty* "I moan," attaching the initial *mem* to the preceding word as enclitic
cxl 13 *yd't* (MT *yāda'ti*) for *yd'ty* "I know"

Defective spelling
of other verbal forms

Ps ix 18 *kl* (MT *kol*) for *klw* "let them perish"
x 4 *'lhym mkl* (MT *'*^{e}*lōhīm kol*) for *'lhym mklh* "God will (not) upset"
xvi 5 *mnt* (MT *m*^{e}*nāt*) for *mnyt* "you have portioned out"
xviii 15 *rb* (MT *rāb*) for *rbh* "he multiplied"
lxv 6 *mbṭḥ* (MT *mibṭāḥ*) for *mbṭyḥ* "who pacified"
lxxii 2 *ydyn* (MT *yādīn*) for *ydynh* "that he may govern" (subjunctive)

Defective spelling
of the suffix *-ī/ -nī*

Ps xvi 6 *nḥlt* (MT *naḥ*^{a}*lāt*) for *nḥlty* "my property"
lxxi 20 *hr'ytn* (MT *hir'ītanīw*), attaching the final *waw* to the next word as emphatic, for *hr'ytny* "you made me see"

Defective spelling
of the suffix *-ekā, -ēkem*

Ps xvii 14 *ṣpynk for ṣpynyk* "your treasured ones"
xlviii 11 *kšmk* (MT *k*^{e}*šim*^{e}*kā*) for *kšmyk* "as your heavens"
lxiii 5 *bšmk* (MT *b*^{e}*šim*^{e}*kā*) for *bšmyk* "in your heaven"
cxxxiv 2 *ydkm* (MT *y*^{e}*dēkem*) for *ydykm*, "your hands"
cxxxix 5 *kpkh* (MT *kappekāh*) for *kpykh*, "your palms"

Defective spelling
of the suffix *-ō*

Ps liv 7 — *b'mt* (MT *ba'amitekā,* parsing the final *k* as emphatic) for *b'mtw* "in his fidelity"
lxviii 25 — *bqdš* (MT *baqqōdeš*) for *bqdšw* "from his sanctuary"
ciii 5 — *bṭwb* (MT *baṭṭōb*) for *bṭwbw* "with his beauty"

Defective spelling
of the suffix *-āyw*

Ps x 4(5) — *drkw* for *drkyw* "his wealth"
lxviii 5 — *šmw* (MT *šemō*) for *šmyw* "his heavens"
xci 4 — *b'brtw* (MT *be'ebrātō*) for *b'brtyw* "with his pinions"

Defective spelling
of various expressions

b'dy (MT *ba'adī*) for *b'wdy* "as long as I live"
Pss iii 4, cxxxviii 8
'dyk (MT *'edyēk*) for *'wdyk* "your eternity"
Ps ciii 5
't (MT *'ēt*) for *'th* "now"
Pss iv 8, lxix 14
'k (MT *'ak*) for *'yk* "O how!"
Ps lxxv 9
'lymw (MT *'ēlēmō*) for *'ylymw* "their rams," i.e., lieutenants
Ps ii 5
'lm (MT *'ēlem*) for *'ylym* "rams=leaders"
Ps lviii 2
h'mnm (MT *ha'umnām*) for *h'mwnym* "O counselors!"
Ps lviii 2
rhbm (MT *rohbām*) for *rhbym* "arrogance"
Ps xc 10
ḥsd (MT *ḥesed*) for *ḥsyd* "the Kind One"
Ps cxli 5
'mrtk (MT *'imrātekā*) for *'mrwtyk* "your words"
Ps cxix 103

Single writing of consonant
where morphology requires two

Ps x 4 — *'yn 'lhym kl* for *'yn 'lhym mkl;* read *'ēn 'elōhīm mekalle,* "God will not upset" (MT *'ēn 'elōhīm kol*)
lxv 10 — *wtšqqh rbt* for *wtšqqh hrbt;* read *witešōqeqehā harribbōtā,* "make her skip with mirth, rain down" (MT *wattešōqeqehā rabbat*)
lxxxi 14 — *lw 'my šm' ly* for *lw 'my yšm' ly;* read *lū 'ammī yišma' lī,* "If only my people would listen to me" (MT *lū 'ammī šōmēa' lī*)
lxxxiv 6 — *'dm 'wz lw bk* for *'dm m'wz lw bk;* read *'ādām mā'ōz lō bāk,* "the man whose refuge is in you" (MT *'ādām 'ōz lō bāk*)
lxxxviii 6 — *ḥllym škby* for *ḥllym mškby;* read *ḥalālīm miškābī* "the slaughtered / My couch" (MT *ḥalālīm šōkebē*)

lxxxix 43 *kl 'wybyw* for *kl' 'wybyw;* read *kelē' 'ōyebāyw* "both hands of his foes" (MT *kol 'ōyebāyw*)

48 *'ny mh ḥld* for *'ny ym hḥld;* read *'ōnī yemē haḥāled,* "my sorrow, the few days of my life" (MT *'anī meh ḥāled*)

xciv 10 *'dm d't* for *'dm md't;* read *'ādām middā'at,* "mankind without knowledge" (MT *'ādām dā'at*)

civ 12–13 *qwl mšqh* for *qwlm mšqh;* read *qōlām mašqeh,* "their voice. Who waters . . ." (MT *qōl mašqeh*)

cv 40 *š'l wyb'* for *š'lw wyb';* read *šā'alū wayyābē',* "they asked and he brought" (MT *šā'al wayyābē'*)

cvii 20 *wymlṭm mšḥytwtm* for *wymlṭ mšḥytwtm;* read *wīmalleṭēm miššeḥītōtām,* "To relieve them of their boils" (MT *wīmmalleṭ miššeḥītōtām*).

cxiv 3 *r'h wyns* for *r'hw wyns;* read *rā'āhū wayyānōs,* "(When the sea) saw him, it fled" (MT *rā'āh wayyānōs*)

cxxxvii 5 *'m 'škḥk yrwšlm* for *'m 'škḥky yrwšlm;* read *'im 'eškāḥēkī yerūšālēm,* "Should I forget you, O Jerusalem" (MT *'im 'eškāḥēk yerūšālāim*)

cxxxix 14 *nwr'wt* for *nwr' 't;* read *nōrā' 'attā,* "you are awesome" (MT *nōrā'ōt;* 11QPs[a] *nwr' 'th*)

cxli 5 *'l yny r'šy* for *'l ynyr r'šy;* read *'al yānīr rō'šī,* "never let my head glisten" (MT *'al yānī rō'šī*)

II. PHONETICS

Consonants:
Prothetic *aleph*

Ps li 9 *'āzōb* (MT *'ēzōb*) "gushing water" from *zwb* "to gush, flow"

lviii 3 *'āreṣ* "caprice" from *rāṣāh* "to be pleased with"

lxviii 22 *'ašāmāyw* "his heavens"

lxix 5 *'āz* "this"

cii 24(25) *'emar* (MT *'ōmar*) "vigor" from *mrr* "to strengthen"

Consonants:
Interchange of *b* and *p*

zarzīp=zarzīb (<*zārab* "to be burned, scorched) scorched land"
Ps lxxii 6 *zarzīpē 'āreṣ* (MT *zarzīp 'āreṣ*) "scorched lands"

ḥāpaš=ḥābaš "to bind up, heal"
Ps lxxviii 7 *wīḥuppaš* (MT *wayeḥappēś*) *rūḥī,* "that my spirit might be healed"

kelōb=kēlūp "ax"
Ps xxii 21 *miyyad kelōb* (MT *keleb*) "from the blade of the ax"

nābak=nāpak "to pour, gush forth"
Pss lxix 11 *wā'ebbōkāh* (MT *wā'ebkeh*) "so I poured out"
lxxxiv 7 *hibbīkā'* (MT *habbākā'*) "may he cause to flow"

nāṭab=nāṭap "to drop, drip, discourse"
Ps xxxix 3 *miṭṭōb* "(I refrained) from speaking"

'arābōt=Ugar. *'rpt* "clouds"
Ps lxviii 5 *lārōkēb bā'arābōt* "for the Rider of the Clouds"

šēpeṭ=šēbeṭ "tribe"
Ps cxlviii 11 *wekol šipṭē 'āreṣ* (MT *wekol šōpeṭē 'āreṣ*) "and all tribes of earth"

šāpar=*šābar* "to measure, trace out"
Ps xvi 6 *šāp*^{e}*rāh* "he has traced out (my property)"

Consonants:
Interchange of *d* and *z*

ḥdy=*ḥāzāh*, "to see, gaze"
Ps iv 9 *yaḥdāw*, "his face"
xxi 7 *t*^{e}*ḥaddēhū*, "you will make him gaze"
xxii 21 *y*^{e}*ḥīdāh*, "face,"//*nepeš*, "neck"
xxxiii 15 *yeḥde* (MT *yaḥad*), "he inspects"
xxxv 17 *y*^{e}*ḥīdāh*, "face,"//*nepeš*, "neck"
xlix 11 *yaḥad*, "he gazes,"//*yir'eh*, "he sees"
cxxxix 16 *lō' 'eḥāde* (MT *lō' 'eḥad*), "I was not seen"

mē'ād (MT *m*^{e}*'ōd*)=*mē'āz*, "of old"
Pss xciii 5
cxxxix 14

dnb=*znb*
Ps cx 6 *y*^{e}*dannēb gōyīm* (MT *yādīn baggōyīm*), "he routed nations"

Vowels:
Shift from *ā* to *ō*

Ps xxii 9 *gōl* for classical Heb. *gāl*, "let (El Yahweh) rejoice"; *gōl* parses as precative perfect of *gīl* (revised analysis)
lxix 21 *nwd* (MT *nūd*) to be read *nōd*=classical Heb. *nād* the qal participle of *nūd*, "to grieve, lament." *nōd*/*nād* "a comforter"
lxxxiii 8 *w*^{e}*'immōnnū '*^{a}*mālēq* (MT *w*^{e}*'ammōn wa'*^{a}*mālēq*), "and with it Amalek"; *'immōnnū*=*'immānnū*<*'immān-hū*
lxxxvii 6 *k*^{e}*tōb* for classical Heb. *k*^{e}*tāb* "register"
xcvi 2 *miyyōm l*^{e}*yōm* for classical Heb. *miyyām l*^{e}*yām* "from sea to sea"
xcix 4 *'ōz melek* for classical Heb. *'āz melek* "the strongest king"
cxxvi 4 *šōbāh* (MT *šūbāh*)=*šābāh* "he restored," third person masculine *qatala*

Vowels:
Shift from *ō* to *ū* in infinitives absolute

Ps xlix 4 *hāgūt* for *hāgōt* (revised analysis proposed at Ps ciii 14)
ciii 14 *zākūr* for *zākōr*
cxii 7 *bāṭū*^{a}*ḥ* for *bāṭō*^{a}*ḥ*
cxxxix 20 *nāśū'* for *nāśō'*

Diphthongs:
ay reduced to *ē*

In Northern duals:
'ād "hand"
Ps xvii 4 *p*^{e}*'ullōt 'ādēm* (MT *'ādām*), "the works of (your) hands"
lxviii 19 *bā'ādēm* (MT *bā'ādām*), "from their hands"

yād "hand"
Ps xvi 4 *middēm* (MT *middām*), "from (my) hands"
leḥī "jaw, cheek"
Ps lvi 2 *leḥēm* (MT *lōḥēm*), "both jaws"
cii 5(6) *leḥēm* (MT *laḥmī*), "my jaws," attaching the final *yod* to the next word

In other substantives:
Ps cxxvii 2 *šēnā'*, "prosperity," instead of *šaynā'*

Diphthongs:
aw reduced to *ō*

Ps lviii 3, lxiv 7 *'ōlōt* for classical Heb. *'awlāh* "malice, crime"
xcii 16 Ketiv: *'ōlātāh* for classical Heb. *'awlātāh* "iniquity"
lxviii 26 *betōk* for classical Heb. *battāwek* "in the middle"

III. PRONOUNS

Independent personal pronoun in the oblique case

Ps lxiii 2 *'attāh 'ašaḥēr kī* (MT *'ašaḥareka*) *ṣāme'āh lekā napšī*, "For you I long, my soul ardently thirsts for you"
cxxxvii 1 *bezokrēnū 'att* (MT *'et*) *ṣiyyōn*, "When we remembered you, Zion"
6 *'im lō' 'ezkerēkī 'im lō' 'a'aleh 'att* (MT *'et*) *yerūšālaim*, "Should I remember you not! If I do not raise you, O Jerusalem!"

Polite substitutes for pronouns

1. *'ebed* "servant"

In parallelism with suffix:
Ps xix 14 "Above all keep your servant (*'abdekā*) from the presumptuous ones, lest they rule over me (*yimšelū bī*)"
xxvii 9 "Turn not your face from me (*mimmēnnī*), repel not in anger your servant (*'abdekā*)"
xxxi 17 "Let your face shine upon your servant (*'al 'abdekā*); save me (*hōšī'ēnī*) in your kindness"
lxix 18 "Turn not your face from your servant (*mē'abdekā*); because distress is mine (*ṣar lī*), quickly answer me (*mahēr 'anēnī*)"
lxxxvi 2 "Protect my life (*napšī*) for I am (*'ānī*) devoted to you, save your own servant (*'abdekā 'attāh*) who trusts in you, my God"
cxix 135 "Make your face shine upon your servant (*be'abdekā*), and teach me (*welammedēnī*) your statutes"

Not in parallelism with suffix:
Pss xix 12, xc 13

2. *ḥāsīd* "the devoted one"

In parallelism with suffix:

Ps iv 4 "And recognize that Yahweh will work wonders for the one devoted to him (*ḥāsīd lō*), Yahweh will hear me when I call (*b^eqor'ī*) to him"

3. *ṣaddīq* "the just man"

Ps v 13 "For you will bless the just man (*ṣaddīq*) yourself, O Yahweh, as with a shield you will surround him (*ta'ṭ^erennū*) with your favor"

Note the use of the first person in vss. 2–9 and the Syr. reading "you will surround me"

4. *nepeš* "soul"="me"

In parallelism with suffix:

Ps lxix 19 "Draw near, O El (*'ēl* for MT *'el*), redeem me (*napšī go'lāh* for MT *napšī g^e'ālāh*); ransom me (*p^edēnī*) from the abode (*lim^e'ōn* for MT *l^ema'an*) of my Foe"

5. *melek* "king"

Ps lxi 7 "Add days to the king's days (*y^emē melek*)"

Note the use of the first person in vss. 2–6, 9

6. *'ōśēh ṣ^edāqāh* "the doer of justice"

Ps cvi 3 "How blest the alert to what is right, the doer of justice (*'ōśēh ṣ^edāqāh*) at all times!" Cf. vs. 4: *zokrēnī*, "remember me," and *poqdēnī*, "visit me"

Possessive suffixes:
third person singular suffix *-ī/-y*

Ps ii 6	*malkī* "his king"
	har qodšī "his holy mountain"
xiv 4	*'ammī* "his people" (cf. Isa liii 8)
xvi 7	*kilyōtāy* (vocalize *kilyōtēy*) "his kidneys"
8	*mīmīnī* "from his right hand"
xviii 33	*darkī* "his dominion"; cf. II Sam xxii 33 *drkw*
34	*bāmōtay* (vocalize *bāmōtēy*) "his heights"
xxiv 4	*napšī* "his mind"
xxv 17	*l^ebābī* "his throat" (revised translation: "My Adversary [Death] opened wide his throat)
xxvii 8	*pānāy* (vocalize *pānēy*) "his face"
xxxii 9	*q^erōb 'ly* (MT *'ēlekā*) "approach him"
xxxvi 2	*b^eqereb libbī* "within his heart"
xlii 5	*w^e'ešp^ekā 'ālay* (vocalize *'ālēy*) *napšī* "and I shall pour out my soul before him"
xlvi 5	*mišk^enī* (MT *mišk^enē*) "his habitation"
l 5	*lī* "before him"
	ḥ^asīdāy (vocalize *ḥ^asīdēy*) "his devoted ones"
	b^erītī "a covenant with him"
lxi 3	*mimmennī* "from it"
lxviii 11	*'ānēy* (MT *'ānī*) "its inhabitants"
31	*'eglēy* "its calves"

brṣy "in his lust"
34 *lārōkēb biš^{e}mēy* "Behold the Rider of his heavens"
36 *mimmiqdāšey* (MT *mimmiqdāšekā*) "for his sanctuary"
lxxvi 4 *riš^{e}pēy* "his thunderbolts"
lxxvii 3 *yādī* "his hand"
napšī "his mind"
lxxvii 11 *ḥ^{a}lōtī* (MT *ḥallōtī*) "his sickness"
lxxviii 9 *nōš^{e}qēy* "his bowmen"
49 *mal'^{a}kēy* "his angels"
xcvii 10 *'hby* "who loves," *-y* expressing the dative of advantage
ci 5 *m^{e}lōš^{e}nī* (Ketiv), "whoever . . . slandered," *-y* expressing the dative of advantage
civ 13 *ma'^{a}śēy* (parsing the final *k* of MT *ma'^{a}śēkā* as emphatic), "his storehouses"
cvii 41 *m^{e}'ōnī* (MT *mē'ōnī*) "his habitation"
cix 31 *miššōp^{e}ṭī* (MT *miššōp^{e}ṭē*) "from his judge"
cx 4 *'al dibrātī* "according to his pact"
malkī ṣedeq "his legitimate king"
cxvi 1 *qōlī taḥ^{a}nūnēy* (MT *taḥ^{a}nūnāy*) "my plea for his mercy"
12 *kol tagmūlōhī* "all his favors"
15 *b^{e}'ēnēy* "in his eyes"
cxli 6 *'^{a}mārēy* (MT *'^{a}māray*) "his words"

Parallelism between the third person suffixes *-ō* and *-i/-y*

Ps xviii 24 *'immō//'^{a}wōnī,* "with him//offend him"
civ 13 *mē'^{a}liyyōtāyw//mipp^{e}rī ma'^{a}śēy* (MT *ma'^{a}śekā*), "from his upper chambers//with the supplies from his storehouses"
Note: The final *k* of *m'šyk* parses as emphatic introducing the next colon
cv 6 *'abdō//b^{e}ḥīrī* (MT *b^{e}ḥīrāyw*), "his servant//his chosen one"
18 *raglēy* (MT *raglāyw*)//*napšō,* "his feet//his neck"
cvi 12 *d^{e}bārēy* (MT *d^{e}bārāyw*)//*t^{e}hillātō,* "his words//his praise"
13 *ma'^{a}śēy* (MT *ma'^{a}śāyw*//*'^{a}ṣātō,* "his works//his advice"
cxiii 8 *l^{e}hōšībī . . . 'ammō,* "to seat him . . . his people"
cxiv 2 *qodšō//memš^{e}lōtī* (MT *mamš^{e}lōtāyw*), "his sanctuary//his dominion"
cxix 2 *'ēdōtēy* (MT *'ēdōtāyw*) . . . *yidr^{e}šūhū,* "his stipulations . . . (they) search for him"
cxxxi 2 *'immō//'ālēy* (MT *'ālay*), "his mother//with him"
cxliv 10 *lammalkī-m* (MT *lamm^{e}lākīm*)//*'abdō,* "to his king//his servant"

Dative suffixes:
with substantives

Ps ii 8 *še'al māmōnī* (MT *mimmennī*) "ask wealth of me"
xvi 4 *niskēhem* "(I surely will not pour) libations to them"
xx 3 *yišlaḥ 'ezr^{e}kā* "May he send you help"
l 5 *kōr^{e}tē b^{e}rītī* "who made a covenant with him"

lxxvii 9 *'ōmer* "visions from him," with *'ōmer* sharing the suffix of *ḥasdō* in the first colon

14 *gedōlekā 'elōhīm* (MT *gādōl kē'lōhīm*) "(What god) is greater than you, O God?"

civ 27 *lātēt 'oklām*, "to give them food"

cv 19 *'ad 'ēt bō' debārō*, "Till the moment the word came to him (i.e., to Pharaoh)"

cix 21 *'aśēh 'ōtī* (MT *'ittī*), "Work a miracle for me!"

cxv 7 *yedēhem welō' yemīšūn*, "They have hands, but do not feel"

raglēhem welō' yehallēkū, "They have feet, but do not walk"

cxxi 1 *mē'ayin yābō' 'ezrī*, "whence will help come to me?"

cxlviii 14 *'am qerōbō*, "the people close to him"

Dative suffixes:
with verbs

Ps v 5 *lō' yegūrekā rā'* "an evil man cannot be your guest"

xviii 29 *kī 'attāh tā'īr* "indeed you shine for me," the dative suffix is to be logically supplied from *nērī*, "my lamp"

xxi 4 *kī teqaddemennū* "but you set before him (the blessings of prosperity)"

7 *kī tešītēhū* "indeed you will give him (blessings forever)"

xxii 26 *mī'ētīkā* (MT *mē'ittekā*) "one hundred times will I repeat to you"

xxxii 5 *'ōdī'akā* "(my sin) I made known to you"

lō' kissītī "I did not hide (my guilt) from you," with the suffix supplied from *'ōdī'akā*

xxxv 8 *tebō'ēhū šō'āh* "may the pit come upon him"

xxxvi 12 *'al tebō'ēnī* "let not (the foot of the presumptuous) overtake me"

xliv 16 *kussetanī* (for MT *kissātenī*) "(my shamefacedness) is exposed before me"

18 *bā'atnū* "(Every indignity) has come upon us"

lvii 10 *'azammerekā* "I will sing to you"

lx 3, 12 *zenaḥtānū* "you were angry with us"

3 *peraṣtānū* "and you ran from us"

11 *mī yōbīlēnī* "Who will bring me (the Rock City)?"

mī nāḥanī "Who will offer me (Edom's throne) as tribute?" Cf. Ps cviii 11

lxiv 9 *wayyakšīlūhū* "(The Most High) shall make (slanderers) stumble"

lxvii 2 *'ātānū* (MT *'ittānū*) "may he come to us"

lxix 36 *wīrūšūhā* (MT *wīrēšūhā*) "those expelled from it"

lxxiii 27 *reḥēqekā* "those who go far from you"

lxxiv 9 *welō' 'ātānū* (MT *'ittānū*) "and has not come to us"

lxxviii 55 *wayyappīlēm* "and (with a measuring cord) made (their patrimony) fall to them"

lxxx 4, 8, 20 *hašībēnū* "return to us!"

lxxxv 5	*šûbēnû* "return to us!"
lxxxix 27	*hû' yiqrā'ēnî* "he shall cry to me"
xc 17	*kônenēhû* "may he sustain for his good (the work of our hands)," the suffix *-hû* is understood as expressing the dative of advantage
xciv 20	*hayeḥobrekā* "Can (the seat of iniquity) associate with you?"
xcvii 10	*'hby* "who loves," *y* expressing dative of advantage
xcix 8	*'alîlōtām* "you dealt severely with them," the suffix expresses here the dative of disadvantage
cii 17	*nir'āhā* (MT *nir'āh*) *bikebōdō,* "he appears to her (i.e., Zion) in his glory"
cvii 39	*wayyāšōḥûm 'ōṣer* (MT *wayyāšōḥû mē'ōṣer*) *rā'āh weyāgōn* "and declined from them oppression, peril, and sorrow"
cviii 11	*mî yōbîlēnî,* "Who will bring me (the Fortress City?)"
	mî nāḥanî, "Who will offer me (Edom's throne) as tribute?" Cf. Ps lx 11
12	*halō' 'elōhîm zenaḥtānû,* "But you, O God—will you be angry with us?"
cix 17	*wayye'ehab qelālāh wattebō'ēhû,* "Since he has loved cursing, it has come to him"
cxix 14	*śāśîkā 'al* (attaching the *k* of MT *ke'al* to the preceding word) *kol hôn,* "I rejoice in you more than in all riches"
41	*wîbō'ēnî* (MT *wîbō'ûnî*) *ḥasdekā* (MT *ḥasādekā*), "And let your kindness come to me"
77	*yebō'ûnî raḥamekā,* "Let your mercies come to me"
121	*'āśîtāy* (MT *'āśîtî*) *mišpāṭ wāṣedeq,* "Defend for me my right and my just cause"
cxxxviii 1	*'azammerekā,* "I sing to you"
cxxxix 10	*gam šām yādekā tenîḥēnî* (MT *tanḥēnî*), "Even there your left hand you would lower upon me"
12	*welaylāh kayyôm ye'îrekā* (MT *yā'îr ka-*), "since the Night shines for you like the day"

Dative suffixes:
expressing the agent

Ps xxxvii 22	*mebōrākāyw* "those blessed by him"
	ûmequllālāyw "but those cursed by him"
l 15	*tekubbedēnî* (MT *tekabbedēnî*) "you will be feasted by me"
23	*yekubbedānenî* (MT *yekabbedānenî*) "he will be feasted by me"
lxiii 11	*ygyrhw* "may they be smitten by him"
lxxii 17	*ye'uššerûhû* (MT *ye'aššerûhû*) "by him (all nations) made happy"
lxxiv 19	*nepeš tûrekā* (MT *tōrekā*) "those taught by you"
lxxxi 8	*'ebbāḥēnekā* (MT *'ebḥānekā*) "I was provoked by you"
lxxxvii 1	*yesûdātō* "founded by him"
cv 9	*šebû'ātō,* "(his covenant) sworn by him"
19	*'imrat yhwh ṣerûpathû* (MT *ṣerāpātehû*), "Yahweh's promise was proved true by him"

Interchange of suffix and article:
suffix serving as article

Ps xvii 11–12	*bā'āreṣ dimyōnō* "into the very Land of Perdition"
xxxi 20	*ṭūbekā* "the good things"
xlix 6	*'ōqebay* (MT *'aqēbay*) "the slanderers"
liii 4	*kullō* "each one"; cf. Ps xiv 3, *hakkōl*
lvi 5	*dōberō* (MT *debārō*) "O slanderer!"

Interchange of suffix and article:
article serving as suffix

Ps iii 9	*hayešū'āh//birekāteka,* "your salvation//your blessing"
xxxii 17	*hassūs//ḥēlō,* "his horse//his might"
lv 23	*haššōlēk* (MT *hašlēk*)//*yōhēbekā* (MT *yehābekā*), "Your Provider//Your Benefactor"
lxxxv 13	*haṭṭōb//yebūlāh,* "his rain//its produce"
lxxxix 48	*'ōnī* (MT *'anī*)//*haḥāled* (MT *meh ḥāled*), "my sorrow//(the few days) of my life"
xc 16	*po'olekā//hadderek* (MT *hadārekā*), "your achievement//your dominion"
cxxvi 6	*mešek hazzāra'//'alummōtāyw,* "his seed pouch//his sheaves"

IV. NOUNS

Feminine absolute singulars:
in *-t*

Ps x 3	*ta'awat* "desire"
lviii 5	*ḥēmāt* (MT *ḥamat*) "venom"
9	*'ēšet* "woman"
lx 13	*'ezrāt* "help"
lxi 1	*negīnat* "a stringed instrument"
lxxiv 19	*leḥayyāt* (MT *leḥayyat*) "to a wild beast"
cxxxii 4	*šēnāt* (MT *šenat*) "sleep"

Feminine absolute singulars:
in *-ōt*

Note: The symbol * indicates that this substantive may be an intensive plural

Ps x 7	*mirmōt* "deceit"
xii 4 / lxxiii 18	*ḥalāqōt** "Perdition"
xlv 15	*betūlōt* "maiden"
xlix 4	*ḥokmōt* "wisdom"
	tebūnōt "insight"=Ps lxxviii 72
12	*'adāmōt* "earth"
liii 7	*yešū'ōt* "salvation"=Ps lxxiv 12
lv 22	*mēḥem'ōt* (MT *maḥmā'ōt*)<*ḥem'ōt* "cream, butter"
lviii 3	*'ōlōt* "malice"

lxviii 12 *'imrāh m^{e}baśś^{e}rōt* (MT *'ōmer ham^{e}baśś^{e}rōt*) "the word rejoicing"
21 *mōšā'ōt* "salvation"
tōṣā'ōt "escape"
36 *ta'^{a}ṣūmōt* "valor"
lxxiii 18 *maššū'ōt** "Desolation"
22 *b^{e}hēmōt** "beast"
lxxviii 15 *t^{e}hōmōt rabbāh* "the vast wasteland"
lxxxviii 9 *tō'ēbōt* "abomination"
lxxxix 26 *n^{e}hārōt* "river"
civ 8 *b^{e}qā'ōt* "the nether chasm"
cvi 2 *g^{e}būrōt* "might"
cxiv 2 *memš^{e}lōt* "dominion"
cxvi 13 *kōs y^{e}šū'ōt* "the chalice of salvation"
cxix 98 *miṣwōt* "commandment"
cxxxii 12 *'ēdōt* "stipulation"
cxl 11 *mah^{a}mōrōt* "the Miry Bog"
12 *madḥēpōt* "Exile"
cl 2 *g^{e}būrōtō* (MT *g^{e}būrōtāyw*), "his might"

Preservation of case endings:
the nominative *-ū*

Note: In all examples marked *, the use of the nominative after a preposition, which requires the genitive, is incorrect

Ps lix 10 *'uzzū* (MT *'uzzō*) *'ēlī kī 'eššāmērāh* (MT *'ēlekā 'ešmōrāh*), "My God is a fortress, truly am I protected"
11 *'^{e}lōhay ḥasdū* (MT *'^{e}lōhēy ḥasdīw*), "a rampart is my God"
lxxix 2 *l^{e}ḥay^{e}tū* (MT *l^{e}ḥay^{e}tō*) *'āreṣ*,* "to the beasts of the earth"
cxiv 8 *l^{e}ma'y^{e}nū* (MT *l^{e}ma'y^{e}nō*) *māyim*,* "into a flowing spring"
cxxii 3 *lāhū yāḥīdū* (MT *lāh yaḥdāw*),* "by him alone" (here the nominative ending has been preserved for metrical reasons)
cxl 9 *yārūmū*, "O Exalted!"

Preservation of case endings:
the genitive *-ī*

Ps xxvi 10 *bydyhm* "in whose left hand"
xliv 13 *bim^{e}ḥīrīhem* (MT *bim^{e}ḥīrēhem*) "(and you did not grow rich) from their price"
lxv 6 *w^{e}yam* (MT *yām*) *r^{e}ḥōqī-m* "(all the ends of the earth) and of the distant sea"; *mem* is enclitic
lxix 27 *ḥ^{a}lālī-kā* (MT *ḥ^{a}lālekā*) "(and told stories about the pain) of him you wounded"
lxxiv 13 *rā'šē tannīnī* (MT *tannīnīm*) "the heads of Tannin"
20 *mēḥōšēkī* (MT *maḥ^{a}šakkē*) "(the city is filled) with darkness"
lxxxiii 4 *'al ṣ^{e}pūnī-kā* (MT *ṣ^{e}pūnekā*) "against your treasure"
lxxxiv 11 *bḥrty* "in the Cemetery"
cv 27 *b^{e}midbāri* (MT *bām dibrē*) "in the wilderness"

30 *malkīhem* (MT *malkēhem*) "of their king"

cvi 7 *rōb ḥasdīkā* (MT *ḥ^{a}sādekā*) "an abundance of your kindness= your abounding kindness"

cxiii 5 *kayhwh . . . hammagbīhī lāšebet,* "like Yahweh . . . the One who is enthroned on high"

6 *hammašpīlī* "the One who stoops"

7 *m^{e}qīmī* "he lifts"

9 *mōšībī* "he founds"

cxiv 8 *hahōp^{e}kī* "who turns," in apposition with genitives *'ādōn* and *'^{e}lō^{a}h* in vs. 7

cxxiii 1 *'ēlekā . . . hayyōš^{e}bī baššāmāyim,* "to you . . . , who are enthroned in heaven"

cxxxviii 6 *mimmerḥāqī* (the final *-ī* coming from the following word *y^{e}yēdā'*) "from a distance"

Preservation of case endings:
the accusative *-ā*

Ps viii 8 *ṣōnāh* (MT *ṣōneh*) "(you put) small cattle"

lx 5 *qāšāh* "(you made your people drain) the cup"

lxviii 7 *baytāh* "(God who established) a home"

ṣ^{e}ḥīḥāh "the Wasteland"; this form is the direct object of *šāk^{e}nū,* "they were entombed." The nominative form is *ṣāḥīḥ,* "glaring surface," Ezek xxiv 7

lxxx 6 *dim'āh* "(You have fed us) tears (as our food)"

cxvi 15 *hammōtāh* (MT *hammāwtāh*) "(Yahweh considers precious) the death (of his devoted ones)"

The construct chain
with intervening preposition

Ps ix 10 }
x 1 } *l^{e}'ittōt baṣṣārāh,* "in times of trouble"

lxxiv 12 *malkē* (MT *malkī*) *miqqedem,* "the kings from the East"

Note: In this text the *mem* of *miqqedem* can be shifted to *malkē,* and parsed as enclitic: *malkē-m qedem.* Cf. H. D. Hummel, JBL 76 (1957), 97

lxxxiv 7 *'ibrē* (MT *'ōb^{e}rē*) *b^{e}'ēmeq,* "brooks in the valley"

xcii 13 *k^{e}'erez ball^{e}bānōn,* "like the cedar of Lebanon"

The construct chain
with intervening suffix

Ps xvi 8 *lin^{e}gīdī* (MT *l^{e}negdī*) *tāmīd,* "(I have chosen Yahweh) as my perpetual Leader." See second NOTE on Ps liv 5

xviii 18 *mē'ōy^{e}bay 'ōz* (MT *mē'ōy^{e}bī 'āz*) "from my powerful Foe"

xxxv 16 *lō'^{a}gay mā'ōg* (MT *la'^{a}gē mā'ōg*) "my encircling mockers"

19 *'ōy^{e}bay šeqer* "my treacherous foes"=Ps lxix 5

śōn^{e}'ay ḥnm "my stealthy enemies"=Ps lxix 5

xxxviii 20 *'ōy^{e}bay ḥayyīm* "my mortal foes"

śōn^{e}'ay šeqer "my treacherous enemies"

xlviii 15 *'^{e}lōhēnū 'ōlām wā'ed* "our eternal and everlasting God"
lxi 5 *b^{e}'ohol^{e}kā 'ōlāmīm* "in your eternal tent"
lxvi 7 *big^{e}būrātō 'ōlām* "from his eternal fortress"
lxxi 6 *t^{e}hillātī tāmīd* "my perpetual praise"
7 *maḥ^{a}sī 'ōz* "my fortress of refuge"
lxxxviii 16 *'ēmekā 'ōpānāh* (MT *'āpūnāh*) "the terrors of your wheel"
cii 24–25 *yāmay 'emār* (MT *yāmāy 'omar*) "my vigorous days"
cv 4 *pānāyw tāmīd,* "his perpetual presence"
cx 4 *malkī ṣedeq,* "his legitimate king"
cxl 10 *m^{e}sibbay 'āmāl* (MT *m^{e}sibbāy '^{a}mal*), "the mischief-makers who surround me"

The construct chain
with intervening suffix and preposition

Ps xvii 9 *'ōy^{e}bay b^{e}nepeš* "my deadly foes"

The construct chain
with intervening emphatic *kī*

Ps xxiv 6 *p^{e}nē-kī ya'^{a}qōb* (MT *pānekā ya'^{a}qōb*), "The Presence of Jacob"
lxviii 25 *hlykwty-k '^{e}lōhīm,* "the marches of God"
lxix 30 *y^{e}šū'āt^{e}-kī* (MT *y^{e}šū'āt^{e}kā*) *'^{e}lōhīm,* "God's help"
cxvi 19 *b^{e}tōkēkī y^{e}rūšālāim,* "in the midst of Jerusalem"
cxxii 2 *bš'ryk* (MT *biš^{e}'ārayik*) *y^{e}rūšālāim,* "within the gates of Jerusalem"
cxxxv 9 *b^{e}tōkēkī miṣrāyim,* "into the midst of Egypt"

The construct chain
with intervening enclitic *mem*

Ps xviii 16 *'^{a}pīqē-m yām* (MT *'^{a}pīqē mayim*), "the fountainheads of the sea"; cf. II Sam xxii 16, *'^{a}pīqē yām*
xxxviii 4, 8 *'ēn-m tōm* (MT *'ēn m^{e}tōm*), "there is no soundness"
xlv 7, lii 10 *'^{e}lōhē-m 'ōlām wā'ed* (MT *'^{e}lōhīm 'ōlām wā'ed*), "The eternal and everlasting God"
lix 6, lxxx 5, 8, 15, 20 *'^{e}lōhē-m ṣ^{e}bā'ōt* (MT *'^{e}lōhīm ṣ^{e}bā'ōt*), "God of Hosts"
lx 11 *'īr-m ṣōr* (MT *'īr māṣōr*), "Rock City"
lxiv 8 *'^{e}lōhē-m ḥēṣ* (MT *'^{e}lōhīm ḥēṣ*), "The God of the Arrow"
lxix 16 *šibbōlet-m yām* (MT *šibbōlet mayim*), "the vortex of the sea"
lxxxi 2 *'^{e}lōhē-m 'ūzzēnū* (MT *'^{e}lōhīm 'ūzzēnū*), "The God of our Fortress"
lxxxix 51 *kol rabbē-m* (MT *rabbīm*) *'ammīm,* "all the shafts of pagans"
civ 18 *sal'ē-mi maḥseh* (MT *s^{e}lā'im maḥseh*), "the sheltering crags"

cx 2, cxxviii 5, cxxxiv 3, cxxxv 21 — *yahweh-m ṣiyyōn* (MT *yahweh miṣṣiyyōn*), "Yahweh of Zion"

cxv 16 — *haššᵉmē-m šāmayim* (MT *haššāmayim šāmayim*), "the heaven of heavens"

cxix 18 — *nipl^{e}'ōt-m tōrātekā* (MT *niplā'ōt mittōrātekā*), "the wonders of your law"

cxxvi 1 — *k^{e}ḥōl-m yām* (MT *k^{e}ḥōl^{e}mīm*), "like the sands of the sea"

The construct chain
with intervening vocative

Ps cxlv 7 *zēker rab ṭūb^{e}kā,* "the record, O Master, of your goodness"

Substantives in genitive to
express "excellent, superb"

'ēl

Ps xxxvi 7, l 10 — *har^{e}rē 'ēl* "the towering mountains"; *har^{e}rē 'ēl* (MT *har^{e}rē 'ālep*)

lxxx 11 *'arzē 'ēl* "the towering cedars"

'^{e}lōhīm

Ps li 19 *zibḥē '^{e}lōhīm* "the finest sacrifices"

lxviii 16 *har '^{e}lōhīm* "mighty mountain"

lxxxiii 13 *n^{e}'ōt '^{e}lōhīm* "the very finest meadows"

yāh

Ps xxxix 3 *dūmīyah* "total silence"

lxv 2, lxii 2 *dūmiyyāh* "the mighty castle"

lxxvii 12 *ma'al^{e}lē yāh* "magnificent deeds"

midbār

Ps lxv 13 *n^{e}'ōt midbār* "the boundless meadows"; cf. Ps lxxxiii 13

māwet

Ps xxiii 4 *ṣalmāwet* "total darkness"

neṣaḥ

Ps lxxiv 3 *maššū'ōt neṣaḥ* "the total ruins"

Metaphorical use of animal names

'abbīr=wild bull

Ps lxviii 31 *'^{a}dat 'abbīrīm* "the herd of wild bulls"

'ayil=ram

Ps ii 5 *'ēlēmō* "their lieutenants"

lviii 2 *'ēlīm* (MT *'ēlem*) "leaders"

'aryēh=lion

Ps xxii 22 psalmist's adversary

ḥᵃzir=boar
Ps lxxx 14 *ḥᵃzīr miyyāʿar* "the boar from the forest," Israel's enemies

kᵉpīr=young lion
Ps xxxiv 11 means the rich
xxxv 17 means the psalmist's enemies

ʿēgel=calf
Ps lxviii 31 here "calves" are Pharaoh's soldiers

rᵉʾēm=buffalo
Ps xxii 22 *rēmīm*=simplified spelling for *rᵉʾēmīm;* means puissant adversaries

tōlēʿāh=worm
Ps xxii 7 the worm is used here to suggest the suffering psalmist

Names of habitations plural in form, singular in meaning

ʾōhālīm "tent"
Ps lxxxiv 11
ʾarmᵉnōt "citadel"
Ps xlviii 4, 14
bottīm "home"
Ps xlix 12
gᵉbūrōt "fortress"
Ps xx 7
ḥᵃṣērīm/ḥᵃṣērōt "court"
Pss lxv 5, lxxxiv 3, 11, xcii 14, xcvi 8, c 4
miqdāšīm "sanctuary"
Pss lxviii 36, lxxiii 17
miškānōt "dwelling"
Pss xliii 3, xlix 12, lxxxiv 2, cxxxii 5, 7

V. VERBS

Denominatives
from names of parts of the body

ʾnp (*ʾap* "nostril, nose, face, anger")
Qal "to be angry" Pss ii 12, lx 3, lxxix 5, lxxxv 6
ʾšd (Ugar. *ʾšd* "leg")
Qal "to stalk" Ps xci 6 *yēšōd* (MT *yāšūd*). On the elision of initial *aleph* cf. GK §69h–k; J. T. Milik in *Biblica* 38 (1957), 251
ʾšr (*ʾᵃšūr* "foot, leg")
Qal "to proceed, march" Ps lvi 7 *kᵉōšēr* (MT *kaʾᵃšēr*), "like a footpad"
blʿ (*blʿ* "gorge, throat" in Prov xxiii 2)
Qal "to swallow" Pss lxix 16, cvi 17, cxxiv 3
Pi "to engorge" Pss xxi 10, xxxv 25
Pi "to worship" Pss x 3, xlix 19 (appetite), xxvi 12 (Yahweh)
brk (*berek* "knee")
Qal "to kneel" Ps xcv 6 (before Yahweh)

dbr (*dbr* "back")
Hiph, Pi "to render supine" Pss xviii 48 (nations), xlvii 4, lxxvii 5 (oneself)

dnb (*zānāb*, Ugar. *ḏnb* "tail")
Pi "to de-tail, attack the rear" Ps cx 6 *yᵉdannēb gōyīm* (MT *yādīn baggōyīm*), "he routed nations"

kr' (*kera'* "leg, shinbone")
Qal "to kneel" Pss xxii 30, lxxii 9, xcv 6
"to slump" Ps xx 9
Hiph "to bring low" Pss xvii 13, xviii 40, lxxviii 31

lšn (*lāšōn* "tongue")
Pi "to slander" Ps lxiv 9 *mᵉlaššᵉnīm* (MT *lᵉšōnām*), attaching the *mem* from the preceding MT *'ālēmō*, "slanderers"
Poel "to slander" Ps ci 5 *mᵉlōšᵉnī* "whoever slandered." (The final *-ī* parses as third person singular suffix expressing the dative of advantage)

ngd (*neged* "front, face")
Hiph "to hold in front" Ps xxxviii 19, *kī 'ᵃwōnī 'aggīd*, "Indeed, I hold my guilt before me"

'yn (*'ayin* "eye")
Hiph "to show" Ps lxv 6 object *nōrā'ōt*, "wondrous deeds"

'nq (*'ᵃnāq* "neck")
Qal "to serve as a necklace" Ps lxxiii 6

'qb (*'āqēb* "heel")
Qal "to malign" Ps lvi 7 *'ōqᵉbay* (MT *'ᵃqēbay*), "my maligners"

p'm (*p'm* "foot")
Ni "to pace" Ps lxxvii 5

qdm (*qedem* "front")
Pi "to set in front" Ps xxi 4
"to come in front" Ps lxxxviii 14

rgl (*regel* "leg")
Qal "to trip" Ps xv 3

šwq (*šōq* "thigh")
Pilpel "to make skip" Ps lxv 10 *witᵉšōqᵉqehā* (MT *wattᵉšōqᵉhā*)

šqq (*šōq* "thigh")
Qal "to leap, spring" Ps cvii 9 *nepeš šōqēqāh* "the throbbing throat"

Denominatives
from various substantives

'lm (*'elem* "muzzle, bridle")
Ni "to be muzzled" Pss xxxi 19, xxxix 3, 10

bqr (*bōqer* "morning, dawn")
Pi "to awake at dawn" Ps xxvii 4

gbr (*geber* "man, hero")
Hiph "to be powerful" Ps xii 5

dbš (*dᵉbaš* "honey")
Qal "to be sweet" Ps cxix 103 *ma dābᵉšū* (MT *middᵉbāš*), "How sweet"

dgl (*degel* "banner")
Pi "to hold high the banner(s)" Ps xx 6 *nᵉdaggēl* (MT *nidgōl*), "we will hold high the banners"

hbl (*hebel* "idol")
Pi "to idolize" Ps lxii 11 *'al tᵉhabbᵉlū* (MT *tehbālū*) *ḥayil*, "do not idolize wealth"

hwt (Ugar. *hwt* "word")
Polel "to bluster" Ps lxii 4

zkr (*zākār* "male")
Hiph "to be strong" Ps xx 8

ḥtk (Ugar. *ḥtk* "father/son")
Pi (privative) "to unchild" Ps lii 7 *yᵉḥattēk* (MT *yaḥtᵉkā*)

ks' (*kissē'* "throne")
Pi "to enthrone" Ps xlv 7 *kissē'ᵃkā* (MT *kis'ᵃkā*)

nyn (*nīn* "offspring, posterity")
Pi "to bear offspring" Ps lxxii 17 *yᵉnayyēn* (MT *yinnyōn*)

n'r (*na'ar* "boy, lad")
Ni "to lose one's youth" Ps cix 23

'zr (Ugar. *ǵzr* "lad, warrior")
Ni "to be rejuvenated" Ps xxviii 7

'ms (Ugar. *'ms* "load")
Pi (privative) "to unburden" Ps lxviii 20 *yᵉ'ammēs* (MT *ya'ᵃmos*)

qrh (*qōrāh* "plank, boarding, storeroom")
Pi "to store" Ps civ 3

šḥr (*šaḥar* "dawn")
Pi "to long" Ps lxiii 2 *'ᵃšaḥēr* (MT *'ᵃšaḥᵃrekā*), detaching the final *k* and parsing it as emphatic "I long"

tpp (*tōp* "drum, tambour")
Qal "to beat tambours" Ps lxviii 26

Denominatives
from numerals

m'h (*mē'āh* "hundred")
Pi "to repeat, retell hundred times"
Ps xxii 26 *mī'ētīkā* (MT *mē'ittᵉkā*), "one hundred times will I repeat to you"
Ps lxvi 20 *wᵉḥasdō mī'ētī* (MT *mē'ittī*), "And his kindness will I repeat a hundred times" (revised translation)

ḥṣh (*ḥᵃṣī* "half")
Qal "to live out a half" Ps lv 24

Preservation of inflectional endings:
qatala third person masculine singular

Ps iv 7 *nāsāh* (MT *nᵉsāh*), "(the light) has fled"
xi 5 *śānᵉ'āh*, "(he who loves injustice) hates (his own life)"
xvi 6 *šāpᵉrāh*, "(The Most High) has traced out (my property)"
xviii 35 *niḥᵃtā*, "he lowered"; cf. II Sam xxii 35 *niḥat*
xx 10 *hōšī'āh*, "(Yahweh) has given victory"
lxxxiv 7 *hibbīkā'* (MT *habbakā'*), "May he cause to flow"
lxxxix 8 *rabbāh*, "he is great"
xc 17 *kōnᵉnāh*, "may he sustain"

xciii 5 *na'^{a}wāh,* "will laud," the subject being the collective singular *qōdeš,* "the holy ones"

ciii 19 *māšālā,* "he rules"

cxxvi 4 *šābāh* or *šōbāh* (*ā*>*ō*) for MT *šūbāh,* "(Yahweh) restored"

Preservation of inflectional endings:
qatalā third person feminine plural/dual

Ps xlv 10 *niṣṣ^{e}bāh* "(daughters of kings) shall be stationed"

lxviii 14 *neḥpāh* "(the two wings) are plated"

lxxiii 2 *šūp^{e}kāh* (MT *šupp^{e}kūh*) "(my legs) were poured out"

lxxxviii 10 *'ēnay* (MT *'ēnī*) *dā'^{a}bāh* "my eyes grow dim"

Preservation of inflectional endings:
yaqtulu imperfect singular in *-u*

Ps x 2 *yittāpāšū* (MT *yittāp^{e}šū*), "he pantingly pursues"

xxxii 9 *'al tihyū* "Don't be!" (singular)

lxiv 7 *yaḥp^{e}śū* "he will investigate"

9 *yakšīlūhū* "he shall make stumble"; the imperfect ending is present in *-lū,* and *-hū* is the dative suffix

lxviii 31 *yeḥpāṣū* "he (the Pharaoh) delighted (in battle)"

lxxii 5 *yiyrā'ūkā* "may he revere you," but here the form may be parsed as a plural of majesty

16 *piryō w^{e}yāṣīṣū* "let his fruit blossom"; the *waw* in *w^{e}yāṣīṣū* is emphatic

lxxxiv 7 *y^{e}šītūhū* "may he turn it"

cxxvii 5 *lō' yēbōšū kī y^{e}dabb^{e}rū,* "He shall not be humiliated but shall drive back"

cxl 11 *yāmīṭū* (Ketiv; MT *yimmōṭū*), "may he heap"

tqtl third person masculine plural

Ps lxviii 3 *tinnādēpu* (MT *tindōp*), "they are driven"

14 *tškbwm,* "may they empty out"(?)

cvi 38 *watteḥen^{e}pū* (MT *watteḥ^{e}nap*), "and they desecrated"

The energic mood

Ps ii 8 *w^{e}'ettannāh* (MT *w^{e}'ett^{e}nāh*), "and I will give"

viii 2 *'^{a}šār^{e}tannāh* (MT *'^{a}šer t^{e}nāh*), "I will adore"
Pi from *šērēt,* "to serve, worship, adore"

xx 4 *y^{e}daššannāh* (MT *y^{e}dašš^{e}neh*), "may he consider generous"
Pi declarative from *dšn* "to be fat"

xxxix 7 *yeh^{e}māyannā* (MT *yeh^{e}māyūn*), "he is in turmoil"

xlv 16 *tūbālannāh* (MT *tūbalnāh*), "let her be led"
Hoph from *ybl,* "to bring"
tūbā'annāh (MT *t^{e}bō'ēnāh*), "let her be brought"
Hoph from *bw',* "to come, enter"

l 23 *y^{e}kubb^{e}dān^{e}nī* (MT *y^{e}kabb^{e}dān^{e}nī*), "he will be feasted by me";

pual of *kbd* followed by the first person singular suffix expressing the agent

lxv 13 *taḥgōrannāh* (MT *taḥgōrnāh*), "gird!" energic imperfect form functioning as an imperative

cxlv 6 *'ᵃsappᵉrannāh* (MT *'ᵃsappᵉrennāh*), "I will number"

Qal passive

Ps iii 7 *šītū* (MT *šātū*), "were deployed"

xvii 10 *sūgārū* (pausal for MT *sāgᵉrū*), "they are clogged"

xviii 7 *yušma'* (MT *yišma'*), "(my voice) was heard"

xlix 15 *šītū* (MT *šattū*), "they will be put"

l 23 *śīm* (MT *śām*), "who is set"

lx 4 *pᵉṣūmᵉtāh* (MT *pᵉṣamtāh*), "and (the land) went to pieces"; *pᵉ* is the conjunction "and"

lxi 8 *mūnū* (MT *man*), "may they be appointed"

lxxi 13 *yū'ᵃṭū* (MT *ya'ᵃṭū*), "may they be robed"

lxxii 15 *yuttān* (MT *yitten*), "may (gold) be given"

lxxiii 2 *šūpᵉkāh* (MT *šuppᵉkūh*), "(my legs) were poured out"

19 *sūpū* (MT *sāpū*), "they will be swept away"; this verb derives from *sāpāh*, not from *sūp*, "to come to an end"

lxxiv 8 *śūrāpū* (MT *śārᵉpū*), "may they be burned"

lxxv 9 *yumṣū* (MT *yimṣū*), "(dregs) will be drained"

lxxvi 6 *wᵉlō' mūṣā'ū* (MT *māṣᵉ'ū*), "and they were found no more"

lxxvii 10 *qūpaṣ* (MT *qāpaṣ*), "(his bosom) shrunk"

xc 5 *keḥāṣīr yuḥlāp* (MT *yaḥᵃlōp*), "like cut grass"

6 *wᵉḥūlāp* (MT *wᵉḥālāp*), "(grass) is cut"

xcii 11 *bullōtī* (MT *ballōtī*), "I have been anointed"

xciv 20 *yuṣṣār* (MT *yōṣēr*), "he will be protected," the verb deriving from *nāṣar*

cix 2 *'ālay pūtāḥū*, "(the mouth of the wicked, and the mouth of the deceitful) are opened against me." MT reads *pātāḥū*

10 *dūrᵉšū mōḥēr bōtēhem*, "May their houses be investigated by the appraiser." MT reads *wᵉdoršū mēḥorbōtēhem*

22 *wᵉlibbī ḥūlal* (MT *ḥālal*) *bᵉqirbī*, "and my heart has been pierced within me"

The infixed *-t-* conjugation
without a direct object

yāšan, "to dry up, become old"

Ps lxxiii 21 *wᵉkilyōtay 'eštōnān*, "and emotionally (i.e., as regards my innards) I dried up"

nāpaš, "to pant after"

Ps x 2 *yittāpāšū* (MT *yittāpᵉśū*), "he pantingly pursues"

Note: *-ū* is the old indicative ending of the imperfect in singular *-u*, which the Masoretes took for the plural ending *sūr,* "to turn aside"

Ps xix 7 *we'ēn nistār,* "And never turning aside (from its pavilion)"

13 *nistārōt* "aberrations"

xxxviii 10 *lō' nistārāh,* "(and my groaning) never leaves (your presence)"

lxxxix 47 *tstr,* "will you estrange yourself?"

The infixed *-t-* conjugation
with a direct object

sūr, "to turn aside"

object: *pānīm,* i.e., "to turn away the face"; cf. LXX, *apostréphein to prósopon,* Vulg., *avertere faciem*

Pss x 11, xiii 2, xxii 25, xxvii 9, xxx 8, xliv 25, li 11, lxix 18, lxxxviii 15, cii 3, civ 29, cxliii 7

pūḥ, "to blow, breathe"

Ps xlix 5 *'eptāḥ . . . ḥīdātī,* "I will breathe out . . . my riddle"

Shaphel, Ishtaphel, and Aphel

Shaphel

from *kālāh* "to be spent, destroyed"

Ps xxxv 12 *šaklēl napšī* (MT *šekōl lenapšī*) "(they repay me evil for good) ravaging my soul," infinitive absolute shaphel continuing a finite verb

lviii 9 *kemō šaklūl* (with some manuscripts; MT *šablūl*) "like one ravaged"

Ishtaphel

from *ḥāšak* "to be or grow dark"

Ps xviii 12 *yištaḥšēk* (MT *yāšet ḥōšek*) *sitrō sebībōtāyw,* "Dark grew his canopy around him" (revised translation proposed at Ps civ 20)

civ 20 *tištaḥšēk* (MT *tāṣet ḥōšek*) *wīhī laylāh,* "It grows dark and night comes on"

Aphel

Ps lv 3 *'ōrēd* or *'ōrīd* (MT *'ārīd*) *beśīḥī,* "descend at my complaint," masculine singular imperative from *yārad,* "to descend." *'ōrīd* literally means "bring yourself down"

cv 22 *le'ōsīr* (MT *le'sōr*), "to instruct," aphel infinitive construct of *yāsar,* "to discipline, instruct"

Hiphil
internal

Ps lvi 7 *yaṣpīnū* (Ketiv; Qere *yiṣpōnū*), "they conceal themselves"

lxvi 7 *hassōrerīm 'al yārīmū* (Ketiv; Qere *yārūmū*) *lāmō,* "lest the rebels rise up against him"

lxxx 4 *'elōhīm hašībēnū,* "O God, return to us!" Cf. vss. 8, 20

Hiphil
elative

Ps xlv 4–5 *wehadrēk hadārekā* (MT *wahadārekā wahadārekā*), "and conquer completely by your majesty"

li 9 *tekabbesēnī ūmiššeleg 'albīn*, "Wash me, and I'll be much whiter than snow"

xcii 14 *beḥaṣrōt 'elōhēnū yapriḥū*, "they will richly flourish in the court of our God"

cxiii 5 *hammagbīhī lāšābet*, "the One who is enthroned on high"

6 *hammašpīlī*, "the One who stoops"

cxxvi 2, 3 *higdīl yhwh*, "Yahweh showed his greatness"

cxxxix 12 *gam ḥōšek lō' yaḥšīk mimmekā*, "Even Darkness is not very dark for you"

Piel
privative

Ps li 9 *teḥaṭṭe'ēnī*, "unsin me!"

lii 7 *yeḥattēk* (MT *yaḥtekā*), "may (El) unchild you!"

wešērešekā, "and may he snatch your sons"

lxviii 20 *ye'ammēs lānū* (MT *ya'amos lānū*), literally "he removed from us the burden"

cxviii 12 *dē'akū* (MT *dō'akū*), "they crackled"

Pual
privative

Ps xliv 16 *ūbōšet pānay kussetanī* (MT *kissātenī*), "and my shamefacedness is exposed before me"

cxliii 9 *'ēlī kī kussētī* (MT *'ēlekā kissītī*), "my God, truly am I being submerged"

VI. PREPOSITIONS

'aḥar "with"

Ps xlv 15 "let her companions be brought after/with her (*'aḥarehā*)"

xlix 18 "his wealth will not descend with him (*'aḥarāyw*)"

lxxiii 24 *we'aḥar kābōd tiqqāḥēnī*, "and with glory take me to yourself"

xciv 15 "But the tribunal of justice will restore equity (*mišpāṭ*), and with it (*we'aḥarāyw*) all upright hearts"

b "before"

Ps cii 25 *'al ta'alēnī baḥaṣī yāmāy*, "Do not take me away before half my days"

b "after"

Ps xxvii 5 "Indeed he will treasure me in his abode, after the evil day (*beyōm rā'āh*)"

cvi 7 "After Egypt (*b^emiṣrayim*) our fathers considered not your wonders"
"And from the Reed Sea (*b^eyam sūp*) they defied the Most High"
cxiv 1 *b^eṣē't yiśrā'ēl mimmiṣrāyim,* "After Israel went out of Egypt"

bō "then"

Ps civ 20 "then (*bō*) all the beasts of the forest prowl"

bāh "then, thereupon"

Ps lxviii 15 "When Shaddai covered the kings, then snow fell (*bāh tašlēg*) on Zalmon"

bāhem "then"

Ps xix 6 "Then (*bāhem*) like a bridegroom it (i.e., the sun) goes forth from its bower"
xc 10 "Our life, then (*bāhem*), lasts seventy years"

b^ezō't "then"

Ps xxvii 3 *b^ezō't '^anī bōṭēaḥ,* "even then will I be confident"
xli 12 "Then (*b^ezō't*) shall I know that you love me, if my Foe does not triumph over me"

b "against"

Ps xxxiv 17 *p^enē yhwh bē'ōśē rā',* "The fury of Yahweh is with the evildoers"
lxxiii 8 *yāmīqū wīdabb^erū b^erā',* "They scoff and speak against the Evil One"
lxxiv 1 *lāmāh . . . ye'šan 'app^ekā b^eṣō'n mar'īteka,* "Why do your nostrils smoke against the sheep of your pasture?"
lxxv 6 *'al . . . t^edabb^erū b^eṣū'r 'attīq* (MT *b^eṣawwā'r 'ātāq*), ". . . nor speak against the Ancient Mountain!"
lxxviii 45 *y^ešallaḥ bāhem 'ārōb,* "He sent flies against them"
49 *y^ešallaḥ bām ḥ^arōn 'appō,* "He sent against them his blazing anger"
lxxxix 23 *lō' yiśśā'* (MT *yaššī'*) *'ōyēb bō,* "No foe shall rise up against him"
cxxiv 3 *baḥ^arōt 'appām bānū,* "when their wrath blazed against us"
cxli 5 *kī 'ōd ūt^epillātī b^erā'ōtēhem,* "nay, my constant prayer will be against their evil customs"

b "from"

Ps i 2 *b^etōrat yahweh ḥepṣō,* "from the law of Yahweh is his delight"
ūb^etōrātō yehgeh, "and from his law he recites"
ii 4 *yōšēb baššāmayim yiśḥāq,* "The Enthroned laughs down from heaven"
iii 3 *'ēn y^ešū'ātāh lō bē'lōhīm,* "No salvation for him from God"

ix 15 *l^{e}ma'an '^{a}sapp^{e}rāh . . . b^{e}ša'^{a}rē bat ṣiyyōn,* "That I may recount . . . from the gates of Daughter Zion"

x 1 *lāmāh . . . ta'^{a}mōd b^{e}rāḥōq,* "Why . . . do you stand afar off?"

14 *lātēt b^{e}yādekā,* "by giving from your own hand"

xi 2 *līrōt b^{e}mō 'ōpel,* "to shoot from ambush"

xv 2 *w^{e}dōbēr '^{e}met bil^{e}bābō,* "and speaks the truth from his heart"

4 *b^{e}'ēnāyw nim'as* (MT *nim'ās*), "is rejected from his presence"

xvii 5 *b^{e}ma'g^{e}lōtekā bal nāmōṭū p^{e}'āmāy,* "From your tracks my feet never swerved"

xviii 14 *wayyar'ēm baššāmayim yahweh,* "Yahweh thundered from the heavens"; cf. II Sam xxii 14, *min šāmayim*

xxi 8 *ūb^{e}ḥesed 'elyōn bal yimmōṭ,* "and from the love of the Most High he will never swerve"

xxxi 10 *'āš^{e}šāh b^{e}ka'as 'ēnī,* "My eye is wasted with sorrow"

22 *kī hiplī' ḥasdō lī b^{e}'īr māṣōr,* "for he has shown me wondrous kindness from the fortified city"

xxxv 15 *w^{e}lō' dammū b^{e}ḥonpī* (MT *b^{e}ḥanpē*), "And they did not desist from slandering me"

xxxvi 6 *yahweh b^{e}haššāmayim ḥasdekā,* "From the heavens, O Yahweh, is your kindness"

xxxviii 15 *w^{e}'ēn b^{e}pīū tōkāḥōt,* "And from whose mouth no recriminations come"

xliv 13 *w^{e}lō' ribbītā bim^{e}ḥīrīhem* (MT *bim^{e}ḥīrēhem*), "Nor did you grow rich from their price." For the explanation of this text, see *Psalms II,* p. XXVI

xlv 3 *hūṣaq ḥēn b^{e}śiptōtekā,* "Charm flows from your lips"

6 *b^{e}lēb,* "senseless"

lv 16 *rā'ōt bim^{e}gūrām b^{e}qirbām,* "venomous words proceed from their throat and breast"

lviii 7 *h^{a}ros šinnēmō b^{e}pīmō,* "rip their teeth from their mouths"

11 *p^{e}'āmāyw yirḥaṣ b^{e}dam hārāšā',* "He will wash his feet of the blood of the wicked"

lix 8 *yabbī'ūn b^{e}pīhem ḥ^{a}rābōt b^{e}śiptōtēhem,* "They belch from their mouth, swords from their lips"

12 *h^{a}nī'ēmō b^{e}ḥēl^{e}kā,* "send them staggering from your bastion!"

14 *'^{e}lōhīm mōšēl b^{e}ya'^{a}qōb l^{e}'apsē hā'āreṣ,* "God rules from Jacob to the edges of the earth"

lx 8 *'^{e}lōhīm dibber b^{e}qodšō,* "God spoke from his sanctuary"

lxiv 5 *līrōt bammistārīm tām,* "To shoot from ambush at the innocent"

lxvi 7 *mōšēl big^{e}būrātō 'ōlām,* "He rules from his eternal fortress"

lxviii 6 "Father of the fatherless, and defender of the widows is God from his holy habitation (*bim^{e}'ōn qodšō*)"

19 *lāqaḥtā mattānōt bā'ādēm* (MT *bā'ādām*), "You received gifts from their hands"

22 *mithallēk ba'^{a}šāmāyw,* "as he marched from his heavens"

25 "Behold the marches of God, the marches of my God, of my King from his sanctuary (*baqqōdeš*)"

lxxviii 26 "He let loose (*yassa'*) the east wind from heaven (*baššāmāyim*), and led forth (*wayenahēg*) the south wind from his fortress (*be'uzzō*)"

lxxxi 8 *'e'enekā beséter ra'am,* "I answered you from the hiding place of thunder"

lxxxiii 11 *nišmedū be'ēn dō'r,* "Let them be exterminated from the surface of the globe"

lxxxiv 6 *mesillōt bilebābām,* "from whose heart are your extolments"

xc 1 *hāyītāl lānū bedōr wādōr,* "Be ours from age to age!"

xci 15 *beṣārāh 'aḥalleṣēhū,* "From anguish will I rescue him"

16 *we'ar'ēhū bīšū'ātī,* "And I will make him drink deeply of my salvation"

xcix 7 *be'ammūd 'ānān yedabbēr 'alēhem,* "From the pillar of cloud he spoke to them"

cii 9 *mehōlelay* (MT *mehōlālay*) *bī nišbā'ū,* "my Mocker feasts on me." Cf. Pss lxv 5, lxxxviii 4

10 *wešiqqūway bibekī māsāktī,* "And from my tears I draw my drink"

cvi 15 *wayešallaḥ rāzōn benapšām,* "and (he) cast out leanness from their throats"

cvii 5 *napšām bāhem tit'aṭṭāp,* "their life ebbed from them"

cviii 8 *'elōhīm dibber beqodšō,* "God spoke from his sanctuary"

cix 13 *bedōr 'aḥēr yimmaḥ šmm* (MT *šemām*), "from the age to come may his name be erased" (parsing the final *mem* of *šmm* as enclitic balancing the pronominal suffix of *'aḥarītō,* "his future life," of the first colon)

cxiii 6 *hammašpīlī lir'ōt baššāmayim ūbā'āreṣ,* "The One who stoops to look from heaven to earth"

cxv 7 *lō' yehgū bigerōnām,* "They emit no sound from their throats"

cxix 87 *kim'aṭ killūnī bā'āreṣ,* "They almost exterminated me from the earth"

cxxvii 5 *yedabberū . . . baššā'ar,* "(he) shall drive back . . . from the gate"

cxxxix 4 *kī 'ēn millāh bilešōnī,* "The word is not even off my tongue"

13 *tesukkēnī bebeṭen 'immī,* "you have sheltered me from the womb of my mother"

16 *welō' 'eḥāde* (MT *'eḥad*) *bāhem,* "when I was not yet seen by them." Note: 11QPs[a] reads *mhmh,* and three manuscripts read *mhm*

cxl 11 *bemahamōrōt bal yāqūmū,* "From the Miry Bog let them not rise!"

cxliv 12 *meguddālīm bine'ūrēhēm,* "carefully trained from their youth"

Partitive *b*

Ps lxxx 6 *wattašqēmō bidmā'ōt šālīš,* "and you have given us tears to drink by the bowl"

xciv 8 *bīnū bō'arīm bā'ām,* "learn some sagacity, you dolts"

cxxxviii 5 *weyašīrū bedarkē yhwh,* "And they will sing of Yahweh's dominion"

cxli 4 *ūbal 'elḥam beman'ammēhem,* "never will I dine on their delicacies"

Comparative *b* "than"

Ps xxxvii 20 "More quickly than smoke (*be'āšān*) shall they vanish"
li 8 *'^{e}met ḥāpaṣtā baṭṭūḥōt ūb^{e}sātūm,* "You prefer truth to both cleverness and secret lore"
lxiii 2 ". . . my soul ardently thirsts for you, my body pines for you more than parched earth (*b^{e}'ereṣ ṣiyyāh*) yearns for drops of water"
lxxiii 16 *'āmāl hī' b^{e}'ēnāy,* "it was too difficult for my mind"
lxxviii 33 "Their days he made vanish more quickly than vapor (*bahebel*), and their years more quickly than a fleeting phantom (*babbehālā*)"
lxxxix 3 *tākīn '^{e}mūnāt^{e}kā bāhem,* "You made your fidelity more steadfast than these"
8 *'ēl na'^{a}rāṣ b^{e}sōd q^{e}dōšīm,* "An El too dreadful for the council of holy ones"
38 *baššaḥaq ne'^{e}mān,* "stabler than the sky"
xcix 2 *yahweh b^{e}ṣiyyōn gādōl,* "Yahweh is too great for Zion"
cii 4 *kī kālū b^{e}'āšān yāmāy,* "For my days are more transitory than smoke"
cxix 89 *d^{e}bār^{e}kā niṣṣāb baššāmāyim,* "Your word is more stable than the heavens!"

l "against"

Ps xvii 4 *bal ya'^{a}bor pī lip'ullōt 'ādēm* (MT *'ādām*), "My mouth has not transgressed against the works of your hands"
xli 6 *yō'm^{e}rū ra' lī,* "They speak maliciously against me"
8 *yaḥš^{e}bū rā'āh lī,* "They plot evil against me"
lxxv 6 *'al tārīmū lammārōm qarn^{e}kem,* "Raise not your horn against the Exalted One!"
cxviii 6 *mah ya'^{a}śeh lī 'ādām,* "What can man do against me?"

l "from"

Ps ix 8 *yahweh l^{e}'ōlām yēšēb,* "Yahweh has reigned from eternity"
xii 7 *lā'āreṣ m^{e}zuqqāq,* "of clay refined"
xv 4 *nišba' l^{e}hāra',* "He swore to do no wrong"
xviii 20 *wayyōṣī'ēnī lammerḥāb,* "He brought me out of the broad domain"
xxix 10 *yahweh lammabbūl yāšāb wayyēšeb yahweh melek l^{e}'ōlām,* "Yahweh has sat enthroned from the flood, And Yahweh has sat enthroned, the king from eternity"
xxxiii 11 *'^{a}ṣat yahweh l^{e}'ōlām ta'^{a}mōd,* "The plan of Yahweh has stood fixed from eternity"
xl 11 *lō' kiḥadtī . . . l^{e}qāhāl rāb,* "I did not hide (your kindness, nor your fidelity) from the great congregation"
xlv 3 ". . . because God has blessed you from eternity (*l^{e}'ōlām*)"
15 *l^{e}būšāh l^{e}rōqāmōt* (MT *lirqāmōt*), "Her wardrobe comes from the women who weave threads of gold"
lx 3 *t^{e}šōbēb lānū,* "You turned away from us"
lxvi 12 *wattōṣī'ēnū lār^{e}wāyāh,* "After you had led us out of abundance"

lxviii 20 *y^eʿammēs* (MT *yaʿ^amos*) *lānū,* "He removed from us the burden"
21 *lammāwet tōṣāʾōt,* "escape from death"
lxix 19 *limeʿōn* (MT *l^emaʿan*) *ʾōy^ebay p^edēnī,* "Ransom me from the abode of my Foe"
lxxiv 3 *hārīmāh . . . l^emaššūʾōt neṣaḥ,* "Raise up . . . from the total ruins"
lxxviii 69 *k^eʾereṣ y^esādāh l^eʿōlām,* "like the earth he established from eternity"
lxxix 13 *l^edōr wādōr n^esappēr t^ehillāteka,* "From generation to generation we will tell your praise"
lxxxi 5 *mišpāṭ lēʾlōhē yaʿ^aqōb,* "an ordinance from the God of Jacob"
lxxxiv 12 *yahweh lōʾ yimnaʿ ṭōb lahōl^ekīm b^etāmīm,* "Yahweh will not withhold his rain from those who walk with integrity"
cii 13 *w^eʾattāh yahweh l^eʿōlām tēšēb w^ezikr^ekā l^edōr wādōr,* "But you, Yahweh, from eternity have sat enthroned, and your throne endures from age to age"
cxi 5 *yizkōr l^eʿōlām b^erītō,* "He remembered his covenant of old (literally, from eternity)"
cxix 152 *kī l^eʿōlām y^esadtām,* "Because you established them from eternity"
cxlviii 6 *wayyaʿ^amīdēm lāʿad l^eʿōlām,* "He stationed them from all time to eternity"
14 *t^ehillāh l^ekol ḥ^asīdāyw,* "Praise from all his devoted ones"

l "in"

Ps xvi 10 *lōʾ taʿ^azōb napšī lišeʾōl,* "You will not put me in Sheol"
li 12 *b^erāʾ lī,* "create in me," in parallelism with *ḥaddēš b^eqirbī,* "re-create within me"
lxvi 9 *w^elōʾ nātan lammōṭ raglēnū,* ". . . and he did not put our foot in the Quagmire"
xciii 5 *l^ebēt^ekā,* "in your temple"

l "than"

Ps xxx 8 ". . . you made me more stable than the mighty mountains (*l^ehar^erī ʿōz*)"
lxii 10 *b^emōʾznayim lʿlwt hemmāh,* "On scales they are lighter than leaves"
cxix 96 *l^ekol tiklāh rāʾītī . . . r^eḥābāh miṣwāt^ekā,* "Than all the perfection I have seen . . . your commandment is more extensive"

min "after"

Ps xxx 4 *ḥiyyītanī miyyōr^edī bōr,* "You restored me to life after my descent to the Pit" (revised translation)
lxxiii 20 *kaḥ^alōm mēhāqīṣ,* "like a dream after awaking"
lxxviii 65 *mitrōnēn miyyāyin,* "(a warrior) resting after wine"
xciv 13 *l^ehašqīṭ lō mīmē rāʿ,* "Giving him respite after the evil days"

min "in"

Ps xviii 7 *yušmaʿ* (or *yiššāmēᵃʿ* for MT *yišmaʿ*) *mēhēkālō qōlī,* "My voice was heard in his palace"

Ps lxviii 27 *mimmeqōr yiśrā'ēl,* "in the convocation of Israel"
Ps cxviii 26 *mibbēt yhwh,* "in the house of Yahweh"

'al "from"

Ps iv 7 *nāsāh* (MT *nesāh*) *'ālēnū 'ōr pānekā,* "The light of your face has fled from us"
xv 5 *weśōḥad 'al nāqī lō' lāqāḥ,* "and he does not accept compensation from the hungry"
lvi 8 *'al 'āwen palleṭ lāmō,* "From malice deliver us!"
lxxxi 6 *beṣē'tō 'al 'ereṣ miṣrāyim,* "When he went from the land of Egypt"
cxlii 4 *behit'aṭṭēp 'ālay rūḥī,* "As my spirit ebbs from me"
cxliii 4 *wattit'aṭṭēp 'ālay rūḥī,* "My spirit ebbed from me"

'al "near, in presence of"

Ps i 3 *'al palegē māyim,* "near streams of water"
xxiii 2 *'al mē menūḥōt yenahalēnī,* "Near tranquil waters will he guide me"
xlii 5 *we'ešpekā 'ālay* (vocalize *'ālēy*) *napšī,* "and I shall pour out my soul before him"
l 5 *'alē zābaḥ,* "in the presence of a sacrifice"
lxvi 5 *nōrā' 'alīlāh 'al benē 'ādām,* "terrifying in action before men"
lxxxi 8 "I was provoked by you near Meribah's waters (*'al mē merībāh*)"
civ 12 *'alēhem,* "near them"
34 *ye'erab 'ālāyw śīḥī,* "when my hymn enters his presence"
cxxxvii 1 *'al naharōt bābel,* "beside the rivers in Babylon"
2 *'al 'arābīm,* "beside the poplars"
cxxxviii 2 *kī higdaltā 'al kōl* (MT *kol*) *šimekā 'imrātekā,* "you surely glorified before all your Name, your promise"
7 *teḥayyēnī 'al 'ap 'ōyebāy,* "keep me alive before the fury of my foes"

'im "from"

Ps lxxxv 5 *hāpēr ka'asekā 'immānū,* "Banish from us your indignation!"

'im "like, on a par with"

Ps lxxii 5 *yīrā'ūkā 'im šemeš,* "May he revere you as long as the sun"
lxxiii 5 *we'im 'ādām lō' yenūgā'ū,* "they are not buffeted like others"
cvi 6 *ḥāṭā'nū 'im 'abōtēnū,* "We have sinned like our fathers"
cxx 4 *'im gaḥalē retāmīm,* "like glowing coals of broom"
cxliii 7 *wenimšaltī 'im yōredē bōr,* "I would resemble those who have descended the Pit"

'im "to, toward"

Ps xviii 24 *wā'ehī tāmīm 'immō,* "I have always been candid toward him." Cf. II Sam xxii 24, *tāmīm lō* xxvi 4 *we'im na'alāmīm lō' 'ābō'*, "and I have not entered the home of the benighted"

xlii 9 "By day Yahweh had sent (*yeṣawweh*) his grace and his vision to me (*'immī*) at night"

lxxviii 37 *welibbām lō' nākōn 'immō*, "And their heart was not steadfast toward him"

taḥat "at, at the feet of"

Ps viii 7 *kol šattāh taḥat raglāyw*, "you put all things at his feet"

xviii 39 *yippelū taḥat raglāy*, "they fell at my feet"

xviii 40 *takrīa' qāmay taḥtāy*, "you made my assailants kneel at my feet"

xviii 48 *wayyadbēr 'ammīm taḥtāy*, "and he made nations bend their back at my feet"

xlv 6 *'ammīm taḥtekā yippelū*, "the peoples shall fall at your feet"

xlvii 4 *yadbēr 'ammīm taḥtēnū ūle'ummīm taḥat raglēnū*, "He made peoples prostrate before us, and nations at our feet"

cxliv 2 *hārōdēd 'ammē* (MT *'ammī*) *taḥtāy*, "the one who prostrated the peoples at my feet"

taḥat "on"

Ps lxvi 17 *wrwmm taḥat lešōnī*, "and sounds of music were on my tongue"

Interchange of *b* and *min*
in the sense of "from"

Ps xvii 14 *memītām* (MT *mimetīm*) *mēḥeled/ḥalleqēm* (MT *ḥelqām*) *baḥayyīm*, "Slay them from the earth/make them perish from among the living!"

xviii 9 *'ālāh 'āšān be'appō/we'ēš mippīw tō'kēl*, "Smoke rose from his nostrils/and fire from his mouth devoured"

xx 7 *ya'anēhū miššemē qodšō/bigebūrōt yōšīa' yemīnō*, "He has granted him triumph from his sacred heaven/and from his fortress has given victory with his right hand"

xxxiii 19 *lehaṣṣīl mimmāwet napšām/ūleḥayyōtām bārā'āb*, "To rescue them from Death/to preserve their lives from the Hungry One"

lv 12 *beqirbāh hawwōt/beqirbāh welō' yāmīš/mēreḥōbāh tōk ūmirmāh*, "From its center, pernicious deeds/from its center, they never leave/from its square, oppression and fraud"

lxxxix 34 *weḥasdī lō' 'āpīr mē'immō/welō' 'ašaqqēr be'emūnātī*, "But I will never banish from him my love/or be false to my fidelity"

cxviii 5 *min hammēṣar qārā'tī yāh/'ānānī bammerḥāb yāh*, "From Confinement I called Yah/Yah answered me from the Broad Domain"

cxlviii 1 *halelū 'et yhwh min haššāmayim halelūhū bammerōmīm*, "Praise Yahweh from the heavens, praise him from the heights"

Interchange of *b* and *min*
in the sense of "than"

Ps li 9 *teḥaṭṭe'ēnī b'zwb we'eṭhār/tekabbesēnī ūmiššeleg 'albīn*, "Unsin me, I'll indeed be purer than gushing water/Wash me, and I'll be whiter than snow"

lxviii 35–36 "Whose majesty and might are too great for heaven (*baššeḥāqīm*); Too awesome is God for his sanctuary (*mimmiqdāšēy;* MT *mimmiqdāšēkā*)"

xciii 4 "Stronger than thundering waters (*miqqōlōt mayim*), Mightier than breakers of the sea (*mišberē yām*), Mightier than high heaven (*bammārōm*) was Yahweh"

Interchange of *b* and *min*
in the sense of "on account of"

Ps v 11 *yippelū mimmō'aṣōtēhem/berōb pišʻēhem haddīḥēmō,* "let them fall because of their schemes/for their numerous crimes hurl them down"

vi 8 *ʻāšešāh mikkaʻas ʻēnī/ʻāteqāh bekālā* (MT *bekol*) *ṣrry,* "My eye is dimmed with sorrow/my heart has grown old from pining"

lix 13 *bige'ōnām ūmē'ālāh ūmikkaḥaš yissāpērū* (MT *yesapperū*), "for their presumption, curses, and lies, let them be proscribed"

Interchange of *b* and *min*
in the sense of "in"

Ps lxviii 27 *bemaqhēlōt//mimmeqōr yiśrā'ēl,* "in the congregation//in the convocation of Israel"

cxviii 26 *bārūk habbā' bešēm yhwh/bēraknūkem mibbēt yhwh,* "Blessed be he who enters in the name of Yahweh/we bless you in the house of Yahweh"

Interchange of *min* and *l*
in the sense of "from"

Ps xviii 44 *tepalleṭēnī mērabbē* (MT *mērībē*) *ʻām/tišmerēnī* (MT *teśīmēnī*) *lerō'š gōyīm,* "You delivered me from the shafts of people/protected me from the venom of nations"

Interchange of *ʻal* and *min*
in comparisons

Ps lxxxix 20 "I made a lad king in preference to a warrior (*ʻal gibbōr*), I exalted a youth above a hero (*mēʻām*)"

Heaping up of prepositions

Ps xvii 2 *millepāneka,* "before you"

cviii 5 *mēʻal šāmayim,* "above the heavens"

VII. PARTICLES

'al "lest"

Ps ix 20 *qūmāh yahweh 'al yāʻōz 'enōš,* "Arise, O Yahweh, lest men should boast" xix 14 "Above all, keep your servant from the presumptuous ones, lest they rule over me (*'al yimšᵉlū bī*)"

xxxv 25 *'al yō'mᵉrū* (twice), "Lest they boast"

lxvi 7 ". . . his eyes keep watch on the nations lest the rebels rise up against him (*hassōrᵉrīm 'al yārīmū lāmō*)"

lxix 15 ". . . rescue me, lest I be submerged by the mire (*miṭṭīṭ wᵉ'al 'eṭbā'āh*)"

28 "Charge them with crime upon crime, lest they enter (*wᵉ'al yābō'ū*) your meadow"

cxix 122 "Assure your servant, O Good One, lest the presumptuous oppress me (*'al ya'ašqūnī zēdīm*)"

'ap "and"

Ps xvi 6 *'ap naḥᵃlāt šāpᵉrāh 'ēlī* (MT *'ālāy*), "And the Most High has traced out my property"

9 *'ap bᵉśārī yiškōn lābeṭaḥ,* "and my body dwells at ease"

xviii 49 *'ap min qāmay tᵉrōmᵉmēnī,* "and above my assailants you exalted me." Cf. II Sam xxii 49, *ūmiqqāmay*

lxv 14 *yitrō'ᵃ'ū 'ap yāšīrū,* "May they jubilate and sing!"

lxxxix 12 *lᵉkā šāmayim 'ap lᵉkā 'āreṣ,* "Yours are the heavens and yours is the earth"

'ap "but"

Ps xliv 10 *'ap zānaḥtā,* "But you rejected/were angry"; cf. first NOTE on Ps lx 3

lviii 3 *'ap bᵉlēb 'ōlōt tip'ālūn,* "But no, you act with a heart of malice"

'ap "surely"

Ps xciii 1 *'ap tikkōn tēbēl bal timmōṭ,* "Surely established is the world, no more shall it totter"

Emphatic *beth*

Ps xii 6 *'āšīt bᵉyēša',* "I will give my help." Here the emphatic *beth* functions as the possessive suffix

xvii 10 *pīmō dibbᵉrū bᵉgē'ūt,* "with their mouth they speak arrogance itself"

xxix 4 *qōl yahweh bakkōᵃḥ . . . behādār,* "The voice of Yahweh is strength itself . . . is very splendor"

xxxiii 4 *wᵉkol ma'ᵃśēhū be'ᵉmūnāh,* "and every work of his is truth itself"

xxxix 7 *'ak bᵉṣelem yithallek 'īš,* "Alas, as a mere phantom does man go about"

xli 4 *hāpaktā bᵉḥōlī* (MT *bᵉḥolyō*), "overthrow the sickness itself!"

l 19 *pīkā šālaḥtā bᵉrā'āh,* "With your mouth you forge evil itself"

liv 6 *'ᵃdōnāy bᵉsōmᵉkē napšī,* "the Lord (became) the true Sustainer of my life"

lv 19 *bᵉrabbīm hāyū 'immādī,* "full many were against me"

lxii 8 *maḥsī bē'lōhīm,* "God himself is my refuge"

lxxviii 31 *wayyah^{a}rōg b^{e}mišmannēhem,* "he slew their sturdiest"

cxviii 7 *yahweh lī b^e'ōz^{e}rāy,* "Yahweh is for me, my Great Warrior"

h^{a}lō' "look!"

Ps liv 2 *b^{e}bō' hazzīpīm wayyō'm^{e}rū l^{e}šā'ūl h^{a}lō' dāwīd mistattēr 'immānū,* "when the Ziphites came and told Saul, 'Look, David is hiding among us'"

lx 12 *h^{a}lō' 'attāh '^{e}lōhīm z^{e}naḥtānū,* "But you, O God—will you be angry with us?"

cxxxix 21 *h^{a}lō' m^{e}śan'ekā yhwh 'eśnā',* "Look, those who hate you, Yahweh, have I hated"

hēm/hēmmāh "look! behold!"

Ps ix 7–8 *hēmmāh yahweh* (MT *wyhwh*) *l^e'ōlām yēšēb,* "Behold Yahweh who has reigned from eternity!"

xxiii 4 *hēmmāh ynḥmny,* "behold, they will lead me." The verb derives from *nāḥāh,* "to lead," and contains an "internal" enclitic *mem.* See below Ps xliii 3

xxvii 2 *hēmmāh kāš^{e}lū w^{e}nāpālū,* "Lo! they stumble and fall"

xxxvii 9 *hēmmāh yīr^{e}šū 'āreṣ,* "Lo, they shall inherit the land"

xxxviii 11 *gam hēm 'ēn 'ittī,* "Alas, even this has left me"

xliii 3 *hēmmāh yanḥūnī,* "behold, let them lead me"

xlviii 6 *hēmmāh rā'ū,* "Lo! they looked"

lvi 7 *hēmmāh 'ōq^{e}bay* (MT *'^{a}qēbay*) *yišmōrū,* "see how my maligners watch!"

Emphatic *waw*
with postposition of the verb

Ps iv 5 *'al miškab^{e}kem w^{e}dommū,* "upon your beds weep!"

v 4 *bōqer 'e'^{e}rōk/l^{e}kā wa'^{a}ṣappeh,* "at dawn I will draw up my case,/ for you will I watch"

xlix 21 *'ādām bīqār w^{e}lō' yābīn,* "Man in the Mansion will nothing sense"

li 9 *t^{e}ḥaṭṭ^e'ēnī b'zwb w^e'eṭhār,* "Unsin me, I'll indeed be purer than gushing water"

18 *kī lū'* (MT *lō'*) *taḥpōṣ zebaḥ w^e'ettēnāh,* "For should you be pleased, a sacrifice indeed would I offer"

lv 12 *b^{e}qirbāh w^{e}lō' yāmīš,* "From its center, they never leave"

lix 13 *ḥaṭṭa't pīmō d^{e}bar ś^{e}pātēmō w^{e}yillākēdū* (MT *w^{e}yillāk^{e}dū*), "By the sin of their mouth, the gossip from their lips, let them be caught"

lxii 5 *'ak maššū'ōt* (MT *miśś^e'ētō*) *w^{e}yā'^{a}ṣū,* "Craft alone do they propose"

b^{e}pī (MT *b^{e}pīw*) *wībārēkū* (MT *y^{e}bārēkū*), "With their mouth indeed they bless"

lxix 15 *haṣṣīlēnī miṭṭīṭ w^e'al 'eṭbā'āh,* "Rescue me, lest I be submerged by the mire" lxxii 16   *kall^ebānōn piryō w^eyāṣīṣū*, "Let his fruit blossom like Lebanon"

lxxvii 2   *qōlī . . . w^e'eṣ'āqāh*, "With my voice . . . I desperately cry"

         qōlī . . . w^eha'^azīn, "To my voice . . . give ear at once"

lxxix 9   *'al d^ebar k^ebōd šim^ekā* (MT *š^emekā*) *w^ehaṣṣīlēnū*, "Because of your glorious name rescue us!"

lxxxi 11   *harḥīb pīkā* (MT *harḥeb pīkā*) *wa'^amal^e'ēhū*, "What is more, I filled your wide-open mouth"

lxxxix 20   *laḥ^asīdekā wattō'mer*, "to your devoted one indeed you said"

    44   *ḥarbō w^elō' h^aqēmōtā* (MT *h^aqēmōtō*), and you did not sustain his sword"

cvi 9   *sūp wayyaḥrēb* (MT *wayyeḥ^erāb*), "the Reeds he dried up"

cxix 46   *. . . neged m^elākīm w^elō' 'ēbōš*, ". . . before kings, And (I shall) not be humiliated"

    90   *'ereṣ watta'^amōd*, "more firmly than earth shall it stand"

cxli 5   *ḥāsīd* (MT *ḥesed*) *w^eyōkīḥēnī*, "May the Kind One chastise me"

Emphatic *waw*
without postposition of the verb

Ps vii 2–3   *w^ehaṣṣīlēnī pen yiṭrōp*, "Rescue me lest he tear me apart"

xvi 4   *ūbal 'assīk niskēhem* (the *waw* having been detached from the preceding *mhrw*), "Surely not will I pour libations to them" (revised wording)

xxv 11   *w^esālaḥtā la'^awōnī*, "forgive my iniquity!"

lxxx 19   *w^elō' nāsōg mimmekā*, "We have never turned away from you"

cii 5   *wayyībaš libbī*, "my heart has withered indeed"

cix 5   *t^epillāh wayyāšīmū 'ālāy*, "My prayer they set down to my debit"

cxviii 27   *'ēl yhwh wayyā'er lānū*, "El Yahweh has truly shone upon us"

cxli 4   *ūbal 'elḥam b^eman'ammēhem*, "never will I dine on their delicacies"

cxlii 4   *w^e'attāh yāda'tā n^etībātī*, "yes, you know my path"

Emphatic *waw*
with other parts of speech

Ps xxvii 8   *lēk* (MT *l^ekā*) *'āmar libbī baqqēš ūpānēy* (MT *baqq^ešū pānāy*), "Come, said my heart, seek his face!"

xxxi 12   *w^eliš^akēnay*, "even to my neighbors"

lix 5–6   *ūr^e'ēh w^e'attāh*, "and see for yourself"

lxiv 7   *w^elēb 'āmōq*, "even the deep heart"

lxix 21   *wa'^anūšāh* (MT *wā'ānūšāh*), "rank disease"

lxxi 20   *w^eṣārōt* (MT *ṣārōt*), "full many tribulations"; the *waw* has been detached from the preceding *hr'ytnw*; read with Qere *hir'ītani*, "you made me see"

lxxix 3   *w^e'ēn*, "with no one"

lxxxiii 17   *wībaqqēš ūšim^ekā* (MT *wībaq^ešū šim^ekā*), "And let your Name avenge itself"

cix 4   *yiśṭ^enūnī wā'ānī* (MT *wa'^anī*), "they slander me, even me"

cxvi 2   *ūbīmēy* (MT *ūb^eyāmay*) *'eqrā'*, "even as I called"

cxx 7   *šālōm w^ekī '^adabbēr*, "peace indeed did I talk" cxxi 8, cxxv 2 — *mē'attāh we'ad 'ōlām*, "from now unto eternity"

cxxxix 14 *wenapšī*, "my soul itself"

cxlii 5 *we'ēn*, "not one"

waw explicativum
functioning as a relative pronoun

Ps iii 4 *kebōdī ūmērīm rō'šī*, "my Glorious One who lifts high my head"

xlix 20 *dōr 'abōtī we'ad* (MT *'abōtāyw 'ad*) *nēṣaḥ lō' yir'ū 'ōr*, "the circle of your fathers, who will never more see the light"

lv 13 *yeḥārepēnī we'śśā'*, "he heaped on me the insults that I bear" Here *waw* explains the noun "insults" implicitly contained in the first verb

lxix 36 *weyāšūbū* (MT *weyāšebū*) *šam wīrūšūhā* (MT *wīrēšūhā*), "Those expelled from it will there return"

lxxii 12 *we'ānī we'ēn 'ōzēr lō*, "and the oppressed who has no helper"

lxxiii 12 *rešā'īm wešalwē 'ōlām hiśgū ḥāyil*, "the wicked, who, heedless of the Eternal, increased their wealth"

xciv 12 *haggeber 'ašer teyasserennū yāh ūmittōrātekā telammedennū*, "the man whom you have instructed, Yah, whom you have taught from your law"

cvii 25 *se'ārāh watterōmēm gallāyw*, "a storm which lifted high his waves"

Vocative *waw*

Ps lxxiv 12 *kallēh* (attached from vs. 11) *we'lōhīm malkē* (MT *malkī*) *miqqedem*, "Destroy, O God, the kings from the East!"

lxxv 2 *hōdīnū weqārōb šemekā*, "We praise your Name, O Near One!"

lxxxvi 10 *kī gādōl 'attāh we'ōśēh niplā'ōt*, "How great you are, O Worker of Marvels!"

cxxxix 19 *we'anšē dāmīm sūrū mennī*, "O men of idols, turn away from me!"

cxlv 6 *we'izzūz* (MT *we'ezūz*) *nōr'ōtekā yō'mēru*, "O Strong One, they shall announce your awesome acts"

Emphatic *kī*
with pronouns

Ps xci 3 *kī hū' yaṣṣīlekā mippaḥ*, "He alone will free you from the snare"

cxlviii 5 *kī hū' ṣiwwāh wenibrā'ū*, "he alone commanded, and they were created"

Emphatic *kī*
with personal pronouns in sentences expressing commands or wishes

Ps x 14 *rā'ītāh kī 'attāh*, "See for yourself!"

xxxix 10 *kī 'attāh 'āśītā*, "Oh that you would act!"

lxi 6 *kī 'attāh 'elōhīm šāma'tā*, "O that you yourself, O God, would hear!"

lxxxii 8 *kī 'attāh tinḥal bekol haggōyim,* "rule over all the nations yourself!"

lxxxvi 17 *kī 'attāh yahweh 'azartanī weniḥamtānī,* "O that you yourself, Yahweh, would help me and console me!"

Emphatic *kī*
with substantives

Ps lix 10, 18 *kī 'elōhīm miśgabbī,* "God himself is my bulwark"

lxviii 29 *ṣawwēh 'elōhay kā'uzzekā* (MT *ṣiwwāh 'elōhekā 'uzzekā*), "Send, my God, your strength!"

lxxviii 15 *wayyašq kī tehōmōt rabbāh,* "and he watered the vast wasteland (feminine singular with the Phoenician ending!) itself"

lxxx 17 *bā'ēš kī sōḥāh* (MT *kesūḥāh*), "with a full blazing fire"

cii 10 *kī 'ēper kalleḥem 'ākāltī,* "Ashes I eat as my food"

cv 12 *kime'aṭ,* "a mere handful," balancing *metē mispār,* "few in number," of the first colon

Emphatic *kī*
with postposition of the verb

Ps xlix 16 *miyyad še'ōl kī yiqqāḥēnī,* "from the hand of Sheol will he surely snatch me"

liv 7 *ba'amittō* (with defective spelling of *-ō*) *kī hiṣmītām* (MT *ba'amittekā haṣmītēm*), "in his fidelity he annihilated them completely"

lvi 13 *nedāray kī* (MT *nedārekā*) *'ašallēm,* "Indeed will I pay my vows"

lix 10 *'uzzū* (MT *'uzzō*) *'ēlī kī* (MT *'ēlekā*) *'eššāmērāh* (MT *'ešmōrāh*), "My God is a fortress, truly am I protected"

18 *'uzzī 'ēlī kī* (MT *'ēlekā*) *'ezzāmērāh* (MT *'azammērāh*), "My God is my fortress, truly am I safeguarded"

lx 4 *'ereṣ . . . kī māṭāh,* "the land . . . much did it totter"

lxxxix 3 *bepī kī 'āmartī,* "With my mouth I clearly admit: . . ."

xc 4 *'elep šānīm . . . kī ya'abōrū* (MT *ya'abōr we*), "a thousand years . . . just pass"

cix 23 *keṣēl kī nāṭawtī* (MT *kinṭōtō*), "Like a shadow indeed have I tapered"

nin'artī kī 'erbeh (MT *kā'arbeh*), "I have lost my youth, truly I have aged"

cxviii 10, 11, 12 *bešēm yhwh kī 'amīlam,* "but in Yahweh's name indeed I cut off their foreskins"

cxx 7 *'anī šālōm wekī 'adabbēr,* "As for me, peace indeed did I talk"

cxxviii 2 *yegīa' kappekā kī tō'kēl,* "the fruit of your toil indeed shall you eat"

cxliii 9 *'ēlī kī kussētī* (MT *'ēlekā kissītī*), "my God truly am I being submerged"

Emphatic *kī*
without postposition of the verb

Ps lxiii 2 *kī ṣāme'āh lekā napšī,* "my soul ardently thirsts for you"; the suffix of MT *'ašaḥarekkā* has been detached and pointed as defectively written emphatic *kī*.

lxxi 23 *kī 'azammerāh lāk,* "indeed will I sing to you"

lxxv 3 *kī 'eqqaḥ mō'ēd,* "Indeed, I will summon the assembly"

lxxvii 12 *kī 'ezkerāh miqqedem pil'ekā,* "indeed will I recite your marvels of old"

lxxxv 9 *yahweh kī yedabbēr šālōm,* "Yahweh indeed has promised well-being"

xc 7 *kī kālīnū be'appekā,* "Indeed we are consumed by your wrath"

cii 5 *kī šākaḥtī mē'ōkēl* (MT *mē'akōl*), "I am utterly wasted by the Devourer"

11 *kī neśā'tanī wattašlīkēnī,* "you lifted me up and threw me down"

14 *kī bā' mō'ēd,* "indeed the appointed time has come"

civ 13 *kī tiśba' hā'āreṣ,* "the earth is fully imbued." The *k* has been detached from the preceding word

cxvi 1 "Out of love for me Yahweh did hear (*kī yišma' yhwh*) my plea for his mercy"

2 *kī hiṭṭāh 'oznō lī,* "Truly he inclined his ear to me"

cxix 161 *ūmedabberay kī* (MT *ūmiddebāreykā*) *pāḥad libbī,* "and my heart indeed dreaded my pursuers"

cxxxviii 2 *kī higdaltā 'al kōl* (MT *kol*) *šimekā 'imrāteka,* "you surely glorified before all your Name, your promise"

Emphatic *kī*
with precative perfect

Ps ix 5 *kī 'āśītā,* "Oh that you would defend!"

lvi 14 *kī hiṣṣaltā napšī mimmāwet,* "Would that you rescue me from Death"

lxi 4 *kī hāyītā maḥseh lī,* "O that you would be my refuge!"

lxiii 8 *kī hāyītā 'ezrātāhl lī,* "O that you would be my help!"

lxxi 24 *kī bōšū,* "O that they would be humiliated!"

kī ḥāperū, "O that they would be put to confusion!"

Emphatic *kī*
with precative perfect and independent personal pronoun

Ps iii 8 *kī hikkītā 'attā* (MT *'et*), "O that you yourself would smite!"

Emphatic *kī*
with jussive

Ps xvii 6 *kī ta'anēnī 'ēl,* "O that you would answer me, O El!"

lxxxvi 7 *kī ta'anēnī,* "O that you would answer me!"

Emphatic *kī*
with prepositions

Ps lxxxvi 3 *ḥonnēnī 'adōnāy kī 'ēlekā 'eqrā' kol hayyōm,* "Have pity on me, my Lord; it is to you I cry all day long"

4 *kī 'ēlekā 'adōnāy napšī 'eśśā'*, "it is to you, my Lord, I lift up my soul"

Emphatic *kī*
introducing a whole sentence

Ps xvi 8 *kī mīmīnī bal 'emmōṭ*, "indeed, from his right hand I will never swerve"

xxii 29 *kī lyhwh hammelūkāh*, "In truth—Yahweh's is the kingship" (revised translation)

xxvi 1 *kī 'anī betummī hālaktī*, "On my word, I have walked in my integrity"

lxii 6 *kī mimmennū tiqwātī*, "from him truly comes my hope"

lxviii 36 *kī 'ēl yiśrā'ēl hū'*, "Truly is he the God of Israel"; the suffix *-kā* has been detached from the preceding word and vocalized as the emphatic *kī*

lxxvi 11 *kī ḥamat 'ādām tōdekkā*, "Truly will they praise you for your rage with other men"

lxxxiv 12 *kī šemeš ūmāgān* (MT *ūmāgēn*) *yahweh 'elōhīm*, "Truly Sun and Suzerain is Yahweh God"

lxxxix 18 *kī tip'eret 'uzzāmō 'āttāh*, "Indeed, you are our glorious triumph"

cxvi 16 *kī 'anī 'abdekā*, "truly am I your servant"

cxix 43 *kī lemišpāṭekā yiḥāltī*, "Indeed I wait for your ordinances"

111 *kī śešōn libbī hēmmāh*, "Truly they are my heart's joy"

cxxv 3 *kī lō' yānūaḥ šēbeṭ hārešaʻ*, "The scepter of the wicked will certainly not rest . . ." Note: *rešaʻ*, "wickedness," assumes concrete meaning because of its parallelism with *ṣaddīqīm*, "the just," in the second colon

cxxxv 5 *kī 'anī yādaʻtī*, "Indeed I acknowledge"

cxxxix 4 *kī 'ēn millāh bilešōnī*, "The word is not even off my tongue"

13 *kī 'attāh qānītā kilyōtāy*, "Yes, you created my inmost self"

cxli 5 *kī 'ōd ūtepillātī berā'ōtēhem*, "nay, my constant prayer will be against their evil customs"

Emphatic *kī*
functioning as interjection

Ps xxxii 10 *kī rabbīm mak'ōbīm lārāšā'*, "How many are the torments of the wicked!"; the *kī* has been attached from the last word of the preceding line

lii 11 *wa'aqawweh šimekā kī ṭōb neged ḥasīdekā*, "And I will proclaim your Name, so good to your devoted ones!"

liv 8 *'ōdeh šimekā yahweh kī ṭōb*, "I will praise your Name, Yahweh, truly good"

lvi 2 *kī še'āpanī 'enōš*, "How men hound me!"

3 *kī rabbīm lōḥamīm lī*, "How many are battling against me!"

lxiii 4 *kī ṭōb ḥasdekā mēḥayyāy* (MT *mēḥayyīm*), "How much sweeter your kindness than my life!"

lxxxiv 11 *kī ṭōb yōm baḥaṣērekā mē'ālep bḥrty*, "How much better is one day in your court than a thousand in the Cemetery!"

lxxxvi 10 *kī gādōl 'attāh*, "How great you are!"
cii 15 *kī rāṣū ʿ^{a}bādekā 'et '^{a}bānehā*, "How your servants love her stones!"
cviii 4 *kī gādōl*, "O truly Great One!"
cix 21 *l^{e}maʿan šim^{e}kā* (MT *š^{e}mekā*) *kī ṭōb*, "For the sake of your Name, truly good"
cxxviii 4 *hinnēh kī kēn y^{e}bārēk* (MT *y^{e}bōrak*) *geber y^{e}rē' yhwh*, "Observe how the Reliable blesses the man who fears Yahweh"
cxxxv 3 *lišmō kī nāʿīm*, "to his Name, truly pleasant"
cxxxviii 5 *kī gādōl k^{e}bōd yhwh*, "How great is the glory of Yahweh!"
cxlvii 1 *kī ṭōb zamm^{e}rāh . . . kī nāʿīm nā'wah . . .*, "How good to hymn . . . How pleasant to laud!"

Emphatic *lamedh*
with substantives

Ps lxii 6 *lē'lōhīm dūmī* (MT *dōmmī*), "God himself is my castle"
lxix 11 *watt^{e}hī laḥ^{a}rāpōt lī*, "and abuse itself was mine"
23 *liš^{e}lūmīm* (MT *liš^{e}lōmīm*), "even their companions"; the suffix is forthcoming from *lipnēhem* of the first colon on the principle of double-duty suffix
lxxxi 4 *l^{e}yōm ḥaggēnū*, "the very day of our feast"
lxxxix 19 *liqdōš yiśrā'ēl malkēnū*, "the Holy One of Israel is our King!"
cvi 46 *wayyittēn 'ōtām l^{e}raḥ^{a}mīm*, "He granted them untold mercies"
cix 11 *y^{e}naqqēš nōšeh l^{e}kol '^{a}šer lō*, "May the creditor seize everything he has"
cxiv 1 *bēt yaʿ^{a}qōb mēʿam l^{e}ʿāz* (MT *lōʿēz*), "the house of Jacob from a barbaric people"
cxx 7 *hēmmāh l^{e}milḥāmāh* (MT *lammilḥāmāh*), "but they, only war"
cxxxv 11 *l^{e}sīḥōn*, "even Sihon" } =Ps cxxxvi 19, 20
ūl^{e}ʿōg, "and Og himself" }
ūl^{e}kōl maml^{e}kōt k^{e}nāʿan, "yes, all the kings of Canaan"

Emphatic *lamedh*
with postposition of the verb

Ps xxv 14 *ūb^{e}rītō l^{e}hōdīʿām*, "and his covenant he truly reveals to them"
xxxi 3 *l^{e}bēt m^{e}ṣūdōt l^{e}hōšīʿēnī*, "O fortified citadel, save me!"
lxx 2 *'^{e}lōhīm l^{e}haṣṣīlēnī*, "O God, rescue me!"
lxxi 3 *lābō' tāmīd ṣiwwītā l^{e}ḥōšīʿēnī*, "To come, Perpetual One, you promised; save me!" (revised translation; cf. Ps cxix 44)
ci 5 *'ōtō l' '^{a}kalle* (MT *lō' 'ūkāl*), "of such I made an end indeed"
cix 16 *w^{e}nik'ēh lēbāb l^{e}mōtēt*, "and the brokenhearted he seeks even to slay"
cxix 20 *gār^{e}sāh napšī l^{e}tā'^{a}bāh* (MT *l^{e}ta'^{a}bāh*), "My soul craves, truly longs"
38 *'^{a}šer līrē'tīkā* (MT *l^{e}yir'ātekā*), "because I indeed fear you"
128 *kol piqqūdekā l^{e}yiššartī* (MT *kol piqqūdē kōl yiššartī*), "All your precepts I consider truly right"

Emphatic *lamedh*
without postposition of the verb

Ps lxviii 19 *we'ap sōrerīm lešikkēn* (MT *liškōn*) *yāh 'elōhīm,* "But Yahweh God completely entombed the stubborn"

lxxxv 10 *lešākēn* (MT *liškōn*) *kābōd be'arṣēnū,* "Indeed his glory dwells in our land"

14 *wyśm* (MT *weyāśēm*) *ledōrēk* (MT *lederek*) *pe'āmāyw,* "beauty will indeed tread in his steps"

xcii 8 *lehišmīdām* (MT *lehiššāmedām*) *'adē 'ad,* "He completely destroyed them for all time!"

civ 14 *lehōṣī' leḥem min hā'āreṣ,* "Indeed he brings forth grain from the earth"

15 *lehiṣhīl* (MT *lehaṣhīl*) *pānīm mešumman* (MT *miššāmen*) "Truly he makes the full face resplendent"

Vocative *lamedh*
with divine appellatives

le'ēl ḥāy, "O living God!" Ps xlii 3 (cf. fifth NOTE on Ps lxxxiv 3)

le'ēl sal'ī, "O El, my Rock!" Ps xlii 10

lē'lōhīm, "O God!" Pss xlii 3 (cf. fourth NOTE on Ps lxxxiv 3), lxix 4 (*lē'lōhāy,* "O my God!" forms an inclusion with vocative *'elōhīm* of vs. 2) "O gods!" Pss xlvii 2//*kol hā'ammīm,* "All you strong ones!" lxviii 5// *šāmāw* (MT *šemō*), "O his heavens!" 33//*mamlekōt hā'āreṣ,* "O kings of the earth!"

lebēt meṣūdōt, "O fortified citadel!" Ps xxxi 3

leṭōb, "O Good One!" Ps cxix 122

leṭōbāh, "O Good One!" Ps lxxxvi 17

lyhwh, "O Yahweh!" Pss iii 9, xvi 2, xxxii 5//*'ēlī* (MT *'alē*), "O Most High!" xci 2, xcii 2//*'elyōn,* "O Most High!" cxix 126, cxl 7//*yhwh* (vocative)

lemārōm (MT *lammārōm*), "O Exalted One!" Ps vii 8

lāneṣaḥ, "O Conqueror!" Pss xliv 24//*'adōnāy,* "O Lord!" (cf. last NOTE on Ps lxxiv 10), lxxiv 10//*'elōhīm,* "O God!" 19, lxxxix 47//*yhwh,* "O Yahweh!"

le'ōlām, "O Eternal One!" Pss xxxi 2 (=lxxi 1)//*yhwh,* "O Yahweh!", lii 11, lxxxvi 12//*'adōnāy 'elōhay,* "my Lord, my God!", cxix 111, 142, 144, 160

le'ōlām wā'ed, "O Eternal and Everlasting!" Ps cxlv 1//*'elōhay hammelek,* "my God, O King!"

leṣūr mā'ōz, "O mountain of refuge!" Ps xxxi 3

leṣūr mā'ōn, "O mountain of succor!" Ps lxxxi 3

lešadday (MT *lešaddī*), "O Shaddai!" Ps xxxii 4//*'ēli* (MT *'alay*), "O Most High!"

With other nouns

lebēt yiśrā'ēl, "O house of Israel!" Ps xcviii 3
libnē 'edōm, "O sons of Edom!" Ps cxxxvii 7
ledāwīd, "O David!" Ps cxxxii 1, 11, 17//*limšīḥī,* "O my anointed!"
lahōlelīm, "O boastful!" Ps lxxv 5//*lārešā'īm,* "O wicked!"

l^eyiśrā'ēl, "O Israel!" Pss lxxiii 1, lxxxi 5, cxxii 4
lay^ešārīm, "O upright!" Ps xxxiii 1//*ṣaddīqīm*, "you just!"
l^emelek, "O king!" Ps xlv 2
limšīḥī, "O my anointed!" Ps cxxxii 17//*l^edāwīd*, "O David!"
lā'ām, "O people!" Ps lxviii 36
lār^ešā'īm, "O wicked!" Ps lxxv 5//*lahōl^elīm*, "O boastful!"

Enclitic *mem*
appended to pronominal suffix

Ps iv 8	*b^elibbī-m* (adding the *mem* of the following *mē'ēt*), "in my heart"
xxii 16	*ūl^ešōnī-m dōbēq* (MT *ūl^ešōnī mudbāq*), "and my tongue sticks"
xxx 4	*ḥiyyītanī-m yār^edī bōr* (MT *ḥiyyītanī miyyōr^edī bōr*), "You restored me to life after my descent to the Pit" (revised translation)
xxxi 12	*w^elišᵃkēnay-m* (attaching the *mem* of the following *m^e'ōd*), "even to my neighbors"
lv 19	*napšī-m* (attaching the *mem* of the following *mqrb*), "my life"
lxviii 24	*l^ešōn k^elābekā-m* (attaching the *mem* of the following *mē'ōy^ebīm*), "the tongues of your dogs"
29	*lānū-m* (attaching the *mem* of the opening word of the next line *mēhēkāleka*), "for us"
lxix 8	*pānāy-m* (attaching the *mem* of the first word of the next line *mwzr*), "my face"
cxi 10	*'ōśēhā-m* (MT *'ōśēhem*), "those who acquire it," i.e., wisdom
cxliv 10	*lammalkī-m* (MT *lamm^elākīm*), "to his king"
cxxx 6	*la'dōnay-mi* (MT *la'dōnāy mi*), "toward my Lord"

Enclitic *mem*
balancing pronominal suffix

Ps v 10	*pīhū//qirbō-m* (MT *qirbām*), "his mouth//his belly"
x 17	*lbm* (MT *libbām*)//*'ozneka*, "your attention//your ear"
xii 8	*tišm^erēm//tiṣṣ^erennū*, "you have protected us//you have guarded us"
lxv 10	*dagna-m* (MT *d^egānām*) . . . *t^ekīnehā*, "her grain . . . you brought her into being"
lxxx 6	*h'kltm* (MT *he'^ekaltām*)//*wattašqēmō*, "you have fed us//you have made us drink"
lxxxi 13	*wā'ᵃšall^eḥēhū* . . . *lbm* (MT *libbām*), "So I repudiated him . . . his heart"
lxxxiv 6	*lō//blbbm* (MT *bil^ebābām*), "to him//from his heart"
civ 29	*pāneka//rūḥm* (MT *rūḥām*), "your face//your spirit"
cix 13	*'aḥᵃrītō//šmm* (MT *š^emām*), "his future life//his name"

Enclitic *mem*
with nouns

Ps xlix 9	*napšō-m* (MT *napšām*), "his soul"
liv 5	*'^elōhīm lin^egīdī-m* (MT *l^enegdām*), "God is my Leader"
lxv 6	*w^eyam r^eḥōqī-m*, "and of the distant sea" (MT *w^eyam r^eḥōqīm*)

lxviii 23 *'āmar '^{a}dōnay-m bāšān* (MT *'^{a}dōnāy mibbāšān*) *'aššīb* (MT *'āšīb*), "The Lord said: 'I stifled the Serpent' "

lxxviii 15 *ṣūr-m* (MT *ṣurīm*), "the rock"; cf. vs. 20

lxxxvi 14 *w^{e}lō' śāmūkā lin^{e}gīdī-m* (MT *l^{e}negdām*), "And they do not consider you my Leader"

cvi 7 *'ēlīm* (MT *'al yām*), "the Most High"

cix 15 *zikrō-m* (MT *zikrām*), "his memory"

cxxxix 16 *gīlay-mī* (MT *golmī*), "my life stages"

Enclitic *mem*
with verbs

Ps xviii 22 *w^{e}lō' rāša'tī-m '^{e}lōhāy* (MT *w^{e}lō' rāša'tī mē'^{e}lōhāy*), "and I have not been guilty, O my God"

41 *ūm^{e}śan^{e}'ay 'aṣmītēm*, "and my enemies I exterminated"

46 *w^{e}yaḥr^{e}gū-m misg^{e}rōtēhem* (MT *w^{e}yaḥr^{e}gū mimmisg^{e}rōtēhem*), "and their hearts are seized with anguish"

xxii 2 *rāḥōq-m šaw'ātī* (MT *rāḥōq mīšū'ātī*), "dismissing my plea"

xxvi 8 *'āhabtī-m 'ūn* (MT *'āhabtī m^{e}'ōn*) *bēteka*, "I love to live in your house"

xxix 6 *wayyarqēd-mi* (MT *wayyarqīdēm*), "he makes skip"

xxxi 11 *wa'^{a}ṣāmay 'āšēšū-m* (attaching the *mem* of the first word of the following line), "and my bones are wasted away"

xxxviii 9 *šā'agtī-m nāhamtī* (MT *šā'agtī minnah^{a}mat*) *libbī*, "I groan and moan in my heart"

xlii 5 *'eddaddēm*, "I prostrate myself"

xlvi 9 *ḥ^{a}zū-m p^{e}'ullōt yahweh* (MT *ḥ^{a}zū mip'^{a}lōt yahweh*), "observe the works of Yahweh!" See below Ps lxvi 5

lv 20 *wayya'an-m* (MT *w^{e}ya'^{a}nēm*), "and he answered"

lxvi 5 *ūr^{e}'ū-m p^{e}'ullōt '^{e}lōhīm* (MT *ūr^{e}'ū mip'^{a}lōt '^{e}lōhīm*), "and see the works of God!"

lxvii 5 *ūl^{e}'ummīm bā'āreṣ tanḥēm*, "and peoples into the land you will lead"

lxxii 16 *piryō w^{e}yāṣīṣū-m* (attaching the *mem* of the following word *mē'īr*), "let his fruit blossom"

lxxiii 10 *yiśb^{e}'ū-m* (MT *yāšīb 'ammō*), "they gorged themselves"

lxxxi 7 *h^{a}sīrōtī-m sēbel* (MT *h^{a}sīrōtī missēbel*) *šikmō*, "I removed the burden on his shoulder"

lxxxiii 12 *šītēmō n^{e}dībēmō*, "Make their nobles!"

lxxxv 4 *h^{e}šībōtā-m ḥ^{a}rōn* (MT *h^{e}šībōtā mēḥ^{a}rōn*) *'appekā*, "abate your blazing wrath!"

lxxxviii 16 *gō'ē-m nō'ēr* (MT *gōwē^{a}' minnō'ar*), "groaning I die"

cxix 152 *yāda'tī-m 'ēdōtekā* (MT *yāda'tī mē'ēdōtekā*), "I acknowledge your stipulations"

Enclitic *mem*
with prepositions

Ps cxlvii 15 *'ad-m hērāh* (MT *'ad m^{e}hērāh*), "toward the mountain"

The conjunction
pa "and"

Ps xlviii 14 *pa-sīgū* (MT *pass^egū*), "and examine!"
l 10–11 . . . *b^ehar^erē-'ēl;* 11. *pa-yāda'tī* . . . (MT *b^ehar^erē 'ālep;* 11. *yāda'tī*), ". . . in the towering mountains; 11. For I know . . ."
lx 3 *p^e-raṣtānū*, "and you ran from us"
4 *p^e-ṣūm^etāh* (MT *p^eṣamtāh*), "and she went to pieces"
lxiv 8 *pa-tō'ēm* (MT *pit'ōm*), "and double (be their wounds)!"
lxxii 16 *pa-sūt bar* (MT *pissat bar*), "a very mantle of wheat"
lxxiv 3 *hārīmāh p^e'amm^ekā* (MT *pē'āmekā*), "Raise up your own people!"
cxxxix 6 *p^elā'^eyāh* (MT *pl'yh*) *da'at mimmennī*, "Too overpowering for me is your knowledge"

šām "behold!"

Ps xiv 5 *šām pāḥ^adū pāḥad*, "See how they have formed a cabal!"
xxxvi 13 *šām nāp^elū pō'^alē 'āwen*, "See how the evildoers will fall!"
xlviii 7 *šām*, "alas" and not "there" because it has no correlative
liii 6 *šām pāḥ^adū paḥad*, "See how they marshaled their troops!"
lxvi 6 *šām niśm^eḥāh bō*, "Come, let us rejoice in him!"
lxviii 28 *šām binyāmīn ṣā'īr rōdēm*, "Look, little Benjamin leads them"

Heaping up of emphatic particles *kī lā*, "truly, verily"

Ps xlvii 10 *kī lē'lōhīm magnē* (MT *māginnē*) *'ereṣ*, "truly God is Suzerain of the earth"
lxxxix 19 *kī lyhwh m^egānēnū* (MT *māginnēnū*), "Truly Yahweh is our Suzerain"

VIII. SYNTAX AND POETIC DEVICES

Prospective suffix

Ps lxix 4 *kālū 'ēnay m^eyaḥēl*, "My eyes grow bleary as I wait"
lxxxvi 11 *ba'^amittekā yāḥīd* (MT *yaḥēd*), "in fidelity to you alone"
lxxxviii 9 *šattanī . . . kālū'* "you put me . . . as I am imprisoned"
18 *hiqqīpū 'ālay yāḥīd* (MT *yāḥad*), "they close in on me alone"

Omission of the suffix with names of parts of the body

Note: Only those examples are listed whose lack of the suffix cannot be explained by the principle of double-duty suffix

kābēd "liver, heart"

Ps xxx 13 *l^ema'an y^ezammer^ekā kābēd* (MT *kābōd*), "So that my heart might sing to you"

kap "hand"

Ps xlvii 2 *kol hā'ammīm tiq'ū kāp*, "All you strong ones, clap your hands"
xcviii 8 *n^ehārōt yimḥ^a'ū kāp*, "Let the ocean currents clap their hands"

lēb "heart"

Ps cv 3 *yiśmaḥ lēb mᵉbaqᵉšē yhwh,* "let your heart rejoice, O seekers of Yahweh!"

cxi 1 *'ōdeh yhwh bᵉkol lēbāb,* "I will thank Yahweh with all my heart"

cxix 2 *ūbᵉkol* (attaching the *waw* of the preceding word) *lēb yidrᵉšūhū,* "and with all their heart search for him"

cxl 3 *'ᵃšer ḥāšᵉbū rā'ōt bᵉlēb,* "Because they plan evil things in their heart"

lāšōn "tongue"

Ps lii 6 *lᵉšōn mirmāh,* "your tongue of deceit"="your deceitful tongue"

nepeš "neck"

Ps lxix 2 *kī bā'ū mayim 'ad nepeš,* "for the waters have reached my neck"

'ayin "eye"

Ps xxxv 19 *śōnᵉ'ay ḥinnām yiqrᵉṣū 'āyin,* "my stealthy enemies wink their eye"

qeren "horn"

Ps lxxv 5 *lārᵉšā'īm 'al tārīmū qāren,* "O wicked, do not raise your horn!"

Abstract noun balanced by concrete noun:
abstract noun//concrete noun

Ps vi 6	*zikrekā//mī yōdeh lāk,* "memory of you=one who remembers you//who praises you?"
xxii 12	*ṣārāh//'ōzēr,* "adversity=adversary//helper"
xxvi 10	*zimmāh//šōḥad,* "idolatry=idols//bribes"
12	*mīšōr//qᵉhālīm,* "uprightness=the upright//congregations"
xxxvi 12	*ga'ᵃwāh//rᵉšā'īm,* "presumption=the presumptuous//the wicked"
xxxvii 28	*mišpāṭ//ḥᵃsīdāyw,* "justice=the just man//his devoted ones"
xl 18	*'ezrātī//mᵉpalᵉṭī,* "my help=my helper//my deliverer"
liv 9	*ṣārāh//'ōyᵉbay,* "adversity=my adversaries//my foes"
lxviii 33	*mamlᵉkōt hā'āreṣ//'ᵉlōhīm,* "kingdoms of the earth=kings of the earth//gods"
lxx 6	*'ezrī//mᵉpalᵉṭī,* "my help=my helper//my deliverer"
lxxviii 61	*šᵉbī//ṣār,* "captivity=the captors//adversary"
lxxxii 2	*'āwel//rᵉšā'īm,* "injustice=the unjust//the wicked"
cvii 42–43	*kol 'awlāh//mī ḥākām,* "all evil=every evil man//whoever is wise." On the chiastic parallelism here, consult *Psalms III*
cxix 139	*qin'ātī//ṣārāy,* "my zeal=my antagonists//my adversaries"
150	*zimmāh//tōrātᵉkā,* "idolatry=idols//your law"
cxxv 3	*šēbeṭ hārešaʿ//haṣṣaddīqīm,* "the scepter of wickedness=the scepter of the wicked//the just"
cxxxviii 7, cxliii 11–12	*ṣārāh//'ōyᵉbay,* "adversity=my adversaries//my foes"
cxli 4	*rešaʿ//'īšīm pō'ᵃlē 'āwen,* "wickedness=the wicked//men who are evildoers"
cxliv 10–11	*rā'āh//bᵉnē nēkar,* "evil=the Evil One//foreigners"

Abstract noun balanced by concrete noun:
concrete noun//abstract noun

Ps xii 2 — *ḥāsīd//'emūnīm,* "the devoted man//fidelity=faithful men"
xxv 19 — *'ōyebay//śin'at ḥāmās,* "my foes//treacherous enmity=treacherous enemies"
xxviii 8 — *'ōz . . . mā'ōz//yešū'ōt,* "stronghold . . . refuge//salvation=the Savior"
xxxi 24 — *ḥasīdāyw//'emūnīm,* "devoted to him//his fidelity=his faithful ones"
xlvi 2 — *maḥseh* (MT *maḥaseh*) *wā'ōz//'ezrāh,* "refuge and stronghold//liberation=Liberator" (revised translation)
li 16 — *'elōhīm 'elōhay* (MT *'elōhē*)*//tešū'ātī,* "O God, my God//my salvation=my Savior"
lx 6 — *yerē'ekā//qōšeṭ,* "those who fear you//archery=bowmen"
lxviii 20 — *hā'ēl//yešū'ātēnū,* "El himself//our salvation=our Savior"
lxxxviii 2 — *'elōhay* (MT *'elōhē*)*//yešū'ātī,* "my God//my salvation=my Savior"
cii 23 — *'ammīm//mamlākōt,* "peoples//kingdoms=kings"
cix 2 — *rāšā'//mirmāh,* "the wicked//deceit=the deceitful"
cx 3 — *'ammekā//nedābōt,* "your Strong One//your generosity=your Valiant"
cxxxv 11 — *sīḥōn . . . 'ōg//mamlekōt kenā'an,* "Sihon . . . Og//kingdoms=kings of Canaan"

Concrete sense of an abstract noun required by the context

Ps v 8 — "I will worship in your holy temple, among those who fear you (*beyir'ātekā,* 'in the fear of you'), O Yahweh"
xxiv 4 — "who has not raised his mind to an idol (*šāw',* 'emptiness, vanity') nor sworn by a fraud (*mirmāh,* 'deceit')"
xxvii 9 — "Be my helper (*'ezrātī,* 'my help')!
Do not reject me nor abandon me,
O God who can save me (*'elōhē yiš'ī*)"
lxxxix 14 — "Yours is a powerful arm, O Warrior (*gebūrāh,* 'strength, force')!
your left hand is triumphant,
your right hand raised in victory!"
xc 11 — "Who can understand the violence of your wrath, or that those who fear you (*kī yir'ātekā,* 'the fear of you,' for MT *keyir'ātekā*) can be the object of your fury?"
cxxxvi 8–9 — "The sun as ruler (*memšelet,* 'rule') over the day . . .
The moon and stars as rulers (*memšālōt,* 'rule'; MT *memšelōt*) over the night"

Concrete noun having an abstract meaning

Ps cxi 8 — *'aśūyīm be'emet weyāšār,* "made of truth and uprightness" (literally, "an upright man")

Breakup of stereotyped phrases

'eben pinnāh "cornerstone"
  Jointly: Jer li 26; Job xxxviii 6
  Separated: Ps cxviii 22 *'eben//pinnāh*

'ereṣ k^{e}na'an "the Land of Canaan"
  Jointly: Gen xi 31, xii 5, xiii 12, xvi 3, etc.
  Separated: Pss cv 11 *'ereṣ//k^{e}na'an* (MT *k^{e}nā'an*), cvi 38 *k^{e}nā'an//hā'āreṣ*

'ēš lehābāh "fire of flame"
  Jointly: Isa iv 5; Hos vii 6
  Separated: Pss lxxxiii 15 *k^{e}'ēš//ūk^{e}lehābāh,* cvi 18 *'ēš//lehābāh*

'ašmūrāh ballaylāh "watch in the night"
  Jointly: Ps xc 4
  Separated: Ps cxix 55 *ballaylāh//w^{e}'ašmūrāh* (MT *wā'ešm^{e}rāh*)

b^{e}bēt yhwh "in the house of Yahweh"
  Jointly: Pss xxiii 6, xxvii 4, xcii 14, cxvi 19, cxxxv 2
  Separated: Ps cxxxiv 1 *b^{e}bēt//yhwh*

b^{e}yōm q^{e}rāb "on the day of battle"
  Jointly: Zech xiv 3; Ps lxxviii 9
  Separated: Ps cx 2–3 *biqrab 'ōy^{e}bekā* (MT *beqereb 'ōy^{e}bekā*)//*b^{e}yōm ḥēlekā* "in the battle with your foes//on the day of your conquest"

ḥesed we'^{e}met "kindness and fidelity"
  Jointly: Pss xxv 10, xl 12, lxi 8, lxxxv 11, lxxxvi 15, lxxxix 15
  Separated: Pss xxvi 3 *ḥasd^{e}kā//ba'^{a}mittekā,* xl 11 *ḥasd^{e}kā//wa'^{a}mitt^{e}kā,* lvii 11 *ḥasdekā//'^{a}mittekā* (=cviii 5, cxv 1, cxxxviii 2), cxvii 2 *ḥasdō//we'^{e}met*

yōmām wālaylāh "day and night"
  Jointly: Pss i 2, xxxii 4, xlii 4, lv 11
  Separated: Pss xxii 3 *yōmām//w^{e}laylāh,* xlii 9 *yōmām//ūballaylāh,* lxxviii 14 *yōmām//w^{e}kol hallaylāh,* xci 5 *lāylāh//yōmām,* cxxi 6 *yōmām//ballāylāh*

yam sūp "the Reed Sea"
  Jointly: Pss cvi 7, 22, cxxxvi 13, 15
  Separated: Ps cvi 9 *bayyām* (MT *b^{e}yam*)//*sūp*

kablē barzel "iron shackles"
  Jointly: Ps cxlix 8
  Separated: Ps cv 18 *bakkebel//barzel*

kissē' qodšō "his holy throne"
  Jointly: Ps xlvii 9
  Separated: Ps xi 4 *qodšō//kis^{e}'ō*

'ēgel massēkāh "a molten young bull"
  Jointly: Exod xxxii 4, 8; Deut ix 16; Neh ix 18
  Separated: Ps cvi 19 *'ēgel//l^{e}massēkāh*

'am naḥ^{a}lāh "people of patrimony"
Jointly: Deut iv 20
Separated: Pss xxviii 9 *'ammekā//naḥ^{a}lātekā*, lxxviii 62 *'ammō//ūb^{e}naḥ^{a}lātō*, 71 *'ammō//naḥ^{a}lātō*, xciv 5 *'amm^{e}kā//w^{e}naḥ^{a}lāt^{e}kā*, 14 *'ammō//w^{e}naḥ^{a}lātō*, cvi 40 *b^{e}'ammō//naḥ^{a}lātō*

ṣūr ḥallāmīš "flinty rock"
Jointly: Deut viii 15 *miṣṣūr haḥallāmīš*, xxxii 13 *mēḥalmīš ṣūr*
Separated: Ps cxiv 8 *haṣṣūr//ḥallāmīš*

qōl šaw'āh "voice of cry"
Jointly: Jer viii 19
Separated: Ps xviii 7 *qōlī//w^{e}šaw'ātī*

rū^{a}ḥ s^{e}'ārāh "storm wind"
Jointly: Ps cxlviii 8
Separated: Ps cvii 25 *rū^{a}ḥ//s^{e}'ārāh*

šūb 'āḥōr "to turn back"
Jointly: Ps ix 4 *b^{e}šūb 'ōy^{e}bay 'āḥōr*, "when my foes turn back"
Separated: Ps lvi 10 *yāšūbū//'āḥōr* (qal absolute infinitive)

šēm k^{e}bōdō "the glory of his name"
Jointly: Ps lxxii 19
Separated: Ps cii 16 *šēm//k^{e}bōdekā*

t^{e}hōmōt hā'āreṣ "the depths of the nether world"
Jointly: Ps lxxi 20
Separated: Ps cxlviii 7 *hā'āreṣ//t^{e}hōmōt*

tōm wāyōšer "integrity and uprightness"
Jointly: Ps xxv 21
Separated: Ps xxxvii 37 *tām//yāšār*

Two different conjugations of one verb in the same verse

Ps xxiv 7	*nāśā'*, "to lift," qal *ś^{e}'ū* and niphal *hinnāś^{e}'ū*
xxix 5	*šābar*, "to shiver," qal *šōbēr* and piel *y^{e}šabbēr*
xxxviii 3	*nāḥat*, "to descend," niphal *niḥ^{a}tū* and qal *tinḥat*
lxiv 5	*yārāh*, "to shoot," qal *līrōt* and hiphil *yōrūhū*
lxix 15	*nṣl*, "to rescue," hiphil *haṣṣīlēnī* and niphal *'innāṣ^{e}lāh*
lxxvii 12	*zākar*, "to recite," hiphil *'azkīr* (Ketiv) and qal *'ezk^{e}rāh*
cxxxix 21	*śānē'*, "to hate," piel *m^{e}śān^{e}'ekā* and qal *'eśnā'*

Precative perfect of the third person

Ps iv 8	*rābbū*, "let (their wheat and their wine) increase"
ix 7	*tammū*, "may they be destroyed"
	'ābad, "may (their memory) perish"
16	*ṭāb^{e}'ū*, "may (the nations) be mired"

nilkedāh, "may (their feet) get caught"
17 *nōda'*, "may (Yahweh) be known"
nōqēš, "let (the wicked man) be snared"
x 16 *'ābedū*, "let (the heathen) perish"
xxii 9 *gōl 'ēl* (MT *'el*) *yhwh*, "Let El Yahweh rejoice" (revised translation)
xlvii 10 *ne'esāpū*, "let (the nobles of the peoples) gather round." Cf. Isa xliii 9
me'ōd na'alāh, "let (God) be greatly exalted"
lii 7 *šērešekā*, "may (El) snatch your sons"
lvii 7 *nāpelū*, "may they fall"
lviii 9 *bal ḥāzū*, "may they never see"
lxiii 9 *dābeqāh*, "may (my soul) cling fast (to you)"
tāmekāh, "may (your right hand) grasp (me)"
lxiv 8 *hāyū*, "(double) be (their wounds)"
11 *ḥāsāh bō*, "let (the just man) fly to him for refuge"
lxv 14 *lābešū*, "may (the hollows) be dressed"
lxvii 7 *nātenāh*, "May (the earth) yield (her produce)"
lxxiv 8 *śūrāpū* (MT *śārepū*), "let (all their progeny) be burned"
lxxxiii 11 *nišmedū*, "let them be exterminated"
hāyū, "may they become"
xc 17 *kōnenāh*, "may he sustain"
kōnenēhū, "may he sustain for his good"; the suffix *-ēhū* expresses the dative of advantage
xcvii 8 *šāme'āh*, "let (Zion) hear"
civ 35 *'ēnām*, "exist no more"
cvi 48 *we'āmar kol hā'ām 'āmēn*, "And let all the people say, 'Amen'"
cvii 42 *qāpeṣāh*, "let (every evil man) clap shut his mouth"
cix 28 *qāmū*, "let them rise up!"
cxxii 6 *šā'alū* (MT *ša'alū*), "may they pray"
cxxix 4 *qiṣṣēs*, "May (Yahweh the Just) snap!"
cxli 6 *nišmeṭū*, "let (their judges) drop"
wešāme'ū, "and let them hear"
cxliv 12 *'iššēr* (MT *'ašer*), "may he bless"

Precative perfect
of the second person

Ps iii 8 *šibbartā*, "smash!"
iv 2 *hirḥabtā lī*, "set me at large!"
vii 7 *ṣiwwītā*, "appoint!"
ix 5 *yāšabtā*, "sit!"
6 *gā'artā*, "rebuke!"
'ibbadtā, "destroy!"
māḥītā, "blot out!"
7 *nātaštā*, "root out!"
x 17 *šāmā'tā*, "hear!"

xvii 3 *bāḥantā*, "examine!"
pāqadtā, "probe!"
ṣeraptanī, "test me with fire!"

xxii 22 *'anītānī*, "make me triumph!"

xxv 11 *wesālaḥtā la'awōnī*, "forgive my iniquity!"
Note: here the precative perfect is preceded by emphatic *waw*

xxvii 9 *'ezrātī hāyītā*, "be my helper!"
Note: here the abstract *'ezrātī*, "my help," must be understood and translated concretely

xxx 12 *hāpaktā*, "turn (my weeping)!"
pittaḥtā, "unlace (my sackcloth)!"

xli 4 *hāpaktā*, "overthrow!"
13 *tāmaktā bī*, "grasp me!"

xlv 8 *'āhabtā*, "you must love"

lxi 6 *nātattā*, "grant!"

lxv 10 *pāqadtā*, "visit!"
haribbōtā (MT *rabbat*), "rain down!"
12 *'iṭṭartā*, "crown!"

lxxiii 23 *'āḥaztā*, "take hold!"

lxxiv 2 *gā'altā*, "redeem!"

lxxvii 16 *gā'altā*, "redeem!"
21 *nāḥītā*, "lead!"

lxxix 10 *nāqamtā* (MT *niqmat*), "avenge!"

lxxxv 2 *rāṣītā*, "favor!"
šabtā, "restore!"
3 *nāśā'tā 'awōn*, "forgive the guilt!"
kissītā, "cover!"
4 *'āsaptā*, "withdraw!"
hešībōtā-m ḥarōn (MT *mēḥarōn*) *'appekā*, "abate your blazing wrath!"

xc 1 *hāyītāl lānū*, "be ours!"

cxvi 16 *pittaḥtā lemōsērāy*, "Loose my fetters!"

cxix 21 *gā'artā*, "Rebuke!"
65 *ṭōb 'āśītā 'im 'abdekā*, "Do good to your servant!"
118 *sālītā*, "make a mound!"
121 *'āśītāy* (MT *'āśītī*) *mišpāṭ wāṣedeq*, "Defend for me my right and my just cause!"

cxxxix 1 *ḥaqartanī*, "examine me!"

cxliii 12 *weha'abadtā*, "and destroy!"

Precative perfect
of the second person with full spelling of the final vowel

Ps iv 8 *nātattāh*, "put (happiness)!" Cf. Ps lx 6
x 14 *rā'ītāh*, "see!" Cf. Ps xxxv 22
xxxi 6 *pādītāh*, "ransom!"
xxxv 22 *rā'ītāh*, "look!" Cf. Ps x 14

xliv 27 *'āzartāh* (MT *'ezrātāh*), "help!"
lvi 9 *sāpartāh*, "write down!"
lx 6 *nātattāh*, "give!" Cf. Ps iv 8
lxxiii 27 *hiṣmattāh*, "annihilate!"
cxl 8 *sakkōtāh*, "shelter!"

Precative perfect
of the first person

Ps lxiii 3 *ḥazītīkā*, "may I gaze on you"
cxxxix 18 *heqīṣōtī*, "may I rise"

yqtl expressing past time

Ps xxi 9–13 Nine *yqtl* forms describing past narrative action. On the importance of this observation for the classification of this passage, see introductory NOTE to Ps xxi

xxvi 6 *'erḥaṣ*, "I have washed." The action thus expressed belongs to the psalmist's protestation of innocence (vss. 3–7), in which *qtl* and *yqtl* forms are used alternatively

11 *'ēlēk*, "I have walked." Verses 11–12 are a reaffirmation of psalmist's innocence. In the next verse *qtl* (*'āmedāh*) is balanced in the second colon by *yqtl* (*'abārēk*)

lii 9 "So this is the man who would not consider (*lō' yāśīm*) God his refuge, but trusted (*wayyibṭaḥ*) in his great wealth, relied (*yā'ōz*) on his perniciousness!"

lv 13 "It was not a rival who heaped on me the insults (*yeḥārepēnī*) that I bear (*we'eššā'*); It was not my enemy who defamed me (*'ālay higdīl*), that I should hide from him (*we'essātēr mimmennū*)." In this line the betrayer's hostile action has been described by *yqtl* and *qtl*

15 *namtīq sōd*, "we used to take sweet counsel"
nehallēk berāgeš, "we used to mingle among the throngs"

lxv 10 *tākīn dagna-m* (MT *degānām*) *kī kēn tekīnehā*, "Provide her grain; for this you brought her into being"

lxviii 23 "The Lord said (*'āmar—qtl*): 'I stifled (*'aššīb* for MT *'āšīb*) the Serpent, muzzled (*'ešbōm* for MT *'āšīb m-*) the Deep Sea' "

lxviii 24 "Thus your foot churned (*timḥaṣ*) in blood"

lxxi 8 "My mouth has been filled (*yimmālē'*) with your praise." That the *yqtl* refers to the past, is indicated by the *qtl* form *hāyītī*, "I have been," of the preceding verse

lxxiii 10 "And so they quickly gorged themselves (*yiśbe'ū-m* for MT *yāšīb 'ammō*), and sucked up (*yāmōṣṣū* for MT *yimmāṣū*) the waters of the full sea"

lxxviii 38 "But the Merciful forgave (*yekappēr*) their sin, and did not destroy them (*welō' yašḥīt*)"

40 "How often they defied him (*yamrūhū*) in the wilderness, and grieved him (*ya'aṣībūhū*) in the desert"

47 *yahārōg babbārād gapnām*, "He killed their vines with hail"

49 *yešallaḥ bām ḥārōn 'appō*, "He sent against them his blazing anger"

58 *ūbip^{e}sīlēhem yaqnī'ūhū,* "and with their idols they roused his jealousy"

72 *ūbit^{e}būnōt kappāyw yanḥēm,* "and with skillful hands he guided them"

lxxx 12 *t^{e}šallaḥ q^{e}ṣīrehā,* "You caused its branches to shoot forth"

14 "The boar from the forest ravaged it (*y^{e}kars^{e}mennāh*), and what moves in the field fed on it (*yir'ennāh*)"

19 *w^{e}lō' nāsōg mimmekā,* "We have never turned away from you!"

lxxxi 6 *ś^{e}pat lō' yāda'tī 'ešma',* "I heard the speech of one unknown to me"

8 "In distress you called (*qārā'tā—qtl*), and I delivered you (*wā'^{a}ḥall^{e}ṣekā*—consec. *yqtl*); I answered you (*'e'en^{e}kā*) from the hiding place of thunder, though I was provoked by you (*'ebbāḥēn^{e}kā* for MT *'ebḥān^{e}kā*) near Meribah's waters"

lxxxi 13 *yēl^{e}kū b^{e}mō'^{a}ṣōtēhem,* "they followed their own designs"

lxxxv 9 *'ašmī'āh* (MT *'ešm^{e}'āh*) *mah y^{e}dabbēr hā'ēl,* "Let me announce what El himself has spoken"

yhwh kī y^{e}dabbēr šālōm, "Yahweh indeed has promised well-being"

lxxxix 3 "Eternal One, your love created (*yibneh* for MT *yibbāneh*) the heavens, but you made your fidelity more steadfast than these (*tākīn '^{e}mūnāt^{e}kā bāhem*)"

xcii 10 "For see how your foes, Yahweh,
For see how your foes have perished (*yō'bēdū*), how all evildoers have been scattered (*yitpār^{e}dū*)!"

12 *tišma'nāh 'oznāy,* "My ears have heard," a formula introducing vss. 13–16 which contain what must have been traditional teaching in Israel about the immortality of the just. Cf. *Psalms II,* NOTE ad loc.

xciv 5–6 Four *yqtl* forms expressing past events

12 "Blest the man whom you have instructed (*t^{e}yass^{e}rennū*), Yah, Whom you have taught (*t^{e}lamm^{e}dennū*) from your law"

16 "Who rose up (*mī yāqūm*) for me against the wicked?
Who took a stand (*mī yityaṣṣēb*) for me against evildoers?"

18 "When I said (*'im 'āmartī—qtl*), 'My foot is sinking' (*māṭāh—qtl*), your love, Yahweh, supported me (*yis'ādēnī*)"

19 "When my cares grew rife (*b^{e}rōb śar'appay*) within me, your consolations delighted (*y^{e}ša'aš^{e}'ū*) my soul"

21 "They banded together (*yāgōddū*) against the life of the just, and secretly condemned (*yaršī'ū*) the innocent"

xcix 6 "Moses and Aaron were among his priests (*b^{e}kōh^{a}nāyw*), and Samuel among those who invoked his name (*b^{e}qōr^{e}'ē š^{e}mō*); They called to Yahweh (*qōr^{e}'īm 'el yhwh*), and he himself answered them (*ya'^{a}nēm*)." Cf. vs. 8

ci 2c–8 Eleven *yqtl* forms describing past events

cii 1 Two *yqtl* forms referring to the past

cvi 18 ". . . flames devoured (*t^{e}lahēṭ*) the wicked"

cvii 5 ". . . their life ebbed from them (*bāhem tit'aṭṭāp*)"

6 ". . . from their straits he rescued them (*yaṣṣīlēm*)"

13, 19 ". . . from their straits he saved them (*yōšī'ēm*)"

14 "He brought them out (*yōṣī'ēm*) of gloomy darkness, and their bonds he snapped (*y^{e}nattēq*)"

17 ". . . for their iniquities they were afflicted (*yit'annū*)"

20 *yišlaḥ d^{e}bārō,* "He sent his word"

26 "They went up (*ya'^{a}lū*) to heaven, they went down (*yēr^{e}dū*) to the depths, their throats trembled (*titmōgāg*) from the peril"

27 "They gyrated (*yāḥūgū* for MT *yāḥōggū*) and teetered (*w^{e}yānū'ū*) like a drunkard, and all their skill was swallowed up (*titballā'*)"

28 ". . . from their straits he brought them forth (*yōṣī'ēm*)"

30 "They rejoiced (*wayyiśm^{e}ḥū*) when they grew calm (*kī yištōqū*)"

33 "He changed (*yāśēm*) rivers into desert"

38 "And their cattle he never let diminish (*lō' yam'īṭ*)"

cx 1 "A seat have I made (*'āšīt*) your foes"

7 "The Bestower of Succession set him (*y^{e}šītēhū* for MT *yišteh*) on his throne, the Most High Legitimate One lifted high (*yārīm*) his head"

cxiv 3 "The Jordan turned (*yissōb*) back"

5 "What ailed you, O sea, that you fled (*kī tānūs*)? O Jordan, that you turned (*tissōb*) back?"

cxvi 1 "Out of love for me Yahweh did hear (*kī yišma'*) my plea for his mercy"

4 "but I invoked (*'eqrā'*) the name of Yahweh"

cxviii 17 *lō' 'āmūt kī 'eḥyeh,* "I did not die but lived." Cf. vs. 18

cxix 171 "May my lips pour forth (*tabba'nāh*) your praise, because you have taught me (*kī t^{e}lamm^{e}dēnī*) your statutes"

cxxvi Five *yqtl* forms describing past events

cxxxix 21 The two *yqtl* verbs seem to express the same past time as the two *qtl* forms of the next line

yqtl followed by consecutive *yqtl*

Ps lv 18 *'āśīḥāh w^{e}'eh^{e}meh wayyišma' qōlī pōdeh* (MT *pādāh*), "I complained and moaned; and the Ransomer heard my voice"

20 *yišma' 'ēl wayya'an-m* (MT *w^{e}ya'^{a}nēm*), "El heard me and answered"

lxxviii 15 *y^{e}baqqa' ṣūr-m* (*mem* enclitic for MT *ṣūrīm*) *bammidbār wayyašq kīt^{e}hōmōt* (*kī* emphatic for MT *ki-*) *rabbāh,* "He split the rock in the wilderness, and watered the vast wasteland itself"

26 *yassa' qādīm baššāmāyim way^{e}nahēg b^{e}'uzzō tēmān,* "He let loose the east wind from heaven, and led forth the south wind from his fortress"

45 *y^{e}šallaḥ bāhem 'ārōb wayyō'k^{e}lēm ūṣ^{e}pardē^{a}' wattašḥītēm,* "He sent flies against them to devour them, and frogs to destroy them"

lxxx 9 "You brought (*tassī^{a}'*) a vine out of Egypt, drove out the nations and planted it (*t^{e}gārēš gōyīm wattiṭṭā'ehā*)" xcii 10–11 “. . . all evildoers have been scattered (*yitpār^{e}dū*)! But you exalted my horn (*wattārem . . . qarnī*) as if I were a wild ox”

xciv 21–22 “. . . and secretly condemned (*yaršī‘ū*) the innocent. But Yahweh became (*way^{e}hī*) a bulwark for me”

21, 23 “. . . and secretly condemned (*yaršī‘ū*) the innocent. He made . . . recoil (*wayyāšeb*) upon them”

xcv 10 “Forty years I loathed (*’āqūṭ*) a generation until I said (*wā’ōmar*)”

cvi 17 “The earth opened up (*tippātaḥ* for MT *tiptaḥ*) and swallowed (*wattibla‘*) Dathan, it covered (*watt^{e}kas*) over the faction of Abiram”

19 “They made (*ya‘^{a}śū*) a young bull at Horeb, and worshiped (*wayyištaḥ^{a}wū*) a molten image”

43 “Many times he rescued them (*yaṣṣīlēm*), but they hardened (*yēmārū* for MT *yamrū*) in their purpose, and so collapsed (*wayyāmōkkū*) in their iniquity”

cvii 5–6 “. . . their life ebbed from them (*bāhem tit‘aṭṭāp*). Then they cried (*wayyiṣ‘^{a}qū*) to Yahweh in their distress”

18 “All food their throat found so loathsome (*t^{e}ta‘ēb*), that they reached (*wayyaggī‘ū*) the gates of Death”

27–28 “. . . and all their skill was swallowed up (*titballā‘*). Then they cried (*wayyiṣ‘^{a}qū*) to Yahweh in their distress”

29 “He stilled (*yāqēm*) the storm to a whisper, the waves that roared were hushed (*wayyeḥ^{e}šū*)”

35–36 “He changed (*yāśēm*) desert into pools of water. . . . He settled (*wayyōšeb*) the hungry there, and they established (*way^{e}kōn^{e}nū*) a town to dwell in”

The sequence *qtl–yqtl* referring to the past

Ps vi 10 “Yahweh has heard (*šāma‘*) my plea, Yahweh has accepted (*yiqqāḥ*) my prayer”

xx 7 “Now I know that Yahweh has given his anointed victory (*hōšī^{a}‘ yahweh m^{e}šīḥō*), has granted him triumph (*ya‘^{a}nēhū*) from his sacred heaven, and from his fortress has given victory (*yōšī^{a}‘* for MT *yēša‘*) with his right hand”

10 “Yahweh has given the king victory (*hōšī‘āh hammelek*), granted him triumph (*ya‘^{a}nennū* for MT *ya‘^{a}nēnū*) when we called”

xxvi 4 “I have not sat (*lō’ yāšabtī*) with idol-worshipers, nor entered (*lō’ ’ābō’*) the home of the benighted”

5 “I have hated (*śānē’tī*) the company of evildoers, and with the wicked never sat down (*lō’ ’ēšēb*)”

12 “My foot has stood firm (*‘ām^{e}dāh*) among the upright, in the congregations I have adored (*’^{a}bārēk*) Yahweh”

lx 3 “O God, you were angry with us (*z^{e}naḥtānū*), and you ran from us (*p^{e}raṣtānū*); You were wrathful (*’ānaptā*), you turned away from us (*t^{e}šōbēb lānū*)”

lxvi 6 “He turned (*hāpak*) the sea into dry land, they passed (*ya‘ab^{e}rū*) through the river dry-shod” lxxi 17 "O God, you have taught me (*limmadtanī*) from my youth, and till now I have recounted (*w*^{e}*'ad hēnnāh 'aggīd*) your wondrous deeds"

lxxiii 3 "When I envied (*kī qinnē'tī*) the boasters, begrudged (*'er'eh*) the prosperity of the wicked"

9 "They set (*šattū*) their mouth against heaven, and their tongue swished (*tih*^{a}*lak*) through the nether world"

lxxiv 14 "It was you who crushed (*riṣṣaṣtā*) the heads of Leviathan, who gave him (*titt*^{e}*nennū*) as food to be gathered by desert tribes"

lxxvii 17 "When the waters saw you (*rā'ūkā*), O God, when the waters saw you (*rā'ūkā*), they trembled (*yāḥīlū*), even the depths shook with fear (*yirg*^{e}*zū*)"

18 "The massed clouds streamed (*zōr*^{e}*mū*) with water, the heaven echoed (*nāt*^{e}*nū*) your voice, and your arrows shot back and forth (*yithallākū*)"

lxxviii 64 "Their priests fell (*nāpālū*) by the sword, and their widows sang no dirges (*lō' tibkēnāh*)"

lxxxi 7 "I removed (*h*^{a}*sīrōtī-m;* with enclitic *mem* instead of the following preposition of *missēbel*) the burden on his shoulder, his hands were freed from the basket (*middūd ta'*^{a}*bōrnāh*)"

xcii 5 "Because you, Yahweh, made me happy (*śimmaḥtanī*) by your work, at your handiwork I sang for joy (*'*^{a}*rannēn*)"

xciii 3 "Ocean currents raised (*nāś*^{e}*'ū*), Yahweh, ocean currents raised (*nāś*^{e}*'ū*) their thunderous roar, ocean currents raised (*yiś*^{e}*'ū*) their pounding waves"

cix 23 "Like a shadow indeed have I tapered (*kī nāṭawtī* instead of MT *kinṭōtō*) . . . I have lost my youth (*nin'artī*), truly I have aged (*kī 'erbeh* for MT *kā'arbeh*)"

cxi 5 "Nourishment he gave (*nātan*) to those who fear him, he remembered (*yizkōr*) his covenant of old"

cxvi 2 "Truly he inclined (*hiṭṭah*) his ear to me even as I called (*ūbīmēy 'eqrā'* for MT *ūb*^{e}*yāmay 'eqrā'*)"

3 "The bands of Death encompassed me (*'*^{a}*pāpūnī*), and emissaries of Sheol overtook me (*m*^{e}*ṣā'ūnī*). By anguish and grief was I overtaken (*'immāṣē'* for MT *'emṣā'*)"

6 *dallōtī w*^{e}*lī y*^{e}*hōšī*^{a}*'*, "I was brought low but he saved me"

10 *he'*^{e}*mantī kī '*^{a}*dubbār* (MT *'*^{a}*dabbēr*), "I remained faithful though I was pursued"

cxviii 10, 11, 12 "All nations surrounded me (*s*^{e}*bābūnī*), but in Yahweh's name indeed I cut off their foreskins (*kī '*^{a}*mīlam*)"

cxxxi 1 "I have not meddled (*w*^{e}*lō' hillaktī*) with lofty matters, nor with thoughts too wondrous for me have I been filled (*'immālē'* for MT *'im lō'*)"

cxxxix 13 "Yes, you created (*qānītā*) my inmost self, have sheltered me (*t*^{e}*sukkēnī*) from the womb of my mother"

16 "Your eyes beheld (*rā'ū*) my life stages, upon your scroll all of them were inscribed (*yikkātēbū*); my days were shaped (*yuṣṣārū*), when I was not yet seen (*w*^{e}*lō' 'eḥāde;* MT *'eḥad*) by them"

cxliii 5 "I remembered (*zākartī*) the days primeval, numbered (*hāgītī*) your deeds completely, on the works of your hands I meditated (*'ᵃśōḥēᵃḥ*)"

cxlvii 20 "He has not dealt (*lō' 'āśāh*) thus with any other nation, and has never taught them (*bal yōdī'ūm;* MT *bal yᵉdā'ūm*) his ordinances"

The sequence *qtl–yqtl*
referring to the present

Ps l 19 "With your mouth you forge (*šālaḥtā*) evil itself, and with your tongue you weave (*taṣmīd*) deceit"

lvi 2 "How men hound me (*šᵉ'āpanī*)! All day long they harass me (*yilḥāṣēnī*) with both jaws"

lxiii 7 "When on my couch I think of you (*zᵉkartīkā*), and through my vigils muse on you (*'ehgeh bāk*)"

lxxvii 6 "I consider (*ḥiššabtī*) the days of old, I remember (*'ezkᵉrāh*) the years long past"

7 "Through the night I play the lyre (*nigganti* for MT *nᵉgīnātī*), with my heart I commune (*'āśīḥāh*)"

cii 15 *kī rāṣū . . . yᵉḥōnēnū,* "How (they) love . . . are moved to pity"

cxxxix 5 "Behind and before you encompass me (*ṣartānī*), and you lay (*wᵉtāšīt;* MT *wattāšet*) your palms upon me"

cxl 3 "Because they plan (*ḥāšᵉbū*) evil things in their heart, all the day conspire (*yāgūrū*) warfare"

The sequence *qtl–yqtl*
referring to the future

Ps iv 4 "And recognize that Yahweh will work wonders (*hiplāh*) for the one devoted to him, Yahweh will hear me (*yišma'*) when I call to him"

The sequence *qtl–yqtl*
to express an optative

Ps vii 14 "O that he would prepare (*wᵉlū hēkīn* for MT *wᵉlō hēkīn*) his lethal weapons, make (*yip'āl*) his arrows into flaming shafts!"

The sequence *yqtl–qtl*
referring to the past

Ps viii 7 "You gave him dominion (*tamšīlēhū*) over the works of your hands, put (*šattāh*) all things at his feet"

ix 8 "Behold Yahweh who has reigned (*yēšēb*) from eternity, has established (*kōnēn*) his throne for judgment"

liv 7 "He made the evil recoil (*yāšīb hāra'*) on my defamers, in his fidelity he annihilated them (*hiṣmītām* for MT *haṣmītēm*) completely"

lxviii 22 "God indeed smote (*yimḥaṣ*) the heads of his foes, split (*šā'ar* for MT *śē'ār*) their skulls . . ."

lxxxix 44 "In your wrath you turned back (*tāšīb*) his blade, and did not sustain (*hᵃqēmōtā* for MT *hᵃqēmōtō*) his sword" xcix 7 "From the pillar of cloud he spoke (*yedabbēr*) to them, they observed (*šāmerū*) his commands, and the law he gave (*nātan*) them"

cx 2 "He has forged (*yišlaḥ*) your victorious mace, Yahweh of Zion has hammered it (*rādāhu* for MT *redēh*)"

6 "he routed nations (*yedannēb gōyīm* for MT *yādīn baggōyīm*); he heaped corpses high (*millē'* for MT *mālē'*)"

The sequence *yqtl–qtl* referring to the present

Ps xxxviii 12 "My friends and fellows stand (*ya'amōdū*) far off from my plague, and my neighbors stand (*'āmādū*) far off"

xlvi 5 "God brings happiness (*yeśammeḥū*) to his city, the Most High sanctifies (*qiddēš* for MT *qedōš*) his habitation"

10 "The bow he breaks (*yešabbēr*), and snaps (*weqiṣṣēṣ*) the spear, the shields he burns (*yiśrōp*) with fire"

lv 5 "My heart's fluttering (*yāḥīl*) in my breast, and Death's terrors assail me (*nāpelū 'ālāy*)"

lxxxiii 3 "For look, your foes raise a tumult (*yehemāyūn*), and your enemies lift (*nāśe'ū*) their head"

cii 5–6 "My jaws fester (*leḥēm yāmaqqū* for MT *laḥmī miqqōl*)/my skeleton clings (*dābeqāh*)"

The sequence *yqtl–qtl* referring to the future

Ps lxxiii 18 "Surely to Perdition will you transplant them (*tištelēmō* for MT *tāšīt lāmō*), making them fall (*hippaltām*) into Desolation"

cxxxii 17 "There I will make the horn glow (*'aṣmīaḥ*), O David, I will trim (*'āraktī*) the lamp, O my anointed!"

cxxxviii 4 "All the kings of the earth will praise you (*yōdūkā*), Yahweh, when they hear (*kī šāme'ū*) the words of your mouth"

cxlvi 4 "When his breath departs (*tēṣē'*), he returns (*yāšūb*) to his land; on that day his projects perish (*'ābedū*)"

The sequence *yqtl–qtl* to express an optative

Ps vii 13 "O that the Victor would again (*yāšūb*) sharpen his sword (*ḥarbō yilṭōš*), draw (*dārak*) and aim (*wayekōnenehā*) his bow"

lxviii 10 "Your generous rain pour down (*tānīp*), O God, your patrimony and dominion yourself restore (*kōnantāh*)!"

The imperative–jussive sequence

Ps v 4 *tišma' qōlī*, "hear my voice!" following three imperatives of vss. 2–3

x 15 *šebōr . . . tidrōš*, "Break . . . requite!"

xvii 8 *šomrēnī . . . tastīrēnī*, "Guard me . . . hide me!"

xxxii 7 *pallēṭ tesōbebēnī*, "save me, enfold me!"

xliii 1 *šopṭēnī . . . rībāh . . . tᵉpallᵉṭēnī,* "Defend me . . . plead (my case) . . . deliver me!"

li 14 *hāšībāh lī . . . tismᵉkēnī,* "Give me again . . . sustain me!"

20 *hēṭībāh . . . tibneh,* "make (Zion) beautiful . . . rebuild (the walls of Jerusalem)!"

liv 3 *hōšīʻēnī . . . tᵉdīnēnī,* "Save me . . . defend me!"

lix 2 *haṣṣīlēnī . . . tᵉśaggᵉbēnī,* "Rescue me . . . be my bulwark!"

lxiv 2 *šᵉmaʻ . . . tiṣṣōr,* "Hear . . . protect!"

lxv 10 *mallē* (MT *mālē'*) . . . *tākīn,* "fill . . . provide!"

lxxxii 8 *qūmāh . . . šopṭāh . . . tinḥal bᵉkol haggōyīm,* "Arise . . . govern . . . rule over all the nations!"

lxxxiii 17 *mallē' . . . wībaqqēš ūšimᵉkā* (MT *wībaqqᵉšū šimᵉkā*), "Fill . . . and let your Name avenge itself!"

lxxxv 8 *har'ēnū . . . titten lānū,* "Show us (your kindness) . . . give us (your prosperity)!"

cii 2 *šimʻāh . . . wᵉšawʻātī 'ēlekā tābō',* "hear . . . let my cry come to you!"

cv 3 *hithalᵉlū . . . yiśmaḥ lēb,* "Glory . . . let your heart rejoice!"

cix 6 *hapqēd ʻālāyw rāšāʻ/wᵉśāṭān yaʻamōd ʻal yᵉmīnō,* "Appoint the Evil One against him/and let Satan stand at his right hand"

cxl 2 *ḥallᵉṣēnī yhwh mē'ādām rāʻ/mē'īš ḥamāsīm tinṣᵉrēnī,* "Rescue me, Yahweh, from the evil man/from the man of violence protect me"

5 *šomrēnī yhwh mīdē rāšāʻ/mē'īš ḥamāsīm tinṣᵉrēnī,* "Guard me, Yahweh, from the hands of the wicked/from the man of violence protect me"

The jussive–imperative sequence

Ps vii 8 *tᵉsōbᵉbekkā . . . šūbāh,* "Surround yourself . . . preside!" cf. third NOTE on Ps lxxxii 8

lix 12 *taharᵉgēm . . . hanīʻēmō . . . hōrīdēmō,* "slay them . . . send them staggering . . . bring them down!"

lxxi 2 *taṣṣīlēnī ūtᵉpallᵉṭēnī haṭṭēh 'ēlay 'oznᵉkā wᵉhōšīʻēnī,* "Deliver me and rescue me! Incline your ear to me and save me!"

cxix 169 *tiqrab rinnātī . . . habīnēnī,* "May my cry reach . . . give me insight!"

170 *tābō' tᵉḥinnātī . . . haṣṣīlēnī,* "May my supplication come . . . rescue me!"

Subjunctive without *waw* depending on verbal forms expressing command or wish

Ps xxii 22–23 *hōšīʻēnī . . . ʻanītānī . . . 'asappᵉrāh,* "Save me . . . make me triumph (precative perfect) . . . that I might proclaim"

xxxix 5 *hōdīʻēnī . . . 'ēdᵉʻāh,* "teach me . . . that I may know"

li 14–15 *hāšībāh . . . tismᵉkēnī . . . 'alammᵉdāh,* "give again . . . sustain me . . . that I may teach"

lvii 9 *ʻūrāh . . . 'āʻīrāh,* "Awake . . . that I might awake" lxi 4–5 *kī hāyītā* (precative perfect) *maḥseh lī . . . 'āgūrāh,* "O that you would be my refuge . . . that I might dwell"

lxix 30–31 *t^{e}śagg^{e}bēnī '^{a}hal^{e}lāh,* "may (God's help) bulwark me that I might praise"

lxxii 1–2 *tēn . . . yādīnā* (MT *yādīn*), "give . . . that he may govern"

lxxxvi 11 *hōrēnī . . . '^{a}hallēk,* "teach me . . . that I may walk"

Infinitive absolute:
continuing a finite verb

Ps xi 1 "How can you lie in wait (*'ēk tō'm^{e}rū*) for my life, and pursue me (*nidhōr* for MT *nūdū harkem*) like a bird?"

xii 9 "On every side the wicked prowl (*yithallākūn*), digging pits (*kārō m^{e}zālōt* for MT *k^{e}rūm zullūt*) for the sons of men"

xvi 11 "You will make me know (*tōdī'ēnī*) the path of life eternal, filling me (*śabbē^{a}'* for MT *ś^{e}ba'*) with happiness before you"

xxii 2 "My God, why have you forsaken me (*lāmāh '^{a}zabtānī*)? dismissing my plea (*rāḥōq-m šaw'ātī* for MT *rāḥōq mīšū'ātī*), the roar of my words?"

xxvi 2 "Examine me (*b^{e}ḥānēnī*), O Yahweh, and try me (*w^{e}nassēnī*), testing (*ṣārōpāh;* MT *ṣorpāh*) my heart and my mind"

xxxv 12 "They repay me (*y^{e}šall^{e}mūnī*) evil for good, ravaging my soul (*šaklēl napšī* for MT *š^{e}kōl l^{e}napšī*)"

lvi 10 "If my foes draw back (*'āz yāšūbū*), recoiling (*'āḥōr*) when I cry out"

lxi 7 "Add (*tōsīp*) days to the king's days, turning (*kammō* for MT *k^{e}mō*) his years into endless generations"

lxxii 16 "Let his fruit blossom (*w^{e}yāṣīṣū*) like Lebanon, flourishing (*'ārō* for MT *mē'īr*) like the grass of the earth"

lxxv 2 "We give thanks to you (*hōdīnū l^{e}kā*), O God, we praise (*hōdīnū*) your Name, O Near One, proclaiming (*sappērū* for MT *sipp^{e}rū*) your wondrous deeds"

ciii 14 "For he knows (*yāda'*) our shape, mindful (*zākūr*) that we are clay"

cxxvi 6 *hālōk yēlēk ūbākōh,* "He went forth weeping." Literally, "He went forth and wept"

cxxxix 20 "Because they gaze upon (*yō'm^{e}rū* for MT *yō'm^{e}rūkā*) every figurine, raise their eyes (*nāśū'*) to vanities arrayed"

Infinitive absolute:
in parallelism with *qtl* to express past action

Ps lxxix 7 "For they have devoured (*'ākōl* for MT *'ākal*) Jacob, and laid waste (*hēšammū*) his habitation"

cvii 4 "They wandered (*tā'ū*) in the wilderness, in the barrens they trod (*dārōk* for MT *derek*)"

cxxxv 10 "It was he who smote (*hikkāh*) great nations, and who slew (*w^{e}hārōg* for MT *w^{e}hārag*) mighty kings"

12 "And he gave (*w^{e}nātōn* for MT *w^{e}nātan*) their land as patrimony." Cf. Ps cxxxvi 21

Infinitive absolute:
preceding the subject

Ps xvii 5 *'orḥōt pārīṣ tāmōk 'ašūray,* "My legs held firmly to the paths of ruggedness"

xlix 4 *wehāgūt libbī tebūnōt,* "And my throat shall proclaim insight" (revised translation)

Infinitive absolute:
following the subject

Ps xxxv 16 *lō'agay mā'ōg* (MT *la'agē mā'ōg*) *ḥārōq šinnēmō,* "My encircling mockers gnashed their teeth"

xlii 2 *ke'ayyelet 'ārōg* (MT *ke'ayyāl ta'arōg*), "As a hind cries aloud"

lxiii 2 *be'ereṣ ṣiyyāh 'āyōp* (MT *we'āyēp*), "More than parched earth yearns" (the conjunction *we* has been omitted as secondary)

Participle functioning as imperative

Ps ix 14 *merōmemī,* "raise me up!"

xvii 14 *memītām* (twice) for MT *mimetīm,* "slay them!"

lxxiv 12 *pō'ēl,* "achieve!"

lxxx 2 *nōhēg,* "lead!"

cxix 130 *mēbīn,* "give insight!"

Conditional sentence without morphological indicator:
with apodosis introduced by *waw*

Ps iii 5 *qōlī 'el yhwh 'eqrā' wayya'anēnī mēhar qodšō,* "If with full voice I call to Yahweh, he answers me from his holy mountain"

xxvii 7 *'eqrā' weḥonnēnī wa'anēnī,* "When I call, have pity on me and answer me"

xci 15 *yiqrā'ēnī we'e'enēhū,* "If he cries to me, I will answer him"

Conditional sentence without morphological indicator:
apodosis without *waw*

Ps iii 6 *'anī šākabtī wā'īšānāh heqīṣōtī,* "If I lie down to sleep, I shall wake up"

lxviii 2 *yāqūm 'elōhīm yāpūṣū 'ōyebāyw,* "When God arises, his foes scatter"

xc 5 *zeramtām šēnāh yihyū babbōqer keḥāṣīr yuḥlāp* (MT *yaḥalōp*), "If you pluck them at night, with the dawn they become like cut grass"

xci 7 *yippōl miṣṣiddekā 'elep ūrebābāh mīmīnekā 'ēlekā lō' yiggāš,* "Though a thousand fall on your left, ten thousand at your right hand, it will not approach you"

civ 28 *tittēn lāhem yilqōṭūn,* "When you give to them, they gather"; *tiptaḥ yādekā yiśbe'ūn,* "when you open your hand, they fill up"

Relative clause without *'ašer*

Ps xviii 28 *kī 'attāh 'am 'ānī tōšīa',* "Indeed you are the Strong One who saves the poor" xxi 5 *ḥayyīm šā'al mimm^{e}kā,* "The life eternal he asked of you" (revised translation)

xxxv 15 *w^{e}lō' yāda'tī,* "And they whom I did not know"

xxxviii 14 *wa'^{a}nī k^{e}ḥērēš lō' 'ešmā' ūk^{e}'illēm lō' yiptaḥ pīw,* "But I am like a deaf man, who does not hear; and like a dumb man, who opens not his mouth." On *'ešma'* expressing third person singular, see *Psalms I*, NOTE ad loc.

l 8 *we'ōlōtekā l^{e}negdī tāmīd,* "(nor for) your burnt offerings that are ever before me"

lviii 8 *k^{e}mō mayim yithall^{e}kū lāmō,* "like water that flows swiftly"

lxiii 10 *w^{e}hēmmāh l^{e}šō'āh y^{e}baq^{e}šū napšī,* "But they who murderously seek my life"

lxviii 11 *ḥayyāt^{e}kā yāš^{e}bū bāh,* "your family that dwells in it"

lxxiv 2 *'^{a}dāt^{e}kā qānītā qedem,* "your flock you acquired of old"

18 *'ōyēb ḥērēp yahweh,* "the foe who blasphemed you, Yahweh," *w^{e}'am nābāl ni'^{a}ṣū š^{e}mekā,* "and the foolish people that reviled your name"

lxxxi 6 *š^{e}pat lō' yāda'tī 'ešmā',* "I heard the speech of one unknown to me"

lxxxv 9 *w^{e}'el* (MT *w^{e}'al*) *yāšūbū l^{e}kislāh,* "and to those who again confide in him"

xc 5 *keḥāṣīr yuḥlāp* (MT *yaḥ^{a}lōp*), "like cut grass"

xcvii 10 *'hby* (MT *'ōh^{a}bē*) *yhwh śān^{e}'ū* (MT *śin^{e}'ū*) *rā',* "Yahweh, who loves those who hate evil"

cxviii 22 *'eben mā'^{a}sū habbōnīm hāy^{e}tāh l^{e}rō'š pinnāh,* "The stone the builders rejected became the cornerstone"

cxix 96 *l^{e}kol tiklāh rā'ītī,* "Than all the perfection I have seen"

130 *p^{e}taḥ* (MT *pētaḥ*) *d^{e}bārekā yā'īrū* (MT *yā'īr*), "Unfold your words which illuminate"

cxli 7 *k^{e}mō pūlaḥ ūbūqa'* (MT *pōlē^{a}ḥ ūbōqē^{a}'*), "like one rent and riven"

9 *mīdē paḥ yāq^{e}šū lī,* "from the clutches of the snare they spread for me"

Accusative of means or material preceding its verb

Ps v 10 *l^{e}šōnām yaḥ^{a}līqūn,* "with their tongue they bring death"

13 *rāṣōn ta'ṭ^{e}rennū,* "you will surround him with your favor"

viii 6 *kābōd w^{e}hādār t^{e}'aṭṭ^{e}rēhū,* "with honor and glory you crowned him"

xvii 10 *ḥelbāmō sūgārū* (MT *sāg^{e}rū*), "they are clogged with their blubber"

pīmō dibb^{e}rū, "with their mouth they speak"

xviii 36 *wīmīn^{e}kā tis'ādēnī,* "with your right hand you sustained me"

w^{e}'anwat^{e}kā tarbēnī, "and by your triumph you made me great"

xxxii 10 *ḥesed y^{e}sōb^{e}bennū,* "with love will he enfold him"

xxxiii 5 *ḥesed yhwh māl^{e}'āh hā'āreṣ,* "of Yahweh's kindness the earth is full"

xxxv 7 *rištām ḥnm* (MT *ḥinnām*) *ḥāp^{e}rū l^{e}napšī,* "with their net they stealthily spied on my life" xlviii 12 *ṣedeq māl^{e}'āh y^{e}mīnekā,* "your right hand is full of generosity"

l 19 *pīkā šālaḥtā b^{e}rā'āh,* "with your mouth you forge evil itself"

ūl^{e}šōn^{e}kā taṣmīd mirmāh, "and with your tongue you weave deceit"

li 14 *w^{e}rū^{a}ḥ n^{e}dībāh tism^{e}kēnī,* "and by your generous spirit sustain me"

lvi 2 *leḥēm* (MT *lōḥēm*) *yilḥāṣēnī,* "they harass me with both jaws"

lix 13 *ḥaṭṭa't pīmō d^{e}bar ś^{e}pātēmō w^{e}yillāk^{e}dū,* "By the sin of their mouth, the gossip from their lips, let them be caught"

lxv 13 *w^{e}gīl g^{e}bā'ōt taḥgōrannāh* (MT *taḥgōrnāh*), "and gird the hills with exultation!"

lxvi 17 *'ēlāyw pī qārā'tī,* "To him I cried with my mouth"

lxxv 9 *w^{e}yayin ḥōmer* (MT *ḥāmar*) *mālē',* "and the bowl is filled with wine"

lxxvii 2 *qōlī . . . w^{e}'eṣ'āqāh,* "With my voice . . . I desperately cry"

lxxix 11 *gōdel* (MT *k^{e}gōdel;* the initial *k* belongs to the preceding word) *z^{e}rō'^{a}kā hōtēr b^{e}nē t^{e}mūtāh,* "with your long arm preserve those condemned to die"

lxxxiv 7 *b^{e}rākōt ya'ṭeh,* "may he cover it with pools"

lxxxviii 8 *w^{e}kol mišbārēkā 'innītā,* "and with all your outbursts you afflict me"

xci 16 *'ōrek yāmīm 'aśbī'ēhū,* "with length of days will I content him"

ciii 19 *ūmalkūtō bakkōl māšālāh,* "and by his royal power he rules over all." Note: *māšālāh* is the third person masculine *qatala* form

civ 6 *t^{e}hōm kall^{e}būš kissītō,* "You covered it with the ocean like a garment"

15 *w^{e}yayin y^{e}śammaḥ l^{e}bab '^{e}nōš,* "and with wine he gladdens the heart of man"

w^{e}leḥem l^{e}bab '^{e}nōš yis'ād, "and with food (he) sustains the heart of man"

cv 40 *w^{e}leḥem šāmayim yaśbī'ēm,* "and with the wheat of heaven he gratified them"

cix 3 *w^{e}dibrē śin'āh s^{e}bābūnī,* "and with words of hate (they) surround me"

21 *ḥasd^{e}kā haṣṣīlēnī,* "by your kindness rescue me"

cxi 6 *kō^{a}ḥ ma'^{a}śāyw higgīd l^{e}'ammō,* "His power by his works he manifested to his people"

cxix 64 *ḥasd^{e}kā yhwh māl^{e}'āh hā'āreṣ,* "With your kindness, Yahweh, the earth is full"

78 *kī šeqer 'iww^{e}tūnī,* "because with guile they sought to pervert me"

86 *šeqer r^{e}dāpūnī,* "by falsehood they persecute me"

cxli 5 *šemen rō'š 'al yānīr* (MT *yānī*) *rō'šī,* "With fine oil never let my head glisten"

cxlii 2 *qōlī . . . 'ez'āq/qōlī . . . 'etḥannān,* "With my voice I cry . . ./ with my voice I beg . . . for mercy"

cxliii 10 *rūḥ^{a}kā ṭōbāh tanḥēnī,* "With your good spirit lead me"

cxlvii 14 *ḥēleb ḥiṭṭīm yaśbī'ēk,* "with the finest wheat he sates you"

Ellipsis:
double-duty pronoun
mī, "who?"

Ps lxiv 6–7 *mī yir'eh lāmō//yaḥp^{e}śū* . . . "Who looks down upon us?//Who can investigate . . . ?"

lxxxix 7 *mī . . . ya'^{a}rōk l^{e}yhwh//yidmeh l^{e}yhwh* . . . , "Who . . . can compare with Yahweh?//Who resembles Yahweh . . . ?"

double-duty suffix
with nouns—
the suffix is omitted in the first colon

Ps iii 4 *māgān* (MT *māgēn*)*//k^{e}bōdī*, "my Suzerain//my Glorious One"

vii 14 *k^{e}lē māwet//ḥiṣṣāyw*, "his lethal weapons//his arrows"

x 3 *ta'^{a}wat//napšō*, "his desire//his appetite"

15 *ra'* (MT *rā'*)*//riš'ō*, "his malice//his wickedness"

xi 2 *qešet//ḥiṣṣām*, "their bow//their arrows"

xvi 4 *middēm* (MT *middām*)*//ś^{e}pātāy*, "from my hands//my lips"

xvii 1 *ṣedeq//rinnātī//t^{e}pillātī*, "my plea for vindication//my cry//my prayer"

xvii 4 *p^{e}'ullōt 'ādēm* (MT *'ādām*)*//d^{e}bar ś^{e}pāteka*, "the works of your hands//the command from your lips"

8 *'āyim//k^{e}nāpekā*, "your eye//your wings"

14 *bānīm//l^{e}'ōl^{e}lēhem*, "their children//to their offspring"

xix 8 *nepeš//pty*, "my soul//my mind"

9 *lēb//'ēnāy* (attaching the final *mem* of MT *'ēnāyim* to the first word of the next line), "my heart//my eyes"

15 *l^{e}rāṣōn//l^{e}pānekā*, "according to your desire//according to your will"

xxv 9 *bammišpāṭ//darkō*, "in his justice//his way"

xxvi 7 *tōdāh//nipl^{e}'ōtekā*, "your praise//your wonders"

xxxvii 14 *ḥereb//qaštām*, "their sword//their bows"

xxxviii 18 *l^{e}ṣela'//negdī*, "at my side//before me"

xxxix 12 *'āwōn//ḥ^{a}mūdō*, "his guilt//his body"

xliv 11 *ṣār//m^{e}śan^{e}'ēnū*, "our adversary//our enemies"

xlvi 5 *'īr//mišk^{e}nī* (MT *mišk^{e}nē*), "his city//his habitation"

l 17 *mūsār//d^{e}bārāy*, "my instruction//my words"

liv 9 *ṣārāh//'ōy^{e}bay*, "my adversaries//my foes"

lvii 6 *rūmāh//k^{e}bōdekā*, "your stature//your glory"

lviii 11 *nāqām//p^{e}'āmāyw*, "his victory//his feet"

lxii 5 *b^{e}pī* (attaching the final *waw* of MT *b^{e}pīw* to the following word as emphatic)*//ūb^{e}qirbām*, "with their mouth//but in their heart"

lxvi 13 *b^{e}'ōlōt//n^{e}dārāy*, "with my burnt offerings//my vows"

lxviii 10 *gešem n^{e}dābōt//naḥ^{a}lāt^{e}kā w^{e}nil'āh*, "your generous rain//your patrimony and dominion"

lxix 34	*'ebyōnīm//'asīrāyw,* "his poor//those bound to him"
lxxi 9	*le'ēt ziqnāh//kiklōt kōḥī,* "in my old age//as my strength fails"
12	*'elōhīm//'elōhay,* "My God//my God"
16	*gebūrōt//ṣidqātekā,* "your mighty house//your fidelity"
lxxvii 12	*ma'alelē yāh//pil'ekā,* "your magnificent deeds//your marvels"
18	*qōl//ḥaṣāṣekā,* "your voice//your arrows"
lxxxvi 2	*ḥāsīd//'abdekā,* "devoted to you//your servant"
lxxxix 2	*ḥasdē yhwh//'emūnātekā,* "Your love, Yahweh//your fidelity"
3	*ḥesed//'emūnātekā,* "your love//your fidelity"
xcvi 13	*beṣedeq//be'emūnātō,* "with his justice//with his truth"
cii 10	*kalleḥem//šiqqūway,* "as my food//my drink"
16	*šēm yhwh//kebōdekā,* "your name, Yahweh//your glory"
cviii 6	*rūmāh//kebōdekā,* "your stature//your glory"
cix 29	*kelimmāh//boštām,* "their disgrace//their humiliation"
cxix 7	*beyōšer lēbāb//mišpeṭē ṣidqekā,* "for your upright heart// your just ordinances"
26	*darkē* (MT *derākay*)*//ḥuqqekā,* "your ways//your statutes"
59	*darkē* (MT *derākāy*)*//'ēdōtekā,* "your ways//your stipulations"
108	*nidbōt pī//mišpāṭekā,* "noble utterances of your mouth// your ordinances"
109	*bekappē* (MT *bekappī*) *tāmīd//tōrātekā,* "in your eternal hands//your law"
155	*yešū'āh//ḥuqqekā,* "your salvation//your statutes"
160	*'emet//ṣidqekā,* "your truth//your justice"
171	*tehillāh//ḥuqqekā,* "your praise//your statutes"
cxxii 6	*šelōm yerūšālāim//'ōhabāyik,* "your peace, Jerusalem//(those) who love you"
cxxxviii 7, cxliii 11–12	*ṣārāh//'ōyebay,* "my adversaries//my foes" Note: abstract *ṣārāh,* "adversity," assumes concrete sense by virtue of the parallelism with concrete "foes"
cxliv 6	*bārāq//ḥiṣṣekā,* "your shafts//your arrows"
cxlix 5	*bekābōd//'al miškebōtām,* "in their Glorious One//on their couches"

Ellipsis: double-duty suffix with nouns— the suffix is omitted in the second colon

Ps xvii 2	*mišpāṭī//mēšārīm,* "my justice//my integrity"
xviii 15	*ḥiṣṣāyw//berāqīm,* "his arrows//his shafts"
xix 6	*ḥuppātō//'ōraḥ,* "its bower//its course"
xx 7	*šemē qodšō//gebūrōt,* "his sacred heaven//his fortress"
xxi 10	*'appō//'ēš,* "his wrath//his fire"
xxvii 5	*'oholō//beṣūr,* "his tent//upon his mountain"

xxxi 21 *b^{e}sēter pānekā//b^{e}sukkāh,* "in the shelter of your presence//in your abode"
24 *ḥ^{a}sīdāyw//'^{e}mūnīm,* "those devoted to him//his faithful ones." The concrete meaning of the latter noun emerges from its balance with concrete "those devoted to him"
xliv 5 *malkī '^{e}lōhay//m^{e}ṣawweh* (MT *'^{e}lōhīm ṣawwēh*), "my King, my God//my Commander"
xlviii 4 *'arm^{e}nōtehā//miśgāb,* "her citadel//her bulwark"
li 14 *yiš'ekā//w^{e}rū^{a}ḥ n^{e}dībāh,* "your salvation//your generous spirit"
lix 4–5 *lō' piš'ī//w^{e}lō' ḥaṭṭā'tī//b^{e}lī 'āwōn,* "no guilt of mine//and no sin of mine//no misdeed of mine"
lxiii 7 *y^{e}ṣū'āy//'ašmūrōt,* "my couch//my vigils"
lxiv 4 *l^{e}šōnām//dābār mār,* "their tongue//their poisonous remark"; cf. *Psalms III*, in connection with Ps cxx 4
lxix 23 *lipnēhem//liš^{e}lūmīm* (MT *liš^{e}lōmīm*), "before them//even their companions"
lxxiii 7 *'ēnēmō//lēbāb,* "their eyes//their heart"
lxxiv 3 *p^{e}'amm^{e}kā* (MT *p^{e}'āmekā*)*//baqqōdēš,* "your own people//in your sanctuary"
lxxvii 9 *ḥasdō//'ōmer,* "his kindness//visions from him"
19 *qōl ra'am^{e}kā/b^{e}rāqīm,* "your pealing thunder//your lightning bolts"
lxxix 3 *dāmām//w^{e}'ēn qōbēr,* "their blood//with no one to bury them"
lxxxv 10 *yiš'ō//kābōd,* "his prosperity//his glory"
xcviii 1 *y^{e}mīnō//z^{e}rō^{a}',* "his right hand//his arm"
cv 27 *'ōtōtāyw//ūmōp^{e}tīm,* "his miracles//and his prodigies"
cvii 41 *m^{e}'ōnī* (MT *mē'ōnī*)*//mišpāḥōt,* "his habitation//his clans"
cx 3 *'ammekā* (MT *'amm^{e}kā*)*//n^{e}dābōt,* "your Strong One//your Valiant"
cxix 138 *'ēdōtekā//we'^{e}mūnāh,* "your stipulations//and fidelity to you"
160 *d^{e}bār^{e}kā//mišpāṭ* (MT *mišpaṭ*), "your word//your judgment"
cxlv 16 *yādekā//rāṣōn,* "your hand//your favor"
cxlvii 1 *'^{e}lōhēnū//t^{e}hillāh,* "our God//our Glorious One"

Ellipsis:
double-duty suffix
with verbs—
the suffix is omitted in the first colon

Ps xxxii 7 *palleṭ//t^{e}sōb^{e}bēnī,* "save me//enfold me"
xxxv 5–6 *dōḥeh//rōd^{e}pām,* "driving them//pursuing them"
11 *y^{e}qūmūn//yiš'ālūnī,* "they testify against me//they interrogate me"
lix 14 *kallēh//'ayyēnēmō* (MT *'ēnēmō*), "exterminate them// annihilate them"
lx 7 *hōšī'āh//wa'^{a}nēnū,* "give us victory//grant us triumph"
cv 19 *bō'//ṣ^{e}rūpathu* (MT *ṣ^{e}rāpāt^{e}hū*), "came to him//was proved true by him"
40 *wayyābē'//yaśbī'ēm,* "he brought them (quails)//he gratified them"
cxix 108 *r^{e}ṣēh-nā'//lamm^{e}dēnī,* "oblige me//teach me"

Ellipsis:
double-duty suffix
with verbs—
the suffix is omitted in the second colon

Ps xvii 7 *ḥōsᵉdekā* (MT *ḥᵃsādekā*)//*mitqōmᵉmīm,* "those who revile you// your assailants"

11 *sᵉbābūnī//linṭōt,* "they surrounded me//to pitch me"

xxxii 5 *'ōdī'ᵃkā//lō' kissītī,* "I made known to you//I did not hide (my guilt) from you"

xli 3 *wīḥayyēhū//yᵉ'aššēr* (MT *yᵉ'uššar*), "May (Yahweh) give him long life//bless him"

lii 7 *yittāṣekā* (pausal form instead of MT)//*yᵉḥattēk* (MT *yaḥtᵉkā*), "May (El) demolish you//unchild you"

lxxvi 11 *tōdekkā//taḥgōr,* "will they praise you//they will encircle you"

lxxxiv 7 *yᵉšītūhū//ya'ṭeh,* "(May he) turn it//(May he) cover it"

xci 3 *yaṣṣīlᵉkā//yāqūš,* "he will free you//he will shield you"

xciv 20 *hayᵉḥobrᵉkā//yuṣṣār* (MT *yōṣēr*), "(Can the seat of iniquity) associate with you//(the architect of disorder) receive your protection?"

cvii 20 *wᵉyirpā'ēm//wīmallēṭ,* "to heal them//to relieve them"

Ellipsis:
double-duty suffix
with the verb in one colon, with the noun in the other—
the suffix is omitted in the first colon

Ps ix 2 *'ōdeh—kol niplᵉ'ōtekā,* "I will thank you—all your wonderful deeds"

lxxiv 10, 18 *yᵉḥārep—šimᵉkā,* "he will blaspheme you—your name"

cvi 44 *wayyar'—rinnātām,* "yet he looked upon them—their cry"

cxix 39 *yāgōrtī—mišpāṭekā,* "I revere you—your ordinances"

147 *qiddamtī—dᵉbārekā,* "I looked toward you—your words"

148 *qiddᵉmū—bᵉ'imrātekā,* "(my eyes) looked toward you—on your promise"

cxxxix 14 *nāpaltī nāpōl—'āyōm ma'ᵃśekā,* "I fall in adoration before you—so dreadful in your deeds"

Ellipsis:
double-duty suffix
with the verb in one colon, with the noun in the other—
the suffix is omitted in the second colon

Ps xi 1 *napšī—nidhōr kᵉmō* (for MT *nūdū harkem*) *ṣippōr,* "my life—you pursue me like a bird"

xvii 3 *bāḥantā libbī//pāqadtā,* "examine my heart//probe me!"

l 23 *yᵉkubbᵉdānᵉnī* (MT *yᵉkabbᵉdānᵉnī*)—*derek,* "he will be feasted by me—my way"

lvi 9 *nōdī//dim'ātī//hal'ē* (MT *hᵃlō*), "my lament//my tears//my hardship"

lxix 2 *hōšīʿēnī—nāpeš*, "save me—my neck"
lxxx 10 *šorāšehā—wattemallēʾ*, "her roots—you caused her to fill"

Ellipsis:
double-duty suffix
with the preposition in one colon, with the noun in the other—
the suffix is omitted in the first colon

Ps lxxxiv 4 *bayit//qēn lāh*, "her home//a nest for herself"
xc 1 *māʿōn//lānū*, "our mainstay//(be) ours"
ci 1 *ḥesed ūmišpāṭ//lekā*, "your love and justice//to you"
cxxii 3 *keʿīr//lāhū* (MT *lāh*), "as his city//by him"

Ellipsis:
double-duty suffix
with the preposition in one colon, with the verb in the other—
the suffix is omitted in the first colon

Ps lv 4 *ʿālay//beʾap*, "upon me//to my face"
lxviii 21 *lānū—tōṣāʾōt*, "for us—our escape"
cxvi 17 *lekā—ūbešēm*, "to you—and in your name"

Ellipsis:
double-duty suffix
with the preposition in one colon, with the noun in the other—
the suffix is omitted in the second colon

Ps cxxxvii 7 *ʿārū ʿārū ʿad hayesōd bāh*, "strip her, strip her, to her foundation!"

Ellipsis:
double-duty suffix
with the preposition in one colon, with the verb in the other—
the suffix is omitted in the second colon

Ps lxxxviii 8 *ʿālay//ʿinnītā*, "upon me//you afflict me"

Ellipsis:
double-duty suffix—
exceptional cases

Ps v 13 *rāṣōn*, "your favor" (see vs. 12 *šemekā*, "your name")
vii 3 *weʾēn maṣṣīl*, "with none to rescue me" (see *wehaṣṣīlēnī*, "rescue me," and *napšī*, "my neck")
viii 3 *lemāʿōn* (MT *lemaʿan*), "for your habitation" (see vs. 2 *hōdekā*, "your majesty," and vs. 3 *ṣōrerekā*, "your adversaries")
xiii 4 *habbīṭāh ʿanēnī*, "Look at me, answer me!"
xviii 29 *tāʾīr nērī yahweh*, "you shine for me; my lamp is Yahweh"
xxx 8 *heʿemadtāh*, "you made me (more) stable" (see *hāyītī*, "I was," of the second colon)
xxxv 15 *qāreʿū*, "they tore me to pieces" (see *ūbeṣalʿī*, "when I stumbled," *ʿālay*, "about me," *welōʾ yādaʿtī*, "they whom I did not know,"

and *b^{e}ḥonpī* [MT *b^{e}ḥanpē*], "from slandering me," which belongs to vs. 15 and not to vs. 16)

xxxvi 3 *kī heḥ^{e}līq 'ēlāyw*, "But his God will destroy him"

xxxviii 13 *dibb^{e}rū*, "they pursue me" (see the preceding word *rā'ātī*, "my misfortune")

xlv 4 *'al yārēk*, "upon your thigh" (see *ḥarb^{e}kā*, "your sword," *hōd^{e}kā*, "your splendor")

liv 8 *bin^{e}dābāh*, "for your nobility" (with the suffix coming from *lāk*, "to you," of the same colon, and from *šim^{e}kā*, "your Name," of the next)

lvi 3 *šā'^{a}pū šōr^{e}ray*, "my defamers hound me"

6 *dōb^{e}ray* (MT *d^{e}bāray*) *y^{e}'aṣṣ^{e}bū*, "my slanderers vex me"

lxiii 3 *baqqōdeš ḥ^{a}zītīkā*, "in your sanctuary may I gaze on you"

lxxii 3 *lā'ām*, "to your people" (see vs. 2 *'amm^{e}kā*, "your people")

lxxiv 2 *šēbeṭ*, "your club" (see the following *naḥ^{a}lāteka*, "your patrimony")

lxxviii 6 *wīsapp^{e}rū libnēhem*, "and might they tell them to their children"

lxxxiv 3 *l^{e}ḥaṣrōt*, "for your court" (see vs. 2 *mišk^{e}nōtekā*, "your dwelling")

lxxxvii 2 *'ōhēb*, "he loves you" (see vs. 3 *bāk*, "in you")

xc 12 *hōda'*, "teach us" (see the preceding *yāmēnū*, "our days")

xciii 5 *na'^{a}wāh*, "(they) will laud you" (see the preceding *l^{e}bēt^{e}kā*, "in your temple")

cvi 23 *mēhašḥīt*, "from ravaging them" (see *l^{e}hašmīdām*, "to exterminate them")

cix 5 *t^{e}pillāh*, "my prayer" (transferred from vs. 4)
ṭōbāh, "my good" (see *'ālay*, "to my debit," and *'ah^{a}bātī*, "my love")

cxi 6 *kō^{a}ḥ*, "his power" (see *ma'^{a}śāyw*, "his works," and *'ammō*, "his people")

cxv 1 *kābōd*, "your glory." The suffix comes from *šim^{e}kā*, "your name"

cxix 49 *dābār l^{e}'abdekā*, "your word to your servant"

132 *mišpāṭ*, "your wont" (see *š^{e}mekā*, "your name")

cxxvii 3 *śākār*, "his reward" (see vs. 2 *līdīdō*, "to his beloved")

5 *'ōy^{e}bīm*, "his foes" (see *'ašpātō*, "his quiver")

cxxxviii 8 *yhwh yigmōr b^{e}'ōdī* (MT *ba'^{a}dī*), "May Yahweh avenge me so long as I live"

cxxxix 1 *yhwh ḥ^{a}qartanī w^{e}tēda'* (MT *wattēdā'*), "Yahweh, examine me, and know me yourself!"

6 *da'at*, "your knowledge." Cf. vs. 5 *kappekāh*, "your palms"

16 *yāmīm*, "my days" (see *gīlay-mī* [MT *golmī*], "my life stages")

cxlvii 20 *ūmišpāṭīm*, "and his ordinances" (see vs. 19 *ḥuqqāyw ūmišpāṭāyw*, "his statutes and his ordinances")

Ellipsis:
omission of the suffix with forms of *šāma'*

Ps iv 4 *yhwh yišma' b^{e}qor'ī 'ēlāyw*, "Yahweh will hear me when I call to him"

xxii 25 *ūb^{e}šaww^{e}ʿō ʾēlāyw šāmē^{a}ʿ*, "but when he cried, he listened to him"
xxxiv 7 *zeh ʿānī qārāʾ wyhwh šāmē^{a}ʿ//. . . hōšīʿō*, "This poor man called and Yahweh heard him//. . . he saved him"
18 *ṣaʿ^{a}qū wyhwh šāmē^{a}ʿ//. . . hiṣṣīlām*, "When they cry, Yahweh hears them//. . . rescues them"
lv 20 *yišmaʿ ʾēl*, "El heard me" (see vs. 19 *ʿimmādī*, "against me")
lix 8 *kī mī šōmē^{a}ʿ*, "For who will hear us?"
lxvi 18 *lōʾ yišmaʿ ʾ^{a}dōnāy*, "my Lord would not have heard me" (see the first colon *b^{e}libbī*, "in my heart")
19 *ʾākēn šāmaʿ ʾ^{e}lōhīm*, "But God did hear me" (see *t^{e}pillātī*, "my prayer," of the second colon)
lxxviii 21 *lākēn šāmaʿ yhwh*, "so when Yahweh heard them"
59 *šāmaʿ ʾ^{e}lōhīm*, "God heard them"

Ellipsis:
double-duty substantives

Ps xii 4 *kol śip^{e}tē ḥ^{a}lāqōt//lāšōn*, "all pernicious lips//every tongue"
lviii 5 *kid^{e}mūt ḥ^{a}mat nāḥāš//k^{e}mō peten*, "like the venom of a serpent//like that of an adder"
lxv 12b–13a *yirʿ^{a}pūn dāšen—yirʿ^{a}pū*, "may (they) drip fatness; May (they) drip fatness"
cxxxv 5 *gādōl yhwh//waʾ^{a}dōnēnū mikkol ʾ^{e}lōhīm*, "Yahweh is great// and our Lord is greater than all gods." Cf. Ps lxxvii 14

Ellipsis:
double-duty verbs

Ps iv 4 *ūd^{e}ʿū kī*, "And recognize that," an introductory formula operating with both halves of the verse
xviii 42 *y^{e}šaww^{e}ʿū w^{e}ʾēn mōšī^{a}ʿ//ʿal yahweh w^{e}lōʾ ʿānām*, "They implored, but the Savior was not there,//the Most High Yahweh, but he did not answer them." Note that here "the Most High Yahweh" of the second colon is the direct object of "they implored" at the beginning of the line
lxvii 5 *ʿammīm mīšōr//ūl^{e}ummīm bāʾāreṣ tanḥēm*, "You will lead nations into the plain,//and peoples into the land"
xci 9 *kī ʾōtōh* (MT *ʾattāh*) *yhwh mḥsy//ʿelyōn śamtā m^{e}ʿōnekā*, "If you consider Yahweh himself your refuge,//the Most High your mainstay"
cxxi 2 *ʿezrī mēʿim yhwh*, "My help will come from the home of Yahweh." The verb *yābōʾ*, "will come," is supplied from the second colon of the preceding line

Ellipsis:
double-duty prepositions—
ʾel, "to"

Ps xl 5 *w^{e}lōʾ pānāh ʾel r^{e}hābīm//w^{e}śāṭē kāzāb*, "and who turns not to pagan idols,//or to fraudulent images"

Ellipsis:
double-duty prepositions—
b^e

Ps xii 3	*śāpōt* (MT *ś^epat*) *ḥ^alāqōt b^elēb wālēb,* "with pernicious lips and a double mind"
xxxiii 1	*b-yhwh//nā'wāh,* "in Yahweh//in lauding"
7	*kōnēs kened* (MT *kannēd*)*//nōtēn b^e'ōṣārōt,* "He gathers into a jar//He puts into storehouses"
xlii 5	*b^eqōl rinnāh w^etōdāh//hāmōn ḥōgēg,* "Amid loud shouts and thanksgiving//amid a festal throng"
lvii 5	*b^etōk l^ebā'īm//lōh^aṭīm,* "amid lions//amid those raging"
lxv 2	*dūmiyyāh//b^eṣiyyōn,* "in the mighty castle//in Zion"
5	*niśb^e'āh b^eṭūb bētekā//q^edōš hēkālekā,* "May we be fully imbued with the beauty of your house,//the holiness of your temple"
lxvii 5	*mīšōr//bā'āreṣ,* "into the plain//into the land"
lxxiii 8	*b^erā'//'ōšeq,* "against the Evil One//against the oppression"
lxxxviii 6	*bammētīm//qeber,* "In Death//in the Grave"
lxxxix 6	*w^eyōdū šāmayim//biqhal q^edōšīm,* "In the heavens they praise //in the congregation of holy ones"
civ 3	*bammayim//'ābīm,* "upon the waters//upon the clouds"
cv 18	*bakkebel//barzel . . . ,* "with shackles//through irons"
30	*'arṣām//b^eḥadrē,* "in their land//in the chambers of"
cxix 55	*ballaylāh//w^e'ašmūrāh* (MT *wā'ešm^erāh*), "in the night//and during the watch"
89–90	*niṣṣāb baššāmāyim . . . 'ereṣ watta'^amōd,* "more stable than the heavens . . . more firmly than the earth shall it stand"
cxxxv 6	*bayyammīm w^ekol t^ehōmōt,* "in the seas and in all the deeps"
cxxxvii 1	*'al nah^arōt bābel,* "Beside the rivers in Babylon." *bābel* shares the preposition *b^e* of *b^etōkāh,* "in her midst," of vs. 2

Ellipsis:
double-duty prepositions—
k^e, "like, as"

Ps xxxvi 7	*k^ehar^erē 'ēl//t^ehōm rabbāh,* "like the towering mountains//like the vast abyss"
xlviii 7b–8a	*ḥīl kayyōlēdāh b^erūaḥ qādīm,* "anguish like a woman in labor. As when by the east wind"
lviii 9	*k^emō šaklūl* (MT *šablūl*)*//nēpel 'ēšet,* "Like one ravaged//like a woman's stillbirth"
xc 4	*k^eyōm 'etmōl . . . 'ašmūrāh* (the initial *waw* having been joined to the preceding verb) *ballāylāh,* "like yesterday . . . like a watch in the night"
cii 8	*k^eṣippōr//bōdēd,* "like a sparrow//like a chatterer"
cxxv 2	*hārīm sābīb lāh wyhwh sābīb l^e'ammō,* "Like the mountains round about her is Yahweh round about his people." *hārīm,* "the mountains," shares the preposition *k^e*, "like," of *k^ehar ṣiyyōn,* "like Mount Zion," of vs. 1

Ellipsis:
double-duty prepositions—
l^{e} "to, for"

Ps xxxviii 23 *ḥûšāh l^{e}'ezrātī//'^{a}dōnāy t^{e}šū'ātī,* "Make haste to help me,//O Lord, to save me!"

lvii 7 *rešet hēkīnū lip'āmay//kpp napšī,* "They spread a net for my feet,//a noose for my neck"

lxxxix 2 *'ōlām 'āšīrāh//l^{e}dōr wādōr 'ōdī^{a}',* "for ever shall I sing,//age after age I shall proclaim"

cxiv 2 *hāy^{e}tāh y^{e}hūdāh l^{e}qodšō//yiśrā'ēl memš^{e}lōtī* (MT *mamš^{e}lōtāyw*), "Judah became his sanctuary,//Israel his dominion"

8 *haṣṣūr '^{a}gam māyim//ḥallāmīš l^{e}ma'y^{e}nū* (MT *l^{e}ma'y^{e}nō*) *māyim,* "(Who turned) rock into a pool of water//flint into a flowing spring"

Ellipsis:
double-duty prepositions—
min, "from, than"

Ps lvii 4 *yišlaḥ miššāmayim w^{e}yōšī'ēnī ḥārēp* (MT *ḥērēp*), "He will send from heaven to save me from the taunts"

lxix 32 *w^{e}tīṭab lyhwh miššōr//pār maqrīn maprīs,* "For this will please Yahweh more than a bull,//than an ox with horns and hoofs"

xciii 4 *miqqōlōt mayim//mišb^{e}rē yām,* "than the thunders of waters// than breakers of the sea"

Ellipsis:
double-duty prepositions—
'al, "upon"

Ps lxxii 6 *yērēd . . . 'al gēz//. . . zarzīpē* (MT *zarzīp*) *'āreṣ,* "May he descend . . . upon the mown grass,//. . . upon the scorched lands!"

lxxix 6 *š^{e}pōk ḥ^{a}māt^{e}kā 'ēl* (MT *'el*) *haggōyim . . .//w^{e}'al mamlākōt . . .,* "Pour out your rage, O God, upon the nations . . .//and upon the kingdoms . . ."

civ 3 *haśśām 'ābīm r^{e}kūbō//ham^{e}hallēk 'al kan^{e}pē rewaḥ* (MT *rū^{a}ḥ*), "Who set his chariot on the clouds,//who travels on wings outstretched"

Ellipsis:
double-duty prepositions—
'im, "like"

Ps cxx 4 *ḥiṣṣē gibbōr š^{e}nūnīm//'im gaḥ^{a}lē r^{e}tāmīm,* "Like sharpened arrows of a warrior//like glowing coals of broom"
(For the retroactive use of double-duty *'im,* "with," in Gen xxx 8, see F. I. Andersen, JBL 88 [1969], 200)

Ellipsis:
double-duty particles—
'al, "not"

Ps xxxviii 2 *'al . . . tōkīḥēnī//t^{e}yass^{e}rēnī,* "do not reprove me//nor chastise me"

lxxv 6 *'al tārīmū//t^{e}dabb^{e}rū,* "Raise not//nor speak"

xc 3 *'al* (transposed from vs. 2) *tāšēb//wattō'mer,* "Do not send back// nor say"

Ellipsis:
double-duty particles—
kī

Ps xlix 11 *kī yir'eh//yāḥad* (MT *yaḥad*), "If he looks//if he gazes"

lxxxiii 19 . . . *kī 'attāh šimekā yhwh//lebaddekā* (MT *lebaddekā*) *'elyōn,* ". . . that your own Name is Yahweh,//that you alone are the Most High"

cxiv 5 *kī tānūs//tissōb,* "that you fled//that you turned"

cxvi 10 *kī 'adubbār* (MT *'adabbēr*)*//'unnētī* (MT *'ānītī*), "though I was pursued//though I was harried"

cxxxviii 6 *kī rām yhwh//wegābōah,* "Though Yahweh is the Exalted//and though the Lofty"

Ellipsis:
double-duty particles—
lō', "not"

Ps ix 19 *lō' lāneṣaḥ yiššākaḥ 'ebyōn//tiqwat . . . tō'bad lā'ad,* "For not forever shall the needy be forgotten//nor the hope of . . . eternally perish"

xxxi 9 *lō' hisgartanī . . .//he'emadtā . . . ,* "You did not put me . . .// nor set . . ."

xliv 19 *lō' nāsōg 'āḥōr . . .//wattēṭ . . .* "has (masculine) not turned back . . .//nor strayed (feminine) . . ."

lix 16 *lō' yiśbe'ū wayyālīnū,* "not sated, they retire not"

cxxxi 1 *welō' hillaktī//'immālē'* (MT *'im lō'*), "I have not meddled//nor have I been filled"

Ellipsis:
double-duty particles—
lāmāh, "why"

Ps ii 1–2 *lāmmāh rāgešū gōyīm/. . . .*
yityaṣṣebū malkē 'ereṣ/. . . .
"Why do the nations forgather,/. . . ?
Why do kings of the earth take their stand,/ . . . ?"

lxxiv 1 *lāmāh . . . zānaḥtā lāneṣaḥ//ye'šan 'appekā . . . ,* "Why . . . are you eternally angry?//Why do your nostrils smoke . . . ?"

lxxxviii 15 *lāmāh . . . tiznaḥ napšī//tastīr pānekā mimmennī,* "Why . . . do you rebuff me,//why do you turn your face from me?"

Ellipsis:
double-duty particles—
mah, "how!" "why"

Ps iii 2–3 *māh rabbū . . .//rabbīm . . .//rabbīm . . . ,* "how many are . . .// how many . . .//how many . . . !"

lii 3–4 *mah tithallēl . . .// . . . hawwōt taḥšōb,* "Why do you boast . . .// . . . why do you harbor pernicious thoughts?"

xcii 6 *mah gādelū . . .//'āmequ . . . ,* "How great . . .//How deep . . . !"

Ellipsis:
double-duty particles—
'ad māh, "How long?"

Ps lxxix 5 *'ad māh yhwh. . . .//tib'ar . . . qin'ātekā,* "How long, O Yahweh? . . .//how long will your zeal burn . . . ?"

lxxxix 47 *'ad māh yhwh . . .//lāneṣaḥ . . . ,* "How long, O Yahweh . . . ?// How long, O Conqueror . . . ?"

Ellipsis:
double-duty particles—
'ad mātay, "How much longer?"

Ps xciv 3–4 *'ad mātay . . ./'ad mātay . . . ya'alōzū*
yabbī'ū yedabberū 'ātāq/. . .
"How much longer . . .//How much longer shall . . . (they) exult?
How much longer shall they pour forth defiant words/. . . ?"

Ellipsis:
double-duty particles—
pen, "lest"

Ps xiii 5 *pen yō'mar . . .//. . . yāgīlū,* "Lest he should boast . . .//. . . lest he should exult"

Ellipsis:
other double-duty expressions

Ps l 8 *lō' 'al zebāḥekā//weōlōtēkā,* "Not for your sacrifices//nor for your burnt offerings (do I reprove you)"

Prosody:
double-duty modifier:
vocative placed in middle

Ps lvii 8 *nākōn libbī*
'elōhīm
nākōn libbī
Firm is my resolve,
O God,
Firm is my resolve"

10 *'ōdekā bā'ammīm*
'adōnāy
'azammerekā bale'ummīm
"I will thank you among peoples,
O Lord,
I will sing to you among nations"

lxxxix 50 *'ayyēh ḥasādekā hārī'šōnīm*
'adōnāy
nišba'tā ledāwīd be'emūnātekā
"Where are those earlier acts of love,
O Lord,
Which you promised on your fidelity to David?"

cxix 43 *we'al taṣṣēl mippī debar 'emet*
'ad mā'ēd (MT *me'ōd*)
kī lemišpāṭekā (MT *lemišpāṭekā*) *yiḥaltī*

"So do not remove the true word from my mouth,
Everlasting Grand One!
Indeed I wait for your ordinances."

55 *zākartī ballaylāh šimekā*
yhwh
we'ašmūrāh (MT *wā'ešmerāh*) *tōrātekā*

"I remember your name in the night,
Yahweh,
And during the watch your law"

104 *mippiqqūdekā 'etbōnān*
'al kēn
śānē'tī kol 'ōraḥ šāqer

"Through your precepts I acquire insight,
Most High Reliable One,
I hate every false way"

107 *na'anētī 'ad mā'ēd* (MT *me'ōd*)
yhwh
ḥayyēnī kidebārekā

"I am afflicted to Calamity,
Yahweh,
Preserve my life according to your word"

111 *nāḥaltī 'ēdōtekā*
le'ōlām
kī śeśōn libbī hēmmāh

"I have inherited your stipulations,
O Eternal One,
Truly they are my heart's joy"

(The same pattern with the vocative *le'ōlām* "O Eternal One!" placed in the middle recurs in vss. 142, 144, 160)

140 *ṣerūpāh 'imrātekā*
mā'ēd (MT *me'ōd*)
we'abdekā 'ahēbāh

"Your word is tested,
O Grand One,
And your servant loves it"

149 *qōlī šim'āh keḥasdekā*
yhwh
kemišpāṭekā ḥayyēnī

"In your kindness hear my voice,
Yahweh,
In your justice preserve my life"

(The same pattern recurs in vss. 166 and 174)

169 *tiqrab rinnātī lepānekā*
yhwh
kidebarekā habīnēnī

"May my cry reach your presence,
Yahweh,
According to your word, give me insight"

cxxxvii 5 *'im 'eškāḥēkī* (MT *'eškaḥēk*)
yerūšālēm (MT *yerūšālāim*)
tiškaḥ yemīnī

"Should I forget you,
O Jerusalem,
Let my right hand wither"

6 *'im lō' 'a'aleh 'att* (MT *'et*)
yerūšālēm (MT *yerūšālāim*)
'al rō'š śimḥātī

"If I do not raise you,
O Jerusalem,
Upon my head in celebration!"

Prosody:
double-duty modifiers

Ps vi 11 *yēbōšū weyibbāhalū mā'ēd* (MT *me'ōd*)
kol 'ōyebāy
yāšūbū yēbōšū rāga'

"May they be humiliated and discomfited by Calamity—
all my foes—
May they return and be humiliated by Perdition!"
(revised translation)

vii 3 *wehaṣṣīlēnī pen yiṭrōp*
ke'aryeh
napšī pōrēq we'ēn maṣṣīl

"Rescue me lest he tear me apart
like a lion
Rending my neck with none to rescue me"

xxi 5 *ḥayyīm šā'al mimmekā*
nātattāh lō
'ōrek yāmīm 'ōlām wā'ed

"The life eternal he asked of you
you gave him
Length of days, O Eternal and Everlasting"
(revised translation)

xxii 26 *mī'ētīkā* (MT *mē'ittekā*) *tehillātī*
beqāhāl rāb
nedāray 'ašallēm nāgīd (MT *neged*)

"One hundred times will I repeat to you my song of praise
in the great congregation
I will fulfill my vows, O Prince!"
(revised translation)

xxvii 4a *'aḥat šā'altī*
mē'ēt yhwh
'ōtāh '^{a}baqqēš
"One thing I have asked
of Yahweh
This do I seek"

(revised translation)

lv 15 *'^{a}šer yaḥdāw namtīq sōd*
b^{e}bēt '^{e}lōhīm
n^{e}hallēk b^{e}rāgeš
"We used to take sweet counsel together—
in God's house—
We used to mingle among the throngs"

lvi 5 *bē'lōhīm bāṭaḥtī*
lō' 'īrā'
mah ya'^{a}śeh bāśār lī
"In God I put my trust,
I fear not,
What can flesh do to me?"
(Identical arrangement is present in vs. 12)

lvii 5 *napšī b^{e}tōk l^{e}bā'īm*
'ešk^{e}bāh
lōh^{a}ṭīm b^{e}nē 'ādām
"Myself amid lions
I must lie
Amid those raging for human prey"

lxix 14 *b^{e}rob ḥasdekā*
'^{a}nēnī
be'^{e}met yiš'ekā
"In your great kindness
answer me
With your faithful help"

lxxiii 25 *mī lī baššāmāyim*
w^{e}'imm^{e}kā
lō' ḥāpaṣtī bā'āreṣ
"What shall I lack in heaven
with you
I shall want nothing on earth"

lxxxiii 18 *yēbōšū w^{e}yibbāh^{a}lū*
'^{a}dē 'ad
w^{e}yaḥp^{e}rū w^{e}yō'bēdū
"May they be humiliated and discomfited
for ever and ever
May they perish in utter disgrace"

lxxxiv 3 *niks^{e}pāh w^{e}gam kāl^{e}tāh napšī*
l^{e}ḥaṣ^{e}rōt yhwh
libbī ūb^{e}śārī y^{e}rann^{e}nū
"My soul longs and pines aloud
for your court, O Yahweh!
My heart and my flesh cry out"

lxxxvi 12 *'ōd^{e}kā '^{a}dōnāy '^{e}lōhay*
b^{e}kol l^{e}bābī
'^{a}kabb^{e}dāh šim^{e}kā l^{e}'ōlām
"I will thank you, my Lord, my God,
with all my heart
I will glorify your name, O Eternal!"
(Note: The *waw* of *wa'^{a}kabb^{e}dāh* has been omitted as secondary.)

lxxxviii 6 *bammēṯīm ḥopšī*
k^{e}mō ḥ^{a}lālīm
miškābī (MT *šōk^{e}bē*) *qeber*
"In Death is my cot
like the slaughtered
My couch is in the Grave"

18 *sabbūnī kammayim*
kol hayyōm
hiqqīpū 'ālay yāḥīd (MT *yāḥad*)
"They surround me like a flood
all day long
They close in on me alone"

xcii 6 *mah gād^{e}lū ma'^{a}śekā*
yhwh mā'ēd (MT *m^{e}'ōd*)
'ām^{e}qū maḥš^{e}bōtekā
"How great your works,
Yahweh the Grand,
How deep your thoughts!"
(revised translation)

xcviii 2 *hōdī^{a}' yhwh y^{e}šū'ātō*
l^{e}'ēnē haggōyīm
gillāh ṣidqātō
"Yahweh made known his victory
before the eyes of the nations
He revealed his vindication"

9 *lip^{e}nē yhwh*
kī bā'
lišpōṭ hā'āreṣ
"Before Yahweh
when he comes
To govern the earth"

cii 3b *haṭṭēh 'ēlay 'oznekā*
b^{e}yōm 'eqrā'
mahēr '^{a}nēnī
"Turn your ear toward me
when I call
Quickly answer me"

20 *kī hišqīp mimm^{e}rōm qodšō*
yhwh
miššāmayim 'el 'ereṣ hibbīṭ
"From his holy height looked down
Yahweh
From heaven to earth gazed"

cix 14 *yizzākēr ʿ^{a}wōn ʾ^{a}bōtāyw*
ʾēl (MT *ʾel*) *yhwh*
w^{e}ḥaṭṭaʾt ʾimmō ʾal timmāḥ

"Recorded be the iniquity of his father
by El Yahweh,
And his mother's sin not be erased!"

20 *zōʾt p^{e}ʿullat śōṭ^{e}nay*
mēʾēt yhwh
(*w^{e}*)*haddōb^{e}rīm rāʿ ʿal napšī*

"Let ignominy be the recompense of my slanderers
from Yahweh,
Of those speaking evil about me"

cxix 103 *mah niml^{e}ṣū l^{e}ḥikkī*
ʾimrōtekā (MT *ʾimrātekā*)
ma dāb^{e}šū (MT *midd^{e}baš*) *l^{e}pī*

"How tasty to my palate
your words,
How sweet to my mouth!"

140 *ṣ^{e}rūpāh ʾimrāt^{e}kā*
māʾēd (MT *m^{e}ʾōd*)
w^{e}ʿabd^{e}kā ʾ^{a}hēbāh

"Your word is tested,
O Grand One,
And your servant loves it"

cxxi 6 *yōmām haššemeš*
lōʾ yakkekā
w^{e}yārē^{a}ḥ ballāylāh

"By day the sun
will not strike you
The moon at night"

7 *yhwh yišmor^{e}kā*
mikkol rāʿ
yišmōr ʾet napšekā

"Yahweh will guard you
from every evil
He will guard your life"

cxxxviii 2 *ʿal ḥasd^{e}kā w^{e}ʿal ʾ^{a}mittekā*
kī higdaltā
ʿal kōl (MT *kol*) *šim^{e}kā ʾimrātekā*

"Through your kindness and through your fidelity
you surely glorified
Before all your Name, your promise"

cxliii 1
be^{e}ʾ^{e}mūnātekā
ʿ^{a}nēnī
b^{e}ṣidaqātekā
"In your fidelity
answer me
In your justice"

IX. PAIRS OF PARALLEL WORDS IN THE PSALTER AND IN UGARITIC

Scholars agree that these provide a sound criterion for assessing the literary relationships between the Psalter and Ugaritic literature. From this list of some one hundred and fifty-seven pairs of parallel words (strict parallelism is indicated by the symbol //), collocations, and juxtapositions, the reader may judge to what extent the psalmists and Canaanite poets drew from a common literary fund. The order of the parallel pairs listed is alphabetic according to Hebrew spelling.

'by "my father"//*ṣwr* "the Mountain" Ps lxxxix 27	*ab ǵr b'l ṣpn* UT, 125:6–7
'dny "O Lord" . . . *'my* "my mother" Ps lxxi 5–6	*adn//um* UT, 77:33–34
1. Juxtaposition of *'hl* "tent" and *škn* "to dwell" Pss lxxviii 55 (in reverse order), 60b, cxx 5 (in reverse order)	
2. *mškn* "dwelling"//*'hl* "tent" Ps lxxviii 60	*ahl//mšknt* UT, 128:III:18–19; 2 Aqht:v:32–33
'ḥ "brother"//*bn 'm* "mother's son" Pss l 20; lxix 9	*aḫ//bn um* UT, 49:VI:10–11, 14–15; Krt:8–9
'ḥ "brother"//*r'* "friend" Pss xxxv 14 (in reverse order), cxxii 8	*aḫ//r'* UT, 1019:8, 10
1. *'yb* "foe"//*ṣr* "adversary" Pss lxxxi 15; lxxxix 43 (in reverse order),	
2. *ṣrh* "adversity-adversary"//*'yb* "foe" Pss liv 9, cxxxviii 7, cxliii 11–12	*ib* "foe"//*ṣrt* "adversity-adversary" UT, 68:9; 'nt:III:34;IV:48, 49–50
'yby "my foes"//*mtqwmmy* "my attackers" Ps lix 2	*ib* "foe"//*qm* "attacker" UT, 76:II:24–25
1. *'wyb* "foe"//*śwn'* "enemy" Pss xxi 9, cvi 10 (in reverse order)	*ib* "the foes of"//*šnu* "the haters of"
2. *'wyb* "foe"//*mśn'* "enemy" Pss xviii 41, lxviii 2	UT, 51:VII:35–36
'kl "to eat"//*šth* "to drink" Ps l 13	*'kl//šty* UT, 2003:3
'lmnwt "widows" . . . *yḥydym* "the solitary" Ps lxviii 6–7	*yḥd//almnt* UT, Krt:96–97

'lp "a thousand"//*rbbh* "ten thousand"
Pss xci 7, cxliv 13

'lp//rbt
UT, 51:I:28–29; v:86.118–19; VIII:25; 77:20; 2 Aqht:v:9–10; Krt:92–93.180–181; 'nt:I:15–17; IV:82; VI:4–5.17; 1019:4–5

'nh "where?"//*w'nh* "Oh where?"
Ps cxxxix 7

an lan "where, Oh where?"
UT, 49:IV:46–47

Ps lxxv 3b (*'ny*), 4b (*'nky*)

UT, 51:IV:59 (*an*), 60 (*ank*)

'rṣ "earth"//*'lhym* "gods"
Ps xcvii 9

ilm arṣ "gods of the underworld"
UT, 62:18; 67:v:6; 1 Aqht:112, 127, 141

1. *'rṣ* "the earth"//*hrym* "mountains"
Pss xlvi 3, lxxii 16, cxlvii 8, 15 (*'d-m hrh,* "toward the mountain," for MT *'d mhrh*)
2. *hrym//'rṣ*
Pss xc 21, civ 13
3. *'rṣ . . . hrym*
Ps civ 5–6

hrm//arṣ
UT, 608:7, 9, 19

'rṣ "the nether world"//*ym* "the sea"
Ps xlvi 3

arṣ . . . ym
UT, 52:61–63

'rṣ "ground"//*'pr* "dust"
Pss vii 6, xxii 30, xliv 26 (in reverse order)

arṣ//'pr
UT, 68:5; 76:II:24–25; 2 Aqht:I:28–29; 'nt:III:11–12; IV:52–53, 67, 72–73

'rṣ "land"//*śdh* "plain"
Ps lxxviii 12b

arṣ//šd
UT, 49:II:16–17, 19–20; 67:VI:6–7, 27–28, 29; 126:III:5–6, 7–8; 'nt:III:13–14; IV:54, 68–69, 74–75

1. a) *'rṣ* "earth"//*šmym* "heaven"
Pss lxviii 9, lxxxv 12
b) *šmym//'rṣ*
Ps lxxiii 9
2. a) *'rṣ wšmym* "earth and heaven"
Ps cxlviii 13
b) *šmym w'rṣ* "heaven and earth"
Pss lxix 35, cxv 15, cxxxv 6, cxlvi 6

arṣ//šmm
UT, 52:62; 67:II:2
šmm//arṣ
'nt:II:39; IV:87
arṣ wšmm
UT, 126:III:2; 609:5
šmm . . . arṣ
'nt:III:21; pl. ix:III:14

1. *h'rṣ* "the nether world"//*thwmwt* "depths"
Ps cxlviii 7
2. *thmwt h'rṣ* "the depths of the nether world"
Ps lxxi 20
3. *'rṣ . . . thwm*
Ps xlii 7–8

arṣ//thmt
'nt:III:21–22; IV:60–61

'šh "wife"//*bn* "son, child" Pss cix 9 (in reverse order), cxxviii 3	UT, 2068:19, *w atth w bnh* "and his wife and his children"
b "in"//*bqrb* "in the midst of" Ps lxxxii 1	*b//bqrb* UT, 51:v:75–76, 123–24, 126–27; vi:5–6, 8–9; 2 Aqht i:26
b//btwk Pss cix 30, cxvi 19	*b//btk* UT, 75:i:20–21; 'nt:iii:26–27
btwk//b Ps cxxxv 9	*btk//b* UT, 128:iii:14–15
b//l Ps cv 2 (*l . . . l . . . b . . .*), 15 (*b . . . l . . .*)	2 Aqht:v:26–27 *bd* "in the hands of" //*lbrkh* "on his knees"
b "with"//*tḥt* "under" Ps xci 4	*b//tḥt* 2 Aqht:v:6
1. *byt* "house"//*ḥṣr* "court" Pss xcii 14, cxxxv 2	*bt//ḥẓr* UT, 51:iv:50–51, 62–63; v:90; 128:ii:22–23; 129:19; Krt:132–33, 203–5, 260–61, 279–80; 'nt:v:46–47
2. *ḥṣr//byt* Ps lxxxiv 11a, c 3. *ḥṣrwt byt* "the courts of the house" Pss cxvi 19, cxxxv 2b	
byt "house"//*šlḥn* "table" Ps cxxviii 3b, d *šlḥn . . . byt* Ps xxiii 5–6	*bt//ṯlḥnm* "two tables" 'nt:ii:29–30
byt "the house of" . . . *š'ry* "the gates of" Ps cxxii 1–2	*ṯǵrt bht* "the gates of the house" 'nt:ii:3–4 *bt//ṯǵr* UT, 1007:5–6
bny "my son"//*yldtyk* "I have begotten you" Ps ii 7	*ybn ašld* "O sons I have begotten!" UT, 52:65
bny hn'wrym "the sons of one's youth" Ps cxxvii 4	*n'r//bn* UT, 2068:25–26
b'dy "so long as I live"//*l'wlm* "for ever" Ps cxxxviii 8	*b'd 'lm* "so long as eternity perdures" UT, 1019:6
bšn (MT *mbšn*) "the Serpent"// *ym* "of the Sea" Ps lxviii 23	*ym . . . bṯn* 'nt:iii:36–38

wyd’ ‘l knpy rwḥ “and he soared on wings outstretched” Ps xviii 11b	*knp* “wings”//*diy* “pinions” 1 Aqht:114–15, 118–19, 122–23, 128–29, 132–33, 136–37, 142–43, 148–49
dyn “to judge” . . . *špṭ* “to try” Ps vii 8–9 *špṭ* “to govern”//*dyn* “to judge” Ps ix 9 *dyn* “cause”//*mšpṭ* “rights” Ps cxl 13 *mšpṭ—dyn* Ps ix 5 *dyn* “sentence” . . . *mšpṭ* “judgment” Ps lxxvi 9–10	*dyn*//*ṯpṭ* UT, 127:33–34, 45–47; 1 Aqht: 23–25; 2 Aqht:v:7–8
dkym “their pounding waves” . . . *rbym* “stronger” Ps xciii 3–4	*rbm* “the Strong One”//*dkym* “the Pounder” UT, 49:v:2–3
dl wytwm “the weak and the fatherless” Ps lxxxii 3	*dl* “the weak” . . . *ytm* “the fatherless” UT, 127:48–49
dm‘h “tears” . . . *bkh* “weeping” Ps cxxvi 5–6	*bky* “to weep”//*dm‘* “to shed tears” UT, 62:9–10; 1 Aqht:34–35, 173–74; Krt:26–27, 31–32, 39–40, 60–61
bhykl “in the temple”//*ks’w* “his throne” Ps xi 4	*lksi* “upon the throne” . . . *bhkl* “in the palace” UT, 123:23, 25
hrh “he is pregnant”//*yld* “he gives birth” Ps vii 15	*w[th]rn wtldn* in UT, 67:v:22 *hry wyld* in UT, 132:5
zqnh wśybh “hoary old age” Ps lxxi 18	*šbt dqnk* “the hoariness of your beard” UT, 51:v:66
wyštḥww “they will prostrate themselves”//*wykbdw* “and they will glorify” Ps lxxxvi 9 *ḥwh . . . kbd* Ps cvi 19b–20a	*tštḥwy wtkbdnh* “she prostrates herself and honors him” UT, 49:I:10; 51:IV:26
ḥwšh ly “hasten to me!”//*’l t’ḥr* “do not tarry!” Ps lxx 6	*aḥš* “I shall hasten . . . *iḫr* “I shall tarry” UT, 2009:11–12
ḥyym “life eternal”//*’rk ymym* Ps xxi 5 *kl ymy ḥyy* “all the days of my life//*l’rk ymym* “for length of days” Ps xxiii 6	*ḥy np[š]* *wurk ym* “and length of days” UT, 1018:18–20 *ḥwt . . . wnark* “may you live . . . and enjoy length of days” UT, 76:II:20

ḥmr "bowl"//*msk* "he will draw" Ps lxxv 9	*ḫmr* "bowl"//*ymsk* "he drew" 'nt:I:16–17
ḥn "favors" . . . *ntn* "to give, bestow" Ps lxxxiv 12	*yḥnnn* "graces him"//*ytn* "gives" UT, 76:I:12–13
ḥsyl "grasshopper"//*'rbh* "locust" Ps lxxviii 46	*irby*//*ḥsn* Krt:103–5, 192–93
ḥṣym "the arrows" . . . *'šptw* "his quiver" Ps cxxvii 4–5	*uṯpt ḥẓm* "a quiver of arrows" UT, 1124:1, 2, 3
1. *ḥrb* "sword"//*yd* "hand" Ps xxii 21; cxliv 10–11 2. *wḥrb . . . bydm* "but a . . . sword in their hand" Ps cxlix 6	*yd* "hand"//*ḥrb* "a large knife" UT, 128:IV:24–25
ṭwbtk "your rain"//*dšn* "fatness" Ps lxv 12	*dšn* "plump"//*ṭbm* "merry" UT, 602:5
ṭwb "good"//*n'ym* "pleasant" Pss cxxxiii 1, cxxxv 3, cxlvii 1	*n'm* "the Pleasant One"// *ṭb ql* "the good/sweet voiced" 'nt:I:19–20
ybl "to bring"//*nḥh* "to offer" Ps lx 11	*ybl . . . mnḥyk* UT, 137:38
ydy "my hands"//*'ṣb'wty* "my arms" Ps cxliv 1	*ydh* "his hands"//*uṣb'th* "his arms" Krt:157–58
yd "left hand"//*ymyn* "right hand" Pss xxvi 10, lxxiv 11, lxxxix 14, 26, cxxxviii 7, cxxxix 10	*yd*//*ymn* UT, 51:VII:40–41; 76:II:6–7; 125:41–42, 47–48; 137:39; 1 Aqht:216, 217–18; Krt:66–67
ydy "my hands"//*npšy* "my throat" Ps cxliii 6	*npš . . . ydy* UT, 67:I:18–20
1. *yd'* "to know"//*byn* "to understand" Pss lxxxii 5, cxxxix 2 2. Juxtaposition in Ps cxix 125	*yd'*//*byn* 'nt:III:24
ywd'y "those who know"//*yhlkwn* "(those) who walk" Ps lxxxix 16	*yd't hlk kbkbm* "she who knows the course of the stars" 1 Aqht:51–52, 56, 200
yd'ty "I know"//*'mdy* "(present) before me" Ps l 11	*yd'm l yd't 'my špš b'lk* UT, 2060:14–15
ywm "one day"//*'lp* "a thousand" Ps lxxxiv 11	*alp ymm* "thousand days" UT, 1019:4
ymym "days"//*šnwt* "years" Pss lxi 7, lxxvii 6, lxxviii 33	*ymm*//*šnt* UT, 1019:4–5

ymwt "days"//*šnwt* "years" Ps xc 15	*ymt*//*šnt* UT, 602:rev.:11–12
yldw "they were born"//*wtḥwll* "and came to birth" Ps xc 2	*ḫl ld* "go into labor, bear" UT, 75:I:25
ymym "seas"//*l’mym* "peoples" Ps lxv 8	*lim ḫp y[m]* "the peoples of the seashore" ‘nt:II:7
ym "sea"//*nhr* "river" Pss xxiv 2, lxvi 6, lxxii 8, lxxxviii 12, lxxxix 26	*ym*//*nhr* UT, 51:II:6–7; 68:12–13, 14–15, 16–17, 19–20, 21–22, 24–25, 27, 29–30; 129:7, 9, 21, 23; 137:22, 26, 28, 30, 33–34, 41, 44; ‘nt:III:36
ym "sea"//*thwmwt* "deeps" Pss xxxiii 7, cxxxv 6	*ym*//*thm* UT, 52:30
ym "the sea"//*r’šy tnyny* (MT *tnynym*) "the heads of Tannin" Ps lxxiv 13	*ym . . . tnn* ‘nt:III:36–37; 1003:7–8
yšb ‘l ks’ qdšw "(God) has taken his seat upon his holy throne" Ps xlvii 9	*yṯb lksi mlk* "he has taken his seat upon the throne of his kingship" UT, 127:23
šb "sit enthroned" . . . *mṭh* "mace" Ps cx 1–2	*yṯb* "he sits" . . . *ḫṭ* "staff, scepter" UT, 52:8–9
šb "sit enthroned!" . . . *‘d* "a seat" Ps cx 1	*yṯb . . . l‘dh* "he sat upon his throne" UT, 127:22
yšb "(Yahweh) has reigned"//*lmšpṭ* "for judgment" Ps ix 8	*ṯbtk* "your throne"//*mṯpṭk* "your rule" UT, 49:VI:28–29
1. *šnt* "sleep"//*tnwmh* "slumber" Ps cxxxii 4 2. *nwm* "to slumber"//*yšn* "to sleep" Ps cxxi 4	*yšn* "sleeping"//*nhmmt* "slumber" Krt:31–32 *šnt* "sleep"//*nhmmt* "slumber" Krt:33–34
1. *ytwm* "fatherless"//*’lmnh* "widow" Pss lxviii 6, cix 9 2. *ytwm w’lmnh* "the fatherless and the widow" Ps cxlvi 9	*ytm* "fatherless"//*almnt* "widow" UT, 127:49–50; in reverse order in UT, 1 Aqht:I:24–25; 2 Aqht:V:8
kdmwt "like"//*kmw* "like" Ps lviii 5 *kmw*//*k* Ps lxxviii 69	*kirby* "like locusts"//*km ḥsn* "like grasshoppers" Krt:103–5
k . . . k . . . kn Ps lxxxiii 15–16, ciii 15, cxxiii 2	*k . . . k . . . km* UT, 49:II:28–30

nkwn "(your throne) was established"//*m'wlm* "from eternity" Ps xciii 2	*'l[m]* "the Eternal"//*dyknn* "he who brought us into being" UT, 76:III:6–7
klh Pi "to annihilate" . . . *mḥṣ* "to smite" Ps xviii 38b–39a	*mḫṣ*//*kly* 67:I:1–2; 1 Aqht:196–97, 201–2
ks'w "his throne"//*mlkwtw* "his royal power" Ps ciii 19	*ks' mlk* "the throne of kingship" UT, 49:V:5; VI:28; 127:23; 'nt:IV:46
ksp "silver"//*yrqrq ḥrwṣ* "yellow gold" Ps lxviii 14	*ksp wyrq ḫrṣ* "silver and yellow gold" Krt:126, 138, 250–51, 269–70, 282–83
l//*b* Ps lxxviii 61, cv 5 (in reverse order)	*l*//*b* UT, 'nt:II:12–13, pl. ix:III:8–9
lyhwh "to Yahweh"//*lmw r'* "to the One Who Sees" Ps lxxvi 12 *lngdk* "before you"//*lm 'wr pnyk* "in the light of your face" Ps xc 8	*lṯn* "to another"//*lm nkr* "to a stranger" Krt:101–2
l//*'l* Ps ciii 10, 17 (in reverse order), cxv 1, cxxiv 2, cxlv 9	*l*//*'l* UT, 608:7, 9, 19
lb "heart"//*kbd* (MT *kbwd*) "liver" Pss xvi 8, lvii 8–9	*lb*//*kbd* UT, 75:I:13; 1 Aqht:34–35; 3 Aqht:rev.:17–18; 'nt:II:26–27
lbm "their heart"//*lhtnkl* "to double-dealing" Ps cv 24	*nklb* personal name UT, 152:rev.:6; 301:rev.:IV:20
lbnwn "Lebanon" . . . *ly'lym* "to the wild goats" Ps civ 16, 18	*dlbnn* "of Lebanon" . . . *by'lm* "from wild goats" 2 Aqht:VI:21–22
lbnwn "Lebanon"//*śryn* "Sirion" Ps xxix 6	*lbnn*//*šryn* UT, 51:VI:18–19, 20–21
klbwš ksytw "(you) covered it like a garment" Ps civ 6	*lpš yks mizrtm* "For clothing, he is covered with a double garment" UT, 67:VI:16–17
lḥm "grain" . . . *yyn* "wine" . . . *šmn* "oil" Ps civ 14–15	*lḥm*//*yn*//*šmn* UT, 126:III:13–16
lḥm "food"//*šqh* Hiph "to cause to drink" Ps lxxx 6 *lḥm* "food"//*šqwy* "my drink" Ps cii 10	*lḥm* "to eat"//*šqy* "to drink" 2 Aqht:I:3–4, 8–9, 11, 13–14, 22–23 *lḥm—šqy* 2 Aqht:II:30–38; V:19, 29

bmdbr "in the wilderness"//*kthmwt* "the wasteland itself" Ps lxxviii 15	*bmdbr*//*thmt* UT, 2001:3–5
mwt Pi "to slay"//*ḥlq* Pi "to make perish" Ps xvii 14	*mt*//*ḫlq* UT, 49:I:13–14; 67:VI:9–10
mṭr "rain"//*rwḥ* "wind" Ps cxxxv 7	*rḥk*//*mṭrtk* "your wind . . .//your rains" UT, 67:v:7–8
mym "water"//*šmn* "oil" Ps cix 18	*mh* "her water" . . . *šmn* "oil" ʻnt:II:38–39; IV:86–87
mlk "king"//*m'rṣw* "from his earth" Ps x 16	*mlk* . . . *arṣ* UT, 49:I:37; 51:VII:43–44
mlk . . . *drk* Pss cii 23–24, cxxxviii 4–5, cxlvi 9–10	*mlk* "kingship"//*drkt* "dominion" UT, 68:10
mlk "to be king"//*yšb* "to sit enthroned" Pss xlvii 9, xcix 1	*mlk*//*yṯb* UT, 127:52–54
mwnh mspr "who assigns a number" Ps cxlvii 4	*sprhn* "their number"//*mnthn* "their count" UT, 77:45–47
ndrw "make vows!"//*šy* "gifts" Ps lxxvi 12	*bm ṯy ndr* "with a gift it was vowed" UT, 117:14
mnwḥty "my resting place"//*'šb* "I will sit" Ps cxxxii 14	*aṯbn* . . . *wanḫn* "I will sit and rest" UT, 49:III:18
nḥltk wnl'h "your patrimony and dominion" Ps lxviii 10	*bǵr nḥlty* "upon the mountain of my patrimony"//*bgbʻ tliyt* "upon the hill of my dominion/victory" ʻnt:III:27–28
nḥš "serpent"//*ḥmt ʻkšwb* "viper's venom" Ps cxl 4 *ḥmt nḥš* "venom of a serpent" Ps lviii 5	*ḥmt* "venom"//*nḥš* "serpent" UT, 607:11–12
nḥš "serpent"//*ptn* "adder" Ps lviii 5	*nḥšm* "serpents"//*bn btn* "snakes" UT, 607:75–76
lhtnkl bʻbdyw "to double-dealing with his servants" Ps cv 25	*ʻbdnkl* personal name UT, 321:II:43
npšm "their lives"//*dmm* "their blood" Ps lxxii 14	*dm* . . . *npšh* 3 Aqht:obverse 24–25

npš šqqh "the throbbing throat"// *npš rʻbh* "the hungry throat" Ps cvii 9	*npš*//*npš* UT, 49:II:17–18
nwšqy "his bowmen"//*rwmy qšt* "his treacherous archers" Ps lxxviii 9	*qšt . . . nṯq* UT, 1123:1–3
ntn "he gave"//*'š* "he produced" Ps cv 32	*ytnt* "present"//*ušn* "gift" Krt:135
ntn "to give"//*šlḥ* "to send" Pss lxxviii 24b–25b, cvi 15, cxlvii 15a–16b (in reverse order)	*ytn*//*šlḥ* 2 Aqht:VI:17–18, 27–28
spr ḥyym "the scroll of life eternal" Ps lxix 29	*ḥym* "eternal life" . . . *aššprk* "I will make you number" 2 Aqht:VI:26–29
spr "scroll" . . . *ktb* "to write" Pss lxix 29, cxxxix 16	*ktb spr hnd* "he has written this letter" UT:1005:9
lʻd "on his seat"//*ks'w* "his throne" Ps lxxxix 30	*lʻdh* "upon his seat"//*lksi mlk* "upon his royal throne" UT, 127:22–23
ʻd ʻwlm "forever" . . . *ʻlmwt* (MT *ʻl mwt*) "eternally" Ps xlviii 9, 15	*ʻd ʻlm šḥr ʻlmt* "forever an eternal dawn" UT, 1008:14–15
ʻwlm "eternity"//*d*(*w*)*r wd*(*w*)*r* Pss lxxxv 6, lxxxix 5, c 5, cxxxv 13, cxlv 13	*ʻlm*//*drdr* UT, 68:10; 1 Aqht:154, 161–62, 167–68
ʻwp "to fly"//*d'h* "to soar" Ps xviii 11	*diy hmt . . . hm tʻpn* "their pinions . . . if they fly" 1 Aqht:149–50
ʻzy wzmrt "my fortress and my sentinel" Ps cxviii 14	*ʻzk ḏmrk* UT, 602:rev.:9
ʻz "triumph/stronghold"//*m'd* "the Grand One" Pss xxi 2, xlvi 2	*ʻz mid* "very strong" UT, 54:13
ʻzb "to put"//*ntn* "to give, allow" Ps xvi 10	*ytn*//*ʻdb* 2 Aqht:v:26–27
ʻzr "to save"//*plṭ* "to rescue" Ps xxxvii 40	*plṭ*//*ʻḏr* 3 Aqht:rev.:13–14
mʻyn "spring"//*brkwt* "pools" Ps lxxxiv 7	*brky* "pool"//*ʻn* "spring" UT, 67:I:16–17; 604:A:6–8
ʻm 'lh "with them" . . . *ʻmnw* "with us" Ps cxxvi 2b–3a	*ʻm*//*ʻm* 2 Aqht:VI:28–29, UT, 1015:14–18

w'mwn "and with it"//*'m* "with" Ps lxxxiii 8	*'m//'mn* 'nt:III:21–22
'nh "to answer"//*hšyb* "to reply" Ps lv 20	*'ny//ṯwb* UT, 121:II:7–8; 1 Aqht:180–81
'ṣ "tree"//*'rz* "cedar" Pss civ 16, cxlviii 9	*'ṣ//arz* UT, 51:VI:18–19, 20–21
pyd'ty "for I know"/*wzyd* "and what moves" Ps l 11 (Note: *p* has been detached from *'lp* of the preceding line; see Note on Ps l 10)	*w'lmh* "and unto eternity"//*pdr.dr* "and for evermore" 1 Aqht:168
pyhm "their mouth"//*ymynm* "their right hand" Ps cxliv 8, 11	*ymn* "right hand" . . . *bphm* "into their mouth" UT, 52:63–64
ph "mouth"//*lšwn* "tongue" Pss lxvi 17, lxxiii 9, lxxviii 36, cxxvi 2	*p//lšn* Palais royal d'Ugarit v:124:2–3
py yspr "my mouth would count" Ps lxxi 15 *sprty* "I proclaim" . . . *pyk* "your mouth" Ps cxix 13	*bpy sprhn* "in my mouth is their count" UT, 77:45–46
ph "mouth"//*śph* "lip" Pss li 17 (in reverse order), lix 8, lxvi 14 (in reverse order), cxix 13, cxli 3	*p//špt* UT, 68:6; 77:45–46; 1 Aqht:75, 113, 127–28, 141–42
ph "here" . . . *šm* "there" Ps cxxxii 14, 17	*p* "here" . . . *ṯmt* "there" UT, 54:12, 18
pḥym/'š, "coals, fire" Ps xi 6 (revised translation)	*išt* "fire"//*pḥmm* UT, 51:II:8–9; 52:41, 44–45, 46, 48
lpnyw "before him"//*p'myw* "(in) his steps" Ps lxxxv 14	*p'n* "foot" . . . *pn* "face" 'nt:III:29–31
ptn "adder"//*tnyn* "serpent" Ps xci 13	*tnn* "Tannin"//*bṯn* "serpent" 'nt:III:37–38
1. *ṣnh w'lpym* "small and large cattle" Ps viii 8 2. *ṣ'wnnw//'lwpynw* "our sheep// our cattle" Ps cxliv 13–14	*alpm* [*ap*] *ṣin* "large and small cattle" UT, 51:VI:40–41 *alp//ṣin* UT, 5:6–7
ṣdq "justice"//*myšrym* "equity" Pss ix 9, lviii 2, xcviii 9 *ṣdyqym* "the just"//*yšrym* "the upright" Ps cxl 14	*ṣdqh* "his righteousness"//*yšrh* "his right" Krt:12–13

ṣdq wšlwm "justice and well-being" Ps lxxxv 11b	*ṣdqšlm* personal name UT, 119:23; 142:4; 300:28; 1116:11; 2039:5 *ṣṭqšlm* personal name UT, 1005:4, 10, 14
yqdmw pnyk "they stand before you" Ps lxxxix 15	*qdmh* "before him"//*wtk pnh* "right in front of him" UT, 51:v:107–8
qdmw "in front"//*btwk* "in the middle" Ps lxviii 26	*qdmh* "before him"//*wtk pnh* "right in front of him" UT, 51:v:107–8
qdš "the holy ones"//*'l* "god" Pss lxxvii 14, lxxxix 6–7	*ilm* "gods"//*bn qdš* "sons of holiness" UT, 137:20–21, 37–38; 2 Aqht: I:3–4, 8–9, 13–14, 22–23
qwl "thunder"//*brqym* "lightning bolts" Ps lxxvii 19	*ql*//*brqm* UT, 51:v:70–71
qšt "bow"//*ḥṣm* "their arrows" Ps xi 2	*qšt*//*ḥẓm* UT, 1123:1–2
r'š "head"//*qdqd* "skull" Pss vii 17, lxviii 22	*riš*//*qdqd* UT, 67:VI:15–16; 127:56–57; 2 Aqht:VI:36–37
r'bym gm ṣm'ym "hungry and thirsty" Ps cvii 5	*rǵb*//*ǵm'* UT, 51:IV:33–34
śdh "field"//*krm* "vineyard" Ps cvii 37	*šd . . . krm* UT, 77:22; 1079:6
1. *śmḥ* "to rejoice"//*gyl* "to leap with joy" Pss xvi 9, xlviii 12, xcvi 11, cxlix 2 2. Juxtaposition: *gyl—śmḥ* Ps cxviii 24	*šmḫ*//*gyl* UT, 125:14–15, 99
śmḥ "he gladdens"//*lhṣhyl* "he truly makes resplendent" Ps civ 15	*šmḫ*//*ṣhl* UT, 2 Aqht:II:9
śph "lip"//*lšwn* "tongue" Pss cxix 171–72, cxx 2, cxl 4 (in reverse order)	*špt* "lip"//[*l*]*šn* "tongue" UT, 67:II:2–3
šb'ym "seventy"//*šmwnym* "eighty" Ps xc 10	*šb'*[*m*]//*ṯmnym* UT, 128:IV:6–7
šbrt r'šy "you smashed the heads of (Tannin)" Ps lxxiv 13	*yṯbr . . . rišk* "may he break/smash your head" UT, 127:55–56; 137:7–8

šyr wzmr "to sing and play" Pss xxi 14, xxvii 6, lvii 8, cviii 2 *šyr//zmr* Pss lxviii 5, ci 1, civ 33, cv 2a, cxliv 9	*yšr wyḏmr* "he sings and plays" UT:602:3
šlwm "peace"//*mlḥmh* "war" Ps cxx 7	*mlḥmt//šlm* 'nt:III:12–13
šlḥn "table"//*kwsy* "my cup" Ps xxiii 5	*bṯlḥny//bks* UT, 51:III:15–16
šmym//'rṣ//ym Ps xcvi 11 *šmym w'rṣ//ym(ym)* Pss lxix 35, cxxxv 6, cxlvi 6	*arṣ//šmm . . . šmm//ym* UT, 52:61–63
šmym "heaven"//*ymym* "seas" Ps lxix 35	*šmm//ym* UT, 1003:6–7
šmw "his heavens"/*lrkb b'rbwt* "for the Rider of the Clouds" Ps lxviii 5	*šmm* "heaven" . . . *rkb 'rpt* "the Rider of the Clouds" 'nt:II:39–40
šmym "heaven"//*thwmwt* "depths" Ps cvii 26	*šmm//thmt* 'nt:III:21–22 *šmm wthm* UT, 607:1
kšmn "like oil"//*kṭl* "like dew" Ps cxxxiii 2a, 3a	*ṭl//šmn* 'nt:II:39; IV:87
šm' "to hear" . . . *'nh* "to answer" Ps lv 20	*šm' . . . 'ny* UT, 129:17–18 *'ny . . . šm'* UT, 3 Aqht: obverse:11–12
1. *yrḥ* "moon"//*šmš* "sun" Ps civ 19 2. *šmš wyrḥ* "sun and moon" Ps cxlviii 3	*špš//yrḫ* UT, 77:3–4 *špš wyrḫ* UT, 5:11, 14; 602:11
špl "to be low"//*rwm* "to be high" Pss lxxv 8, cxxxviii 6	*špl//rwm* UT, 52:32
tšrš šršyh "you made her strike roots"//*'rṣ* "land" Ps lxxx 10	*šršk barṣ al yp'* "May your roots not flourish in the earth" UT, 1 Aqht:159–60

INDEX OF BIBLICAL PASSAGES*

* Since it is furnished with a very detailed table of contents, THE GRAMMAR OF THE PSALTER has not been included in this index.

INDEX OF HEBREW WORDS*

* Since it is furnished with a very detailed table of contents, THE GRAMMAR OF THE PSALTER has not been included in this index.

INDEX OF SUBJECTS*

(GP=The Grammar of the Psalter)

* Since it is furnished with a very detailed table of contents, page references to The Grammar of the Psalter have not been included in this index.

INDEX OF MOTIFS*

* Since it is furnished with a very detailed table of contents, THE GRAMMAR OF THE PSALTER has not been included in this index.